MORPHOTACTICS

The study of morphology is central to linguistics, and morphotactics – the general principles by which the parts of a word form are arranged – is essential to the study of morphology. Drawing on evidence from a range of languages, this is a comprehensive and up-to-date account of the principles of morphotactic analysis. Gregory Stump proposes that the arrangement of word forms' grammatically significant parts is an expression of the ways in which a language's morphological rules combine with one another to form more specific rules. This rule-combining approach to morphotactics has important implications for the synchronic analysis of inflectional and derivational morphology, and it provides a solid conceptual platform for understanding both the processing of morphologically complex words and the paths of morphological change. Laying the groundwork for future research on morphotactic analysis, this is essential reading for researchers and graduate students in linguistics, and anyone interested in understanding language structure.

GREGORY STUMP is Emeritus Professor of Linguistics at the University of Kentucky. His research focuses on the structure of inflectional systems, the nature of inflectional complexity, and the logic of morphotactics. Notable publications include *Inflectional Morphology* (Cambridge University Press, 2001), *Morphological Typology* (Cambridge University Press, 2013, with R. Finkel), and *Inflectional Paradigms* (Cambridge University Press, 2016).

CAMBRIDGE STUDIES IN LINGUISTICS

General Editors: U. ANSALDO, P. AUSTIN, B. COMRIE,
T. KUTEVA, R. LASS, D. LIGHTFOOT, K. RICE, I. ROBERTS,
S. ROMAINE, M. SHEEHAN, I. TSIMPLI

In this series

124 NEIL SMITH: *Acquiring Phonology*
125 NINA TOPINTZI: *Onsets: Suprasegmental and Prosodic Behaviour*
126 CEDRIC BOECKX, NORBERT HORNSTEIN and JAIRO NUNES: *Control as Movement*
127 MICHAEL ISRAEL: *The Grammar of Polarity: Pragmatics, Sensitivity, and the Logic of Scales*
128 M. RITA MANZINI and LEONARDO M. SAVOIA: *Grammatical Categories: Variation in Romance Languages*
129 BARBARA CITKO: *Symmetry in Syntax: Merge, Move and Labels*
130 RACHEL WALKER: *Vowel Patterns in Language*
131 MARY DALRYMPLE and IRINA NIKOLAEVA: *Objects and Information Structure*
132 JERROLD M. SADOCK: *The Modular Architecture of Grammar*
133 DUNSTAN BROWN and ANDREW HIPPISLEY: *Network Morphology: A Defaults-based Theory of Word Structure*
134 BETTELOU LOS, CORRIEN BLOM, GEERT BOOIJ, MARION ELENBAAS and ANS VAN KEMENADE: *Morphosyntactic Change: A Comparative Study of Particles and Prefixes*
135 STEPHEN CRAIN: *The Emergence of Meaning*
136 HUBERT HAIDER: *Symmetry Breaking in Syntax*
137 JOSÉ A. CAMACHO: *Null Subjects*
138 GREGORY STUMP and RAPHAEL A. FINKEL: *Morphological Typology: From Word to Paradigm*
139 BRUCE TESAR: *Output-Driven Phonology: Theory and Learning*
140 ASIER ALCÁZAR and MARIO SALTARELLI: *The Syntax of Imperatives*
141 MISHA BECKER: *The Acquisition of Syntactic Structure: Animacy and Thematic Alignment*
142 MARTINA WILTSCHKO: *The Universal Structure of Categories: Towards a Formal Typology*
143 FAHAD RASHED AL-MUTAIRI: *The Minimalist Program: The Nature and Plausibility of Chomsky's Biolinguistics*
144 CEDRIC BOECKX: *Elementary Syntactic Structures: Prospects of a Feature-Free Syntax*
145 PHOEVOS PANAGIOTIDIS: *Categorial Features: A Generative Theory of Word Class Categories*
146 MARK BAKER: *Case: Its Principles and Its Parameters*
147 WM. G. BENNETT: *The Phonology of Consonants: Dissimilation, Harmony and Correspondence*
148 ANDREA SIMS: *Inflectional Defectiveness*
149 GREGORY STUMP: *Inflectional Paradigms: Content and Form at the Syntax-Morphology Interface*

150 ROCHELLE LIEBER: *English Nouns: The Ecology of Nominalization*
151 JOHN BOWERS: *Deriving Syntactic Relations*
152 ANA TERESA PÉREZ-LEROUX, MIHAELA PIRVULESCU and YVES ROBERGE: *Direct Objects and Language Acquisition*
153 MATTHEW BAERMAN, DUNSTAN BROWN and GREVILLE G. CORBETT: *Morphological Complexity*
154 MARCEL DEN DIKKEN: *Dependency and Directionality*
155 LAURIE BAUER: *Compounds and Compounding*
156 KLAUS J. KOHLER: *Communicative Functions and Linguistic Forms in Speech Interaction*
157 KURT GOBLIRSCH: *Gemination, Lenition, and Vowel Lengthening: On the History of Quantity in Germanic*
158 ANDREW RADFORD: *Colloquial English: Structure and Variation*
159 MARIA POLINSKY: *Heritage Languages and Their Speakers*
160 EGBERT FORTUIN and GETTY GEERDINK-VERKOREN: *Universal Semantic Syntax: A Semiotactic Approach*
161 ANDREW RADFORD: *Relative Clauses: Structure and Variation in Everyday English*
162 JOHN H. ESLING, SCOTT R. MOISIK, ALISON BENNER and LISE CREVIER-BUCHMAN: *Voice Quality: The Laryngeal Articulator Model*
163 JASON ROTHMAN, JORGE GONZÁLEZ ALONSO and ELOI PUIG-MAYENCO: *Third Language Acquisition and Linguistic Transfer*
164 IRINA NIKOLAEVA and ANDREW SPENCER: *Mixed Categories: The Morphosyntax of Noun Modification*
165 ABRAHAM WERNER: *Modality in Syntax, Semantics and Pragmatics*
166 GUGLIELMO CINQUE: *The Syntax of Relative Clauses: A Unified Analysis*
167 HENK J. VERKUYL: *The Compositional Nature of Tense, Mood and Aspect*
168 SANDRO SESSAREGO: *Interfaces and Domains of Contact-Driven Restructuring: Aspects of Afro-Hispanic Linguistics*
169 GREGORY STUMP: *Morphotactics: A Rule-Combining Approach*

MORPHOTACTICS
A RULE-COMBINING APPROACH

GREGORY STUMP
University of Kentucky

CAMBRIDGE
UNIVERSITY PRESS

Shaftesbury Road, Cambridge CB2 8EA, United Kingdom

One Liberty Plaza, 20th Floor, New York, NY 10006, USA

477 Williamstown Road, Port Melbourne, VIC 3207, Australia

314–321, 3rd Floor, Plot 3, Splendor Forum, Jasola District Centre, New Delhi – 110025, India

103 Penang Road, #05–06/07, Visioncrest Commercial, Singapore 238467

Cambridge University Press is part of Cambridge University Press & Assessment, a department of the University of Cambridge.

We share the University's mission to contribute to society through the pursuit of education, learning and research at the highest international levels of excellence.

www.cambridge.org
Information on this title: www.cambridge.org/9781009168199

DOI: 10.1017/9781009168205

© Gregory Stump 2023

This publication is in copyright. Subject to statutory exception and to the provisions of relevant collective licensing agreements, no reproduction of any part may take place without the written permission of Cambridge University Press & Assessment.

First published 2023
First paperback edition 2025

A catalogue record for this publication is available from the British Library

Library of Congress Cataloging-in-Publication data
Names: Stump, Gregory T. (Gregory Thomas), 1954– author.
Title: Morphotactics : a rule-combining approach / Gregory Stump.
Description: First edition. | Cambridge, United Kingdom ; New York, NY : Cambridge University Press, 2022. | Series: Cambridge studies in linguistics ; v. 169 | Includes bibliographical references and index.
Identifiers: LCCN 2022026517 (print) | LCCN 2022026518 (ebook) | ISBN 9781009168212 (hardback) | ISBN 9781009168199 (paperback) | ISBN 9781009168205 (epub)
Subjects: LCSH: Grammar, Comparative and general–Morphology.
Classification: LCC P241 .S786 2022 (print) | LCC P241 (ebook) | DDC 415/.9–dc23/eng/20220822
LC record available at https://lccn.loc.gov/2022026517
LC ebook record available at https://lccn.loc.gov/2022026518

ISBN   978-1-009-16821-2   Hardback
ISBN   978-1-009-16819-9   Paperback

Cambridge University Press & Assessment has no responsibility for the persistence or accuracy of URLs for external or third-party internet websites referred to in this publication and does not guarantee that any content on such websites is, or will remain, accurate or appropriate.

For Marcia and Jorie

Contents

List of Figures	*page* xiv
List of Tables	xvi
Preface and Acknowledgments	xxv
List of Abbreviations	xxvii
List of Symbols and Operators	xxx

1	**Canonical Morphotactics**	1
1.1	Introduction and Objectives	1
1.2	Rule-combining Morphotactics	5
1.3	Past Work Supporting the Morphotactic Holism Hypothesis	8
1.4	Canonical Morphotactics in Rule-based Morphology	15
	1.4.1 The Definitional Uniformity of Individual Rules of Exponence in a Canonical Morphotactic System	17
	1.4.2 The Interactive Uniformity of Rules of Exponence That Apply Together in a Canonical Morphotactic System	17
	1.4.3 The Contrastive Uniformity of Rules of Exponence That Do Not Apply Together in a Canonical Morphotactic System	18
1.5	Examples of Conformity to and Deviation from the Criterial Characteristics of Canonical Morphotactics	19
	1.5.1 The Minimal Rule Criterion	19
	1.5.2 The Rule Independence Criterion	20
	1.5.3 The Parallel Sequence Criterion	21
	1.5.4 The Unique Sequence Criterion	24
	1.5.5 The Compositional Content Criterion	24
	1.5.6 The Stem Operand Criterion	26
	1.5.7 The Intermediate Well-formedness Criterion	27
	1.5.8 The Integral Stem Criterion	28
	1.5.9 The Rule Opposition Criterion	29
	1.5.10 The Affix Directionality Criterion	32
1.6	Prospect	32

x Contents

2	**Rule Combinations**	36
2.1	Some Preliminary Assumptions about Paradigms and Rules of Exponence	37
	2.1.1 Inflectional Morphology	38
	2.1.2 Derivational Morphology	44
2.2	Rule Composition	54
2.3	Holistic Combination	61
2.4	Rule Aggregation	66
2.5	Counterpotentiation	77
2.6	A Rule Combination's Inner and Outer Rules	80
2.7	Conclusion	81
3	**Dependent Rules and Carrier Rules**	83
3.1	Dependent Rules and Rule Composition	84
3.2	Outer Dependent Rules in Limbu Verb Morphology	86
3.3	An Inner Dependent Rule in Sanskrit Verb Morphology	96
3.4	Conclusion	111
4	**Rule Composition and Rule Ordering**	113
4.1	Fixed Deviations from a Default Sequence of Rule Application in Fula	114
4.2	Complementary Sequences of Rule Application in Udmurt	121
4.3	Alternative Acceptable Sequences of Rule Application in Eastern Mari	131
4.4	Conclusion	140
5	**Extending Canonical Morphotactic Criteria to Composite Rules**	141
5.1	An Apparent Case of Nonlocal Morphotactic Conditioning in Sanskrit	141
5.2	Relations of Paradigmatic Opposition and Competition among Morphological Rules	150
	5.2.1 Paradigmatic Opposition of a Simple Rule to Composite Rules without Competition: Latin ⟦-minī⟧	151
	5.2.2 Paradigmatic Opposition of a Simple Rule to a Competing Composite Rule	154
	5.2.2.1 A Simple Rule Overrides a Composite Rule: Limbu ⟦-mʔna⟧	154
	5.2.2.2 A Composite Rule Overrides a Simple Rule: Sanskrit (⟦-hí⟧ ∘ ⟦-nu⟧)	155
5.3	Conclusion	158

6	**Rule Combinations Expressing Holistic Content**	159
6.1	Holistic Content in Breton Verb Inflection	160
6.2	Accounting for Holistic Content by Means of Content Supplementations	165
6.3	Emergent Supplementary Content in Limbu Verb Inflection	171
6.4	Holistic Content in Old English Verb Inflection	173
6.5	Conclusion	181
7	**Rule Aggregation**	182
7.1	Noon	184
	7.1.1 Adjective Inflection in Noon	184
	7.1.2 Rule Aggregation in Noon	190
7.2	Lithuanian	193
	7.2.1 Lithuanian Reflexive Verbs	193
	7.2.2 Rule Aggregation in Lithuanian Reflexive Verb Forms	198
7.3	Discussion	211
7.4	The Interaction of Aggregation with True Ambifixation in Italian	218
7.5	Conclusion	223
8	**Complex Morphotactic Interactions in Swahili**	224
8.1	The Morphotactics of Swahili Verb Inflection	225
	8.1.1 The Polyfunctionality of the Verbal Concords in Swahili	227
	8.1.2 The Morphotactics of Negation in Swahili Verb Inflection	229
	8.1.3 The Morphotactics of Relative Verb Forms in Swahili	231
8.2	The Subject/Object Polyfunctionality of Verbal Concords in Swahili Verb Morphology: Fragment I	233
8.3	The Morphotactics of Negation in Swahili Verb Morphology: Fragment II	242
8.4	The Morphotactics of Relativization in Swahili Verb Morphology: Fragment III	247
8.5	Discussion and Conclusions	253
9	**The Nonassociativity of Rule Composition in Murrinhpatha**	259
9.1	Rule Composition Is Nonassociative	259
9.2	Murrinhpatha Verb Inflection	262
	9.2.1 Classifier Inflection in Murrinhpatha Verbs	263
	9.2.2 Concordial Exponents in Murrinhpatha Verb Forms	264

xii *Contents*

	9.2.3	The Joint Expression of a Subject's Person and Number in a Murrinhpatha Verb Form	267
	9.2.4	The Joint Expression of an Object's Person and Number in a Murrinhpatha Verb Form	268
	9.2.5	The Complex Morphotactics of Subject Concord in Murrinhpatha Verb Forms	269
9.3	A Rule-combining Morphotactic Analysis of Murrinhpatha Verbs		273
	9.3.1	FERs Conforming to the Simple Rule Pattern (21a)	277
	9.3.2	FERs Conforming to the Two-rule Pattern (21b)	278
	9.3.3	FERs Conforming to the Nested Pattern (21c)	282
	9.3.4	FERs Conforming to the Nested Pattern (21d)	285
	9.3.5	Accounting for the Morphotactic Facts in (14)	287
	9.3.6	The Nonassociativity of Rule Composition in Murrinhpatha	289
	9.3.7	Extending the Analysis of Murrinhpatha Verbal Morphotactics	290
9.4	Conclusion		297

10 Potentiation and Counterpotentiation   298
10.1 Rule Composition and Potentiation   299
10.2 Counterpotentiation   302
    10.2.1 Compositionally Motivated Counterpotentiations and Composites Whose Domains-of-definition Differ in a Lexically Arbitrary Way   305
    10.2.2 Compositionally Motivated Counterpotentiations and Composites Whose Domains-of-definition Differ Systematically   311
10.3 Affixal Discontinuity, Parasynthesis, Synaffixes, and Domains-of-definition   315
10.4 Conclusion   319

11 Rule Combinations and Morphological Simplicity   321
11.1 Formulaic Rule Combinations   322
    11.1.1 Frequent Rule Combinations   323
    11.1.2 Conventional Rule Combinations   325
    11.1.3 Semantically Noncompositional Rule Combinations   333
11.2 Affix Telescoping   334
    11.2.1 *-ic-al*   338
    11.2.2 *-ist-ic*   339
    11.2.3 *-at-ion*   340
    11.2.4 *-ic-ian*   342
11.3 Conclusion   343

		Contents xiii
12	**Rule-combining Morphotactics and Morphological Theories**	**344**
12.1	Paradigm Function Morphology	344
12.2	Construction Morphology	345
12.3	Word-skeletal vs. Exponence-driven Morphotactics	349
12.4	A Parsimonious Inventory of Morphological Operations	351
12.5	Rule Combinations vs. Morph-position Templates	354
	12.5.1 Analyzing Relative Verb Forms in Swahili	362
	12.5.2 Analyzing Verbal Concord in Fula	369
	12.5.3 Analyzing the Inflection of Eastern Mari Nouns	373
	12.5.4 Differences between FER Patterns and Templates	381
12.6	Conclusion	389
13	**Conclusions**	**391**
13.1	Problematic Morphotactic Patterns and Their Resolution	391
13.2	Canonical and Noncanonical Characteristics of a Language's Morphotactics	393
13.3	A Formal Synopsis of Rule Combinations	397
	13.3.1 Composition (Operator ∘)	398
	13.3.2 Potentiation (Operator Ⓟ)	400
	13.3.3 Counterpotentiation (Operator $\boxed{\text{CP}}$)	400
	13.3.4 Content Supplementation (Operator Ⓢ)	401
	13.3.5 Aggregation (Operator Ⓐ)	401
	13.3.6 Inflectional Rule Combinations vs. Derivational Rule Combinations	403
	13.3.7 The Category Determination Principle	403
13.4	Looking Ahead	405
	References	406
	Index	415

Figures

2.1	The *registered-to-vote-in* function	page 45
4.1	The intersecting sets of A cases and B cases in Eastern Mari	136
5.1	The realization of Latin *audīminī* 'you are heard' and *audiuntur* 'they are heard'	154
7.1	The structure of the prefixal domain of the Lithuanian verb. Adapted by permission of Peter Arkadiev from a table appearing in his unpublished lecture handout (2012a), '"External" verbal prefixes in Lithuanian,' presented at the Scuola Normale Superiore di Pisa, December 14, 2012	196
8.1	Two distinct patterns of paradigmatic opposition	230
8.2	Individual affixes of Swahili verb inflection categorized according to the rule group by which they are defined	234
11.1	The parts of the Turkish word form in (1a)	323
11.2	The parts of the Turkish word form in (1b)	324
12.1	Word skeleta in the 'syntax of words' theory of Selkirk. Reproduced by permission of the MIT Press from tree diagram (3.10.b) on p. 67 of Elisabeth O. Selkirk (1982), *The syntax of words* (Cambridge, MA: MIT Press)	349
12.2	The realization rule introducing the Swahili past-tense affix *li* in an IbM analysis	355
12.3	Feature structure of Swahili *aliyenipiga* 'who (sg.) struck me' in the IbM approach	356
12.4	Grouping of rules in the Swahili FER in (35)	358
12.5	Indexed morph positions for a fragment of Swahili verb morphology	365
12.6	Two fully instantiated rules defining the morphotactics of the Swahili RA affix *ye* in the IbM approach	365

12.7	Indexed morph positions for a fragment of Fula indicative verb morphology	372
12.8	The intersecting sets of A cases and B cases in Eastern Mari	374
12.9	Indexed morph positions for a fragment of Eastern Mari noun morphology	376
12.10	Underspecified realization-rule schemas for possessor-marking rules in an IbM analysis of Eastern Mari noun inflection	377

Tables

1.1	Ten criterial characteristics of canonical morphotactics	page 19
1.2	Present- and future-tense forms of Breton KAROUT 'love'	25
1.3	Plural personal forms of Swahili KUSOMA 'read' in three tenses	31
2.1	Some disciplinary nouns and the corresponding practitioner nouns in English	49
2.2	An example of mathematical function composition	56
2.3	An example of the composition of two rules of inflectional exponence	57
2.4	An example of the composition of two rules of derivation	57
2.5	The morphotactics of the Swahili forms in (28)	60
2.6	Present indicative and future-tense forms of Breton KAROUT 'love'	62
2.7	Some Breton collective nouns and their singulative derivatives	64
2.8	Other uses of Breton 〚-**enn**〛	64
2.9	Cardinal, ordinal, and fractional numerals in Breton	65
2.10	Instances of counterposition in three languages	66
2.11	Classification of tense/aspect/mood categories in Fula	72
2.12	Examples of nonpreterite vs. preterite forms in Fula	72
2.13	Some nonpreterite and preterite forms of Fula WALL 'help'	73
2.14	The morphotactics of three Fula verb forms	74
2.15	Derivational correspondences involving adjectives in *-istic*	80
3.1	The agent suffixes *-ŋ* and *-m* in the positive nonpreterite paradigm of the Limbu verb HUʔMAʔ 'teach'	87
3.2	FERs for the thirteen Limbu verb forms in Table 3.1	92
3.3	The agent suffixes *-ŋ* and *-m* in the positive preterite paradigm of the Limbu verb HUʔMAʔ 'teach'	93
3.4	The morphotactics of four forms of the Limbu verb HUʔMAʔ 'teach'	95

3.5	Perfect and future indicative active paradigms of two Sanskrit verbs	97
3.6	Future stems of some Sanskrit verbs	98
3.7	First-person plural indicative active forms of eight Sanskrit verbs	99
3.8	Four stem-selection rules for a fragment of Sanskrit verb morphology	101
3.9	Examples of the application of the stem-selection rules (i)–(iv) in Table 3.8	101
3.10	Distinguishing the five aorist exponence classes in Sanskrit by means of THM, SIG, and SEṬ	102
3.11	Inflection-class properties of eight Sanskrit verbs	104
3.12	Third-person plural indicative active forms of eight Sanskrit verbs	105
3.13	The morphotactics of four present indicative forms in the fragment of Sanskrit verb inflection	106
3.14	The morphotactics of four perfect forms in the fragment of Sanskrit verb inflection	107
3.15	The morphotactics of four aorist forms in the fragment of Sanskrit verb inflection	108
3.16	The morphotactics of four future-tense forms in the fragment of Sanskrit verb inflection	109
4.1	Classification of tense/aspect/mood categories in Fula	114
4.2	Series 5 subject affixes and object suffixes in Fula	116
4.3	Composed FERs in a fragment of Fula verb inflection	118
4.4	Examples of the morphotactics of subject agreement and pronominal-object marking in Fula verb inflection	120
4.5	Present indicative forms of Latin AUDĪRE 'hear'	121
4.6	Singular case forms of Udmurt GURT 'village'	122
4.7	Plural case forms of Udmurt GURT 'village'	123
4.8	Rule group for oblique case inflection in Udmurt	126
4.9	Rule group for possessor inflection in Udmurt	127
4.10	The six types of FERs defined by the FER pattern (14)	129
4.11	The morphotactics of six inflected forms of Udmurt GURT 'village' exemplifying the six FER types in Table 4.10	130
4.12	Udmurt FERs of the type ($R_A \circ R_{POSS}$) for singular A-case nouns with possessor marking	132
4.13	Udmurt FERs of the type ($R_{POSS} \circ R_B$) for singular B-case nouns with possessor marking	133
4.14	Declensional paradigm of Eastern Mari PÖRT 'house'	135

4.15	The personal possessor suffixes on the nominative singular form of the Eastern Mari noun PÖRT 'house'	135
4.16	Singular case forms of Eastern Mari PÖRT 'house' with the first-person singular possessor suffix -em	137
4.17	Plural case forms of Eastern Mari PÖRT 'house' with the first-person singular possessor suffix	138
4.18	The FERs defining the forms in Table 4.17	139
5.1	Stem formation in the present-system conjugations in Sanskrit	142
5.2	Second-person singular imperative active forms in Sanskrit (thematic conjugations)	143
5.3	Second-person singular imperative active forms in the second, third, seventh, and eighth conjugations	144
5.4	Second-person singular imperative active forms of some Sanskrit fifth-conjugation verbs	144
5.5	Second-person singular and plural imperative active forms of some Sanskrit ninth-conjugation verbs	145
5.6	The distribution of the second-person singular imperative active termination -hí in the ten present-system conjugations in Sanskrit	146
5.7	The morphotactics of four second-person singular imperative active forms in Sanskrit	148
5.8	Sanskrit second-person singular imperative active forms distinguished according to the type of form cell they realize, the FER by which they are realized, and the phonological condition on that FER	150
5.9	Synthetic passive forms of Latin AUDĪRE 'hear' and their active counterparts in the indicative and subjunctive moods	152
5.10	Second-person singular imperative active forms in Sanskrit	157
6.1	Finite forms of Breton KAROUT 'love'	161
6.2	Suffixes sequences in the inflection of Breton KAROUT 'love'	162
6.3	Relations of form to content among prevocalic, terminal, and portmanteau suffixes in Breton conjugation	163
6.4	Relations of form to content among vocalic suffixes in Breton conjugation	163
6.5	Seven affix sequences exhibiting holistic exponence in Breton regular verb inflection	165
6.6	FERs arising through holistic combination or solitary specialization classified according to their addends	166

6.7	Combined carrier rules for indicative past and irrealis rules and the composite FERs based on them	168
6.8	FERs defining the finite forms of Breton KAROUT in Table 6.1	170
6.9	The morphotactics of four Breton verb forms	171
6.10	Finite paradigms of five Old English verbs	175
6.11	Finite stems of five Old English verbs	176
6.12	FERs for the finite paradigms of five Old English verbs	179
6.13	The morphotactics of five Old English verb forms	180
7.1	The inflection of the Noon adjective YAK 'big'	187
7.2	Components of Noon adjectival inflections according to Soukka 2000	188
7.3	An analysis of the definite location 2 forms of Noon YAK 'big' that conforms to both the minimal rule criterion (Section 1.5.1) and the stem operand criterion	189
7.4	Soukka's analysis of the definite location 2 forms of the Noon adjective YAK 'big'	189
7.5	The morphotactics of four forms of the Noon adjective YAK 'big' from Table 7.1	192
7.6	Differences between reflexives and their nonreflexive counterparts in Lithuanian	194
7.7	Infinitive forms of some unprefixed verbs in Lithuanian	194
7.8	Present indicative active paradigms of three Lithuanian verbs and their reflexive counterparts	195
7.9	Present indicative active paradigms of Lithuanian SU-TIKTI 'to meet, agree' and its reflexive counterpart	195
7.10	Past proximative/avertive paradigm of Lithuanian ATEĨTI 'to come'	197
7.11	Positive and negative present indicative active paradigms of Lithuanian LENKTIS 'to bow'	197
7.12	Some Lithuanian reflexive verb forms in which two prefixes precede the reflexive affix	199
7.13	Some Lithuanian reflexive verb forms in which three prefixes precede the reflexive affix	201
7.14	Aktionsart prefix subclasses of Lithuanian verbs	202
7.15	The orthogonal membership of nine Lithuanian verbs in the three conjugation subclasses and in the *pa-*, *nu-*, and *ap-* prefix subclasses	203
7.16	The orthogonal membership of twenty Lithuanian verbs in ten Aktionsart prefix subclasses and in the reflexivity subclasses	204

7.17	Inflection-class property sets of twenty-six Lithuanian verbal lexemes	205
7.18	Present indicative forms (simple and negative continuative) of four Lithuanian verbs	206
7.19	The morphotactics of five Lithuanian verb forms from Table 7.18	207
7.20	FERs for the verb forms in Table 7.18	211
7.21	The principal patterns of Gurma gender-class morphology	213
7.22	Tone patterns of Gurma nouns	214
7.23	Rules in Groups I–III in the inflection of Gurma nouns	214
7.24	Rules belonging to both Groups I and II in the inflection of Gurma nouns	215
7.25	The morphotactics of two Gurma noun forms from Table 7.21	215
7.26	Italian pronominal affixes	218
7.27	Possible combinations of Italian pronominal affixes	220
7.28	Rules of exponence for Italian pronominal affixes and their suffixational, prefixational, and aggregative instantiations	222
8.1	Real or apparent deviations from six criterial characteristics of canonical morphotactics in Swahili verb inflection	225
8.2	Swahili noun classes	226
8.3	Swahili verbal concords	227
8.4	Swahili relative affixes for noun classes NC3–NC14	228
8.5	Morphosyntactic properties for three cumulative fragments of Swahili verb inflection	236
8.6	The morphotactics of three Swahili verb forms in Fragment I	241
8.7	The morphotactics of five Swahili verb forms in Fragment II	245
8.8	Aggregated relative tense/negation rules defined for Group II by (31)	250
8.9	The morphotactics of five Swahili verb forms in Fragment III	252
8.10	FERs are of either the type ($R_{III} \circ R_{II}$) or the type (($R_{III} \circ R_{II}) \circ R_{I}$) in the morphotactics of Swahili verbs	254
9.1	The Murrinhpatha verbal template	262
9.2	The inflection of the classifier SEE(13) (default stem *ba-*) in Murrinhpatha	264
9.3	The inflection of the classifier SAY(34) (default stem *ma-*) in Murrinhpatha	265
9.4	Five distinct types of concordial exponents in Murrinhpatha verb inflection	266
9.5	The encoding of subject number in the Murrinhpatha verb	268

9.6	Direct-object suffixes in Murrinhpatha	270
9.7	The morphotactics of the Murrinhpatha SBJ.NUM suffixes	271
9.8	The morphotactics of Murrinhpatha *pu-bam-ngkardu* 'they saw her/him' (= (10g))	278
9.9	The three types of composite FERs conforming to the two-rule pattern (Group I ∘ Group III) in (21b)	279
9.10	The morphotactics of Murrinhpatha *pu-bam-ka-ngkardu* 'they (two siblings) saw her/him'	279
9.11	The morphotactics of Murrinhpatha *bam-ngintha-ngkardu* 'they (two female nonsiblings) saw her/him'	280
9.12	The morphotactics of Murrinhpatha *pu-bam-nganku-ngkardu* 'they (two siblings) saw us (two excl siblings)' (= (11))	280
9.13	The two types of composite FERs conforming to the nested pattern ((Group I ∘ Group II) ∘ Group III) in (21c)	282
9.14	The morphotactics of Murrinhpatha *pu-bam-ka-ngkardu-ngime* 'they (paucal female nonsiblings) saw her/him' (= (10f))	283
9.15	The morphotactics of Murrinhpatha *pu-bam-ngi-ngkardu-ngintha* 'they (two female nonsiblings) saw me' (= (10c))	283
9.16	The morphotactics of Murrinhpatha *pu-bam-nganku-ngkardu-ngime* 'they (two siblings) saw us (paucal exclusive female nonsiblings)' (= (12b))	285
9.17	Where R is a DNS rule instantiating 〚**-ngintha**$_{C/L}$〛 or 〚**-nintha**$_{C/L}$〛, R enters into one of three patterns of composition	287
9.18	Composite rule pairs demonstrating the nonassociativity of rule composition in Murrinhpatha	291
9.19	The ambiguity of the verb form in (12)	292
9.20	The morphotactics of the Murrinhpatha forms (30a,c)	293
9.21	The morphotactics of the Murrinhpatha forms (32a) and (34)	294
9.22	The morphotactics of the Murrinhpatha forms (36a) and (37a)	296
10.1	Examples of conformity to the intermediate well-formedness criterion	302
10.2	Apparent examples of "nonpersistent ill-formedness" in English derivation	303
10.3	Counterpotentiation of 〚**-ic**〛 by 〚**-al**〛	304
10.4	Counterpotentiation of 〚**-ist**〛 by 〚**-ic**〛	307
10.5	Some derivative stems in *-ian*	309
10.6	Some derivative stems defined by the composite (〚**-ian**〛 ∘ 〚**-ic**〛)	310

10.7	Instances of the counterpotentiation (23)	310
10.8	Derivative verb stems in -*ate*	312
10.9	Verb stems in which ⟦-**ate**⟧ serves a thematizing function	312
10.10	Instances in which (⟦-**ion**⟧ $\boxed{\text{CP}}_{30}$ ⟦-**ate**⟧) applies to a ⟨lexeme, stem, Verb⟩ triplet	313
10.11	Instances in which (⟦-**ion**⟧ $\boxed{\text{CP}}_{30}$ ⟦-**ate**⟧) applies to a ⟨lexeme, stem, Noun⟩ triplet	313
10.12	Adjectives derived by (⟦-**ive**⟧ ∘ ⟦-**ate**⟧) from verbs thematized by ⟦-**ate**⟧	314
10.13	Adjectives derived by (⟦-**ive**⟧ $\boxed{\text{CP}}_{35}$ ⟦-**ate**⟧) from verbs not thematized by ⟦-**ate**⟧	315
10.14	Circumfixal ordinal marking Kanuri	316
11.1	Some Modern English adjectives in -*ic* and -*ical*	329
11.2	Past and present perfect forms of HUṚ 'see' in Pengo	330
11.3	The morphotactics of two Pengo verb forms	332
11.4	Reconstructed serial verbs in Proto-Pengo	332
11.5	Univerbation and morphological simplification in Pengo	333
12.1	Analysis of the Swahili verb forms in (39) and (40) in the rule-combining approach to morphotactics	363
12.2	The morphotactics of the Swahili relative forms *anipigaye* 'who strikes me' and *aliyenipiga* 'who (sg.) struck me'	363
12.3	Analysis of the Swahili verb forms in (39) and (40) in an IbM approach to morphotactics	366
12.4	Simple rules and rule combinations belonging to the three rule groups defining Swahili verb inflection	368
12.5	Four Fula verb forms in the relative past active tense	369
12.6	Analysis of the verb forms in Table 12.5 in a rule-combining morphotactics	370
12.7	Analysis of the verb forms in Table 12.5 in an IbM approach to morphotactics	373
12.8	Analysis of the Eastern Mari noun forms in (46)–(49) in the rule-combining approach to morphotactics	375
12.9	Analysis of the Eastern Mari noun forms in (46)–(49) in an IbM approach to morphotactics	376
12.10	The morphotactics of the nouns in (51) in a rule-combining analysis of Eastern Mari	378
12.11	The purported structural ambiguity of dative nouns in an IbM approach to Eastern Mari morphotactics	379

12.12	Templatic analysis of seven Swahili verb forms in an IbM approach	382
12.13	A FER pattern instantiated by seven Swahili verb forms	383
12.14	Examples of counterposition in four languages	385
12.15	Second-person singular indicative forms of three Old English verbs	387
12.16	Templatic analysis of the shaded verb forms in Table 12.15	388
12.17	FERs of the shaded verb forms in Table 12.15	388
13.1	How different combinations of two rules R_A, R_B differ from one another	404

Preface and Acknowledgments

In this book, I investigate the morphotactic patterns of natural languages – the ways in which languages arrange their word forms' grammatically significant parts. Specifically, I propose a rule-combining approach to modeling these patterns. According to this approach, the arrangement of word forms' grammatically significant parts is an expression of the ways in which rules of exponence combine with one another to form more complex rules. In general, patterns of rule combination are binary (one rule combines with another rule), such combinations may be nested (a combined rule may combine with another rule), and the modes of rule combination are varied, in the sense that the combinations into which rules of exponence enter may entail different kinds of formal or functional effects.

The rule-combining approach to morphotactics has specific implications for the analysis of both inflectional and derivational morphology. Each inflected word form is the expression of a single inflectional rule, its full exponence rule. In the limiting case, a full exponence rule is just a simple rule, but very often, a full exponence rule is a combination of more than one rule. Many such combinations are just composites of their component rules, but other modes of combination exist alongside composition, including aggregation (where one rule operates on the affixal exponent defined by the other rule) and holistic combination (where together, two rules realize more than just the sum of the content that they realize individually). I demonstrate a wide range of possibilities by presenting detailed analyses of a variety of inflectional systems, including those of Breton, Eastern Mari, Fula, Gurma, Italian, Latin, Limbu, Lithuanian, Murrinhpatha, Noon, Old English, Pengo, Sanskrit, Swahili, and Udmurt.

Derivational rules also enter into combinations. Some combinations are, again, merely composites, but others embody more specific relations between their component rules, as in cases of potentiation (e.g. the combined *-abil-ity* rule, which determines a pocket of high productivity in the use of the otherwise relatively unproductive *-ity* rule) and counterpotentiation (e.g. the combination of the *-ic* and *-al* rules that derives *whimsical* from *whimsy* in the absence of **whimsic*).

As I show, the rule-combining approach to morphotactics provides a solid conceptual platform for understanding both the processing of morphologically complex words and the paths of morphological change. Moreover, it is sufficiently precise in its formulation to afford meaningful comparisons with current theories of morphology, including Paradigm Function Morphology, Construction Morphology, Distributed Morphology, and Information-based Morphology.

In developing these ideas, I have benefitted from the helpful suggestions of a great many students and colleagues over a period of several years. I must particularly thank Peter Arkadiev, Jeremy Bradley, Greville Corbett, Raphael Finkel, Brian Joseph, John Mansfield, Rachel Nordlinger, and Andrew Spencer for comments and advice pertaining to the manuscript itself.

For their help in the realization of this work, I heartily thank Andrew Winnard, Helen Barton, Izzie Collins, and Natasha Whelan at Cambridge University Press, Vinithan Sethumadhavan, and Lesley Hay.

Abbreviations

1	first person
2	second person
3	third person
A	adjective (in labeled bracketings)
ABESS	abessive
ABL	ablative
ABS	absolutive
ACC	accusative
ACT	active
ADJ	adjective
ADVBL	adverbial
AGR	agreement
AGT	agent
ANIM	animate
ANT	anterior aspect
AOR	aorist
APPROX	approximative
ASP	aspect
ATTR	attributive
CLF.n	classifier number n in Murrinhpatha
CNT	continuative
COMIT	comitative
COMPAR	comparative
CONJ.n	conjugation n
CONT.(i)	continuous-(i) aspect in Fula
CS	classifier stem in Murrinhpatha
DAT	dative
DEF	definite
DIM	diminutive
DNS	dual nonsibling

DS	dual sibling
DU	dual
EGR	egressive
ELAT	elative
ERG	ergative
EXCL	exclusive
FEM	feminine
FG	final glottality in Fula
FIN	finite
FUT	future
FV	final vowel in Chichewa
GC*n*	gender class *n*
GEN	genitive
GEN.PST	general past
HAB	habitual
id.fcn	identity function
ILLAT	illative
IMPF	imperfect
IMPS	impersonal
IMP	imperative
INCL	inclusive
IND	indicative
INESS	inessive
INS	instrumental
LAT	lative
LOC	location
LS	lexical stem in Murrinhpatha
MASC	masculine
N	noun
NC*n*	noun class *n*
NEG	negative
NFUT	nonfuture
Nom	nominal
NOM	nominative
NONIND	nonindicative
NONSG	nonsingular
NUM	number
OBJ	object

PASS	passive
PAT	patient
PERMISS	permissive
PFTV	perfective
PFX	prefix
PL	plural
PNS	paucal nonsibling
POS	positive
POSS	possessor
PRET	preterite
PRF	perfect
PROLAT	prolative
PRS	present
PS	paucal sibling
PST	past
PTCP	participle
RA	relativized argument
REFL	reflexive
REL	relative
RSTR	restrictive
SBJ	subject
SBJV	subjunctive
SER.n	Series n
SEṬ	inflecting with the union vowel i
SG	singular
SIG	sigmatic
STAT.(i)	stative-(i) aspect in Fula
TERM	terminative
THM	thematic
TNS	tense
V	verb

NB: In the formal specification of a property set, properties are given in lower-case characters (e.g. {nom sg} 'nominative singular').

Symbols and Operators

$\langle L, \rho \rangle$	the content cell pairing the lexeme L with the property set ρ
$\langle Z, \rho \rangle$	the form cell pairing the stem Z with the property set ρ
$\| \langle L, \rho \rangle \|$	the form correspondent of the content cell $\langle L, \rho \rangle$
$[\![x]\!]$	label of a rule introducing exponent x
$\cap$	set intersection operator
$\in$	set membership operator
$\cup$	set union operator
$\sqcup$	unification operator
ic	function from stems to sets of inflection-class properties
PF	paradigm function
X → Y	operation on X to produce Y
⇒	derivation operator
Ⓐ	aggregation operator
∘	composition operator
$\boxed{CP}_n$	counterpotentiation operator associated with domain μ_n
Ⓟ	potentiation operator
Ⓢ$_\gamma$	supplementation operator having γ as its addend

1 *Canonical Morphotactics*

1.1 Introduction and Objectives

A language's morphology defines two kinds of things. At the level of pure content, it specifies the grammatical categories and properties that its words embody (such as 'plural number', 'agent nominalization', and 'first conjugation') and the combinations into which these categories and properties enter (such as the combination '3rd person plural imperfect indicative passive, first conjugation' embodied by the Latin verb form *laudābantur* 'they were praised'). At the complementary level of morphological realization, a language's morphology identifies the formal exponents of its grammatical categories and properties (affixes, patterns of ablaut, grammatical tone or accent specifications, and so on) and the ways in which these exponents combine with a word's stem in realizing a word form's lexical and grammatical content. Intuitively, a language's **morphotactics** is that part of its morphology that determines the morphological realization of word forms – the system of principles that defines the patterns according to which word forms' grammatically significant parts are arranged as well as the relations among such patterns.[1]

Simple word forms naturally have simple morphotactics: the word form *dogs*, for example, is just the noun stem *dog* followed by the plural suffix -*s*. In such cases, it is hard to argue that the full word form isn't simply listed lexically (or, in psycholinguistic terms, stored and accessed as a unit), with its stem+affix structure simply built in. But as one examines word forms of increasing complexity, it becomes less and less reasonable to assume that a language's word forms are in all cases listed as wholes. A language's morphotactics must comprise means of inferring complex word forms that aren't necessarily listed. Logically, there are many possible frameworks within which

---

[1] It should be noted at the outset that the concept of the morpheme is not a necessary part of this conception of morphotactics, a point to which I return below.

such inferences might be organized, and choosing among these possibilities is essential for the formulation of an adequate theory of grammar.

One possibility is to assume that a language's morphotactics is based on a set of skeletal word structures into which stems and affixes can be systematically inserted, either from the lexicon or by rules that associate stems and affixes with specific skeletal slots. (Such skeletal structures might be argued to be configurations of terminal nodes defined by syntax, or they might be defined by means of an autonomous morphological template.) On a word-skeletal approach of this sort, a language's morphotactic patterns are based on two different kinds of elements: concrete units with phonological content and abstract skeletal structures that determine the kinds of combinations into which those units enter as an effect of their insertion (whether from the lexicon or by rule).

Another possibility is to assume that a language's morphotactics comprises rules of exponence (rules that realize specific grammatical content by means of specific formal exponents) and that the order of these rules' application alone suffices to determine a word form's morphotactics without the help of any predefined skeletal structure. In an exponence-driven theory of this sort, a morphologically complex word's form is purely and simply an expression of the rules that realize its grammatical content with exponents. In fact, two sorts of exponence-driven theories might be distinguished. On the one hand, one might assume that all rules of exponence are minimal, in the sense that each rule introduces a single exponent. On this view, the Latin verb stem *laudā-* 'praise' is related to the imperfect passive verb form *laudābantur* 'they were praised' through the ordered application of three minimal rules of exponence, the first introducing the imperfect suffix *-bā* (short allomorph *-ba*), a second introducing the third-person plural suffix *-nt*, and a third introducing the passive suffix *-ur*. In this approach (the ordered rule approach), a language's morphotactic patterns are again based on two kinds of elements: individual rules of exponence and an overarching specification of the order in which these rules apply in the definition of a full word form.

On the other hand, one might assume that rules of exponence may themselves combine to form more complex rules of exponence, so that the stem *laudā-* is related to *laudābantur* through the application of a single, complex rule that affixes *-bantur*, a rule that is itself the combination of three simpler rules. In this approach (the rule-combining approach), a language's morphotactics simply specifies its inventory of (simple or complex) rules of exponence. (Such specifications might, of course, involve a basic set of simple rules and a set of principles for combining simpler rules to form more complex rules.)

On first consideration, one might suppose that the word-skeletal approach, the ordered rule approach, and the rule-combining approach are all essentially equivalent. Yet, a variety of phenomena can be shown to favor the third, rule-combining approach. In this book, I identify several phenomena of this sort, and I show how they can be accounted for in the context of a new theory of morphotactics. The phenomena at issue include periodic multiple exponence, asymmetrical affix dependencies, exceptional affix order, apparently nonlocal conditions on affix distribution, the paradigmatic opposition of one affix to a sequence of affixes, affix polyfunctionality, affix sequences expressing holistic content, affix counterposition (prefixation to a suffix or suffixation to a prefix), and affix potentiation and counterpotentiation, including parasynthetic derivation.

My objectives in this book are therefore twofold. On the empirical side, I document the wide variety of complexities that arise in the analysis of a language's morphotactics. I propose ten characteristics that canonical morphotactics might be assumed to possess in unremarkable cases, then demonstrate the numerous ways in which morphological systems deviate from these characteristics. Some such deviations are genuine; other phenomena are merely apparent deviations, ultimately conforming to canonical criteria if certain well-motivated assumptions are made.

On the theoretical side, I motivate an exponence-driven theory of morphotactics. I distinguish exponence-driven approaches to modeling a language's morphotactic characteristics from the word-skeletal approach, according to which a word form embodies an abstract skeletal structure or template that logically predefines the order of the particular exponents that give that word form its phonological substance. On the word-skeletal approach, the definition of a language's morphotactics is, in essence, the definition of its word forms' skeleta; many ways of defining such skeleta have been proposed (Selkirk 1982; Lieber 1992; Halle & Marantz 1993; Embick & Noyer 2001; Arregi & Nevins 2012; Crysmann & Bonami 2016). As I shall argue here, there are compelling reasons for favoring an exponence-driven approach to morphotactics over the word-skeletal approach.

In particular, I argue for a rule-combining approach to exponence-driven morphotactics, according to which a word's morphological form is the manifestation of an organized combination of rules of exponence. Crucially, I argue that the combinations into which rules of exponence enter are binary and potentially nested, and may involve any of four different modes of combination (namely composition, holistic combination, aggregation, and counterpotentiation).

I emphasize that the rules at issue here are not input–output rules for converting an underlying phonological representation to its superficial form, nor are they rules for constructing isomorphic representations of a complex word's form and content by putting morphemes together. Rather, the rules at issue here declare the organized expression of details of a complex word's content by details of its phonological form.

In the rule-combining approach to exponence-driven morphotactics, the central question is: What are the ways in which rules of exponence may combine in order to define the systematic aspects of the association of a complex word's content with its form? The null hypothesis is that in combining to define the association of a complex word's content with its form, rules of exponence always combine in the same way. I contend that this is not the case – that rules of exponence may in fact combine in at least four different ways in defining the correspondence between words' content and their form. Rules, in other words, are of different kinds. Simpler rules may combine to form more complex rules, and the patterns of such combination are various. Morphotactics, on this view, might instead be called ***regulatactics*** (< Latin *rēgula* 'rule'), the patterns of contact and arrangement among a word form's defining rules of exponence.

The rule-combining approach to exponence-driven morphotactics has important implications for both inflectional and derivational morphology. In the domain of inflection, the rule-combining approach makes it possible to regard every inflected word form as the expression of a single rule; in very many cases, this is a complex combination of simpler rules of inflectional exponence. I refer to a complex rule of this sort as a ***full exponence rule***; as I shall show, the definition of a language's system of full exponence rules may involve a variety of modes of rule combination, with ordinary rule composition being the default mode but by no means the only mode.

In the domain of derivation, the rule-combining approach makes it possible to postulate complex rules of derivation that result from the combination of simpler rules of derivational exponence. The existence of such complex rules is motivated by a variety of considerations. These include the phenomenon of potentiation; a contrary phenomenon of counterpotentiation; and instances in which a combination of derivational rules expresses more than the summed content of its component rules. As with inflection, the default mode of rule combination is that of composition, but the evidence discussed here motivates the postulation of additional modes.

The details of exponence-driven morphotactics are sometimes intricate, but the ultimate argument that motivates this approach is very simple: that a theory of morphotactics requires rules of exponence, and by Occam's Razor, no further stipulations about the purported skeletal or templatic structure of words are needed, since rules of exponence in various combinations alone suffice to define a language's morphotactic patterns.

In this chapter, I discuss the preliminary assumptions of the rule-combining approach to morphotactics and advance the two fundamental hypotheses that underlie it: the morphotactic holism hypothesis and the morphotactic variety hypothesis (Section 1.2). In Section 1.3, I review previous proposals that provide empirical support for the morphotactic holism hypothesis, which (unlike the morphotactic variety hypothesis) is not a novel idea. In Section 1.4, I discuss the nature of canonical morphotactics, for which I introduce ten criterial characteristics, construed in rule-based terms. In Section 1.5, I give examples of phenomena that possess these characteristics as well as of phenomena that do not apparently possess them. The morphotactic phenomena to be analyzed in the following chapters deviate from some of these canonical characteristics but reinforce conformity to others provided that a rule-combining approach is assumed. In Section 1.6, I anticipate the range of topics to be discussed in subsequent chapters.

1.2   Rule-combining Morphotactics

The systematic word-internal relations exhibited by the components of a language's complex word forms constitute that language's morphotactics. In the morpheme-based approaches to morphology popular in the mid-twentieth century, a language's morphotactic principles are seen as constraints on the concatenation of a word form's morphemes. By contrast, rule-based conceptions of morphology represent a language's morphotactic principles as constraints on the interaction of the rules of exponence by means of which a word's form is defined. In this book, I examine a wide range of morphotactic phenomena in a variety of languages. The systematic patterns embodied by this evidence necessitate a more richly structured conception of the nature of morphotactics than follows from current assumptions (whether these be articulated in morpheme-based or rule-based terms). I therefore propose a new set of assumptions about morphotactics that is motivated by the need to provide an explanatory account of these numerous phenomena.

I develop this new conception of morphotactics in the context of a rule-based perspective on morphology. I favor the rule-based approach for reasons of descriptive precision, but the exponence-driven conception of morphotactics developed here could be profitably adapted to certain other kinds of formal frameworks; for example, it has clear implications for the refinement of a construction-based approach to morphology (a point to which I shall return).

The rules at issue throughout the following discussion are declarative in nature – that is, they are clauses in the static definition of a language's morphology. They are not rules for converting underlying forms into superficial forms, nor are they rules for combining smaller form/meaning pairings to build larger form/meaning pairings. Rather, they are systematic generalizations of two kinds.

In the domain of inflection, a rule of exponence is a generalization about the relation between a word form's abstract representation and its concrete representation. Consider, for example, the two representations of the word *shoes* in (1). Elsewhere (Stump 2016), I have referred to an abstract representation such as (1a) as a content cell: a word form's content cell is the pairing of the lexeme that it expresses (e.g. SHOE)[2] with the morphosyntactic property set that it expresses (e.g. {plural}); a word form's content cell is what determines its syntactic distribution and its semantic interpretation. Lexemes are not units of form. Rather, they are units that possess lexicosemantic properties and are realized by stems and word forms; the lexeme SHOE, for example, possesses the lexicosemantic property 'count noun', denotes the set of shoes, and is realized by the stem *shoe-* as well as by the word forms *shoe* and *shoes*. The relation between the abstract representation in (1a) and its concrete representation (1b) is expressed by a default rule of exponence according to which ⟨L, {plural}⟩ is realized as ⟨Z-*s*, {plural}⟩, where Z is L's stem.

(1) Two representations of the word *shoes*
    a.   Abstract: ⟨SHOE, {plural}⟩
    b.   Concrete: ⟨*shoes*, {plural}⟩

In the domain of derivation, a rule of exponence is a generalization about the relation between the abstract and concrete characteristics of one lexeme and those of a related lexeme. Consider, for example, the lexemes SHOE and SHOELESS: the former has the property 'count noun', denotes the set of shoes, and has *shoe-* as its stem; the latter has the property 'privative adjective', denotes the set of things lacking shoes, and has *shoeless* as its stem. The relation between SHOE and SHOELESS is expressed by a default rule of exponence according to which a count noun L_1 with stem Z is related to a privative adjective L_2 with stem Z-*less*.

---

[2] Throughout, a lexeme's name is given in small caps.

In formal terms, rules of exponence should be likened to mathematical functions: just as the squaring function f^2 denotes the relation between 2 and 4, between 3 and 9, between 3.5 and 12.25 (and so on), so the rule ⟦**-ed**⟧ in (2) denotes the relation between the weak stem /pɪk/ and the past-tense form /pɪkt/, between the weak stem /hʌm/ and the past-tense form /hʌmd/, between the weak stem /æd/ and the past-tense form /ædəd/, and so on. As this example shows, generalizations about superficial forms may perfectly well incorporate abstractions such as 'weak' or 'voiceless'; doing so in no way diminishes their fundamentally declarative nature. (Throughout, I use ⟦**x**⟧ as the label for a rule that introduces the exponent x. I use this sort of label to represent both inflectional rules, according to which x is the exponent of some morphosyntactic property set, and derivational rules, according to which x is the exponent of some derivational category. I introduce formal representations for the definition of rules of inflectional and derivational exponence in Section 2.1.)

(2)   ⟦**-ed**⟧:   In the inflection of a weak verb stem /X/, the property set {past} is expressed as
/X/-**ed** (where /YZ/-**ed** = /YZəd/ if Z is an oral alveolar stop,
otherwise   = /YZt/ if Z is voiceless,
otherwise   = /YZd/).

Rules serve two functions in a language's morphology.[3] First, they define form/content relations that are not listed in the lexicon. For example, an inflectional rule may define the form/content pairings of completely regular forms that are not frequent enough in their use to have induced lexical listing (e.g. forms such as the plural *shrikes* or the present participle *repaving*); in the derivational domain, a rule might be employed to create a novel lexeme such as BAGELIZE, which I have just now made up for use in sentences such as *They bagelized the traditional grilled-cheese sandwich*.[4]

Not all rules of exponence are sufficiently productive to be used to define form/content relations that are not listed in the lexicon. But even those that are not may still serve to simplify the lexicon. As Bochner (1993) has argued, lexical items that conform to rules are less "costly" to learn and to store than lexical items that deviate from rules in one way or another. For instance, verbs such as *ripen*, *sweeten*, and *toughen* conform to a regular (if unproductive) pattern that allows their lexical entries to be simplified in relation to those of the

---

[3] Jackendoff & Audring (2020: 52) make fundamentally this same point in distinguishing between the generative and relational uses of a morphological schema.
[4] Google shows that I am not the first person to have used the ⟦**-ize**⟧ rule to create a novel lexeme BAGELIZE.

adjectives *ripe*, *sweet*, and *tough*; by contrast, the verb *christen* conforms less well to this pattern, so that its lexical entry requires more special stipulations.[5]

I argue here that a satisfactory synchronic account of a language's morphotactics must be one that allows the (potentially recursive) combination of simpler rules of exponence to form more complex rules of exponence. In my discussion, I pursue two fundamental hypotheses. The first of these, the **morphotactic holism hypothesis** in (3), is not a new idea, as I shall show presently. The second of them, the **morphotactic variety hypothesis** in (4), is an idea that has never before been investigated in a systematic way.

(3) Morphotactic holism hypothesis
     A combination of rules of exponence may possess characteristics that do not follow from the characteristics of its simpler component rules.

(4) Morphotactic variety hypothesis
     Rules of exponence may enter into different kinds of combinations possessing different characteristics.

In Section 1.3, I review a number of past proposals that support the morphotactic holism hypothesis. In Sections 1.4–1.5, I show that the content of hypotheses (3) and (4) can be most clearly elucidated in the context of a set of assumptions about the canonical characteristics of a language's morphotactics. As I shall show, such canonical characteristics are of two main kinds: those from which the postulation of morphological rule combinations constitutes a noncanonical deviation, and those that are reconciled with apparent deviations through the postulation of morphological rule combinations.

1.3 Past Work Supporting the Morphotactic Holism Hypothesis

A number of people have, in past work, suggested that the combination of two rules (or of two affixes) sometimes possesses characteristics that are not predictable from the characteristics of the individual rules (or affixes) constituting that combination.

Studies of the morphology of the Romance languages have long drawn attention to the phenomenon of parasynthesis (Darmesteter 1874: 80ff.; Corbin 1980; Scalise 1986: 21, 147ff.; Fradin 2003: 288–292; Fábregas & Scalise 2012: 62f.; Serrano-Dolader 2015). The label 'parasynthesis' is applied to two distinct but related phenomena. On the one hand, parasynthetic compounding

---

[5] Derivational rules may also simplify the lexicon by serving a stem-defining function, applying to a lexeme's "substem" to yield that lexeme's stem (see Section 2.1).

1.3 Past Work Supporting Morphotactic Holism 9

(Bisetto & Melloni 2007) refers to patterns of compounding that involve the integral presence of an affix (e.g. the suffix *-olo* in Italian *pesci-vend-olo* 'fish seller'). On the other hand, parasynthesis may also refer to derivational patterns such as that of Italian *imburrare* 'to butter', whose derivation involves conversion of the stem of the noun *burro* 'butter' to a verb stem (cf. *zuccher-o* 'sugar' → *zuccher-are* 'to sugar, sweeten'), but involves the integral presence of the prefix *in-* (Masini & Iacobini 2018). What these two kinds of patterns have in common is that they involve the inseparability of two logically distinct morphological operations. In *pescivendolo*, the compounding of *pesci* 'fish' goes hand-in-hand with the addition of the nominalizing suffix *-olo*; it is not plausible to think of *pescivendolo* either as the result of compounding *pesci* with a nonexistent noun *vendolo (purportedly meaning 'seller') or as the result of suffixing *-olo* to the stem of a nonexistent verb *pescivendere (purportedly 'to sell fish'). Similarly, it is not plausible to think of *imburrare* either as arising through the prefixation of *in-* to a nonexistent verb *burrare or as arising by conversion from a nonexistent prefixed noun *imburro; in *imburrare*, prefixation and conversion go hand in hand.

Bauer (1988) draws attention to the frequent incidence of cases in which two morphological markings work together to express a single piece of content. In English, for example, causative verbs are derived from adjectives in some cases by means of the suffix *-en* (e.g. *weak* → *weaken*), in other cases by means of the prefix *en-* (*able* → *enable*), and in still other cases by means of *-en* together with *en-* (*bold* → *embolden*). As Bauer shows, cooperative combinations of this kind not only involve all kinds of affixation but may also involve nonaffixal morphology; for example, the derivation of *bathe* from *bath* (/bæθ/ → /beɪð/) involves both ablaut (cf. *food* → *feed*) and consonant gradation (cf. *wreath* /riθ/ → *wreathe* /rið/). Bauer proposes the term 'synaffix' as a label for combined morphology of this sort; circumfixation and parasynthesis may accordingly be thought of as kinds of synaffixation. As Bauer shows, the components of a synaffix may or may not have uses apart from one another. Even if they do, labeling their combination a synaffix is nevertheless apt if the content expressed by their combination is not simply the composition of the content that they express when used separately; for instance, the Dutch synaffix *ge-* + *-te* expresses a collective meaning (*been* 'bone' → *ge-been-te* 'skeleton'), and although *ge-* and *-te* are used separately in other contexts, the collective meaning associated with the synaffix cannot be attributed to either affix on its own. In rule-based terms, this means that a combination of two rules may express holistic content that is not directly deducible from the rules' individual content.

Bochner (1993) argues that morphological simplicity is best assessed not by reference to a symbol-counting evaluation metric (which favors generalizations that minimize the amount of information that must be stored in the lexicon), but rather by reference to a pattern-matching metric (which favors generalizations that minimize the unpredictability of the information that is stored in the lexicon). In this context, he draws attention to many cases in which greater predictiveness can be attained by simultaneous reference to the patterns associated with distinct rules. Consider, for example, the rules in (5): (5a) defines deverbal adjectives in *-able* and (5b) defines deadjectival nominalizations in *-ity*. The fact that (5b) can in general apply to adjectives defined by (5a) might be expressed by means of the more specific rule in (5c), which makes simultaneous reference to the patterns associated with (5a) and (5b); (5c) is what Bochner terms a subset rule, since it specifies a subset of instances of the application of rule (5b). Rules (5a) and (5b) might be thought to make (5c) redundant in a morphological description of English; but in fact, (5b) is much less regular than the subset rule (5c). Rule (5b) isn't very regular; the adjectives *main* and *plain*, for example, are not nominalized as *manity and *planity. For this reason, the existence of *vanity* alongside *vain* in the English lexicon is not too predictable; by contrast, given the high regularity of (5c), the existence of *acceptability* alongside *acceptable* is highly predictable, a fact that presumably makes *acceptability* easier to learn and less "expensive" to store than *vanity*. Thus, as a kind of rule combination, (5c) contributes to the simplicity (i.e. to the predictability) of the English lexicon to an extent that (5a) and (5b) on their own do not.[6]

(5) a. $\begin{bmatrix} /X/ \\ V \\ Z \end{bmatrix} \leftrightarrow \begin{bmatrix} /Xable/ \\ A \\ \text{ABLE to be Zed} \end{bmatrix}$

b. $\begin{bmatrix} /X/ \\ A \\ Z \end{bmatrix} \leftrightarrow \begin{bmatrix} /Xity/ \\ N \\ \text{STATE of being Z} \end{bmatrix}$

c. $\begin{bmatrix} /Xable/ \\ A \\ \text{ABLE to be Zed} \end{bmatrix} \leftrightarrow \begin{bmatrix} /Xability/ \\ N \\ \text{STATE of being ABLE to be Zed} \end{bmatrix}$

(Bochner 1993: 72, 88)

Stump (1993, 2001: 139–144) proposes that a portmanteau rule expressing a combination of inflectional categories α + β may compete with a

---

[6] In the context of somewhat different theoretical assumptions, Raffelsiefen 1992 and Booij 2010: 47–50 both argue for a similar conclusion.

1.3 Past Work Supporting Morphotactic Holism

default pattern combining a rule expressing category α with a rule expressing category β. He develops this proposal in the context of a theory in which affixes belonging to the same position class are introduced by a block of rules in paradigmatic opposition to one another. The proposal entails that within a rule block, a portmanteau rule may compete with the Function Composition Default, a default rule inducing the composition of two separate rules. The case at issue is that of indicative negation in Swahili. In (6a), indicative negation and first-person singular subject agreement are expressed by a single portmanteau prefix *si-*. Otherwise, indicative negation and subject agreement are expressed by separate prefixes, as in (6b). According to Stump's proposal, the rule of *si-* prefixation involved in the definition of (6a) belongs to a rule block in which the Function Composition Default otherwise realizes indicative negation and subject agreement through the composition of the negative indicative rule of *ha-* prefixation with a separate rule of subject agreement (e.g. the rule of *tu-* prefixation in example (6b)). In this analysis, relations of paradigmatic opposition within a rule block may, in effect, involve the opposition of a simple rule with a combination of two rules.

(6) a. *si-ta-soma*   b. *ha-tu-ta-soma*
         IND.NEG.SBJ:1SG-FUT-read   IND.NEG-SBJ:1PL-FUT-read
         'I will not read'   'we will not read'

Luís & Spencer (2005) present an analysis of European Portuguese pronominal object affixes that makes essential use of the notion of rule combination. In European Portuguese, a pronominal object affix may appear in three different positions: in the default case, it appears at the end of a verb form, as in (7a); but in the future indicative and in the conditional, it instead appears in "mesoclitic" position, before the affixal morphology expressing tense/mood and subject agreement, as in (7b); moreover, in the presence of certain kinds of preverbal constituents, it is in any event attracted to a proclitic position, as in (7c,d). In view of these distributional facts, Luís & Spencer draw a distinction between affix exponence and affix directionality (a distinction first considered by Stump 1993: 174f.). Crucially, if there are two pronominal object affixes, they appear in the same sequence relative to one another, whichever of the three positions they occupy. In (8), for example, the sequence *no-lo* appears in suffixal, 'mesoclitic', and proclitic positions. Luís & Spencer therefore propose that a rule introducing a dative pronominal affix (such as the first-person plural affix *no(s)* in (8)) may compose with a rule introducing an accusative pronominal affix (such as the third-person singular masculine affix *(l)o* in (8)) to produce a composite rule introducing an affix sequence (such as *no-lo* in (8)) whose prefixal vs. suffixal directionality conforms to the usual patterns. See Spencer (2005) for additional details concerning the formalization of this kind of analysis.

(7)   a.   *cantamo-lo*
              sing.PRS.IND.SBJ:1PL-ACC:3SG.MASC
              'we sing it'
     b.   *cantá-lo-emos*
              sing-ACC:3SG.MASC-FUT.IND.SBJ:1PL
              'we will sing it'
     c.   *não   o   cantamos*
              not   ACC:3SG.MASC   sing.PRS.IND.SBJ:1PL
              'we do not sing it'
     d.   *não   o   cantaremos*
              not   ACC:3SG.MASC   sing.FUT.IND.SBJ:1PL
              'we will not sing it'

(8)   a.   *O   Paulo   deu-no-lo.*
              the   Paulo   gave.SBJ:3SG-DAT:2PL-ACC:3SG.MASC.
              'Paulo gave it to us.'
     b.   *O   Paulo   dar-no-lo-á.*
              the   Paulo   give-DAT:2PL-ACC:3SG.MASC-FUT.IND.SBJ:3SG
              'Paulo will give it to us.'
     c.   *O   Paulo   não   no-lo   deu.*
              the   Paulo   not   DAT:2PL-ACC:3SG.MASC   gave.SBJ:3SG
              'Paulo didn't give it to us.'

In the framework of Construction Morphology, the phonological, grammatical, and semantic characteristics of morphological constructions are represented as morphological schemas. Booij (2007, 2010: 41ff.) has drawn attention to two kinds of evidence reflecting the unification of two simpler schemas into a single, more complex schema. The first kind of evidence is the fact that a derived lexeme may be related to a base lexeme via an intermediate derivative that is not itself in actual use, existing only as a potential lexeme. For example, the *on*-prefixed negative adjectives in (9) are related to verbal bases through intermediate adjectival derivatives in *-baar* that are not in regular use (though nothing excludes the possibility of their coming into use). Such facts show that schema (10b) unifies with schema (10a) to form the complex schema in (11), which in effect associates negative adjectives with their verbal bases in a single complex step, without entailing that the implied intermediate step is anything more than a potential lexeme.

(9)   Dutch evidence for schema unification (Booij 2007: 38, 2010: 42f.)
        verb   (potential deverbal adjective)   *on*-adjective
    a. *bedwing*   (*bedwing-baar*)   *on-bedwing-baar*
        'suppress'   'suppressable')   'unsuppressable'
    b. *bestel*   (*bestel-baar*   *on-bestel-baar*
        'deliver'   'deliverable')   'undeliverable'
    c. *blus*   (*blus-baar*   *on-blus-baar*
        'extinguish'   'extinguishable')   'unextinguishable'
    d. *verwoest*   (*verwoest-baar*   *on-verwoest-baar*
        'destroy'   'destroyable')   'undestroyable'

(10)   Two schemas in Dutch derivational morphology
    a. [[X]_V -*baar*]_A   b. [*on*- [X]_A]_A
        Interpretation: 'able to be Xed'   Interpretation: 'not X'
        e.g. *hoor-baar* 'audible'   e.g. *on-rein* 'unclean'

(11)   Unified schema for negative adjectives in Dutch
        [*on*- [[X]_V -*baar*]_A]_A
        Interpretation: 'not able to be Xed'
        e.g. *on-hoor-baar* 'inaudible'

The second kind of evidence of schema unification is the fact that the combination of two simpler schemas may take on formal or semantic properties that are not directly attributable to either one of them on its own. Booij (2010: 45) cites derivatives such as those in (12), which come from nouns but are participle-like in their morphology. He proposes that such derivatives involve the unified schema in (13c), which combines the noun-to-verb conversion schema (13a) with the past participle schema (13b). As the examples in (14) show, noun-to-verb conversions are extremely variable in their meaning in Dutch; but the unified schema in (13c) has special semantics not deducible from either of the component schemas in (13a,b); this semantic peculiarity – meaning 'having X', where X is the meaning of the base noun – must be associated directly with (13c).

(12)   "Participia praeverbalia" in Dutch
        Base   Derivative
        tand 'tooth'   *ge-tand*   'toothed, having teeth'
        tak   'branch'   *ge-tak-t*   'branched, having branches'
        spits 'point'   *ge-spits-t*   'pointed, having a point'

(13)   a. [[X]_N]_V
            Interpretation: variable
        b. [*ge*- [X]_V -*d*]_V
            Interpretation: past participle of X
        c. Unification of (13a,b): [*ge*- [[X]_N]_V -*d*]_V
            Interpretation: 'having X'

(14) Examples of noun-to-verb conversion in Dutch (Booij 1979: 995f.)

noun	gloss	gloss of verbal conversion
carnaval	'carnival'	'to celebrate carnival'
dieet	'diet'	'to be on a diet'
klei	'clay'	'to play with clay'
lift	'elevator'	'to go by elevator'
tafel	'table'	'to have a meal'

The notion that combinations of bound morphological markings (or combinations of rules of exponence) can be theoretically indispensable units of analysis implies that the morphology of a language may comprise entire subsystems that serve to define bound elements of considerable complexity. Subsystems of this sort are in fact widely observable. Nordlinger (2010, 2015), for example, describes the conjugational system of Murrinhpatha (Southern Daly; Australia) as primarily involving bipartite forms comprising both a classifier stem and a lexical stem such that inflected forms of the classifier stem themselves serve in the inflection of the lexical stem to which they are bound. Of the thirty-eight classifier stems in this system, only eleven have independent status as verb stems. The remaining twenty-seven classifier stems are in effect prefixes, yet they themselves exhibit inflectional patterns that are definable independently of the particular lexical stems in whose inflection they participate. Descriptive grammars of specific languages abound with cases in which affixes are themselves analyzed as complexes consisting of smaller affixes; examples are E. Ashton's grammar of Swahili (Ashton 1947), D. W. Arnott's account of the nominal and verbal systems of Fula (Arnott 1970), and Maria Soukka's grammar of Noon (Soukka 2000), all of which will figure in the chapters below.

These proposals to take combinations of morphological markings (or combinations of rules of exponence) as theoretically indispensable units of analysis are based on various kinds of insights.

- Bauer's notion of synaffixation, traditional parasyntheses, and Booij's unified schema (13c) are based on the insight that a combination of morphological markings may express holistic content.
- Bochner's subset rules are based on the insight that a rule's regularity may vary according to whether its application is in combination with that of another rule.
- Stump's analysis of portmanteau affixes and Luís & Spencer's analysis of European Portuguese pronominal object affixes are both based on the insight that the distribution of a combination of affixes may parallel that of a simple affix.
- Booij's unified schema (11) is based on the insight that a combination of derivational patterns may itself constitute an independent derivational pattern.

These various insights may be seen as supporting a single, more general claim: that two rules of exponence R_1 and R_2 may combine to form a larger rule R_3, and that when this happens, the characteristics of R_3 may be deducible by default from those R_1 and R_2 but may also include special characteristics that are peculiar to R_3. This claim is the morphotactic holism hypothesis (3). In pursuing this hypothesis in the chapters that follow, I present evidence in support of an additional hypothesis – that rules of exponence may enter into different kinds of combinations with different sorts of consequences for the characteristics of the resulting combination (= the morphotactic variety hypothesis (4)).

The conception of morphotactics that I motivate here focuses on relations among the declarative rules that define the distribution of individual morphological markings. The relations at issue are of two basic kinds: relations of paradigmatic opposition (certain rules are disjunctive in their application) and relations of syntagmatic combination (if their application is not disjunctive, compatible rules apply in a certain sequence). In general, relations of paradigmatic opposition and syntagmatic combination among rules correspond to cognate relations among the markings defined by these rules; for instance, if two rules of exponence are paradigmatically opposed (or must apply in a particular sequence), then the exponents whose distribution they define may likewise be said to stand in paradigmatic opposition (or to stand in a particular syntagmatic relation).

Morphotactic systems vary widely in the complexity of their relations of paradigmatic opposition and syntagmatic combination. In order to appreciate the nature and extent of this variation, it is helpful to begin by considering the unremarkable morphotactics of canonical systems that conform fully to the expectations arising from basic assumptions about morphological form. Once the characteristics of a plain vanilla system of morphotactics are explicit, it is then possible to compare actual morphotactic systems according to the directions and degrees of their deviation from these characteristics. (Such comparisons embody the general strategy of canonical typology elucidated by Corbett 2005, 2015, and Brown et al. 2013.)

1.4 Canonical Morphotactics in Rule-based Morphology

In rule-based approaches to morphology, a language's lexicon is assumed to house lexemes and their stems,[7] but not individual affixes. An affix is instead

---

[7] Throughout, I use 'stem' to refer to any formal expression of a lexeme on which a rule of exponence may operate. A morphologically unanalyzable stem is a root. The form resulting when a morphological rule operates on a stem may be (a) a stem but not a word form (e.g.

seen as the mark of a particular rule of exponence operating on a stem; for example, the application of the rule of exponence realizing the plural form of the stem *shoe-* is marked by the suffix *-s* in *shoes*. Affixes are not the only possible marks of the application of rules of exponence; a wide range of nonaffixal markings is also possible, such as the rime substitution effected by the rule converting French *national-* /nasjɔnal/ to its masculine plural form *nationaux* /nasjɔno/. Rule-based morphology does not entail that a word form is a constellation of morphemes organized in a quasi-syntactic constituent structure; indeed, the exponence-driven approach to morphotactics advanced here is based on the assumption that word forms do not possess the sort of skeletal structure ordinarily associated with phrases in syntax. In addition, rule-based morphology is in no way committed to the idea that a word form's meaning is compositionally computable from the meanings of its individual morphemes. (See Matthews 1972, Anderson 1992, and Stump 2001, 2016 for arguments against this untenable idea.)

In a rule-based conception of morphology, morphotactics is not simply a system of principles regulating the sorts of combinations in which morphemes may appear; it is instead a system of principles regulating the organization and interaction of rules of exponence. Thus, in rule-based morphology, canonical morphotactics involves the canonical organization and interaction of rules of exponence.

In a canonical morphotactic system, rules of exponence are wholly unremarkable in that they are highly uniform. Actual morphotactic systems can thus be described and compared by reference to the direction and degree of their deviations from a wholly canonical system. I assume that a fully canonical morphotactic system possesses a number of criterial characteristics reflecting three kinds of uniformity. Its individual rules of exponence are definitionally uniform; rules of exponence that apply together in the definition of a given word form are interactively uniform; and rules of exponence that do not apply together because they realize contrasting content are contrastively uniform. Consider these three sorts of uniformity in greater detail.

---

laudā-v-, the perfect active stem of Latin LAUDĀRE 'praise'), (b) a word form but not a stem (e.g. *laudābant-ur*, the third-person plural imperfect indicative passive form of LAUDĀRE), or (c) both a stem and a word form (e.g. *lauda-nt*, the third-person present indicative form of LAUDĀRE, which is an active word form on its own but serves as a stem for the formation of the corresponding passive through the suffixation of *-ur*).

1.4.1 The Definitional Uniformity of Individual Rules of Exponence in a Canonical Morphotactic System

Rules of exponence relate parts of a word form's content to parts of its form, in effect realizing content through form. I assume that the ***definitional uniformity*** of a morphotactic system's rules of exponence resides in the extent to which they are alike in their definition. Definitional uniformity is enhanced by conformity to four canonical characteristics. First, each rule is minimal, in the sense that it realizes a single property or coherent set of properties by means of a single exponent; a morphological system whose rules exhibit this characteristic thereby conforms to the ***minimal rule criterion***. Second, a given rule of exponence canonically performs the same operation in all of its uses. In particular, each rule of affixation has a fixed directionality, so that the affix that it introduces is always ordered in the same way with respect to its operand; a morphological system whose rules exhibit this characteristic thereby conforms to the ***affix directionality criterion***. Third, a rule of exponence canonically operates on a stem, not on some other sort of operand; a morphological system whose rules possess this characteristic thereby conforms to the ***stem operand criterion***. Finally, the applicability of a rule of exponence is canonically sensitive to characteristics of the stem X on which it operates but not to characteristics of a proper part of X that do not persist as characteristics of X as a whole; a morphological system whose rules possess this characteristic thereby conforms to the ***integral stem criterion***. In Section 1.5, I present examples of conformity to and of deviation from the minimal rule criterion, the affix directionality criterion, the stem operand criterion, and the integral stem criterion.

1.4.2 The Interactive Uniformity of Rules of Exponence That Apply Together in a Canonical Morphotactic System

In all but the simplest cases, the realization of a word form's content is effected by more than one rule of exponence. I assume that a morphotactic system's rules of exponence exhibit ***interactive uniformity*** to the extent that, in jointly determining a word form's realization, they interact in the same way. Interactive uniformity is enhanced by conformity to four canonical characteristics. First, they are canonically independent, in the sense that the applicability of one rule is never directly dependent on the application of some other rule; a morphological system in which rules possess this characteristic thereby conforms to the ***rule independence criterion***. Second, given any two rules of inflectional exponence that both apply in the definition of some word form, those two rules always apply in the same relative order; a morphological system whose rules exhibit this characteristic thereby conforms to the *unique sequence criterion*. Third, where R_1 and R_2 are two rules of exponence, the content realized by the successive application of R_1 and R_2 is the simple sum of the content realized by the application of R_1 and that realized by the application of R_2; a morphological system whose rules exhibit this characteristic thereby conforms to the *compositional content criterion*. Finally, where R_1 and R_2 are two rules of exponence, if the expression defined by the successive operation of R_1 and R_2 on stem X is well-formed, then the expression defined by the operation of R_1 on X is well-formed; a morphological system whose rules possess this characteristic thereby conforms to the *intermediate well-formedness criterion*. In Section 1.5, I present examples of conformity to and of deviation from the rule independence criterion, the unique sequence criterion, the compositional content criterion, and the intermediate well-formedness criterion.

1.4.3 The Contrastive Uniformity of Rules of Exponence That Do Not Apply Together in a Canonical Morphotactic System

I assume that a morphotactic system's rules of inflectional exponence exhibit **contrastive uniformity** to the extent that when rules realize contrasting values of the same inflectional category (or set of categories), there is a simple contrast in their application. Contrastive uniformity is enhanced by conformity to two canonical characteristics. First, rules of exponence realizing contrasting values of the same inflectional category (or categories) exhibit the same order of application relative to other rules of exponence; a morphological system whose rules exhibit this characteristic thereby conforms to the *parallel sequence criterion*. Second, the application of one rule of exponence may be contrastively opposed to that of another rule of exponence but not to that of a sequence of rules of exponence; a morphological system whose rules exhibit this characteristic thereby conforms to the *rule opposition criterion*. In Section 1.5, I present examples of conformity to and of deviation from the parallel sequence criterion and the rule opposition criterion.

Summarizing, a morphotactic system is canonical to the extent that it conforms to the ten criteria in Table 1.1.[8] Actual systems of morphotactics may be

---

[8] See Crysmann & Bonami (2016) for an alternative conception of canonical morphotactics; I discuss this alternative conception in Section 12.5.

Table 1.1 *Ten criterial characteristics of canonical morphotactics*

Criteria having deviations that reflect rule combinations	Criteria conformity to which is enhanced by the postulation of rule combinations
Minimal rule criterion (Section 1.5.1) Rule independence criterion (Section 1.5.2) Parallel sequence criterion (Section 1.5.3) Unique sequence criterion (Section 1.5.4) Compositional content criterion (Section 1.5.5) Stem operand criterion (Section 1.5.6) Intermediate well-formedness criterion (Section 1.5.7)	Integral stem criterion (Section 1.5.8) Rule opposition criterion (Section 1.5.9) Affix directionality criterion (Section 1.5.10)

compared and contrasted in a precise way according to the manner in which they deviate from the idealized point of reference defined by the criteria in this table. We shall see that the postulation of rule combinations affords an accurate means of modeling genuine deviations from the seven canonical properties on the lefthand side of Table 1.1; at the same time, certain phenomena that seem to deviate from the three canonical properties on the righthand side can be reconciled with these criteria through the postulation of rule combinations.

1.5 Examples of Conformity to and Deviation from the Criterial Characteristics of Canonical Morphotactics

In this section, I exemplify each of the ten criteria in Table 1.1 by morphology that is canonical in satisfying the criterion as well as by morphology that, prima facie, is noncanonical by virtue of its apparent failure to satisfy it.

1.5.1 The Minimal Rule Criterion

This criterion relates to rules of both inflectional and derivational exponence – that is, rules that either specify the morphological realization of a given morphosyntactic property set or specify derived membership in a given lexicosemantic category. According to the minimal rule criterion, rules of exponence are minimal, that is, they cannot be analyzed into smaller, component rules of exponence.[9] The English rule [[-**ize**]] by means

---

[9] In morpheme-based terms, the minimal rule criterion might be likened to the assumption that all affixes are monomorphemic; see Stump (2020a).

of which inchoative/causative verbs such as *vaporize* are derived satisfies the minimal rule criterion since it cannot be plausibly factored into smaller, simpler rules of exponence. By contrast, Bochner's rule (5c) and Booij's unified schemas (11) and (13c) may be seen as deviations from the minimal rule criterion. In the chapters below, I present extensive cross-linguistic evidence for the existence of combined rules of exponence that do not conform to the minimal rule criterion. Deviations from the minimal rule criterion are extremely varied, embodying a number of different kinds of rule combination. In general, postulating these deviations from the minimal rule criterion serves two purposes. On the one hand, it sometimes affords the most explanatory way of modeling deviations from other canonical criteria. On the other hand, it sometimes facilitates conformity to other canonical morphotactic criteria. In the chapters that follow, I will examine several cases of each type.

1.5.2   The Rule Independence Criterion

According to this criterion, the application of a rule operating on a stem is conditioned only by that stem's characteristics (e.g. the stem's phonological properties, the morphological or morphosyntactic properties with which it is associated, the lexicosemantic properties of the lexeme that it realizes, and so on); it is not directly sensitive to the concurrent application of some other rule. In Swahili, the past tense is realized by the ⟦**li-**⟧ rule in affirmative forms but by ⟦**ku-**⟧ in negative forms (e.g. *ni-li-soma* 'I read', *tu-li-soma* 'we read' but *si-ku-soma* 'I didn't read', *ha-tu-ku-soma* 'we didn't read'). The choice between ⟦**li-**⟧ and ⟦**ku-**⟧ in the expression of past tense is therefore determined by the morphosyntactic properties of tense and polarity whose association with a verb stem (e.g. *-soma* 'read') is being realized. The property of negative polarity conditions the application of an additional rule (either the default negative rule ⟦**ha-**⟧ or by the portmanteau rule ⟦**si-**⟧; cf. Section 1.3), but the application of ⟦**ku-**⟧ is not directly sensitive to that of either ⟦**ha-**⟧ or ⟦**si-**⟧; independently of those rules, it is sensitive only to the property of negative polarity associated with the stem being realized. For this reason, ⟦**ku-**⟧ satisfies the rule independence criterion.

By contrast, Kipacha (2006: 83), citing Maganga (1990: 33), observes that in the Unguja dialect of Swahili, anterior aspect is expressed either by the prefix *me-* or by the lack of any tense/aspect prefix. In addition, anterior forms involve two alternative rules for the expression of class 1 subject agreement: if anteriority is expressed by *me*-prefixation, then class 1 subject agreement is expressed by means of the 〚**a-**〛 rule, as in (15a); but if anteriority is expressed without *me*-prefixation, then class 1 subject agreement is instead expressed by means of the 〚**ka-**〛 rule, as in (15b). Insofar as (15a) and (15b) are identical in content, one could argue that whether subject agreement is expressed by 〚**a-**〛 or by 〚**ka-**〛 is sensitive to the prior application of *me*-prefixation and therefore deviates from the rule independence criterion.

(15)   a.   *mw-alimu*   *a-me-sema*
            NC1-teacher   NC1-ANT-say
            'the teacher has said'
       b.   *mw-alimu*   *ka-sema*
            NC1-teacher   NC1-ANT.say
            'the teacher has said'

(Kipacha 2006: 83)

In Chapter 3, I present a precise account of rule combinations in Limbu and Sanskrit whose definition deviates from the rule independence criterion.

1.5.3 The Parallel Sequence Criterion

According to this criterion, rules that express the same inflectional category canonically occupy the same position in any sequence of rule applications in which they serve in the definition of an inflected word form. The parallel sequence criterion might be seen as a manifestation of the universal probabilistic tendency toward category clustering, which Mansfield, Stoll, & Bickel (2020: 256) define as in (16).

(16)   Category clustering: Morphological categories tend to cluster in positions, that is,
       a.   markers of the same category tend to be expressed in the same morphological position, and
       b.   morphological positions tend to be filled by markers of the same category.

Given two rules that are in paradigmatic opposition because they realize alternative properties in the same inflectional category, those rules conform to the parallel sequence criterion if they always apply in the same sequence relative to other rules; thus, if both are rules of prefixation (or both rules of suffixation), they fill the same slot in a word form's sequence of affixes. Two rules may, however, fail to conform to the parallel sequence criterion: they may be in paradigmatic opposition, realizing alternative properties in the same category, yet differ in their applicational sequence, so that if both are rules of prefixation (or both rules of suffixation), they fail to fill the same slot.

In the inflection of nouns in Udmurt (Uralic; Russia), the suffixation rules in (17) express plural possessors and are paradigmatically opposed to one another; they are also alike in their applicational sequence, applying after the plural rule in (18a) and before the case rules in (18b–d). The possessor suffixes are therefore situated farther from the noun stem than the plural suffix but closer to it than the genitive, ablative, and dative case suffixes, as the examples in (19)–(21) show. The possessor rules in (17) therefore conform to the parallel sequence criterion.

(17) ⟦-mi̯⟧ : the first-person plural possessor property is expressed through the suffixation of -mi̯.
      ⟦-di̯⟧ : the second-person plural possessor property is expressed through the suffixation of -di̯.
      ⟦-zi̯⟧ : the third-person plural possessor property is expressed through the suffixation of -zi̯.

(18) a. ⟦-jos⟧ : plural number is expressed through the suffixation of -jos.
      b. ⟦-len⟧ : genitive case is expressed through the suffixation of -len.
      c. ⟦-leś⟧ : ablative case is expressed through the suffixation of -leś.
      d. ⟦-li̯⟧ : dative case is expressed through the suffixation of -li̯.

(19) a. *gurt-jos-mi̯-len*   b. *gurt-jos-ti̯-len*
          village-PL-POSS:1PL-GEN   village-PL-POSS:2PL-GEN
          'of our villages'   'of your villages'
      c. *gurt-jos-si̯-len*
          village-PL-POSS:3PL-GEN
          'of their villages'

(20) a. *gurt-jos-mi̯-leś*   b. *gurt-jos-ti̯-leś*
          village-PL-POSS:1PL-ABL   village-PL-POSS:2PL-ABL
          'from our villages'   'from your villages'
      c. *gurt-jos-si̯-leś*
          village-PL-POSS:3PL-ABL
          'from their villages'

(21) a. *gurt-jos-mi̯-li̯*   b. *gurt-jos-ti̯-li̯*
          village-PL-POSS:1PL-DAT   village-PL-POSS:2PL-DAT
          'to our villages'   'to your villages'
      c. *gurt-jos-si̯-li̯*
          village-PL-POSS:3PL-DAT
          'to their villages'

Udmurt noun inflection does, however, present a phenomenon that fails to conform to this criterion. Although the Udmurt rules of case inflection are paradigmatically opposed to one another, they do not all exhibit the same applicational sequence. Thus, although the application of the genitive, ablative, and dative rules in (18b–d) follows that of the possessor rules in (17), the application of the instrumental, elative, and egressive rules in (22) precedes that of the possessor rules, as the examples in (23)–(25) show. The case rules in (18b–d) and those in (22) are in paradigmatic opposition, but they differ from one another in their sequence of application relative to other rules, interacting in opposite ways with rules of possessor marking.

(22) a. 〚**-ini**〛 : instrumental case is expressed through the suffixation of -*ini*.
 b. 〚**-iśti**〛 : elative case is expressed through the suffixation of -*iśti*.
 c. 〚**-iśeni**〛 : egressive case is expressed through the suffixation of -*iśeni*.

(23) a. *gurt-jos-ini-mi*   b. *gurt-jos-ini-di*
 village-PL-INS-POSS:1PL   village-PL-INS-POSS:2PL
 'by means of our villages'   'by means of your villages'
 c. *gurt-jos-ini-zi*
 village-PL-INS-POSS:3PL
 'by means of their villages'

(24) a. *gurt-jos-iśti-mi*   b. *gurt-jos-iśti-di*
 village-PL-ELAT-POSS:1PL   village-PL-ELAT-POSS:2PL
 'out of our villages'   'out of your villages'
 c. *gurt-jos-iśti-zi*
 village-PL-ELAT-POSS:3PL
 'out of their villages'

(25) a. *gurt-jos-iśeni-mi*   b. *gurt-jos-iśeni-di*
 village-PL-EGR-POSS:1PL   village-PL-EGR-POSS:2PL
 'starting from our villages'   'starting from your villages'
 c. *gurt-jos-iśeni-zi*
 village-PL-EGR-POSS:3PL
 'starting from their villages'

The parallel sequence criterion relates specifically to rules realizing alternative properties in the same inflectional category; accordingly, it is not a canonical characteristic of rules of derivational exponence. I examine rule combinations that fail to conform to the parallel sequence criterion in Chapter 4, where the Udmurt facts are taken up in greater detail, along with evidence from Fula and Eastern Mari.

1.5.4 The Unique Sequence Criterion

According to this criterion, rules of inflectional exponence that may apply in the definition of the same word always apply in the same sequence relative to one another. The analyzability of a language's affixes into position classes reflects the conformity of the corresponding rules of affixation to this criterion. In the Swahili verb form *a-ta-soma* 's/he will read', the fixed ordering of the subject-agreement prefix *a-* and the future-tense prefix *ta-* reflects the fact that in the verb form's definition, two prefixation rules apply in a fixed sequence: the future-tense rule of *ta*-prefixation applies before the third-person singular subject-agreement rule of *a*-prefixation. It is typical for a language's inflectional rules to satisfy the unique sequence criterion in this way. Nevertheless, not all inflection satisfies this criterion. The Chintang language (Kiranti; Nepal) is rather spectacular in its failure to do so, exhibiting verb inflection in which the ordering of prefixes is remarkably free (Bickel et al. 2007); for example, the verb form in (26a) exhibits all of the prefixal ordering alternatives in (26b).

(26)   a.   *u-kha-ma-cop-yokt-e.*
             3.NONSG.AGT-1.NONSG.PAT-NEG-see-NEG-PST
             'They didn't see us.'
     b.   *kha-u-ma-cop-yokt-e.*
             kha-ma-u-cop-yokt-e.
             u-ma-kha-cop-yokt-e.
             ma-u-kha-cop-yokt-e.
             ma-kha-u-cop-yokt-e.

The formulation of a language's derivational rules may allow them to apply in more than one order (e.g. *commun-ist-ic* but *class-ic-ist*); the unique sequence criterion is therefore a canonical characteristic of inflection rather than of morphology generally. In Chapter 4, I present a precise account of rule combinations in Eastern Mari nominal inflection, whose definition deviates from the unique sequence criterion.

1.5.5 The Compositional Content Criterion

According to this criterion, the content expressed by a word form's morphology is always compositional, that is, a function of the content expressed by the individual rules defining that morphology. For example, the third-person plural imperfect passive content expressed by the morphology of the Latin verb form *laudābantur* 'they were praised' is a function of the content expressed by the imperfect 〚**-ba**〛 rule, the third-person plural 〚**-nt**〛 rule, and the passive 〚**-ur**〛 rule. Deviations from this criterion are of two types.

Table 1.2 *Present- and future-tense forms of Breton* KAROUT *'love'*

	Present		Future
	Indicative	Irrealis	
1SG	kar-an	kar-fe-n	kar-i-n
2SG	kar-ez	kar-fe-s	kar-i
3SG	kar	kar-fe	kar-o
1PL	kar-o-mp	kar-fe-mp	kar-i-mp
2PL	kar-i-t	kar-fe-c'h	kar-o-t
3PL	kar-o-nt	kar-fe-nt	kar-i-nt
IMPS	kar-e-r	kar-fe-d	kar-o-r

(Kervella 1976: 124)

In instances of **holistic combination**, the content expressed by a combination of rules includes content that cannot be attributed to any of the component rules on its own. In instances of **solitary specialization**, the content expressed by a rule applying on its own includes content that is not expressed by that rule when it applies in combination with other rules. Consider a case of conformity to this criterion and cases of both sorts of deviation from it.

Among the rules involved in the conjugation of Breton regular verbs are the three rules in (27), whose use is exemplified in the (partial) paradigm of KAROUT 'love' in Table 1.2. In the definition of the present irrealis form *kar-fe-mp* 'we would love', the rule sequence ⟨⟦**-fe**⟧, ⟦**-mp**⟧⟩ unambiguously expresses the content {1pl present irrealis}, in accordance with the compositional content criterion.[10] By contrast, the rule sequence ⟨⟦**-o**⟧, ⟦**-mp**⟧⟩ unambiguously expresses the content {1pl present indicative} even though neither ⟦**-o**⟧ nor ⟦**-mp**⟧ expresses the present indicative on its own; this rule sequence is therefore an instance of holistic combination and fails to conform to the compositional content criterion. In addition, when the ⟦**-o**⟧ rule applies on its own, it always expresses the third-person singular future, even though it doesn't express that content in combination with other rules; uncombined ⟦**-o**⟧ is therefore an instance of solitary specialization, a second kind of deviation from the compositional content criterion.

---

[10] In Section 6.1, it will be seen that ⟦**-fe**⟧ is itself a composite rule, though that fact is not important for the example at hand.

(27)   Three rules of Breton verb inflection
       In the finite inflection of a regular verb,
       ⟦-fe⟧ :   the property set {present irrealis} is expressed through the suffixation of -fe.
       ⟦-o⟧ :   there is no fixed content associated with the suffix -o, which, by stipulation, appears in several contexts.
       ⟦-mp⟧ :   the subject-agreement property set {1 pl} is expressed through the suffixation of -mp.

In Chapter 6, I present a precise formal account of rule combinations in Breton, Limbu, and Old English that deviate from the compositional content criterion.

1.5.6   The Stem Operand Criterion

According to this criterion, the formal operation associated with a morphological rule is an operation on stems. The ⟦-ize⟧ rule conforms to this criterion, operating on noun stems such as *burglar*, *color*, *crystal*, *magnet*, and *vapor*; on adjective stems such as *familiar*, *random*, *stable*, *trivial*, and *western*; and arguably on bound stems such as *euthan-*, *monet-*, *ostrac-*, *recogn-*, and *tantal-*. Some languages, however, present cases of ***affix counterposition*** – instances in which a rule introducing one affix operates on another affix. Affix counterposition has a particular signature: affix A exhibits a particular directionality D (prefixal or suffixal) with respect to a stem with which it joins, but in the presence of some affix B possessing the opposite directionality, A exhibits directionality D with respect to B, to which it is adjacent.

Logically, affix counterpositions may be of two types. In a ***prefixational counterposition***, a rule of suffixation has a prefix as its operand, operating on that prefix to produce a complex prefix; in Lithuanian, for example, the rule of reflexive suffixation ⟦-si⟧ operates on the verb stem in (28a) but operates on the negative verbal prefix *ne-* in (28b), producing the complex prefix *ne-si-*.

(28)   a.   *lenkia-si*   b.   *ne-si-lenkia*
            bows-**REFL**   **NEG**-**REFL**-bows
            's/he bows'   's/he doesn't bow'

In a ***suffixational counterposition***, by contrast, a rule of prefixation has a suffix as its operand, operating on that suffix to produce a complex suffix. In Noon (Cangin; Senegal), for example, adjectives carry a concordial noun-class prefix, and if the noun they modify is definite, they additionally carry a definite suffix expressing spatial deixis. This suffix carries the same concordial noun-class prefix as the adjectival stem itself (Soukka 2000: 86ff.); the examples in (29) illustrate.

(29) a. *waas-um* *w-i-yak-w-um*
        road-NEAR.HEARER NC1-ADJ.PFX-big-NC1-NEAR.HEARER
        'the big road (near you)'
    b. *ŷaal-ii* *y-i-yaanaaw-y-ii*
        man-NEAR.SPEAKER NC.ANIM-ADJ.PFX-white-NC.
        ANIM-NEAR.SPEAKER
        'the white man (here)'
    c. *kedik-k-ii* *k-i-sewiñ-k-ii*
        tree-NC4-NEAR.SPEAKER NC4-ADJ.PFX-thin-NC4-NEAR.SPEAKER
        'the thin tree (here)'
    d. *pëlkít-p-aa* *p-i-yo'oh-p-aa*
        thread-NC5-DISTANT NC5-ADJ.PFX-red-NC5-DISTANT
        'the red thread (there)'

(Soukka 2000: 89)

In Chapters 7 and 8, I present precise accounts of affix counterpositions in Noon, Lithuanian, and Swahili; all of these are defined by rule combinations that deviate from the stem operand criterion.

1.5.7 The Intermediate Well-formedness Criterion

This criterion entails that if the form resulting from the application of a rule operating on stem Z is well-formed, then Z itself is well-formed. In English, an adjective in *-ical* ordinarily exists alongside a similar adjective in *-ic*, from which it presumably derives; thus, when the [[-al]] rule operates on the well-formed stems in (30a) to produce the well-formed derivatives in (30b), the application of the [[-al]] rule conforms to the intermediate well-formedness criterion. By contrast, some adjectives in *-ical* are apparently unaccompanied (in my speech, at least) by well-formed bases in *-ic*, as the judgments in (31) show.

(30) a. *classic, cyclic, electric, historic, satiric*
     b. *classical, cyclical, electrical, historical, satirical*

(31) a. **identic, *lexic, *nonsensic, *surgic, *whimsic*
     b. *identical, lexical, nonsensical, surgical, whimsical*

Contrasts such as *whimsical/*whimsic* apparently deviate from the intermediate well-formedness criterion. A couple of complicating issues do, however, arise in this connection. First, adjectives such as *whimsical* are sometimes claimed as evidence for a suffix *-ical* that is synchronically separate from both *-ic* and *-al* (Bauer, Lieber, & Plag 2013: 289, 318ff.; cf. Marchand 1966: 185ff.; Dixon 2014: 251f., 261); if this is so, then the examples in (31b) do not actually deviate from the intermediate well-formedness criterion. (I return to this issue in Chapter 11.) Second, Rainer (2012) draws a distinction between two sorts of nonactual words in the domain of derivational morphology. On one hand, a **virtual** word is a word whose existence is blocked by that of a synonymous actual word, in the way that **famosity* is blocked by *fame*; on the other hand, a **potential** word is a word whose nonexistence has a purely pragmatic motivation that is subject to override in the right circumstances; *odorize*, for example, is not an actual word, but it is a well-formed potential word by dint of which *deodorize*, like *demagnetize*, might be said to conform to the intermediate well-formedness criterion. In applying this criterion, one must therefore take care to distinguish intermediate forms that are nonactual merely because they are potential forms (like *odorize*, which nothing actually blocks) from intermediate forms that are nonactual because they are virtual (like **whimsic*, whose deviation from the intermediate well-formedness criterion stems from the fact that it is in some sense blocked by *whimsical* itself); only in the latter case can one say that the nonactual intermediate form is ill-formed. (I return to this issue in Chapter 10.)

1.5.8 The Integral Stem Criterion

By this locality criterion, the application of a rule operating on a stem is conditioned by characteristics of the stem as a whole, not by characteristics of a proper part of the stem that do not persist to the stem as a whole. In English, the application of the verb-deriving ⟦-en⟧ rule is constrained in two ways by the phonology of the stem to which it suffixes *-en*. First, the stem must end with an obstruent; second, it must be monosyllabic. The examples in (32a) satisfy both conditions; the first condition accounts for the ungrammaticality of the examples in (32b); and the second condition, for the ungrammaticality of the examples in (32c). Thus, the ⟦-en⟧ rule only operates on stems of the type [...[obstruent]]$_\sigma$, in accordance with the integral stem criterion.

(32) a. black   blacken   b. fine   *finen   c. candid   *candiden
       fat   fatten   dull   *dullen   potent   *potenten
       loose   loosen   high   *highen   active   *activen
       stiff   stiffen   long   *longen   nervous   *nervousen
       wide   widen   low   *lowen   squeamish *squeamishen

By contrast, Aronoff (1976: 53f.) claims that the denominal adjective suffix *-al* "does not attach to the class of nouns of the form $X_V ment$ (i.e. the class of nouns of the form *Xment*, where *X* is an independently occurring verb)," citing the evidence in (33) in support of this claim. If this is a solid generalization, then it constitutes an apparent deviation from the integral stem criterion, since it entails that when the adjective-forming [[-**al**]] rule operates on a noun stem in *-ment*, its application is sensitive to the status of a proper part of that stem as an independently occurring verb (a characteristic that does not persist to the noun stem itself).[11]

(33)
ornament	*$orna_V$	ornamental
excrement	*$excre_V$	excremental
regiment	*$regi_V$	regimental
fragment	*$frag_V$	fragmental
employment	employ	*employmental
discernment	discern	*discernmental
containment	contain	*containmental
derangement	derange	*derangemental

In Chapter 5, I examine an apparent deviation from the integral stem criterion in Sanskrit verb morphology; this deviation proves to be merely apparent in a rule-combining approach to Sanskrit morphotactics.

1.5.9 The Rule Opposition Criterion

According to this criterion, relations of paradigmatic opposition among rules of inflectional exponence are, canonically, relations among individual rules. In applying this criterion, it is important to be clear about the nature of paradigmatic opposition. In syntax, constituents that have the same distribution are in paradigmatic opposition; for instance, *dog* and *cat* are in paradigmatic opposition because they are distributionally alike. In inflectional morphology, by contrast, paradigmatic opposition refers to two different things.

First, the word forms realizing different cells of a lexeme's paradigm are in paradigmatic opposition, not because they are distributionally alike (which in general they are not), but precisely because they are different realizations of the same lexeme; in this sense, *sings* and *sung* are in paradigmatic opposition.

Second, the individual rules of exponence available for a lexeme's inflection are in paradigmatic opposition if the application of one excludes the

---

[11] The well-formedness of *developmental*, *governmental*, and *judgmental* raises doubts about the claimed pattern of sensitivity.

application of the other(s); thus, the ⟦-en⟧ and ⟦-ing⟧ rules that introduce the suffixes -en and -ing in *eaten* and *eating* are in paradigmatic opposition. In some instances, rules of exponence are in paradigmatic opposition because they realize incompatible content; thus, ⟦-en⟧ and ⟦-ing⟧ are mutually exclusive in their application because the properties that they realize ('past participle' and 'present participle') are incompatible properties. In other instances, the rules of exponence are in paradigmatic opposition not as an effect of incompatible content, but because one rule overrides the other(s) in accordance with Pāṇini's principle; thus, the rules ⟦-t⟧ and ⟦-ed⟧ that realize the property 'past participle' through the suffixation of *-t* and *-ed* are mutually exclusive in their application because the domain-of-application of ⟦-t⟧ is narrower than that of the default rule ⟦-ed⟧, which it therefore overrides in the inflection of verbs such as MEAN, LEAVE, and FEEL (with past participles *meant*, *left*, and *felt*).

The inclination is to assume that rules of inflectional affixation are in paradigmatic opposition if they fill (or compete to fill) the same "slot" in a linear sequence of affix positions. In many instances, this is a harmless assumption; thus, in Swahili verb inflection, the rules of tense prefixation are in paradigmatic opposition and they fill the same linear slot, represented as Slot –II in Table 1.3. In some instances, however, rules that are in paradigmatic opposition situate affixes in different linear positions. In Fula (Senegambian; Nigeria), for example, the subject-agreement rules employed in certain tenses are prefixal for some types of subjects and suffixal for others (as e.g. in the relative past active, where *'o-looti* 's/he washed', *min-looti* 'we washed' contrast with *lootu-mi* 'I washed', *lootu-ɗaa* 'you (sg) washed'; Arnott 1970: 191); these rules are in paradigmatic opposition not because they fill the same slot in a linear sequence of affix positions (they don't), but because they occupy the same position in the sequence of rule applications defining Fula verb forms.

According to the rule opposition criterion, relations of paradigmatic opposition among rules are, canonically, relations among individual rules, such as the ⟦-t⟧ rule defining the form *mean-t* and the ⟦-en⟧ rule defining the form *eat-en*. There are, however, apparent deviations from this canonical pattern – instances in which a relation of paradigmatic opposition seems to exist between a single rule and a sequence of rules, where a single rule appears to compete with some sequence of rules for the same position in the succession of rule applications defining a language's inflection. An example is the Latin rule expressing the second-person plural passive by means of *-minī* in *laudā-minī* 'you (PL) are praised'; on first consideration, the rule of *-minī* suffixation

Table 1.3 *Plural personal forms of Swahili* KUSOMA *'read' in three tenses*

('we are reading it', etc., with Class 7 object concord)

		Present					Past					Future				
		-IV	-III	-II	-I	STEM	-IV	-III	-II	-I	STEM	-IV	-III	-II	-I	STEM
Positive	1PL		tu-	na-	ki-	soma		tu-	li-	ki-	soma		tu-	ta-	ki-	soma
	2PL		m-	na-	ki-	soma		m-	li-	ki-	soma		m-	ta-	ki-	soma
	3PL		wa-	na-	ki-	soma		wa-	li-	ki-	soma		wa-	ta-	ki-	soma
Negative	1PL	ha-	tu-	na-	ki-	soma	ha-	tu-	ku-	ki-	soma	ha-	tu-	ta-	ki-	soma
	2PL	ha-	m-	na-	ki-	soma	ha-	m-	ku-	ki-	soma	ha-	m-	ta-	ki-	soma
	3PL	ha-	wa-	na-	ki-	soma	ha-	wa-	ku-	ki-	soma	ha-	wa-	ta-	ki-	soma

appears to stand in paradigmatic opposition to rule sequences consisting of a rule expressing subject agreement followed by a rule expressing passive voice, as in the definition of *laudā-t-ur* 's/he is praised', *lauda-nt-ur* 'they are praised', and so on.

In Chapter 5, I examine this apparent deviation from the rule opposition criterion in Latin and other apparent deviations in Limbu and Sanskrit; a rule-combining approach to morphotactics reveals these deviations to be merely apparent.

1.5.10 The Affix Directionality Criterion
According to the affix directionality criterion, the affix introduced by a rule is always in the same linear order with respect to its operand (i.e. to the expression on which the rule operates). The rule that introduces the indicative negative affix *ha-* in the definition of Swahili *ha-tu-ta-ki-soma* 'we shall not read it' is canonical with respect to this criterion, since it invariably places *ha-* in prefixal position. By contrast, the rule introducing the preterite affix *no* in Fula seems not to satisfy this criterion, apparently serving in some instances as a suffix (as in *'o-wallii-no* 'he had helped', a general past active form of the verb WALL 'help') and in other instances as a prefix (as in *'o-don-no-walla'* 'he was helping', a continuous-(i) active form of WALL); see Arnott (1970: 217f.).

In Chapters 7 and 8, I examine apparent deviations from the affix directionality criterion in Noon, Lithuanian, and Swahili; the rule-combining approach to morphotactics reveals every one of these deviations to be merely apparent.

1.6 Prospect

The ten morphotactic criteria discussed in Section 1.5 are canonical criteria; they do not exclude the incidence of noncanonical phenomena that deviate from them. In the chapters that follow, I discuss a range of morphotactic phenomena involving combinations of rules of inflectional or derivational exponence. Some such combinations entail genuine deviations from the canonical morphotactic criteria; others have the effect of reconciling superficially recalcitrant phenomena with these criteria.

In Chapter 2 ('Rule Combinations'), I present a formal basis for discussing rule combinations. Ordinary composition is the simplest, default mode of rule combination, but other modes of combination also exist; these include holistic combinations (a type of rule combination that expresses special content), aggregations (a type of rule combination in which one rule operates on the other rule's affix), and counterpotentiations (a type of rule combination whose domain-of-definition is disjoint from that of its 'inner' rule).

In Chapter 3 ('Dependent Rules and Carrier Rules'), I discuss the rule-based equivalent of the distinction (Harris 2017: 54) between dependent affixes and carrier affixes. A dependent rule is a rule whose applicability depends on the application of a carrier rule. The morphotactics of dependent rules fails to conform to the rule independence criterion; because dependent rules often participate in the expression of periodic multiple exponence (Harris 2017: 55), they may also deviate from the unique sequence criterion. I discuss examples of dependent rules from Limbu and Sanskrit. In such cases, the relation between a dependent rule and its carrier rule can be modeled as a relation of rule composition.

In Chapter 4 ('Rule Composition and Rule Ordering'), rule composition is shown to account for an important class of deviations from the parallel sequence and unique sequence criteria. These include (i) cases in which the applicational sequence of rules realizing different properties in the same inflectional categories depends on which properties they realize, and (ii) cases in which the same rules may apply in more than one sequence. In cases of type (i), different rules participate in different patterns of composition; in cases of type (ii), distinct patterns of composition exist as equivalent alternatives.

If the integral stem criterion and the rule opposition criterion are taken as criteria relating purely to simple rules of exponence, a number of deviations arise. In Chapter 5 ('Extending Canonical Morphotactic Criteria to Composite Rules'), I draw on evidence from Sanskrit, Latin, and Limbu to show that such deviations can be resolved by extending the coverage of these two criteria to include composite rules as well as simple rules.

One kind of evidence supporting the morphotactic holism hypothesis (3) is the fact that two rules of exponence may combine to express content that neither rule expresses on its own. In Chapter 6 ('Rule Combinations Expressing Holistic Content'), I examine a number of rule combinations of this sort; these deviate from the compositional content criterion. I show that Breton verb inflection presents numerous instances of holistic rule combination; I propose a general formal means of modeling such combinations. I further show that holistic content is an emergent property of some rule combinations, illustrating with evidence from Limbu verb inflection; and I show that the same rules may enter into more than one holistic combination, exemplifying with evidence from Old English verb inflection.

In Chapter 7 ('Rule Aggregation'), I discuss rule aggregation, a noncanonical mode of rule combination in which one rule takes another rule's affix as its operand. I examine two instances of this phenomenon in detail, one involving adjective inflection in Noon, the other involving the inflection of reflexive verbs in Lithuanian. Rule aggregations deviate from the stem operand criterion but resolve certain apparent deviations from the affix directionality criterion. Rule aggregations therefore differ from "ambifixal" rules of exponence that define alternative directionalities for the same affix, which conform to the stem operand criterion but deviate from the affix directionality criterion; I exemplify this contrast with evidence from Gurma (Gur; Burkina Faso).

In Chapters 8 and 9, I discuss the morphotactics of verb inflection in Swahili and Murrinhpatha. Both systems of verb inflection are highly complex, but scrutiny reveals them to be complex in quite different ways. The analysis in Chapter 8 ('Complex Morphotactic Interactions in Swahili') focuses on the polyfunctionality of a verb's argument-coding rules, on the rules expressing verbal negation, and on the rules by which a relative verb form inflects for the properties of its relativized argument. The richness of the Swahili patterns of rule combination stems from the fact that they involve the extensive interaction of two different modes of rule combination (composition and aggregation). These interactions engender deviations from the rule independence criterion, the parallel sequence criterion, the unique sequence criterion, and the stem operand criterion; at the same time, they produce apparent deviations from the rule opposition criterion and the affix directionality criterion that prove to be merely apparent under a rule-combining approach to morphotactics.

The Murrinhpatha analysis in Chapter 9 ('The Nonassociativity of Rule Composition in Murrinhpatha') involves a dimension of complexity very different from that of Swahili. Where Swahili verb inflection involves the complex interaction of different modes of rule combination, Murrinhpatha verb inflection involves only a single mode of combination (composition), but allows the same rules to compose in more than one way to express contrasting content. The Murrinhpatha system presents evidence that the composition of three rules of inflectional morphology isn't invariably associative – an unexpected finding, given the associativity of function composition in set theory. This peculiarity of inflectional rule composition results from the fact that certain rules of Murrinhpatha verb inflection express either subject concord or object concord depending upon the rule with which they compose. This fact affords an unprecedented account for a widely observable pattern of ambiguity in Murrinhpatha verb forms.

1.6 Prospect

In Chapter 10 ('Potentiation and Counterpotentiation'), I turn to the analysis of rule combinations in the domain of derivational morphology. I show that potentiation (Williams 1981) is a subcase of rule composition in which the domain-of-definition of the composite rule's 'inner' rule is that of the composite itself. I contrast potentiation (e.g. the relation between *-able* and *-ity* in *reliable/reliability*) with counterpotentiation (e.g. the relation between *-al* and *-ic* in *whimsical/*whimsic*), in which the domain-of-definition of a combined rule is not a subset of that of its inner rule. Counterpotentiations may be pleonastic or compositionally motivated.

In Chapter 11 ('Rule Combinations and Morphological Simplicity'), I discuss the relation between rule combinations and morphological simplicity both from the perspective of language processing and from that of language change. I cite experimental psycholinguistic evidence that demonstrates the existence of formulaic rule combinations, whose storage facilitates morphological processing. I argue that, like word combinations in syntax, morphological rule combinations are likely to be formulaic if they are especially frequent, or have a conventional character, or are semantically noncompositional. Rule combinations may also simplify historically by the process of "affix telescoping."

In Chapter 12 ('Rule-combining Morphotactics and Morphological Theories'), I discuss the exponence-driven, rule-combining approach to morphotactics within the wider context of current morphological theories. Certain theories (e.g. Paradigm Function Morphology, Construction Morphology) easily accommodate this approach and could benefit by incorporating it. At the same time, certain other theories (Distributed Morphology, Information-based Morphology) are committed to a word-skeletal approach to morphotactics that is less obviously compatible with the rule-combining approach. The rule-combining approach affords a more parsimonious typology of morphological operations than is assumed in word-skeletal theories, and it affords a more explanatory account of a range of morphotactic phenomena.

In Chapter 13 ('Conclusions'), I summarize the variety of problematic phenomena that motivate the rule-combining approach to morphotactics, showing the particular ways in which these phenomena deviate from canonical morphotactics and the means by which their characteristics may be elucidated. I provide a closing synopsis of the set of formal definitions on which the rule-combining approach is based.

2 *Rule Combinations*

Grammatical theory has long been dominated by the assumption that affixes are morphologically minimal (or 'monomorphemic') in the sense that they are insusceptible to division into smaller grammatically significant forms. Although this assumption has sometimes been questioned in the theoretical literature and although descriptive grammars often implicitly abandon it, it remains a matter of wide consensus across the theoretical landscape. Yet, evidence suggests that affixes do in fact combine to form more complex affixes.[1] In this book, I examine some of this evidence and discuss its considerable significance from the perspective of rule-based morphology; I therefore focus less on principles of affix combination per se than on the principles by which simpler rules of exponence are combined to form more complex rules.

One might suppose that all rule combinations are alike; obviously they are alike in deviating from the minimal rule criterion (Section 1.5.1). We shall see, however, that the evidence discussed here confirms the morphotactic variety hypothesis (Section 1.2), according to which rules of exponence combine in different ways, such that the different modes of rule combination involve different kinds of deviation from the nine other criterial characteristics of canonical morphotactics discussed in Sections 1.4–1.5.

Before considering these different modes of combination, it is important to be clear about the nature of the individual rules that enter into combination. I discuss my assumptions about the characteristics of individual rules in Section 2.1, then proceed to discuss the different ways in which they combine in Sections 2.2–2.5.

In Section 2.2, I discuss rule composition, the default mode of rule combination. As I show in Chapters 3 and 4, certain patterns of rule composition constitute deviations from the rule independence criterion (Section 1.5.2), the parallel sequence criterion (Section 1.5.3), and the unique sequence criterion

---

[1] The arguments developed here are an outgrowth of several recent articles: Stump 2017a–c, 2019a, 2019c, 2020a, 2021, 2022.

(Section 1.5.4); at the same time, the postulation of rule composition makes it possible to reconcile superficially problematic phenomena with the integral stem criterion (Section 1.5.8) and the rule opposition criterion (Section 1.5.9), as I show in Chapter 5.

Although composition is the default mode of rule combination, other sorts of combination are also possible; these differ from ordinary rule composition in exhibiting unexpected patterns in the content that they express, in their morphological operands, or in their domains-of-definition. I refer to these other sorts of rule combinations as ***special rule combinations***, among which I distinguish holistic combinations, aggregations, and counterpotentiations.

In Section 2.3, I discuss holistic rule combination, a mode of rule combination that accounts for deviations from the compositional content criterion (Section 1.5.5) – cases in which a combination of rules realizes more than the sum of the content that those rules realize individually.

In Section 2.4, I discuss rule aggregation, a mode of rule combination that accounts for deviations from the stem operand criterion (Section 1.5.6); these are cases in which a rule operates not on a stem, but on the affix introduced by the rule with which it is aggregated. The postulation of rule aggregation also has the effect of reconciling the affix directionality criterion (Section 1.5.10) with certain apparent deviations from it.

In Section 2.5, I discuss counterpotentiation, a mode of rule combination that accounts for deviations from the intermediate well-formedness criterion (Section 1.5.7) – cases in which the result of applying one rule is ill-formed unless its application is followed by that of another particular rule.

Rules of exponence can themselves be classified according to the ways in which they participate in a given mode of rule combination (Section 2.6).

In Section 2.7, I outline the elaboration of these ideas in the chapters that follow, in which I scrutinize each mode of rule combination more closely and identify its characteristics more precisely, exemplifying with detailed evidence from a variety of languages.

2.1 Some Preliminary Assumptions about Paradigms and Rules of Exponence

Before considering the varied ways in which rules of exponence combine with one another, it is important to be precise about the characteristics that the rules in question possess on their own. I assume an inferential-realizational theory of morphology embodying the fundamental principles and assumptions of Paradigm

Function Morphology (PFM).[2] This theory makes an essential distinction between rules of inflection (Section 2.1.1) and rules of derivation (Section 2.1.2).[3]

2.1.1 Inflectional Morphology

A language's inflectional morphology specifies the word forms that realize a given lexeme when it is associated with different sets of morphosyntactic properties. The full set of such forms constitutes the lexeme's paradigm. I follow Stump (2016) in assuming that a lexeme's paradigm can be represented in three different ways, corresponding to three different levels of abstraction. A lexeme's content paradigm specifies exactly the information relevant to the syntactic distribution and semantic interpretation of its word forms; by contrast, its form paradigm specifies exactly the information relevant to the morphological realization of its word forms, and its realized paradigm accordingly specifies the fully realized forms determined by the information in its form paradigm. Two lexemes may have content paradigms that are alike but have form paradigms (hence realized paradigms) that are significantly different. For example, the content paradigms of the verbal lexemes STEER and DRIVE are alike, since their word forms are completely parallel in their syntax and semantics, yet these lexemes have significantly different form paradigms and realized paradigms, since their word forms differ in their morphological realization. The verb STEER has the single stem *steer-*, and the morphological realization of both its past-tense form *steered* and its past-participial form *steered* involves the ⟦-**ed**⟧ rule. By contrast, the verb DRIVE has the three stems *drive-*, *drove-*, and *driv-*, and the morphological realization of its past-tense and past-participial forms does not involve the ⟦-**ed**⟧ rule: the past-tense form *drove* simply involves the selection of its second stem, and the past-participial form *driven* involves the selection of its third stem together with the ⟦-**en**⟧ rule. Because the distinction between content

---

[2] Some of the principal references relating to PFM are Stump 1991, 1993, 2001, 2012, 2016, 2019b, 2020b; Stewart & Stump 2007; Spencer 2005, 2013; and Spencer & Stump 2013.

[3] It is sometimes asserted that the distinction between inflection and derivation cannot be theoretically motivated. It is true that an inflectional rule and a derivational rule may involve the same operation (e.g. the operation of *-s* suffixation employed in the inflection of *dogs* and in such playful adjectival derivations as *bonkers* and *preggers*); that classes of derivational stems may be characterized by membership in a particular inflection class (e.g. the fact that derived causatives in Sanskrit generally belong to the tenth conjugation; Stump 2005); that derivational morphology may be pressed into service in the formation of a lexeme's inventory of inflectional stems (e.g. the use of the noun-forming suffix *-enn* of Breton *uhel* 'high' → *uhel-enn* 'elevated place' to form the singular stem of a noun such as *spilh-enn* 'pin', pl. *spilh-où*; Stump 1990); and so on. But such phenomena in no way alter the fact that on a theoretical plane, rules of inflection and rules of derivation do different things. Inflectional rules specify the forms assumed by a given lexeme in different syntactic and semantic contexts; derivational rules specify differences in form and content between related lexemes.

paradigms, form paradigms, and realized paradigms will prove recurrently useful in the analysis of a language's morphotactics, I maintain the following formal distinction among them.

A lexeme L's ***content paradigm*** is a set of ***content cells***, each the pairing of L with a morphosyntactic property set with which L may be associated in syntax and relative to which it may be interpreted semantically.

> *Examples:* The content paradigm of the English nominal lexeme SHOE is the set {⟨SHOE, {sg}⟩, ⟨SHOE, {pl}⟩}; that of LEAF is the set {⟨LEAF, {sg}⟩, ⟨LEAF, {pl}⟩}.
>
> The content paradigm of the English verbal lexeme WALK is the set {⟨WALK, {3sg prs ind}⟩, ⟨WALK, {prs ind}⟩, ⟨WALK, {pst ind}⟩, ⟨WALK, {irr}⟩, ⟨WALK, {pst ptcp}⟩,⟨WALK, {prs ptcp}⟩, ⟨WALK, {inf}⟩}; that of WRITE is the set {⟨WRITE, {3sg prs ind}⟩, ⟨WRITE, {prs ind}⟩, ⟨WRITE, {pst ind}⟩, ⟨WRITE, {irr}⟩, ⟨WRITE, {pst ptcp}⟩,⟨WRITE, {prs ptcp}⟩, ⟨WRITE, {inf}⟩}.

A lexeme L's ***form paradigm*** is a set of ***form cells***, each the pairing of some stem Z of L with a property set σ such that ⟨Z, σ⟩ determines L's morphological realization as a particular word form.

> *Examples:* The form paradigm of the English nominal lexeme SHOE is the set {⟨*shoe-*, {sg}⟩, ⟨*shoe-*, {pl}⟩}; that of LEAF is the set {⟨*leaf-*, {sg}⟩, ⟨*leav-*, {pl}⟩}.
>
> The form paradigm of the English verbal lexeme WALK is the set {⟨*walk-*, {3sg prs ind}⟩, ⟨*walk-*, {prs ind}⟩, ⟨*walk-*, {pst ind}⟩, ⟨*walk*, {irr}⟩, ⟨*walk-*, {pst ptcp}⟩, ⟨*walk-*, {prs ptcp}⟩, ⟨*walk-*, {inf}⟩}; that of WRITE is the set {⟨*write-*, {3sg prs ind}⟩, ⟨*write-*, {prs ind}⟩, ⟨*wrote-*, {strong pst ind}⟩, ⟨*wrote-*, {strong irr}⟩, ⟨*writt-*, {strong pst ptcp}⟩, ⟨*write-*, {prs ptcp}⟩, ⟨*write-*, {inf}⟩}.

For each form cell ⟨Z, σ⟩ in a lexeme's form paradigm, there is a word form *w* such that ⟨Z, σ⟩ has the ***realized cell*** ⟨*w*, σ⟩ as its realization; the full set of realized cells realizing the cells in a lexeme L's form paradigm constitute L's ***realized paradigm***.

> *Examples:* The realized paradigm of the English nominal lexeme SHOE is the set {⟨*shoe*, {sg}⟩, ⟨*shoes*, {pl}⟩}; that of LEAF is the set {⟨*leaf*, {sg}⟩, ⟨*leaves*, {pl}⟩}.
>
> The realized paradigm of the English verbal lexeme WALK is the set {⟨*walks*, {3sg prs ind}⟩, ⟨*walk*, {prs ind}⟩, ⟨*walked*, {pst ind}⟩, ⟨*walked*, {irr}⟩, ⟨*walked*, {pst ptcp}⟩, ⟨*walking*, {prs ptcp}⟩, ⟨*walk*, {inf}⟩}; that of WRITE is the set {⟨*writes*, {3sg prs ind}⟩, ⟨*write*, {prs ind}⟩, ⟨*wrote*, {strong pst ind}⟩, ⟨*wrote*, {strong irr}⟩, ⟨*written*, {strong pst ptcp}⟩, ⟨*writing*, {prs ptcp}⟩, ⟨*write*, {inf}⟩}.

Once these three sorts of paradigms are distinguished, a language's inflectional morphology can be seen as a system of principles relating the three sorts of paradigm: a principle of form correspondence relates each cell in a lexeme L's content paradigm with a corresponding cell in L's form paradigm, and a paradigm function relates each cell in L's form paradigm (and by extension, the corresponding cell in L's content paradigm) with the cell in L's realized paradigm by which it is realized. Consider these notions in somewhat more detail.

Generally, each content cell $\langle L, \rho \rangle$ has a *form correspondent*; this is a form cell $\langle Z, \sigma \rangle$ in which Z is a stem of L. Where $\langle Z, \sigma \rangle$ is the form correspondent of $\langle L, \rho \rangle$, the property sets σ and ρ are, in the simplest cases, the same property set. But in some cases, the form correspondent's property set σ may include purely morphological properties that are absent from ρ; for instance, σ may include a property specifying the inflection class of the stem Z. In such cases, σ and ρ aren't identical, but ρ is instead a proper subset of σ.

> *Examples:* The content cell $\langle \text{SHOE}, \{\text{pl}\} \rangle$ has the form cell $\langle \textit{shoe-}, \{\text{pl}\} \rangle$ as its form correspondent.
> The content cell $\langle \text{LEAF}, \{\text{pl}\} \rangle$ has the form cell $\langle \textit{leav-}, \{\text{pl}\} \rangle$ as its form correspondent.
> The content cell $\langle \text{WALK}, \{\text{pst ptcp}\} \rangle$ has the form cell $\langle \textit{walk-}, \{\text{pst ptcp}\} \rangle$ as its form correspondent, since by default, *walk-* inflects as a weak verb.
> The content cell $\langle \text{WRITE}, \{\text{pst ptcp}\} \rangle$ has the form cell $\langle \textit{writt-}, \{\text{strong pst ptcp}\} \rangle$ as its form correspondent, since *writt-* inflects as a strong verb.

I use the notation $\| \langle L, \rho \rangle \|$ to represent the form correspondent of the content cell $\langle L, \rho \rangle$.

> *Examples:* $\| \langle \text{SHOE}, \{\text{pl}\} \rangle \| = \langle \textit{shoe-}, \{\text{pl}\} \rangle$.
> $\| \langle \text{LEAF}, \{\text{pl}\} \rangle \| = \langle \textit{leav-}, \{\text{pl}\} \rangle$.
> $\| \langle \text{WALK}, \{\text{pst ptcp}\} \rangle \| = \langle \textit{walk-}, \{\text{pst ptcp}\} \rangle$.
> $\| \langle \text{WRITE}, \{\text{pst ptcp}\} \rangle \| = \langle \textit{writt-}, \{\text{strong pst ptcp}\} \rangle$.

In the cases at issue in this book, $\| \langle L, \rho \rangle \|$ (i.e. the form correspondent of $\langle L, \rho \rangle$) is a form cell $\langle Z, [\rho \cup \textit{ic}(Z)] \rangle$, where Z is a stem of L and $\textit{ic}(Z)$ is the (possibly empty) set of inflection-class properties associated with Z.[4] In any given case, the particular identity of stem Z is determined by a stem-selection rule.

---

[4] The maximally general account of inflectional morphology developed by Stump 2016 also accommodates special cases in which a content cell $\langle L, \rho \rangle$ has a form correspondent $\langle Z, \sigma \rangle$ such that ρ is not a subset of σ. These are cases in which there is a mismatch between the property set ρ determining a word form's syntax and semantics and the property set σ determining that word form's morphological realization; phenomena such as syncretism and deponency involve mismatches of this sort. See Stump (2016: 252ff.) for detailed discussion.

A stem-selection rule has the form in (1), in which τ is a morphosyntactic property set and f is a function from lexemes to stems. Rule (1) is applicable to the content cell ⟨L, ρ⟩ only if ρ is an extension[5] of τ, and the result of applying (1) to ⟨L, ρ⟩ is ⟨f(L), [ρ ∪ ic(f(L))]⟩; thus, if f(L) = Z, the result of applying (1) to ⟨L, ρ⟩ is ⟨Z, [ρ ∪ ic(Z)]⟩. If two or more stem-selection rules are applicable to a content cell, it is the narrowest of these that determines that cell's form correspondent. Given the two stem-selection rules in (1) and (2), (1) is narrower than (2) if and only if τ' is a proper subset of τ; in that case, (1) overrides (2) in determining the form correspondent of any content cell to which (1) and (2) are both applicable.

(1)   Stem-selection rule: τ, f

(2)   Stem-selection rule: τ', g

   Example: Where (3) is the narrowest stem-selection rule that is applicable to ⟨WRITE, {pst ptcp}⟩, then assuming that ic(writt-) = {strong}, (3) entails that ‖ ⟨WRITE, {pst ptcp}⟩ ‖ = ⟨writt-, {strong pst ptcp}⟩.

(3)   Stem-selection rule: {pst ptcp}, {WRITE → writt-; WALK → walk-; etc.}

   Example: Where (4) is the narrowest stem-selection rule that is applicable to ⟨LEAF, {pl}⟩, then assuming that ic(leav-) = { }, (4) entails that ‖ ⟨LEAF, {pl}⟩ ‖ = ⟨leav-, {pl}⟩.

(4)   Stem-selection rule: {pl}, {LEAF → leav-; SHOE → shoe-; etc.}

Form correspondence is the central relation between the cells in a lexeme's content paradigm and the cells in its form paradigm. A language's paradigm function in turn relates each cell in a lexeme L's form paradigm (and by extension, the corresponding cell in L's content paradigm) to a cell in L's realized paradigm. Let $\mathcal{L}$ be any language in which the realized cell ⟨w, σ⟩ is the realization of ‖ ⟨L, ρ⟩ ‖; in that case, the *paradigm function* PF of $\mathcal{L}$ is such that PF(⟨L, ρ⟩) = PF(‖ ⟨L, ρ⟩ ‖) = ⟨w, σ⟩. The definition of a language's inflectional morphotactics is, in effect, nothing other than the definition of its paradigm function.

   Examples: The inflectional morphotactics of English is a paradigm function whose definition entails the following equations (among innumerable others):

   PF(⟨SHOE, {pl}⟩) = PF(⟨shoe-, {pl}⟩) = ⟨shoes, {pl}⟩.
   PF(⟨LEAF, {pl}⟩) = PF(⟨leav-, {pl}⟩) = ⟨leaves, {pl}⟩.
   PF(⟨WALK, {pst ptcp}⟩) = PF(⟨walk-, {pst ptcp}⟩)
                                              = ⟨walked, {pst ptcp}⟩.
   PF(⟨WRITE, {pst ptcp}⟩) = PF(⟨writt-, {strong pst ptcp}⟩)
                                              = ⟨written, {strong pst ptcp}⟩.

---

[5] The extension relation is similar (though not identical) to the superset relation. 'Extension' is defined in (25a).

A language's paradigm function is defined by means of rules of inflectional exponence such that for any content cell ⟨L, ρ⟩, the rules apply to ‖ ⟨L, ρ⟩ ‖ to produce the realized cell ⟨w, σ⟩, which realizes both ‖ ⟨L, ρ⟩ ‖ and ⟨L, ρ⟩. In order to formulate rules of inflectional exponence with the necessary precision, it is useful to draw upon some basic set-theoretic notions.

In set theory, a function f from set P to set Q is a function that associates each member of P with at most one member of Q. In the particular case in which P and Q are the same set – in which a function f associates each member of set P with at most one member of the same set P – f is said to be a ***function in the set P***. If f associates every member of P with a member of Q, then f is a ***total function*** from P to Q; a total function in the set P is a function that associates every member of P with exactly one member of P. If f associates some members of P but not others with members of Q, then f is a ***partial function*** from P to Q; a partial function in the set P is a function that associates some but not all members of P with members of P.

In the analyses developed here, every rule of inflectional exponence is seen as a partial function in the set of ⟨form, property set⟩ pairings. A rule of inflectional exponence has the form in (5), where τ is the property set representing the content realized by the rule, f is the morphological operation by means of which this content is realized, and C is the category of forms on which f operates in default uses of the rule. (This default is overridden in instances of aggregation; Section 2.4.)

(5)   ***Format for a rule of inflectional exponence:*** [C, τ : f]

Given the pairing ⟨Z, σ⟩ of a stem Z with a property set σ, a rule having the form in (5) is applicable to ⟨Z, σ⟩ if and only if Z belongs to category C and σ is an extension of τ. Where ⟨Z, σ⟩ is such a pairing, the result of applying (5) to ⟨Z, σ⟩ is the pairing ⟨f(Z), σ⟩. In the particular case in which f is an operation of -*x* suffixation or *y*- prefixation, I represent f as '-*x*' or '*y*-', respectively.

> *Example:* Part of the definition of the English paradigm function is the rule of inflectional exponence in (6), which applies to the form cell ⟨*walk*, {pst ptcp}⟩ (= the form correspondent of ⟨WALK, {pst ptcp}⟩) to yield the realized cell ⟨*walked*, {pst ptcp}⟩.
>
> (6)   ⟦**-ed**⟧ : [V, {pst} : -*ed*]

If two realization rules are both applicable to the pairing ⟨Z, σ⟩, this competition is resolved in favor of the narrower rule by Pāṇini's principle (Stump 2001: 22), for which I assume the formulation in (7).

(7) Pāṇini's principle: If the domain of Rule R_1 is a proper subset of that of Rule R_2, the application of R_1 prevails over that of R_2 in any instance in which they compete.

> *Example:* In the definition of the English paradigm function, the realization rules (6) and (8) compete in the realization of ⟨*writt-*, {strong pst ptcp}⟩; because it is restricted to the realization of strong verbs' past participles, (8) overrides (6) in applying to the form cell ⟨*writt-*, {strong pst ptcp}⟩, licensing the equation (9).
>
> (8) ⟦**-en**⟧ : [V, {strong pst ptcp} : *-en*]
>
> (9) PF(⟨WRITE, {pst ptcp}⟩) = PF(⟨*writt-*, {strong pst ptcp}⟩)
> $\qquad\qquad\qquad\quad$ = ⟨*written*, {strong pst ptcp}⟩

Throughout, I make an important set of assumptions about morphosyntactic properties and the inflectional categories to which they belong. First, I assume that an ***atomic*** property (one which isn't itself a set of other properties) unambiguously belongs to a particular inflectional category; for example, the property 'past' is an unambiguous member of the TENSE category, that the property 'plural' is an unambiguous member of the NUMBER category, and so on. In instances in which there may be some doubt about the inflectional category to which a property belongs, I specify the inflectional category as part of the property's name; for example, the property of noun class 1 in Swahili is abbreviated as 'NC1' rather than simply as '1'.

A property may also be ***set-based*** – that is, it may itself be a set of other properties. A set-based property P may be determinate or indeterminate with respect to its inflectional category membership. A set-based property P is ***category-determinate*** if and only if P contains a property that uniquely determines P's inflectional category membership; for example, the set-based property {subject 1 sg} is category-determinate, since the property 'subject' makes it an unambiguous member of the SUBJECT AGREEMENT category. By contrast, a set-based property P is ***category-indeterminate*** if and only if P lacks any property that uniquely determines P's inflectional category membership. Thus, in a language whose verbs inflect for both subject agreement and object agreement, the set-based property {1 sg} is category-indeterminate, since it has well-formed extensions belonging to different inflectional categories: the extension {subject 1 sg} belongs to the SUBJECT AGREEMENT category, but the extension {object 1 sg} belongs to the OBJECT AGREEMENT category.

44 *Rule Combinations*

In Chapters 8 and 9, I propose analyses of the conjugational systems of Swahili and Murrinhpatha that make important use of the distinction between set-based properties that are category-determinate and those that are category-indeterminate. In these analyses, I assume the **Category Determination Principle** in (10).[6] In informal terms, this is the principle that a rule whose morphosyntactic content is ambiguous (because it contains a category-indeterminate property) is disambiguated by the first rule with which it composes. More precisely, a rule realizing a category-indeterminate property P always combines with another rule to produce a rule that realizes a category-determinate extension of P.

(10) Category Determination Principle
If R is a rule of inflectional exponence that realizes a category-indeterminate property P, R always combines with a rule that realizes a set-based property Q such that the unification [P ⊔ Q] is a set-based property that is well-formed and category-determinate.

2.1.2 *Derivational Morphology*

Because rules of derivation relate one lexeme's characteristics to those of a distinct lexeme, it is necessary to represent rules of derivational exponence differently from rules of inflectional exponence. At the root of this difference is the distinction between a function's domain and its domain-of-definition.

The ***domain*** of a function f is the set P containing the elements to which f may apply. The members of P to which f actually applies (i.e. for which it supplies a defined value) is the function's ***domain-of-definition***. Total and partial functions can be distinguished by reference to the difference between a function's domain and its domain-of-definition. If f is a total function, its domain-of-definition equals its domain; if f is a partial function, its domain-of-definition is a proper subset of its domain.

The nonlinguistic (and nonmathematical) example in Figure 2.1 can be used to illustrate. The ***registered-to-vote-in*** function applies to a US citizen (a member of set C) to give the state (the member of set S) in which they are registered to vote in a presidential election: applying this function to me gives the value Kansas, the state where I am registered to vote. This is a partial function, since not all US citizens are registered to vote. The domain of this function is the set C of US citizens; the domain-of-definition is R, the proper subset of US citizens who are registered to vote.

---

[6] The definition of unification relevant to (10) is presented in (25b).

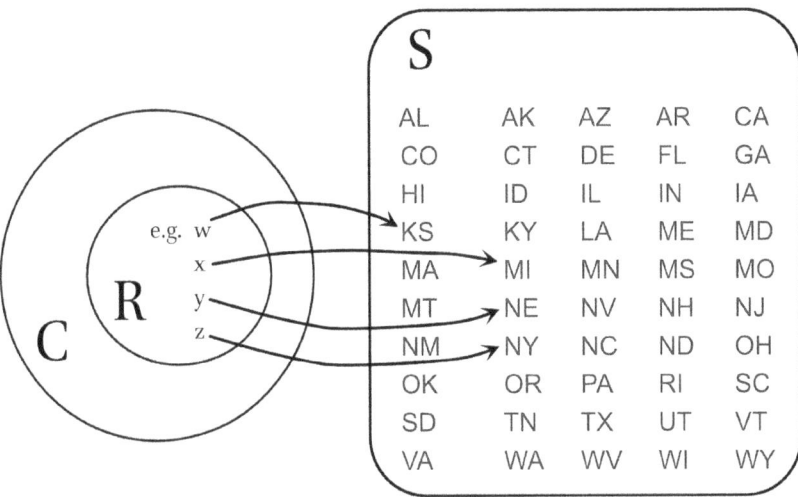

Figure 2.1 The **registered-to-vote-in** function

In the formalism assumed here, rules of inflectional exponence and rules of derivational exponence are both treated as partial functions; that is, a rule of either sort has a domain-of-definition that is a proper subset of the rule's domain. I assume, however, that in the formulation of a rule of inflectional exponence, it is sufficient to specify the domain without specifying the domain-of-definition because the latter is strictly deducible from the manner in which the rule interacts with other rules. Consider again rule (6), which defines English past-tense verb forms in *-ed*. The domain of this rule is that of ⟨form, content⟩ pairings of the type ⟨Z, τ⟩, where Z is a verb stem and {pst} ⊆ τ; some of the members of this domain are the pairings in (10). Although all of the pairings in (10) belong to the domain of (6), not all belong to its domain-of-definition: (10a) does, but (10b) and (10c) do not. Still, this fact about the domain-of-definition of (6) need not figure in its formulation. Instead, one need only acknowledge that (6) coexists with competing rules that override it in the inflection of form cells such as (10b) and (10c). In general, if competing inflectional rules are applicable to a given ⟨form, content⟩ pairing, then it is the rule with the narrowest domain that prevails (= Pāṇini's principle (7)).

(10) a. ⟨*walk-*, {pst ind}⟩ (= ‖ ⟨WALK, {pst ind}⟩ ‖)
 b. ⟨*mean-*, {*t*-class pst ind}⟩ (= ‖ ⟨MEAN, {pst ind}⟩ ‖)
 c. ⟨*wrote-*, {strong pst ind}⟩ (= ‖ ⟨WRITE, {pst ind}⟩ ‖)

Verb stems of the *t*-class conjugation (e.g. the stems *leave*, *lose*, and *mean*) are subject to rule (11), whose domain (pairings of the type ⟨Z, τ⟩, where Z is a *t*-class verb stem and {*t*-class pst} ⊆ τ) is a proper subset of that of rule (6); verb stems belonging to the strong class (e.g. the stems *wrote*, *dug*, and *sang*) are subject to rule (12), whose domain (pairings of the type ⟨Z, τ⟩, where Z is a strong verb stem and {strong pst} ⊆ τ) is a proper subset of that of rule (6); and so on. The fact that (6) competes with the rules in (11) and (12) makes it unnecessary to delineate its domain-of-definition as part of its formulation, since overriding rules such as (11) and (12) suffice to distinguish its domain-of-definition from its full domain in ways that are completely predictable (by means of Pāṇini's principle).

(11)   ⟦-t⟧ : [V, {*t*-class pst} : X → X′-*t*],

   where X′ is the result of laxing and lowering any tense vowel in the final syllable of X.

(12)   ⟦X → X⟧ : [V, {strong pst} : X → X]

The situation is different with derivational rules. Consider, for example, the derivational rule that defines denominal verbs in -*ize*. This rule defines the relation between nominal lexemes (such as the adjective STABLE and the noun FOSSIL) and the corresponding inchoative/causative verbs (STABILIZE, FOSSILIZE). The rule's domain is the set of ⟨lexeme, stem, lexicosemantic category⟩ triplets of the types ⟨L, Z, Adjective⟩ and ⟨L, Z, Noun⟩, of which its domain-of-definition is a proper subset. Here, however, the members of the full domain that are not members of the domain-of-definition are not deducible by reference to competing rules. Although the triplets in (13a,b) belong to the -*ize* rule's domain-of-definition (hence the derivation of STABILIZE, FOSSILIZE), those in (13c,d) do not. We cannot account for the absence of *tiny-ize or *soupize by appealing to an override of the -*ize* rule by some other rule; instead, we must simply assume that the -*ize* is indexed for a particular domain-of-definition.

(13)   a.   ⟨STABLE, *stable*, Adjective⟩
        b.   ⟨FOSSIL, *fossil*, Noun⟩
        c.   ⟨TINY, *tiny*, Adjective⟩
        d.   ⟨SOUP, *soup*, Noun⟩

Building on this reasoning, I assume that every rule of derivational morphology is a partial function in the set of ⟨lexeme, stem, lexicosemantic category⟩ triplets and has the form schematized in (14), whose components μ, Q and *f* are as in (15).

(14)   *Format for a rule of derivational exponence*: [μ ⇒ Q : *f*]

(15) The parts of a derivational rule as schematized in (14)
   a. μ is the rule's domain-of-definition (the specific set of triplets for which it is defined). Each such triplet is of the type ⟨lexeme, stem, lexicosemantic category⟩, e.g. ⟨STABLE, *stable*, Adjective⟩. While some rules have domains-of-definition in which all triplets contain the same lexicosemantic category, others have domains-of-definition encompassing triplets of more than one type; the domain-of-definition μ_{17} of the ⟦-**ize**⟧ rule, for example, includes both ⟨STABLE, *stable*, Adjective⟩ and ⟨FOSSIL, *fossil*, Noun⟩.
   b. Q is the lexicosemantic category of the derivative lexeme in the derivational relation defined by the rule. Q may itself be a disjunction of more specific lexicosemantic categories; the ⟦-**ize**⟧ rule, for example, defines derivatives belonging to the disjunctive category Inchoative/causative verb.
   c. *f* is the morphological operation relating the stem of the base lexeme to that of the derivative lexeme.

A rule R having the form in (14) is applicable to a triplet ⟨L, Z, P⟩ only if (a) lexeme L is a member of category P having Z as a stem, and (b) triplet ⟨L, Z, P⟩ belongs to R's domain-of-definition μ. If R is applicable to ⟨L, Z, P⟩, the result of applying R to this triplet is ⟨L', *f*(Z), Q⟩, where lexeme L' is a member of category Q having *f*(Z) as a stem.

   Example: English ordinal numerals are derived by means of the rule of derivational exponence in (16), which applies to the triplet ⟨SEVEN, *seven*, Cardinal numeral⟩ to define the triplet ⟨SEVENTH, *seventh*, Ordinal numeral⟩. The set μ_{16} is this rule's domain-of-definition; this set includes the triplet ⟨SEVEN, *seven*, Cardinal numeral⟩, but not the triplet ⟨THREE, *three*, Cardinal numeral⟩.

   (16) ⟦-**th**⟧ : [μ_{16} ⇒ Ordinal numeral : -*th*]

   Example: Members of one class of inchoative/causative verbs are derived by means of the rule of derivational exponence in (17), which applies to the triplets ⟨STABLE, *stable*, Adjective⟩ and ⟨FOSSIL, *fossil*, Noun⟩ to define the triplets ⟨STABILIZE, *stabilize*, Inchoative/causative verb⟩ and ⟨FOSSILIZE, *fossilize*, Inchoative/causative verb⟩. The set μ_{17} is this rule's domain-of-definition, which includes the triplets ⟨STABLE, *stable*, Adjective⟩ and ⟨FOSSIL, *fossil*, Noun⟩ but not the triplets ⟨TINY, *tiny*, Adjective⟩ and ⟨SOUP, *soup*, Noun⟩.

   (17) ⟦-**ize**⟧ : [μ_{17} ⇒ Inchoative/causative verb : -*ize*]

As a matter of convention, I shall often represent the lexeme in a ⟨lexeme, stem, lexicosemantic category⟩ triplet simply as 'L' with the understanding that in any such triplet ⟨L, Z, P⟩, L designates that lexeme that is a member of category P and that has Z as a stem. For example, the L in ⟨L, *face*, Noun⟩ represents the nominal lexeme FACE, while the L in ⟨L, *faceless*, Privative adjective⟩ represents the adjectival lexeme FACELESS. Thus, in a sentence such as "⟨L, *faceless*, Privative adjective⟩ derives from ⟨L, *face*, Noun⟩," the two instances of L designate distinct lexemes.

In discussing rules of derivational morphology, I assume that the formulation of a rule of derivation often underdetermines a derivative's content. In the general case, three distinct factors participate in determining the semantic interpretation of a derived lexeme. First, there is a compositional factor: where lexeme D derives from lexeme B by means of rule R, R may be associated with a semantic function $\mathcal{F}$ such that the meaning of D is the result of applying $\mathcal{F}$ to the meaning of B. For example, if ⟦**-less**⟧ is the rule of derivational exponence by which an adjective derives from a noun through the suffixation of *-less*, then it is reasonable to assume that ⟦**-less**⟧ is associated with a semantic function $\mathcal{F}$ such that $\mathcal{F}('X') =$ 'without any X, lacking any X' (e.g. *driverless* 'without any driver, lacking any driver').

Second, there is a lexical factor: where one lexeme derives from another, the two lexemes may, as a matter of convention, participate in a fixed lexicosemantic relationship. For instance, the lexicon of English includes a number of nouns naming disciplines of human activity, and a disciplinary noun typically has a corresponding practitioner noun denoting a person who works in that discipline; examples are the noun pairs on the different rows of Table 2.1. As these examples show, the difference between a disciplinary noun and its corresponding practitioner noun is morphologically variable: the disciplinary nouns don't share a common affix, nor do the practitioner nouns; the practitioner noun's stem may derive from that of the corresponding disciplinary noun (*logic* → *logician*), or the disciplinary noun's stem may derive from that of the corresponding practitioner noun (*linguist* → *linguistics*), or neither may derive from the other (*geography/geographer*). What is not variable is the semantic relation between the two nouns, which remains constant from row to row in the table. The particular morphology exhibited by a practitioner noun need not always express practitioner semantics; for instance, even though *geographer* denotes a practitioner of a particular discipline, *New Yorker*, *whiner*, and *goner* do not. Instead, the rule deriving personal nouns in *-er* must be assumed to confer only a very general meaning ('person or instrument associated with X' or the like) so that the status of *geographer* as a practitioner noun is not a direct effect of the ⟦**-er**⟧ rule but rather an effect of its lexical relation to *geography* (which is essentially the same as the lexical relation

Table 2.1 Some disciplinary nouns and the corresponding practitioner nouns in English

	Disciplinary nouns	Practitioner nouns							
		In -ic	In -e	In -icist	In -ician	In -ist	In ∅	In -er, -or	In -ian
In -ics	academ-ics	academ-ic							
	athlet-ics		athlet-e						
	phys-ics			phys-icist					
	mathemat-ics				mathemat-ician				
	econom-ics					econom-ist			
	gymnast-ics						gymnast		
In -y	geolog-y					geolog-ist			
	geograph-y							geograph-er	
	histor-y								histor-ian
In ∅	art					art-ist			
In -ure	grammar								grammar-ian
	architect-ure						architect		
	sculpt-ure							sculpt-or	
In -ic	log-ic				log-ician				
In -istics	lingu-istics					lingu-ist			

49

between *logic* and *logician* or between *linguistics* and *linguist*, notwithstanding their morphological difference). The ⟦-er⟧ rule doesn't determine the meaning of *geographer*, but at most constrains it.

Third, there is a pragmatic factor: where lexeme D derives from lexeme B, the semantic relation between B and D may be a very convoluted one, but one that language users have just agreed on. For instance, the verb *posterize* may mean 'to convert (an image) to a limited, nongradient color scheme', but it may also mean 'to humiliate (an opposing player in basketball) by executing a slam-dunk past them in a manner worthy of commemoration on a poster'. The latter meaning is not supplied by the ⟦-ize⟧ rule, but is simply an agreed-upon use of the verb among people who are in on the gag.

The ⟦-ize⟧ rule itself derives inchoative/causative verbs whose precise meaning it does not fully specify. Whether the derivative is inchoative or causative is not determined by ⟦-ize⟧ itself, which allows both possibilities. The actual sense of a given verbal derivative in *-ize* is determined pragmatically, by the intentions and inferences of language users. (For a similar perspective, see Clark & Clark 1979; Hanks 2013: 65; Spencer 2013: 213–219; Lieber 2016: 7ff.) The verb *vaporize* is used both inchoatively and causatively; the verb *hospitalize* is only used causatively. Among causative derivatives in *-ize*, the nature of the semantic relation between the verb and its nominal base is widely variable, as the examples in (18) show. It is possible to classify the different kinds of semantic relations exhibited by derivatives in *-ize*, but such classifications relate to lexicalized content that is not generally attributable to the ⟦-ize⟧ rule itself. This does, of course, point to a challenge for the analysis of derivational rules: if part of a derivative's content stems from a rule but part of it instead stems from language users' intentions and inferences, how does one draw the line between these parts? Certainly if there is a piece of content that is shared by all of the derivatives defined by means of a rule of derivation R, then that piece of content should likely be attributed to R itself. But derivational rules also seem to present options. As we have seen, the base on which the ⟦-ize⟧ rule operates may be an adjective or a noun (*industrialize*, *unionize*) and the verb resulting from its application may be inchoative or causative (*They economized*, *They customized their cars*). The formulation of the ⟦-ize⟧ rule in (17) accommodates the former option by means of its domain-of-definition μ_{17}, which includes triplets both of type ⟨L, Z, Adjective⟩ and of type ⟨L, Z, Noun⟩; it accommodates the latter option by means of the disjunctiveness of the derived lexicosemantic category 'inchoative/causative verb'. Thus, ⟦-ize⟧ underdetermines the content of its derivative ⟨L, *hospitalize*, Inchoative/causative verb⟩ insofar as it doesn't predict its lack of inchoative semantics, which is therefore purely a matter of lexical stipulation.

(18)   Some verbal derivatives in *-ize* and their semantic diversity
         fossilize   become or cause to become a fossil
         hospitalize   put (someone) into a hospital for treatment
         pasteurize   detoxify (a substance) by heating, a method developed by
                         L. Pasteur
         posterize   (ambiguous)
                         convert (an image) to a limited, nongradient color scheme;
                         humiliate (an opponent) with an offensive move deserving
                         commemoration on a poster
         terrorize   inspire terror in (someone)
         victimize   make (someone) a victim, i.e. harm (someone) intentionally

Rules of derivational exponence very often present an additional complication. In the simplest instances, a rule of derivational exponence defines the default stem of a derived lexeme from the default stem of its base lexeme. In other instances, however, a rule of derivational exponence defines the form of a lexeme's default stem without deriving that lexeme from another lexeme. And in still other instances, a rule of derivational exponence defines the "combining stem" of a lexeme L – the stem on which the default stem of a lexeme derived from L is based. Consider, for instance, the three uses of the English ⟦**-ate**⟧ rule. First, ⟦**-ate**⟧ derives the lexemes ACTIVATE and HYPHENATE from the base lexemes ACTIVE and HYPHEN, forming the derivatives' default stems *activate* and *hyphenate* from the base lexemes' default stems *active* and *hyphen* through the suffixation of *-ate*. Second, ⟦**-ate**⟧ simply defines the default stem of INSINUATE from its "substem" *insinu-* without deriving it from another lexeme.[7] Third, ⟦**-ate**⟧ defines the combining stem *variat-* of the lexeme VARY on which the default stem *variation* of its nominalization is based.

I shall therefore distinguish three kinds of uses to which a rule of derivational exponence may be put: its ***true derivational*** use (e.g. the use of ⟦**-ate**⟧ to derive ⟨ACTIVATE, *activate*, Verb⟩ from ⟨ACTIVE, *active*, Adj⟩), its ***thematizing*** use (e.g. the use of ⟦**-ate**⟧ to define the stem of ⟨INSINUATE, *insinuate*, Verb⟩ on the basis of ⟨INSINUATE, *insinu-*, Verb⟩), and its use in ***forming a combining stem*** (e.g. the use of ⟦**-ate**⟧ in combination with the nominalizing rule ⟦**-ion**⟧ in the derivation of ⟨VARIATION, *variation*, Noun⟩ from ⟨VARY, *vary*, Verb⟩). This means that the domain-of-definition of the ⟦**-ate**⟧ rule includes triplets of at least three types. In its true derivational use, ⟦**-ate**⟧ applies to triplets of the types ⟨L, Z, Adjective⟩ and ⟨L, Z, Noun⟩ to

---

[7] Related lexemes may share a substem even if neither directly derives from the other; for example, AMBITION and AMBITIOUS share the substem /æmˈbɪʃ/. See Jackendoff & Audring (2020: 106f.) for relevant discussion.

yield triplets of the type ⟨L, Z-*ate*, Verb⟩. In its thematizing use, ⟦**-ate**⟧ applies to triplets of the type ⟨L, Z, Verb⟩ in which Z is a substem: ⟦**-ate**⟧ applies to triplets of this type simply to convert the substem Z to the stem Z-*ate*, without implying the existence of a derived lexeme – applying, for instance, to ⟨INSINUATE, *insinu-*, Verb⟩ to yield ⟨INSINUATE, *insinuate*, Verb⟩, where *insinu-* and *insinuate* are substem and stem of the same verbal lexeme INSINUATE. In its use in forming a combining stem, ⟦**-ate**⟧ combines with ⟦**-ion**⟧ to form a rule that applies to triplets of the type ⟨L, Z, Verb⟩ (in which Z is L's default stem, as in ⟨VARY, *vary*, Verb⟩) to yield triplets of the type ⟨L, Z-*ation*, Noun⟩. Note that triplets such as ⟨VARY, *vary*, Verb⟩ are in the domain-of-definition not of ⟦**-ate**⟧ itself, but of the rule arising from the combination of ⟦**-ate**⟧ with ⟦**-ion**⟧; we will return to combinations of this sort in Section 2.5.

The foregoing assumptions about the characteristics of rules of exponence make it desirable to be precise about the terminology of rule application. I assume that rules of inflectional exponence apply to what I call ***stem pairings*** (i.e. to ⟨stem, property set⟩ pairings such as ⟨*drive*, {3sg prs ind}⟩ and ⟨*driv-*, {pst ptcp}⟩) and that derivational rules apply to what I call ***stem triplets*** (i.e. to ⟨lexeme, stem, lexicosemantic category⟩ triplets such as ⟨DRIVE, *drive*, transitive verb⟩ and ⟨DRIVER, *driver*, agent noun⟩). Technically, neither sort of rule applies to stems *tout court*. Instead, I will say that when a rule R applies to a stem pairing ⟨Z, ρ⟩ or to a stem triplet ⟨L, Z, C⟩, R ***operates on*** the stem Z. For example, because rule (20) applies to the stem pairing ⟨*driv-*, {pst ptcp strong}⟩, I will say that (20) operates on the stem *driv-*.

(20) ⟦**-en**⟧ : [V, {pst ptcp strong} : *-en*]

A final word is necessary about the rule formats in (5) and (14) and rule representations such as (20). I assume that the operation that introduces an affix may also effect various morphophonological modifications, of the affix that it introduces, of the stem on which it operates, or of both. For instance, besides introducing the suffix *-ion*, the operation *f* referenced in the formulation of the English ⟦**-ion**⟧ rule in (21a) induces a number of changes in the stem on which it operates, causing a stem-final alveolar obstruent to appear as a palatal fricative (*commit* → *commission*, *invade* → *invasion*, *discuss* → *discussion*, *fuse* → *fusion*), causing stress to appear on the stem-final syllable (*exhíbit* → *exhibítion*, *inítiate* → *initiátion*), causing /aɪ/ to monophthongize as /ɪ/ (*collide* → *collision*, *ignite* → *ignition*, *incise* → *incision*), and so on. Because this set of modifications is associated with the suffixation of *-ion*, the representation of ⟦**-ion**⟧ in (21b) should be interpreted as implicitly invoking these modifications, and similarly for all other rules of affixation.

(21) a. ⟦**-ion**⟧ : [μ$_{20}$ ⇒ Action nominalization : *f*], where *f*(X) = X′*-ion* and X′ differs from X as an effect of a particular set of morphophonological rules (including palatal spirantization, stress attraction, monophthongization, and so on).
b. ⟦**-ion**⟧ : [V, μ$_{20}$ ⇒ Action nominalization : *-ion*]

Representative members of μ$_{20}$:
⟨L, *commit*, Verb⟩, ⟨L, *invade*, Verb⟩, ⟨L, *discuss*, Verb⟩, ⟨L, *fuse*, Verb⟩, ⟨L, *exhibit*, Verb⟩, ⟨L, *initiate*, Verb⟩, ⟨L, *collide*, Verb⟩, ⟨L, *ignite*, Verb⟩, ⟨L, *incise*, Verb⟩

The key conclusion from the discussion in this section is that inflectional rules and derivational rules differ in their formulation: rules of inflectional exponence conform to the format in (5) but rules of derivational exponence conform to the format in (14). As we shall see, these formats are valid both for simple rules and for combined rules.

In a purely canonical system of morphotactics, rules would conform to each of the ten criteria detailed in Section 1.5, repeated here in (22). In the chapters that follow, I discuss a range of phenomena all of which deviate from the minimal rule criterion – phenomena that entail that simpler rules may combine to form more complex rules whose characteristics are not necessarily deducible from those of their component rules. Taken together, the rule-combination phenomena that arise in actual systems of morphotactics deviate from all of the canonical morphotactic criteria listed in (22a); at the same time, they allow apparent deviations from the criteria listed in (22b) to be reconciled with them. As we shall see, rule combinations are of a range of different types.

(22) Ten criterial properties of canonical morphotactics
a. Minimal rule criterion   b. Rule opposition criterion
    Compositional content criterion   Integral stem criterion
    Intermediate well-formedness   Affix directionality
      criterion   criterion
    Stem operand criterion
    Rule independence criterion
    Parallel sequence criterion
    Unique sequence criterion

In the following sections, I give an overview of the kinds of rule combination that languages exploit in their morphotactics. At least four modes of rule combination are discernible. Not all languages give evidence of all four of these modes of combination. Rule composition (Section 2.2) is the most common mode of rule combination and can be seen as the default mode. But there is also evidence for three special modes of rule combination: holistic combination (Section 2.3), aggregation (Section 2.4), and counterpotentiation

(Section 2.5). In the chapters that follow, I exemplify each of these modes of rule combination extensively and elaborate on their characteristics in precise terms. I examine both combinations of inflectional rules and combinations of derivational rules, focusing largely (though not exclusively) on rules of affixation.

2.2 Rule Composition

Rule composition is the simplest mode of rule combination. In English, for example, the rule [[**-ate**]] allows the verbal lexeme HYPHENATE to be derived from the noun HYPHEN, and the rule [[**-ion**]] in turn allows the nominalization HYPHENATION to be derived from the verb HYPHENATE. Together, these facts imply a derivational relation between HYPHEN and HYPHENATION; this relation can be modeled as involving ([[**-ion**]] ∘ [[**-ate**]])—the composite of the [[**-ion**]] rule with the [[**-ate**]] rule.

As will be seen in subsequent chapters, instances of rule composition vary with respect to their conformity to the canonical morphotactic criteria outlined in Section 1.5. Some instances deviate from the rule independence criterion; these are cases in which the application of a given rule is directly dependent upon that of another rule (with which it enters into composition). Other patterns of composition constitute deviations from the parallel sequence criterion; these are cases in which a rule realizing a particular inflectional category composes with other rules in an order that is atypical for rules realizing that category. Rules deviate from the unique sequence criterion if they compose in more than one order. At the same time, the postulation of rule composition makes it possible for apparent deviations from the integral stem criterion or from the rule opposition criterion to be reconciled with these criteria.

Given the essential difference between rules of inflection and rules of derivation, it is important to distinguish the effects of rule composition in these two domains. Suppose, first, that R_1 and R_2 are rules of inflectional exponence with the characteristics in (23). The composite of the two inflectional rules in (23) is then as defined in (24). Crucially, just as the individual rules in (23) conform to the inflectional rule format in (5), so, too, does the definition of their composite in (24).

(23) Two rules of inflectional exponence
    a. Rule R_1 realizes content τ_1 by means of operation f_1 on expressions belonging to class C_1:
        $R_1 : [C_1, \tau_1 : X \rightarrow f_1(X)]$.

b. Rule R_2 realizes content τ_2 by means of operation f_2 on expressions belonging to class C_2:
$R_2 : [C_2, \tau_2 : X \to f_2(X)]$.

(24) Composite inflectional rules
Where R_1 and R_2 are as in (23), the composite inflectional rule $(R_2 \circ R_1)$ is that partial function F in the set of ⟨form, content⟩ pairs such that for any stem $Z \in [C_2 \cap C_1]$ and any extension σ of $[\tau_2 \sqcup \tau_1]$, $F(\langle Z, \sigma \rangle)$ has the value $\langle f_2(f_1(Z)), \sigma \rangle$.

$(R_2 \circ R_1)$ is thus equivalent to $[[C_2 \cap C_1], [\tau_2 \sqcup \tau_1] : X \to f_2(f_1(X))]$.

In the definition in (24), '$[C_2 \cap C_1]$' represents the **intersection** of C_2 with C_1 (= the set containing only and all elements that are members of both C_2 and C_1) and '$[\tau_2 \sqcup \tau_1]$' represents the unification of τ_2 and τ_1. Following Gazdar et al. (1985: 27), I assume that unification is defined in terms of extension, as in (25).[8]

(25) Extension and unification of property sets
a. Given two sets ρ, σ each of whose members may be an atomic property or a set-based property: ρ is an **extension** of σ if and only if for each member m of σ,
either (i) m is an atomic property and is a member of ρ
or (ii) m is a set-based property and an extension of m is a member of ρ.

Examples: {1 pl} is an extension of {pl}.
{{1 pl} pst sbjv} is an extension of {{pl} pst}.

b. Given two sets ρ, σ each of whose members may be an atomic property or a set-based property: the **unification** [ρ ⊔ σ] is the smallest well-formed extension of both ρ and σ (i.e. that well-formed extension of both ρ and σ that is lower in cardinality than any other well-formed extension of ρ and σ). The unification [ρ ⊔ σ] is undefined if there is no well-formed extension of both ρ and σ; it is likewise undefined if the set of well-formed extensions of both ρ and σ does not contain a single member whose cardinality is lower than that of all other members.

Examples: [{1} ⊔ {pl}] is {1 pl}.
[{{sbj 3 sg} pst} ⊔ {{sbj fem}}] is {{sbj 3 sg fem} pst}.
[{{sbj pl} pst} ⊔ {{1} pst sbjv}] is {{sbj 1 pl} pst sbjv}.

Consider in turn the composition of two derivational rules. Suppose that R_3 and R_4 are rules of derivational exponence with the characteristics in (26). The

---

[8] The definitions of extension and unification in (25) treat all set-based properties alike, whether or not they are category-determinate. The analyses proposed in Chapters 8 and 9 depend upon this characteristic of these definitions, as will be seen.

composite of the two derivational rules in (26) is then as defined in (27). Crucially, just as the individual rules in (26) conform to the derivational rule format in (14), so, too, does the definition of their composite in (27).

(26) Two rules of derivational exponence
   a. Rule R_3 derives a lexeme belonging to the lexicosemantic category D by means of operation f_3 on the stem Z_a of a lexeme L_a belonging to the lexicosemantic category C_a provided that $\langle L_a, Z_a, C_a \rangle$ belongs to the domain-of-definition μ_3: $R_3 : [\mu_3 \Rightarrow D : X \rightarrow f_3(X)]$.
   b. Rule R_4 derives a lexeme belonging to the lexicosemantic category E by means of operation f_4 on the stem Z_b of a lexeme L_b belonging to the lexicosemantic category C_b provided that $\langle L_b, Z_b, C_b \rangle$ belongs to the domain-of-definition μ_4 and μ_4 includes triplets of type $\langle$lexeme, stem, D$\rangle$: $R4 : [\mu 4 \Rightarrow E : X \rightarrow f_4(X)]$.

(27) Composite derivational rules
Where R_3 and R_4 are as in (26), the composite derivational rule $(R_4 \circ R_3)$ is that function F in the set of $\langle$lexeme, stem, lexicosemantic category$\rangle$ triplets such that for any triplet t in the domain-of-definition μ_3 of R_3, F(t) is the result of applying R_4 to the result of applying R_3 to t, if this is defined. F(t) is defined only if (a) t is in the domain-of-definition μ_3 of R_3 and (b) the result of applying R_3 to t is in the domain-of-definition μ_4 of R_4. The domain-of-definition of $(R_4 \circ R_3)$ is thus a subset of (potentially identical to) that of R_3.

$(R_4 \circ R_3)$ is thus equivalent to $[\mu_{27} \Rightarrow E : X \rightarrow f_4(f_3 (X))]$, where the domain-of-definition μ_{27} is the smallest set such that for each triplet t in μ_3, t belongs to μ_{27} if and only if the result of applying R_3 to t belongs to μ_4.

The notion of rule composition at issue in (24) and (27) is similar to that of function composition in mathematics, where the function $(g \circ f)$ is the composition of the functions g and f if and only if for any x in the domain of f, $(g \circ f)(x) = g(f(x))$. Thus, just as the composition of the function g with the function f produces the function $(g \circ f)$ in Table 2.2, so the composition of the [[-ur]] rule with the [[-nt]] rule produces the composed inflectional rule ([[-ur]] $\circ$ [[-nt]])

Table 2.2 *An example of mathematical function composition*

	Definition	Examples		
		Function(argument)	$\rightarrow$	value
Function f	$f(n) = n \times 2$	$f(2)$	$\rightarrow$	4
Function g	$g(n) = n + 1$	$g(4)$	$\rightarrow$	5
Composition of g with f	$(g \circ f)(n) = (n \times 2) + 1$	$(g \circ f)(2)$	$\rightarrow$	5

2.2 Rule Composition   57

Table 2.3 *An example of the composition of two rules of inflectional exponence* (where σ = {{sbj 3pl} prs ind pass})

		Examples
Rule		Argument → value
⟦-nt⟧ :	[V, {{sbj 3pl}} : -nt]	⟨amā-, σ⟩ → ⟨amant-, σ⟩
⟦-ur⟧ :	[V, {pass} : -ur]	⟨amant-, σ⟩ → ⟨amantur, σ⟩
(⟦-ur⟧ ∘ ⟦-nt⟧) :	[V, {pass {sbj 3pl}} : -nt-ur]	⟨amā-, σ⟩ → ⟨amantur, σ⟩

Table 2.4 *An example of the composition of two rules of derivation*

		Examples
Rule		Argument → value
⟦-ate⟧ : [μ$_I$ ⇒ V : -ate]		⟨L, *valid*, Adj⟩ → ⟨L, *validate*, Verb⟩
		⟨L, *hyphen*, Noun⟩ → ⟨L, *hyphenate*, Verb⟩
⟦-ion⟧ : [μ$_{II}$ ⇒ N : -ion]		⟨L, *hyphenate*, Verb⟩ → ⟨L, *hyphenation*, Noun⟩
		⟨L, *validate*, Verb⟩ → ⟨L, *validation*, Noun⟩
(⟦-ion⟧ ∘ ⟦-ate⟧) : [μ$_{III}$ ⇒ N : -at-ion], where μ$_{III}$ ⊆ μ$_I$		⟨L, *valid*, Adj⟩ → ⟨L, *validation*, Noun⟩
		⟨L, *hyphen*, Noun⟩ → ⟨L, *hyphenation*, Noun⟩

in Table 2.3 and the composition of the ⟦-ion⟧ rule with the ⟦-ate⟧ rule produces the composed derivational rule (⟦-ion⟧ ∘ ⟦-ate⟧) in Table 2.4.

The notion of rule composition proposed here is closely akin to the notion of schema unification in Construction Morphology (Booij 2007, 2010, 2018). The three other modes of rule combination discussed below differ from ordinary rule composition; thus, the evidence motivating the postulation of these other modes of rule combination motivates the postulation of cognate alternatives to schema unification in Construction Morphology. I return to this point in Section 12.2.

I assume that composition is the default sort of rule combination. This assumption affords an important modification of the architecture of the theory of Paradigm Function Morphology (PFM). In earlier versions of PFM, it was assumed (following Anderson 1992) that a language's rules of inflectional exponence are organized into blocks such that when a form cell's inflectional realization involves the successive application of more than one rule of exponence, the order of application of these individual rules is determined by the ordering of the blocks to which they belong. The theory of morphotactics that I develop here, however, builds on the idea that rules may combine recursively to form a larger rule, so that invariably, only a single rule is needed to map a given form cell onto the corresponding realized cell.

Consider the fragment of Swahili verb morphology in (28). Uncontroversially, the stem on which these affirmative finite verb forms are based is *-piga*, and each form contains a sequence of three prefixes – the first expressing subject agreement, the second expressing tense, and the third encoding a pronominal object. The rules defining the prefixes in these verb forms might be formulated as in (29)–(31).

(28)　Some Swahili verb forms
　　a.　*atakupiga* 's/he will strike you (sg.)'
　　b.　*utampiga* 'you (sg.) will strike her/him'
　　c.　*alikupiga* 's/he struck you (sg.)'
　　d.　*ulimpiga* 'you (sg.) struck him/her'

(29)　Group III (subject agreement rules)
　　a.　⟦**u-**⟧ :　[V, {{sbj 2sg}} : *u*-]
　　b.　⟦**a-**⟧ :　[V, {{sbj 3sg}} : *a*-]

(30)　Group II (tense rules)
　　a.　⟦**ta-**⟧ :　[V, {fut} : *ta*-]
　　b.　⟦**li-**⟧ :　[V, {pst} : *li*-]

(31)　Group I (pronominal object rules)
　　a.　⟦**ku-**⟧ :　[V, {{obj 2sg}} : *ku*-]
　　b.　⟦**m-**⟧ :　[V, {{obj 3sg}} : *m*-]

In earlier versions of PFM, each of the rule groups in (29)–(31) was seen as belonging to a separate rule block participating in the definition of the Swahili paradigm function PF; on this assumption, PF has the (partial) definition in (32). Here, however, I assume that the rules in (29)–(31) combine to form larger rules, including, for example, the composite rules in (33), which supply the prefix sequences exhibited in (28). By virtue of the principles of rule combination proposed here, the definition of the word form realizing a particular form cell need never involve more than one rule of inflectional exponence. That is, for any form cell ⟨Z, σ⟩, there is a *full exponence rule* (FER) – call it R – that is the narrowest rule of exponence that is applicable to ⟨Z, σ⟩, and is therefore such that PF(⟨Z, σ⟩) is the result of applying R to ⟨Z, σ⟩. In more general terms, I assume the Full Exponence Principle in (34); according

2.2 *Rule Composition* 59

to this principle, every FER in a language is a subfunction[9] of that language's paradigm function.

(32) For any positive finite cell ⟨Z, σ⟩ in the form paradigm of a Swahili verb,

PF(⟨Z, σ⟩) = [(29) NAR [(30) NAR [(31) NAR ⟨Z, σ⟩]]],

where for any rule block B, [B NAR ⟨X, σ⟩] represents the result of applying to ⟨X, σ⟩ the narrowest applicable rule in block B.

(33) Full exponence rules (FERs) for the Swahili forms in (28)
 a. ((〚a-〛 ∘ 〚ta-〛) ∘ 〚ku-〛) : [V, {{sbj 3sg} fut {obj 2sg}} : *ataku-*]
 b. ((〚u-〛 ∘ 〚ta-〛) ∘ 〚m-〛) : [V, {{sbj 2sg} fut {obj 3sg}} : *utam-*]
 c. ((〚a-〛 ∘ 〚li-〛) ∘ 〚ku-〛) : [V, {{sbj 3sg} pst {obj 2sg}} : *aliku-*]
 d. ((〚u-〛 ∘ 〚li-〛) ∘ 〚m-〛) : [V, {{sbj 2sg} pst {obj 3sg}} : *ulim-*]

(34) Full Exponence Principle
The realization PF(⟨L, σ⟩) of a content cell ⟨L, σ⟩ is the result of applying the narrowest applicable FER to ∥ ⟨L, σ⟩ ∥. This FER is, in other words, a subfunction of PF.

In accordance with the Full Exponence Principle, the Swahili paradigm function defines each of the forms in (28) through the application of a single, composite rule to the corresponding form cell. Thus, in each of the four parts (a)–(d) of Table 2.5, the Swahili paradigm function realizes the form cell (i) through the application of one of the FERs in (33) to produce the corresponding realized cell (ii).

In many cases, whole classes of FERs can be defined by a general ***FER pattern***. In Swahili, for example, the composite rules in (33) are among the many rules defined for positive finite verb forms by the FER pattern in (35).[10] Given this pattern, it is unnecessary for the grammar of Swahili to comprise separate, individual stipulations of the composite rules in (33).

(35) FER pattern for positive finite verb forms in Swahili
For each positive finite cell ⟨Z, σ⟩ in the form paradigm of a Swahili verb, the FER for ⟨Z, σ⟩ is ((R$_{III}$ ∘ R$_{II}$) ∘ R$_{I}$), where R$_{III}$, R$_{II}$, and R$_{I}$ are, respectively, the narrowest rules in Groups III, II, and I (in (29)–(31)) that are applicable to ⟨Z, σ⟩.

The notion of rule composition affords an account of numerous otherwise problematic phenomena in morphotactics. Some of these are phenomena

---

[9] Function *g* is a subfunction of function *f* if and only if for every member *x* of *g*'s domain-of-definition, (i) *x* is a member of *f*'s domain-of-definition and (ii) *g(x)* = *f (x)*.
[10] I discuss an elaboration of this pattern in Chapter 8.

Table 2.5 *The morphotactics of the Swahili forms in (28)*

(a) (i) Form cell: ⟨-piga, {{sbj 3sg} fut {obj 2sg}}⟩ 's/he will strike you (sg.)'
 |
 FER ((⟦a-⟧ ∘ ⟦ta-⟧) ∘ ⟦ku-⟧) (= (33a))
 ↓
 (ii) Realized cell: ⟨atakupiga, {{sbj 3sg} fut {obj 2sg}}⟩

(b) (i) Form cell: ⟨-piga, {{sbj 2sg} fut {obj 3sg}}⟩ 'you (sg.) will strike her/him'
 |
 FER ((⟦u-⟧ ∘ ⟦ta-⟧) ∘ ⟦m-⟧) (= (33b))
 ↓
 (ii) Realized cell: ⟨utampiga, {{sbj 2sg} fut {obj 3sg}}⟩

(c) (i) Form cell: ⟨-piga, {{sbj 3sg} pst {obj 2sg}}⟩ 's/he struck you (sg.)'
 |
 FER ((⟦a-⟧ ∘ ⟦li-⟧) ∘ ⟦ku-⟧) (= (33c))
 ↓
 (ii) Realized cell: ⟨alikupiga, {{sbj 3sg} pst {obj 2sg}}⟩

(d) (i) Form cell: ⟨-piga, {{sbj 2sg} pst {obj 3sg}}⟩ 'you (sg.) struck him/her'
 |
 FER ((⟦u-⟧ ∘ ⟦li-⟧) ∘ ⟦m-⟧) (= (33d))
 ↓
 (ii) Realized cell: ⟨ulimpiga, {{sbj 2sg} pst {obj 3sg}}⟩

that genuinely deviate from the canonical morphotactic criteria in (22). In Chapter 3, I show how rule composition illuminates the distinction (proposed by Harris 2017) between dependent affixes and carrier affixes. Dependent affixes deviate from the rule independence criterion, in that their application is directly sensitive to the concurrent application of a carrier rule; in a rule-combining theory of morphotactics, dependent affixes are introduced by rules whose sole application is in composition with an appropriate carrier rule. In Chapter 4, I examine phenomena that fail to conform to the parallel sequence criterion and the unique sequence criterion. In a rule-combining approach to morphotactics, these are instances in which two contrasting sequences of rule composition coexist, standing in either a relation of complementarity, a default/override relation, or a relation of optionality.

Although the notion of rule composition can be appealed to in order to account for divergences from the canonical morphotactic criteria in (22), it also sometimes helps reconcile otherwise problematic phenomena with these criteria. In Chapter 5, I examine apparent deviations from the integral stem criterion and the rule opposition criterion and show that they in fact conform to these criteria if the criteria are seen as pertaining not only to simple rules but also to composite rules.

Ultimately, though, a key question is whether composition is the only way in which rules of inflectional or derivational exponence may combine. Is rule composition the only mode of rule combination by means of which a lexeme's FERs are defined, or do some FERs in some languages involve other modes of rule combination? The simplest hypothesis is that every instance of rule combination is simply an instance of rule composition – that where rule R_1 is such that $R_1(x) = y$ and rule R_2 is such that $R_2(y) = z$, the combination of R_2 with R_1 is the rule composition $(R_2 \circ R_1)$, whose application to x yields the value z: $(R_2 \circ R_1)(x) = R_2(R_1(x)) = z$. We shall see, however, that this hypothesis is inadequate: that a language's morphotactics may employ other modes of rule combination. Chapters 6–10 are devoted to a detailed discussion of these modes of rule combination that go beyond mere composition. In the following sections, I discuss the fundamental properties of these other modes of combination, characterizing them in terms of their differences from ordinary composition.

2.3 Holistic Combination

Many languages present instances in which the content expressed by the joint application of two rules is more than the sum of the content that those rules express on their own. ***Holistic combination*** is the mode of rule combination that accounts for this additional content.

According to the compositional content criterion, the content expressed by a word form's morphology is canonically compositional – a function of the content expressed by the individual rules defining that morphology. As noted earlier, deviations from this criterion are of two kinds. In instances of holistic combination, the content expressed by a combination of rules includes content that cannot be attributed to either one of the component rules on its own; in instances of solitary specialization, a rule expresses more content on its own than when it combines with other rules. I assume that both kinds of deviation from the compositional content criterion involve an operation of content supplementation.

Consider first the hypothetical rule of inflectional exponence in (36). While the content expressed by this rule is the property set τ, this rule may, in certain circumstances, be used to express a proper extension of τ. In definitions of

62   *Rule Combinations*

Table 2.6 *Present indicative and future-tense forms of Breton* KAROUT *'love'*

	Present indicative	Future
1SG	kar-an	kar-i-n
2SG	kar-ez	kar-i
3SG	kar	kar-o
1PL	kar-o-mp	kar-i-mp
2PL	kar-i-t	kar-o-t
3PL	kar-o-nt	kar-i-nt
IMPS	kar-e-r	kar-o-r

(Kervella 1976: 124)

inflectional content supplementation of this sort, the **content supplementation operator** Ⓢ has the schematic interpretation in (37). According to (37), the rule Ⓢ$_\gamma$(R) is like the rule R except that it has γ as part of the content that it realizes. If R is a simple rule, the rule Ⓢ$_\gamma$(R) is a solitary specialization; if R is a composite rule, the rule Ⓢ$_\gamma$(R) is a holistic combination. In either case, I refer to γ as the **addend** of the rule Ⓢ$_\gamma$(R). Just as the individual rule R in (36) conforms to the inflectional rule format in (5), so, too, does the definition of the inflectional content supplementation Ⓢ$_\gamma$(R) in (37).

(36)   A hypothetical rule of inflectional exponence
        R : [C, τ : X → f(X)]

(37)   Inflectional content supplementation
        Where the inflectional rule R is as in (36), the rule Ⓢ$_\gamma$(R) is an inflectional content supplementation that is by definition equivalent to [C, [τ ⊔ γ] : X → f(X)].

Consider some examples from Breton. Among the rules defining the regular conjugation of Breton verbs are the two rules in (38), some of whose uses are seen in the present indicative and future-tense subparadigms of the verb KAROUT 'love' in Table 2.6. Although *-mp* can in general be seen as the expression of first-person plural subject agreement, the suffix *-o* has a variety of uses; overall, the forms in which it appears have no morphosyntactic property in common. In Table 2.6, for example, the *-o* suffix expresses the present indicative in combination with *-mp* (*karomp* 'we love') and with the third-person plural suffix *-nt* (*karont* 'they love'), but expresses the future tense in combination with the second-person plural suffix *-t* (*karot* 'you (pl.) will love') and with the impersonal suffix *-r* (*karor* 'one will love'); and on its own,

2.3 Holistic Combination 63

it expresses the third-person singular of the future tense (*karo* 's/he will love'). Thus, the composition in (39a) expresses extra content that cannot be directly attributed to either of its component rules (i.e. to the rules in (38)), and when serving as a FER on its own, the ⟦**-o**⟧ rule expresses extra content that it doesn't possess when it combines with other rules, as in (39b). To account for these facts, I assume that in the definition of Breton morphotactics, the content supplementations in (40) act as FERs; (40a) is a holistic combination, and (40b) is a solitary specialization.

(38) Two rules of Breton verb inflection
  ⟦**-o**⟧ : [V, { } : *-o*]   ⟦**-mp**⟧ : [V, {1pl} : *-mp*]

(39) a. (⟦**-mp**⟧ ∘ ⟦**-o**⟧) : [V, {1pl} : *-omp*]   Extra content: present indicative
  b. ⟦**-o**⟧ : [V, { } : *-o*]   Extra content: 3sg future tense

(40) Some content supplementations serving as FERs in Breton
  a. Ⓢ$_{\{prs\ ind\}}$(⟦**-mp**⟧ ∘ ⟦**-o**⟧) : [V, {1pl prs ind} : *-omp*] (a holistic combination)
  b. Ⓢ$_{\{3sg\ fut\}}$(⟦**-o**⟧) : [V, {3sg fut} : *-o*] (a solitary specialization)

The Breton content supplementations in (40) are inflectional rules. Content supplementations may also be derivational rules. Thus, consider the rule of derivational exponence in (41).

(41) A hypothetical rule of derivational exponence
  R : [μ ⇒ D : X → *f*(X)]

When applying to a derivational rule, the supplementation operator Ⓢ has the schematic interpretation in (42).

(42) Derivational content supplementation
  Where the derivational rule R is as in (41), the rule Ⓢ$_E$(R) is a derivational content supplementation that is by definition equivalent to [μ ⇒ [D ∪ E] : X → *f*(X))].

Consider another example from Breton. The derivation of fractional numerals in Breton involves a holistic combination of the ordinal rule ⟦**-ved**⟧ in (43) and the singulative rule ⟦**-enn**⟧ in (44) (Trépos 1968: 128f.; Kervella 1976: 270). The general function of the ⟦**-enn**⟧ rule is to express individuation: one of its uses, exemplified in Table 2.7, is that of deriving feminine nouns with singular reference from collective nouns (e.g. *logodenn* 'mouse' from *logod* 'mice'); as the examples in Table 2.8 show, the ⟦**-enn**⟧ rule also serves to derive nouns denoting countable units from mass nouns, to derive one count

Table 2.7 *Some Breton collective nouns and their singulative derivatives*

Collective noun		Singulative noun	
buzhug	'worms'	*buzhugenn*	'worm'
c'hwibu	'gnats'	*c'hwibuenn*	'gnat'
gwer	'glasses'	*gwerenn*	'glass'
gwez	'trees'	*gwezenn*	'tree'
kraon	'nuts'	*kraonenn*	'nut'
logod	'mice'	*logodenn*	'mouse'
per	'pears'	*perenn*	'pear'
sivi	'strawberries'	*sivienn*	'strawberry'

Table 2.8 *Other uses of Breton* ⟦**-enn**⟧

a.	Mass noun		Count noun	
	douar	'earth, soil'	*douarenn*	'plot of land'
	geot	'grass'	*geotenn*	'blade of grass'
	kafe	'coffee'	*kafeenn*	'coffee bean'
	kolo	'straw'	*koloenn*	'piece of straw'
b.	Count noun		Related count noun	
	boutez	'shoe'	*botezenn*	'kick'
	enez	'island'	*enezenn*	'island'
	lagad	'eye'	*lagadenn*	'eyelet'
	lost	'tail'	*lostenn*	'dress'
c.	Adjective		Related count noun	
	bas	'shallow'	*basenn*	'shoal'
	koant	'pretty'	*koantenn*	'pretty girl'
	lous	'dirty'	*lousenn*	'grubby woman (pejorative)'
	uhel	'high'	*uhelenn*	'elevated place'

noun from another in the expression of sundry semantic relations, and to derive count nouns from adjectives.[11]

(43) ⟦**-ved**⟧ : [μ_{43} ⇒ Ordinal numeral : *-ved*]
(where μ_{43} includes triplets of the type ⟨L, Z, Cardinal numeral⟩)

---

[11] One might suppose that ⟦**-enn**⟧ is an inflectional rule expressing singular number, but it is not; derivative nouns in *-enn* are themselves subject to inflectional pluralization, even those deriving from collective nouns (Stump 1990; Trépos 1957).

Table 2.9 *Cardinal, ordinal, and fractional numerals in Breton*

Cardinal		Ordinal		Fractional	
unan	'1'	*kentañ*	'first'		
daou	'2'	*eil*	'second'	*hanter*	'half'
tri	'3'	*trede*	'third'	*trederenn*	'1/3'
pevar	'4'	*pevare*	'fourth'	*palevarz, kard*	'1/4'
pemp	'5'	*pempved*	'fifth'	*pempvedenn*	'1/5'
c'hwec'h	'6'	*c'hwec'hved*	'sixth'	*c'hwec'hvedenn*	'1/6'
seiz	'7'	*seizved*	'seventh'	*seizvedenn*	'1/7'
eiz	'8'	*eizved*	'eighth'	*eizvedenn*	'1/8'
nao	'9'	*naoved*	'ninth'	*naovedenn*	'1/9'
deg	'10'	*degved*	'tenth'	*degvedenn*	'1/10'
unneg	'11'	*unnegved*	'eleventh'	*unnegvedenn*	'1/11'
daouzeg	'12'	*daouzegved*	'twelfth'	*daouzegvedenn*	'1/12'
ugent	'20'	*ugentved*	'twentieth'	*ugentvedenn*	'1/20'

(44) 〚**-enn**〛 : [µ$_{44}$ ⇒ Feminine count noun : *-enn*]
(where µ$_{44}$ includes triplets of the types ⟨L, Z, Noun⟩, ⟨L, Z, Adjective⟩, and ⟨L, Z, Ordinal numeral⟩)

As the examples in Table 2.9 show, most Breton ordinal numerals derive from the corresponding cardinal through the application of 〚**-ved**〛 (e.g. *pempved* 'fifth' from *pemp* '5'). (As is true in many languages, the low ordinals involve morphology that is instead irregular or suppletive; Stump 2010.) Aside from the lowest ones, fractionals arise from the corresponding ordinal through the application of 〚**-enn**〛; see again Table 2.9. Neither 〚**-ved**〛 nor 〚**-enn**〛 expresses fractional content; this is instead a property of the combination of the two rules. In order to account for this fact, I assume that the Breton rules of derivational morphology include the derivational content supplementation in (45), a holistic combination.

(45) A derivational content supplementation in Breton (a holistic combination)
Ⓢ$_{fractional}$(〚**-enn**〛 ∘ 〚**-ved**〛) : [µ$_{45}$ ⇒ Feminine fractional count noun : *-vedenn*]

In Chapter 7, I investigate the phenomenon of inflectional content supplementation, examining its role in Breton verb morphology at greater length, as well as its role in the verb morphology of Limbu and Old English. Throughout, I regard holistic combination as a mode of rule combination distinct from composition, aggregation, and counterpotentiation; note, however, that unlike the latter three modes of rule combination, holistic combination is not directly formalized as a binary relation, but rather as the effect of the monadic content supplementation operator Ⓢ on a composite rule.

2.4 Rule Aggregation

Canonically, a rule of affixation operates on a stem; this is the stem operand criterion. Surprisingly often, however, one encounters cases of affix counterposition – instances in which a rule of affixation operates on the affix introduced by another rule; the examples in Table 2.10 illustrate.

As noted in Section 1.5.6, affix counterposition has a specific signature: affix A exhibits a particular directionality D (prefixal or suffixal) with respect to a stem with which it joins, but in the presence of some affix B possessing the opposite directionality, A exhibits directionality D with respect to B, to which it is adjacent. In such cases, aggregation is the mode of combination of the A rule with the B rule. Though instances of rule aggregation are noncanonical with respect to the stem operand criterion, they conform to the affix directionality criterion. That is, if R is a rule of affixation, the directionality of R's affix remains the same whether R's operand is a stem or another rule's affix: if R's affix is a prefix, it precedes R's operand, but if it is a suffix, it follows R's operand.

On first consideration, the very idea of rules affixing affixes to affixes might seem like a paradoxical notion. What makes it seem paradoxical is the mistaken idea that the stem operand criterion (according to which the formal operation associated with a morphological rule is an operation on stems) is a

Table 2.10 *Instances of counterposition in three languages*

	[Suffix] not in counterposition	[Prefix-suffix] in counterposition
Fula	'o-warii[-no] AGR-come.TNS[-PRET] 's/he had come'	'o-[don-no]-wara' AGR-[ASP-PRET]-come.TNS 's/he was coming'
Lithuanian	lenkia[-si] bows[-REFL] 's/he bows'	[ne-si]-lenkia [NEG-REFL]-bows 's/he doesn't bow'
Swahili	a-soma[-ye] SBJ.NC1-read[-REL.NC1] 'who reads'	a-[taka-ye]-soma SBJ.NC1-[FUT-REL.NC1]-read 'who will read'

rigid grammatical principle that categorically excludes the possibility that a rule of affixation might operate on an affix; but the stem operand criterion merely identifies a canonical morphotactic pattern from which deviations exist. The strongest arguments for the existence of such deviations are based on synchronic evidence; at the same time, it is helpful to recognize the kinds of diachronic patterns that give rise to such deviations. Consider two hypothetical examples.

First, a language might possess a suffix -Suff that appears after a verb stem or after a preverbal auxiliary, as in (46a). Speakers of that language might subsequently reanalyze the auxiliary as a verbal prefix, as in (46b). After this reanalysis, -Suff still has the status of a suffix in Verb-Suff word forms. But what about Aux-Suff-Verb word forms? If one assumes that the stem operand criterion constitutes an inviolable grammatical principle, then one must assume that the reanalysis of Aux as a prefix in Aux-Suff-Verb word forms is accompanied by a simultaneous reanalysis of -Suff as a prefix in these forms, notwithstanding its clearly suffixal status is Verb-Suff word forms; thus, the reanalysis of Aux as a prefix entails a complication of the rule introducing -Suff – in particular, it becomes noncanonical with respect to the affix directionality criterion. Alternatively, if one assumes that affixation to an affix exists as a noncanonical possibility, then the reanalysis of Aux as a prefix doesn't entail any complication of the rule introducing -Suff, which remains a rule of suffixation in the definition of both Verb-Suff forms and Aux-Suff-Verb forms (and thus remains canonical with respect to the affix directionality criterion). As we will see below, Fula verb inflection presents precisely the synchronic situation in (46b); see Harris (2017: 115–130) for other similar cases. This is an instance of prefixational counterposition (Section 1.5.6), in which rule aggregation engenders a complex rule of prefixation (specifically, a rule that prefixes a suffixed prefix).

(46)   Hypothetical historical development
        a.   Stage I.   Verb-Suff   Aux-Suff Verb
        b.   Stage II.   Verb-Suff   Aux-Suff-Verb

Consider now the possibility that a language with noun-class (NC) prefixes exhibits postnominal demonstratives that agree with respect to noun class, as in (47a). Speakers of that language might reanalyze the demonstrative as a suffix, as in (47b). In that case, what becomes of the noun-class prefix NC? If the stem operand criterion is an inviolable principle, one must assume that the reanalysis of the demonstrative as a suffix is accompanied by a simultaneous reanalysis of some instances of

NC as suffixes, notwithstanding the continued existence of prefixal instances of NC in prenominal position; thus, the reanalysis of Dem as a suffix entails a puzzling complication of the NC rule (again a deviation from the affix directionality criterion). Alternatively, if one assumes that affixation to an affix exists as a noncanonical possibility, then the reanalysis of Dem as a suffix doesn't affect the NC rule, which remains a rule of prefixation in all of its uses (thus remaining canonical with respect to the affix directionality criterion). As we will see in Chapter 7, Noon adjective inflection presents forms of exactly the kind hypothesized in (47b). (Cf. also Greenberg 1977, 1978; Harris 2017: 130–136.) This is an instance of suffixational counterposition (Section 1.5.6), in which rule aggregation engenders a complex rule of suffixation (specifically, a rule that suffixes a prefixed suffix).

(47) Hypothetical historical development
    a. Stage I.   NC-Noun NC-Dem
    b. Stage II.   NC-Noun-NC-Dem

Rule aggregation[12] is the combination of a rule R_2 that uses operation f_2 to affix b to its operand with a rule R_1 that uses operation f_1 to affix a to its operand to form a rule R_3 that uses operation f_2 to affix b to a and uses operation f_1 to affix the resulting affixal aggregation to its operand. Canonically, a rule of inflectional exponence has a stem as its operand; but in the aggregation of R_2 to R_1, the operand of R_2 is the affix introduced by R_1. A rule aggregation is therefore a special rule combination that deviates from ordinary composition with respect to the operands of the rules in terms of which it is defined. According to the stem operand criterion, rules of affixation canonically involve operations on stems. Rule aggregations, however, deviate from this canonical criterion in that they involve two rules one of which operates on the affix introduced by the other rule. Given the affixational

---

[12] In a series of papers leading to the preparation of this book (Stump 2017a–c, 2019a, 2019c, 2020a), I used the term ***rule conflation*** to refer to a hybrid kind of rule combination that is like rule aggregation when the combining rules differ in their direction of affixation (one being prefixational, the other suffixational) but like composition when the combining rules are alike in their direction of affixation (both being prefixational or both suffixational). In the particular analyses presented in those papers, this hybrid quality made it possible to regard any instance of either rule composition or rule aggregation as an instance of rule conflation. In the richer set of analyses developed here, it has been important to assume that rules that differ in their direction of affixation are subject to both composition and aggregation (with different results); I therefore here abandon the notion of rule conflation in favor of the more generally useful distinction between composition and aggregation.

2.4 Rule Aggregation

inflectional rules R_1 and R_2 in (48a,b), the composite rule $(R_2 \circ R_1)$ has the definition in (48c). I now introduce an ***aggregation operator*** Ⓐ such that the aggregated rule $(R_2 \; Ⓐ \; R_1)$ has the definition in (48d). Just as the individual rules in (48a,b) conform to the inflectional rule format in (5), so, too, does the definition of their aggregation in (48d).

(48) Composite vs. aggregated inflectional rules
    a. $R_1 : [C_1, \tau_1 : X \to f_1(a, X)]$, where f_1 is an affixation operation.
    b. $R_2 : [C_2, \tau_2 : X \to f_2(b, X)]$, where f_2 is an affixation operation.
    c.   The composite rule $(R_2 \circ R_1) = [[C_2 \cap C_1], [\tau_2 \sqcup \tau_1] : X \to f_2(b, f_1(a, X))]$
    d.   The aggregation $(R_2 \; Ⓐ \; R_1) = [[C_2 \cap C_1], [\tau_2 \sqcup \tau_1] : X \to f_1(f_2(b, a), X))]$

Thus, suppose 〚**c-**〛 and 〚**-d**〛 are the affixational inflectional rules in (49); in that case, the composite (〚**-d**〛 ∘ 〚**c-**〛) is as in (50a). Given a form–content pairing ⟨Z, σ⟩ such that Z belongs to category C and σ is an extension of both γ and δ, the application of the composite rule (〚**-d**〛 ∘ 〚**c-**〛) to ⟨Z, σ⟩ is ⟨c-Z-d, σ⟩, where c-Z-d is the result of suffixing -d to the result of prefixing c- to Z. By contrast, the aggregation (〚**-d**〛 Ⓐ 〚**c-**〛) is as in (50b). The application of (〚**-d**〛 Ⓐ 〚**c-**〛) to ⟨Z, σ⟩ is ⟨cd-Z, σ⟩, where cd-Z is the result of prefixing to Z the result of suffixing -d to c-.

(49)   a.   Rule 〚**c-**〛 : [C, γ : c-]
       b.   Rule 〚**-d**〛 : [C, δ : -d]

(50)   a.   The composition of 〚**-d**〛 with 〚**c-**〛: (〚**-d**〛 ∘ 〚**c-**〛) : [C, [γ ⊔ δ] : X → c-X-d]
       b.   The aggregation of 〚**-d**〛 with 〚**c-**〛: (〚**-d**〛 Ⓐ 〚**c-**〛) : [C, [γ ⊔ δ] : cd-]

Five characteristics of rule aggregation should be carefully noted:

- Rule R_1 has a dominant role in the interpretation of the aggregated rule $(R_2 \; Ⓐ \; R_1)$, since the direction of affixation of R_1 determines that of $(R_2 \; Ⓐ \; R_1)$, as in (50b).
- In the application of $(R_2 \; Ⓐ \; R_1)$ to a pairing ⟨Z, ρ⟩, R_2's affix is always sequenced primarily with respect to R_1's affix, which alone determines the sequence of affixation with respect to Z.
- The definition of rule aggregation does not exclude the possibility that an aggregated rule might itself enter into the aggregation of a still more complex rule; that is, rule aggregation may be recursive. We shall see examples of this in Chapter 8.
- Rule aggregation is an operation on rules rather than on affixes; nevertheless, if 〚**c-**〛 and 〚**-d**〛 are rules introducing the respective affixes c- and -d, one can, as a kind of shorthand, refer to the prefix cd- introduced by the aggregated rule (〚**-d**〛 Ⓐ 〚**c-**〛) as an ***aggregated affix***.

70 *Rule Combinations*

- When rules R_1 and R_2 are both rules of prefixation or both rules of suffixation, ($R_2 \circ R_1$) and (R_2 Ⓐ R_1) are, in extensional terms, the same rule; on the other hand, if R_1 and R_2 differ in their direction of affixation (i.e. if one is prefixational and the other suffixational), ($R_2 \circ R_1$) and (R_2 Ⓐ R_1) are distinct rules. The hypothetical examples in (51) and (52) show this. Thus, crucially: when a prefixational rule composes with a suffixational rule (in either order), the result is a rule that effects both prefixation and suffixation, as in (52a.i) and (52b.i); but when a prefixational rule aggregates with a suffixational rule, the result is a suffixational rule aggregation (as in (52a.ii)), and when a suffixational rule aggregates with a prefixational rule, the result is a prefixational rule aggregation (as in (52b.ii)).

(51) The composite of two rules is equivalent to the aggregation of those rules
    a. Combinations of two prefixation rules: $[\![y\text{-}]\!] : [C, \rho : y\text{-}]$
                                                             $[\![z\text{-}]\!] : [C, \sigma : z\text{-}]$
        by composition: $([\![z\text{-}]\!] \circ [\![y\text{-}]\!]) : [C, [\rho \sqcup \sigma] : zy\text{-}]$
        by aggregation: $([\![z\text{-}]\!]$ Ⓐ $[\![y\text{-}]\!]) : [C, [\rho \sqcup \sigma] : zy\text{-}]$

    b. Combinations of two suffixation rules: $[\![\text{-}y]\!] : [C, \rho : \text{-}y]$
                                                            $[\![\text{-}z]\!] : [C, \sigma : \text{-}z]$
        by composition: $([\![\text{-}z]\!] \circ [\![\text{-}y]\!]) : [C, [\rho \sqcup \sigma] : \text{-}yz]$
        by aggregation: $([\![\text{-}z]\!]$ Ⓐ $[\![\text{-}y]\!]) : [C, [\rho \sqcup \sigma] : \text{-}yz]$

(52) The composite of two rules is not equivalent to the aggregation of those rules
    a. Combinations of a
        prefixation rule: $[\![z\text{-}]\!] : [C, \sigma : z\text{-}]$
        with a suffixation rule: $[\![\text{-}y]\!] : [C, \rho : \text{-}y]$
        i.   by composition: $([\![z\text{-}]\!] \circ [\![\text{-}y]\!]) : [C, [\rho \sqcup \sigma] : X \to z\text{-}X\text{-}y]$
        ii.   by aggregation: $([\![z\text{-}]\!]$ Ⓐ $[\![\text{-}y]\!]) : [C, [\rho \sqcup \sigma] : \text{-}zy]$

    b. Combinations of a
        suffixation rule: $[\![\text{-}z]\!] : [C, \sigma : \text{-}z]$
        with a prefixation rule: $[\![y\text{-}]\!] : [C, \rho : y\text{-}]$
        i.   by composition: $([\![\text{-}z]\!] \circ [\![y\text{-}]\!]) : [C, [\rho \sqcup \sigma] : Y \to y\text{-}X\text{-}z]$
        ii.   by aggregation: $([\![\text{-}z]\!]$ Ⓐ $[\![y\text{-}]\!]) : [C, [\rho \sqcup \sigma] : yz\text{-}]$

Given that composition is the default mode of rule combination and that ($R_2 \circ R_1$) is equivalent to (R_2 Ⓐ R_1) whenever R_1 and R_2 are both prefixational or both suffixational, I will ordinarily appeal to aggregation only in the analysis of combinations of rules that contrast in their direction of affixation.[13]

---

[13] There are, however, cases in which the definition of a morphotactic pattern is most simply seen as involving the aggregation of a rule with members of a class of rules some of which are

2.4 Rule Aggregation

The aggregation operation is clearly motivated in the morphotactic systems of many languages. Consider an example from Fula (Senegambian; Nigeria).[14] Fula possesses an elaborate system of tense/aspect/mood (TAM) categories, whose morphology is sensitive to the three-way grouping in Table 2.11 (Arnott 1970: 179–182).[15] Within most of the categories in this system, Fula distinguishes preterite forms from nonpreterite forms. (Those categories that don't exhibit this distinction are marked by an asterisk in Table 2.11; Arnott 1970: 216.) Preterite forms are marked by an affix realized as -no-, -noo-, or -noo' according to context. In the fragment of Fula verb morphology pertinent to the present discussion, the long alternant -noo- appears in the relative tenses (appearing as -noo-', with final glottality, if it is word-final) and the short alternant appears elsewhere.[16] I use -nO- to denote the preterite affix independently of its realization as one or another of its alternant forms. Examples of the use of -nO- for distinguishing preterite forms are given in Table 2.12. As a comparison of these forms reveals, -nO- generally follows the verb stem, but precedes it in the presence of the aspectual prefix *don-* (used in both stative-(i) and continuous-(i) forms); the general past active and continuous-(i) active subparadigms of 'help' further exemplify this contrast in the placement of the -nO- affix (Table 2.13).[17]

These facts might be taken as evidence that -nO- functions sometimes as a suffix and sometimes as a prefix. But the notion of rule aggregation affords a

---

prefixational and others of which are suffixational; we will see a case of this sort from Italian in Section 7.4.

[14] The evidence discussed here is from Arnott (1970), who focuses on the Gombe dialect of northeastern Nigeria.

[15] The stative-(i) and stative-(ii) categories both "indicate a *state* resulting from the action or process" denoted by the verb; the continuous-(i) and continuous-(ii) categories "indicate a *continuing* action or process" (Arnott 1970: 181). There is no synchronic semantic difference between the stative-(i) and stative-(ii), nor between the continuous-(i) and continuous-(ii); rather, they differ in their morphotactics. The stative-(i) and continuous-(i) involve the aspectual marker *don-* (which follows the subject-agreement prefix) and may appear in the preterite; by contrast, the stative-(ii) and continuous-(ii) involve the aspectual marker '*e-* (which precedes the subject-agreement prefix) and do not appear in the preterite (Arnott 1970: 194f., 237f.).

[16] For a fuller account of the distribution of the three alternants, see Arnott (1970: 219–21, 232).

[17] Arnott (1970: 194f.) analyzes *don-* as a recurrent feature of the subject-concord prefixes belonging to Series 2, the series employed in the stative-(i) and continuous-(i) tenses, but notes that in the Gombe variety of Fula under discussion here, it might alternatively be seen as a "pre-radical tense element," a position for which McIntosh (1984: 187ff.) argues in her analysis of Kaceccereere Fula. I assume this alternative analysis here, though nothing strictly hinges on this assumption; rather than assume that the Fula preterite rule aggregates with an aspectual rule of *don-* prefixation, one could just as easily assume that it aggregates with Series 2 subject-concord rules of the kind advocated by Arnott.

Table 2.11 *Classification of tense/aspect/mood categories in Fula*

TAM group A		TAM group B
Subgroup (i)	Subgroup (ii)	
General past	Stative-(i)	Relative past
Emphatic past	Stative-(ii)*	Relative future
General future	Continuous-(i)	Subjunctive*
Vague future*	Continuous-(ii)*	
Desiderative*		
Negative past		
Negative future		
Negative of quality		

* Tenses that do not exhibit preterite forms (Arnott 1970: 216)
(Arnott 1970: 179–182)

Table 2.12 *Examples of nonpreterite vs. preterite forms in Fula*

TAM group	Tense/mood	Nonpreterite	Preterite
A (i)	General past active	'o-warii SBJ.3SG.NC1-come.TNS 's/he came'	'o-warii-**no** SBJ.3SG.NC1-come.TNS-PRET 's/he had come'
	General future active	'o-waray SBJ.3SG.NC1-come.TNS 's/he will come'	'o-waray-**no** SBJ.3SG.NC1-come.TNS-PRET 's/he was going to come'
A (ii)	Stative-(i) middle	'o-don-joodii-' SBJ.3SG.NC1-ASP-be. seated.TNS-FG 's/he is seated'	'o-don-**no**-joodii-' SBJ.3SG.NC1-ASP-PRET-be. seated.TNS-FG 's/he was seated'
	Continuous-(i) active	'o-don-wara-' SBJ.3SG. NC1-ASP-come. TNS-FG 's/he is coming'	'o-don-**no**-wara-' SBJ.3SG. NC1-ASP-PRET-come. TNS-FG 's/he was coming'
B	Relative past active	'o-wari-' SBJ.3SG.NC1-come. TNS-FG 's/he came'	'o-war-**noo**-' SBJ.3SG.NC1-come. TNS-PRET-FG 's/he had come'

(Arnott 1970: 216f.)

Table 2.13 *Some nonpreterite and preterite forms of Fula* WALL *'help'*

		'helped/had helped' General past active			'is/was helping' Continuous-(i) active			
		SBJ	STEM	PRET	SBJ	ASP-	PRET	STEM
Nonpreterite	1SG	mi-	wallii		mi-	ɗon-		walla'
	2SG	'a-	wallii		'a-	ɗon-		walla'
	3SG.NC1	'o-	wallii		'o-	ɗon-		walla'
	1PL	min-	wallii		min-	ɗon-		walla'
	2PL INCL	'en-	wallii		'en-	ɗon-		walla'
	2PL EXCL	'on-	wallii		'on-	ɗon-		walla'
	3PL.NC2	ɓe-	wallii		ɓe-	ɗon-		walla'
Preterite	1SG	mi-	wallii	-no	mi-	ɗon-	-no-	walla'
	2SG	'a-	wallii	-no	'a-	ɗon-	-no-	walla'
	3SG.NC1	'o-	wallii	-no	'o-	ɗon-	-no-	walla'
	1PL	min-	wallii	-no	min-	ɗon-	-no-	walla'
	2PL INCL	'en-	wallii	-no	'en-	ɗon-	-no-	walla'
	2PL EXCL	'on-	wallii	-no	'on-	ɗon-	-no-	walla'
	3PL.NC2	ɓe-	wallii	-no	ɓe-	ɗon-	-no-	walla'

(Arnott 1970: 217f)

different conception of the distribution of *-nO-*; in the following analysis, ⟦**-nO**⟧ is strictly a rule of suffixation.

I assume that the affixes in Table 2.13 are defined by the simple rules in (53). The suffixational ⟦**-nO**⟧ rule and the prefixational ⟦**ɗon-**⟧ rule both belong to Group I and are defined as in (53a); the rules in (53b) belong to Group II and express personal subject agreement by means of the Series 1 prefixes used in the TAM categories in Table 2.13 and others (Arnott 1970: 193ff.).

(53) Rules of exponence for a fragment of Fula verb inflection
    a. Group I
        ⟦**-nO**⟧ : [V, {tns.α pret} : *-nO*],
           where *-nO* represents *-noo* (word-finally, *-noo-'*) if α is a relative tense, and otherwise represents *-no*.
        ⟦**ɗon-**⟧ : [V, {stat.(i)/cont.(i)} : *ɗon-*]
    b. Group II (representative Series 1 subject-agreement rules)
        ⟦**mi-**⟧ : [V, {{sbj 1 sg ser.1}} : *mi-*] ⟦**min-**⟧ : [V, {{sbj 1 pl}} : *min-*]
        ⟦**'a-**⟧ : [V, {{sbj 2 sg ser.1}} : *'a-*] ⟦**'en-**⟧ : [V, {{sbj 2 pl incl ser.1}} : *'en-*]
        ⟦**'o-**⟧ : [V, {{sbj 3 sg nc1}} : *'o-*] ⟦**'on-**⟧ : [V, {{sbj 2 pl excl ser.1}} : *'on-*]
           ⟦**ɓe-**⟧ : [V, {{sbj 3 pl nc2}} : *ɓe-*]

Table 2.14 *The morphotactics of three Fula verb forms*

(a)	Form cell:	⟨*wallii*, {{sbj 3 sg nc1 ser.1} gen.pst act pret}⟩	's/he had helped'
	FER ↓	(⟦'o-⟧ ∘ ⟦-nO⟧) :	(= (55c))
	Realized cell:	⟨*'owalliino*, {{sbj 3 sg nc1 ser.1} gen.pst act pret}⟩	
(b)	Form cell:	⟨*-walla'*, {{sbj 3 sg nc1 ser.1} cont.(i) act –pret}⟩	's/he is helping'
	FER ↓	(⟦'o-⟧ ∘ ⟦ ɗon-⟧) :	(= (55j))
	Realized cell:	⟨*'oɗonwalla'*, {{sbj 3 sg nc1 ser.1} cont.(i) act –pret}⟩	
(c)	Form cell:	⟨*-walla'*, {{sbj 3 sg nc1 ser.1} cont.(i) act pret}⟩	's/he was helping'
	FER ↓	(⟦'o-⟧ ∘ (⟦-nO⟧ Ⓐ ⟦ɗon-⟧))	(=(57c))
	Realized cell:	⟨*'oɗonnowalla'*, {{sbj 3 sg nc1 ser.1} cont.(i) act pret}⟩	

The rules in (53b) are, on their own, FERs for the nonpreterite forms of the general past active in Table 2.13. In accordance with the FER pattern in (54), Group II rules compose with Group I rules to produce composite FERs. When they compose with ⟦-nO⟧, they produce the composite FERs in (55a–g); these FERs define the preterite forms of the general past active in Table 2.13. For example, in the realization of the preterite general past active form *'o-wallii-no* 's/he had helped', the composite FER (⟦'o-⟧ ∘ ⟦-nO⟧) in (55c) applies to the form cell in part (a) of Table 2.14 to yield the corresponding realized cell; the morphotactic definition of the other preterite general past active forms of 'help' in Table 2.13 follows similarly from the other composite rules in (55a–g). When Group II rules compose with ⟦ɗon-⟧, they produce the composite FERs in (55h–n); these FERs define the nonpreterite forms of the continuous-(i) active in Table 2.13. For instance, the nonpreterite continuous-(i) active form *'o-ɗon-walla'* 's/he is helping' in Table 2.13 involves the composite FER (⟦'o-⟧ ∘ ⟦ ɗon-⟧) in (55j), which applies to the form cell in part (b) of Table 2.14 to yield the corresponding realized cell; the morphotactic definition of the other nonpreterite continuous-(i) active forms of 'help' in Table 2.13 proceeds similarly.

2.4 Rule Aggregation   75

(54)   FER pattern for Fula verb forms
        Where R_I is a Group I rule and R_{II} a Group II rule, the composite rule
        ($R_{II} \circ R_I$) is a FER.

(55)   FERs defined by FER pattern (54)

   Composites of ⟦-nO⟧
   a.   (⟦mi-⟧ ∘ ⟦-nO⟧) :   [V, {{sbj 1 sg ser.1} pret} : X → mi-X-nO]
   b.   (⟦'a-⟧ ∘ ⟦-nO⟧) :   [V, {{sbj 2 sg ser.1} pret} : X → 'a-X-nO]
   c.   (⟦'o-⟧ ∘ ⟦-nO⟧) :   [V, {{sbj 3 sg nc1} pret} : X → 'o-X-nO]
   d.   (⟦min-⟧ ∘ ⟦-nO⟧) :   [V, {{sbj 1 pl} pret} : X → min-X-nO]
   e.   (⟦'en-⟧ ∘ ⟦-nO⟧) :   [V, {{sbj 2 pl incl ser.1} pret} : X → 'en-X-nO]
   f.   (⟦'on-⟧ ∘ ⟦-nO⟧) :   [V, {{sbj 2 pl excl ser.1} pret} : X → 'on-X-nO]
   g.   (⟦ɓe-⟧ ∘ ⟦-nO⟧) :   [V, {{sbj 3 pl nc2} pret} : X → ɓe-X-nO]

   Composites of ⟦ɗon-⟧
   h.   (⟦mi-⟧ ∘ ⟦ɗon-⟧) :   [V, {{sbj 1 sg ser.1} stat.(i)/cont.(i)} : miɗon-]
   i.   (⟦'a-⟧ ∘ ⟦ɗon-⟧) :   [V, {{sbj 2 sg ser.1} stat.(i)/cont.(i)} : 'aɗon-]
   j.   (⟦'o-⟧ ∘ ⟦ɗon-⟧) :   [V, {{sbj 3 sg nc1} stat.(i)/cont.(i)} : 'oɗon-]
   k.   (⟦min-⟧ ∘ ⟦ɗon-⟧) :   [V, {{sbj 1 pl} stat.(i)/cont.(i)} : minɗon-]
   l.   (⟦'en-⟧ ∘ ⟦ɗon-⟧) :   [V, {{sbj 2 pl incl ser.1} stat.(i)/cont.(i)} : 'enɗon-]
   m.   (⟦'on-⟧ ∘ ⟦ɗon-⟧) :   [V, {{sbj 2 pl excl ser.1} stat.(i)/cont.(i)} : 'onɗon-]
   n.   (⟦ɓe-⟧ ∘ ⟦ɗon-⟧) :   [V, {{sbj 3 pl nc2} stat.(i)/cont.(i)} : ɓeɗon-]

The FERs for the preterite forms of the general past active and those for the nonpreterite forms of the continuous-(i) active involve the composition of simple rules in (53). The morphotactic definition of the preterite continuous-(i) active forms of 'help' in Table 2.13 is marginally more complex, involving both aggregation and composition. In particular, the preterite ⟦-nO⟧ rule aggregates with the aspectual ⟦ɗon-⟧ rule to produce the rule of *ɗonnO-* prefixation in (56). Like its members, this aggregation belongs to Group I; thus, (⟦-nO⟧ Ⓐ ⟦ɗon-⟧), like ⟦-nO⟧, is a Group I rule realizing the preterite property. In accordance with the FER pattern in (54), the Group II rules in (53b) therefore compose not only with ⟦-nO⟧ and ⟦ɗon-⟧ but also with the aggregation (⟦-nO⟧ Ⓐ ⟦ɗon-⟧), to produce the additional composite FERs in (57). These FERs define the preterite forms of the continuous-(i) active in Table 2.13. For example, in the definition of the preterite continuous-(i) active form *'o-don-no-walla* 's/he was helping', the FER in (57c) applies to the form cell in part (c) of Table 2.14 to yield the corresponding realized cell. The morphotactic definition of the other preterite continuous-(i) active forms of 'help' in Table 2.13 follows similarly from the other composite rules in (57).

76 *Rule Combinations*

(56) A rule aggregation in Group I
([[-nO]] Ⓐ [[ɗon-]]) : [V, {stat.(i)/cont.(i) pret} : *ɗonno-*]

(57) Additional FERs defined by FER pattern (54)
    a. ([[mi-]] ∘ ([[-nO]] Ⓐ [[ɗon-]])) : [V, {{sbj 1 sg ser.1} stat.(i)/cont.(i) pret} : *miɗonno-*]
    b. ([['a-]] ∘ ([[-nO]] Ⓐ [[ɗon-]])) : [V, {{sbj 2 sg ser.1} stat.(i)/cont.(i) pret} : *'aɗonno-*]
    c. ([['o-]] ∘ ([[-nO]] Ⓐ [[ɗon-]])) : [V, {{sbj 3 sg nc1} stat.(i)/cont.(i) pret} : *'oɗonno-*]
    d. ([[min-]] ∘ ([[-nO]] Ⓐ [[ɗon-]])) : [V, {{sbj 1 pl} stat.(i)/cont.(i) pret} : *minɗonno-*]
    e. ([['en-]] ∘ ([[-nO]] Ⓐ [[ɗon-]])) : [V, {{sbj 2 pl incl ser.1} stat.(i)/cont.(i) pret} : *'enɗonno-*]
    f. ([['on-]] ∘ ([[-nO]] Ⓐ [[ɗon-]])) : [V, {{sbj 2 pl excl ser.1} stat.(i)/cont.(i) pret} : *'onɗonno-*]
    g. ([[ɓe-]] ∘ ([[-nO]] Ⓐ [[ɗon-]])) : [V, {{sbj 3 pl nc2} stat.(i)/cont.(i) pret} : *ɓeɗonno-*]

This analysis allows the preterite affix *-nO* to be seen as a suffix in both *'o-looti-nO* 's/he washed' and *'o-ɗon-nO-joodii* 's/he was seated': the difference is that in the former case, *-nO* is suffixed to the verb stem *looti-*, but in the latter case, as an effect of aggregation, it is instead suffixed to the aspectual prefix *ɗon-*. This synchronic analysis doubtless reflects the origins of *ɗon* as an auxiliary verb, whose historical reanalysis as a prefix has not yet robbed it of its ability to serve as an operand for the suffixation of *-nO* in the Gombe dialect of Fula (cf. the discussion of Pengo in Section 11.1.2).

According to the aggregation analysis, the Fula preterite suffix fails to conform to the stem operand criterion, since by definition, aggregation involves affixation to an affix rather than to a stem. At the same time, this analysis shows that although the Fula preterite affix seems to diverge from the affix directionality criterion, this divergence is merely apparent: although it seems to be a suffix in *'o-wallii-no* 's/he had helped' but a prefix in *'o-ɗon-no-walla'* 's/he was helping', it is in fact a suffix in both cases, being suffixed to the stem *wallii-* in one instance and to the prefix *ɗon-* in the other. In Chapters 7 and 8 I examine other, similar cases of affix counterposition, in each of which rule aggregation plays a role in the definition of a language's morphotactics.

As I have not encountered any convincing examples of rule aggregation in the derivational domain, I shall assume here that aggregation is a mode of combination restricted to rules of inflectional exponence.

2.5   Counterpotentiation

According to the intermediate well-formedness criterion, a lexeme that derives from some base through the successive application of two derivational rules canonically implies the existence of an intermediate lexeme, as the derivation of FOOLISHLY from FOOL implies the existence of FOOLISH. Languages

2.5 Counterpotentiation

sometimes present derived lexemes that deviate from this criterion; such cases involve two rules of derivation whose mode of combination is that of counterpotentiation.

The types of rule combination considered so far – composite rules, holistic combinations, and aggregations – are alike in that each has a domain-of-definition that is a subset of (and possibly identical to) the domain-of-definition of its righthand member. That is, the domain-of-definition of a composite rule ($R_2 \circ R_1$), that of a holistic combination $\circledS_y(R_2 \circ R_1)$, and that of an aggregation ($R_2 \circledA R_1$) are all subsets of the domain-of-definition of R_1. Another type of rule combination – that of *counterpotentiations* – diverges from these other types of rule combination in this respect.

Above (Section 2.1.2), three uses of a rule of derivational exponence are distinguished: the true derivational use (e.g. the use of ⟦-ate⟧ in deriving HYPHENATE from HYPHEN), the thematizing use (e.g. the use of ⟦-ate⟧ in defining the stem of INSINUATE), and the use in forming a combining stem (e.g. the use of ⟦-ate⟧ together with ⟦-ion⟧ in deriving VARIATION from VARY). Counterpotentiations account for the third of these uses.

Suppose that R_1 and R_2 are rules of derivational exponence possessing the characteristics in (58a,b). In that case, rules R_1 and R_2 may enter into a counterpotentiation (R_2 ⟦CP⟧$_n$ R_1), in which the *counterpotentiation operator* ⟦CP⟧$_n$ has the schematic interpretation in (58c).

(58) Counterpotentiation
    a. Let R_1 be the derivational rule [$\mu_1 \Rightarrow D : X \rightarrow f_1(X)$], whose domain-of-definition μ_1 is a subset of some set $\mathbb{C}$ of ⟨lexeme, stem, lexicosemantic category⟩ triplets, so that R_1 is a partial function from $\mathbb{C}$ to the set $\mathbb{D}$ of triplets of the type ⟨lexeme, stem, D⟩.
    b. Let R_2 be a derivational rule [$\mu_2 \Rightarrow E : X \rightarrow f_2(X)$] that defines members of the set $\mathbb{E}$ of triplets of type ⟨lexeme, stem, E⟩.
    c. In that case, the counterpotentiation
(R_2 ⟦CP⟧$_n$ R_1) : [$\mu_n \Rightarrow E : X \rightarrow f_2(f_1(X))$]
is a partial function from $\mathbb{C}$ to $\mathbb{E}$ whose domain-of-definition μ_n is disjoint from the domain-of-definition μ_1 of R_1.

According to this definition:

- the morphological operation associated with the counterpotentiation (R_2 ⟦CP⟧$_n$ R_1) is the combination of the operations f_2 and f_1 associated with R_2 and R_1;

78   *Rule Combinations*

- the domain of (R$_2$ ⌊CP⌋$_n$ R$_1$) is the same as the domain of R$_1$;
- by contrast, the domain-of-definition μ$_n$ of (R$_2$ ⌊CP⌋$_n$ R$_1$) is disjoint from the domain-of-definition μ$_1$ of R$_1$;
- the counterpotentiation (R$_2$ ⌊CP⌋$_n$ R$_1$), like R$_2$, defines triplets of type ⟨lexeme, stem, E⟩; and
- just as the individual rules R$_1$ and R$_2$ in (58a,b) conform to the derivational rule format in (14), so, too, does the definition of the counterpotentiation (R$_2$ ⌊CP⌋$_n$ R$_1$) in (58c).

The rule pairs entering into counterpotentiations seem to be of two main types: **pleonastic** and **compositionally motivated**. On one hand, it is possible that in (58), $\mathbb{D} = \mathbb{E}$ and μ$_1$, μ$_2$, and μ$_n$ are disjoint subsets of $\mathbb{C}$; in such cases, R$_1$, R$_2$, and (R$_2$ ⌊CP⌋$_n$ R$_1$) are all partial functions from $\mathbb{C}$ to $\mathbb{E}$, as in (59). Here, the counterpotentiation has a pleonastic quality.

(59)   Pleonastic counterpotentiation, where μ$_1$, μ$_2$, and μ$_n$ are disjoint subsets of $\mathbb{C}$
    a.   R$_1$: [μ$_1$ ⇒ E : X → f_1(X)]
    b.   R$_2$: [μ$_2$ ⇒ E : X → f_2(X)]
    c.   (R$_2$ ⌊CP⌋$_n$ R$_1$) : [μ$_n$ ⇒ E : X → $f_2(f_1$ (X))]

In English, for example, some causative verbs derive from an adjectival or nominal base by means of the prefixational 〚**en-**〛 rule (*able, rapture → enable, enrapture*); others, by means of the suffixational 〚**-en**〛 rule (*sad, strength → sadden, strengthen*); and still others, by means of the two rules in concert (*bold, light → embolden, enlighten*). As their definitions in (60)–(62) show, the 〚**en-**〛 rule, the〚**-en**〛 rule, and the counterpotentiation (〚**en-**〛 ⌊CP⌋$_{62}$ 〚**-en**〛) are alike in that all three are partial functions from the set $\mathbb{C}$ that includes triplets of types ⟨lexeme, stem, Adj⟩ and ⟨lexeme, stem, Noun⟩ to the set $\mathbb{E}$ of ⟨lexeme, stem, Causative verb⟩ triplets. The shaded triplets in (60) are in the domain-of-definition of the partial function 〚**en-**〛 but not in those of the partial functions 〚**-en**〛 or (〚**en-**〛 ⌊CP⌋$_{62}$ 〚**-en**〛) – hence the ungrammaticality of **ablen, *rapturen, *enablen,* and **enrapturen*. The shaded triplets in (61) are in the domain-of-definition of the partial function 〚**-en**〛 but not in those of the partial functions 〚**en-**〛 or (〚**en-**〛 ⌊CP⌋$_{62}$ 〚**-en**〛) – hence the ungrammaticality of **ensad, *enstrength, *ensadden,* and **enstrengthen*. The shaded triplets in (62) are in the domain-of-definition of the partial function (〚**en-**〛 ⌊CP⌋$_{62}$ 〚**-en**〛) but not in those of the partial functions 〚**en-**〛 or 〚**-en**〛 – hence the ungrammaticality of **embold, *enlight, *bolden,* and (in the relevant sense) **lighten*.

⟦**en-**⟧ : [μ_{60} ⇒ Causative verb : *en-*]

(60)   Representative members of μ_{60}: ⟨L, *able*, Adj⟩, ⟨L, *rapture*, Noun⟩

(61)   ⟦**-en**⟧ : [μ_{61} ⇒ Causative verb : *-en*]

Representative members of μ_{61}: ⟨L, *sad*, Adj⟩, ⟨L, *strength*, Noun⟩

(62)   (⟦**-en**⟧ $\boxed{CP}_{62}$ ⟦**en-**⟧) : [μ_{62} ⇒ Causative verb : X → *en*-X-*en*], where μ_{62} is disjoint from μ_{60}

Representative members of μ_{62}: ⟨L, *bold*, Adj⟩, ⟨L, *light*, Noun⟩

In addition to the counterpotentiations of the pleonastic type, there are also counterpotentiations that define affix combinations that appear elsewhere as an effect of ordinary composition. That is, two rules that enter into a composite rule may also enter into a compositionally motivated counterpotentiation, as in (63). This represents the possibility that in the scenario described in (58), ($R_2 \circ R_1$) and (R_2 $\boxed{CP}_n$ R_1) are both partial functions from $\mathbb{C}$ to $\mathbb{E}$.

(63)   Compositionally motivated counterpotentiation
    a. R_1 : [μ_1 ⇒ D : X → $f_1(X)$], where μ_1 is a subset of $\mathbb{C}$
    b. R_2 : [μ_2 ⇒ E : X → $f_2(X)$], where μ_2 is a subset of $\mathbb{D}$
    c.   ($R_2 \circ R_1$) : [μ_3 ⇒ E : X → $f_2(f_1(X))$], where μ_3 is a subset of μ_1
    d.   (R_2 $\boxed{CP}_n$ R_1) : [μ_n ⇒ E : X → $f_2(f_1(X))$], where μ_n is a subset of $\mathbb{C}$ disjoint from μ_1

Consider an example. In English, the ⟦**-ic**⟧ rule in (64) composes with ⟦**-ist**⟧ rule in (65), yielding derivational correspondences such as those in part (a) of Table 2.15. At the same time, there are adjectives in *-istic* for which there is no intermediate form in *-ist*; examples are the adjectives in part (b) of Table 2.15. Thus, whereas the adjectives in part (a) are defined by the composite rule (⟦**-ic**⟧ ∘ ⟦**-ist**⟧) in (66), those in part (b) are defined by the counterpotentiation (⟦**-ic**⟧ $\boxed{CP}_{67}$ ⟦**-ist**⟧) in (67). The counterpotentiation in (67) is unlike a counterpotentiation of the pleonastic type (e.g. the counterpotentiation (⟦**en-**⟧ $\boxed{CP}_{62}$ ⟦**-en**⟧) in (62)) in that it parallels an existing composite, namely (⟦**-ic**⟧ ∘ ⟦**-ist**⟧). The rules (⟦**-ic**⟧ ∘ ⟦**-ist**⟧) and (⟦**-ic**⟧ $\boxed{CP}_{67}$ ⟦**-ist**⟧) define forms that are affixally alike, but their domains-of-definition μ_{66} and μ_{67} are disjoint.

⟦**-ic**⟧ : [μ_{64} ⇒ Relational Adj : *-ic*]

Representative members of μ_{64}: ⟨L, *scene*, Noun⟩, ⟨L, *artist*, Noun⟩, ⟨L, *nationalist*, Adj⟩

80   *Rule Combinations*

Table 2.15 *Derivational correspondences involving adjectives in -istic*

	Base	Noun in *-ist*	Adjective in *-istic*
a.	art	artist	artistic
	journal	journalist	journalistic
	national	nationalist	nationalistic
b.	cannibal	*cannibalist	cannibalistic
	character	*characterist	characteristic
	probable	*probabilist	probabilistic

(65)   ⟦**-ist**⟧ : [μ_{65} ⇒ Noun/Adj : *-ist*]

   Representative members of μ_{65}: ⟨L, *art*, Noun⟩, ⟨L, *journal*, Noun⟩, ⟨L, *national*, Adj⟩

(66)   (⟦**-ic**⟧ ∘ ⟦**-ist**⟧) : [μ_{66} ⇒ Relational Adj : *-istic*]

   Representative members of μ_{66}: ⟨L, *art*, Noun⟩, ⟨L, *journal*, Noun⟩, ⟨L, *national*, Adj⟩

(67)   (⟦**-ic**⟧ $\boxed{\text{CP}}_{67}$ ⟦**-ist**⟧) : [μ_{67} ⇒ Relational Adj : *-istic*]

   Representative members of μ_{67}: ⟨L, *cannibal*, Noun⟩, ⟨L, *character*, Noun⟩, ⟨L, *probable*, Adj⟩

I return to the topic of counterpotentiation in Chapter 10.

2.6   A Rule Combination's Inner and Outer Rules

In general, the order in which two rules of morphology are combined is significant.[18] For instance, the composite rule (⟦**-al**⟧ ∘ ⟦**-ic**⟧) suffixes *-ical*, but the composite rule (⟦**-ic**⟧ ∘ ⟦**-al**⟧) suffixes *-alic*. It is therefore useful to be able to distinguish a combined rule's **inner rule** from its **outer rule**; in (⟦**-al**⟧ ∘ ⟦**-ic**⟧), for example, ⟦**-ic**⟧ is the inner rule and ⟦**-al**⟧ is the outer rule. Analogously, R_1 is the inner rule and R_2 the outer rule in the holistic combination $\text{Ⓢ}_y(R_2 \circ R_1)$, the aggregation ($R_2$ Ⓐ R_1), and the counterpotentiation (R_2 $\boxed{\text{CP}}_\zeta$ R_1).

---

[18] But given a prefixational rule ⟦**g-**⟧ and a suffixational rule ⟦**-h**⟧ having the same domain, the composition (⟦**-h**⟧ ∘ ⟦**g-**⟧) and the composition (⟦**g-**⟧ ∘ ⟦**-h**⟧) are extensionally equivalent.

In the discussion of rule combinations in the following chapters, it will frequently be observed that when two rules combine, they play different roles in that combination. A rule combination's inner rule determines three characteristics of the combination itself: (i) the domain of the rule combination is always that of its inner rule; (ii) the domain-of-definition of a rule combination is a subset of that of its inner rule unless the combination is itself a counterpotentiation, whose domain-of-definition is disjoint from that of its inner rule; and (iii) the operation defined by a rule aggregation is the same kind of operation (prefixational or suffixational) as that defined by its inner rule.

2.7 Conclusion

According to the morphotactic variety hypothesis (Section 1.2), rules of exponence may enter into different kinds of combinations possessing different characteristics. The present chapter has pursued this hypothesis, surveying a variety of modes of rule combination that can be plausibly claimed to figure in the morphotactics of the world's languages: these are the modes of composition, holistic combination, aggregation, and counterpotentiation.

These concepts lay the foundation for the chapters that follow, in which I provide extensive empirical evidence that the definition of a language's morphology makes essential reference to the modes of rule combination distinguished here. The first part of this discussion focuses on the properties of rule composition in the analysis of dependent rules and their carrier rules (Chapter 3), in the analysis of unexpected rule orderings (Chapter 4), and in the analysis of apparently noncanonical patterns of morphotactic conditioning and paradigmatic opposition among rules of inflectional exponence (Chapter 5). In Chapter 6, I examine rule combinations in Breton, Limbu, and Old English that express holistic content; these must be represented as holistic combinations rather than as ordinary composite rules. Chapter 7 is devoted to instances of rule aggregation in the morphology of Noon and Lithuanian; Chapters 8 and 9 present detailed morphotactic analyses of verb inflection in Swahili and Murrinhpatha, in which patterns of rule combination interact in complex ways. In Chapter 10, I examine the contrary phenomena of potentiation and counterpotentiation in the derivational morphology of English.

Chapters 11 and 12 discuss rule combinations in broader contexts. Chapter 11 concerns both the kinds of synchronic simplifications that rule combinations afford in a morphotactic system and the kinds of diachronic simplifications that result from the erosion of such combinations. In Chapter 12, I discuss the significance of exponence-based, rule-combining morphotactics for the broader landscape of current morphological theory. I summarize my conclusions in Chapter 13.

3 Dependent Rules and Carrier Rules

In this chapter and the two that follow, I develop the claim that the definition of a language's morphology makes essential reference to the composition of rules. The truth of this claim is not self-evident, given that the result of applying a composite rule ($R_2 \circ R_1$) is seemingly indistinguishable from the result of successively applying the inner rule R_1 and the outer rule R_2 without composition. Nevertheless, at least three kinds of evidence reveal that rule composition is an essential feature of a language's morphotactics:

- A rule's application may be dependent on that of a carrier rule, and composition is the appropriate expression of this dependency. Such dependencies are deviations from the rule independence criterion (Section 1.5.2).
- If rules realizing inflectional category A ordinarily apply before rules realizing inflectional category B, there may be special cases in which a particular B rule is licensed to apply before a particular A rule, and composition is the appropriate expression of this licensing. Special orderings of this sort are deviations from the parallel sequence criterion (Section 1.5.3).
- Certain phenomena appear not to conform to canonical morphotactic criteria if they are seen as involving simple rules but come into conformity with these criteria once they are seen as potentially involving composite rules. Examples include apparent deviations from the integral stem criterion (Section 1.5.8) and the rule opposition criterion (Section 1.5.9).

In this chapter and in the two subsequent chapters, I discuss evidence of these sorts and demonstrate how the proposed representation of rule composition accounts for it.

In the present chapter, I show that rule composition makes it possible to model an important kind of deviation from the rule independence criterion – cases in which the application of one rule is directly dependent on that of another, carrier rule. In such cases, the only use of the dependent rule is as part of a composite rule incorporating both the dependent rule and its carrier. In case the definition of a word form involves two carrier rules, it can further happen that the same dependent rule composes with both of them, engendering a pattern of multiple exponence that deviates from the unique sequence criterion (Section 1.5.4). I begin (Section 3.1) by relating the notion of dependent rules to the notion of dependent affixes introduced by Harris (2017). I then discuss two patterns of rule dependency. First, I show that Limbu possesses a pattern in which a dependent rule composes with its carrier rule to produce a composite ($R_{dependent} \circ R_{carrier}$). Second, I show that Sanskrit possesses a pattern of the reverse sort, in which a carrier rule composes with its dependent to produce a composite ($R_{carrier} \circ R_{dependent}$).

Before proceeding, let me concisely recapitulate the assumed conception of rule composition given in Section 2.2. Given two rules of morphology, the composition of those two rules is itself a composite rule. In accordance with the proposals in Section 2.3, I assume that the composite ($[\![-b]\!] \circ [\![-a]\!]$) of the inflectional rules in (1) is as defined in (2), and that the composite ($[\![-d]\!] \circ [\![-c]\!]$) of the derivational rules in (3) is as defined in (4).

(1) Two inflectional rules $[\![-a]\!] : [C, \alpha : -a]$
$[\![-b]\!] : [C', \beta : -b]$

(2) $([\![-b]\!] \circ [\![-a]\!]) : [[C \cap C'], [\alpha \sqcup \beta] : -ab]$

(3) Two derivational rules $[\![-c]\!] : [\mu_3 \Rightarrow Q : -c]$
$[\![-d]\!] : [\nu_3 \Rightarrow R : -d]$

(4) $([\![-d]\!] \circ [\![-c]\!]) : [\mu_4 \Rightarrow R : -cd]$
(NB: The domain-of-definition μ_4 of ($[\![-d]\!] \circ [\![-c]\!]$) is the smallest set such that for any triplet t in the domain-of-definition μ_3 of $[\![-c]\!]$, μ_4 contains t if the result of applying $[\![-c]\!]$ to t belongs to the domain-of-definition ν_3 of $[\![-d]\!]$.)

3.1 Dependent Rules and Rule Composition

In the 1970s, P. H. Matthews introduced the term **extended exponence** (or **multiple exponence**) to describe a situation "in which a category, if positively identified at all, would have exponents in each of two or more distinct positions" within a word (1974: 149). In her book *Multiple exponence*, Harris (2017) identifies the four frequent types of multiple exponence. One of these – periodic multiple exponence – is of particular interest here. According to Harris (pp. 55f.), periodic multiple exponence "occurs when a bound morpheme must be accompanied by an exponent of feature F, while the stem must also be accompanied by an exponent of F. In addition to the base and the multiple exponents, we can identify a carrier morpheme, a bound morpheme that requires the presence of one of the multiple exponents."

Noon (Cangin; Senegal) provides a clear example. In Noon, an indefinite noun carries its noun-class marker as a prefix (*k-edik* 'tree', *t-edik* 'trees') and a definite noun additionally has a deictic suffix (*-ii* proximal, *-um* medial, or *-aa* distal) which itself serves as the carrier for a second instance of the noun's noun-class marker (*k-edik-k-ii* 'the tree (near me)', *t-edik-t-um* 'the trees (near you)'. Thus, Noon noun-class marking exhibits a pattern of periodic multiple exponence in which a definite noun's deictic suffix acts as a carrier morpheme (cf. pp. 57f.)

As this example shows, periodic multiple exponence involves four elements: a stem, a carrier morpheme, and two dependent morphemes (= the multiple exponents), one associated with the stem and the other associated with the carrier morpheme. Periodic multiple exponence might therefore be represented as the schematic pattern (5a). But the concepts 'dependent morpheme' and 'carrier morpheme' are not logically restricted to the phenomenon of periodic multiple exponence. Whenever the incidence of morpheme A depends directly on that of morpheme B, it is reasonable to think of A as a dependent morpheme and of B as its carrier morpheme, whether they form part of a larger pattern of periodic multiple exponence (as in (5a)) or not (as in (5b)). By the same token, one can imagine a word form exhibiting multiple exponence in which none of the dependent morphemes is directly associated with the stem but in which each dependent morpheme is associated with its own carrier morpheme distinct from the stem, as in the schematic pattern in (5c); though (5c) is not strictly the same as the pattern in (5a), the notion of periodic multiple exponence might reasonably be seen as subsuming both (5a) and (5c). In any event, I shall, in the following discussion, use the terms 'dependent' and 'carrier' in the less restricted sense encompassing all three of the patterns schematized in (5).

(5) a. [[Stem-dependent][Carrier-dependent]]   (periodic multiple exponence)
     b. [Stem [Carrier-dependent]]
     c. [Stem [Carrier-dependent][Carrier-dependent]]

In a rule-based conception of morphology, the distinction between dependent morphemes and carrier morphemes can be recast as a difference between dependent rules and carrier rules. A dependent rule is then a rule that is only used in composition with some other rule, which is thus its carrier. (Somewhat less categorically, one could, alternatively, say that a rule is dependent to the extent that its use is restricted to composite rules involving some other, carrier rule.) Logically, the dependent member of a composite rule might be either the outer rule in that composite (with the inner rule its carrier, as in the composite type ($R_{dependent} \circ R_{carrier}$)) or the composite's inner rule (with the outer rule its carrier, as in the composite type ($R_{carrier} \circ R_{dependent}$)); instances of both sorts exist, as I now show.

3.2 Outer Dependent Rules in Limbu Verb Morphology

Limbu (Kiranti; Nepal) presents clear examples of composite rules of the type ($R_{dependent} \circ R_{carrier}$), in which the dependent rule composes with its carrier rule. Limbu verb inflection involves a complex system of agreement that encodes both subject and object. At issue here are two suffixes: the first-person singular agent concord *-ŋ* and the nonthird-person plural agent concord *-m*, whose use is exemplified in the positive nonpreterite paradigm of HU?MA? 'teach' in Table 3.1. These suffixes are special in two ways. First, they may appear in two different positions in a verb form's morphology (in affix positions 5 and 9, in the numbering employed in Table 3.1),[1] and second, they appear in these positions only if a carrier affix appears in the immediately preceding affix position (positions 4 and 8).[2] As a consequence of these peculiarities, these affixes can participate in a verb form's morphotactics in three distinct ways. If a word form has carrier affixes in both position 4 and position 8, then the agent suffix appears in both position 5 and position 9, as in *hu?ruŋsiŋ* 'I teach them' (rows (e), (g), (j), (m) of Table 3.1); if a word form has a carrier affix in position 4 but not position 8, then the agent suffix only appears in position 5, as in *hu?ruŋ* 'I teach her/him' (rows (b), (c), (d), (f), (i), (l) of Table 3.1); and if a carrier affix appears in neither position 4 nor position 8, then no agent suffix appears, as in *hu?nɛ* 'I teach you (sg.)' (row (a) of

---

[1] The placement of *-m* and *-ŋ* in Table 3.1 differs slightly from what is assumed by van Driem (1987: 368). He situates the *-ŋ* in forms such as *hu?-nɛ-tchi₁-ŋ* 'I teach you (du.)' and *hu?-n-i-ŋ* 'I teach you (pl.)' (but not that in *hu?r-u-ŋ* 'I teach him/her') in suffix position 9 rather than in position 5; and he situates the first *-m* in a form such as *a-hu?r-u-m-si-m* 'we (incl.) teach them' in suffix position 7 rather than in position 5. It is not clear, however, that there is synchronic motivation for these assumed deviations of *-m* and *-ŋ* from the simpler distributional pattern represented in Table 3.1.

[2] Zimmerman (2012) attributes the appearance of *-ŋ* and *-m* more than once in the same word form to a phonological copying process; cf. also van Driem (1987: 102). This implies an implausible depth of interaction between phonology and morphology and fails to account for the dependency of *-ŋ* and *-m* on a carrier affix even in forms in which no doubling appears. See Section 12.4 for additional relevant discussion.

Table 3.1 *The agent suffixes -ŋ and -m in the positive nonpreterite paradigm of the Limbu verb HUʔMAʔ 'teach'* (prevocalic stem *huʔr*, default stem *huʔ*)

	agent → patient	Prefix positions		Stem	Suffix positions						
		−2	−1		1	4	5	7	8	9	10
a.	1SG → 2SG			*huʔ*	nɛ						
b.	1SG → 2DU			*huʔ*	nɛ	*tchi₁*					
c.	1SG → 2PL			*huʔ*	n(ɛ)*	*i*	*ŋ*				
d.	1SG → 3SG			*huʔr*		*u*	*ŋ*				
e.	1SG → 3NONSG			*huʔr*		*u*	*ŋ*		*si*	*ŋ*	
f.	1PL.INCL → 3SG	*a*		*huʔr*		*u*	*m*				
g.	1PL.INCL → 3NONSG	*a*		*huʔr*		*u*	*m*		*si*	*m*	
h.	1NONSG.EXCL → 2			*huʔ*	nɛ			*tchi₂*			*ge*
i.	1PL.EXCL → 3SG			*huʔr*		*u*	*m*				*be*****
j.	1PL.EXCL → 3NONSG			*huʔr*		*u*	*m*		*si*	*m*	*be*****
k.	2 → 1	*a*	*ge*†	*huʔ*							
l.	2PL → 3SG		*kɛ*	*huʔr*		*u*	*m*				
m.	2PL → 3NONSG		*kɛ*	*huʔr*		*u*	*m*		*si*	*m*	

* The parenthesized vowel ɛ is elided prevocalically (van Driem 1987: 89).
** The suffix *-be* arises from *-ge* through assimilation to preceding *-m* (van Driem 1987: 102).
† The prefix *gɛ-* arises from *kɛ-* through intervocalic voicing (van Driem 1987: 2).
(van Driem 1987: 367–374)

Table 3.1). In this way, the agent suffixes *-ŋ* and *-m* are wholly dependent on carrier affixes to enable them to appear.[3]

In order to account for the morphotactic patterns in Table 3.1, I assume that the individual affixes in this table are introduced by the simple rules of exponence in (6) and (7) and that these rules combine in specific ways to form the full exponence rules (FERs) that define the table's thirteen word forms. The rules in (6) belong to six specific groups; as will be seen presently, the numbering of these groups corresponds to the order in which their member rules compose. Among these groups, Groups 4 and 6 are special, since they contain both the individual rules in (6) and the composite rules in (8). Group 4 contains the carrier rules 〚**-u**〛, 〚**-tchi₁**〛, and 〚**-i**〛 (whose affixes occupy position 4 in Table 3.1) but also contains their carrier+dependent composites in (8a); Group 6 contains the carrier rule 〚**-si**〛 (whose affix occupies position 8 in Table 3.1) but also contains its carrier+dependent composites in (8b). The rules 〚**-ŋ**〛 and 〚**-m**〛 in (7) are dependent rules whose only use is in the composites in (8); they themselves don't belong to any group, but their composites do.[4] Each of the composites in (8) belongs to the same rule group as its carrier rule, and because each composite is narrower than its carrier rule, the composites in (8) override the simple carrier rules in (6) in any instance in which they come into competition.

(6) Basic rules of exponence for Limbu verb inflection (part I; part II is in (13))
Group 1 〚**kɛ-**〛 :   [V, {{2}} : *kɛ-*]   (cf. van Driem 1987: 80f.)
         〚**-nɛ**〛 :   [V, {{agt 1}{pat 2}} : *-nɛ*] (pp. 88f.)
Group 2 〚**a-**〛 :   [V, {{1}} : *a-*]   (pp. 77ff.)
Group 3 [to be discussed in connection with (13) below.]
Group 4 〚**-u**〛 :   [V, {{pat 3}} : *-u*]   (p. 82)
         〚**-tchi₁**〛 : [V, {{pat/sbj du}} : *-tchi*] (pp. 94f.)
         〚**-i**〛 :   [V, {{pat/sbj 1/2 pl}} : *-i*] (pp. 95f.)
Group 5 〚**-tchi₂**〛 : [V, {{agt 1 –sg}{pat 2}} : *-tchi*] (p. 100)
Group 6 〚**-si**〛 :   [V, {{pat 3 –sg}} : *-si*]   (pp. 101f.)
Group 7 〚**-ge**〛 :   [V, {{1 excl}} : *-ge*]   (pp. 102f.)

---

[3] The possibility that a carrier affix may appear in position 8 but not in position 4 is not realized in Table 3.1 (nor in Table 3.3), but this possibility is realized in negative preterite forms such as (i), where the first-person singular agent suffix *-ŋ* appears only in position 8; cf. van Driem (1987: 98, 369).

(i) *mɛ-n-huʔ-baŋ-si-ŋ*
     NEG-NEG-teach-AGT:1SG.PAT:3.NEG.PRET-PAT:3NONSG-AGT:1SG
     'I did not teach them'

[4] Some of the rules in (6)–(8) involve disjunctive notation (e.g. pat/sbj and 1/2). Here and throughout, this notation is a convention for abbreviating parallel rules; thus, [V, {{pat/sbj du}} : *-tchi*] abbreviates the two rules [V, {{pat du}} : *-tchi*] and [V, {{sbj du}} : *-tchi*].

3.2 *Outer Dependent Rules in Limbu*   89

(7) Dependent rules for Limbu verb inflection (cf. van Driem 1987: 99f.)
⟦-ŋ⟧ : [V, {{agt 1 sg}} : -ŋ]   ⟦-m⟧ : [V, {{agt 1/2 pl}} : -m]
Dependency constraint: These rules must compose with carrier rules in Groups 4 and 6 in (6).

(8) Rules composing ⟦-ŋ⟧ and ⟦-m⟧ with the carrier rules in Groups 4 and 6 in (6)
a. Group 4 (⟦-ŋ⟧ ∘ ⟦-u⟧) :   [V, {{agt 1 sg}{pat 3}} : -uŋ]
             (⟦-ŋ⟧ ∘ ⟦-tchi$_1$⟧) : [V, {{agt 1 sg}{pat du}} : -tchiŋ]
             (⟦-ŋ⟧ ∘ ⟦-i⟧) :   [V, {{agt 1 sg}{pat 2 pl}} : -iŋ]
             (⟦-m⟧ ∘ ⟦-u⟧) :   [V, {{agt 1/2 pl}{pat 3}} : -um]
b. Group 6 (⟦-ŋ⟧ ∘ ⟦-si⟧) :   [V, {{agt 1 sg}{pat 3 –sg}} : -siŋ]
             (⟦-m⟧ ∘ ⟦-si⟧) :   [V, {{agt 1/2 pl}{pat 3 –sg}} : -sim]

The composite rules in (8) model the Limbu deviation from the independent rule criterion, representing the dependency of ⟦-ŋ⟧ and ⟦-m⟧ on their carrier rules as a relation of rule composition. When a Limbu word form involves the application of two rules from (8) – one from Group 4, the other from Group 6 – the resulting pattern of multiple exponence also constitutes a deviation from the unique sequence criterion; in the definition of *huʔruŋsiŋ* 'teach them', for example, the ⟦-ŋ⟧ rule applies both before the ⟦-si⟧ rule and after it. This becomes clear once the FERs defining the forms in Table 3.1 are projected from the rules in (6)–(8). But projecting the FERs involves a couple of complications.

Before taking up these complications, consider first what most of the FERs for the verb forms in Table 3.1 will be like. The FERs for these forms are of three types: those consisting of a rule from a single group, those in which rules from two groups are composed, and those in which rules from three groups are composed. The order of composition in all cases conforms to the numbering of the rule groups involved, as in (9).

(9) Licensed types of FERs for the Limbu verb forms in Table 3.1 (where i, j, k ∈ {1, 2, 4, 5, 6, 7} and i < j < k)
a. Rules of Type R_i : rules belonging to Group i.
b. Rules of Type (R_j ∘ R_i) : composites of a Group j rule with a Group i rule.
c. Rules of Type (R_k ∘ (R_j ∘ R_i)): composites of a Group k rule, a Group j rule, and a Group i rule.

This is a generally accurate characterization of the types of FERs necessary to define the forms in Table 3.1. One complication, however, is that some of the logically possible ways of composing the rules in (6)–(8) are excluded; that is, there are rules in (6)–(8) that are logically compatible with composition but which never participate as part of the same FER. Among these are the rules listed in (10). Van Driem (1987:

77f.) points out that the affix combinations listed in (10a–c) would lead to redundancy if they occurred. Because ⟦a-⟧ expresses the category-indeterminate property set {{1}} (as in (6, Group 2)), its application is rendered redundant by that of ⟦-nɛ⟧, which expresses the property set {{agt 1}{pat 2}} (as in (6, Group 1)); by that of ⟦-ŋ⟧, which expresses the property set {{agt 1 sg}} (as in (7)); and by that of ⟦-ge⟧, which expresses the property set {{1 excl}} (as in (6, Group 7)). Perhaps as a consequence of these facts, composites involving the ⟦-nɛ⟧, ⟦-ŋ⟧, and ⟦-ge⟧ rules do not include the ⟦a-⟧ rule. The failure of the rule pairs in (10a–c) to participate in composite rules cannot, however, be seen as evidence of a general anti-redundancy principle in Limbu morphology, since many of the forms in Table 3.1 are defined by redundant rule combinations (most obviously, those involving a repetition of the same rule); for instance, the composite rule ((⟦-ŋ⟧ ∘ ⟦-si⟧) ∘ (⟦-ŋ⟧ ∘ ⟦-u⟧)) introduces redundant expressions of {{pat 3}} and {{agt 1 sg}}, and (⟦-ge⟧ ∘ (⟦-tchi$_2$⟧ ∘ ⟦-nɛ⟧)) introduces redundant expressions of {{agt 1}{pat 2}}. Thus, the fact that the rules in (10) are redundant may be a part of the explanation for the fact that they are not licensed to enter into the same compositions, but it cannot be the whole explanation. The restriction in (10) must simply be seen as the effect of a stipulation to the effect that the rules paired in (10) do not enter into the same compositions.

(10) Rules that never participate in the same composite rule
    a. ⟦a-⟧ and ⟦-nɛ⟧   (cf. van Driem 1987: 78)
    b. ⟦a-⟧ and ⟦-ŋ⟧   (p. 78)
    c. ⟦a-⟧ and ⟦-ge⟧   (p. 77)

Thus, the first complication is that not all of the composite rules characterized by (9b,c) are licensed. An additional complication is that one of the forms in Table 3.1 is likely defined by a noncompositional rule combination: specifically, the definition of the form *a-gɛ-hu?* 'you teach me/us' is best seen as involving the holistic combination Ⓢ$_{\{\{agt\ 2\}\{pat\ 1\}\}}$(⟦a-⟧ ∘ ⟦kɛ-⟧). (I defer discussion of this fact to Section 6.3.)

These complications make it desirable to supplement the characterization of licensed types of FERs in (9) with the stipulations in (11).

(11)   a. The holistic rule combination Ⓢ$_{\{\{agt\ 2\}\{pat\ 1\}\}}$(⟦a-⟧ ∘ ⟦kɛ-⟧) is licensed.
    b. **Licensing constraint:** Among rules of the types in (9), only those not involving the rule pairs in (10a–c) are licensed.

Assuming this mode of licensing for the relevant FER types, the FER pattern for the forms in Table 3.1 may be characterized as in (12).

(12)   FER pattern for the Limbu verb forms in Table 3.1
For each cell ⟨Z, σ⟩ in the form paradigm of a verb in the fragment of Limbu verb inflection represented in Table 3.1, the FER for ⟨Z, σ⟩ is that licensed rule belonging to one of the types in (9)/(11) that contains the narrowest applicable rule (if such exists) from each of the rule groups in (6) and (8).

The thirteen forms in Table 3.1 are thus defined by means of the FERs in Table 3.2, each of which instantiates the characterization in (12). Of the thirteen FERs in this table, ten deviate from the rule independence criterion because they involve composites from (8); of these, four additionally deviate from the unique sequence criterion because they simultaneously involve two composites from (8), with the same dependent rule (either ⟦-ŋ⟧ or ⟦-m⟧) composing with more than one carrier rule.

The preterite inflection of transitive verbs presents another striking case in which the composition of compatible rules is not licensed. Thus, consider the positive preterite paradigm of HUʔMAʔ 'teach' in Table 3.3. The forms in this paradigm involve two additional basic suffixes. Most involve the preterite suffix -ε; those that do not instead involve the portmanteau suffix -mʔna, an expression of the property set {pret {agt 1 pl excl}{pat 3}}. The ⟦-ε⟧ and ⟦-mʔna⟧ rules are formulated in (13).

(13)   Basic rules of exponence for Limbu verb inflection (part II; part I is in (6))
Group 3   ⟦-ε⟧ :   [V, {pret} : -ε]   (cf. van Driem 1987: 89)
          ⟦-mʔna⟧ :   [V, {pret {agt 1 pl excl}{pat 3}} : -mʔna]   (pp. 100f.)

These rules both belong to a new, seventh rule group, Group 3; in order to accommodate this addition, the FER types in (11) and the FER pattern in (12) must be supplemented. The ⟦-ε⟧ rule composes straightforwardly with existing rules. The ⟦-mʔna⟧ rule, by contrast, is quite idiosyncratic. The ⟦-si⟧ rule composes with it as in (14); on the other hand, it fails to participate in composite rules involving any of ⟦-u⟧, ⟦-m⟧, or ⟦-ge⟧. (Compare rows (i), (j) of Table 3.3.) The application of the ⟦-mʔna⟧ rule makes that of these three other rules redundant; note, by contrast, that the composite rule (⟦-si⟧ ∘ ⟦-mʔna⟧) in (14) is nonredundant. To account for these facts, I assume that Limbu verb morphology licenses the FER in (14) but that it doesn't license composite rules involving ⟦-mʔna⟧ together with any of ⟦-u⟧, ⟦-m⟧, or ⟦-ge⟧. This fact about the morphotactics of Limbu verbs is surprising in at least one respect: even though ⟦-si⟧ elsewhere acts as a carrier of ⟦-m⟧, it cannot carry ⟦-m⟧ when it enters into composition with ⟦-mʔna⟧.

(14)   (⟦-si⟧ ∘ ⟦-mʔna⟧) : [V, {pret {agt 1 pl excl}{pat 3 –sg}} : -mʔnasi]

Table 3.2 *FERs for the thirteen Limbu verb forms in Table 3.1*

(where R_n represents a rule in Group n)

FER type	FER label	FER definition	Form in Table 3.1	
R_1	[**-nɛ**] :	[V, {{agt 1}{pat 2}} : *-nɛ*]	*huʔnɛ*	in row (a)
$(R_4 \circ R_1)$	(([**-ŋ**] ∘ [**-tchi₁**]) ∘ [**-nɛ**]) :	[V, {{agt 1 sg}{pat 2 du}} : *-netchiŋ*]	*huʔnetchiŋ*	(b)
$(R_4 \circ R_1)$	(([**-ŋ**] ∘ [**-i**]) ∘ [**-nɛ**]) :	[V, {{agt 1 sg}{pat 2 pl}} : *-niŋ*]	*huʔniŋ*	(c)
R_4	([**-ŋ**] ∘ [**-u**]) :	[V, {{agt 1 sg}{pat 3}} : *-uŋ*]	*huʔruŋ*	(d)
$(R_6 \circ R_4)$	(([**-ŋ**] ∘ [**-si**]) ∘ ([**-ŋ**] ∘ [**-u**])) :	[V, {{agt 1 sg}{pat 3 –sg}} : *-uŋsiŋ*]	*huʔruŋsiŋ*	(e)
$(R_4 \circ R_2)$	(([**-m**] ∘ [**-u**]) ∘ [**a-**]) :	[V, {{agt 1 pl –excl}{pat 3}} : $X \to a$-X-*um*]	*ahuʔrum*	(f)
$(R_6 \circ (R_4 \circ R_2))$	(([**-m**] ∘ [**-si**]) ∘ (([**-m**] ∘ [**-u**]) ∘ [**a-**])) :	[V, {{agt 1 pl –excl}{pat 3 –sg}} : $X \to a$-X-*umsim*]	*ahuʔrumsim*	(g)
$(R_7 \circ (R_5 \circ R_1))$	([**-ge**] ∘ ([**-tchi₂**] ∘ [**-nɛ**])) :	[V, {{agt 1 –sg excl}{pat 2}} : *-netchige*]	*huʔnetchige*	(h)
$(R_7 \circ R_4)$	([**-ge**] ∘ ([**-m**] ∘ [**-u**])) :	[V, {{agt 1 excl pl}{pat 3}} : *-umbe*]	*huʔrumbe*	(i)
$(R_7 \circ (R_6 \circ R_4))$	([**-ge**] ∘ (([**-m**] ∘ [**-si**]) ∘ ([**-m**] ∘ [**-u**]))) :	[V, {{agt 1 excl pl}{pat 3 –sg}} : *-umsimbe*]	*huʔrumsimbe*	(j)
[see §6.3]	Ⓢ({{agt 2}{pat 1}})([**a-**] ∘ ⟦**kɛ-**⟧) :	[V, {{agt 2}{pat 1}} : *agɛ-*]	*agɛhuʔ*	(k)
$(R_4 \circ R_1)$	(([**-m**] ∘ [**-u**]) ∘ [**kɛ-**]) :	[V, {{agt 2 pl}{pat 3}} : $X \to k\varepsilon$-X-*um*]	*kɛhuʔrum*	(l)
$(R_6 \circ (R_4 \circ R_1))$	(([**-m**] ∘ [**-si**]) ∘ (([**-m**] ∘ [**-u**]) ∘ [**kɛ-**])) :	[V, {{agt 2 pl}{pat 3-sg}}] : $X \to$ $k\varepsilon$-X-*umsim*]	*kɛhuʔrumsim*	(m)

Table 3.3 *The agent suffixes -ŋ and -m in the positive preterite paradigm of the Limbu verb* HU?MA? *'teach'*
(prevocalic stem *hu?r*, default stem *hu?*)

	agent → patient	Prefix positions		Stem	Suffix positions							
		−2	−1		1	2	4	5	7	8	9	10
a.	1SG → 2SG			*hu?*	n(ε)*	ε						
b.	1SG → 2DU			*hu?*	n(ε)	ε	tchi₁					
c.	1SG → 2PL			*hu?*	n(ε)	(ε)	i	ŋ				
d.	1SG → 3SG			*hu?r*		(ε)	u	ŋ				
e.	1SG → 3NONSG			*hu?r*		(ε)	u	ŋ		si	ŋ	
f.	1PL.INCL → 3SG	a		*hu?r*		(ε)	u	m				
g.	1PL.INCL → 3NONSG	a		*hu?r*		(ε)	u	m		si	m	
h.	1PL.EXCL → 2			*hu?*	n(ε)	ε			tchi₂			ge
i.	1PL.EXCL → 3SG			*hu?*		m?na		m				
j.	1PL.EXCL → 3NONSG			*hu?*		m?na		m		si		
k.	2 → 1	a	ge**	*hu?r*		ε						
l.	2PL → 3SG		kε	*hu?r*		(ε)	u	m				
m.	2PL → 3NONSG		kε	*hu?r*		(ε)	u	m		si	m	

* The parenthesized vowel *ε* is elided prevocalically (van Driem 1987: 89).
** The prefix *gε-* arises from *kε-* through intervocalic voicing (van Driem 1987: 2).
(van Driem 1987: 367–374)

94 *Dependent Rules and Carrier Rules*

In order to revise the proposed morphotactic analysis to accommodate the forms in Table 3.3 along with those in Table 3.1, it is necessary to extend the set of licensed FER types, as in (15), and to make the the FER pattern sensitive to this extension, as in (16).

(15) Licensed types of FERs for the Limbu verb forms in Tables 3.1 and 3.3 (where h, i, j, k ∈ {1, 2, 3, 4, 5, 6, 7} and h < i < j < k)
   a. Rules of Type R_h : rules belonging to Group h.
   b. Rules of Type ($R_i \circ R_h$) : composites of a Group i rule with a Group h rule.
   c. Rules of Type ($R_j \circ (R_i \circ R_h)$): composites of a Group j rule, a Group i rule, and a Group h rule.
   d. Rules of Type ($R_k \circ (R_j \circ (R_i \circ R_h))$): composites of a Group k rule, a Group j rule, a Group i rule, and a Group h rule.
   e. The holistic combination $Ⓢ_{\{\{agt\ 2\}\{pat\ 1\}\}}(\llbracket a\text{-}\rrbracket \circ \llbracket kɛ\text{-}\rrbracket)$.
   Constraints: Among the rules of these types, the Group 6 rule $\llbracket\text{-si}\rrbracket$ is the only rule whose composition with the Group 3 rule $\llbracket\text{-m?na}\rrbracket$ is licensed; otherwise, only those rules not involving the rule pairs in (10a–c) are licensed.

(16) FER pattern for the Limbu verb forms in Tables 3.1 and 3.3
   For each cell ⟨Z, σ⟩ in the form paradigm of a verb in the fragment of Limbu verb inflection in Tables 3.1 and 3.3, the FER for ⟨Z, σ⟩ is that licensed rule belonging to one of the types in (15) that contains the narrowest applicable rule (if such exists) from each of the groups in (6), (8), and (13).

This analysis of Limbu verb inflection models its deviation from the rule independence criterion, insofar as it makes the application of rules $\llbracket\text{-ŋ}\rrbracket$ and $\llbracket\text{-m}\rrbracket$ entirely conditional on that of a carrier rule. In this way, it accounts for a variety of facts for which no alternative explanation is obvious. Consider the Limbu verb forms in (17). These forms all have a first-person singular agent; yet, the first-person singular agent rule $\llbracket\text{-ŋ}\rrbracket$ doesn't apply at all in (17a), it applies once in (17b), and it applies twice in (17c). The proposed analysis accounts for this difference as in parts (a)–(c) of Table 3.4. In each of these parts, the form cells are realized by the narrowest applicable FER in Table 3.2. In part (a), the FER for (17a) is $\llbracket\text{-nɛ}\rrbracket$; because this FER doesn't contain a carrier rule for $\llbracket\text{-ŋ}\rrbracket$, the $\llbracket\text{-ŋ}\rrbracket$ rule doesn't apply at all here. In part (b) of Table 3.4, the FER for (17b) is ($\llbracket\text{-ŋ}\rrbracket \circ \llbracket\text{-u}\rrbracket$) – the composite of $\llbracket\text{-ŋ}\rrbracket$ with the carrier rule $\llbracket\text{-u}\rrbracket$. In part (c) of Table 3.4, the FER for (17c) is (($\llbracket\text{-ŋ}\rrbracket \circ \llbracket\text{-si}\rrbracket$) ∘ ($\llbracket\text{-ŋ}\rrbracket \circ \llbracket\text{-u}\rrbracket$)), in which $\llbracket\text{-ŋ}\rrbracket$ applies twice because $\llbracket\text{-u}\rrbracket$ and $\llbracket\text{-si}\rrbracket$ are both carrier rules; here, the analysis entails a deviation from the unique sequence criterion, since $\llbracket\text{-ŋ}\rrbracket$ applies both before and after $\llbracket\text{-si}\rrbracket$ in the definition of the realized cell in part (c).

Table 3.4 *The morphotactics of four forms of the Limbu verb* HUʔMAʔ *'teach'*

(a)	Form cell:	⟨ huʔ-, { pos –pret {agt 1 sg} {pat 2 sg} } ⟩		'I teach you (sg.)'
	|			
	FER	⟦-nɛ⟧		(cf. (6))
	↓			
	Realized cell:	⟨ huʔnɛ, { pos –pret {agt 1 sg} {pat 2 sg} } ⟩		
(b)	Form cell:	⟨ huʔr-, { pos –pret {agt 1 sg} {pat 3 sg} } ⟩		'I teach her/him'
	|			
	FER	(⟦-ŋ⟧ ∘ ⟦-u⟧)		(cf. (8))
	↓			
	Realized cell:	⟨ huʔruŋ, { pos –pret {agt 1 sg} {pat 3 sg} } ⟩		
(c)	Form cell:	⟨ huʔr-, { pos –pret {agt 1sg} {pat 3 –sg} } ⟩		'I teach them'
	|			
	FER	((⟦-ŋ⟧ ∘ ⟦-si⟧) ∘ (⟦-ŋ⟧ ∘ ⟦-u⟧))		(cf. Table 3.2)
	↓			
	Realized cell:	⟨ huʔruŋsiŋ, { pos –pret {agt 1sg} {pat 3 –sg} } ⟩		
(d)	Form cell:	⟨ huʔ-, { pos pret {agt 1 pl excl} {pat 3 –sg} } ⟩		'we taught them'
	|			
	FER	(⟦-si⟧ ∘ ⟦-mʔna⟧)		(= (14))
	↓			
	Realized cell:	⟨ huʔmʔnasi, { pos pret {agt 1 pl excl} {pat 3 –sg} } ⟩		

(17)   a.   *huʔ-nɛ*   'I teach you (sg.)'
        b.   *huʔr-u-ŋ*   'I teach her/him'
        c.   *huʔr-u-ŋ-si-ŋ*   'I teach them'

Consider finally the form *huʔ-mʔna-si* 'we (excl.) taught them', which realizes the form cell in part (d) of Table 3.4. Here, the verb's agent is first-person plural, so we might expect it to be expressed by means of ⟦-m⟧, particularly since the definition of this form involves the carrier rule ⟦-si⟧; yet, ⟦-m⟧ does not apply in this form, for which the only licensed FER is the composite rule (⟦-si⟧ ∘ ⟦-mʔna⟧) in (14). Although ⟦-m⟧ would be an appropriate expression for the subject properties of *huʔ-mʔna-si*, and although the definition of *huʔ-mʔna-si* involves the carrier rule ⟦-si⟧, the morphotactic system of Limbu does not license the appearance of ⟦-m⟧ and ⟦-mʔna⟧ as part of the same composite rule. Perhaps this should be related to the fact that the composition of (⟦-m⟧ ∘ ⟦-si⟧) with ⟦-mʔna⟧ would in any event express the same morphosyntactic content as the simpler composite rule in (14), but again, this cannot be seen as the effect of a general redundancy-avoidance principle in Limbu morphotactics. If such a principle existed, it would wholly exclude the striking patterns of multiple exponence presented by forms such as *huʔr-u-ŋ-si-ŋ* 'I teach them', *kɛ-huʔr-u-m-si-m* 'you (pl.) teach them', and so on.

In summary, the Limbu system of verb inflection reveals two kinds of deviation from the ten criterial characteristics of canonical morphotactics. First, the 〚-ŋ〛 and 〚-m〛 rules in (7) do not conform to the rule independence criterion: in order to apply in the definition of a given verb form, they must compose with a carrier rule, as in (8). Second, the 〚-ŋ〛 and 〚-m〛 rules fail to conform to the unique sequence criterion insofar as they may compose with carrier rules occupying more than one position in a sequence of rule applications, in some cases yielding patterns of multiple exponence.

3.3   An Inner Dependent Rule in Sanskrit Verb Morphology

In Limbu, composite rules involving a dependent rule and a carrier rule take the form ($R_{dependent} \circ R_{carrier}$) – the composition of the dependent rule with its carrier rule. The question therefore arises whether this is a general fact about composite rules involving dependent rules and carrier rules or whether such composites might sometimes take the form ($R_{carrier} \circ R_{dependent}$) – the composition of a carrier rule with a dependent rule. In fact, there do seem to be composite rules of this second kind. Sanskrit verb morphology provides a clear example.

In Sanskrit, some verb forms exhibit what Whitney (1889: §254) terms a **union vowel**. This vowel – ordinarily *i* – appears between a consonant-final verb root and a suffix beginning with a consonant other than *y*; for example, the union vowel appears preconsonantally in *vad-i-ṣyati* 's/he will speak' but not prevocalically in *vad-ati* 's/he speaks'.

Consider the perfect and future indicative active paradigms of the two verbal lexemes in Table 3.5. The verb JĪV 'live' has *jijīv-* as its perfect stem, and whenever this is followed by a suffix with an initial consonant, the union vowel separates that consonant from the final *v* of *jijīv-*; similarly, when the future-tense suffix *-sya* is added to the root *jīv-*, the union vowel separates the suffix-initial *s* from the final *v*. (As a matter of automatic sandhi, the *s* of *-sya* is made retroflex by the preceding *i*.) In the inflection of the verb STHĀ 'stand', by contrast, the union vowel rarely shows up, and this is precisely because the juncture of STHĀ's perfect stem with an inflectional suffix is only rarely the juxtaposition of two consonants, and that of the root *sthā-* with the future-tense suffix *-sya* never is. Thus, from the evidence in Table 3.5, one might try to

3.3 An Inner Dependent Rule in Sanskrit

Table 3.5 *Perfect and future indicative active paradigms of two Sanskrit verbs*

			Singular	Dual	Plural
JĪV	Perfect	1	jijī́v-a	jijīv-i-vá	jijīv-i-má
'live'		2	jijī́v-i-tha	jijīv-áthus	jijīv-á
		3	jijī́v-a	jijīv-átus	jijīv-úr
	Future	1	jīv-i-syā́mi	jīv-i-syā́vas	jīv-i-syā́mas
		2	jīv-i-syási	jīv-i-syáthas	jīv-i-syátha
		3	jīv-i-syáti	jīv-i-syátas	jīv-i-syánti
STHĀ	Perfect	1	tasth-áu	tasth-i-vá	tasth-i-má
'stand'		2	tasthā́-tha, tasth-i-thá	tasth-áthus	tasth-á
		3	tasth-áu	tasth-átus	tasth-úr
	Future	1	sthā-syā́mi	sthā-syā́vas	sthā-syā́mas
		2	sthā-syási	sthā-syáthas	sthā-syátha
		3	sthā-syáti	sthā-syátas	sthā-syánti

(Whitney 1885; Deshpande 1997)

conclude that the union vowel is a phonologically conditioned epenthetic vowel. Further evidence, however, reveals three reasons why this is not a sustainable analysis – why the union vowel should be seen as an affix rather than as a purely phonological adjustment (Renou 1996: §§285–286).

First, phonologically similar verb roots vary lexically with respect to whether or not they exhibit the union vowel. Thus, the roots in the lefthand column of Table 3.6 do not exhibit the union vowel in their future-tense stem; by contrast, the phonologically similar roots in the righthand column of the table have a future-tense stem that does exhibit the union vowel.

Second, the very same root may exhibit the union vowel in some parts of its paradigm but not in others. In Classical Sanskrit, a verb's paradigm of finite forms has four subsystems:

- the present system (incorporating the present and imperfect indicative and their corresponding modal forms);
- the perfect system (incorporating the perfect indicative);
- the aorist system (incorporating aorist indicative); and
- the future system (incorporating the future indicative and the conditional).

The same verb root may exhibit the union vowel in one of these subsystems but not in another; moreover, verb roots vary widely according to which of

98 Dependent Rules and Carrier Rules

Table 3.6 *Future stems of some Sanskrit verbs*

Root		Future stem without union vowel	Root		Future stem with union vowel
√*muc*	'release'	*mok-ṣyá-*	√*ruc*	'shine'	*roc-i-ṣyá-*
√*pac*	'cook'	*pak-ṣyá-*	√*rac*	'produce'	*rac-i-ṣyá-*
√*yaj*	'offer'	*yak-ṣyá-*	√*vraj*	'proceed'	*vraj-i-ṣyá-*
√*yuj*	'join'	*yok-ṣyá-*	√*vij*	'tremble'	*vij-i-ṣyá-, vej-i-ṣyá-*
√*nud*	'push'	*not-syá-*	√*mud*	'be merry'	*mod-i-ṣyá-*
√*pad*	'go'	*pat-syá-*	√*vad*	'speak'	*vad-i-ṣyá-*
√*rudh*	'obstruct'	*rot-syá-*	√*bādh*	'oppress'	*bādh-i-ṣyá-*
√√*vyadh*	'pierce'	*vet-syá-*	√*vadh*	'slay'	*vadh-i-ṣyá-*
√*āp*	'obtain'	*āp-syá-*	√*lap*	'prate'	*lap-i-ṣyá-*
√*gup*	'protect'	*gop-syá-*	√*śap*	'curse'	*śap-i-ṣyá-*
√*rabh*	'take hold'	*rap-syá-*	√*śubh*	'beautify'	*śobh-i-ṣyá-*
√*ram*	'be/make content'	*raṁ-syá-*	√*gam*	'go'	*gam-i-ṣyá-*
√*diś*	'point'	*dekṣ-yá-*	√*aś*	'eat'	*aś-i-ṣyá-*
√*dṛś*	'see'	*drakṣ-yá-*	√*daṅs*	'bite'	*daś-i-ṣyá-*
√√*viṣ*	'be active'	*vekṣ-yá-*	√*bhāṣ*	'speak'	*bhāṣ-i-ṣyá-*
√√*vas*	'clothe'	*vat-syá-*	√*has*	'laugh'	*has-i-ṣyá-*
√*duh*	'milk, derive'	*dhokṣ-yá-*	√*gāh*	'plunge'	*gāh-i-ṣyá-*

(Whitney 1885)

their subsystems exhibit the union vowel. The first-person plural indicative active forms of the eight verbal lexemes[5] in Table 3.7 exemplify this variability.[6]

---

[5] No significance should be attributed to the relative ordering of the rows in Table 3.7, which follow Devanagari alphabetical order. Note that the shaded cells in Table 3.7 involve stems that end in *ā*, after which the union vowel is not possible for phonological reasons. But some stems ending in other vowels (or in syllabic *ṛ*) have consonant-final alternants that are compatible with the appearance of the union vowel; for instance, the perfect stem *dudru-* has the consonant-final alternant *dudruv-*, which appears with the union vowel in the third-person plural perfect middle form *dudruv-i-ré* 'they moved'. For this reason, some cells with stem-final vowels are unshaded.

[6] This variability highlights an important difference between the synchrony and the diachrony of the Sanskrit union vowel. In Indo-European linguistics, the Sanskrit union vowel is often treated as the reflex of a root-final laryngeal; cf. Meier-Brügger (2003: 106ff.). Thus, Sanskrit verbs ordinarily

3.3 An Inner Dependent Rule in Sanskrit   99

Table 3.7 *First-person plural indicative active forms of eight Sanskrit verbs*

Verb root		Present	Perfect	Aorist	Future
√dru	'run'	drávā-mas	dudru-má	ádudruvā-ma	dro-syā́mas
√pac	'cook'	pácā-mas	pec-**i**-má	ápāk-ṣma	pak-syā́mas
√yā	'go'	yā-más	yay-**i**-má	áyās-**i**-ṣma	yā-syā́mas
√vad	'speak'	vádā-mas	ūd-**i**-má	ávād-**i**-ṣma	vad-**i**-syā́mas
√sr̥	'move'	sárā-mas	sasr̥-má	ásār-ṣma	sar-**i**-syā́mas
√smr̥	'remember'	smárā-mas	sasmar-**i**-má	ásmār-ṣma	smar-**i**-syā́mas
√svap	'sleep'	svap-**i**-más	suṣup-**i**-má	ásvāp-sma	svap-syā́mas
√hiṁs	'kill'	hiṁs-más	jihiṁs-**i**-má	áhiṁs-**i**-ṣma	hiṁs-**i**-syā́mas

☐ = forms exhibiting the union vowel
▨ = forms in which the union vowel cannot appear for phonological reasons

(Whitney 1885; Deshpande 1997)

Third, the notion that the union vowel is simply an epenthetic *i* cannot be reconciled with the fact that other vowels sometimes serve as union vowels (by which I mean suffixal vowels that are devoid of morphosyntactic content and that appear before consonant-initial terminations but not elsewhere). In the

> exhibit the full-grade form of their root in the infinitive but the zero-grade form in the past passive participle: √*ji* 'conquer', infinitive *je-tum*, past passive participle *ji-ta-*. Some verbs, however, exhibit the full-grade form of their root plus the union vowel in the infinitive but the zero-grade form plus vowel lengthening in the past passive participle: √*bhū* 'be', infinitive *bhav-i-tum*, past passive participle *bhū-ta-*. One historical explanation for this anomaly is that the root of the verb 'be' ended in a laryngeal H in pre-Sanskrit, and that the laryngeals in the fully regular pre-Sanskrit forms (*bheu̯H-tum, *bhuH-to-) underwent two sound changes (*$_H$ > i, *V$_H$ > V̄) to yield the attested Sanskrit forms. This historical explanation might be used to argue for an abstract synchronic analysis according to which the Sanskrit union vowel is but one manifestation of a root-final morphophoneme realized variously as *i* (in *vad-i-ṣyati* 's/he will speak'), as vowel length (in the past passive participle *bhū-ta-*), or as zero (in *vad-ati* 's/he speaks'), depending on its context.
> This sort of abstract synchronic analysis cannot be plausibly reconciled with the variability in Table 3.7, which shows that Sanskrit verb roots cannot simply be sorted into two groups (those taking the union vowel and those not); the same root may be accompanied by the union vowel in one tense but not in another. This variability is presumably the outcome of analogical changes that have significantly modified the distributional properties of the union vowel. These changes have also engendered forms in which the union vowel is separated from the verb root, as in the *siṣ*-aorist (e.g. *áyā-s-i-ṣ-ma* 'we went', with root √*yā*) and in sundry other forms (e.g. the desiderative causative (i)).

(i)   *pi-pād-ay-i-ṣa-ti* (√*pad* 'fall')
      REDUP-ROOT-CAUS-UNION.VOWEL-DESID-3SG.IND.ACT
      's/he wants to cause to fall'

inflection of √*brū* 'say' and √*grah* 'seize', for example, long *ī* appears as a union vowel (Whitney 1889: §§632, 900, 936), and in the inflection of certain forms of √*rud* 'weep', √*svap* 'sleep' √*an* 'breathe', and √*śvas* 'blow', *a* sometimes serves as a union vowel (Whitney 1889: §631).

In short, the Sanskrit union vowel is not a simple manifestation of phonological epenthesis, but is a suffix whose highly complex distribution is sensitive to lexical differences (*not-syáti* 's/he will push' from the root √*nud* vs. *mod-i-ṣyáti* 's/he will be merry' from the root √*mud*) and to morphosyntactic differences (future *smar-i-ṣyā́mas* 'we will remember' vs. aorist *ásmār-ṣma* 'we remembered') as well as to phonological differences (*sváp-i-ti* 's/he sleeps' vs. *svap-ánti* 'they sleep'). The rule 〖**-i**〗 introducing the union-vowel suffix *-i* never applies alone, but is invariably dependent on a carrier rule introducing a following suffix. In each such case, it is the carrier rule that composes with the dependent rule (e.g. (〖**-mas**〗 ∘ 〖**-i**〗)). A general phonological feature of the 〖**-i**〗 rule is that its carrier rule must introduce a consonant-initial suffix. Thus, in the forms in Table 3.7, the carrier rules for 〖**-i**〗 are 〖**-mas**〗, 〖**-ma**〗, 〖**-s**〗, 〖**-syá**〗, all of which introduce consonant-initial suffixes. But these rules don't always carry the 〖**-i**〗 rule; whether or not they do instead depends on the lexical properties of the verb form being inflected and on the morphosyntactic properties being realized.

In order to elucidate this analysis of the union vowel as the mark of a dependent inflectional rule 〖**-i**〗, it is important to be precise both about stem selection and about the characteristics of the inflection-class function in Sanskrit. Recall from Section 2.1 that a stem-selection rule having the form (18) is applicable to a content cell ⟨L, ρ⟩ only if $\tau \subseteq \rho$, and where $f(L) = Z$, the result of applying (18) to ⟨L, ρ⟩ is the form cell ⟨Z, [ρ ∪ ***ic***(Z)]⟩, where ***ic*** is the inflection-class function, to be discussed presently.

(18) τ, f

The stem-selection rules relevant for the fragment of Sanskrit under discussion are the four rules (i)–(iv) in Table 3.8; these apply to content cells to yield form cells, as illustrated in Table 3.9 with examples from the content and form paradigms of VAD 'speak'.

The value of the category CONJ in the form cells in Table 3.9 depends on the definition of the Sanskrit inflection-class function ***ic***. Recall from Section 2.1 that a language's inflection-class function ***ic*** applies to stem Z to give the set of inflection-class properties associated with Z. I assume that the ***ic*** function has the following characteristics in Sanskrit.

If Z is a present-system stem, then ***ic***(Z) = {CONJ:{α β}}, where α is a specification of the present-system conjugation class to which Z belongs (i.e.

Table 3.8 *Four stem-selection rules for a fragment of Sanskrit verb morphology*

	Stem–selection rules				
	(i) {prs}, f_1	(ii) {prf}, f_2	(iii) {aor}, f_3	(iv) {fut}, f_4	
L	$f_1(L)$	$f_2(L)$	$f_3(L)$	$f_4(L)$	
DRU	dráva-	dudru-	ádudruva-	dro-	'run'
PAC	páca-	pec-	ápāk-	pak-	'cook'
YĀ	yā-$_1$	yay-	áyās-	yā-$_2$	'go'
VAD	váda-	ūd-	ávād-	vad-	'speak'
SR̥	sára-	sasr̥-	ásār-	sar-	'move'
SMR̥	smára-	sasmar-	ásmār-	smar-	'remember'
SVAP	svap-$_1$	suṣup-	ásvāp-	svap-$_2$	'sleep'
HIM̐S	him̐s-$_1$	jihim̐s-	áhim̐s-	him̐s-$_2$	'kill'

Table 3.9 *Examples of the application of the stem-selection rules (i)–(iv) in Table 3.8*

Rule	applies to Content cell	to yield Form cell
(i)	⟨VAD, {1pl prs ind act}⟩	⟨váda-, {CONJ:{I, SET:−} 1pl prs ind act}⟩
(ii)	⟨VAD, {1pl prf ind act}⟩	⟨ūd-, {CONJ:{SET:+} 1pl prf ind act}⟩
(iii)	⟨VAD, {1pl aor ind act}⟩	⟨ávād-, {CONJ:{THM:−, SIG:+, SET:+} 1pl aor ind act}⟩
(iv)	⟨VAD, {1pl fut ind act}⟩	⟨vad-, { CONJ:{SET:+} 1pl fut ind act}⟩

one of I through X) and β is a specification of whether the inflection of Z involves the union vowel (SET:+) or not (SET:−). (Note that *seṭ* is a Pāṇinian label signifying 'with i'.)

If Z is an aorist-system stem, then $ic(Z) = \{\text{CONJ}:\{\alpha\}\}$, where $\{\alpha\}$ is a well-formed instantiation of the property set {THEMATIC:±, SIGMATIC:±, SET:±}. Traditionally, aorist forms are treated as falling into seven conjugations in Sanskrit (Whitney 1889: §824); in the analysis proposed here, these are grouped into five aorist exponence classes by means of the categories

- THEMATIC (where a stem is THM:+ if it ends in a short *a*),
- SIGMATIC (where a stem is SIG:+ if it inflects with a sibilant suffix), and
- SET (where a stem is SET:+ if it inflects with the union vowel *i*), as in Table 3.10.

102 *Dependent Rules and Carrier Rules*

Table 3.10 *Distinguishing the five aorist exponence classes in Sanskrit by means of* THM, SIG, *and* SET

Traditional aorist-system conjugations	THEMATIC (THM)	SIGMATIC (SIG)	SET
root aorist	−	−	−
thematic aorist, reduplicated aorist	+	−	−
s-aorist	−	+	−
iṣ-aorist, *siṣ*-aorist	−	+	+
sa-aorist	+	+	−

Stems that belong to the root aorist conjugation (e.g. that of *á-gan-ta* 'you (pl.) went') are neither thematic nor sigmatic, nor do they take the union vowel -*i*; they therefore belong to the exponence class CONJ:{THM:−, SIG:−, SET:−}. Stems belonging to the traditional thematic and reduplicated aorist conjugations (e.g. those of *á-sica-ta* 'you (pl.) poured', *á-jījana-ta* 'you (pl.) gave birth') are thematic but not sigmatic, nor do they inflect with the union vowel *i*; they therefore belong to the exponence class CONJ:{THM:+, SIG:−, SET:−}.[7] Stems belonging to the *s*-aorist conjugation (e.g. that of *á-bhār-ṣ-ṭa* 'you (pl.) carried') are sigmatic but are athematic and do not inflect with the union vowel *i*; hence their exponence class is CONJ:{THM:−, SIG:+, SET:−}. Stems that belong to the *iṣ*-aorist and *siṣ*-aorist conjugations (e.g. those of *á-kram-iṣ-ṭa* 'you (pl.) strode', *á-naṁs-iṣ-ṭa* 'you (pl.) bowed') are athematic but are sigmatic and do involve the union vowel *i*; hence their exponence class is CONJ:{THM:−, SIG:+, SET:+}.[8] Stems belonging to the *sa*-aorist conjugation (e.g. that of *á-dik-ṣa-ta* 'you (pl.) showed') are thematic and sigmatic but do not involve the union vowel *i*; they therefore belong to the exponence class CONJ:{THM:+, SIG:+, SET:−}.

If Z is a perfect-system or future-system stem, *ic*(Z) = {CONJ:{α}}, where α = SET:+ or SET:− according to whether or not the inflection of Z involves the union vowel *i*; no additional conjugation-class specification is necessary, since neither the perfect system nor the future system involves conjugation-class distinctions in Sanskrit.

---

[7] The traditional thematic and reduplicating aorist conjugations correspond to a single aorist exponence class CONJ:{THM:+, SIG:−, SET:−}: although they differ with respect to the formation of their member stems (specifically, with respect to the absence or presence of initial reduplication), they are alike in the ways in which these stems are marked by rules of inflectional exponence.

[8] The traditional *iṣ*-aorist and *siṣ*-aorist conjugations correspond to a single aorist exponence class CONJ:{THM:−, SIG:+, SET:+}; although their member stems differ with respect to the absence or presence of a stem-final *s*, they too are alike in the ways in which these stems are marked by the rules of inflectional exponence that operate on them. I follow Whitney (1889: §912) in characterizing the *siṣ*-aorist as a subtype of the *iṣ*-aorist.

3.3 An Inner Dependent Rule in Sanskrit

Construed in this way, the inflection-class function *ic* applies to the stems of the eight verbs in Table 3.7 to yield the values in Table 3.11.

The rules of exponence that define a Sanskrit verb form are sensitive both to its morphosyntactic properties and to the inflection-class properties in Table 3.11. For purposes of illustration, I shall focus on that fragment of Sanskrit consisting of the first-person plural indicative active forms in Table 3.7 and their third-person plural counterparts in Table 3.12, which, for phonological reasons, exhibit the union vowel less widely than the first-person plural forms.

The basic rules of inflectional exponence for the forms in this fragment of Sanskrit verb inflection are those in (19) and (20). The ⟦-s⟧ and ⟦-syá⟧ rules in (19) express tense; the rules in (20) express subject agreement and voice (and sometimes also tense).[9] The subject agreement rules in (20) serve as default FERs for the fragment's present indicative and perfect forms (e.g. the present indicative form *hiṁs-ánti* 'they kill' and the perfect form *dudru-má* 'we ran'). The rules in (20) also compose with the tense rules in (19) to yield the composite rules in (21), which serve as default FERs for the fragment's aorist and future-tense forms (e.g. the aorist form *ápāk-ṣ-ma* 'we cooked' and the future-tense form *dro-ṣyá-nti* 'they will run'). (Note that here and elsewhere, *s* is subject to automatic retroflexion to *ṣ* after *r*, *o*, *k*, and *i*.) The rules in (20) and (21) in turn serve as carrier rules for the dependent ⟦-i⟧ rule in (22), composing with it as in (23). Because ⟦-i⟧'s carrier rule must define a consonant-initial affix, the ⟦-anti⟧, ⟦-ur⟧, and ⟦-an⟧ rules in (20) cannot serve as ⟦-i⟧'s carrier.

(19) Simple rules of exponence for tense in the fragment of Sanskrit in Tables 3.7 and 3.12
⟦-s⟧ :   [V, {CONJ:{SIG:+} aorist} : -s]
⟦-syá⟧ : [V, {fut} : -syá]

(20) Simple rules of exponence for subject agreement in the fragment
a. ⟦-mas⟧ : [V, {prs/fut 1pl act} : X → X'-mas]
              (where X' = Yā if X = Ya; otherwise X' = X)
b. ⟦-ma⟧ :   [V, {1pl act} : X → X'-ma]
              (where X' is as above)
c. ⟦-anti⟧ : [V, {prs/fut 3pl act} : X → X-(a)nti]
              (where (a) is absent if X ends in ă)
d. ⟦-ur⟧ :   [V, {3pl act} : -ur]
e. ⟦-an⟧ :   [V, {3pl act} : Xa → Xan]

---

[9] I follow Renou (1996: §281) in representing the third-person plural active agreement suffix as *-ur* rather than *-us*; cf. Whitney (1889: §169b, §550c).

Table 3.11 *Inflection-class properties of eight Sanskrit verbs*

	Present-system stems		Perfect-system stems	
'run'	$ic(dráva\text{-}) =$	CONJ:{I, SEṬ:−}	$ic(dudru\text{-}) =$	CONJ:{SEṬ:−}
'cook'	$ic(páca\text{-}) =$	CONJ:{I, SEṬ:−}	$ic(pec\text{-}) =$	CONJ:{SEṬ:+}
'go'	$ic(yā\text{-}_1) =$	CONJ:{II, SEṬ:−}	$ic(yay\text{-}) =$	CONJ:{SEṬ:+}
'speak'	$ic(váda\text{-}) =$	CONJ:{I, SEṬ:−}	$ic(ūd\text{-}) =$	CONJ:{SEṬ:+}
'move'	$ic(sára\text{-}) =$	CONJ:{I, SEṬ:−}	$ic(sasr\text{-}) =$	CONJ:{SEṬ:−}
'remember'	$ic(smára\text{-}) =$	CONJ:{I, SEṬ:−}	$ic(sasmar\text{-}) =$	CONJ:{SEṬ:+}
'sleep'	$ic(svap\text{-}_1) =$	CONJ:{II, SEṬ:+}	$ic(suṣup\text{-}) =$	CONJ:{SEṬ:+}
'kill'	$ic(hiṁs\text{-}_1) =$	CONJ:{VII, SEṬ:−}	$ic(jihiṁs\text{-}) =$	CONJ:{SEṬ:+}
	Aorist-system stems		Future-system stems	
'run'	$ic(ádudruva\text{-}) =$	CONJ:{THM:+, SIG:−, SEṬ:−}	$ic(dro\text{-}) =$	CONJ:{SEṬ:−}
'cook'	$ic(ápāk\text{-}) =$	CONJ:{THM:−, SIG:+, SEṬ:−}	$ic(pak\text{-}) =$	CONJ:{SEṬ:−}
'go'	$ic(áyās\text{-}) =$	CONJ:{THM:−, SIG:+, SEṬ:+}	$ic(yā\text{-}_2) =$	CONJ:{SEṬ:−}
'speak'	$ic(ávād\text{-}) =$	CONJ:{THM:−, SIG:+, SEṬ:+}	$ic(vad\text{-}) =$	CONJ:{SEṬ:+}
'move'	$ic(ásār\text{-}) =$	CONJ:{THM:−, SIG:+, SEṬ:−}	$ic(sar\text{-}) =$	CONJ:{SEṬ:+}
'remember'	$ic(ásmār\text{-}) =$	CONJ:{THM:−, SIG:+, SEṬ:−}	$ic(smar\text{-}) =$	CONJ:{SEṬ:+}
'sleep'	$ic(ásvāp\text{-}) =$	CONJ:{THM:−, SIG:+, SEṬ:−}	$ic(svap\text{-}_2) =$	CONJ:{SEṬ:−}
'kill'	$ic(áhiṁs\text{-}) =$	CONJ:{THM:−, SIG:+, SEṬ:+}	$ic(hiṁs\text{-}_2) =$	CONJ:{SEṬ:+}

Table 3.12 *Third-person plural indicative active forms of eight Sanskrit verbs*

Verb root		Present	Perfect	Aorist	Future
√*dru*	'run'	*dráva-nti*	*dudruv-úr*	*ádudruva-n*	*dro-ṣyánti*
√*pac*	'cook'	*páca-nti*	*pec-úr*	*ápāk-ṣur*	*pak-ṣyánti*
√*yā*	'go'	*yā́-nti*	*yay-úr*	*áyās-i-ṣur*	*yā-syánti*
√*vad*	'speak'	*váda-nti*	*ūd-úr*	*ávād-i-ṣur*	*vad-i-ṣyánti*
√*sṛ*	'move'	*sára-nti*	*sasr-úr*	*ásār-ṣur*	*sar-i-ṣyánti*
√*smṛ*	'remember'	*smára-nti*	*sasmar-úr*	*ásmār-ṣur*	*smar-i-ṣyánti*
√*svap*	'sleep'	*svap-ánti*	*suṣup-úr*	*ásvāp-sur*	*svap-syánti*
√*hiṁs*	'kill'	*hiṁs-ánti*	*jihiṁs-úr*	*áhiṁs-i-ṣur*	*hiṁs-i-ṣyánti*

☐ = forms exhibiting the union vowel

= forms in which the union vowel cannot appear for phonological reasons

(Whitney 1885; Deshpande 1997)

(21) Composite rules of tense and subject agreement
    a. (⟦-mas⟧ ∘ ⟦-syá⟧) : [V, {fut 1pl act} : -syā́mas]
    b. (⟦-ma⟧ ∘ ⟦-s⟧) : [V, {CONJ:{SIG:+} aorist 1pl act} : -sma]
    c. (⟦-anti⟧ ∘ ⟦-syá⟧) : [V, {fut 3pl act} : -syánti]
    d. (⟦-ur⟧ ∘ ⟦-s⟧) : [V, {CONJ:{SIG:+} aorist 3pl act} : -sur]

(22) Dependent union vowel rule
⟦-i⟧ : [V, { CONJ:{SEṬ:+}} : -i]
Dependency constraint: ⟦-i⟧ is such that a carrier rule defining a consonant-initial suffix must compose with it.

(23) (Carrier ∘ ⟦-i⟧) composites
    a. (⟦-mas⟧ ∘ ⟦-i⟧): [V, { CONJ:{SEṬ:+} prs/fut 1pl act} : -imas]
    b. (⟦-ma⟧ ∘ ⟦-i⟧): [V, { CONJ:{SEṬ:+} 1pl act} : -ima]
    c. ((⟦-mas⟧ ∘ ⟦-syá⟧) ∘ ⟦-i⟧): [V, { CONJ:{SEṬ:+} fut 1pl act} : -iṣyā́mas]
    d. ((⟦-ma⟧ ∘ ⟦-s⟧) ∘ ⟦-i⟧): [V, { CONJ:{ SIG:+ SEṬ:+} aorist 1pl act} : -iṣma]
    e. ((⟦-anti⟧ ∘ ⟦-syá⟧) ∘ ⟦-i⟧) : [V, { CONJ:{SEṬ:+} fut 3pl act} : -iṣyánti]
    f. ((⟦-ur⟧ ∘ ⟦-s⟧) ∘ ⟦-i⟧): [V, { CONJ:{ SIG:+ SEṬ:+} aorist 3pl act} : -iṣur]

While rules in (20) and (21) serve as default FERs for the forms in the fragment under consideration, these are overridden by the rules in (23) in the realization of many forms associated with the inflection-class specification CONJ:{SEṬ:+} (e.g. the present indicative form *svap-i-más* 'we sleep', the perfect form *sasmar-i-má* 'we remembered', the aorist form *ávād-i-ṣur* 'they

Table 3.13 *The morphotactics of four present indicative forms in the fragment of Sanskrit verb inflection*

(a)	Content cell:	⟨SMR, {ind prs act 1pl}⟩	'we remember'
	Form cell:	⟨smára-, {CONJ:{I SEṬ:−} ind prs act 1pl}⟩	
	|		
	FER	⟦-mas⟧	(= (20a))
	↓		
	Realized cell:	⟨smárāmas, {CONJ:{I SEṬ:−} ind prs act 1pl}⟩	
(b)	Content cell:	⟨SVAP, {ind prs act 1pl}⟩	'we sleep'
	Form cell:	⟨svap-, {CONJ:{II SEṬ:+} ind prs act 1pl}⟩	
	|		
	FER	(⟦-mas⟧ ∘ ⟦-i⟧)	(= (23a))
	↓		
	Realized cell:	⟨svapimás, {CONJ:{II SEṬ:+} ind prs act 1pl}⟩	
(c)	Content cell:	⟨SMR, {ind prs act 3pl}⟩	'they remember'
	Form cell:	⟨smára-, {CONJ:{I SEṬ:−} ind prs act 3pl}⟩	
	|		
	FER	⟦-anti⟧	(= (20c))
	↓		
	Realized cell:	⟨smáranti, {CONJ:{I SEṬ:−} ind prs act 3pl}⟩	
(d)	Content cell:	⟨SVAP, {ind prs act 3pl}⟩	'they sleep'
	Form cell:	⟨svap-, {CONJ:{II SEṬ:+} ind prs act 3pl}⟩	
	|		
	FER	⟦-anti⟧	(= (20c))
	↓		
	Realized cell:	⟨svapánti, {CONJ:{II SEṬ:+} ind prs act 3pl}⟩	

spoke', and the future-tense form *sar-i-ṣyánti* 'they moved'). On the other hand, because the rules ⟦**-anti**⟧, ⟦**-ur**⟧, and ⟦**-an**⟧ introduce vowel-initial suffixes and so cannot compose with ⟦**-i**⟧, these three rules act as FERs in the inflection of certain forms associated with the inflection-class specification CONJ:{SEṬ:+} (e.g. the present indicative form *svap-ánti* 'they sleep' and the perfect form *sasmar-úr* 'they remembered').

Overall, the forms in the fragment conform to the FER pattern in (24).

(24) FER pattern for the forms in Tables 3.7 and 3.12
For each cell ⟨Z, σ⟩ in the form paradigm of a verb in the fragment of Sanskrit verb inflection represented in Tables 3.7 and 3.12, the FER for ⟨Z, σ⟩ is the narrowest applicable rule in the set of rules comprising (20), (21), and (23).

Representative instances of the application of the FERs conforming to this pattern are given in Tables 3.13 through 3.16. Table 3.13 shows the

3.3 An Inner Dependent Rule in Sanskrit   107

Table 3.14 *The morphotactics of four perfect forms in the fragment of Sanskrit verb inflection*

(a)	Content cell:	⟨SR, {ind prf act 1pl}⟩	'we moved'
	Form cell:	⟨sasr-, {CONJ:{SEṬ:−} ind prf act 1pl}⟩	
	|		
	FER	⟦-ma⟧	(= (20b))
	↓		
	Realized cell:	⟨sasrmá, {CONJ:{SEṬ:−} ind prf act 1pl}⟩	
(b)	Content cell:	⟨SMR, {ind prf act 1pl}⟩	'we remembered'
	Form cell:	⟨sasmar-, {CONJ:{SEṬ:+} ind prf act 1pl}⟩	
	|		
	FER	(⟦-ma⟧ ∘ ⟦-i⟧)	(= (23b))
	↓		
	Realized cell:	⟨sasmarimá, {CONJ:{SEṬ:+} ind prf act 1pl}⟩	
(c)	Content cell:	⟨SR, {ind prf act 3pl}⟩	'they moved'
	Form cell:	⟨sasr-, {CONJ:{SEṬ:−} ind prf act 3pl}⟩	
	|		
	FER	⟦-ur⟧	(= (20d))
	↓		
	Realized cell:	⟨sasrúr, {CONJ:{SEṬ:−} ind prf act 3pl}⟩	
(d)	Content cell:	⟨SMR, {ind prf act 3pl}⟩	'they remembered'
	Form cell:	⟨sasmar-, {CONJ:{SEṬ:+} ind prf act 3pl}⟩	
	|		
	FER	⟦-ur⟧	(= (20d))
	↓		
	Realized cell:	⟨sasmarúr, {CONJ:{SEṬ:+} ind prf act 3pl}⟩	

morphotactic definition of the first- and third-person plural present indicative active forms of SMR 'remember' and SVAP 'sleep'. The first-person plural forms are defined by means of the FERs ⟦-mas⟧ and (⟦-mas⟧ ∘ ⟦-i⟧), respectively (as in parts (a) and (b) of the table); only the form 'we sleep' involves ⟦-i⟧, since the present-tense stem of SVAP is associated with the inflection-class property SEṬ:+ while that of SMR is not. (See again Table 3.11.) On the other hand, the corresponding third-person plural forms are both defined by means of ⟦-anti⟧, since this is not a carrier rule for ⟦-i⟧, and thus applies indiscriminately in the realization of both SEṬ:− and SEṬ:+ forms (as in parts (c) and (d) of the table).

Table 3.14 gives the morphotactic definition of the first- and third-person plural perfect active forms of SR 'move' and SMR 'remember'. The first-person plural forms are defined by means of the FERs ⟦-ma⟧ and (⟦-ma⟧ ∘ ⟦-i⟧),

Table 3.15 *The morphotactics of four aorist forms in the fragment of Sanskrit verb inflection*

(a)	Content cell:	⟨SVAP, {ind aor act 1pl}⟩	'we slept'
	Form cell:	⟨*ásvāp-*, {CONJ:{THM:−, SIG:+, SEṬ:−} ind aor act 1pl}⟩	
	|		
	FER	([[-**ma**]] ∘ [[-**s**]])	(= (21b))
	↓		
	Realized cell:	⟨*ásvāpsma*, {CONJ:{THM:−, SIG:+, SEṬ:−} ind aor act 1pl}⟩	
(b)	Content cell:	⟨HIṀS, {ind aor act 1pl}⟩	'we killed'
	Form cell:	⟨*áhiṁs-*, {CONJ:{THM:−, SIG:+, SEṬ:+} ind aor act 1pl}⟩	
	|		
	FER	(([[-**ma**]] ∘ [[-**s**]]) ∘ [[-**i**]])	(= (23d))
	↓		
	Realized cell:	⟨*áhiṁsiṣma*, {CONJ:{THM:−, SIG:+, SEṬ:+} ind aor act 1pl}⟩	
(c)	Content cell:	⟨SVAP, {ind aor act 3pl}⟩	'we slept'
	Form cell:	⟨*ásvāp-*, {CONJ:{THM:−, SIG:+, SEṬ:−} ind aor act 3pl}⟩	
	|		
	FER	([[-**ur**]] ∘ [[-**s**]])	(= (21d))
	↓		
	Realized cell:	⟨*ásvāpsur*, {CONJ:{THM:−, SIG:+, SEṬ:−} ind aor act 3pl}⟩	
(d)	Content cell:	⟨HIṀS, {ind aor act 3pl}⟩	'we killed'
	Form cell:	⟨*áhiṁs-*, {CONJ:{THM:−, SIG:+, SEṬ:+} ind aor act 3pl}⟩	
	|		
	FER	(([[-**ur**]] ∘ [[-**s**]]) ∘ [[-**i**]])	(= (23f))
	↓		
	Realized cell:	⟨*áhiṁsiṣur*, {CONJ:{THM:−, SIG:+, SEṬ:+} ind aor act 3pl}⟩	

respectively (as in parts (a) and (b) of the table); only the form 'we remembered' involves [[-**i**]], since the perfect stem of SMṚ is associated with the inflection-class property SEṬ:+ while that of SṚ is not. On the other hand, the corresponding third-person plural forms are both defined by means of [[-**ur**]], since this is not a carrier rule for [[-**i**]], and thus applies indiscriminately in the realization of both SEṬ:− and SEṬ:+ forms (as in parts (c) and (d) of the table).

Table 3.15 shows the morphotactic definition of the first- and third-person plural aorist active forms of SVAP 'sleep' and HIṀS 'kill'. The first-person plural forms are defined by means of the FERs ([[-**ma**]] ∘ [[-**s**]]) and (([[-**ma**]] ∘ [[-**s**]]) ∘ [[-**i**]]), respectively (as in parts (a) and (b) of the table); only the form 'we

Table 3.16 *The morphotactics of four future-tense forms in the fragment of Sanskrit verb inflection*

(a)	Content cell:	⟨ SVAP, { ind fut act 1pl } ⟩	'we will sleep'
	Form cell:	⟨ svap-, { CONJ:{SEṬ:−} ind fut act 1pl } ⟩	
	|		
	FER	(⟦**-mas**⟧ ∘ ⟦**-syá**⟧)	(= (21a))
	↓		
	Realized cell:	⟨ svapsyā́mas, { CONJ:{SEṬ:−} ind fut act 1pl } ⟩	
(b)	Content cell:	⟨ VAD, { ind fut act 1pl } ⟩	'we will speak'
	Form cell:	⟨ vad-, { CONJ:{SEṬ:+} ind fut act 1pl } ⟩	
	|		
	FER	((⟦**-mas**⟧ ∘ ⟦**-syá**⟧) ∘ ⟦**-i**⟧)	(= (23c))
	↓		
	Realized cell:	⟨ vadiṣyā́mas, { CONJ:{SEṬ:+} ind fut act 1pl } ⟩	
(c)	Content cell:	⟨ SVAP, { ind fut act 3pl } ⟩	'they will sleep'
	Form cell:	⟨ svap-, { CONJ:{SEṬ:−} ind fut act 3pl } ⟩	
	|		
	FER	(⟦**-anti**⟧ ∘ ⟦**-syá**⟧)	(= (21c))
	↓		
	Realized cell:	⟨ svapsyánti, { CONJ:{SEṬ:−} ind fut act 3pl } ⟩	
(d)	Content cell:	⟨ VAD, { ind fut act 3pl } ⟩	'they will speak'
	Form cell:	⟨ vad-, { CONJ:{SEṬ:+} ind fut act 3pl } ⟩	
	|		
	FER	((⟦**-anti**⟧ ∘ ⟦**-syá**⟧) ∘ ⟦**-i**⟧)	(= (23e))
	↓		
	Realized cell:	⟨ vadiṣyánti, { CONJ:{SEṬ:+} ind fut act 3pl } ⟩	

killed' involves ⟦**-i**⟧, since the aorist stem of HIṀS is associated with the inflection-class property SEṬ:+ while that of SVAP is not. For the same reason, the corresponding third-person plural forms are defined by means of the FERs (⟦**-ur**⟧ ∘ ⟦**-s**⟧) and ((⟦**-ur**⟧ ∘ ⟦**-s**⟧) ∘ ⟦**-i**⟧), respectively (as in parts (c) and (d) of the table).

Table 3.16 gives the morphotactic definition of the first- and third-person plural future active forms of SVAP 'sleep' and VAD 'speak'. The first-person plural forms are defined by means of the FERs (⟦**-mas**⟧ ∘ ⟦**-syá**⟧) and ((⟦**-mas**⟧ ∘ ⟦**-syá**⟧) ∘ ⟦**-i**⟧), respectively (as in parts (a) and (b) of the table); only the form 'we will speak' involves ⟦**-i**⟧, since the future stem of VAD is associated with the inflection-class property SEṬ:+ while that of SVAP is not. For the same reason, the corresponding third-person plural forms are defined by means of the FERs

([[-anti]] ∘ [[-syá]]) and (([[-anti]] ∘ [[-syá]]) ∘ [[-i]]), respectively (as in parts (c) and (d) of the table).

The Sanskrit union-vowel rule [[-i]] and the Limbu agent rules rules [[-ŋ]] and [[-m]] are similar in some ways and different in others. Their fundamental similarity is that they are all dependent rules: none can apply unless it is part of a composite with an appropriate carrier rule.

Although Sanskrit [[-i]] and Limbu [[-ŋ]] and [[-m]] are all dependent rules, the [[-i]] rule differs from the [[-ŋ]] and [[-m]] rules in that it is always the inner rule in a composite in which it combines with a carrier rule; the [[-ŋ]] and [[-m]] rules, by contrast, are invariably the outer rule in combinations with a carrier rule.

Another difference between Sanskrit [[-i]] and Limbu [[-ŋ]] and [[-m]] is that [[-i]] never applies more than once in the definition of a given word form. By contrast, Limbu [[-ŋ]] and [[-m]] may apply more than once in the definition of the same word form (e.g. *huʔr-u-ŋ-si-ŋ* 'I teach them', *kɛhuʔr-u-m-si-m* 'you (pl.) teach them'); that is, one composite of [[-ŋ]] or [[-m]] may compose with another, as in part (c) of Table 3.4.

A final difference between Sanskrit [[-i]] and Limbu [[-ŋ]] and [[-m]] is that [[-ŋ]] and [[-m]] always take a simple rule as their carrier (any of the rules [[-u]], [[-tchi$_1$]], [[-i]], and [[-si]] in (6)); in the proposed analysis of Sanskrit, by contrast, the carrier of [[-i]] is sometimes a simple rule ([[-mas]] or [[-ma]] in (20)) and sometimes a composite rule (one of those in (21)). One might propose a different analysis of the Sanskrit fragment in which [[-i]] only has simple carriers ([[-mas]], [[-ma]], [[-s]], or [[-syá]]), but such an analysis would be complicated by the need to avoid defining nonexistent forms such as **ávād-i-ṣ-i-ma*, in which [[-i]] applies twice, carried once by [[-s]] and again by [[-ma]].

Together, the facts surrounding Sanskrit [[-i]] and Limbu [[-ŋ]] and [[-m]] raise two questions, neither of which can be definitively answered without further research:

(i) Is the relation between a dependent rule and its carrier always a relation of rule composition?

(ii) Are the affixes introduced by a dependent rule and its carrier always adjacent?

Consider first question (i). In the Sanskrit and Limbu cases, the relation between a dependent rule and its carrier is always a relation of rule composition. But could this ever be a different relation? One might view instances of what I am calling aggregation (Section 2.4) – instances in which a rule of suffixation aggregates with a rule of prefixation, or a rule of prefixation with a rule of suffixation – as involving a dependent/carrier relation between a rule and the rule with which it aggregates. Typically, however, a rule that applies as part of a rule aggregation in the definition of some word forms also applies unaggregated in the definition of other word forms. Thus, if aggregation, like composition, is a possible expression of rule dependency, it may be necessary to regard some rules as "semi-dependent," in the sense that they aggregate with a carrier rule if one applies, but otherwise apply unaggregated. The Noon consonantal marker rules (Section 7.1), the Lithuanian reflexive rule (Section 7.2), and the Swahili relativized-argument rules (Section 8.4) would all be examples of such semi-dependent rules.

Consider now question (ii). In the Sanskrit and Limbu cases, the affix introduced by a dependent rule is always adjacent to the affix introduced by its carrier rule; and if there are dependent/carrier relations expressed by aggregation, these too involve dependent and carrier affixes in adjacent positions. But if a prefixation rule 〚**x-**〛 were dependent on a suffixational carrier rule 〚**-y**〛, the composite of those rules would put the *x-* and *-y* affixes in nonadjacent positions. I know of no convincing examples of this sort, so it may be that question (ii) is to be answered in the affirmative; if so, this is an important result, since nothing logically necessitates the adjacency of the affixes introduced by a dependent/carrier rule pair.

3.4 Conclusion

The evidence presented in this chapter has shown that various kinds of constraints on the interaction of rules of exponence can be modeled as constraints on the composition of these rules. A language's morphology may prevent seemingly compatible rules from applying together in the definition of the same word form; such cases may be seen as involving rules whose composition is not licensed. Some rules are dependent in the sense that they are only applicable in the definition of a given word form if a suitable carrier rule also applies; in such cases, a dependent rule can be seen as a rule that only applies as part of a composite with an appropriate carrier. In this way, rule composition models a deviation from the rule independence criterion. Multiple exponence arises when the same dependent rule composes with more than one carrier rule in the definition of the same word form; the pattern of rule composition in such cases models a deviation from the unique sequence criterion, since it involves one rule applying both before and after another rule. In a composite rule embodying a dependent/carrier relation, the dependent may compose with the carrier (as in Limbu verb inflection) or the carrier may compose with the dependent (as with the Sanskrit union vowel).

In the next chapter, rule composition is further shown to afford a precise way of modeling another noncanonical morphotactic pattern, one which (contrary to the parallel sequence criterion) involves an inconsistency in the order in which distinct inflectional categories are expressed.

4 *Rule Composition and Rule Ordering*

Very often, the sequence in which rules of inflectional exponence apply in a word form's definition conforms to the universal probabilistic tendency toward category clustering (Mansfield, Stoll, & Bickel 2020; Section 1.5.3). Consider, for example, the verb form *u-ta-m-piga* 'you (sg.) will hit him' in Swahili. In the definition of this form, the three prefixation rules follow a fixed sequence, with the application of the pronominal object-coding ⟦**m-**⟧ rule preceding that of the tense-coding ⟦**ta-**⟧ rule, whose application in turn precedes that of the subject-agreement rule ⟦**u-**⟧. This sequence of application is not a narrow peculiarity of these three rules; instead, it reflects a general pattern in which the applicational sequence of all pronominal object-coding rules is like that of ⟦**m-**⟧, that of all tense-coding rules is like that of ⟦**ta-**⟧, and that of all subject-agreement rules is like that of ⟦**u-**⟧. Such patterns conform to the parallel sequence criterion (Section 1.5.3), according to which rules that express the same inflectional category canonically occupy the same position in any sequence of rule applications in which they serve in the definition of an inflected word form. The rules that define the inflected form *u-ta-m-piga* also conform to the unique sequence criterion (Section 1.5.4), according to which, canonically, rules of inflectional exponence that may apply in the definition of the same word form always apply in the same sequence relative to one another. Fixed rule-ordering patterns of this sort are what facilitate the postulation of affix-ordering templates in many languages (Good 2016).

Nevertheless, languages do sometimes deviate from both of these canonical criteria. Contrary to the parallel sequence criterion, rules realizing different properties in the same inflectional category may differ in their applicational sequence: in some such cases, one applicational sequence is clearly identifiable as the default, and the other, as an override of that default; in other cases, the contrasting applicational sequences do not clearly stand in a default/override relation. In this chapter, I discuss both sorts of deviation from the parallel sequence criterion. In Section 4.1, I discuss patterns of subject and object marking in Fula; I show that these patterns involve a default applicational

114 *Rule Composition and Rule Ordering*

sequence that is overridden in specific circumstances by the opposite sequence of application. I show that the rule-combining approach to morphotactics affords a straightforward means of modeling this deviation, as one in which one pattern of rule composition stands in a default/override relation to another. In Section 4.2, I discuss rules of case marking in Udmurt, which, despite their paradigmatic opposition to one another, do not all exhibit the same applicational sequence in the definition of Udmurt case forms; here, however, it is not clear that either sequence of application is a default overridden by the opposite sequence. I propose a rule-combining analysis in which Udmurt case-marking involves two complementary patterns of rule composition.

Both the Fula evidence in Section 4.1 and the Udmurt evidence in Section 4.2 conform to the unique sequence criterion. But contrary to this criterion, inflectional rules sometimes exhibit alternative acceptable sequences of application. In Section 4.3, I discuss alternative acceptable sequences of rule application in the declensional morphology of Eastern Mari; the rule-combining approach to morphotactics allows these to be seen as involving alternative patterns of rule composition for realizing the same set of morphosyntactic properties.

4.1 Fixed Deviations from a Default Sequence of Rule Application in Fula

As was seen in Section 2.4, tense/aspect/mood categories in Fula fall into the three groupings in Table 4.1; each grouping has its own morphological

Table 4.1 *Classification of tense/aspect/mood categories in Fula*

TAM group A		TAM group B
Subgroup (i)	Subgroup (ii)	
General past	Stative-(i)	Relative past
Emphatic past	Stative-(ii)*	Relative future
General future	Continuous-(i)	Subjunctive*
Vague future*	Continuous-(ii)*	
Desiderative*		
Negative past		
Negative future		
Negative of quality		

* Tenses that do not exhibit preterite forms (Arnott 1970: 216); cf. Section 2.4.
(Arnott 1970: 179–182)

peculiarities. Verb forms in the 'Group B' categories exhibit subject-agreement prefixes in the series that Arnott (1970: 193ff.) labels Series 4 and 5. The Series 5 affixes, in particular, appear in active, middle, and passive forms of the relative past as well as in middle and passive forms of the relative future; the full inventory of Series 5 affixes is listed in Table 4.2 along with the corresponding pronominal object suffixes. Note that the morphophonology of Fula causes some verb forms to be pronounced with final glottality (Arnott 1970: 231ff.). Most of the object markers in Table 4.2 are represented with -' or -^{h}, respectively indicating the usual presence or absence of final glottality in the forms in which they appear. The subject-agreement suffix *-mi* and the pronominal-object suffix *-maa* are verb-final in some forms and not in others; the diacritic $^{(\,\prime)}$ on these affixes represents glottality if in word-final position and its absence otherwise.

In the definition of a verb form in the relative past tense, the rule introducing the pronominal object marker ordinarily applies after the rule introducing the Series 5 subject marker; a subject suffix therefore precedes an accompanying pronominal object suffix, as in (1). Yet, when the rule introducing the first-person singular subject suffix *-mi* applies with a rule introducing a singular personal object suffix (the second-person singular object suffix *-maa* or the third-person singular Class 1 object suffix *-mo(o)*), the rules apply in the opposite order, causing the object marker to precede the subject suffix; the examples in (2) illustrate.

(1) a. *mballu-mi-ɓe-'*
       help.REL.PST.ACT-SBJ.1SG-OBJ.3PL.NC2-FG
       'I helped them'
    b. *mballu-daa-mo-'*
       help.REL.PST.ACT-SBJ.2SG-OBJ.3SG.NC1-FG
       'you (sg.) helped her/him'

(2) a. *mballu-maa-mi-'*
       help.REL.PST.ACT-OBJ.2SG-SBJ.1SG-FG
       'I helped you (sg.)'
    b. *mballu-moo-mi-'*
       help.REL.PST.ACT-OBJ.3SG.NC1-SBJ.1SG-FG
       'I helped her/him'

(Arnott 1970: Appendix 15)

Stump (1993) suggested that this phenomenon reflects the possibility that in the realization of certain combinations of morphosyntactic properties, two rule blocks might reverse their order of application. The notion of rule composition,

Table 4.2 Series 5 subject affixes and object suffixes in Fula

Person, number	Subject affix (Series 5)	Object suffix	3SG noun class	Subject affix (Series 5)	Object suffix
1SG	-mi-(ʼ)	-yam-ʰ	NC1**	ʼo- ~ mo-	-mo-ʼ ~ -moo-
2SG*	-aa-(ʼ) ~ -daa-(ʼ)	-maa-(ʼ)	NC3	ŋgel-	-ŋgel-ʼ
1PL	min-	-min-ʰ	NC4	kal-	-kal-ʼ
2PL INCL*	-en-(ʼ) ~ -den-(ʼ)	-ʼen-ʰ	NC5	ŋgum-	-ŋgum-ʼ
2PL EXCL*	-on-(ʼ) ~ -don-(ʼ)	-ʼon-ʰ	NC7	ŋga-	-ŋga-ʼ
			NC9	nde-	-nde-ʼ
			NC10	ndi-	-ndi-ʼ
			NC11	ndu-	-ndu-ʼ
			NC12	ŋga-	-ŋga-ʼ
			NC13	ŋge-	-ŋge-ʼ
			NC14	ŋgo-	-ŋgo-ʼ
			NC15	ŋgu-	-ŋgu-ʼ
			NC16	ŋgal-	-ŋgal-ʼ
			NC17	ŋgol-	-ŋgol-ʼ
			NC18	ka-	-ka-ʼ
			NC19	ki-	-ki-ʼ
			NC20	ko-	-ko-ʼ
			NC21	kol-	-kol-ʼ
			NC22	dam-	-dam-ʼ
			NC23	dum-	-dum-ʼ

3PL noun class	Subject affix (Series 5)	Object suffix
NC2	be-	-be-ʼ
NC6	kon-	-kon-ʼ
NC8	ko-	-ko-ʼ
NC24	de-	-de-ʼ
NC25	di-	-di-ʼ

* Concerning the distribution of the alternant forms of the second-person subject affixes in Series 5, see Arnott (1970: 196).
** Concerning the distribution of the alternant forms of the NC1 subject affix in Series 5, see Arnott (1970: 193). Arnott (1970: 194, 212)

however, affords an alternative analysis in which composite rules define argument-coding suffix sequences such as those in (1) and (2). Thus, suppose that the verb morphology of Fula includes the subject-agreement rules in (3) and the pronominal object rules in (4).[1]

(3)　　Series 5 subject-agreement rules (partial)
　　　a.　⟦-mi⟧ :　　[V, {{sbj 1 sg SER.5}} : -mi-⁽'⁾]
　　　b.　⟦-ɗaa⟧ :　[V, {{sbj 2 sg SER.5}} : -ɗaa-⁽'⁾]
　　　c.　⟦'o-⟧ :　　[V, {{sbj 3 sg nc1}} : 'o-]
　　　d.　⟦min-⟧ :　[V, {{sbj 1 pl SER.5}} : min-]
　　　e.　⟦-ɗen⟧ :　[V, {{sbj 2 pl incl SER.5}} : -ɗen-⁽'⁾]
　　　f.　⟦-ɗon⟧ :　[V, {{sbj 2 pl excl SER.5}} : -ɗon-⁽'⁾]
　　　g.　⟦ɓe-⟧ :　　[V, {{sbj 3 pl nc2}} : ɓe-]

(4)　　Pronominal object rules (partial)
　　　a.　⟦-yam⟧ :　[V, {{obj 1 sg}} : -yam-^{h}]
　　　b.　⟦-maa⟧ :　[V, {{obj 2 sg}} : -maa-⁽'⁾]
　　　c.　⟦-mO⟧ :　[V, {{obj 3 sg nc1}} : -mO'][2]
　　　d.　⟦-min⟧ :　[V, {{obj 1 pl}} : -min-^{h}]
　　　e.　⟦-'en⟧ :　[V, {{obj 2 pl incl}} : -'en-^{h}]
　　　f.　⟦-'on⟧ :　[V, {{obj 2 pl excl}} : -'on-^{h}]
　　　g.　⟦-ɓe⟧ :　[V, {{obj 3 pl nc2}} : -ɓe-']

Composites of the rules in (3) and (4) are as defined by the full exponence rule (FER) patterns in (5). In the default case defined in (5b), a pronominal object rule composes with a subject agreement rule, producing a composite rule such as those in (6); but in the particular cases in which the subject-agreement rule ⟦-mi⟧ in (3a) interacts with a singular personal pronominal object rule (⟦-maa⟧ or ⟦-mO⟧ in (4b,c)), then it is the subject-agreement rule that composes with the pronominal object rule, producing the composite rules in (7) in accordance with (5a). On the basis of the rules in (3) and (4), the FER patterns in (5) define the composite rules in Table 4.3; each of these composite rules is a FER. All FERs conform to the default pattern of composition in (5b) except the two that are shaded, which instead conform to the opposite, overriding pattern of composition in (5a).

---

[1] Here, I follow Arnott in treating the 'you and I' rule ⟦-ɗen⟧ and the 'you and me' rule ⟦-'en⟧ as expressing the inclusive of the second-person plural (so that 'inclusive' here means 'includes the speaker'); see Arnott (1970: 134) for the rationale for this decision.
[2] In (4c), -mO' represents -moo when followed by -mi-' and -mo-' otherwise; see Arnott (1970: 213ff.).

Table 4.3 Composed FERs in a fragment of Fula verb inflection

Series 5 subject agreement rules	Pronominal object rules						
	(4a) [-yam]	(4b) [-maa]	(4c) [-mO]	(4d) [-min]	(4e) [-'en]	(4f) [-'on]	(4g) [-ɓe]
(3a) [-mi]	▓	([-mi]∘[-maa]) *-maami*	([-mi]∘[-mO]) *-moomi*	▓	▓	([-'on]∘[-mi]) *-mi'on*	([-ɓe]∘[-mi]) *-miɓe*
(3b) [-ɗaa]	([-yam]∘[-ɗaa]) *-ɗaayam*	▓	([-mO]∘[-ɗaa]) *-ɗaamo*	([-min]∘[-ɗaa]) *-ɗaamin*	▓	▓	([-ɓe]∘[-ɗaa]) *-ɗaaɓe*
(3c) ['o-]	([-yam]∘['o-]) X → 'o-X-yam	([-maa]∘['o-]) X → 'o-X-maa	([-mO]∘['o-]) X → 'o-X-mo	([-min]∘['o-]) X → 'o-X-min	([-'en]∘['o-]) X → 'o-X-'en	([-'on]∘['o-]) X → 'o-X-'on	([-ɓe]∘['o-]) X → 'o-X-ɓe
(3d) [min-]	▓	([-maa]∘[min-]) X → min-X-maa	([-mO]∘[min-]) X → min-X-mo	▓	▓	([-'on]∘[min-]) X → min-X-'on	([-ɓe]∘[min-]) X → min-X-ɓe
(3e) [-ɗen]	▓	▓	([-mO]∘[-ɗen]) *-ɗenmo*	▓	▓	▓	([-ɓe]∘[-ɗen]) *-ɗenɓe*
(3f) [-ɗon]	([-yam]∘[-ɗon]) *-ɗonyam*	▓	([-mO]∘[-ɗon]) *-ɗonmo*	([-min]∘[-ɗon]) *-ɗonmin*	▓	▓	([-ɓe]∘[-ɗon]) *-ɗonɓe*
(3g) [ɓe-]	([-yam]∘[ɓe-]) X → ɓe-X-yam	([-maa]∘[ɓe-]) X → ɓe-X-maa	([-mO]∘[ɓe-]) X → ɓe-X-mo	([-min]∘[ɓe-]) X → ɓe-X-min	([-'en]∘[ɓe-]) X → ɓe-X-'en	([-'on]∘[ɓe-]) X → ɓe-X-'on	([-ɓe]∘[ɓe-]) X → ɓe-X-ɓe

(5) FER patterns
Where R_{SBJ} is a rule in (3) and R_{OBJ} is a rule in (4),
a. ($R_{SBJ} \circ R_{OBJ}$) is a FER if R_{SBJ} = ⟦-mi⟧ and R_{OBJ} = ⟦-maa⟧ or ⟦-mO⟧;
b. otherwise, ($R_{OBJ} \circ R_{SBJ}$) is a FER, provided that it realizes a well-formed property set.[3]

(6) Some default composites in Fula verb morphology
a. (⟦-ɓe⟧ ∘ ⟦-mi⟧) : [V, {{sbj 1 sg SER.5} {obj 3 pl nc2}} : -miɓe']
b. (⟦-mO⟧ ∘ ⟦-ɗaa⟧) : [V, {{sbj 2 sg SER.5} {obj 3 sg nc1}} : -ɗaamo']

(7) Two overriding composites in Fula verb morphology
a. (⟦-mi⟧ ∘ ⟦-maa⟧) : [V, {{sbj 1 sg SER.5} {obj 2 sg}} : -maami']
b. (⟦-mi⟧ ∘ ⟦-mO⟧) : [V, {{sbj 1 sg SER.5} {obj 3 sg nc1}} : -moomi']

As the evidence discussed here shows, Fula morphotactics is noncanonical in that it fails to conform to the parallel sequence criterion. In a rule-combining approach to exponence-driven morphotactics, this divergence from canonicity can be represented as the coexistence of opposite sequences of rule composition in the inflectional morphology of Fula verbs. One sequence of composition – that of ($R_{OBJ} \circ R_{SBJ}$) – is the default; the other – that of ($R_{SBJ} \circ R_{OBJ}$) – overrides this default. The default pattern accounts for forms such as those in (1), as parts (a) and (b) of Table 4.4 show; the overriding pattern accounts for forms such as those in (2), as in parts (c) and (d) of Table 4.4.

Fixed deviations from a default sequence of rule application are by no means unusual in inflectional morphology. In the verb inflection of European Portuguese, for example, pronominal-object morphology ordinarily follows tense/mood and subject-agreement morphology, as in (8a); in the future indicative and the conditional, however, pronominal-object morphology precedes tense/mood and subject-agreement morphology, as in (8b).[4] Thus, the form in (8a) is defined by the composite (⟦-(l)o⟧ ∘ (⟦-mo(s)⟧ ∘ ⟦-va⟧)), which conforms to the default pattern ($R_{OBJ} \circ (R_{SBJ} \circ R_{T/M})$); the form in (8b), by contrast, is defined by the composite ((⟦-mo(s)⟧ ∘ ⟦-e⟧) ∘ ⟦-(l)o⟧), which conforms to the overriding pattern (($R_{SBJ} \circ R_{T/M}) \circ R_{OBJ}$).

---

[3] The ill-formed property sets are those involving subject and object properties that are (i) both first-person or second-person inclusive, or (ii) both second-person. Middle voice forms are instead used to express reflexiveness (Arnott 1970: 255–257).

[4] Luís & Spencer 2005 develop an analysis of the enclitic/mesoclitic alternation exemplified by (8) that is the basis for the cursory analysis sketched here. The European Portuguese facts are, however, complicated by the additional, proclitic placement of pronominal-object morphology in certain contexts; to account for this additional dimension of European Portuguese pronominal-object morphology, Luís & Spencer argue for a distinction between affix exponence and affix directionality in the definition of a language's morphology. See Section 7.3 for relevant discussion. See also Luís & Otoguro (2004, 2011).

120   *Rule Composition and Rule Ordering*

Table 4.4 *Examples of the morphotactics of subject agreement and pronominal-object marking in Fula verb inflection*

(a)	Form cell:	⟨ *mballu-*, {{rel.pst act {sbj 1 sg SER.5} {obj 3 pl nc2}} ⟩		'I helped them'
	FER	([[-ɓe]] ∘ [[-mi]])		(= (6a))
	↓			
	Realized cell:	⟨ *mballumiɓe'*, {rel.pst act {sbj 1 sg SER.5} {obj 3 pl nc2}} ⟩		
(b)	Form cell:	⟨ *mballu-*, {rel.pst act {sbj 2 sg SER.5} {obj 3 sg nc1}} ⟩		'you helped her'
	FER	([[-mO]] ∘ [[-ɗaa]])		(= (6b))
	↓			
	Realized cell:	⟨ *mballuɗaamo'*, {rel.pst act {sbj 2 sg SER.5} {obj 3 sg nc1}} ⟩		
(c)	Form cell:	⟨ *mballu-*, {rel.pst act {sbj 1 sg SER.5} {obj 2 sg}} ⟩		'I helped you'
	FER	([[-mi]] ∘ [[-maa]])		(= (7a))
	↓			
	Realized cell:	⟨ *mballumaami'*, {rel.pst act {sbj 1 sg SER.5} {obj 2 sg}} ⟩		
(d)	Form cell:	⟨ *mballu-*, {rel.pst act {sbj 1 sg SER.5} {obj 3 sg nc1}} ⟩		'I helped her'
	FER	([[-mi]] ∘ [[-mO]])		(= (7b))
	↓			
	Realized cell:	⟨ *mballumoomi'*, {rel.pst act {sbj 1 sg SER.5} {obj 3 sg nc1}} ⟩		

(8)   a.   *mostrá-va-mo-lo*
           show-IMPF.IND-SBJ.1PL-ACC:3SG.MASC
           'we showed it'
    b.   *mostrá-lo-e-mos*
           show-ACC:3SG.MASC-FUT-SBJ.1PL
           'we will show it'

A similar example is that of the Latin rule [[-(u)r]] realizing passive voice. In the morphological definition of most passive forms, the application of this rule follows that of the accompanying subject-agreement rule; thus, the *-(u)r* suffix follows the subject-agreement suffix in most of the passive forms in Table 4.5.[5] In the definition of second-person singular passive forms, however, the application of the [[-(u)r]] rule precedes that of the rule expressing subject agreement. Thus, the default ordering relation between the passive [[-(u)r]] rule and an accompanying subject-agreement rule R follows the pattern ([[-(u)r]] ∘ R); but this default is overridden by the composite ([[-(i)s]] ∘ [[-(u)r]]) in the definition of second-person singular forms.

---

[5] Concerning the absence of *-(u)r* from the second-person plural form *audīminī* 'you (pl.) are heard', see Section 5.2.1.

Table 4.5 *Present indicative forms of Latin* AUDĪRE *'hear'*

	Active		Passive	
	Singular	Plural	Singular	Plural
1	audi-ō	audī-mus	audi-o-r	audī-mu-r
2	audī-s	audī-tis	audī-r-is	audī-minī
3	audi-t	audi-unt	audī-t-ur	audi-unt-ur

To summarize the principal conclusion of this section: languages often exhibit default patterns of affix ordering that are, in specific instances, overridden by a reverse pattern; reverse patterns of this sort are morphotactically noncanonical, involving a deviation from the parallel sequence criterion. In a rule-combining approach to morphotactics, such deviations can be seen as the effect of a special pattern of rule composition that overrides a general pattern of composition.

4.2 Complementary Sequences of Rule Application in Udmurt

In the Fula case considered in Section 4.1, overrides of a default sequence of rule application constitute a deviation from the parallel sequence criterion. But deviations from this criterion may also involve cases that do not obviously involve any default/override relation. These are cases in which rules that are in paradigmatic opposition to one another fall into two groups of more or less equal size, participating complementarily in opposite sequences of rule application.

In Section 1.5.3, I alluded to a case of this sort presented by the declensional system of Udmurt (Uralic; Russia), which I now consider in greater detail. In Udmurt, nouns inflect for fifteen cases in the singular and the plural, and may additionally inflect for the person and number of a possessor. The singular and plural paradigms of the noun GURT 'village' in Tables 4.6 and 4.7 exemplify this system.[6]

For purposes of this discussion of Udmurt, I distinguish the nominative and accusative cases from the thirteen remaining cases, which I shall call the oblique cases. Nominative case is unmarked. Accusative case forms are complicated by the peculiarities in (9); these are not central to the morphotactic phenomenon at issue here, which primarily concerns the oblique cases. (For additional details on accusative morphology, see Winkler 2001: 20–21, 28.)

---

[6] The paradigms in Tables 4.6 and 4.7 are based on forms downloaded from the Udmurt paradigm generator (www.copius.eu/udm-paradigm.php) created by the Department of Finno-Ugric Studies at the University of Vienna and hosted by the strategic partnership COPIUS "Community of Practice in Uralic Studies."

Table 4.6 Singular case forms of Udmurt GURT 'village'

				Possessor			
	none	1sg	2sg	3sg	1pl	2pl	3pl
Nominative	gurt	gurt-e	gurt-ed	gurt-ez	gurt-mı̈	gurt-tı̈	gurt-sı̈
Accusative	gurt-ez	gurt-me	gurt-te	gurt-se	gurt-me-s	gurt-te-s	gurt-se-s
Genitive	gurt-len	gurt-e-len	gurt-ed-len	gurt-ez-len	gurt-mı̈-len	gurt-tı̈-len	gurt-sı̈-len
Ablative	gurt-leś	gurt-e-leś	gurt-ed-leś	gurt-ez-leś	gurt-mı̈-leś	gurt-tı̈-leś	gurt-sı̈-leś
Dative	gurt-lı̈	gurt-e-lı̈	gurt-ed-lı̈	gurt-ez-lı̈	gurt-mı̈-lı̈	gurt-tı̈-lı̈	gurt-sı̈-lı̈
Abessive	gurt-tek	gurt-e-tek	gurt-ed-tek	gurt-ez-tek	gurt-mı̈-tek	gurt-tı̈-tek	gurt-sı̈-tek
Adverbial	gurt-ja	gurt-e-ja	gurt-ed-ja	gurt-ez-ja	gurt-mı̈-ja	gurt-tı̈-ja	gurt-sı̈-ja
Approximative	gurt-lań	gurt-e-lań	gurt-ed-lań	gurt-ez-lań	gurt-mı̈-lań	gurt-tı̈-lań	gurt-sı̈-lań
Instrumental	gurt-en	gurt-enı̈-m	gurt-enı̈-d	gurt-enı̈-z	gurt-enı̈-mı̈	gurt-enı̈-dı̈	gurt-enı̈-zı̈
Inessive	gurt-ı̈n	gurt-a-m	gurt-a-d	gurt-a-z	gurt-a-mı̈	gurt-a-dı̈	gurt-a-zı̈
Illative	gurt-e	gurt-a-m	gurt-a-d	gurt-a-z	gurt-a-mı̈	gurt-a-dı̈	gurt-a-zı̈
Elative	gurt-ı̈ś	gurt-ı̈śtı̈-m	gurt-ı̈śtı̈-d	gurt-ı̈śtı̈-z	gurt-ı̈śtı̈-mı̈	gurt-ı̈śtı̈-dı̈	gurt-ı̈śtı̈-zı̈
Egressive	gurt-ı̈śen	gurt-ı̈śenı̈-m	gurt-ı̈śenı̈-d	gurt-ı̈śenı̈-z	gurt-ı̈śenı̈-mı̈	gurt-ı̈śenı̈-dı̈	gurt-ı̈śenı̈-zı̈
Prolative	gurt-(e)ti	gurt-(e)ti-m	gurt-(e)ti-d	gurt-(e)ti-z	gurt-(e)ti-mı̈	gurt-(e)ti-dı̈	gurt-(e)ti-zı̈
Terminative	gurt-oź	gurt-oźa-m	gurt-oźa-d	gurt-oźa-z	gurt-oźa-mı̈	gurt-oźa-dı̈	gurt-oźa-zı̈

Table 4.7 *Plural case forms of Udmurt GURT 'village'*

		Possessor				
	none	1sg	2sg	3sg	1pl	2pl	3pl
Nominative	gurt-jos	gurt-jos-y	gurt-jos-yd	gurt-jos-yz	gurt-jos-my	gurt-jos-ty	gurt-jos-sy
Accusative	gurt-jos-ty ~ gurt-jos-yz	gurt-jos-me	gurt-jos-te	gurt-jos-se	gurt-jos-me-s	gurt-jos-te-s	gurt-jos-se-s
Genitive	gurt-jos-len	gurt-jos-y-len	gurt-jos-yd-len	gurt-jos-yz-len	gurt-jos-my-len	gurt-jos-ty-len	gurt-jos-sy-len
Ablative	gurt-jos-leś	gurt-jos-y-leś	gurt-jos-yd-leś	gurt-jos-yz-leś	gurt-jos-my-leś	gurt-jos-ty-leś	gurt-jos-sy-leś
Dative	gurt-jos-ly	gurt-jos-y-ly	gurt-jos-yd-ly	gurt-jos-yz-ly	gurt-jos-my-ly	gurt-jos-ty-ly	gurt-jos-sy-ly
Abessive	gurt-jos-tek	gurt-jos-y-tek	gurt-jos-yd-tek	gurt-jos-yz-tek	gurt-jos-my-tek	gurt-jos-ty-tek	gurt-jos-sy-tek
Adverbial	gurt-jos-ja	gurt-jos-y-ja	gurt-jos-yd-ja	gurt-jos-yz-ja	gurt-jos-my-ja	gurt-jos-ty-ja	gurt-jos-sy-ja
Approximative	gurt-jos-lań	gurt-jos-y-lań	gurt-jos-yd-lań	gurt-jos-yz-lań	gurt-jos-my-lań	gurt-jos-ty-lań	gurt-jos-sy-lań
Instrumental	gurt-jos-yn	gurt-jos-yny-m	gurt-jos-yny-d	gurt-jos-yny-z	gurt-jos-yny-my	gurt-jos-yny-dy	gurt-jos-yny-zy
Inessive	gurt-jos-yn	gurt-jos-a-m	gurt-jos-a-d	gurt-jos-a-z	gurt-jos-a-my	gurt-jos-a-dy	gurt-jos-a-zy
Illative	gurt-jos-y	gurt-jos-a-m	gurt-jos-a-d	gurt-jos-a-z	gurt-jos-a-my	gurt-jos-a-dy	gurt-jos-a-zy
Elative	gurt-jos-yś	gurt-jos-yśty-m	gurt-jos-yśty-d	gurt-jos-yśty-z	gurt-jos-yśty-my	gurt-jos-yśty-dy	gurt-jos-yśty-zy
Egressive	gurt-jos-yśen	gurt-jos-yśeny-m	gurt-jos-yśeny-d	gurt-jos-yśeny-z	gurt-jos-yśeny-my	gurt-jos-yśeny-dy	gurt-jos-yśeny-zy
Prolative	gurt-jos-ti	gurt-jos-ti-m	gurt-jos-ti-d	gurt-jos-ti-z	gurt-jos-ti-my	gurt-jos-ti-dy	gurt-jos-ti-zy
Terminative	gurt-jos-oź	gurt-jos-oźa-m	gurt-jos-oźa-d	gurt-jos-oźa-z	gurt-jos-oźa-my	gurt-jos-oźa-dy	gurt-jos-oźa-zy

(9) Peculiarities of Udmurt accusative morphology
   a. The accusative case suffix is absent in indefinite forms.
   b. In the absence of possessor marking, the accusative case suffix exhibits four alternants:
      Singular: -ez after a consonant, -jez after a vowel (e.g. gurt-ez 'the village', busɨ-jez 'the field');
      Plural: -tɨ ~ -ɨz (e.g. gurt-jos-tɨ ~ gurt-jos-ɨz 'the villages').
   c. In possessor-marked forms, the accusative case and the possessor properties are together marked as follows:

   with first-person possessor: -me (singular possessor),   -mes (plural possessor);
   with second-person possessor: -de (singular possessor),   -des (plural possessor);
   with third-person possessor: -ze (singular possessor),   -zes (plural possessor).

   d. The initial obstruents of the suffixes -de(s), -ze(s) assimilate to the voicelessness of a preceding voiceless consonant, as in Tables 4.6 and 4.7.

4.2 Complementary Sequences in Udmurt 125

Inspection of the oblique case affixes in Tables 4.6 and 4.7 reveals a number of systematic complexities. These include alternations in form and in ordering.

An oblique case may have as many as four different exponents; the choice of a particular exponent for a given oblique case may depend on (i) the presence or absence of possessor marking, (ii) the presence or absence of plural marking, or (iii) both. In the inventory of oblique case rules in Table 4.8, column I lists the default rule for each case; column II lists the rule that instead applies in the definition of possessorless forms (if this is different from the default rule); column III lists the rule that instead applies in the definition of plural forms (if this is different from the default rule); and column IV lists the rule that instead applies in the definition of plural possessorless forms (if this is different from the column II rule that would otherwise apply).

As the forms in Tables 4.6 and 4.7 show, oblique case affixes are ordered in two different ways with respect to an accompanying possessor affix. In what I shall call the A cases (the genitive, ablative, dative, abessive, adverbial, and approximative cases), the case suffix follows an accompanying possessor suffix. In the remaining oblique cases (the B cases, shaded in Tables 4.6 and 4.7), the case suffix precedes an accompanying possessor suffix. The rules in Table 4.8 are grouped according to whether the case they realize is an A case or a B case. The distinction between A cases and B cases is fundamentally morphomic (Aronoff 1994); its only effect is precisely to condition this morphotactic contrast. In formalizing the distinction between A cases and B cases, I assume the property coöccurrence restrictions in (10). These restrictions guarantee that the property set associated with an oblique case form is well-formed only if it contains either the property 'A.case' or the property 'B.case' – that it is ill-formed if it contains neither property or if it contains both.

(10)   Property coöccurrence restrictions
      a.   Only and all nouns specified for an A case have the morphomic property 'A.case'.
      b.   Only and all nouns specified for a B case have the morphomic property 'B.case'.

Unlike the plural possessor affixes, the singular possessor affixes vary in form according to their context: for each type of singular possessor, there is an affix used in singular A-case forms, another used in plural A-case forms, and a third used in B-case forms regardless of their number. Thus, in the inventory of possessor rules in Table 4.9, column I lists the default possessor rule for each type of possessor; column II lists the singular possessor rules used in the definition of plural A-case forms; and column III lists the singular possessor rules used in the definition of B-case forms.

Table 4.8 *Rule group for oblique case inflection in Udmurt*

		I Default rules		II Possessorless case rules		III Plural case rules		IV Plural possessorless case rules	
A cases		[**-len**]] :	[N, {gen} : -*len*]						
		[**-leś**]] :	[N, {abl} : -*leś*]						
		[**-lỵ**]] :	[N, {dat} : -*lỵ*]						
		[**-tek**] :	[N, {abess} : -*tek*]						
		[**-ja**] :	[N, {advbl} : -*ja*]						
		[**-lań**] :	[N, {approx} : -*lań*]						
B cases		[**-enỵ**]:	[N, {ins} : -*enỵ*]	[**-en**]] :	[N, {−poss ins} : -(*j*)*en*]	[**-ỵnỵ**] :	[N, {ins pl} : -*ỵnỵ*]	[**-ỵn**]]₁ :	[N, {−poss ins pl} : -*ỵn*]
		[**-a**]]₁ :	[N, {iness} : -(*j*)*a*]	[**-ỵn**]]₂ :	[N, {−poss iness} : -*ỵn*]				
		[**-a**]]₂ :	[N, {illat} : -(*j*)*a*]	[**-e**]] :	[N, {−poss illat} : -(*j*)*e*]			[**-i**]] :	[N, {−poss illat pl} : -*i*]
		[**-ỵśtỵ**]] :	[N, {elat} : -*ỵśtỵ*]	[**-ỵś**]] :	[N, {−poss elat} : -*ỵś*]				
		[**-ỵśenỵ**]] :	[N, {egr} : -*ỵśenỵ*]	[**-ỵśen**]] :	[N, {−poss egr} : -*ỵśen*]				
		[**-eti**] :	[N, {prolat} : -(*j*)(*e*)*ti*]			[**-ti**] :	[N, {prolat pl} : -*ti*]		
		[**-oźa**]] :	[N, {term} : -*oźa*]	[**-oź**]] :	[N, {−poss term} : -*oź*]				

The parenthesized (*j*) is present postvocalically, absent otherwise.

Table 4.9 *Rule group for possessor inflection in Udmurt*

I Default rules		II Rules used in plural A-case forms		III Rules used in B-case forms	
[[-**e**]] :	[N, {{poss 1 sg}} : -(*j*)*e*]	[[-**ĭ**]] :	[N, {{poss 1 sg} pl A.case} : -*ĭ*]	[[-**m**]] :	[N, {{poss 1 sg} B.case} : -*m*]
[[-**ed**]] :	[N, {{poss 2 sg}} : -(*j*)*ed*]	[[-**ĭd**]] :	[N, {{poss 2 sg} pl A.case} : -*ĭd*]	[[-**d**]] :	[N, {{poss 2 sg} B.case} : -*d*]
[[-**ez**]] :	[N, {{poss 3 sg}} : -(*j*)*ez*]	[[-**ĭz**]] :	[N, {{poss 3 sg} pl A.case} : -*ĭz*]	[[-**z**]] :	[N, {{poss 3 sg} B.case} : -*z*]
[[-**mĭ**]] :	[N, {{poss 1 pl}} : -*mĭ*]				
[[-**dĭ**]] :	[N, {{poss 2 pl}} : -*dĭ*]				
[[-**zĭ**]] :	[N, {{poss 3 pl}} : -*zĭ*]				

The parenthesized (*j*) is present postvocalically, absent otherwise.
Suffix-initial obstruents assimilate to the voicelessness of a preceding consonant.

128 *Rule Composition and Rule Ordering*

Unlike the oblique case suffixes and the possessor suffixes, the Udmurt plural suffix is simple: it has the invariant form *-jos* and invariably precedes accompanying oblique case and possessor suffixes. The rule introducing the plural suffix is as in (11).

(11)   Udmurt plural rule: ⟦-**jos**⟧ : [N, {pl} : *-jos*]

When the oblique case rules in Table 4.8, the possessor rules in Table 4.9, and the plural rule combine, they compose in accordance with the constraints in (12).

(12)   Constraints on the composition of Udmurt rules of noun inflection
   a.   Simple A-case rules compose with simple possessor rules.
   b.   Simple possessor rules compose with simple B-case rules.
   c.   Simple or composite rules expressing an oblique case compose with the plural rule ⟦-**jos**⟧.

Consider some examples. In accordance with (12a), the approximative rule ⟦-**lań**⟧ in Table 4.8, an A-case rule, composes with the default first-person plural possessor rule ⟦-**mị̇**⟧ in Table 4.9 to produce the composite rule in (13a). In accordance with (12b), the default first-person plural possessor rule ⟦-**mị̇**⟧ composes with the instrumental rule ⟦-**enị̇**⟧, a B-case rule, to produce the composite rule in (13b). In accordance with (12c), the abessive rule ⟦-**tek**⟧ composes with the plural rule ⟦-**jos**⟧ to produce the composite rule in (13c). In accordance with (12a), the ablative rule ⟦-**leś**⟧, an A-case rule, composes with the second-person singular possessor rule ⟦-**i̱d**⟧ reserved for plural A-case forms; in accordance with (12c), the resulting composite rule (⟦-**leś**⟧ ∘ ⟦-**i̱d**⟧) composes with the plural rule ⟦-**jos**⟧ to produce the composite rule in (13d). In accordance with (12b), the second-person singular possessor rule ⟦-**d**⟧ reserved for B-case forms composes with the elative rule ⟦-**i̱śti̱**⟧, a B-case rule; in accordance with (12c), the resulting composite rule (⟦-**d**⟧ ∘ ⟦-**i̱śti̱**⟧) composes with the plural rule ⟦-**jos**⟧ to produce the composite rule in (13e).

(13)   Some composite rules for the oblique case forms in Tables 4.6 and 4.7
   a.   (⟦-**lań**⟧ ∘ ⟦-**mị̇**⟧) :   [N, {{poss 1 pl} approx} : *-mị̇lań*]
   b.   (⟦-**mị̇**⟧ ∘ ⟦-**enị̇**⟧) :   [N, {{poss 1 pl} ins} : *-enị̇mị̇*]
   c.   (⟦-**tek**⟧ ∘ ⟦-**jos**⟧) :   [N, {abess pl} : *-jostek*]
   d.   ((⟦-**leś**⟧ ∘ ⟦-**i̱d**⟧) ∘ ⟦-**jos**⟧) :   [N, {{poss 2 sg} abl pl A.case} : *-josi̱dleś*]
   e.   ((⟦-**d**⟧ ∘ ⟦-**i̱śti̱**⟧) ∘ ⟦-**jos**⟧) :   [N, {{poss 2 sg} elat pl B.case} : *-josi̱śti̱d*]

The constraints in (12) determine the composite rules defined by the FER pattern in (14).

(14)   FER pattern for the Udmurt oblique case forms in Tables 4.6 and 4.7
         For each oblique cell ⟨Z, σ⟩ in the form paradigm of a noun in the fragment of Udmurt noun inflection represented in Tables 4.6 and 4.7, the FER for ⟨Z, σ⟩ is involves at most three simple rules:

4.2 Complementary Sequences in Udmurt   129

- the case rule in Table 4.8 that is most narrowly applicable to ⟨Z, σ⟩,
- the possessor rule in Table 4.9 that is most narrowly applicable to ⟨Z, σ⟩ (unless –poss ∈ σ), and
- the plural rule ⟦-jos⟧ (unless sg ∈ σ).

These rules are composed in accordance with the constraints in (12).

In accordance with (14), the FER that realizes a given oblique cell ⟨Z, σ⟩ in a noun's form paradigm is based on the narrowest applicable case rule from Table 4.8 and the narrowest applicable possessor rule from Table 4.9. For this reason, certain composite rules that are compatible with the constraints in (12) do not constitute FERs. Consider, for example, the composite rule in (15a). This is compatible with constraints in (12), but it is not a FER, since ⟦-e⟧ is not the narrowest applicable possessor rule for realizing instrumental singular forms with a first-person singular possessor. Instead, ⟦-m⟧ is the narrowest applicable possessor rule for the realization of such forms, for which the FER is therefore (15b) rather than (15a).

(15)   a.   (⟦-e⟧ ∘ ⟦-eni̯⟧) : [V, {{poss 1 sg} ins} : -enije]
       b.   (⟦-m⟧ ∘ ⟦-eni̯⟧) : [V, {{poss 1 sg} ins B.case} : -eni̯m]

The FER pattern in (14) defines the six types of FERs in Table 4.10.

The six FER types (a)–(f) in Table 4.10 are exemplified by the morphotactic definitions in parts (a)–(f) of Table 4.11. In part (a) of Table 4.11, the form cell of the singular possessorless genitive form *gurt-len* 'of the village' is simply realized by the genitive case rule ⟦-len⟧ from Table 4.8, a FER of type R_{CASE}. In part (b), the form cell of the plural possessorless abessive form *gurt-jos-tek* 'without the villages' is realized by the composite rule (⟦-tek⟧ ∘ ⟦-jos⟧) in (13c), a FER of type (R_{CASE} ∘ ⟦-jos⟧). In part (c), the form cell of the singular possessor-marked A-case (approximative) form *gurt-mi̯-lań* 'toward our village' is realized by the composite rule (⟦-lań⟧ ∘ ⟦-mi̯⟧) in (13a), a FER of type

Table 4.10 *The six types of FERs defined by the FER pattern (14)*

(Where R_{CASE} is a case rule, R_A is an A-case rule, and R_B is a B-case rule (Table 4.8); R_{POSS} is a possessor rule (Table 4.9); and ⟦-jos⟧ is the plural rule (11).]

	FER type	Form cells realized by that type
(a)	R_{CASE}	singular possessorless
(b)	(R_{CASE} ∘ ⟦-jos⟧)	plural possessorless
(c)	(R_A ∘ R_{POSS})	singular possessor-marked A cases
(d)	((R_A ∘ R_{POSS}) ∘ ⟦-jos⟧)	plural possessor-marked A cases
(e)	(R_{POSS} ∘ R_B)	singular possessor-marked B cases
(f)	((R_{POSS} ∘ R_B) ∘ ⟦-jos⟧)	plural possessor-marked B cases

Table 4.11 *The morphotactics of six inflected forms of Udmurt* GURT *'village' exemplifying the six FER types in Table 4.10*

(a)	Form cell:	⟨ gurt-, {–poss gen sg A.case} ⟩	'of the village'
	|		
	FER	⟦-len⟧	(cf. Table 4.8)
	↓		
	Realized cell:	⟨ gurtlen, {–poss gen sg A.case} ⟩	
(b)	Form cell:	⟨ gurt-, {–poss abess pl A.case} ⟩	'without the villages'
	|		
	FER	(⟦-tek⟧ ∘ ⟦-jos⟧)	(= (13c))
	↓		
	Realized cell:	⟨ gurtjostek, {–poss abess pl A.case} ⟩	
(c)	Form cell:	⟨ gurt-, {{poss 1 pl} approx sg A.case} ⟩	'toward our village'
	|		
	FER	(⟦-lań⟧ ∘ ⟦-mị⟧)	(= (13a))
	↓		
	Realized cell:	⟨ gurtmịlań, {{poss 1 pl} approx sg A.case} ⟩	
(d)	Form cell:	⟨ gurt-, {{poss 2 sg} abl pl A.case} ⟩	'from your (sg.) villages'
	|		
	FER	((⟦-leś⟧ ∘ ⟦-ịd⟧) ∘ ⟦-jos⟧)	(= (13d))
	↓		
	Realized cell:	⟨ gurtjosịdleś, {{poss 2 sg} abl pl A.case} ⟩	
(e)	Form cell:	⟨ gurt-, {{poss 1 pl} ins sg B.case} ⟩	'by means of our village'
	|		
	FER	(⟦-mị⟧ ∘ ⟦-enị⟧)	(= (13b))
	↓		
	Realized cell:	⟨ gurtenịmị, {{poss 1 pl} ins sg B.case} ⟩	
(f)	Form cell:	⟨ gurt-, {{poss 2 sg} elat pl B.case} ⟩	'out of your (sg.) villages'
	|		
	FER	((⟦-d⟧ ∘ ⟦-ịśtị⟧) ∘ ⟦-jos⟧)	(= (13e))
	↓		
	Realized cell:	⟨ gurtjosịśtịd, {{poss 2 sg} elat pl B.case} ⟩	

($R_A \circ R_{POSS}$). In part (d), the form cell of the plural possessor-marked A-case (ablative) form *gurt-jos-ịd-leś* 'from your (sg.) villages' is realized by the composite rule ((⟦-leś⟧ ∘ ⟦-ịd⟧) ∘ ⟦-jos⟧) in (13d), a FER of type (($R_A \circ R_{POSS}$) ∘ ⟦-jos⟧). In part (e), the form cell of the singular possessor-marked B-case (instrumental) form *gurt-enị-mị* 'by means of our village' is realized by the composite rule (⟦-mị⟧ ∘ ⟦-enị⟧) in (13b), a FER of type ($R_{POSS} \circ R_B$). In part (f), the form cell of the plural possessor-marked B-case (elative) form *gurt-jos-ịśtị-d* 'out of your (sg.) villages' is realized by the composite rule ((⟦-d⟧ ∘ ⟦-ịśtị⟧) ∘ ⟦-jos⟧) in (13e), a FER of type (($R_{POSS} \circ R_B$) ∘ ⟦-jos⟧).

The composites into which the oblique case and possessor rules enter in Table 4.10 are noncanonical: they do not conform to the parallel sequence criterion because the relative sequence of their application in defining the morphology of nouns overtly inflecting for both categories depends on a form's specific case. The Udmurt facts differ from the Fula facts in Section 4.1 insofar as the opposite sequences of rule application in Udmurt do not clearly involve a default/override relation. That is, while the Fula case involves a default rule-composition pattern of the type ($R_{OBJ} \circ R_{SBJ}$) that is overridden by the opposite pattern ($R_{SBJ} \circ R_{OBJ}$) in a mere two instances (see again Table 4.3), the Udmurt case involves a complementary relation between the two opposite patterns ($R_A \circ R_{POSS}$) and ($R_{POSS} \circ R_B$), neither of which clearly acts as a default overridden by a more narrowly observed pattern. Both of the Udmurt patterns are extensively instantiated: compare the instantiations of ($R_A \circ R_{POSS}$) in Table 4.12 with those of ($R_{POSS} \circ R_B$) in Table 4.13.

Thus, in general: when one order of rule composition contrasts with the reverse order of composition, this may involve the override of a default pattern, or it may simply involve the existence of complementary patterns of composition that do not strictly stand in a default/override relation.

4.3 Alternative Acceptable Sequences of Rule Application in Eastern Mari

Although the Fula and Udmurt cases are both noncanonical with respect to the parallel sequence criterion, both are canonical[7] with respect to the unique sequence criterion, according to which rules of inflectional exponence that may apply in the definition of the same word always apply in the same sequence relative to one another. But there are also cases that fail to conform to either criterion. In the Eastern Mari language (Uralic; Russia), nouns inflect for case and number and may additionally inflect for the person and number of an associated possessor; this inflection is effected by the simple rules in (16). The declensional paradigm of PÖRT 'house' in Table 4.14 exemplifies the case and plural rules in (16a,b) and the various nominative singular forms of PÖRT in

---

[7] The Udmurt terminative case may be an exception to this generalization; that is, it may actually deviate from the unique sequence criterion. According to Winkler (2001: 29), the terminative case suffix may precede or follow a possessor suffix (e.g. gurt-oźa-mi ~ gurt-mi-oź 'to our village'). Whether this is a genuine deviation from the unique sequence criterion depends on whether -oźa and -oź are variant forms introduced by the same rule of exponence (hence a deviation) or are introduced by distinct rules of exponence (hence not a deviation). Winkler (2011: 63) presents the ordering of the terminative case suffix before a possessor suffix as the only order.

Table 4.12 *Udmurt FERs of the type* ($R_A \circ R_{POSS}$) *for singular A-case nouns with possessor marking*

Possessor	Case	FER	
First-person singular	GEN	([[-len]] ∘ [[-e]]) :	[N, {{poss 1sg} gen} : -elen]
	ABL	([[-leś]] ∘ [[-e]]) :	[N, {{poss 1sg} abl} : -eleś]
	DAT	([[-li̯]] ∘ [[-e]]) :	[N, {{poss 1sg} dat} : -eli̯]
	ABESS	([[-tek]] ∘ [[-e]]) :	[N, {{poss 1sg} abess} : -etek]
	ADVBL	([[-ja]] ∘ [[-e]]) :	[N, {{poss 1sg} advbl} : -eja]
	APPROX	([[-lań]] ∘ [[-e]]) :	[N, {{poss 1sg} approx} : -elań]
Second-person singular	GEN	([[-len]] ∘ [[-ed]]) :	[N, {{poss 2sg} gen} : -edlen]
	ABL	([[-leś]] ∘ [[-ed]]) :	[N, {{poss 2sg} abl} : -edleś]
	DAT	([[-li̯]] ∘ [[-ed]]) :	[N, {{poss 2sg} dat} : -edli̯]
	ABESS	([[-tek]] ∘ [[-ed]]) :	[N, {{poss 2sg} abess} : -edtek]
	ADVBL	([[-ja]] ∘ [[-ed]]) :	[N, {{poss 2sg} advbl} : -edja]
	APPROX	([[-lań]] ∘ [[-ed]]) :	[N, {{poss 2sg} approx} : -edlań]
Third-person singular	GEN	([[-len]] ∘ [[-ez]]) :	[N, {{poss 3sg} gen} : -ezlen]
	ABL	([[-leś]] ∘ [[-ez]]) :	[N, {{poss 3sg} abl} : -ezleś]
	DAT	([[-li̯]] ∘ [[-ez]]) :	[N, {{poss 3sg} dat} : -ezli̯]
	ABESS	([[-tek]] ∘ [[-ez]]) :	[N, {{poss 3sg} abess} : -eztek]
	ADVBL	([[-ja]] ∘ [[-ez]]) :	[N, {{poss 3sg} advbl} : -ezja]
	APPROX	([[-lań]] ∘ [[-ez]]) :	[N, {{poss 3sg} approx} : -ezlań]
First-person plural	GEN	([[-len]] ∘ [[-mi̯]]) :	[N, {{poss 1pl} gen} : -mi̯len]
	ABL	([[-leś]] ∘ [[-mi̯]]) :	[N, {{poss 1pl} abl} : -mi̯leś]
	DAT	([[-li̯]] ∘ [[-mi̯]]) :	[N, {{poss 1pl} dat} : -mi̯li̯]
	ABESS	([[-tek]] ∘ [[-mi̯]]) :	[N, {{poss 1pl} abess} : -mi̯tek]
	ADVBL	([[-ja]] ∘ [[-mi̯]]) :	[N, {{poss 1pl} advbl} : -mi̯ja]
	APPROX	([[-lań]] ∘ [[-mi̯]]) :	[N, {{poss 1pl} approx} : -mi̯lań]
Second-person plural	GEN	([[-len]] ∘ [[-di̯]]) :	[N, {{poss 2pl} gen} : -di̯len]
	ABL	([[-leś]] ∘ [[-di̯]]) :	[N, {{poss 2pl} abl} : -di̯leś]
	DAT	([[-li̯]] ∘ [[-di̯]]) :	[N, {{poss 2pl} dat} : -di̯li̯]
	ABESS	([[-tek]] ∘ [[-di̯]]) :	[N, {{poss 2pl} abess} : -di̯tek]
	ADVBL	([[-ja]] ∘ [[-di̯]]) :	[N, {{poss 2pl} advbl} : -di̯ja]
	APPROX	([[-lań]] ∘ [[-di̯]]) :	[N, {{poss 2pl} approx} : -di̯lań]
Third-person plural	GEN	([[-len]] ∘ [[-zi̯]]) :	[N, {{poss 3pl} gen} : -zi̯len]
	ABL	([[-leś]] ∘ [[-zi̯]]) :	[N, {{poss 3pl} abl} : -zi̯leś]
	DAT	([[-li̯]] ∘ [[-zi̯]]) :	[N, {{poss 3pl} dat} : -zi̯li̯]
	ABESS	([[-tek]] ∘ [[-zi̯]]) :	[N, {{poss 3pl} abess} : -zi̯tek]
	ADVBL	([[-ja]] ∘ [[-zi̯]]) :	[N, {{poss 3pl} advbl} : -zi̯ja]
	APPROX	([[-lań]] ∘ [[-zi̯]]) :	[N, {{poss 3pl} approx} : -zi̯lań]

4.3 Alternative Sequences in Eastern Mari 133

Table 4.13 *Udmurt FERs of the type* ($R_{POSS} \circ R_B$) *for singular B-case nouns with possessor marking*

Possessor	Case	FER	
First-person singular	INS	(〚-m〛 ∘ 〚-eni̯〛) :	[N, {{poss 1 sg} ins B.case} : -eni̯m]
	INESS	(〚-m〛 ∘ 〚-a〛) :	[N, {{poss 1 sg} iness B.case} : -am]
	ILLAT	(〚-m〛 ∘ 〚-a〛) :	[N, {{poss 1 sg} illat B.case} : -am]
	ELAT	(〚-m〛 ∘ 〚-iśti̯〛) :	[N, {{poss 1 sg} elat B.case} : -iśti̯m]
	EGR	(〚-m〛 ∘ 〚-iśeni̯〛) :	[N, {{poss 1 sg} egr B.case} : -iśeni̯m]
	PROLAT	(〚-m〛 ∘ 〚-eti〛) :	[N, {{poss 1 sg} prolat B.case} : -etim]
	TERM	(〚-m〛 ∘ 〚-oźa〛) :	[N, {{poss 1 sg} term B.case} : -oźam]
Second-person singular	INS	(〚-d〛 ∘ 〚-eni̯〛) :	[N, {{poss 2 sg} ins B.case} : -eni̯d]
	INESS	(〚-d〛 ∘ 〚-a〛) :	[N, {{poss 2 sg} iness B.case} : -ad]
	ILLAT	(〚-d〛 ∘ 〚-a〛) :	[N, {{poss 2 sg} illat B.case} : -ad]
	ELAT	(〚-d〛 ∘ 〚-iśti̯〛) :	[N, {{poss 2 sg} elat B.case} : -iśti̯d]
	EGR	(〚-d〛 ∘ 〚-iśeni̯〛) :	[N, {{poss 2 sg} egr B.case} : -iśeni̯d]
	PROLAT	(〚-d〛 ∘ 〚-eti〛) :	[N, {{poss 2 sg} prolat B.case} : -etid]
	TERM	(〚-d〛 ∘ 〚-oźa〛) :	[N, {{poss 2 sg} term B.case} : -oźad]
Third-person singular	INS	(〚-z〛 ∘ 〚-eni̯〛) :	[N, {{poss 3 sg} ins B.case} : -eni̯z]
	INESS	(〚-z〛 ∘ 〚-a〛) :	[N, {{poss 3 sg} iness B.case} : -az]
	ILLAT	(〚-z〛 ∘ 〚-a〛) :	[N, {{poss 3 sg} illat B.case} : -az]
	ELAT	(〚-z〛 ∘ 〚-iśti̯〛) :	[N, {{poss 3 sg} elat B.case} : -iśti̯z]
	EGR	(〚-z〛 ∘ 〚-iśeni̯〛) :	[N, {{poss 3 sg} egr B.case} : -iśeni̯z]
	PROLAT	(〚-z〛 ∘ 〚-eti〛) :	[N, {{poss 3 sg} prolat B.case} : -etiz]
	TERM	(〚-z〛 ∘ 〚-oźa〛) :	[N, {{poss 3 sg} term B.case} : -oźaz]
First-person plural	INS	(〚-mi̯〛 ∘ 〚-eni̯〛) :	[N, {{poss 1 pl} ins} : -eni̯mi̯]
	INESS	(〚-mi̯〛 ∘ 〚-a〛) :	[N, {{poss 1 pl} iness} : -ami̯]
	ILLAT	(〚-mi̯〛 ∘ 〚-a〛) :	[N, {{poss 1 pl} illat} : -ami̯]
	ELAT	(〚-mi̯〛 ∘ 〚-iśti̯〛) :	[N, {{poss 1 pl} elat} : -iśti̯mi̯]
	EGR	(〚-mi̯〛 ∘ 〚-iśeni̯〛) :	[N, {{poss 1 pl} egr} : -iśeni̯mi̯]
	PROLAT	(〚-mi̯〛 ∘ 〚-eti〛) :	[N, {{poss 1 pl} prolat} : -etimi̯]
	TERM	(〚-mi̯〛 ∘ 〚-oźa〛) :	[N, {{poss 1 pl} term} : -oźami̯]

Table 4.13 (*cont.*)

Possessor	Case	FER	
Second-person plural	INS	(⟦-di⟧ ∘ ⟦-eni⟧) :	[N, {{poss 2 pl} ins} : -*enidi*]
	INESS	(⟦-di⟧ ∘ ⟦-a⟧) :	[N, {{poss 2 pl} iness} : -*adi*]
	ILLAT	(⟦-di⟧ ∘ ⟦-a⟧) :	[N, {{poss 2 pl} illat} : -*adi*]
	ELAT	(⟦-di⟧ ∘ ⟦-iśti⟧) :	[N, {{poss 2 pl} elat} : -*iśtidi*]
	EGR	(⟦-di⟧ ∘ ⟦-iśeni⟧) :	[N, {{poss 2 pl} egr} : -*iśenidi*]
	PROLAT	(⟦-di⟧ ∘ ⟦-eti⟧) :	[N, {{poss 2 pl} prolat} : -*etidi*]
	TERM	(⟦-di⟧ ∘ ⟦-oźa⟧) :	[N, {{poss 2 pl} term} : -*oźadi*]
Third-person plural	INS	(⟦-zi⟧ ∘ ⟦-eni⟧) :	[N, {{poss 3 pl} ins} : -*enizi*]
	INESS	(⟦-zi⟧ ∘ ⟦-a⟧) :	[N, {{poss 3 pl} iness} : -*azi*]
	ILLAT	(⟦-zi⟧ ∘ ⟦-a⟧) :	[N, {{poss 3 pl} illat} : -*azi*]
	ELAT	(⟦-zi⟧ ∘ ⟦-iśti⟧) :	[N, {{poss 3 pl} elat} : -*iśtizi*]
	EGR	(⟦-zi⟧ ∘ ⟦-iśeni⟧) :	[N, {{poss 3 pl} egr} : -*iśenizi*]
	PROLAT	(⟦-zi⟧ ∘ ⟦-eti⟧) :	[N, {{poss 3 pl} prolat} : -*etizi*]
	TERM	(⟦-zi⟧ ∘ ⟦-oźa⟧) :	[N, {{poss 3 pl} term} : -*oźazi*]

Table 4.15 exemplify the use of the possessor rules in (16c).[8] Each of the rules in (16) is, on its own, a FER: those in (16a) are FERs for non-nominative case forms that are singular and possessorless (e.g. the forms in the singular column of Table 4.14); the ⟦-βlak⟧ rule in (16b) is the FER for possessorless nominative plural forms (e.g. *pört-βlak* 'houses' in Table 4.14); and the rules in (16c) are FERs for nominative singular forms with a possessor (e.g. the forms in Table 4.15).

(16)   Simple rules of Eastern Mari nominal inflection[9]
  a. Case rule group   b. Plural rule group
      ⟦-(ə)n⟧ : [N, {gen} : -(ə)n]   ⟦-βlak⟧ : [N, {pl} : -βlak][10]
      ⟦-(ə)m⟧ : [N, {acc} : -(ə)m]   c. Possessor rule group
      ⟦-lan⟧ : [N, {dat} : -lan]   ⟦-em⟧ : [N, {POSS:1sg} : -em]
      ⟦-eš⟧ : [N, {lat} : -eš]   ⟦-et⟧ : [N, {POSS:2sg} : -et]
      ⟦-(ə)škE⟧ : [N, {illat} : -(ə)š(kE)]   ⟦-žE⟧ : [N, {POSS:3sg} : -žE]
      ⟦-(ə)štE⟧ : [N, {iness} : -(ə)štE]   ⟦-na⟧ : [N, {POSS:1pl} : -na]
      ⟦-la⟧ : [N, {compar} : -la]   ⟦-da⟧ : [N, {POSS:2pl} : -da]
      ⟦-ge⟧ : [N, {comit} : -ge]   ⟦-(ə)št⟧ : [N, {POSS:3pl} : -(ə)št]

---

[8] The paradigms in Tables 4.14–16 are based on forms downloaded from the Mari paradigm generator (http://paradigm.mari-language.com) hosted by the Mari Web Project.

[9] In the rules in (16), the parenthesized (ə) is an epenthetic vowel; it is absent postvocalically, but otherwise represents ə /ə/. The vowel E in the rules ⟦-(ə)škE⟧, ⟦-(ə)štE⟧, and ⟦-žE⟧ is realized as *e*, *o*, or *ö*, in accordance with the principles of Eastern Mari vowel harmony. The initial consonants of the suffixes introduced by the rules ⟦-ge⟧, ⟦-žE⟧, and ⟦-da⟧ are devoiced after a voiceless obstruent.

[10] The expression of plural number in Mari nouns is an important locus of dialectal variation (Luutonen 1997: 53ff.); the -βlak suffix in (16b) is typical of the Eastern Mari dialect under discussion here.

Table 4.14 *Declensional paradigm of Eastern Mari* PÖRT *'house'*

	Singular	Plural
Nominative	pört	pört-βlak
Genitive	pört-ǝn	pört-βlak-ǝn
Accusative	pört-ǝm	pört-βlak-ǝm
Dative	pört-lan	pört-βlak-lan
Lative	pört-eš	pört-βlak-eš
Illative	pört-ǝš(kö)	pört-βlak-ǝš(ke)
Inessive	pört-ǝštö	pört-βlak-ǝšte
Comparative	pört-la	pört-βlak-la
Comitative	pört-ge	pört-βlak-ge

Table 4.15 *The personal possessor suffixes on the nominative singular form of the Eastern Mari noun* PÖRT *'house'*

		Number of possessor	
		Singular	Plural
Person of possessor	1	pört-em	pört-na
	2	pört-et	pört-da
	3	pört-šö	pört-ǝšt

When the rules in (16) combine, their relative ordering is fixed in some respects, but flexible in others; even if there is a favored ordering, this is not necessarily exclusive. In general, the plural suffix precedes an accompanying case suffix, as the examples in Table 4.14 show; cf. Luutonen (1997: 17), Alhoniemi (2010: 69). Accordingly, the case rules in (16a) compose with the plural rule in (16b) as in the FER pattern (17), which defines the composite rules in (18b–i); together with the simple ⟦-βlak⟧ rule in (18a) (= (16b)), they serve as FERs for possessorless plural forms such as those in Table 4.14.

(17) FER pattern for possessorless case-marked plurals in Eastern Mari
Where R_{CASE} is a simple case rule in (16a), (R_{CASE} ∘ ⟦-βlak⟧) is a FER.

(18) The FERs defining the possessorless plural forms in Table 4.14
    a. ⟦-βlak⟧ : [N, {pl} : -βlak]   (= (16b))
    b. (⟦-(ǝ)n⟧ ∘ ⟦-βlak⟧) :   [N, {gen pl} :   -βlakǝn]   ((18b–i) defined by (17))
    c. (⟦-(ǝ)m⟧ ∘ ⟦-βlak⟧) :   [N, {acc pl} :   -βlakǝm]

136   *Rule Composition and Rule Ordering*

    d. ([[-lan]] ∘ [[-βlak]]) :   [N, {dat pl} :   -βlaklan]
    e. ([[-eš]] ∘ [[-βlak]]) :   [N, {lat pl} :   -βlakeš]
    f. ([[-(ə)škE]] ∘ [[-βlak]]) :   [N, {illat pl} :   -βlakə̂š(ke)]
    g. ([[-(ə)štE]] ∘ [[-βlak]]) :   [N, {iness pl} :   -βlakə̂šte]
    h. ([[-la]] ∘ [[-βlak]]) :   [N, {compar pl} : -βlakla]
    i. ([[-ge]] ∘ [[-βlak]]) :   [N, {comit pl} :   -βlakge]

In a case-marked singular form inflected for a possessor by means of one of the rules in (16c), the sequence in which the case rule composes with the possessor rule depends on the particular case being realized. I will say that Eastern Mari cases fall into two intersecting sets, the A cases and the B cases. The A cases are what might be loosely called the "grammatical" cases, which include the nominative, genitive, accusative, and comitative; the B cases might be called the "local" cases, which include the lative, illative, and inessive. Crucially for what follows, the dative and comparative cases serve as both A cases and B cases, as in Figure 4.1.

In case-marked forms inflected for a possessor, the possessor suffix precedes a suffix marking an A case, but follows a suffix marking a B case. The forms in Table 4.16 illustrate; note that in the dative and comparative forms in Table 4.16, the possessor suffix and the case suffix may appear in either order. In order to account for this fact, one must assume that in the definition of the A-case forms in Table 4.16, the case rule composes with the possessor rule, as in (19a), but that in the definition of the B-case forms, it is instead the possessor rule that composes with the case rule, as in (19b). This pattern is exemplified by the composite rules in (20), which involve the first-person singular possessor rule [[-em]].

(19)   FER patterns for singular possessor-marked case forms in Eastern Mari
    a. If R_A is a simple rule realizing an A case, then (R_A ∘ R_{POSS}) is a FER.
    b. If R_B is a simple rule realizing a B case, then (R_{POSS} ∘ R_B) is a FER.

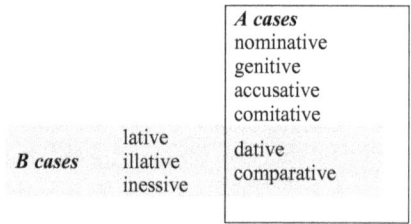

Figure 4.1 *The intersecting sets of A cases and B cases in Eastern Mari*

4.3 Alternative Sequences in Eastern Mari

Table 4.16 *Singular case forms of Eastern Mari* PÖRT *'house' with the first-person singular possessor suffix* -em

	Stem-POSS-CASE	Stem-CASE-POSS
Nominative	pört-em	
Genitive	pört-em-ə̂n	
Accusative	pört-em-ə̂m	
Dative	pört-em-lan	pört-lan-em
Lative		pört-eš-em
Illative		pört-ə̂šk-em
Inessive		pört-ə̂št-em
Comparative	pört-em-la	pört-la-m
Comitative	pört-em-ge	

(20) The FERs defining the singular possessor-marked case forms in Table 4.16

a. ⟦-em⟧ : [N, {POSS:1sg} : -em] (from (16c))
b. (⟦-(ə̂)n⟧ ∘ ⟦-em⟧) : [N, {gen POSS:1sg} : -emə̂n] ((20b–f) defined by (19a))
c. (⟦-(ə̂)m⟧ ∘ ⟦-em⟧) : [N, {acc POSS:1sg} : -emə̂m]
d. (⟦-lan⟧ ∘ ⟦-em⟧) : [N, {dat POSS:1sg} : -emlan]
e. (⟦-la⟧ ∘ ⟦-em⟧) : [N, {compar POSS:1sg} : -emla]
f. (⟦-ge⟧ ∘ ⟦-em⟧) : [N, {comit POSS:1sg} : -emge]
g. (⟦-em⟧ ∘ ⟦-lan⟧) : [N, {dat POSS:1sg} : -lanem] ((20g–k) defined by (19b))
h. (⟦-em⟧ ∘ ⟦-eš⟧) : [N, {lat POSS:1sg} : -ešem]
i. (⟦-em⟧ ∘ ⟦-(ə̂)škE⟧) : [N, {illat POSS:1sg} : -(ə̂)škem]
j. (⟦-em⟧ ∘ ⟦-(ə̂)štE⟧) : [N, {iness POSS:1sg} : -(ə̂)štem]
k. (⟦-em⟧ ∘ ⟦-la⟧) : [N, {compar POSS:1sg} : -lam]

In nominative plural forms inflected for a possessor, the plural suffix and the possessor suffix may appear in either order; there is no overt nominative suffix in these forms. In other plural forms inflected for a possessor, the three coöccurring inflectional suffixes – the case suffix, the plural suffix, and the possessor suffix – may appear in as many as three alternative orders, depending on the particular case involved. The forms in Table 4.17 illustrate the possibilities, with the first-person singular possessor suffix -em serving as the possessor marker. I follow Luutonen in omitting the comparative and comitative cases; Jeremy Bradley (personal communication) notes the extreme infrequency of these cases among plural possessor-marked nouns in the existing corpora of Eastern Mari. In all of the other cases, the pattern

138 *Rule Composition and Rule Ordering*

Table 4.17 *Plural case forms of Eastern Mari* PÖRT *'house' with the first-person singular possessor suffix*

	I	II	III
	Stem-POSS-PL-CASE	Stem-PL-POSS-CASE	Stem-PL-CASE-POSS
Nominative	pört-em-βlak	pört-βlak-em	
Genitive	pört-em-βlak-ǝn	pört-βlak-em-ǝn	
Accusative	pört-em-βlak-ǝm	pört-βlak-em-ǝm	
Dative	pört-em-βlak-lan	pört-βlak-em-lan	pört-βlak-lan-em
Lative	pört-em-βlak-eš		pört-βlak-eš-em
Illative	pört-em-βlak-ǝš(ke)		pört-βlak-ǝšk-em
Inessive	pört-em-βlak-ǝšte		pört-βlak-ǝšt-em

Based on Luutonen 1997

Stem-POSS-PL-CASE is possible, as in column I of Table 4.17. The Stem-PL-POSS-CASE pattern in column II is additionally possible for the A cases, and the Stem-PL-CASE-POSS pattern in column III is instead additionally possible for the B cases. Because the dative case is both an A case and a B case, it exhibits all three of the patterns in Table 4.17. In his extensive investigation of these patterns, Luutonen (1997: 32ff.) observes that speakers readily accept alternative forms conforming to these regularities, but generally reject forms exhibiting other imaginable orderings, including some that are historically attested.

An important regularity concerning nominal forms with three inflectional suffixes is what Luutonen calls the Variable Morphotactics Reduction Principle. According to this principle, "the acceptability relations among [three-suffix strings] can be reduced to the corresponding relations between their constituent strings" (Luutonen 1997: 151). The acceptability of all of the three-suffix sequences in column I of Table 4.17 follows from that of the corresponding two-suffix sequences in the 'Plural' column of Table 4.14. Thus, given that the FERs in (18) define the forms in the 'Plural' column of Table 4.14, the corresponding forms in column I of Table 4.17 follow the FER pattern (21); these are the FERs in the top half of Table 4.18. The acceptability of all of the three-suffix sequences in columns II and III of Table 4.17 follows from that of the corresponding two-suffix sequences in Table 4.16. Thus, given that the FERs in (20) define the forms in Table 4.16, the corresponding forms in columns II and III of Table 4.17 follow the FER pattern (22); these are the FERs in the bottom half of Table 4.18. Each of the composite rules in

Table 4.18 *The FERs defining the forms in Table 4.17*

	FERs following pattern (21)	
Nominative (no case rule)	([[-βlak]] ∘ [[-em]])	
Genitive	(([[-(ə)n]] ∘ [[-βlak]]) ∘ [[-em]])	
Accusative	(([[-(ə)m]] ∘ [[-βlak]]) ∘ [[-em]])	
Dative	(([[-lan]] ∘ [[-βlak]]) ∘ [[-em]])	
Lative	(([[-eš]] ∘ [[-βlak]]) ∘ [[-em]])	
Illative	(([[-(ə)škE]] ∘ [[-βlak]]) ∘ [[-em]])	
Inessive	(([[-(ə)štE]] ∘ [[-βlak]]) ∘ [[-em]])	
	FERs following pattern (22)	
Nominative (no case rule)	([[-em]] ∘ [[-βlak]])	
Genitive	(([[-(ə)n]] ∘ [[-em]]) ∘ [[-βlak]])	
Accusative	(([[-(ə)m]] ∘ [[-em]]) ∘ [[-βlak]])	
Dative	(([[-lan]] ∘ [[-em]]) ∘ [[-βlak]])	(([[-em]] ∘ [[-lan]]) ∘ [[-βlak]])
Lative		(([[-em]] ∘ [[-eš]]) ∘ [[-βlak]])
Illative		(([[-em]] ∘ [[-(ə)škE]]) ∘ [[-βlak]])
Inessive		(([[-em]] ∘ [[-(ə)štE]]) ∘ [[-βlak]])

Table 4.18 serves as a FER for the appropriate case form of a plural noun marked for a first-person singular possessor. Each has a kind of "annexational" structure involving the composition of an existing FER with a simple rule to produce a more complex FER; the more complex FER preserves all of the patterns of relative order and adjacency entailed by the simpler FER on which it is based.

(21)   Three-rule FER pattern based on the possessorless FERs in (18)
       Given any FER in (18) and any simple possessor rule R_{POSS}, (FER ∘ R_{POSS}) is also a FER.

(22)   Three-rule FER pattern based on the singular FERs in (20)
       Given any FER in (20), (FER ∘ [[-βlak]]) is also a FER.

As this evidence shows, Eastern Mari morphotactics is noncanonical in that it fails to conform to either the parallel sequence criterion or the unique sequence criterion. In a rule-combining approach to exponence-driven morphotactics, this divergence from canonicity can be represented as the coexistence of opposite sequences of rule composition neither of which overrides the other[11] but which instead allow the same form cell in a noun's paradigm to be realized in more than one way – and in at least one case, in as many as three ways.

Cross-linguistically, deviations from the unique sequence criterion are widely observable. In general, these can be seen as involving the competition of composite rules which consist of the same rules composed in different sequences and have the same domain-of-definition.

4.4 Conclusion

Rule composition provides a simple way of modeling regularities in the order of rule application. As the evidence discussed in this chapter has shown, deviations from the parallel sequence criterion are of various kinds, all of which reflect well-defined patterns of rule composition. In Fula verb inflection, the order of concordial suffixes reveals a default order of rule composition that is overridden by the opposite order of composition in combinations of certain specific rules. Udmurt noun inflection presents two complementary rule orderings (neither of which is obviously a default) that contrast with respect to the order in which case rules and possessor-coding rules compose, with some cases inducing one order of composition and others inducing the opposite order. In Eastern Mari noun inflection, case rules, possessor-coding rules, and the plural rule compose in more than one acceptable order; thus, rule composition makes it possible to model deviations from both the parallel sequence criterion and the unique sequence criterion.

In the following chapter, certain apparent deviations from canonical morphotactic criteria are shown to be reconcilable with them if these criteria are seen as defining canonical morphotactic characteristics of composite as well as simple rules.

---

[11] In Table 4.18, all of the rules realizing a given case have the same domain-of-definition. For this reason, no rule realizing any case in this table overrides the other rule(s) realizing that case; Pāṇini's principle fails to single out a "winner" for any case.

5 *Extending Canonical Morphotactic Criteria to Composite Rules*

In Chapters 3 and 4, rule composition was shown to provide an enlightening way of modeling deviations from the rule independence criterion (Section 1.5.2) in Limbu and Sanskrit, deviations from the parallel sequence criterion (Section 1.5.3) in Fula and Udmurt, and deviations from the unique sequence criterion (Section 1.5.4) in Eastern Mari. In the present chapter, I show that besides affording a way of modeling deviations from canonical morphotactics, rule composition also makes it possible to see apparently recalcitrant morphotactic patterns as conforming to canonical criteria if these are assumed to cover composite rules as well as simple rules. In Section 5.1, I examine an apparent deviation from the integral stem criterion (Section 1.5.8) in Sanskrit; in Section 5.2, I examine apparent deviations from the rule opposition criterion (Section 1.5.9) in Latin, Limbu, and Sanskrit. Each of these phenomena can be reconciled with the canonical criterion from which it apparently deviates if this criterion is assumed to cover composite rules as well as simple rules. All of these are cases in which deviation from the minimal rule criterion (Section 1.5.1) facilitates conformity to other canonical morphotactic criteria.

5.1 An Apparent Case of Nonlocal Morphotactic Conditioning in Sanskrit

Conditions on the application of rules of exponence tend overwhelmingly to be local. One manifestation of this tendency is the integral stem criterion, according to which a rule's operation on a stem is canonically conditioned by characteristics of the stem as a whole, not by characteristics of a proper part of the stem that do not persist to the stem as a whole. That is, the application of a derivational rule to a ⟨lexeme, stem, category⟩ triplet ⟨L, Z, C⟩ may be sensitive to phonological, prosodic, grammatical, or lexical properties of Z as a whole, but it is not canonically sensitive to phonological, prosodic, grammatical, or lexical properties of a proper part of Z that do not persist to Z itself; in the same way, the application of an inflectional rule to a ⟨stem, property set⟩ pairing ⟨Z, σ⟩ may be

Table 5.1 *Stem formation in the present-system conjugations in Sanskrit*

Conjugation		Stem-forming affix	Example	Present-system stem	
Thematic	First	suffix -*a*	BHŪ 'be' :	*bháv-a-*	
	Fourth	suffix -*ya*	NAH 'bind' :	*náh-ya-*	
	Sixth	suffix -*á*	VIŚ 'enter' :	*viś-á-*	
	Tenth	suffix -*áya*	CINT 'think' :	*cint-áya-*	
Athematic	Second	none	DVIṢ 'hate' :	Weak: *dviṣ-*	Strong: *dvéṣ-*
	Third	reduplicative prefix	BHṚ 'carry' :	*bi-bhṛ-*	*bí-bhar-*
	Fifth	suffix -*nu*/-*nó*	SU 'press out' :	*su-nu-*	*su-nó-*
	Seventh	infix -*n*-/-*ná*-	BHID 'split' :	*bhi-n-d-*	*bhi-ná-d-*
	Eighth	suffix -*u*/-*ó*	TAN 'stretch' :	*tan-u-*	*tan-ó-*
	Ninth	suffix -*nī̆*/-*nā̆*	PŪ 'purify' :	*pu-nī̆-*	*pu-nā̆-*

sensitive to properties of Z as a whole, but is not canonically sensitive to impersistent properties of a proper part of Z. In this section, I examine an apparent deviation from the integral stem criterion in Sanskrit; as I show, the Sanskrit facts do not involve any deviation if the integral stem criterion is seen as relating to composite rules as well as to simple rules.

In the inflection of Sanskrit verbs, the termination -*hí* serves as a cumulative expression of the second-person singular imperative active (that is, of the property set {2sg imp act}), as in *i-hí* 'go!' The distribution of this termination is rather intricate, and on first consideration, it seems to involve a deviation from the integral stem criterion; but if one assumes that the integral stem criterion relates to composite rules as well as to simple rules, then the apparent participation of 〚-**hí**〛 in noncanonical morphotactic patterns proves instead to be the participation of composites of 〚-**hí**〛 in perfectly canonical patterns.

In Sanskrit, a verb's imperative forms are part of its present-system conjugation.[1] A verb's conjugation in the present system is based on a stem whose formation and inflection follow one of the ten main conjugations in Table 5.1.

---

[1] Recall from Section 3.3 that in Sanskrit, finite verb forms fall into four systems: the present, the perfect, the aorist, and the future. A verb has a different stem (or set of stem alternants) for use in each of these systems, and the inflection-class distinctions to which the systems are sensitive are generally orthogonal to one another; for instance, the inflection-class membership of a verb's aorist-system stem doesn't necessarily reveal that of its present-system stem. For this reason, dictionaries of Sanskrit generally list (at least) four principal parts for a given verb.

Table 5.2 *Second-person singular imperative active forms in Sanskrit (thematic conjugations)*

Present-system conjugation	Member lexeme and present-system stem		Inflectional realization = bare stem
First	BHŪ 'be':	bháva-	bháva
Fourth	NAH 'bind':	náhya-	náhya
Sixth	VIŚ 'enter':	viśá-	viśá
Tenth	CINT 'think' :	cintáya-	cintáya

In most conjugations, a verbal lexeme's present-system stem is formed from its root through the addition of a suffix; but stems in the second conjugation lack any stem-forming suffix, those in the third conjugation instead exhibit a reduplicative prefix, and those in the seventh conjugation instead involve a stem-forming infix. Verbs in the athematic conjugations generally exhibit distinct weak and strong stem forms whose distribution within a verb's present-system paradigm is grammatically conditioned. In the second and third conjugations, a verb's weak and strong stems are distinguished by apophony of the root vowel; in the fifth, seventh, eighth, and ninth conjugations, a verb's weak and strong stems are distinguished by the vocalism of the stem-forming suffix. The examples in Table 5.1 illustrate.

The distribution of the {2sg imp act} termination *-hí* is intricate. It is altogether absent from the thematic conjugations (i.e. the first, fourth, sixth, and tenth conjugations, all of which are based on a present-system stem ending in the short theme vowel *a*); the imperative forms in Table 5.2 illustrate.

In the athematic conjugations (which always involve a present-system stem not ending in short *a*), the presence of the {2sg imp act} termination *-hí* depends on both morphological and phonological conditions. In the second and third conjugations, *-hí* only appears on a vowel-final stem; with a consonant-final stem, the termination *-dhí* is instead used.[2] In the seventh conjugation, the present-system stem is always consonant-final, so that *-dhí* is invariably used. In the eighth conjugation, the {2sg imp act} form lacks any termination. The imperative forms in Table 5.3 illustrate.

---

[2] Exceptionally, the third-conjugation verb HU 'sacrifice' has *-dhí* postvocalically: *juhu-dhí* 'sacrifice!' Whitney (1889: §652) attributes this to the need to avoid the appearance of *h* in two successive syllables. Note that *dh* is a digraph representing a voiced aspirated plosive.

Table 5.3 *Second-person singular imperative active forms in the second, third, seventh, and eighth conjugations*

Conjugation	Vowel-final stem	Consonant-final stem
Second	i-hí 'go!'	dug-dhí 'milk!'
Third	bibhr-hí 'carry!'	babhas-dhí (→ babho-dhí by sandhi) 'devour!'
Seventh	—	yuṅg-dhí 'join!'
Eighth	tanú 'stretch!'	—

Table 5.4 *Second-person singular imperative active forms of some Sanskrit fifth-conjugation verbs*

aś-nu-hí	'attain!'	vr-nú	'cover!'
āp-nu-hí	'obtain!'	ūr-nu-hí	'cover!'
r̥dh-nu-hí	'thrive!'	vr-nú	'choose!'
kṣi-ṇú	'destroy!'	śak-nu-hí	'be able!'
ci-nú	'gather!'	śr-ṇú	'hear!'
tr̥p-ṇu-hí	'be pleased!'	su-nú	'press out!'
du-nú	'burn!'	stu-nú	'praise!'
dhi-nú	'nourish!'	str-ṇú	'strew!'
dhū-nú	'shake!'	hi-nú	'impel!'
dhr̥ṣ-ṇu-hí	'dare!'	ci-nú	'note, observe!'
mi-nú	'fix!'	jagh-nu-hí	'devour!'
mi-nú	'damage!'	ti-nú	'crush!'
rādh-nu-hí	'succeed!'	pr-ṇú	'fill!'

The retroflexion of suffixal *n* in several of these forms is an effect of automatic phonology; see Whitney (1889: §189).

This leaves the fifth and ninth conjugations, in both of which the distribution of *-hí* involves an apparent deviation from the integral stem criterion. In the fifth conjugation, whose stem-forming suffix is *-nu*, the presence of *-hí* seems to depend on whether the root to which *-nu* is suffixed ends in a consonant: if it does, then the {2sg imp act} form exhibits *-hí* (e.g. *āp-nu-hí* 'obtain!'), but not otherwise (e.g. *su-nú* 'press out!'); the imperative forms in Table 5.4 embody this regularity.

In the ninth conjugation, whose stem-forming suffix is *-nī*, the presence of *-hí* seems to depend on whether the root to which *-nī* is suffixed ends in a vowel: if it does, then the {2sg imp act} form exhibits *-hí* (e.g. *krī-ṇī-hí* 'buy!'); otherwise, the termination *-āná* is instead used on the (consonant-final) root itself, without *-nī* (e.g. *aś-āná* 'eat!'). The imperative forms in

Table 5.5 *Second-person singular and plural imperative active forms of some Sanskrit ninth-conjugation verbs*

Singular	Plural		Singular	Plural	
aś-āná	aś-nī-tá	'eat!'	mr̥d-āná	mr̥d-nī-tá	'rub, crush!'
krī-ṇī-hí	krī-ṇī-tá	'buy!'	lu-nī-hí	lu-nī-tá	'cut!'
gr̥-ṇī-hí	gr̥-ṇī-tá	'sing!'	vr̥-ṇī-hí	vr̥-ṇī-tá	'choose!'
grath-āná	grath-nī-tá	'tie!'	śr̥-ṇī-hí	śr̥-ṇī-tá	'crush!'
gr̥h-āṇá	gr̥h-ṇī-tá	'seize!'	stabh-āná	stabh-nī-tá	'prop!'
jā-nī-hí	jā-nī-tá	'know!'	str̥-ṇī-hí	str̥-ṇī-tá	'strew!'
pu-nī-hí	pu-nī-tá	'purify!'	aś-āná	aś-nī-tá	'attain!'
prī-ṇī-hí	prī-ṇī-tá	'please!'	kuṣ-āṇá	kuṣ-nī-tá	'tear!'
badh-āná	badh-nī-tá	'bind!'	kliś-āná	kliś-nī-tá	'distress!'
math-āná	math-nī-tá	'shake!'	dhū-nī-hí	dhū-nī-tá	'shake!'
muṣ-āṇá	muṣ-nī-tá	'steal!'	puṣ-āṇá	puṣ-nī-tá	'thrive!'

The retroflexion of suffixal *n* in several of these forms is an effect of automatic phonology; see Whitney (1889: §189).

Table 5.5 exhibit this regularity; as the table's plural forms show, *-nī* is not in general restricted to postvocalic contexts.

These facts concerning the distribution of *-hí* are summarized in Table 5.6.

If one attempts to model the distribution of *-hí* as a set of conditions on the ⟦**-hí**⟧ rule itself, these conditions involve a deviation from the integral stem criterion. Suppose that the ⟦**-dhí**⟧ rule is formulated as in (1). This makes it possible to formulate the ⟦**-hí**⟧ rule as in (2).

(1)   ⟦**-dhí**⟧ : [V, {2sg imp act CONJ.n} : XC → XC-*dhí*], where n = 2, 3, or 7

(2)   ⟦**-hí**⟧ : [V, {2sg imp act CONJ.n} : X → X-*hí*], where n $\neq$ 1, 4, 6, 8, or 10 and
   (i)   X is based on a consonant-final root if n = 5;
   (ii)   X is based on a vowel-final root if n = 9.

In the {2sg imp act} inflection of stems belonging to thematic conjugations, neither (1) nor (2) is applicable. In the {2sg imp act} inflection of stems belonging to athematic conjugations, rules (1) and (2) interact in the following ways.

- For a stem Z in the second or third conjugation, (1) overrides (2) if Z is consonant-final; otherwise, (2) applies by default.
- For a stem Z in the seventh conjugation, (1) overrides (2), since Z is consonant-final.
- For a stem in the eighth conjugation, neither (1) nor (2) is applicable.

Table 5.6 *The distribution of the second-person singular imperative active termination -hí in the ten present-system conjugations in Sanskrit*

Thematic conjugations (First, Fourth, Sixth, Tenth): no personal termination		
Athematic conjugations	-hí appears	-hí is absent
Second	if stem is vowel-final, e.g. *i-hí* 'go!'	-*dhí* appears after a consonant-final stem, e.g. *dug-dhí* 'milk!'
Third	if stem is vowel-final, e.g. *bibhr-hí* 'carry!'	-*dhí* appears after a consonant-final stem, e.g. *babhas-dhí* (→ *babho-dhí* by sandhi) 'devour!'
Fifth	if root (≠ stem) is consonant-final, e.g. *āp-nu-hí* 'obtain!'	no personal termination if root (≠ stem) is vowel-final, e.g. *su-nú* 'press out!'
Seventh	—	-*dhí* always appears because stem is always consonant-final, e.g. *yuṅg-dhí* 'join!'
Eighth	—	no personal termination, e.g. *tanú* 'stretch!'
Ninth	after stem X-*nī* if root X is vowel-final, e.g. *krī-ṇī-hí* 'buy!'	-*āná* appears after root (to the exclusion of -*nī*) if root is consonant-final, e.g. *aś-āná* 'eat!' (NB: stem *aś-nī*-)

- For a stem Z in the fifth conjugation, (2) applies only if Z is based on a consonant-final root [...C] (i.e. only if Z = [...C]-*nu*-); otherwise, no rule applies.
- For a stem Z in the ninth conjugation, (2) applies only if Z is based on a vowel-final root [...V] (i.e. only if Z = [...V]-*nī*-); otherwise, the ⟦-**āná**⟧ rule in (3) operates directly to Z's consonant-final root (without -*nī*).

(3)   ⟦-**āná**⟧ : [V, {2sg imp act CONJ.9} : -*āná*]

Conditions (i) and (ii) on rule (2) are deviations from the integral stem criterion: both conditions make the operation of (2) on a verb stem sensitive to the final segment of the root from which the stem arises. This analysis runs afoul of the integral stem criterion because it represents the morphotactic peculiarities of -*hí* as the effect of noncanonical conditions on the ⟦-**hí**⟧ rule. But these deviations from the integral stem criterion can be avoided.

5.1 *An Apparent Case of Nonlocal Conditioning*   147

In particular, these morphotactic peculiarities of -*hí* can instead be seen as the effect of canonical conditions on the application of the composite rule (⟦-**hí**⟧ ∘ ⟦-**nu**⟧) and on the override of the composite rule (⟦-**hí**⟧ ∘ ⟦-**nī**⟧) by the ⟦-**āná**⟧ rule.

The following analysis of the morphotactics of ⟦-**hí**⟧ treats the weak stem in each athematic conjugation as its default stem and entails that {2sg imp act} forms are defined in essentially three ways, as specified by clauses (4a–c) in the definition of the Sanskrit paradigm function. First, there are many verbs for which the {2sg imp act} form is identical to the default present-system stem; these are verbs whose present-system stem belongs either to a thematic conjugation (the first, fourth, sixth, or tenth) or to the eighth athematic conjugation. The {2sg imp act} inflection of such verbs is covered by clause (4a). Second, there are many verbs for which the {2sg imp act} form is the result of applying one or the other of the two full exponence rules (FERs) in (5) to the default present-system stem; these are verbs whose default present-system stem belongs to the second, third, or seventh athematic conjugation and whose inflection is covered by clause (4b). Finally, clause (4c) entails that members of the fifth and ninth athematic conjugations have a {2sg imp act} form that is the result of applying one of the four FERs in (6), not to the present-system stem, but to the verb root.

(4) Clauses in the definition of the Sanskrit paradigm function
Where L is a verbal lexeme with root R and L's default present-system stem Z belongs to present-system conjugation n ($1 \leq n \leq 10$),
a. PF(⟨L, {2sg imp act}⟩) = ⟨Z, {2sg imp act CONJ.n}⟩, provided that n is 1, 4, 6, 8, or 10.
b. PF(⟨L, {2sg imp act}⟩) = the result of applying a FER from (5) to the form cell ⟨Z, {2sg imp act CONJ.n}⟩, provided that n is 2, 3, or 7.
c. PF(⟨L, {2sg imp act}⟩) = the result of applying a FER from (6) to the form cell ⟨R, {2sg imp act CONJ.n}⟩, provided that n is 5 or 9.

(5) FERs for {2sg imp act} forms in (4b)
a. ⟦-**dhí**⟧ : [V, {2sg imp act} : XC → XC-*dhí*]
b. ⟦-**hí**⟧ : [V, {2sg imp act} : -*hí*]

(6) FERs for {2sg imp act} forms in (4c)
a. That subfunction of (⟦-**hí**⟧ ∘ ⟦-**nu**⟧) that is equivalent to:
[V, {2sg imp act CONJ.5} : XC → XC-*nuhí*]
b. ⟦-**nu**⟧ : [V, {CONJ.5} : -*nu*]
c. ⟦-**āná**⟧ : [V, {2sg imp act CONJ.9} : XC→ XC-*āná*]
d. (⟦-**hí**⟧ ∘ ⟦-**nī**⟧) : [V, {2sg imp act CONJ.9} : -*nīhi*] (cf. (7))

(7) ⟦-**nī**⟧ : [V, {CONJ.9} : -*nī*]

Table 5.7 *The morphotactics of four second-person singular imperative active forms in Sanskrit*

(a)	Content cell:	⟨ĀP, {2sg imp act}⟩	'obtain!'
	Form cell:	⟨āp-, {2sg imp act CONJ.5}⟩	
	|		
	FER	subfunction (6a) of (⟦**-hí**⟧ ∘ ⟦**-nu**⟧)	
	↓		
	Realized cell:	⟨āpnuhí, {2sg imp act CONJ.5}⟩	
(b)	Content cell:	⟨SU, {2sg imp act}⟩	'press out!'
	Form cell:	⟨su-, {2sg imp act CONJ.5}⟩	
	|		
	FER	⟦**-nu**⟧	(= (6b))
	↓		
	Realized cell:	⟨sunú, {2sg imp act CONJ.5}⟩	
(c)	Content cell:	⟨AŚ, {2sg imp act}⟩	'eat!'
	Form cell:	⟨aś-, {2sg imp act CONJ.9}⟩	
	|		
	FER	⟦**-āná**⟧	(= (6c))
	↓		
	Realized cell:	⟨aśāná, {2sg imp act CONJ.9}⟩	
(d)	Content cell:	⟨KRĪ, {2sg imp act}⟩	'buy!'
	Form cell:	⟨krī-, {2sg imp act CONJ.9}⟩	
	|		
	FER	(⟦**-hí**⟧ ∘ ⟦**-nī**⟧)	(= (6d))
	↓		
	Realized cell:	⟨krīṇīhí, {2sg imp act CONJ.9}⟩	

Rule (6a) realizes {2sg imp act} by suffixing *-nuhí* to a consonant-final fifth-conjugation root. Rule (6a) is a subfunction of the composite (⟦**-hí**⟧ ∘ ⟦**-nu**⟧); that is, the domain of (6a) is a proper subset of the domain of (⟦**-hí**⟧ ∘ ⟦**-nu**⟧). Specifically, a member ⟨R, σ⟩ of the domain of (⟦**-hí**⟧ ∘ ⟦**-nu**⟧) is a member of the domain of (6a) if and only if R ends in a consonant. Thus, the domain of (6a) is narrower than that of ⟦**-nu**⟧ in (6b). In the {2sg imp act} inflection of a fifth-conjugation verb L, rule (6a) competes with and overrides the simple ⟦**-nu**⟧ rule if L's root ends in a consonant (in accordance with Pāṇini's principle); otherwise, (6a) is inapplicable and ⟦**-nu**⟧ applies by default. In applying to the form cell ⟨āp-, {2sg imp act CONJ.5}⟩, (6a) overrides the ⟦**-nu**⟧ rule to yield the realized cell ⟨āpnuhí, {CONJ.5 2sg imp act}⟩, as in part (a) of Table 5.7. By default, however, ⟦**-nu**⟧ applies to the form cell ⟨su-, {2sg imp act CONJ.5}⟩ to yield the realized cell ⟨sunú, {2sg imp act

5.1 An Apparent Case of Nonlocal Conditioning   149

CONJ.5}), as in part (b) of Table 5.7. (Note that although the ⟦-**nu**⟧ rule in (6b) is a FER in the definition of *sunú* 'press out!', it is not a FER in all of its uses; elsewhere, it serves in the formation of a fifth-conjugation verb's weak present-system stem as well as in the definition of the composite rule in (6a).)

Rule (6c) realizes {2sg imp act} by suffixing *-āná* to a consonant-final ninth-conjugation root; and rule (6d), the composite of ⟦-**hí**⟧ with the ⟦-**nī**⟧ rule in (7), realizes {2sg imp act} by suffixing *-nīhi* to a ninth-conjugation root by default. Thus, the realization of the form cell ⟨*aś-*, {2sg imp act CONJ.9}⟩ is as in part (c) of Table 5.7, while that of ⟨*krī-*, {2sg imp act CONJ.9}⟩ is as in part (d).

In this analysis, the conditions on ⟦-**hí**⟧ in (2) are eliminated, and with them, any deviation from the integral stem criterion; these noncanonical conditions on the application of ⟦-**hí**⟧ are in effect replaced with canonical conditions restricting the application of the composite (6a) and of the simple rule ⟦-**āná**⟧ to consonant-final roots. In the application of composite (6a) to ⟨*āp-*, {2sg imp act CONJ.5}⟩, the root *āp-* is treated as an integral stem, as are

- *su-* in the application of ⟦-**nu**⟧ to ⟨*su-*, {2sg imp act CONJ.5}⟩,
- *aś-* in the application of ⟦-**āná**⟧ to ⟨*aś-*, {2sg imp act CONJ.9}⟩, and
- *krī-* in the application of composite (6d) to ⟨*krī-*, {2sg imp act CONJ.9}⟩.

This analysis reveals an unexpected symmetry in the morphology of {2sg imp act} forms. Where L is a verbal lexeme whose root is R and whose present-system stem Z belongs to conjugation *n*, the {2 sg imp act} form of L realizes the form cell ⟨R, {2sg imp act CONJ.*n*}⟩ if *n* = 5 or 9, but otherwise realizes the form cell ⟨Z, {2sg imp act CONJ.*n*}⟩. Where *n* = 1, 4, 6, 8, or 10, the realized cell is, by default, the same as this form cell. Where *n* = 2, 3, 5, 7, or 9, this form cell is realized through the application of one of two rules: an overriding rule that only operates on consonant-final forms, and a default rule that applies otherwise. Where *n* = 2, 3, or 7, the overriding rule is ⟦-**dhí**⟧ and the default rule is ⟦-**hí**⟧; where *n* = 5, the overriding rule is (⟦-**hí**⟧ ∘ ⟦-**nu**⟧) and the default rule is ⟦-**nu**⟧; and where *n* = 9, the overriding rule is ⟦-**āná**⟧ and the default rule is (⟦-**hí**⟧ ∘ ⟦-**nī**⟧). These patterns are summarized in Table 5.8.

I return to this analysis in Section 5.2.2.2, where I show that besides reconciling apparently recalcitrant morphotactics with the integral stem criterion, the rule-combining approach also reconciles apparent deviations from the rule opposition criterion.

150 *Extending Canonical Morphotactic Criteria*

Table 5.8 *Sanskrit second-person singular imperative active forms distinguished according to the type of form cell they realize, the FER by which they are realized, and the phonological condition on that FER*

For a given verbal lexeme L:		Z is L's present-system stem, Z belongs to conjugation n, R is L's root, and $\sigma = \{2 \text{ sg imp act CONJ.}n\}$.	
Z's conjugation n	Form cell	FER	Phonological condition on the application of the FER
1, 4, 6, 8, 10	⟨Z, σ⟩	none	—
2, 3, 7	⟨Z, σ⟩	〚-dhí〛	Z is consonant-final
		〚-hí〛	none
5	⟨R, σ⟩	(〚-hí〛 ∘ 〚-nu〛)	R is consonant-final
		〚-nu〛	none
9	⟨R, σ⟩	〚-āná〛	R is consonant-final
		(〚-hí〛 ∘ 〚-nī〛)	none

5.2 Relations of Paradigmatic Opposition and Competition among Morphological Rules

Canonically, relations of paradigmatic opposition among rules of morphology are relations among individual rules; this is the rule opposition criterion. Thus, the paradigmatic opposition between the 〚-ing〛 rule that defines the form *eat-ing* and the 〚-en〛 rule that defines the form *eat-en* is morphotactically canonical. A deviation from this canonical pattern would be a case in which the application of rule R_A is paradigmatically opposed to the sequential application of two or more rules $R_1, \ldots, R_n$. But such a deviation becomes merely apparent if the rule opposition criterion pertains not merely to simple rules, but also to composite rules; in that case, the paradigmatic opposition of rule R_A's application to that of a composite rule R_B that combines the effects of rules $R_1, \ldots, R_n$ is canonical with respect to the rule opposition criterion.

Rules that stand in paradigmatic opposition to one another may or may not be in competition with one another. The English rules 〚-en〛 and 〚-ing〛 that define the participial forms *eaten* and *eating* are in paradigmatic opposition, but not in competition, since they realize contrasting content (as in (8)). But the English rules 〚-ed〛 and 〚-t〛 that define the past-tense forms *leaned* and *meant* are paradigmatically opposed and are sometimes in competition, in accordance with their formulation in (9). Because the domain of 〚-t〛 is restricted as in (10a) but the

5.2 Paradigmatic Opposition and Competition 151

domain of the default ⟦-ed⟧ rule is not similarly restricted (being instead as in (10b)), the application of ⟦-t⟧ prevails over that of ⟦-ed⟧ in instances in which both are applicable; this is the outcome predicted by Pāṇini's principle.

(8)   a.   ⟦-en⟧ : [V, {strong pst ptcp} : -en]
         b.   ⟦-ing⟧ : [V, {prs ptcp} : -ing]

(9)   a.   ⟦-t⟧ : [V, {t-class pst} : -t]
         b.   ⟦-ed⟧ : [V, {pst} : -ed]

(10)   a.   Domain of ⟦-t⟧ : the set of ⟨form, content⟩ pairings of the type ⟨Z, τ⟩, where Z is the stem of a *t*-class verb (e.g. *mean, feel, leave*) and {*t*-class pst} ⊆ τ.
         b.   Domain of ⟦-ed⟧ : the set of ⟨form, content⟩ pairings of the type ⟨Z, τ⟩, where Z is a verb stem and {pst} ⊆ τ.

Instances in which a simple rule R_A is paradigmatically opposed to a composite rule R_B that combines the effects of rules $R_1, \ldots, R_n$ are of three types:

(i)   In instances in which rule R_A is paradigmatically opposed to but does not compete with rule R_B, rules R_A and R_B apply in complementary contexts.
(ii)   In instances in which rule R_A is paradigmatically opposed to and competes with rule R_B, the resolution of this competition is not always in the same direction:
    (a) in some cases it is the simple rule R_A that prevails;
    (b) in others, it is the composite rule R_B that prevails.

In cases (ii.a) and (ii.b), Pāṇini's principle is what determines whether it is the simple rule R_A or the composite rule R_B that prevails. In this section, I discuss examples of each of these three sorts – an example from Latin of type (i), an example from Limbu of type (ii.a), and an example from Sanskrit of type (ii.b). The notion of rule composition makes it possible to regard all of these apparent deviations from the rule opposition criterion as merely apparent, since they involve the paradigmatic opposition of a simple rule to a composed rule.

5.2.1   Paradigmatic Opposition of a Simple Rule to Composite Rules without Competition: Latin ⟦-minī⟧

In Latin, the default formation of a synthetic passive verb form is one exhibiting the morphology of the corresponding active form plus a suffixal formative *-(u)r* (together with any morphophonological modifications that this induces, e.g. *audiēbam* → *audiēba-r* 'I was heard'); this pattern is exemplified in Table 5.9. The passive suffix *-(u)r* is ordinarily word-final (e.g. *audiunt-ur* 'they are

Table 5.9 Synthetic passive forms of Latin AUDĪRE 'hear' and their active counterparts in the indicative and subjunctive moods

		Present		Imperfect		Future	
		Active	Passive	Active	Passive	Active	Passive
Indicative		audi-ō	audi-o-r	audiēba-m	audiēba-r	audia-m	audia-r
		audī-s	audī-r-is	audiēbā-s	audiēbā-r-is	audiē-s	audiē-r-is
		audi-t	audī-t-ur	audiēba-t	audiēbā-t-ur	audie-t	audiē-t-ur
		audī-mus	audī-mu-r	audiēbā-mus	audiēbā-mu-r	audiē-mus	audiē-mu-r
		audī-tis	audī-minī	audiēbā-tis	audiēbā-minī	audiē-tis	audiē-minī
		audi-unt	audi-unt-ur	audiēba-nt	audiēba-nt-ur	audie-nt	audie-nt-ur
Subjunctive		audia-m	audia-r	audīre-m	audīre-r		
		audiā-s	audiā-r-is	audīrē-s	audīrē-r-is		
		audia-t	audiā-t-ur	audīre-t	audīre-t-ur		
		audiā-mus	audiā-mu-r	audīrē-mus	audīrē-mu-r		
		audiā-tis	audiā-minī	audīrē-tis	audīrē-minī		
		audia-nt	audia-nt-ur	audīre-nt	audīre-nt-ur		

5.2 Paradigmatic Opposition and Competition

heard'), though in second-person singular forms, it is positioned before rather than after the subject-agreement suffix (e.g. *audī-r-is* 'you (sg) are heard'; cf. Section 4.1). This pattern – corresponding active morphology plus *-(u)r*, in some order – holds for all person/number combinations but one: whereas *-tis* is the usual subject-agreement marker for the second person plural active, the expression of the corresponding passive involves neither *-tis* nor *-(u)r*, but instead involves a special portmanteau suffix *-minī* realizing both second-person plural subject agreement and passive voice (e.g. *audī-minī* 'you (pl.) are heard').

Under the analysis proposed here, the passive ⟦**-(u)r**⟧ rule in (11) is a dependent rule whose carrier rules include the subject-agreement rules in (12a). Thus, in accordance with the pattern in (13), the ⟦**-(u)r**⟧ rule composes with the rules in (12a) to produce the composed passive agreement rules in (14) (with relevant sandhi here taken into account). Exceptionally, note that ⟦**-(u)r**⟧ does not compose with the second-person plural subject-agreement rule ⟦**-tis**⟧ in (12b).[3] Instead, the simple ⟦**-minī**⟧ rule (12c) is paradigmatically opposed to the composed rules in (14); for this reason, the morphology of passive forms such as *audī-minī* 'you (pl.) are heard' and *audi-unt-ur* 'they are heard' is defined in parallel fashion, as in Figure 5.1.

(11) ⟦**-(u)r**⟧ : [V, {passive} : *-(u)r*]

(12) Some subject-agreement rules in Latin
    a. ⟦**-ō**⟧ : [V, {{sbj 1 sg}} : *-ō*]
        ⟦**-t**⟧ : [V, {{sbj 3 sg}} : *-t*]
        ⟦**-mus**⟧ : [V, {{sbj 1 pl}} : *-mus*]
        ⟦**-unt**⟧ : [V, {{sbj 3 pl}} : *-unt*]
    b. ⟦**-tis**⟧ : [V, {{sbj 2 pl}} : *-tis*]
    c. ⟦**-minī**⟧ : [V, {{sbj 2 pl} passive} : *-minī*]

(13) FER pattern for Latin passives
    Where R is a rule in (12a), (⟦**-(u)r**⟧ ∘ R) is a FER.

(14) Default composites defined by (13)
    a. (⟦**-(u)r**⟧ ∘ ⟦**-ō**⟧) :   [V, {{sbj 1 sg} passive} : *-or*]
    b. (⟦**-(u)r**⟧ ∘ ⟦**-t**⟧) :   [V, {{sbj 3 sg} passive} : *-tur*]
    c. (⟦**-(u)r**⟧ ∘ ⟦**-mus**⟧) : [V, {{sbj 1 pl} passive} : *-mur*]
    d. (⟦**-(u)r**⟧ ∘ ⟦**-unt**⟧) : [V, {{sbj 3 pl} passive} : *-untur*]

---

[3] I assume that the second-person singular subject-agreement rule ⟦**-s**⟧ in (i) composes with ⟦**-(u)r**⟧ in the order opposite to (13), as in (ii).

(i) ⟦**-s**⟧ : [V, {{sbj 2 sg}} : *-s*]

(ii) (⟦**-s**⟧ ∘ ⟦**-(u)r**⟧) : [V, {{sbj 2 sg} passive} : *-(u)ris*] (assuming the appropriate sandhi).

	Form cell:	⟨audī, {2 pl prs ind pass}⟩	⟨audī, {3 pl prs ind pass}⟩
Rules of inflectional affixation	simple:	⟦-minī⟧	—
	composed:	—	(⟦-(u)r⟧ ∘ ⟦-unt⟧)
	Realized cell:	⟨audīminī, {2 pl prs ind pass}⟩	⟨audiuntur, {3 pl prs ind pass}⟩

Figure 5.1 *The realization of Latin* audīminī *'you are heard' and* audiuntur *'they are heard'*

In this analysis, the portmanteau ⟦-minī⟧ rule is a simple rule in paradigmatic opposition to each of the composite rules in (14), in conformity with the rule opposition criterion. The ⟦-minī⟧ rule does not compete with any of the rules in (14); given that ⟦-(u)r⟧ is a dependent rule, ⟦-minī⟧ doesn't enter into direct competition with it, either. By contrast, ⟦-minī⟧ does enter into direct competition with ⟦-tis⟧, which is not a dependent rule. By Pāṇini's principle, ⟦-minī⟧ overrides ⟦-tis⟧ whenever the two compete.

5.2.2 Paradigmatic Opposition of a Simple Rule to a Competing Composite Rule

In instances in which a simple rule is paradigmatically opposed to a composite rule with which it competes, there are two logically possible outcomes: either the simple rule prevails or the composite rule prevails. In accordance with Pāṇini's principle, the outcome in any event depends on which rule has the narrower domain. In the Limbu case considered in Section 5.2.2.1, it is the simple rule that overrides the competing composite rule; in the Sanskrit case in Section 5.2.2.2, it is the composite rule that overrides the competing simple rule.

5.2.2.1 A Simple Rule Overrides a Composite Rule: Limbu ⟦-mʔna⟧

In the Limbu verb morphology examined in Section 3.2, it was seen that Limbu transitive verbs inflect for the person and number of both their agent and patient arguments. The inflection of the form huʔrumbe 'we (excl.) teach her/him' is defined by the composite (15a) of rules (15b–d) (in whose realization the suffixal /g/ is assimilated to the place of articulation of the preceding suffixal /m/); thus, (15a) is the FER that applies to the form cell (16a) to yield the realized cell (16b). The form cell (17a) is also in the domain of rule (15a); but because (17a) (unlike (16a)) is likewise in the domain of the narrower rule (18), it is (18) that serves as the FER for (17a), realizing it as (17b) (to yield huʔmʔna 'we (excl.) taught her/him'). Pāṇini's principle predicts this override: the domain of the composite rule (15a) is the set of stem pairings of the type ⟨Z, ρ⟩, where ρ is a well-formed extension of {{agt 1 excl pl}{pat 3}}; by contrast, the domain of the simple rule (18) is the set of stem pairings of the type ⟨Z, σ⟩, where σ is a well-formed extension of {pret {agt 1 pl excl}{pat 3}}. Because the domain of (18) is a proper subset of that of (15a), (18) prevails in instances in which it competes with (15a).[4]

(15)   a.   (⟦-ge⟧ ∘ (⟦-m⟧ ∘ ⟦-u⟧)) : [V, {{agt 1 pl excl}{pat 3}} : -*umbe*]
       b.   ⟦-u⟧ : [V, {{pat 3}} : -*u*]
       c.   ⟦-m⟧ : [V, {{agt 1/2 pl}} : -*m*]
       d.   ⟦-ge⟧ : [V, {{1 excl}} : -*ge*]

(16)   a.   ⟨*huʔr-*, {–pret pos {agt 1 pl excl} {pat 3 sg}}⟩
       b.   ⟨*huʔrumbe*, {–pret pos {agt 1 pl excl} {pat 3 sg}}⟩

(17)   a.   ⟨*huʔ-*, {pret pos {agt 1 pl excl} {pat 3 sg}}⟩
       b.   ⟨*huʔmʔna*, {pret pos {agt 1 pl excl} {pat 3 sg}}⟩

(18)   ⟦-mʔna⟧ : [V, {pret {agt 1 pl excl}{pat 3}} : -*mʔna*]

5.2.2.2 A Composite Rule Overrides a Simple Rule: Sanskrit (⟦-hí⟧ ∘ ⟦-nu⟧)

In Section 5.1, the inflection of Sanskrit second-person singular imperative active forms was seen to present an apparent deviation from the integral stem criterion; the postulation of composite rules was seen to render this deviation merely apparent by allowing what appeared to be noncanonical conditions on the application of the simple rule ⟦-hí⟧ to be modeled as canonical conditions on the application of the composite rule (⟦-hí⟧ ∘ ⟦-nu⟧) and of the simple rule ⟦-āná⟧, an override of the composite rule (⟦-hí⟧ ∘ ⟦-nī⟧). So analyzed, this same body of Sanskrit evidence also presents a case in which a composite rule competes with and overrides a simple rule.

Recall from Section 5.1 that a Sanskrit verb's second-person singular imperative active (= {2sg imp act}) form depends on the form and conjugation-class membership of its stem or of its root. The {2sg imp act} form lacks any personal termination in the thematic conjugations and in the eighth athematic conjugation. In the second, third, and seventh

---

[4] The fact that the composite (⟦-ge⟧ ∘ (⟦-m⟧ ∘ ⟦-u⟧)) doesn't apply in the realization of preterite forms cannot be attributed to any of the three component rules ⟦-ge⟧, ⟦-m⟧, and ⟦-u⟧, each of which sometimes applies in the definition of a preterite form; for example, ⟦-ge⟧ applies in the realization of *huʔnɛtchige* 'we (excl.) taught you'; ⟦-m⟧ applies in the realization of *ahuʔrum* 'we (incl.) taught her/him'; and ⟦-u⟧ applies in the realization of *ahuʔrum* 'we (incl.) taught her/him'.

conjugations, it exhibits either *-dhí* (after a stem-final consonant) or *-hí* (after a stem-final vowel). A fifth-conjugation verb's {2sg imp act} form is the result of suffixing *-hí* to its present-system stem in *-nu* if its root ends in a consonant, and is otherwise the verb's bare stem, lacking any personal termination. A ninth-conjugation verb's {2sg imp act} form is the result of suffixing *-āná* to its root if this ends in a consonant, and is otherwise the result of suffixing *-hí* to its present-system stem in *-nī*. These facts are summarized in Table 5.10.

According to the analysis presented in Section 5.1, the composite rule (19a) and the simple rule (19b) enter into competition in the definition of a fifth-conjugation verb's {2sg imp act} form in those cases in which the verb's root ends in a consonant; in such cases, it is the composite rule that overrides the simple rule. Pāṇini's principle predicts this override: the domain of the simple rule (19b) is the set of stem pairings of the type ⟨R, ρ⟩, where R is a root belonging to the fifth conjugation and ρ is a well-formed extension of {CONJ.5}; by contrast, the domain of the composite rule (19a) is the set of stem pairings of the type ⟨[...C], σ⟩, where [...C] is a consonant-final root belonging to the fifth conjugation and σ is a well-formed extension of {2sg imp act CONJ.5}. Because the domain of (19a) is a proper subset of that of (19b), (19a) competes with and prevails over (19b) whenever it is applicable.

(19)　　FERs for {2sg imp act} forms in the fifth conjugation
　　　　a.　　That subfunction of (⟦-**hí**⟧ ∘ ⟦-**nu**⟧) that is equivalent to:
　　　　　　　　　　　　　　　　[V, {2sg imp act CONJ.5} : XC → XC-*nuhí*]
　　　　b.　　⟦-**nu**⟧ :　　[V, {CONJ.5} : -*nu*]

The analyses presented in this chapter are morphotactically noncanonical to the extent that they deviate from the minimal rule criterion; they all depend on the postulation of rules that are composites of "smaller" rules. At the same time, the phenomena analyzed here can be seen as morphotactically canonical with respect to the integral stem criterion and the rule opposition criterion provided that these criteria are assumed to encompass composite rules as well as simple rules. In Chapters 7 and 8, I discuss morphotactic phenomena that appear to deviate from the affix directionality criterion (Section 1.5.10) but that in fact conform to this criterion if one assumes that rule aggregation (Section 2.4) is a mode of rule combination. At the same time, rule aggregation inherently deviates from the stem operand criterion (Section 1.5.6) as well as from the minimal rule criterion.

Table 5.10 *Second-person singular imperative active forms in Sanskrit*

Present-system conjugation		Member lexeme and present-system stem		Inflectional realization			
				-*dhí* with C-final stem	-*hí* with V-final stem	Bare stem	Portmanteau -*ānā*
Thematic	First	BHŪ 'be' :	*bháv-a-*			*bháv-a*	
	Fourth	NAH 'bind' :	*náh-ya-*			*náh-ya*	
	Sixth	VIŚ 'enter' :	*viś-á-*			*viś-á*	
	Tenth	CINT 'think' :	*cint-áya-*			*cint-áya*	
Athematic	Second	DUH 'milk' :	*duh-*	*dug-dhí**			
		I 'go' :	*i-*		*i-hí*		
	Third	BHAS 'devour' :	*babhas-*	*babho-dhí***			
		BHR 'carry' :	*bíbhr-*		*bibhr̥-hí*		
	Fifth	ĀP 'obtain' :	*āp-nu-*		*āp-nu-hí* (where root is C-final)		
		SU 'press out' :	*su-nu-*			*su-nú* (where root is V-final)	
	Seventh	YUJ 'join' :	*yu-ñ-j-*	*yu-ṅ-g-dhí*†			
	Eighth	TAN 'stretch' :	*tan-u-*			*tan-ú*	
	Ninth	KRĪ 'buy' :	*krī-ṇī-*‡		*krī-ṇī-hí* (where root is V-final)		
		AŚ 'eat' :	*aś-nī-*				*aś-ānā* (where root is C-final)

* By sandhi, *h-dh* → *g-dh*. ** By sandhi, *as-dh* → *o-dh*. † By sandhi, *ñj* → *ṅg* before *dh*. ‡ By sandhi, *krī-nī-* → *krīṇī-*.

5.3 Conclusion

This chapter has examined two different kinds of evidence for the postulation of composite inflectional rules. First, composite rules make it possible to reconcile the integral stem criterion with apparent deviations from this criterion in the inflection of Sanskrit imperatives. Second, composite rules also serve to reconcile the rule opposition criterion with cases in which the application of a single rule seems to be paradigmatically opposed to that of a sequence of rules. Cases of this latter sort involve instances of paradigmatic opposition among rules that are not in competition (e.g. the opposition of the simple second-person plural passive rule ⟦-**minī**⟧ and the composite third-person plural passive rule (⟦-**(u)r**⟧ ∘ ⟦-**unt**⟧) in the inflection of Latin verbs) as well as among competing rules (e.g. the opposition of the simple rule ⟦-**āná**⟧ and the composite rule (⟦-**hí**⟧ ∘ ⟦-**nī**⟧) in the second-person singular imperative active inflection of Sanskrit verbs belonging to the ninth conjugation). In cases of the latter sort, Pāṇini's principle determines whether the competition is resolved in favor of the simple rule or the composite rule.

In the next chapter, I discuss deviations from the compositional content criterion (Section 1.5.5); in order to account for these, a mode of rule combination distinct from ordinary composition will be seen to be necessary – that of holistic combination.

6 *Rule Combinations Expressing Holistic Content*

Canonically, a language's morphotactics conforms to the compositional content criterion (Section 1.5.5), according to which the content expressed by a rule sequence is compositional, that is, a function of the content expressed by the individual rules in that sequence. Thus, consider again the Swahili rules of exponence in (1), first seen in Section 2.2. When these rules compose to produce the full exponence rules (FERs) in (2), the resulting composite rules serve unambiguously to realize the summed content of their component rules.

(1) Some simple rules of Swahili verb inflection
    a.   Subject agreement rules
           ⟦**u-**⟧ : [V, {{sbj 2sg}} : *u-*]
           ⟦**a-**⟧ : [V, {{sbj 3sg}} : *a-*]
    b.   Tense rules
           ⟦**ta-**⟧ : [V, {fut} : *ta-*]
           ⟦**me-**⟧ : [V, {cmpl} : *me-*]
    c.   Pronominal object rules
           ⟦**ku-**⟧ : [V, {{obj 2sg}} : *ku-*]
           ⟦**m-**⟧ : [V, {{obj 3sg}} : *m-*]

(2) Three FERs of Swahili verb morphology
        (((⟦**u-**⟧ ∘ ⟦**ta-**⟧) ∘⟦**m-**⟧) : [V, {{sbj 2sg} {obj 3sg} fut} : *utam-*]
        (((⟦**a-**⟧ ∘ ⟦**me-**⟧) ∘⟦**ku-**⟧) : [V, {{sbj 3sg} {obj 2sg} cmpl} : *ameku-*]
        (((⟦**a-**⟧ ∘ ⟦**ta-**⟧) ∘⟦**m-**⟧) : [V, {{sbj 3sg} {obj 3sg} fut} : *atam-*]

Very often, however, languages present cases in which a FER expresses content some of which cannot be attributed to any of the individual rules that it comprises; indeed, even a simple rule sometimes expresses more content as a FER than when it is used in combination with other rules. In such cases, a language's morphotactics fails to conform to the compositional content criterion because it allows certain FERs to realize ***holistic content***. In this chapter, I show how a sufficiently rich theory of rule combination makes it possible to accommodate this deviation from canonical morphotactics. I examine the inflection of regular verbs in Breton, which exhibit several examples of holistic

160 *Rule Combinations Expressing Holistic Content*

content (Section 6.1). I show how the postulation of holistic combinations – special rule combinations expressing supplementary content – affords a straightforward account of this phenomenon in Breton (Section 6.2).[1]

Some holistic combinations have an emergent character. These are cases in which all of the forms realized by a composite rule ($R_2 \circ R_1$) happen to possess a property P that neither R_1 nor R_2 realizes on its own; in such cases the composite rule ($R_2 \circ R_1$) is open to reanalysis as a holistic combination realizing P. In Section 6.3, I examine a case of this sort from Limbu.

A particularly compelling case for the postulation of holistic combinations arises in systems in which the same two rules express different supplementary content in different contexts. In Section 6.4, I show that Old English verb inflection is a system of this sort.

6.1 Holistic Content in Breton Verb Inflection

The inflection of regular verbs in Breton provides several clear instances of holistic content. Consider, for example, the finite paradigm of the Breton verb KAROUT 'love' in Table 6.1.

The forms in Table 6.1 all arise from the bare stem *kar-* through the application of up to three rules of inflectional exponence. The suffix sequences exhibited by the forms in Table 6.1 are abstracted in Table 6.2. Scrutiny of these sequences reveals the four types of suffixes classified in (3). The irrealis sequences and most of the past indicative sequences show one of the prevocalic suffixes in (3a). Most of the sequences in Table 6.2 exhibit one of the three vocalic suffixes in (3b). In most of the forms containing one of the three vocalic suffixes, this is followed by one of the terminations in (3c). Finally, the portmanteau suffixes in (3d) take the place of an expected suffix sequence in certain forms.

(3) Breton conjugational suffixes
    a. Prevocalic suffixes: *-j, -f*
    b. Vocalic suffixes: *-e, -i, -o*
    c. Terminations: *-n, -s, -mp, -t, -c'h, -nt, -r, -d*
    d. Portmanteau suffixes: *-out, -an, -ez, -is, -as*

Some of the suffixes in (3) stand in a biunique relation to the content that they express; a suffix of this sort always expresses the same content and is the only suffix expressing exactly that content. Suffixes of this sort include the

---

[1] The analysis of Breton in this chapter is a refinement of the earlier analysis presented in Stump (2021).

Table 6.1 *Finite forms of Breton* KAROUT *'love'*

	Indicative				Irrealis		Imperative
	Present	Imperfect	Future	Past	Present	Past	
1SG	kar-an	kar-e-n	kar-i-n	kar-is	kar-f-e-n	kar-j-e-n	
2SG	kar-ez	kar-e-s	kar-i	kar-j-out	kar-f-e-s	kar-j-e-s	kar
3SG	kar	kar-e	kar-o	kar-as	kar-f-e	kar-j-e	kar-e-t
1PL	kar-o-mp	kar-e-mp	kar-i-mp	kar-j-o-mp	kar-f-e-mp	kar-j-e-mp	kar-o-mp
2PL	kar-i-t	kar-e-c'h	kar-o-t	kar-j-o-c'h	kar-f-e-c'h	kar-j-e-c'h	kar-i-t
3PL	kar-o-nt	kar-e-nt	kar-i-nt	kar-j-o-nt	kar-f-e-nt	kar-j-e-nt	kar-e-nt
IMPS	kar-e-r	kar-e-d	kar-o-r	kar-j-o-d	kar-f-e-d	kar-j-e-d	

(Kervella 1976: 124)

162 *Rule Combinations Expressing Holistic Content*

Table 6.2 *Suffixes sequences in the inflection of Breton* KAROUT *'love'*

	Indicative				Irrealis		Imperative
	Present	Imperfect	Future	Past	Present	Past	
1SG	-an	-e-n	-i-n	-is	-f-e-n	-j-e-n	
2SG	-ez	-e-s	-i	-j-out	-f-e-s	-j-e-s	—
3SG	—	-e	-o	-as	-f-e	-j-e	-e-t
1PL	-o-mp	-e-mp	-i-mp	-j-o-mp	-f-e-mp	-j-e-mp	-o-mp
2PL	-i-t	-e-c'h	-o-t	-j-o-c'h	-f-e-c'h	-j-e-c'h	-i-t
3PL	-o-nt	-e-nt	-i-nt	-j-o-nt	-f-e-nt	-j-e-nt	-e-nt
IMPS	-e-r	-e-d	-o-r	-j-o-d	-f-e-d	-j-e-d	

prevocalic suffix -*f*, the terminations -*mp* and -*nt*, and all of the portmanteau suffixes. The prevocalic suffix -*j* and most of the other terminations (-*n*, -*s*, -*c'h*, -*r*, and -*d*) are alike in that each of these always expresses the same content but is not the only suffix expressing that content; for example, -*j* always expresses past tense, but some portmanteaus also express past tense, either to the exclusion of -*j* (-*is* and -*as*) or in combination with it (-*out*). The termination -*t* is ambiguous, expressing second-person plural subject agreement in some forms but third-person singular subject agreement in one form.

The form–content relations involving the prevocalic suffixes in (3a), the terminations in (3c), and the portmanteaus in (3d) are summarized in Table 6.3. While these are comparatively straightforward, the form–content relations involving the vocalic suffixes in (3b) are somewhat more complicated. Forms containing the vocalic suffix -*e* include all irrealis forms, all imperfect indicative forms, the impersonal present indicative form (*karer* 'one loves, on aime'), and the third-person imperative forms (*karet* 's/he must love', *karent* 'they must love'). Forms containing the vocalic suffix -*i* include second-person plural forms of the present indicative and imperative as well as some future-tense forms. Forms containing the vocalic suffix -*o* include some present indicative forms, some future-tense forms, plural and impersonal past indicative forms, and the first-person plural imperative form. The vocalic suffixes' somewhat miscellaneous distribution is summarized in Table 6.4.

In view of these observations about the relation of form to content in Breton verb paradigms, it is reasonable to assume that Breton conjugation is based on the system of simple rules of exponence in (4). Because certain rules in (4) do not express the same content in all of their uses, they are not directly associated with any specific content. For instance, the rule ⟦-**o**⟧ is represented in (4) as

Table 6.3 *Relations of form to content among prevocalic, terminal, and portmanteau suffixes in Breton conjugation*

Prevocalic suffixes	-j	always expresses	pst
	-f	is the biunique expression of	prs irrealis
Terminations	-n	always expresses	1sg
	-s	always expresses	2sg
	-mp	is the biunique expression of	1pl
	-t	expresses	2pl *or* 3sg
	-c'h	always expresses	2pl
	-nt	is the biunique expression of	3pl
	-r	always expresses	imps
	-d	always expresses	imps
Portmanteau suffixes	-out	is the biunique expression of	2sg past ind
	-an	is the biunique expression of	1sg pres ind
	-ez	is the biunique expression of	2sg pres ind
	-is	is the biunique expression of	1sg past ind
	-as	is the biunique expression of	3sg past ind

Table 6.4 *Relations of form to content among vocalic suffixes in Breton conjugation*

-e	appears in	all irrealis forms
		all imperfect indicative forms
		the impersonal present indicative form
		the third-person imperative forms
-i		the second-person plural forms of the present indicative and imperative
		some future-tense forms
-o		some present indicative forms
		some future-tense forms
		the plural and impersonal past indicative forms
		the first-person plural imperative form

applying to a verb to realize the empty set through the suffixation of -*o*. But in combination with the impersonal rule ⟦-**r**⟧, ⟦-**o**⟧ realizes the future indicative (as in *karor* 'one will love'); in combination with first-person plural rule ⟦-**mp**⟧, it realizes the present indicative (*karomp* 'we love'); in combination with both the past-tense rule ⟦-**j**⟧ and the ⟦-**mp**⟧ rule, it realizes the past indicative (*karjomp* 'we loved'); if it serves on its own as a FER, it realizes the third-person singular future indicative (*karo* 's/he will love'); and so on.

(4) Prevocalic suffix rules:
  ⟦-j⟧ :   [V, {pst} : -j]
  ⟦-f⟧ :   [V, {irr prs} : -f]
 Vocalic-suffix rules:
  ⟦-i⟧ :   [V, { } : -i]
  ⟦-o⟧ :   [V, { } : -o]
  ⟦-e⟧ :   [V, { } : -e]
 Termination rules:
  ⟦-n⟧ :   [V, {1sg} : -n]
  ⟦-s⟧ :   [V, {2sg} : -s]
  ⟦-mp⟧ :   [V, {1pl} : -mp]
  ⟦-t⟧ :   [V, { } : -t]
  ⟦-c'h⟧ : [V, {2pl} : -c'h]
  ⟦-nt⟧ :   [V, {3pl} : -nt]
  ⟦-r⟧ :   [V, {imps} : -r]
  ⟦-d⟧ :   [V, {imps} : -d]
 Portmanteau-suffix rules:
  ⟦-out⟧ : [V, {2sg} : -out]
  ⟦-an⟧ :   [V, {ind prs 1sg} : -an]
  ⟦-ez⟧ :   [V, {ind prs 2sg} : -ez]
  ⟦-is⟧ :   [V, {ind pst 1sg} : -is]
  ⟦-as⟧ :   [V, {ind pst 3sg} : -as]

It is clear that in this system, holistic content abounds. Consider the seven affix sequences in Table 6.5. The form of the first-person plural present indicative suffix sequence *-o-mp* in *kar-o-mp* 'we love' is defined by the successive application of the rules ⟦-o⟧ and ⟦-mp⟧, but neither of these rules expresses tense or mood on its own; instead, it is the combination of ⟦-o⟧ and ⟦-mp⟧ that expresses the additional content {ind prs}. By contrast, it is the combination of the rules ⟦-e⟧ and ⟦-r⟧ that expresses the content {ind prs} in the definition of the impersonal present indicative suffix sequence *-e-r* in *kar-e-r* ('one loves, on aime'). And even though ⟦-d⟧ and ⟦-r⟧ are both expressions of an impersonal subject, the combination of ⟦-e⟧ and ⟦-d⟧ expresses different content from the combination of ⟦-e⟧ and ⟦-r⟧: in the definition of the suffix sequence *-e-d* in *kar-e-d* ('one loved, on aimait'), the combination of ⟦-e⟧ and ⟦-d⟧ expresses the content {ind impf}.

The additional content expressed by the combination of two rules may differ from the additional content expressed by those two rules when they are together in combination with some third rule. Thus, the suffix sequence *-j-o-mp* whose form is defined by the successive application of ⟦-j⟧, ⟦-o⟧, and ⟦-mp⟧ expresses the first-person plural past indicative (not the first-person plural present indicative expressed by ⟦-o⟧ and ⟦-mp⟧ in the absence of ⟦-j⟧); similarly, the suffix sequence *-j-e-d* whose form is defined by the successive

Table 6.5 *Seven affix sequences exhibiting holistic exponence in Breton regular verb inflection*

	Affix sequence	Rules	Content	Additional content
Holistic combination	-o-mp	⟦-o⟧	{ }	{ind prs}
		⟦-mp⟧	{1pl}	
	-e-r	⟦-e⟧	{ }	{ind prs}
		⟦-r⟧	{imps}	
	-e-d	⟦-e⟧	{ }	{ind impf}
		⟦-d⟧	{imps}	
	-j-o-mp	⟦-j⟧	{pst}	{ind}
		⟦-o⟧	{ }	
		⟦-mp⟧	{1pl}	
	-j-e-d	⟦-j⟧	{pst}	{irr}
		⟦-e⟧	{ }	
		⟦-d⟧	{imps}	
Solitary specialization	-i	⟦-i⟧	{ }	{2sg fut ind}
	-o	⟦-o⟧	{ }	{3sg fut ind}

application of ⟦-j⟧, ⟦-e⟧, and ⟦-d⟧ expresses the impersonal past irrealis (not the impersonal imperfect indicative expressed by ⟦-e⟧ and ⟦-d⟧ in the absence of ⟦-j⟧).

Finally, a solitary rule may serve as a FER expressing more specific content than that same rule expresses in combination with other rules. As FERs, ⟦-i⟧ and ⟦-o⟧ respectively express the second- and third-person singular future indicative though both appear in rule combinations expressing other person/number/tense/mood combinations. Thus, as FERs, ⟦-i⟧ and ⟦-o⟧ are instances of solitary specialization (Section 1.5.5).

Any adequate theory of morphotactics must account for facts of these sorts, which show that the compositional content criterion is a canonical tendency and not a theorem of some inviolable set of principles.

6.2 Accounting for Holistic Content by Means of Content Supplementations

In order to account for the fact that an inflectional rule may express supplementary content, I employ the supplementation operator Ⓢ defined in Section 2.3. This may apply to a simple inflectional rule serving as a solitary specialization, as in (5a), or to the composition of two inflectional rules serving as a holistic combination, as in (5b).

166 *Rule Combinations Expressing Holistic Content*

(5) Two uses of the supplementation operator Ⓢ
    a. Solitary specialization:
        Given the inflectional rule $R : [C, \tau : X \rightarrow f(X)]$,
        Ⓢ$_\gamma$(R) is the inflectional rule $[C, [\tau \sqcup \gamma] : X \rightarrow f(X)]$.
    b. Holistic combination:
        Given the composite $(R_2 \circ R_1)$ of the inflectional rules
            $R_1 : [C_1, \tau_1 : X \rightarrow f_1(X)]$,
            $R_2 : [C_2, \tau_2 : X \rightarrow f_2(X)]$,
        Ⓢ$_\gamma(R_2 \circ R_1)$ is the inflectional rule $[[C_2 \cap C_1], [\tau_2 \sqcup \tau_1 \sqcup \gamma] :$
                                                $X \rightarrow f_2(f_1(X))]$.

The patterns of content supplementation in (5) afford a straightforward account of the holistic content expressed by the inflectional morphology of Breton regular verbs.

For the inflection of indicative nonpast and imperative forms, the rules in (4) participate in the definition of the FERs specified in Table 6.6; all of these

Table 6.6 *FERs arising through holistic combination or solitary specialization classified according to their addends*

	Addend	Content supplementation	
(a)	{ind prs}	Ⓢ$_{\{ind\ prs\}}$([**-mp**] ∘ [**-o**]) :	[V, {ind prs 1pl} : *-omp*]
		Ⓢ$_{\{ind\ prs\}}$([**-nt**] ∘ [**-o**]) :	[V, {ind prs 3pl} : *-ont*]
		Ⓢ$_{\{ind\ prs\}}$([**-r**] ∘ [**-e**]) :	[V, {ind prs imps} : *-er*]
(b)	{ind fut}	Ⓢ$_{\{ind\ fut\}}$([**-n**] ∘ [**-i**]) :	[V, {ind fut 1sg} : *-in*]
		Ⓢ$_{\{ind\ fut\}}$([**-mp**] ∘ [**-i**]) :	[V, {ind fut 1pl} : *-imp*]
		Ⓢ$_{\{ind\ fut\}}$([**-nt**] ∘ [**-i**]) :	[V, {ind fut 3pl} : *-int*]
		Ⓢ$_{\{ind\ fut\}}$([**-r**] ∘ [**-o**]) :	[V, {ind fut imps} : *-or*]
(c)	{ind impf}	Ⓢ$_{\{ind\ impf\}}$([**-n**] ∘ [**-e**]) :	[V, {ind impf 1sg} : *-en*]
		Ⓢ$_{\{ind\ impf\}}$([**-s**] ∘ [**-e**]) :	[V, {ind impf 2sg} : *-es*]
		Ⓢ$_{\{ind\ impf\}}$([**-mp**] ∘ [**-e**]) :	[V, {ind impf 1pl} : *-emp*]
		Ⓢ$_{\{ind\ impf\}}$([**-c'h**] ∘ [**-e**]) :	[V, {ind impf 2pl} : *-ec'h*]
		Ⓢ$_{\{ind\ impf\}}$([**-nt**] ∘ [**-e**]) :	[V, {ind impf 3pl} : *-ent*]
		Ⓢ$_{\{ind\ impf\}}$([**-d**] ∘ [**-e**]) :	[V, {ind impf imps} : *-ed*]
(d)	{ind}	Ⓢ$_{\{ind\}}$([**-out**] ∘ [**-j**]) :	[V, {ind pst 2sg} : *-jout*]
(e)	addends that include person/number properties	Ⓢ$_{\{ind\ prs\ 2pl\}}$([**-t**] ∘ [**-i**]) :	[V, {ind prs 2pl} : *-it*]
		Ⓢ$_{\{ind\ fut\ 2pl\}}$([**-t**] ∘ [**-o**]) :	[V, {ind fut 2pl} : *-ot*]
		Ⓢ$_{\{imp\ 3sg\}}$([**-t**] ∘ [**-e**]) :	[V, {imp 3sg} : *-et*]
		Ⓢ$_{\{ind\ fut\ 2sg\}}$([**-i**]) :	[V, {ind fut 2sg} : *-i*]
		Ⓢ$_{\{ind\ fut\ 3sg\}}$([**-o**]) :	[V, {ind fut 3sg} : *-o*]
		Ⓢ$_{\{ind\ impf\ 3sg\}}$([**-e**]) :	[V, {ind impf 3sg} : *-e*]

6.2 Accounting for Holistic Content   167

FERs involve supplementary content, and they fall into five main groups according to the nature of their addend (= their supplementary content). The holistic combinations listed in part (a) of the table share the addend {ind prs}; those in part (b), the addend {ind fut}; and those in part (c), the addend {ind impf}. The sole holistic combination in part (d) supplies {ind} as supplementary content for the combination of past-tense ⟦-j⟧ with the rule introducing the second-person singular portmanteau suffix -*out*. In each of the FERs in part (e), the supplementary content includes a person/number specification; note that these FERs include three holistic combinations and three solitary specializations.

The definition of the other indicative past-tense forms and that of the irrealis forms involve the rule combinations in Table 6.7. Three rules function as carrier rules in these combinations: these are the holistic combination Ⓢ$_{\{ind\}}$(⟦-o⟧ ∘ ⟦-j⟧), the composite rule (⟦-e⟧ ∘ ⟦-f⟧), and the holistic combination Ⓢ$_{\{irr\}}$(⟦-e⟧ ∘ ⟦-j⟧) on the left side of the table. Each of these serves as the carrier rule for various termination rules. Termination rules compose with the rule Ⓢ$_{\{ind\}}$(⟦-o⟧ ∘ ⟦-j⟧) in part (a) of the table to provide FERs for the definition of indicative past-tense forms. Termination rules compose with the composite (⟦-e⟧ ∘ ⟦-f⟧) to provide FERs for the definition of irrealis present-tense forms. And termination rules compose with the combination Ⓢ$_{\{irr\}}$(⟦-e⟧ ∘ ⟦-j⟧) to provide FERs for the definition of irrealis past-tense forms. The composite (⟦-e⟧ ∘ ⟦-f⟧) and the holistic combination Ⓢ$_{\{irr\}}$(⟦-e⟧ ∘ ⟦-j⟧) serve on their own as default FERs for two third-person singular forms – specifically, that of the present irrealis (e.g. *karfe* 's/he would love') and that of the past irrealis (e.g. *karje* 's/he would have loved').

The rules in (4) and in Tables 6.6 and 6.7 define all but a handful of the forms of KAROUT 'love' in Table 6.1. To account for the two suffixless forms (the third-person singular present indicative form *kar* 's/he loves' and the second-person singular imperative form *kar* 'love!'), I assume that the definition of the Breton paradigm function PF includes the clause in (6). This assumption excludes the possibility that any otherwise applicable rule of overt affixation in (4) (e.g. ⟦-i⟧, ⟦-o⟧, ⟦-e⟧, ⟦-s⟧, ⟦-t⟧, or ⟦-out⟧) might apply in the definition of these forms.

(6)   Where Z is the bare stem of a verbal lexeme L and σ is {ind prs 3sg} or {imp 2sg}, PF(⟨L, σ⟩) = ⟨Z, σ⟩.

   Examples: PF(⟨KAROUT, {ind prs 3sg}⟩) = ⟨*kar*, {ind prs 3sg}⟩
   PF(⟨KAROUT, {imp 2sg}⟩) = ⟨*kar*, {imp 2sg}⟩

I additionally assume that the plural imperative forms have the shape they do as an effect of systematic syncretism – specifically, that the definition of the

Table 6.7 Combined carrier rules for indicative past and irrealis rules and the composite FERs based on them

	Combined carrier rules for indicative past and irrealis rules	Composite FERs based on these combined carrier rules	
(a)	$\circledS_{\{ind\}}([\mathbf{-o}] \circ [\mathbf{-j}])$:	$([\mathbf{-mp}] \circ \circledS_{\{ind\}}([\mathbf{-o}] \circ [\mathbf{-j}]))$:	[V, {ind pst 1pl}: -*jomp*]
	[V, {ind pst} : -*jo*]	$([\mathbf{-c'h}] \circ \circledS_{\{ind\}}([\mathbf{-o}] \circ [\mathbf{-j}]))$:	[V, {ind pst 2pl}: -*joc'h*]
		$([\mathbf{-nt}] \circ \circledS_{\{ind\}}([\mathbf{-o}] \circ [\mathbf{-j}]))$:	[V, {ind pst 3pl}: -*jont*]
		$([\mathbf{-d}] \circ \circledS_{\{ind\}}([\mathbf{-o}] \circ [\mathbf{-j}]))$:	[V, {ind pst imps}: -*jod*]
(b)	$([\mathbf{-e}] \circ [\mathbf{-f}])$:	$([\mathbf{-n}] \circ ([\mathbf{-e}] \circ [\mathbf{-f}]))$:	[V, {irr prs 1sg}: -*fen*]
	[V, {irr prs} : -*fe*]	$([\mathbf{-s}] \circ ([\mathbf{-e}] \circ [\mathbf{-f}]))$:	[V, {irr prs 2sg}: -*fes*]
		$([\mathbf{-mp}] \circ ([\mathbf{-e}] \circ [\mathbf{-f}]))$:	[V, {irr prs 1pl}: -*femp*]
		$([\mathbf{-c'h}] \circ ([\mathbf{-e}] \circ [\mathbf{-f}]))$:	[V, {irr prs 2pl}: -*fec'h*]
		$([\mathbf{-nt}] \circ ([\mathbf{-e}] \circ [\mathbf{-f}]))$:	[V, {irr prs 3pl}: -*fent*]
		$([\mathbf{-d}] \circ ([\mathbf{-e}] \circ [\mathbf{-f}]))$:	[V, {irr prs imps}: -*fed*]
(c)	$\circledS_{\{irr\}}([\mathbf{-e}] \circ [\mathbf{-j}])$:	$([\mathbf{-n}] \circ \circledS_{\{irr\}}([\mathbf{-e}] \circ [\mathbf{-j}]))$:	[V, {irr pst 1sg}: -*jen*]
	[V, {irr pst} : -*je*]	$([\mathbf{-s}] \circ \circledS_{\{irr\}}([\mathbf{-e}] \circ [\mathbf{-j}]))$:	[V, {irr pst 2sg}: -*jes*]
		$([\mathbf{-mp}] \circ \circledS_{\{irr\}}([\mathbf{-e}] \circ [\mathbf{-j}]))$:	[V, {irr pst 1pl}: -*jemp*]
		$([\mathbf{-c'h}] \circ \circledS_{\{irr\}}([\mathbf{-e}] \circ [\mathbf{-j}]))$:	[V, {irr pst 2pl}: -*jec'h*]
		$([\mathbf{-nt}] \circ \circledS_{\{irr\}}([\mathbf{-e}] \circ [\mathbf{-j}]))$:	[V, {irr pst 3pl}: -*jent*]
		$([\mathbf{-d}] \circ \circledS_{\{irr\}}([\mathbf{-e}] \circ [\mathbf{-j}]))$:	[V, {irr pst imps}: -*jed*]

Breton paradigm function includes the clauses in (7), according to which (i) a regular verb's first- and second-person plural imperative forms are syncretic with the corresponding present indicative forms; and (ii) its third-person plural imperative form is syncretic with the corresponding imperfect indicative form.

(7) For any verbal lexeme L,
    a. if PF(⟨L, {ind prs 1pl}⟩) = ⟨w, {ind prs 1pl}⟩,
        then PF(⟨L, {imp 1pl}⟩) = ⟨w, {imp 1pl}⟩.
    b. if PF(⟨L, {ind prs 2pl}⟩) = ⟨w, {ind prs 2pl}⟩,
        then PF(⟨L, {imp 2pl}⟩) = ⟨w, {imp 2pl}⟩.
    c. if PF(⟨L, {ind impf 3pl}⟩) = ⟨w, {ind impf 3pl}⟩,
        then PF(⟨L, {imp 3pl}⟩) = ⟨w, {imp 3pl}⟩.

With these additional assumptions, it is now possible to account for the definition of every one of the forms of the paradigm of KAROUT 'love' in Table 6.1: each form in Table 6.1 is defined by the corresponding FER in Table 6.8.

This analysis correctly accounts for the fact that combinations of rules may realize content some parts of which cannot be directly attributed to any of the individual rules being combined. That is, it accounts for the possibility that a word's morphology may express holistic content – content that fails to conform to the canonical expectation of compositionality. Notice, in addition, that this analysis correctly accounts for the fact that the mode of combination exhibited by two rules, and hence also the content that they express, may vary with the presence or absence of some additional rule. For instance, the holistic combination $\mathcal{S}_{\{\text{ind prs}\}}(\llbracket\text{-mp}\rrbracket \circ \llbracket\text{-o}\rrbracket)$ expresses {ind prs 1pl} through the suffixation of -o-mp while the composite ($\llbracket\text{-mp}\rrbracket \circ \mathcal{S}_{\{\text{ind}\}}(\llbracket\text{-o}\rrbracket \circ \llbracket\text{-j}\rrbracket)$) expresses {ind pst 1pl} through the suffixation of -j-o-mp. Similarly, the holistic combination $\mathcal{S}_{\{\text{ind impf}\}}(\llbracket\text{-d}\rrbracket \circ \llbracket\text{-e}\rrbracket)$ expresses {ind impf imps} through the suffixation of -e-d while the composite ($\llbracket\text{-d}\rrbracket \circ \mathcal{S}_{\{\text{irr}\}}(\llbracket\text{-e}\rrbracket \circ \llbracket\text{-j}\rrbracket)$) expresses {irr pst imps} through the suffixation of -j-e-d. Such facts show that the same rules may enter into different kinds of combinations, and in doing so, may express different kinds of supplementary content.

Of particular interest here is the fact that in the inflection of a Breton verb, parallel forms may not express parallel content because of the different ways in which the rules defining those forms combine. Given the forms *kar-o-mp* 'we love' and *kar-i-mp* 'we will love', one might expect the parallel forms *kar-o-t* and *kar-i-t* to express the parallel content 'you (pl.) love' and 'you (pl.) will love'. And yet, it is *karot* that means 'you (pl.) will love' and *karit* that means 'you (pl.) love'. The forms *karomp*, *karimp*, *karot*, and *karit* involve the four simple rules $\llbracket\text{-o}\rrbracket$, $\llbracket\text{-i}\rrbracket$, $\llbracket\text{-mp}\rrbracket$, and $\llbracket\text{-t}\rrbracket$, but these rules combine in different

Table 6.8 *FERs defining the finite forms of Breton KAROUT in Table 6.1*

		Present	Imperfect	Future	Past
Indicative mood	1sg	[**-an**]	S$_{\{ind\ impf\}}$([**-n**] ∘ [**-e**])	S$_{\{ind\ fut\}}$([**-n**] ∘ [**-i**])	[**-is**]
	2sg	[**-ez**]	S$_{\{ind\ impf\}}$([**-s**] ∘ [**-e**])	S$_{\{ind\ fut\ 2sg\}}$([**-i**])	S$_{\{ind\}}$([**-out**] ∘ [**-j**])
	3sg	clause (6) of PF	S$_{\{ind\ impf\ 3sg\}}$([**-e**])	S$_{\{ind\ fut\ 3sg\}}$([**-o**])	[**-as**]
	1pl	S$_{\{ind\ prs\}}$([**-mp**] ∘ [**-o**])	S$_{\{ind\ impf\}}$([**-mp**] ∘ [**-e**])	S$_{\{ind\ fut\}}$([**-mp**] ∘ [**-i**])	([**-mp**] ∘ S$_{\{ind\}}$([**-o**] ∘ [**-j**])
	2pl	S$_{\{ind\ prs\ 2pl\}}$([**-t**] ∘ [**-i**])	S$_{\{ind\ impf\}}$([**-c'h**] ∘ [**-e**])	S$_{\{ind\ fut\ 2pl\}}$([**-t**] ∘ [**-o**])	([**-c'h**] ∘ S$_{\{ind\}}$([**-o**] ∘ [**-j**])
	3pl	S$_{\{ind\ prs\}}$([**-nt**] ∘ [**-o**])	S$_{\{ind\ impf\}}$([**-nt**] ∘ [**-e**])	S$_{\{ind\ fut\}}$([**-nt**] ∘ [**-i**])	([**-nt**] ∘ S$_{\{ind\}}$([**-o**] ∘ [**-j**])
	imps	S$_{\{ind\ prs\}}$([**-r**] ∘ [**-e**])	S$_{\{ind\ impf\}}$([**-d**] ∘ [**-e**])	S$_{\{ind\ fut\}}$([**-r**] ∘ [**-o**])	([**-d**] ∘ S$_{\{ind\}}$([**-o**] ∘ [**-j**])

		Present	Past	Imperative mood	
Irrealis mood	1sg	([**-n**] ∘ ([**-e**] ∘ [**-f**]))	([**-n**] ∘ S$_{\{irr\}}$([**-e**] ∘ [**-j**]))		
	2sg	([**-s**] ∘ ([**-e**] ∘ [**-f**]))	([**-s**] ∘ S$_{\{irr\}}$([**-e**] ∘ [**-j**]))	2sg	clause (6) of PF
	3sg	([**-e**] ∘ [**-f**])	S$_{\{irr\}}$([**-e**] ∘ [**-j**])	3sg	S$_{\{imp\ 3sg\}}$([**-t**] ∘ [**-e**])
	1pl	([**-mp**] ∘ ([**-e**] ∘ [**-f**]))	([**-mp**] ∘ S$_{\{irr\}}$([**-e**] ∘ [**-j**]))	1pl	clause (7a) of PF
	2pl	([**-c'h**] ∘ ([**-e**] ∘ [**-f**]))	([**-c'h**] ∘ S$_{\{irr\}}$([**-e**] ∘ [**-j**]))	2pl	clause (7b) of PF
	3pl	([**-nt**] ∘ ([**-e**] ∘ [**-f**]))	([**-nt**] ∘ S$_{\{irr\}}$([**-e**] ∘ [**-j**]))	3pl	clause (7c) of PF
	imps	([**-d**] ∘ ([**-e**] ∘ [**-f**]))	([**-d**] ∘ S$_{\{irr\}}$([**-e**] ∘ [**-j**]))		

6.3 Emergent Supplementary Content in Limbu   171

Table 6.9 *The morphotactics of four Breton verb forms*

(a)	Form cell:	⟨*kar*-, {ind prs 1pl}⟩	'we love'
	⏐		
	FER	ⓢ$_{\{ind\ prs\}}$(⟦**-mp**⟧ ∘ ⟦**-o**⟧)	(Table 6.6a)
	↓		
	Realized cell:	⟨*karomp*, {ind prs 1pl}⟩	
(b)	Form cell:	⟨*kar*-, {ind fut 2pl}⟩	'you (pl.) will love'
	⏐		
	FER	ⓢ$_{\{ind\ fut\ 2pl\}}$(⟦**-t**⟧ ∘ ⟦**-o**⟧)	(Table 6.6e)
	↓		
	Realized cell:	⟨*karot*, {ind fut 2pl}⟩	
(c)	Form cell:	⟨*kar*-, {ind fut 1pl}⟩	'we will love'
	⏐		
	FER	ⓢ$_{\{ind\ fut\}}$(⟦**-mp**⟧ ∘ ⟦**-i**⟧)	(Table 6.6b)
	↓		
	Realized cell:	⟨*karimp*, {ind fut 1pl}⟩	
(d)	Form cell:	⟨*kar*-, {ind prs 2pl}⟩	'you (pl.) love'
	⏐		
	FER	ⓢ$_{\{ind\ prs\ 2pl\}}$(⟦**-t**⟧ ∘ ⟦**-i**⟧)	(Table 6.6e)
	↓		
	Realized cell:	⟨*karit*, {ind prs 2pl}⟩	

ways in the definition of these forms (Table 6.9). The holistic combination of ⟦**-mp**⟧ with ⟦**-o**⟧ has {ind prs} as its addend (as in part (a) of Table 6.9), but the holistic combination of ⟦**-t**⟧ with ⟦**-o**⟧ has {ind fut 2pl} as its addend (as in part (b) of the table); by contrast, the holistic combination of ⟦**-mp**⟧ with ⟦**-i**⟧ has {ind fut} as its addend (as in part (c)), but the holistic combination of ⟦**-t**⟧ with ⟦**-i**⟧ has {ind prs 2pl} as its addend (as in part (d)).[2]

6.3   Emergent Supplementary Content in Limbu Verb Inflection

There are cases in which holistic combinations have an emergent character; these are cases in which the composition of a rule R_2 expressing property P_2 with a rule R_1 expressing property P_1 only applies in the definition of forms that possess an additional property P_3, even though on their own, R_1 and R_2

---

[2] The analysis presented here accounts for the inflectional morphotactics of regular verbs in the conservative variety of Breton described by Trépos (1968) and Kervella (1976). For discussion of possible extensions of this analysis to account for irregular verbs, dialect variation, and inflecting prepositions, see Stump (2021).

172 *Rule Combinations Expressing Holistic Content*

both apply in the definition of forms that do not necessarily possess P_3. In such cases, R_1 and R_2 might be assumed to enter into the holistic combination $⑤_{\{P_3\}}(R_2 \circ R_1)$. **Emergent content supplementations** of this sort are not unusual; consider an example from Limbu.

In the inflection of transitive verbs in Limbu (Section 3.2), the ⟦**a-**⟧ rule in (8a) expresses first-person involvement through the prefixation of *a-*, identifying either the agent argument (as in (9a)) or the patient argument (as in (9b)) as first person; similarly, the ⟦**kɛ-**⟧ rule in (8b) expresses second-person involvement through the prefixation of *kɛ-* (~ *gɛ-* after a vowel), identifying either a second-person agent (as in (10a)) or a second-person patient (as in (10b)). One might therefore expect that a form such as *a-gɛ-huʔ*, which carries both *a-* and *kɛ-* and no other overt morphology, should be ambiguous between a first-person agent/second-person patient interpretation and a second-person agent/first-person patient interpretation; yet, *a-gɛ-huʔ* only means 'you teach me/us' (as in (11a)). The other interpretation is instead expressed by means of the portmanteau rule ⟦**-nɛ**⟧ in (12), which signals a first-person agent acting on a second-person patient, as in (11b); see van Driem (1987: 80). This shows that although the ⟦**a-**⟧ and ⟦**kɛ-**⟧ rules are both indeterminate with respect to the argument whose person they encode, their combination ⟦**a-gɛ-**⟧ is not similarly indeterminate; that is, the combination of ⟦**a-**⟧ with ⟦**kɛ-**⟧, though representable as the composite rule (⟦**a-**⟧ ∘ ⟦**kɛ-**⟧) in (13a), might also be represented as the emergent content supplementation $⑤_{\{\{agt\ 2\}\{pat\ 1\}\}}$(⟦**a-**⟧ ∘ ⟦**kɛ-**⟧) in (13b). Consider these alternatives.

(8)   Two rules of Limbu verb inflection (= (7a,b), Section 3.2)
      a. ⟦**a-**⟧ : [V, {{1}} : *a-*]
      b. ⟦**kɛ-**⟧ : [V, {{2}} : *kɛ-*]

(9)   a. *a-huʔ-s-u-si*
        1-teach-AGT:DU-PAT:3-PAT:NONSG
        'we (DU.INCL) teach them'
    b. *a-m-huʔ-si*
        1-AGT:3NONSG-teach-PAT:DU
        'they teach us (DU.INCL)'

(10)   a. *kɛ-huʔr-u*
        2-teach-PAT:3
        'you (SG) teach him/her'
     b. *kɛ-huʔ*
        2-teach
        's/he teaches you (SG)'

(11) a. *a-gɛ-huʔ*
          1-2-teach
          'you teach me/us'
      b. *huʔ-nɛ*
          teach-AGT:1.PAT:2
          'I teach you (SG)'

(12) ⟦-nɛ⟧ : [V, {{agt 1}{pat 2}} : -nɛ] (= (7c), Section 3.2)

(13) a. (⟦a-⟧ ∘ ⟦kɛ-⟧) : [V, {{1}{2}} : *agɛ-*]
      b. ⑤_{{agt 2}{pat 1}} (⟦a-⟧ ∘ ⟦kɛ-⟧) : [V, {{agr 2}{pat 1}} : *agɛ-*]
          (cf. Table 3.2, Section 3.2)

If the morphotactics of Limbu involves the composite rule (13a) rather than the emergent content supplementation (13b), the realization of the form cell (14a) as the realized cell (14b) involves the competition of (13a) with (12) – a competition that Pāṇini's principle resolves in favor of (12). But if the Limbu system instead involves the emergent content supplementation (13b), this rule doesn't compete with (12); the realization of (14a) by (14b) is, in that case, computationally simpler. That is, the composite rule (13a) is a default that is subject to override by (12), but the emergent content supplementation (13b) is not subject to override by (12), since its domain is disjoint from that of (12). On the assumption that it is more efficient for speakers to memorize frequently recurring form/content correspondences rather than to recompute them extemporaneously, it is reasonable to assume that (13b) would be the preferred mode of combination for ⟦a-⟧ and ⟦kɛ-⟧ in Limbu. (See Section 11.1 for related discussion.)

(14) a. ⟨*huʔ-*, {pos –pret {agt 1 sg} {pat 2 sg}}⟩
      b. ⟨*huʔ-nɛ*, {pos –pret {agt 1 sg} {pat 2 sg}}⟩

6.4 Holistic Content in Old English Verb Inflection

In certain cases, the same two rules may combine to express different holistic content in different contexts. Some striking instances of this sort appear in Old English verb inflection.[3]

The finite inflection of Old English verbs distinguishes three moods (indicative, subjunctive, imperative), two tenses (present, past), and two numbers,

---

[3] The forms discussed here are those of the West Saxon dialect, as presented by Sievers & Cook (1903), Brook (1955), and Quirk & Wrenn (1955).

174 *Rule Combinations Expressing Holistic Content*

with person distinguished in the singular of the indicative (present and past); the imperative is restricted to the present tense. Typically of Germanic languages, Old English makes a distinction between weak verbs (whose past stem is marked by a dental suffix) and strong verbs (whose past stem is instead distinguished by ablaut). The finite paradigms of the five verbs in Table 6.10 are representative.[4]

Each of the verbs in Table 6.10 exhibits three stems in its finite paradigm (Table 6.11): a present stem (in present-tense forms, whether indicative, subjunctive, or imperative), a default past stem (in past-tense forms, both in the subjunctive and in the plural and second-person singular of the indicative), and a singular past stem (in the first and third persons of the singular past indicative). In the inflection of weak verbs, the default past stem and the singular past stem are syncretic.

The suffixal morphology in Table 6.10 exhibits varying patterns of similarity among the five paradigms. In the present tense, the strong verbs SMĪTAN, CLĒOFAN, SINGAN, and the weak class 1 verb DĒMAN are alike, but differ from the weak class 2 verb LEORNIAN. In the singular of the past indicative, the suffixal morphology of the strong verbs differs from that of the weak verbs. In the plural of the past indicative and in the past subjunctive, all five verbs exhibit the same suffixal morphology. Within the context of this variety, the suffixal inflection of Old English verbs presents several instances of holistic content; of particular interest is the fact that in more than one instance, the same two rules may enter into two distinct holistic combinations.

I assume that the fragment of Old English verb morphology in Table 6.10 involves the simple rules of inflectional exponence in (15)–(17). The vocalic suffixes in (15) serve as carrier rules; ⟦-e⟧ also applies on its own, as a FER. The ⟦-e⟧ rule expresses content only in combination with one or more other rules; thus, when ⟦-e⟧ applies on its own, it does so by default, signaling the inapplicability of any other rule. The dependent rules in (16) combine with the carrier rules as in (18)–(21); as we shall see, these combinations involve several examples of the expression of holistic content. The identity rules in (17) override rules of overt suffixation in the definition of particular forms – specifically, in the first and third persons singular of the indicative past of strong verbs and in singular imperatives. (For convenience of reference, I distinguish the two rules in (17) by means of the subscripts 'pst' and 'imp'.)

---

[4] Verbs have been chosen to avoid the irrelevant complications presented by umlaut and geminate alternations.

Table 6.10 *Finite paradigms of five Old English verbs*

(Shaded cells on the same line exhibit the same suffixal morphology as DĒMAN.)

			SMĪTAN 'smite' (strong–1)	CLĒOFAN 'cleave' (strong–2a)	SINGAN 'sing' (strong–3a)	DĒMAN 'judge' (weak–1)	LEORNIAN 'learn' (weak–2)
Present	IND	1SG	smīt-e	clēof-e	sing-e	dēm-e	leorn-i-e
		2SG	smīt-e-st	clief-e-st	sing-e-st	dēm-e-st	leorn-a-st
		3SG	smīt-e-þ	clief-e-þ	sing-e-þ	dēm-e-þ	leorn-a-þ
		PL	smīt-a-þ	clēof-a-þ	sing-a-þ	dēm-a-þ	leorn-i-a-þ
	SBJV	SG	smīt-e	clēof-e	sing-e	dēm-e	leorn-i-e
		PL	smīt-e-n	clēof-e-n	sing-e-n	dēm-e-n	leorn-i-e-n
	IMP	SG	smīt	clēof	sing	dēm	leorn-a
		PL	smīt-a-þ	clēof-a-þ	sing-a-þ	dēm-a-þ	leorn-i-a-þ
Past	IND	1SG	smāt	clēaf	sang	dēmd-e	leornod-e
		2SG	smit-e	cluf-e	sung-e	dēmd-e-st	leornod-e-st
		3SG	smāt	clēaf	sang	dēmd-e	leornod-e
		PL	smit-o-n	cluf-o-n	sung-o-n	dēmd-o-n	leornod-o-n
	SBJV	SG	smit-e	cluf-e	sung-e	dēmd-e	leornod-e
		PL	smit-e-n	cluf-e-n	sung-e-n	dēmd-e-n	leornod-e-n

176 *Rule Combinations Expressing Holistic Content*

Table 6.11 *Finite stems of five Old English verbs*

	SMĪTAN 'smite' (strong–1)	CLĒOFAN 'cleave' (strong–2a)	SINGAN 'sing' (strong–3a)	DĒMAN 'judge' (weak–1)	LEORNIAN 'learn' (weak–2)
Present stem	smīt-	cleof-	sing-	dēm-	leorn-
Default past stem	smit-	cluf-	sung-	dēmd-	leornod-
Singular past stem	smāt-	cleaf-	sang-	dēmd-	leornod-

(15) Carrier rules
⟦-e⟧ : [V, { } : -e]
⟦-o⟧ : [V, {ind pst pl} : -o]
⟦-i⟧ : [V, {weak–2 prs} : -i]
⟦-a⟧ : [V, { } : -a]

(16) Dependent rules
⟦-st⟧ : [V, {ind 2 sg} : -st]
⟦-þ⟧ :   [V, { } : -þ]
⟦-n⟧ : [V, {pl} : -n]

(17) Identity rules
⟦X→X⟧$_{pst}$: [V, {strong ind pst 1/3 sg} : X → X]
⟦X→X⟧$_{imp}$: [V, {imp prs sg} : X → X]

The combined rules in (18) apply in the inflection of all five verbs. Rule (18a) is simply the composite rule (⟦-n⟧ ∘ ⟦-o⟧), which realizes indicative past plural forms through the suffixation of *-on*. In the holistic combination (18b), ⟦-n⟧ combines with ⟦-e⟧ to yield a rule realizing the subjunctive plural through the suffixation of *-en*. This is an example of emergent content supplementation, since neither ⟦-n⟧ nor ⟦-e⟧ realizes subjunctive mood on its own, but in combination, they only realize plural subjunctives. In the inflection of all five verbs, the subjunctive singular is realized by default through the application of ⟦-e⟧.

(18) Combined rules applying to all five verbs
a. (⟦-n⟧ ∘ ⟦-o⟧) : [V, {ind pst pl} : -on]
b. Ⓢ$_{\{sbjv\}}$(⟦-n⟧ ∘ ⟦-e⟧) : [V, {sbjv pl} : -en]

In the singular of the indicative past, strong verbs and weak verbs behave differently. In the inflection of strong verbs, the default rule ⟦-e⟧ realizes the second-person singular of the indicative past; but in the first and third persons of the singular indicative past, the application of this rule is overridden by the

6.4 *Holistic Content in Old English*   177

identity rule ⟦**X→X**⟧~pst~. In the inflection of weak verbs, the default rule ⟦**-e**⟧ applies in the first and third persons of the singular indicative past; in the second person, however, its application is overridden by that of the holistic combination in (19).

(19)   Holistic combination for weak verbs
        Ⓢ~{weak pst}~(⟦**-st**⟧ ∘ ⟦**-e**⟧) : [V, {weak ind pst 2 sg} : *-est*]

In the present tense, strong verbs show the same suffixal morphology as weak class 1 verbs. In the inflection of such verbs, the holistic combinations in (20) define second-person singular indicative present forms in *-est*, third-person singular indicative present forms in *-eþ*, and plural indicative present forms in *-aþ*. Note that two distinct rules combine ⟦**-st**⟧ with ⟦**-e**⟧: the holistic combination in (19) defines *-est* as a second-person singular suffix for the indicative past of weak verbs (*dēmdest* 'you judged', *leornodest* 'you learned'), but the holistic combination (20a) defines *-est* as the default second-person singular suffix for the indicative present (applying in the definition of *smītest* 'you smite', *clīefest* 'you cleave', *singest* 'you sing', and *dēmest* 'you judge' but overridden in *leornast* 'you learn').

(20)   Combined rules for strong verbs and weak class 1 verbs
        a.   Ⓢ~{prs}~(⟦**-st**⟧ ∘ ⟦**-e**⟧) : [V, {ind prs 2 sg} : *-est*]
        b.   Ⓢ~{ind prs 3 sg}~(⟦**-þ**⟧ ∘ ⟦**-e**⟧) : [V, {ind prs 3 sg} : *-eþ*]
        c.   Ⓢ~{ind prs pl}~(⟦**-þ**⟧ ∘ ⟦**-a**⟧) : [V, {ind prs pl} : *-aþ*]

Besides sharing the morphology defined by the rules in (20), strong verbs and weak class 1 verbs are alike in their present-tense inflection in other ways as well:

- their first-person singular indicative present forms and their singular subjunctive present forms are defined by the default rule ⟦**-e**⟧;
- their imperative singular forms are defined by ⟦**X→X**⟧~imp~; and
- their plural subjunctive present forms are defined by means of the same rule (18b) as defines the plural subjunctive forms of all verbs in the past tense.

Verbs belonging to weak class 2 are very different in their present-tense inflection, which involves the combined rules in (21). In the definition of the first-person singular indicative present and singular subjunctive present forms of LEORNIAN, the composite (⟦**-e**⟧ ∘ ⟦**-i**⟧) in (21a) overrides ⟦**-e**⟧; in the definition of the other indicative present forms, the combinations in (21b–d) override those in (20). Note that two distinct rules combine ⟦**-þ**⟧ with ⟦**-a**⟧: the

178 *Rule Combinations Expressing Holistic Content*

holistic combination in (20c) defines *-aþ* as the default suffixal expression of the plural indicative present (*smītaþ* 'we/you/they smite', *clēofaþ* 'we/you/they cleave', *singaþ* 'we/you/they sing', *dēmaþ* 'we/you/they judge'), but the holistic combination in (21c) defines *-aþ* as the suffixal expression of the third person singular indicative present of weak class 2 verbs (*leorn-a-þ* 's/he learns').

(21)   Combined rules for weak class 2 verbs
    a. $(\llbracket\text{-e}\rrbracket \circ \llbracket\text{-i}\rrbracket)$:   [V, {weak–2 prs} : *-ie*]
    b. $Ⓢ_{\{\text{weak–2 prs}\}}(\llbracket\text{-st}\rrbracket \circ \llbracket\text{-a}\rrbracket)$:   [V, {weak–2 ind prs 2 sg} : *-ast*]
    c. $Ⓢ_{\{\text{weak–2 ind prs 3 sg}\}}(\llbracket\text{-þ}\rrbracket \circ \llbracket\text{-a}\rrbracket)$:   [V, {weak–2 ind prs 3 sg} : *-aþ*]
    d. $(Ⓢ_{\{\text{ind prs pl}\}}(\llbracket\text{-þ}\rrbracket \circ \llbracket\text{-a}\rrbracket) \circ \llbracket\text{-i}\rrbracket)$:   [V, {weak–2 ind prs pl} : *-iaþ*]
    e. $(Ⓢ_{\{\text{sbjv}\}}(\llbracket\text{-n}\rrbracket \circ \llbracket\text{-e}\rrbracket) \circ \llbracket\text{-i}\rrbracket)$:   [V, {weak–2 sbjv prs pl} : *-ien*]
    f. $Ⓢ_{\{\text{weak–2 imp prs sg}\}}(\llbracket\text{-a}\rrbracket)$:   [V, {weak–2 imp prs sg} : *-a*]

Outside the weak class 2, the plural present forms of the indicative and subjunctive are defined by the content supplementations (20c) and (18b). In the inflection of weak class 2 verbs, these forms are defined by (21d,e) – the respective composites of (20c) and (18b) with $\llbracket\text{-i}\rrbracket$. Because the domains-of-definition of (21d,e) are narrower than those of (20c) and (18b), (21d,e) override (20c) and (18b) in the definition of plural present forms of weak class 2 verbs. Finally, the solitary specialization in (21f) overrides both $\llbracket X \rightarrow X \rrbracket_{\text{imp}}$ and (21a) in defining imperative singular forms of weak class 2 verbs.

Plural imperative forms are invariably identical to their plural present indicative counterparts. I assume that this is a systematic syncretism enforced by clause (22) in the definition of the Old English paradigm function PF.

(22)   If PF(⟨L, {ind prs pl}⟩) = ⟨w, {ind prs pl}⟩,
          then PF(⟨L, {imp prs pl}⟩) = ⟨w, {imp prs pl}⟩.

This analysis accounts for all of the forms in Table 6.10. For each cell A in Table 6.10, the corresponding cell in Table 6.12 lists the FER defining the form in A.

In this analysis, the suffixal morphology of the forms *leornodest* 'you learned' and *smītest* 'you smite' in both cases involves the simple rules $\llbracket\text{-e}\rrbracket$ and $\llbracket\text{-st}\rrbracket$ in (15) and (16); but because these rules enter into two different holistic combinations, the suffix sequence *-e-st* is an exponent of different property sets in *leornodest* and *smītest*, as parts (a) and (b) of Table 6.13 show. Similarly, the suffixal morphology of the forms *smītaþ* 'we/you/they smite' and *leornaþ* 's/he learns' in both cases involves the rules $\llbracket\text{-a}\rrbracket$ and $\llbracket\text{-þ}\rrbracket$ in (15) and (16); here, too, the rules enter into two different holistic combinations, as in parts (c) and (d) of Table 6.13. Finally, like the analysis of Limbu proposed

Table 6.12 *FERs for the finite paradigms of five Old English verbs*

(Shaded cells on the same line exhibit the same suffixal morphology as DĒMAN.)

			SMĪTAN 'smite' (strong–1)	CLĒOFAN 'cleave' (strong–2a)	SINGAN 'sing' (strong–3a)	DĒMAN 'judge' (weak–1)	LEORNIAN 'learn' (weak–2)
PRS	IND	1SG		[-e]			([-e] ∘ [-i])
		2SG		ⓢ{prs}([-st] ∘ [-e])			ⓢ{weak–2 prs}([-st] ∘ [-a])
		3SG		ⓢ{3 sg}([-b] ∘ [-e])			ⓢ{weak–2 ind prs 3 sg}([-b] ∘ [-a])
		PL		ⓢ{ind prs pl}([-b] ∘ [-a])			ⓢ{ind prs pl}([-b] ∘ [-a]) ∘ [-i]
	SBJV	SG		[-e]			([-e] ∘ [-i])
		PL		ⓢ{sbjv}([-n] ∘ [-e])			ⓢ{sbjv}([-n] ∘ [-e]) ∘ [-i]
	IMP	SG		[X→X]imp clause (22) of PF			[-e]
		PL					ⓢ{weak–2 imp prs sg}([-a]) clause (22) of PF
PST	IND	1SG		[X→X]pst			
		2SG		[-e]			ⓢ{weak pst}([-st] ∘ [-e])
		3SG		[X→X]pst			[-e]
		PL			([-n] ∘ [-o])		
	SBJV	SG			[-e]		
		PL			ⓢ{sbjv}([-n] ∘ [-e])		

179

180 *Rule Combinations Expressing Holistic Content*

Table 6.13 *The morphotactics of five Old English verb forms*

(a)	Content cell:	⟨LEORNIAN, {ind pst 2 sg}⟩	'you learned'
	Form cell:	⟨*leornod*-, {weak–2 ind pst 2 sg}⟩	
		|	
	FER	Ⓢ$_{\{\text{weak pst}\}}$([[-**st**]] ∘ [[-**e**]])	(= (19))
	↓		
	Realized cell:	⟨*leornodest*, {weak–2 ind pst 2 sg}⟩	
(b)	Content cell:	⟨SMĪTAN, {ind prs 2 sg}⟩	'you smite'
	Form cell:	⟨*smīt*-, {strong ind prs 2 sg}⟩	
		|	
	FER	Ⓢ$_{\{\text{prs}\}}$([[-**st**]] ∘ [[-**e**]])	(= (20a))
	↓		
	Realized cell:	⟨*smītest*, {strong ind prs 2 sg}⟩	
(c)	Content cell:	⟨SMĪTAN, {ind prs pl}⟩	'we/you/they smite'
	Form cell:	⟨*smīt*-, {strong ind prs pl}⟩	
		|	
	FER	Ⓢ$_{\{\text{ind prs pl}\}}$([[-**þ**]] ∘ [[-**a**]])	(= (20c))
	↓		
	Realized cell:	⟨*smītaþ*, {strong ind prs pl}⟩	
(d)	Content cell:	⟨LEORNIAN, {ind prs 3 sg}⟩	's/he learns'
	Form cell:	⟨*leorn*-, {weak–2 ind prs 3 sg}⟩	
		|	
	FER	Ⓢ$_{\{\text{weak–2 ind prs 3 sg}\}}$([[-**þ**]] ∘ [[-**a**]])	(= (21c))
	↓		
	Realized cell:	⟨*leornaþ*, {weak–2 ind prs 3 sg}⟩	
(e)	Content cell:	⟨SMĪTAN, {sbjv pst pl}⟩	'we/you/they smote (sbjv)'
	Form cell:	⟨*smit*-, {strong sbjv pst pl}⟩	
		|	
	FER	Ⓢ$_{\{\text{sbjv}\}}$([[-**n**]] ∘ [[-**e**]])	(= (18b))
	↓		
	Realized cell:	⟨*smiten*, {strong sbjv pst pl}⟩	

in Section 6.3, this analysis of Old English verb morphology derives computational simplicity from the use of holistic combination, treating the combination of rules [[-**n**]] and [[-**e**]] not simply as a composite rule spelling out the default exponence of plural number, but as a holistic combination spelling out the (present or past) exponence of the plural subjunctive; the definition of *smiten* 'we/you/they smote (sbjv)' in part (e) of Table 6.13 illustrates this.

The notion of holistic combination highlights an important reason why the morpheme concept (and in particular, its theorem that a word form's content is the sum of the content associated with its component morphemes) is wrong. The morpheme concept entails that a word form is endowed with the summed content of its individual formatives. But holistic combinations show that word forms with different content don't necessarily differ in content because they are composed of different exponents; even if they involve the very same exponents, they may instead differ because the rules introducing those exponents are combined in different ways.

6.5 Conclusion

In this chapter, deviations from the compositional content criterion have been shown to necessitate a mode of rule combination distinct from ordinary composition, namely that of holistic combination. Breton conjugation is an example of an inflectional system whose morphotactics makes extensive use of this mode of combination. I analyze such systems by means of a supplementation operator $Ⓢ_γ$, whose application to a rule R realizing content τ produces the content supplementation $Ⓢ_γ(R)$, a rule whose formal effect is like that of R but which realizes the more specific content [τ ⊔ γ]. If R is a composite rule, the content supplementation $Ⓢ_γ(R)$ is a rule of holistic combination; if R is a simple rule, $Ⓢ_γ(R)$ is instead a solitary specialization. Evidence from Old English shows that the same two rules may enter into more than one holistic combination.

In the following chapter, I present evidence motivating another special mode of rule combination – that of aggregation. Aggregation inherently deviates from the stem operand criterion (Section 1.5.6), but it brings apparent deviations from the affix directionality criterion (Section 1.5.10) into conformity with it.

7 *Rule Aggregation*

In many cases of affixational rule combination, the combining rules are alike in the directionality of their affixation: either both are rules of suffixation or both are rules of prefixation. But there are also cases in which the combined rules differ in their directionality – instances in which a rule of prefixation combines with a rule of suffixation. Logically, combinations of this sort may produce three distinct patterns of affixation.

The first pattern is one in which a rule of x- prefixation and a rule of $-y$ suffixation enter into composition, producing a rule that operates on stem Z to yield the form x-Z-y. Some of the composite rules in the analysis of Limbu verb inflection in Section 3.2 are of this type, and one might argue that rules of circumfixation in general arise through the historical reanalysis of this sort of composite as a simple rule defining a discontinuous affix.

The second and third patterns are ones in which a rule of x- prefixation and a rule of $-y$ suffixation might combine to produce a rule of affix counterposition (Section 1.5.6). Recall again the defining signature of affix counterposition: affix A exhibits a particular directionality D (prefixal or suffixal) with respect to a stem with which it joins, but in the presence of some affix B possessing the opposite directionality, A exhibits directionality D with respect to B, to which it is adjacent. Aggregation is the mode of rule combination that defines affix counterpositions (Section 2.4). A rule of x- prefixation aggregates with a rule of $-y$ suffixation to produce a rule of suffixational counterposition, which operates on stem Z to yield the form Z-x-y (this is the second pattern); by contrast, a rule of $-y$ suffixation aggregates with a rule of x- prefixation to produce a rule of prefixational counterposition, which instead operates on stem Z to yield the form x-y-Z (the third pattern).

In this chapter, I discuss cases of the latter two sorts: as I show, the inflection of adjectives in Noon involves a pattern of suffixational counterposition, and the inflection of reflexive verbs in Lithuanian involves a pattern of prefixational counterposition. According to the proposed analyses, these are cases that deviate from the stem operand criterion (Section 1.5.6); at the same time, these analyses make it possible to regard the dependent rules in Noon and Lithuanian as canonical with respect to the affix directionality criterion (Section 1.5.10), despite the fact that at first appearance, they seem to deviate from it.

The type of rule combination involved in these cases is, again, aggregation rather than composition. Recall that the aggregation of rule R_2 with rule R_1, represented as $(R_2 \circledA R_1)$, is a rule combination possessing the characteristics in (1).[1]

(1)   Aggregated inflectional rules
        Given the inflectional rules R_1 and R_2 –
            $R_1 : [C_1, \tau_1 : X \rightarrow f_1(a, X)]$, where f_1 is an affixation operation
            $R_2 : [C_2, \tau_2 : X \rightarrow f_2(b, X)]$, where f_2 is an affixation operation
        – the aggregation $(R_2 \circledA R_1)$ is the rule
            $[[C_2 \cap C_1], [\tau_2 \sqcup \tau_1] : X \rightarrow f_1(f_2(b, a), X))]$.

Recall from Section 2.4 that rule aggregation is equivalent to rule composition in cases in which R_1 and R_2 are both prefixational or both suffixational; it is therefore reasonable to appeal to aggregation mainly in cases in R_2 with R_1 differ in their direction of affixation, as in the hypothetical example in (2).[2]

(2)   Given the rules
         $[\![\mathbf{y\text{-}}]\!] : [C_1, \tau_1 : y\text{-}]$ and
         $[\![\mathbf{\text{-}z}]\!] : [C_2, \tau_2 : \text{-}z]$,
        $([\![\mathbf{y\text{-}}]\!] \circledA [\![\mathbf{\text{-}z}]\!]) = [[C_2 \cap C_1], [\tau_2 \sqcup \tau_1] : \text{-}yz]$ (a rule of suffixational counterposition)
        and
        $([\![\mathbf{\text{-}z}]\!] \circledA [\![\mathbf{y\text{-}}]\!]) = [[C_2 \cap C_1], [\tau_2 \sqcup \tau_1] : yz\text{-}]$ (a rule of prefixational counterposition).

A language's morphotactics canonically conforms to the stem operand criterion, according to which rules of affixation operate on stems. Rule combinations do not, as a class, deviate from the stem operand criterion: if R_1 and R_2 are morphological rules that conform to the stem operand criterion, then the composite $(R_2 \circ R_1)$ and the holistic combination $\circledS_\gamma(R_2 \circ R_1)$ (for some addend γ) both likewise conform to this criterion. Rule aggregation, however, differs from these other modes of rule combination in that it deviates from the

---

[1] Note that in rule R_2 in (1), f_2 operates by default on an operand belonging to category C_2; but when R_2 is aggregated with R_1, this default is overridden, and f_2 takes the affix a introduced by R_1 as its operand. (See Section 7.1.2 for a specific illustration.)

[2] Nevertheless, a morphotactic pattern is in some cases most simply seen as involving the aggregation of a rule with members of a class of rules some of which are prefixational and others of which are suffixational; see the discussion of Italian pronominal affixes in Section 7.4.

stem operand criterion; aggregation in effect involves a rule of affixation operating not on a stem but on an affix (e.g. most clearly a rule of suffixation operating on a prefix or a rule of prefixation operating on a suffix).

Evidence favoring the postulation of rule aggregation as a mode of rule combination is not unusual. In this chapter, I discuss evidence of this sort from Noon (Section 7.1) and Lithuanian (Section 7.2). In Section 7.3, I discuss a contrasting body of evidence from Gurma. While the analyses proposed for Noon and Lithuanian bring their morphotactics into conformity with the affix directionality criterion, Gurma presents a noncanonical phenomenon that genuinely deviates from this criterion; this is the phenomenon of true ambifixes – affixes that actually do function as prefixes in some word forms but as suffixes in other word forms. Thus, rule aggregation cannot be seen as logically excluding all possible deviations from the affix directionality criterion. Indeed, I show in Section 7.4 that the morphotactics of Italian pronominal affixes involves a significant interaction between true ambifixation and rule aggregation. In Chapter 8, I discuss additional instances of rule aggregation as part of more wide-ranging analysis of the inflectional morphotactics of Swahili.

7.1 Noon

On first consideration, affixation to an affix seems like a strange idea; but as noted earlier (Section 2.4), it isn't difficult to see how such a phenomenon might arise historically. Suppose, for example, that an attributive adjective A and an accompanying determiner D both take a prefix y- expressing agreement with the noun they modify: [N y-A y-D]. Suppose, too, that with the passage of time, the determiner is reanalyzed as an adjective suffix $-x$. Once that happens, the prefix y- has a distribution in which it is prefixed either to an adjective stem or to the suffix $-x$: [N y-A-y-x]. In that case, the ⟦**y-**⟧ rule aggregates synchronically with the ⟦**-x**⟧ rule in the definition of the adjectival form y-A-y-x. The morphotactic system of the Noon language (Cangin; Senegal) exhibits exactly this synchronic pattern of suffixational counterposition.

In this discussion, I draw extensively on the detailed account of the Noon noun-class system presented by Soukka (2000); the focus here is on the manner in which attributive adjectives are integrated within this system.

7.1.1 Adjective Inflection in Noon

In Noon, the ways in which an attributive adjective's inflection relates to the properties of the modified noun are somewhat complex. The overarching generalization is that an adjective agrees with the modified noun in definiteness and number: agreement is expressed by means of an *attributive prefix* expressing number and (in definite forms) by a *definite suffix* expressing both number and definiteness (Soukka 2000: 87). Definite nouns inflect cumulatively both for definiteness and for the position of their referent (location 1 'near the speaker', location 2 'near the addressee', location 3 'near neither speaker nor addressee'); a definite adjective's definite suffix exhibits this same cumulation, expressing agreement with the modified noun's position inflection. Finally, the affixal expression of both number agreement and definiteness agreement in an adjective's inflection depends on the modified noun's diminutivity, animacy, and noun class, in the following way.

(i) If the referent of the modified noun is diminutive, the adjective's inflection expresses this diminutiveness cumulatively with its number. The attributive prefixes and definite suffixes that express diminutiveness are those that express number agreement and definiteness for noun class 6 (the usual class for diminutive nouns in Noon), but an adjective may inflect for diminutiveness even if the modified noun does not itself belong to class 6; thus, in the inflection of the adjective *jijófi'jum* in (3), the singular attributive prefix *ji-* and the location-2 definite suffix *-jum* express the diminutiveness of the modified noun's referent, even though the modified noun *kowukum* itself belongs to noun class 4.

(3) Adjective whose modified noun has a diminutive referent
kowu-kum ji-jófi'-jum
child-DEF.SG.NC4.LOC2 ATTR.SG.DIM-good-DEF.SG.DIM.LOC2
'the good child (near you)'

(Soukka 2000: 91)

(ii) If the referent of the modified noun is nondiminutive, the adjective's inflection depends on whether its referent is animate or inanimate. If it is animate, the adjective's inflection expresses this animacy cumulatively with number, through the use of the special animate attributive prefixes (singular *yi-*, plural *ɓi-*) and the special animate definite suffixes (in the singular, location 1 *-yii*, location 2 *-yum*, location 3 *-yaa*; and in the plural, location 1 *-ɓii*, location 2 *-ɓum*, location 3 *-ɓaa*). Thus, the adjective *yiyaanaawyii* in (4) agrees with the modified noun with respect to number, definiteness, and location and indicates the animacy of its nondiminutive referent; note,

186 *Rule Aggregation*

however, that the adjective inflection does not explicitly specify the modified noun's membership in noun class 1.

(4) Adjective whose modified noun has a nondiminutive animate referent
ɣaal-ii yi-yaanaaw-yii
man-DEF.SG.NC1.LOC1 ATTR.SG.ANIM-white-DEF.SG.ANIM.LOC1
'the white man (here)'

(Soukka 2000: 89)

(iii) If the referent of the modified noun is neither diminutive nor animate, the adjective's inflection depends on the modified noun's noun-class[3] membership, which it expresses cumulatively with its number. Thus, in the inflection of the adjective *fineɓpafii* in (5), the attributive prefix *fi-* and the definite suffix *-fii* express agreement with the modified noun *cuunohfii* with respect to singular number, membership in noun class 2, definiteness, and location 1 (near the speaker).

(5) Adjective whose modified noun has a nondiminutive inanimate referent
cuunoh-fii fi-neɓpa-fii
lunch-DEF.SG.NC2.LOC1 ATTR.SG.NC2-very.tasty-DEF. SG.NC2.LOC1
'the very tasty lunch (here)'

(Soukka 2000: 91)

This inflectional complexity is exemplified by the paradigm of the adjective[4] YAK 'big' in Table 7.1.[5]

Soukka observes that each of the affixes in Table 7.1 is morphologically complex: each attributive prefix consists of a consonantal marker of diminutiveness, animacy, or noun class and a prefixal formative *i-*, and each definite

---

[3] I follow Soukka's system of noun-class numbering, according to which Noon possesses six noun classes such that a typical noun's singular and plural forms are both treated as belonging to the same noun class; thus, Soukka's numbering does not derive from the commonly assumed system of noun-class labels in Meinhof 1906, in which a noun's singular and plural forms typically belong to distinct noun classes.

[4] This adjective belongs to a subclass whose members also function as stative verbs (Soukka 2000: 88f.).

[5] Note that in the inflection of an adjective A for agreement with a noun N, the properties of diminutivity and animacy possessed by the referent of N override N's noun-class property; thus, it is only when N has a nondiminutive, inanimate referent that N's noun-class membership in one of the noun classes 1–6 surfaces in the inflection of A. This does not, however, mean that a noun only belongs to one of these noun classes if it has a nondiminutive, inanimate referent; for instance, the diminutive, animate noun *kowu* 'child' belongs to noun class 4, as is reflected by the fact that it takes the class 4 definite suffix *-kum* in (3). See Soukka (2000: 65–67, 74–77) for discussion.

Table 7.1 The inflection of the Noon adjective YAK 'big'

			Noun class	Indefinite	Location 1	Definite Location 2	Location 3
Nondiminutive	Inanimate	SG	NC1	wi-yak	wi-yak-wii	wi-yak-wum	wi-yak-waa
			NC2	fi-yak	fi-yak-fii	fi-yak-fum	fi-yak-faa
			NC3	mi-yak	mi-yak-mii	mi-yak-mum	mi-yak-maa
			NC4	ki-yak	ki-yak-kii	ki-yak-kum	ki-yak-kaa
			NC5	pi-yak	pi-yak-pii	pi-yak-pum	pi-yak-paa
			NC6	ji-yak	ji-yak-jii	ji-yak-jum	ji-yak-jaa
		PL	NC1–3	ci-yak	ci-yak-cii	ci-yak-cum	ci-yak-caa
			NC4–6	ti-yak	ti-yak-tii	ti-yak-tum	ti-yak-taa
	Animate	SG	yi-yak	yi-yak-yii	yi-yak-yum	yi-yak-yaa	
		PL		ɓi-yak	ɓi-yak-ɓii	ɓi-yak-ɓum	ɓi-yak-ɓaa
Diminutive		SG		ji-yak	ji-yak-jii	ji-yak-jum	ji-yak-jaa
		PL		ti-yak	ti-yak-tii	ti-yak-tum	ti-yak-taa

Table 7.2 *Components of Noon adjectival inflections according to Soukka 2000*

			Noun class	Consonantal marker	Attributive prefix = consonantal marker + prefixal formative
Nondiminutive	Inanimate	SG	NC1	w-	
			NC2	f-	*Prefixal formative:* i-
			NC3	m-	
			NC4	k-	
			NC5	p-	Definite suffix =
			NC6	j-	consonantal marker + positional formative
		PL	NC1–3	c-	
			NC4–6	t-	*Positional formatives:*
	Animate	SG		y-	Location 1 -ii
		PL		6-	Location 2 -um
Diminutive		SG		j-	Location 3 -aa
		PL		t-	

suffix consists of the same consonantal marker and one of the positional formatives -*ii*, -*um*, and -*aa*. These components of the affixes in Table 7.1 are distinguished in Table 7.2.

Soukka's analysis treats both the attributive prefixes and the definite suffixes as being analyzable into smaller grammatically significant parts. In rule-based terms, it treats the rules of attributive prefixation and the rules of definite suffixation as noncanonical deviations from both the minimal rule criterion (they are rules built up from smaller rules) and the stem operand criterion (their definition involves rules operating on affixes). One might try to propose an alternative analysis that conforms to both of these criteria – an analysis in which definite adjectival forms such as those in Table 7.1 are seen as involving the successive operation of four rules (two of them prefixational, the other two suffixational) on an adjective's stem, to produce forms such as those in Table 7.3. Such an analysis, however, would have to involve rules that prefix the consonantal markers in some instances but suffix them in others, a deviation from the affix directionality criterion. Soukka's analysis, by contrast, treats the consonantal markers as conforming to the affix directionality criterion: they are uniformly prefixal, being prefixed to the prefixal formative *i*- in some instances and to the suffixal positional formatives -*ii*, -*um*, and -*aa* in

Table 7.3 *An analysis of the definite location 2 forms of Noon* YAK *'big' that conforms to both the minimal rule criterion (Section 1.5.1) and the stem operand criterion*

			Noun class	Definite Location 2			
				−2	−1	Stem	1	2
Nondiminutive	Inanimate	SG	NC1	w-	i-	**yak**	-w	-um
			NC2	f-	i-	**yak**	-f	-um
			NC3	m-	i-	**yak**	-m	-um
			NC4	k-	i-	**yak**	-k	-um
			NC5	p-	i-	**yak**	-p	-um
			NC6	j-	i-	**yak**	-j	-um
		PL	NC1–3	c-	i-	**yak**	-c	-um
			NC4–6	t-	i-	**yak**	-t	-um
	Animate	SG		y-	i-	**yak**	-y	-um
		PL		ɓ-	i-	**yak**	-ɓ	-um
Diminutive		SG		j-	i-	**yak**	-j	-um
		PL		t-	i-	**yak**	-t	-um

Table 7.4 *Soukka's analysis of the definite location 2 forms of the Noon adjective* YAK *'big'*

			Noun class	Attributive prefix	Stem	Definite suffix (Location 2)
Nondiminutive	Inanimate	SG	NC1	w-i-	**yak**	-w-um
			NC2	f-i-	**yak**	-f-um
			NC3	m-i-	**yak**	-m-um
			NC4	k-i-	**yak**	-k-um
			NC5	p-i-	**yak**	-p-um
			NC6	j-i-	**yak**	-j-um
		PL	NC1–3	c-i-	**yak**	-c-um
			NC4–6	t-i-	**yak**	-t-um
	Animate	SG		y-i-	**yak**	-y-um
		PL		ɓ-i-	**yak**	-ɓ-um
Diminutive		SG		j-i-	**yak**	-j-um
		PL		t-i-	**yak**	-t-um

others, as in Table 7.4. In a rule-based approach to morphology, the economy of Soukka's analysis favors the postulation of rule aggregation as a noncanonical mode of rule combination deviating from both the minimal rule criterion and the stem operand criterion.

190 *Rule Aggregation*

7.1.2 Rule Aggregation in Noon

The availability of rule aggregation as a mode of rule combination affords a straightforward morphotactic analysis of Noon adjective inflection. I assume that the simple rules of inflectional exponence for Noon adjectives are as in (6)–(8). The consonantal marker rules in (6) are dependent, and their carrier rules include the prefixal formative rule (7) and the positional formative rules in (8). The consonantal marker rules combine with the prefixal formative rule ⟦i-⟧ as in (9a) and with the positional formative rules as in (9b). The full exponence rules (FERs) for Noon adjectives are accordingly formulable as in (9c,d).

(6) Consonantal marker rules
  a. ⟦**w-**⟧ :   [Nom, {–dim –anim sg nc1} : *w-*]
  b. ⟦**f-**⟧ :   [Nom, {–dim –anim sg nc2} : *f-*]
  c. ⟦**m-**⟧ :   [Nom, {–dim –anim sg nc3} : *m-*]
  d. ⟦**k-**⟧ :   [Nom, {–dim –anim sg nc4} : *k-*]
  e. ⟦**p-**⟧ :   [Nom, {–dim –anim sg nc5} : *p-*]
  f. ⟦**j-**⟧ :   [Nom, {–dim –anim sg nc6} : *j-*]
  g. ⟦**c-**⟧ :   [Nom, {–dim –anim pl nc1–3} : *c-*]
  h. ⟦**t-**⟧ :   [Nom, {–dim –anim pl nc4–6} : *t-*]
  i. ⟦**y-**⟧ :   [Nom, {–dim +anim sg} : *y-*]
  j. ⟦**ɓ-**⟧ :   [Nom, {–dim +anim pl} : *ɓ-*]
  k. ⟦**j-**⟧$_{dim}$:   [Nom, {+dim sg} : *j-*]
  l. ⟦**t-**⟧$_{dim}$:   [Nom, {+dim pl} : *t-*]

(7) Prefixal formative rule: ⟦**i-**⟧ : [A, { } : *i-*][6]

(8) Positional formative rules
  a. ⟦**-ii**⟧ :   [Nom, {definite loc1} : *-ii*]
  b. ⟦**-um**⟧ :   [Nom, {definite loc2} : *-um*]
  c. ⟦**-aa**⟧ :   [Nom, {definite loc3} : *-aa*]

(9) Combined rules of adjective inflection
  a. Attributive prefix rules
    Given any consonantal marker rule R, the composite (R ∘ ⟦**i-**⟧) is an attributive prefix rule.
  b. Definite suffix rules
    Given any positional formative rule R_1 and any consonantal marker rule R_2, the aggregation (R_2 Ⓐ R_1) is a definite suffix rule.

---

[6] Rule (7) is formulated as realizing the property 'adjective' because Noon attributive prefixes only participate in the inflection of adjectives. This property is not realized by the definite suffixes, since these participate in the inflection of nouns as well as adjectives. (The category Nom in (6) and (8) is thus intended to include both adjectives and nouns.)

c. FER pattern for definite adjectives
Where ⟨Z, σ⟩ is an adjective form cell in the domain of both the attributive prefix rule R_1 and the definite suffix rule R_2, ($R_2 \circ R_1$) is the FER for ⟨Z, σ⟩.
d. FER pattern for indefinite adjectives
Where ⟨Z, σ⟩ is an adjective form cell in the domain of the attributive prefix rule R, and indefinite ∈ σ, R is the FER for ⟨Z, σ⟩.

The attributive prefix rules defined by (9a) are the composite rules in (10).

(10) Composite attributive prefix rules
    a. (⟦**w-**⟧ ∘ ⟦**i-**⟧) :   [A, {–dim –anim sg nc1} : *wi-*]
    b. (⟦**f-**⟧ ∘ ⟦**i-**⟧) :   [A, {–dim –anim sg nc2} : *fi-*]
    c. (⟦**m-**⟧ ∘ ⟦**i-**⟧) :   [A, {–dim –anim sg nc3} : *mi-*]
    d. (⟦**k-**⟧ ∘ ⟦**i-**⟧) :   [A, {–dim –anim sg nc4} : *ki-*]
    e. (⟦**p-**⟧ ∘ ⟦**i-**⟧) :   [A, {–dim –anim sg nc5} : *pi-*]
    f. (⟦**j-**⟧ ∘ ⟦**i-**⟧) :   [A, {–dim –anim sg nc6} : *ji-*]
    g. (⟦**c-**⟧ ∘ ⟦**i-**⟧) :   [A, {–dim –anim pl nc1–3} : *ci-*]
    h. (⟦**t-**⟧ ∘ ⟦**i-**⟧) :   [A, {–dim –anim pl nc4–6} : *ti-*]
    i. (⟦**y-**⟧ ∘ ⟦**i-**⟧) :   [A, {–dim +anim sg} : *yi-*]
    j. (⟦**ɓ-**⟧ ∘ ⟦**i-**⟧) :   [A, {–dim +anim pl} : *ɓi-*]
    k. (⟦**j-**⟧$_{dim}$ ∘ ⟦**i-**⟧) :   [A, {+dim sg} : *ji-*]
    l. (⟦**t-**⟧$_{dim}$ ∘ ⟦**i-**⟧) :   [A, {+dim pl} : *ti-*]

The definite suffix rules defined by (9b) are aggregations of a consonantal marker rule with a positional formative rule. These aggregations include (i) the set of rules in (11), which are based on the location 1 positional formative rule ⟦**-ii**⟧ and (ii) parallel sets of rules (not listed but easily constructed) based on the other positional formative rules ⟦**-um**⟧ and ⟦**-aa**⟧. Note that when a consonantal marker rule in (6) applies, it operates by default on a nominal stem (i.e. an adjective or noun stem); but when that same rule is aggregated with a positional formative rule from (8), this default is overridden, and the consonantal marker rule operates on the positional formative introduced by the rule with which it is aggregated.

(11) Aggregated definite suffix rules
    a. (⟦**w-**⟧ Ⓐ ⟦**-ii**⟧) :   [Nom, {–dim –anim sg nc1 definite loc1} : *-wii*]
    b. (⟦**f-**⟧ Ⓐ ⟦**-ii**⟧) :   [Nom, {–dim –anim sg nc2 definite loc1} : *-fii*]
    c. (⟦**m-**⟧ Ⓐ ⟦**-ii**⟧) :   [Nom, {–dim –anim sg nc3 definite loc1} : *-mii*]
    d. (⟦**k-**⟧ Ⓐ ⟦**-ii**⟧) :   [Nom, {–dim –anim sg nc4 definite loc1} : *-kii*]
    e. (⟦**p-**⟧ Ⓐ ⟦**-ii**⟧) :   [Nom, {–dim –anim sg nc5 definite loc1} : *-pii*]
    f. (⟦**j-**⟧ Ⓐ ⟦**-ii**⟧) :   [Nom, {–dim –anim sg nc6 definite loc1} : *-jii*]
    g. (⟦**c-**⟧ Ⓐ ⟦**-ii**⟧) :   [Nom, {–dim –anim pl nc1–3 definite loc1} : *-cii*]
    h. (⟦**t-**⟧ Ⓐ ⟦**-ii**⟧) :   [Nom, {–dim –anim pl nc4–6 definite loc1} : *-tii*]
    i. (⟦**y-**⟧ Ⓐ ⟦**-ii**⟧) :   [Nom, {–dim +anim sg definite loc1} : *-yii*]

192 *Rule Aggregation*

Table 7.5 *The morphotactics of four forms of the Noon adjective* YAK *'big' from Table 7.1*

(a)	Form cell:	⟨yak, {+dim sg definite loc1}⟩
	$\mid$	
	FER	((⟦j-⟧$_{dim}$ Ⓐ ⟦-ii⟧) ∘ (⟦j-⟧$_{dim}$ ∘ ⟦i-⟧))
	↓	
	Realized cell:	⟨jiyakjii, {+dim sg definite loc1}⟩
(b)	Form cell:	⟨yak, {−dim −anim sg nc2 definite loc2}⟩
	$\mid$	
	FER	((⟦f-⟧ Ⓐ ⟦-um⟧) ∘ (⟦f-⟧ ∘ ⟦i-⟧))
	↓	
	Realized cell:	⟨fiyakfum, {−dim −anim sg nc2 definite loc2}⟩
(c)	Form cell:	⟨yak, {−dim −anim sg nc1 definite loc3}⟩
	$\mid$	
	FER	((⟦w-⟧ Ⓐ ⟦-aa⟧) ∘ (⟦w-⟧ ∘ ⟦i-⟧))
	↓	
	Realized cell:	⟨wiyakwaa, {−dim −anim sg nc1 definite loc3}⟩
(d)	Form cell:	⟨yak, {−dim +anim pl indefinite}⟩
	$\mid$	
	FER	(⟦ɓ-⟧ ∘ ⟦i-⟧)
	↓	
	Realized cell:	⟨ɓiyak, {−dim +anim pl indefinite}⟩

j. (⟦ɓ-⟧ Ⓐ ⟦-ii⟧) : [Nom, {−dim +anim pl definite loc1} : -ɓii]
k. (⟦j-⟧$_{dim}$ Ⓐ ⟦-ii⟧) : [Nom, {+dim sg definite loc1} : -jii]
l. (⟦t-⟧$_{dim}$ Ⓐ ⟦-ii⟧) : [Nom, {+dim pl definite loc1} : -tii]

In accordance with the FER pattern (9c), definite suffix rules such as those in (11) compose with the attributive prefix rules in (10) to form FERs for definite adjective forms. For example, (⟦j-⟧$_{dim}$ Ⓐ ⟦-ii⟧) composes with (⟦j-⟧$_{dim}$ ∘ ⟦i-⟧) to yield the FER realizing the adjective form *jiyakjii* in part (a) of Table 7.5; (⟦f-⟧ Ⓐ ⟦-um⟧) composes with (⟦f-⟧ ∘ ⟦i-⟧) to yield the FER realizing the form *fiyakfum* in part (b) of the table; and (⟦w-⟧ Ⓐ ⟦-aa⟧) composes with (⟦w-⟧ ∘ ⟦i-⟧) to yield the FER realizing the form *wiyakwaa* in part (c) of the table. On their own, the attributive prefix rules in (10) function as FERs for indefinite adjective forms, in accordance with the FER pattern (9d); for example, (⟦ɓ-⟧ ∘ ⟦i-⟧) serves as the FER realizing the indefinite adjective form *ɓi-yak* in part (d) of Table 7.5.

The key feature of this analysis is that it combines the rules of consonantal marker prefixation with other rules in two different ways: they compose with the prefixal formative rule ⟦**i-**⟧ to form attributive prefix rules, and they aggregate with the positional formative rules ⟦**-ii**⟧, ⟦**-um**⟧, and ⟦**-aa**⟧ to form definite suffix rules. Throughout, the consonant marker rules are rules of prefixation, and are therefore canonical with respect to the affix directionality criterion; at the same time, the proposed rule aggregations cause prefixation rules to operate on suffixes, and are therefore noncanonical with respect to the stem operand criterion.

7.2   Lithuanian

The inflection of Noon adjectives involves the aggregation of rules of prefixation with rules of suffixation to produce suffixational counterpositions. Lithuanian presents the opposite possibility, that of a rule of suffixation aggregating with rules of prefixation to produce prefixational counterpositions.

7.2.1   Lithuanian Reflexive Verbs

Reflexive verbs play an important role in the grammar and lexicon of Lithuanian. In the vast majority of cases, a reflexive verb derives from a nonreflexive verb from whose syntax and semantics it may differ in a variety of ways (Ambrazas et al. 1997: 227–234; cf. also Holvoet 2020). For example, a reflexive verb may be interpreted as a transitive verb having a reflexive or reciprocal complement bound by its subject (as in rows (a) and (b) of Table 7.6); it may be interpreted as the unaccusative counterpart of a transitive verb (as in row (c)); or it may be interpreted as having a reflexive dative argument (as in row (d)). In some instances, a reflexive verb is used to describe a habitual property of its subject's referent, without any strictly reflexive sense (as in row (e)). There are, in addition, cases in which a reflexive verb is synonymous with its nonreflexive counterpart (as in row (f)) or differs from its meaning in an idiosyncratic way (as in row (g)). Notwithstanding their syntactic and semantic variety, reflexive verbs are comparatively straightforward in the domain of morphology (Ambrazas et al. 1997: 222f.). Most reflexive verbs are distinguished from their non-reflexive counterpart by the presence of the reflexive affix -*si* or its alternant -*s*. In the case of unprefixed verbs, the reflexive affix appears word-finally: nonreflexive *kelia* 's/he raises' → reflexive *kelia-si* 's/he gets up'. In this

Table 7.6 *Differences between reflexives and their nonreflexive counterparts in Lithuanian*

	Nonreflexive	Reflexive
(a)	*Aprengiau vaiką.* 'I dressed the child.'	*Apsirengiau.* 'I dressed myself.'
(b)	*bučiuoti* 'to kiss'	*bučiuotis* 'to kiss each other'
(c)	*Jie viską pakeitė.* 'They changed everything.'	*Viskas pasikeitė.* 'Everything changed.'
(d)	*Nupirkau sūnui kepurę.* 'I bought (my) son a cap.'	*Nusipirkau kepurę.* 'I bought myself a cap.'
(e)	*Arklys spardo žemę.* 'The horse kicks the ground.'	*Arklys spardosi.* 'The horse kicks (is in the habit of kicking).'
(f)	*apžergti* 'to straddle' *bijoti* 'to be afraid'	*apsižergti* 'to straddle' *bijotis* 'to be afraid'
(g)	*atsakyti* 'to answer' *parvežti* 'to bring home (in a vehicle)'	*atsisakyti* 'to refuse, turn down, resign' *parsivežti* 'to bring along (in a vehicle)'

Table 7.7 *Infinitive forms of some unprefixed verbs in Lithuanian*

Nonreflexive		Reflexive	
imti	'to take, pick up, being'	*imti-s*	'to begin, to undertake'
kelti	'to raise, lift up'	*kelti-s*	'to get up, arise, rise'
rodyti	'to show'	*rodyti-s*	'to seem, appear'
sakyti	'to say'	*sakyti-s*	'to say oneself to be, say that one is'
tikėti	'to believe, trust'	*tikėti-s*	'to expect, hope for'

word-final position, the *-s* alternant is usual in certain forms, including the infinitive (Table 7.7) and first- and second-person plural forms (Table 7.8); the *-s* alternant also regularly appears postconsonantally in word-final position, where it is preceded by an epenthetic *i* (e.g. *kels* 's/he will raise' → *kels-i-s* 's/he will get up'). In prefixed verbs, the reflexive affix, in its full form *-si-*, appears after the prefix; in each of the reflexive forms in the partial paradigm in Table 7.9, for example, the full form of the reflexive affix appears after the Aktionsart prefix *su-*.

Verbal prefixes in Lithuanian are quite heterogeneous in character. Arkadiev (2012a) classifies them according to their function and position

Table 7.8 *Present indicative active paradigms of three Lithuanian verbs and their reflexive counterparts*

	First conjugation		Second conjugation		Third conjugation	
	LENKTI 'to bend' (nonrefl.)	LENKTIS 'to bow' (refl.)	TIKĖTI 'to believe' (nonrefl.)	TIKĖTIS 'to expect, to hope for' (refl.)	MATYTI 'to see' (nonrefl.)	MATYTIS 'to see each other, to meet, to meet socially' (refl.)
1SG	lenkiu	lenkiuo-si	tikiu	tikiuo-si	matau	matau-si
2SG	lenki	lenkie-si	tiki	tikie-si	matai	matai-si
3SG	lenkia	lenkia-si	tiki	tiki-si	mato	mato-si
1PL	lenkiame	lenkiamė-s	tikime	tikimė-s	matome	matomė-s
2PL	lenkiate	lenkiatė-s	tikite	tikitė-s	matote	matotė-s
3PL	lenkia	lenkia-si	tiki	tiki-si	mato	mato-si

(Dambriūnas et al. 1972: 60)

Table 7.9 *Present indicative active paradigms of Lithuanian SU-TIKTI 'to meet, agree' and its reflexive counterpart*

	SU-TIKTI 'to meet, agree' (nonreflexive)	SU-SI-TIKTI 'to meet with s. o.' (reflexive)
1SG	su-tinku	su-si-tinku
2SG	su-tinki	su-si-tinki
3SG	su-tinka	su-si-tinka
1PL	su-tinkame	su-si-tinkame
2PL	su-tinkate	su-si-tinkate
3PL	su-tinka	su-si-tinka

(Dambriūnas et al. 1972: 59)

as in Figure 7.1. The Aktionsart prefixes often have a perfectivizing effect, as in (12), but they may also express more specific modulations in meaning, for example inchoation (*dainuoti* 'to sing' → *už-dainuoti* 'begin to sing') or repetition (*rašyti* 'write' → *per-rašyti* 'rewrite'); for a full account of their functions, see Ambrazas et al. (1997: 234–237) and Arkadiev (2011a).

External prefixes			Internal prefixes		
permissive restrictive affirmative	negation	aspectual and modal meanings	Aktionsart preverbs	reflexive	Verb stem
te-	ne-	be-	12+	-si	

Figure 7.1 *The structure of the prefixal domain of the Lithuanian verb (Arkadiev 2012a)*

(12) Examples of perfectivizing Aktionsart prefixes in Lithuanian

baudžiau	'I was punishing'	nu-baudžiau	'I punished/have punished'
gelbėjau	'I was rescuing'	iš-gelbėjau	'I rescued/have rescued'
rašiau	'I was writing'	pa-rašiau	'I wrote/have written'
stačiau	'I was building'	pa-stačiau	'I built/have built'
vykdžiau	'I was accomplishing'	į-vykdžiau	'I accomplished/have accomplished'

(Ambrazas et al. 1997: 234)

Unlike the internal prefixes in Figure 7.1, the three external prefixes are not lexically conditioned, but have regular grammatical functions. In the permissive mood, *te-* is prefixed to a third-person form, as in (13a); *te-* also serves the restrictive function exemplified in (13b).[7] The prefix *ne-* expresses negation, as in *parašė* 's/he wrote' → *neparašė* 's/he didn't write'.

(13) a. *te-sako*
PERMISS-say.PRS.3
'may he say, let him say' (Dambriūnas et al. 1972: 131)
b. *Te-atėj-o   Jon-as.*
RSTR-come-PST Jonas-NOM.SG
'Only Jonas came.' (Arkadiev 2010: 27)

The prefix *be-* is used to express various aspectual and modal meanings (Arkadiev 2011b). For example, proximative/avertive forms involve the use of a finite form of *būti* 'be' in combination with the appropriate inflected form of a verb's present active participle, prefixed with *be-*; the paradigm in Table 7.10 illustrates. In addition, the prefixes *te-* and *ne-* combine with *be-* in order to express positive and negative polarity in the continuative aspect, as in (14) (Arkadiev 2011b, 2012a).

(14) a. *Pernai   tėvas   te-be-dirb-dav-o   naktimis.*
last.year   father.NOM.SG   POS-CNT-work-HAB-PST   night.INS.PL
'Last year, father still used to work at night.'

---

[7] See Arkadiev 2010 for a detailed discussion of these uses of *te-*.

Table 7.10 *Past proximative/avertive paradigm of Lithuanian* ATEĪTI *'to come'*

	Masculine	Feminine
1SG	*buvau be-at-einąs* 'I was coming'	*buvau be-at-einanti*
2SG	*buvai be-at-einąs*	*buvai be-at-einanti*
3SG	*buvo be-at-einąs*	*buvo be-at-einanti*
1PL	*buvome be-at-einą*	*buvome be-at-einančios*
2PL	*buvote be-at-einą*	*buvote be-at-einančios*
3PL	*buvo be-at-einą*	*buvo be-at-einančios*

(Dambriūnas et al. 1972: 125; Arkadiev 2011b)

Table 7.11 *Positive and negative present indicative active paradigms of Lithuanian* LENKTIS *'to bow'*

	positive	negative
1SG	*lenkiuo-si*	*ne-si-lenkiu*
2SG	*lenkie-si*	*ne-si-lenki*
3SG	*lenkia-si*	*ne-si-lenkia*
1PL	*lenkiamė-s*	*ne-si-lenkiame*
2PL	*lenkiatė-s*	*ne-si-lenkiate*
3PL	*lenkia-si*	*ne-si-lenkia*

(Dambriūnas et al. 1972: 60)

b. *Šiemet   tėvas   dešimtą   valandą   ne-be-dirb-a.*
   this.year father.NOM.SG tenth.ACC.SG hour.ACC.SG NEG-CNT-work-PRS
   'This year father does not work at 10 o'clock any more.'

(Arkadiev 2011b)

Like the Aktionsart prefixes, all three of these grammatical prefixes may host the reflexive affix. Thus, while the reflexive marker is word-final in the positive forms of LEŇKTIS 'to bow', its placement is preverbal in the corresponding negative forms, as in Table 7.11. Similarly, the reflexive marker follows the aspectual *be-* prefix in the past avertive form in (15) and follows the modal *te-* prefix in the permissive form *te-si-moko* 'may he learn, let him learn'.

(15)   *Jis buvo be-si-rengiąs   eiti   pas   mus*[.]
       He was CNT-REFL-get.ready.PRS.ACT.PTCP   to.go chez us
       'He was getting ready to go to our place.'

(Dambriūnas et al. 1972: 125)

198 *Rule Aggregation*

The external prefixes *te-*, *ne-*, and *be-* may all combine with verbs carrying an Aktionsart prefix, to produce verb forms having two or three prefixes; if a verb form of this sort is reflexive, the reflexive marker follows the full prefix sequence.[8] Table 7.12 lists forms in which the reflexive affix is preceded by two prefixes: positive continuative forms with *te-be-*, negative continuative forms with *ne-be-*, negative forms with *ne-* followed by an Aktionsart prefix, and forms with restrictive or permissive *te-* followed by an Aktionsart prefix. Table 7.13 lists forms in which the reflexive affix is preceded by three prefixes: positive continuative forms with *te-be-* followed by an Aktionsart prefix and negative continuative forms with *ne-be-* followed by an Aktionsart prefix.

7.2.2 Rule Aggregation in Lithuanian Reflexive Verb Forms
In the analysis that I shall propose for reflexive marking in Lithuanian, I assume that each stem of a verbal lexeme belongs to a particular inflection class, where membership in a given inflection class involves membership in the intersection three subclasses:

(i) a conjugation subclass (the traditional first, second, and third conjugations),[9]

---

[8] In past work on Lithuanian reflexive morphology, it is sometimes asserted that in the event that a reflexive verb form begins with two or more prefixes, the reflexive marker only follows the first of these (Nevis & Joseph 1992; Embick & Noyer 2001; Arregi & Nevins 2012: 252ff.; Crysmann & Bonami 2016: 367); as support for this claim, forms such as (i) are cited. Closer scrutiny of the evidence, however, reveals that this is an exceptional pattern. Šereikaitė 2017 argues that the *pa-* in *pažinti* 'to be acquainted with' is not a true lexical prefix, but is, in some sense, part of the root; that would account for the fact that it is preceded rather than followed by the reflexive marker in (i). But *pa-* is clearly an Aktionsart prefix in some verb forms (cf. again (12)), and there are even attestations of reflexive forms of *pažinti* in which *pa-* hosts the reflexive affix, as for example in *pa-si-žino* 'they became acquainted with'. Perhaps one should say that *pažin-* is in the process of being reanalyzed as an unprefixed stem; this would account for the attestation both of conservative forms such as *pasižino* and of innovative forms such as (i).

(i) *su-si-pa-žinti*
PRF-REFL-PRF-be.acquainted.with.INF
'to become acquainted with'

[9] The traditional postulation of three conjugations overlooks certain complexities in the analysis of Lithuanian inflection classes (Pakerys 2011, 2021; Arkadiev 2012b); because these are orthogonal to the analysis of reflexive morphotactics proposed here, I assume the traditional analysis as a matter of expository convenience. The aggregation-based analysis in no way depends on this assumption.

Table 7.12 *Some Lithuanian reflexive verb forms in which two prefixes precede the reflexive affix*

(All forms are attested in the Corpus of the Contemporary Lithuanian Language; https://klc.vdu.lt/en/.)

Preceding prefixes	Reflexive verb form		Related infinitive
continuative *te-be-*	*te-be-si-džiaugia*	'[3rd person] still rejoice(s)'	(*džiaugti-s* 'to rejoice')
	te-be-si-matė	'[3rd person] is/are still visible'	(*matyti-s* 'to be visible')
	te-be-si-domiu	'I am still interested'	(*domėti-s* 'to be interested')
	te-be-si-laiko	'[3rd person] still maintain(s)'	(*laikyti-s* 'to abide')
continuative *ne-be-*	*ne-be-si-džiaugia*	'[3rd person]is no longer happy'	(*džiaugti-s* 'to rejoice')
	ne-be-si-matė	'[3rd person] no longer saw'	(*matyti-s* 'to be visible')
	ne-be-si-domiu	'I'm no longer interested'	(*domėti-s* 'to be interested')
	ne-be-si-aiškinu	'I don't explain anymore'	(*aiškinti-s* 'to clarify')
	ne-be-si-laiko	'[3rd person] no longer adhere(s)'	(*laikyti-s* 'to abide')
negative *ne-* + Aktionsart prefix	*ne-ap-si-metu*	'I don't pretend'	(*ap-si-mesti* 'to pretend')
	ne-at-si-bundu	'I don't wake up'	(*at-si-busti* 'to wake up')
	ne-į-si-dėmiu	'I ignore'	(*į-si-dėmėti* 'to take note, pay attention')
	ne-iš-si-aiškinu	'I don't find out'	(*iš-si-aiškinti* 'to find out')
	ne-nu-si-menu	'I don't become sad'	(*nu-si-minti* 'to become sad, get upset')
	ne-pa-si-slėpiau	'I did not hide'	(*pasislėpti* 'to hide')
	ne-par-si-duodu	'I don't give up'	(cf. *parduoti* 'to sell')
	ne-per-si-dirbu	'I don't work'	(*per-si-dirbti* 'to work too much')

Table 7.12 (cont.)

Preceding prefixes	Reflexive verb form		Related infinitive
	ne-pra-si-dedu	'I don't start'	(*pra-si-dėti* 'to begin')
	ne-pri-si-menu	'I don't remember'	(*pri-si-minti* 'to remember')
	ne-su-si-tiksime	'we won't meet up'	(*su-si-tikti* 'to meet up')
	ne-su-si-darau	'I don't form'	(*su-si-daryti* 'to form')
	ne-už-si-būnu	'I don't stay'	(*už-si-būti* 'to linger')
restrictive *te-* + Aktionsart prefix	*te-pa-si-taiko*	'it rarely occurs'	(*pa-si-taikyti* 'to occur')
	te-pa-si-tikiu	'I only trust'	(*pa-si-tikėti* 'to trust')
permissive *te-* + Aktionsart prefix	*te-nu-si-leidžia*	'let [3rd person] land'	(*nu-si-leisti* 'to land')
	te-at-si-mena	'let [3rd person] remember'	(*at-si-minti* 'to remember, keep in mind')
	te-pri-si-mena	'let [3rd person] remember'	(*pri-si-minti* 'to remember')

Table 7.13 *Some Lithuanian reflexive verb forms in which three prefixes precede the reflexive affix*

(All forms are attested in the Corpus of the Contemporary Lithuanian Language; https://klc.vdu.lt/en/.)

Preceding prefixes	Reflexive verb form		Related infinitive
continuative *te-be-* + Aktionsart prefix	*te-be-pa-si-tikiu* *te-be-pri-si-menu*	'I still trust' 'I still remember'	(*pa-si-tikėti* 'to trust') (*pri-si-minti* 'to remember')
continuative *ne-be-* + Aktionsart prefix	*ne-be-at-si-kėlė*	'[3rd person] didn't get up anymore'	(*at-si-kelti* 'to get up')
	ne-be-pa-si-tikiu	'I no longer trust'	(*pa-si-tikėti* 'to trust')
	ne-be-pri-si-menu	'I don't remember anymore'	(*pri-si-minti* 'to remember')
	ne-be-su-si-rinks	'[3rd person] will no longer gather'	(*su-si-rinkti* 'to gather')

(ii) one of the Aktionsart prefix subclasses in Table 7.14, and
(iii) one of the reflexivity subclasses (either the reflexive subclass or the nonreflexive subclass).[10]

What members of the same conjugation subclass have in common is that their morphosyntactic content is realized in the same way. What members of the same Aktionsart prefix subclass have in common is that they exhibit the same

---

[10] One might object to the claim that Lithuanian verbs' Aktionsart prefixes and reflexive affixes are marks of inflection-class membership. One might instead try to claim that these are all derivational affixes; in support of this point of view, one might cite the idiosyncratic semantics of *iš-virsti* 'to fall down' (← *virsti* 'to turn into, become') and *iš-rinkti* 'to elect' (← *rinkti* 'to gather') or the valence change of *pasikeisti* 'to change (intransitive)' (← *pakeisti* 'to change (transitive)') observed in Table 7.6.

Such an argument, however, would embody a confusion between the use of morphology *x* to derive a stem belonging to some inflection class C and the inflectional use of morphology *x* to express a stem's membership in inflection class C. In Lithuanian, reflexive verb forms do not embody a single derivational category; rather, they serve a variety of distinct functions (exemplified in Table 7.6), and therefore constitute a category having the morphomic character of an inflection class (Aronoff 1994). For their part, the Aktionsart prefixes interact with reflexive morphology in the same way as the inflectional prefixes *te-*, *ne-*, and *be-*: the host of a preverbal reflexive affix may be an Aktionsart prefix, as in Table 7.9; an inflectional prefix, as in Table 7.11; or a composite of prefixes of these sorts, as in Table 7.12. The fact that Aktionsart prefixes are composable with the inflectional prefixes *te-*, *ne-*, and *be-* suggests that they, too, are inflectional; but unlike *te-*, *ne-*, and *be-*, the Aktionsart prefixes have the lexically discriminative function of inflection-class markings.

Table 7.14 *Aktionsart prefix subclasses of Lithuanian verbs*

Aktionsart prefix subclass	Sample member		Aktionsart prefix subclass	Sample member	
ap-	*ap-daužyti*	'to damage, beat'	**par-**	*par-vežti*	'to bring home (in a vehicle)'
at-	*at-rasti*	'to find, discover'	**per-**	*per-kelti*	'to move, transfer'
į-	*į-kurti*	'to found'	**pri-**	*pri-dėti*	'to add'
iš-	*iš-rinkti*	'to elect'	**su-**	*su-tikti*	'to meet, agree'
nu-	*nu-pirkti*	'to buy'	**už-**	*už-imti*	'to occupy'
pa-	*pa-rodyti*	'to show'	no prefix	*imti*	'to take, pick up'

(Dambriūnas et al. 1972)

preverb or lack of any preverb. What members of the reflexive subclass have in common is that they exhibit reflexive morphology (whatever the content that this may express), which members of the nonreflexive subclass uniformly lack.

Subclasses of the same type do not intersect; for instance, if a lexeme's stem belongs to the first conjugation, then it does not belong to the second conjugation, or if a lexeme's stem belongs to the *ap-* prefix subclass, then it does not belong to the *at-* prefix subclass. (This does not, however, exclude the possibility that two distinct lexemes might have homophonous stems belonging to distinct Aktionsart prefix classes; for example, APRODYTI 'to show everything' and ATRODYTI 'to seem' both have a stem having the form *rod-*, but as the stem of APRODYTI, *rod-*$_1$ belongs to the *ap-* prefix subclass, and as the stem of ATRODYTI, *rod-*$_2$ instead belongs to the *at-* prefix subclass.)

Subclasses of different types crosscut each other. In Table 7.15, for instance, the membership of the verbs in the three conjugation subclasses is orthogonal to their membership in the *pa-*, *nu-*, and *ap-* prefix subclasses. Similarly, Table 7.16 contrasts nonreflexive verbs in several Aktionsart prefix subclasses with reflexive verbs belonging to the same subclasses.

Recall from Section 2.1 that a stem's inflection-class membership is represented by means of a function ***ic*** from stems to sets of inflection-class properties. This means that in the inflection of a Lithuanian verb stem Z, the value of ***ic***(Z) is a set $\{\alpha\ \beta\ \gamma\}$ of three inflection-class properties: a conjugation subclass property α, an Aktionsart prefix subclass property β, and a reflexivity subclass property γ. Table 7.17 lists the value of ***ic*** for several Lithuanian verb stems.

The illustrative fragment of Lithuanian verb inflection that will form the basis for this analysis is the set of partial paradigms in Table 7.18; these are the

Table 7.15 *The orthogonal membership of nine Lithuanian verbs in the three conjugation subclasses and in the* pa-, nu-, *and* ap- *prefix subclasses*

		Aktionsart prefix subclass to which the form's stem belongs		
		pa- subclass	*nu-* subclass	*ap-* subclass
Conjugation subclass to which the form's stem belongs	First	*pa-béga* 's/he runs'	*nu-krinta* 's/he falls'	*ap-kalba* 's/he slanders'
	Second	*pa-ilsi* 's/he rests'	*nu-gali* 's/he defeats'	*ap-žiūri* 's/he has a look at'
	Third	*pa-daro* 's/he makes'	*nu-krapšto* 's/he pulls off'	*ap-moko* 's/he trains'

(Dambriūnas et al. 1972)

present indicative paradigms (simple and negative continuative) of the unprefixed verb RODYTI 'to show', its reflexive counterpart RODYTI-S 'to show up', the prefixed verb PA-RODYTI 'to show', and its reflexive counterpart PA-SI-RODYTI 'to appear'.

The personal terminations exhibited by the partial paradigms in Table 7.18 are defined by the rules in (16); these are rules of type R_{TERM}. The simple rules 〚**-au**〛 and 〚**-ai**〛 define the first- and second-person singular terminations, and the composite rules (〚**-me**〛 ∘ 〚**-o**〛) and (〚**-te**〛 ∘ 〚**-o**〛) define the first- and second-person plural terminations. In the third conjugation (to which the forms in Table 7.18 belong), the 〚**-o**〛 rule applies by default in third-person forms (whether singular or plural). In the simple inflection of the unprefixed nonreflexive verb RODYTI 'to show', rules (16a–c, f, g) serve as FERs; thus, the content and form cells in part (a) of Table 7.19 are realized through the application of 〚**-au**〛.

(16) Rules of type R_{TERM}: personal termination rules (simple and composite)
    a.   〚**-au**〛 : [V, {CONJ.3 1sg} : -*au*]
    b.   〚**-ai**〛 : [V, {CONJ.3 2sg} : -*ai*]
    c.   〚**-o**〛 : [V, {CONJ.3} : -*o*]
    d.   〚**-me**〛 : [V, {1pl} : -*me*]
    e.   〚**-te**〛 : [V, {2pl} : -*te*]
    f.   (〚**-me**〛 ∘ 〚**-o**〛) : [V, {CONJ.3 1pl} : -*ome*]
    g.   (〚**-te**〛 ∘ 〚**-o**〛) : [V, {CONJ.3 2pl} : -*ote*]

The simple reflexive rules in (17) are rules of type R_{REFL}. For the simple inflection of unprefixed reflexives, a rule of type R_{REFL} composes with a rule of type R_{TERM} to yield a composite rule, in accordance with the FER pattern (18).

Table 7.16 *The orthogonal membership of twenty Lithuanian verbs in ten Aktionsart prefix subclasses and in the reflexivity subclasses*

Aktionsart prefix subclass to which the form's stem belongs	Reflexivity subclass to which the form's stem belongs			
	Nonreflexive subclass		Reflexive subclass	
ap- subclass	*ap-daužyti*	'to damage, beat'	*ap-si-daužyti*	'to bang about'
at- subclass	*at-rasti*	'to find, discover'	*at-si-rasti*	'to appear, to be found'
į- subclass	*į-kurti*	'to found'	*į-si-kurti*	'to establish oneself, to settle down (in a place)'
iš- subclass	*iš-rinkti*	'to elect'	*iš-si-rinkti*	'to choose for oneself'
nu- subclass	*nu-pirkti*	'to buy'	*nu-si-pirkti*	'to buy for oneself'
pa- subclass	*pa-rodyti*	'to show'	*pa-si-rodyti*	'to appear'
par- subclass	*par-vežti*	'to bring home (in a vehicle)'	*par-si-vežti*	'to bring along (in a vehicle)'
per- subclass	*per-kelti*	'to move, transfer'	*per-si-kelti*	'to move, remove (to another place)'
su- subclass	*su-tikti*	'to meet, agree'	*su-si-tikti*	'to meet each other'
už- subclass	*už-imti*	'to occupy'	*už-si-imti*	'to be busy, to be occupied'

Table 7.17 *Inflection-class property sets of twenty-six Lithuanian verbal lexemes*

Lexeme L	Present-tense stem Z of L	Value of $ic(Z)$
AP-KALBĖTI 'to slander'	*kalb-*	{CONJ.1 Aktprf.*ap* −refl}
AT-RASTI 'to find, discover'	*rand-*$_1$	{CONJ.1 Aktprf.*at* −refl}
AT-SI-RASTI 'to appear, to be found'	*rand-*$_2$	{CONJ.1 Aktprf.*at* +refl}
Į-KURTI 'to found'	*kuri-*$_1$	{CONJ.1 Aktprf.*į* −refl}
Į-SI-KURTI 'to settle down (in a place)'	*kuri-*$_2$	{CONJ.1 Aktprf.*į* +refl}
IŠ-RINKTI 'to elect'	*renk-*$_1$	{CONJ.1 Aktprf.*iš* −refl}
IŠ-SI-RINKTI 'to choose for oneself'	*renk-*$_2$	{CONJ.1 Aktprf.*iš* +refl}
LENKTI 'to bend'	*lenki-*$_1$	{CONJ.1 Aktprf.none −refl}
LENKTI-S 'to bow'	*lenki-*$_2$	{CONJ.1 Aktprf.none +refl}
SU-TIKTI 'to meet, agree'	*tink-*$_1$	{CONJ.1 Aktprf.*su* −refl}
SU-SI-TIKTI 'to meet with s. o.'	*tink-*$_2$	{CONJ.1 Aktprf.*su* +refl}
UŽ-IMTI 'to occupy'	*im-*$_1$	{CONJ.1 Aktprf.*už* −refl}
UŽ-SI-IMTI 'to be busy, to be occupied'	*im-*$_2$	{CONJ.1 Aktprf.*už* +refl}
TIKĖTI 'to believe'	*tiki-*$_1$	{CONJ.2 Aktprf.none −refl}
TIKĖTI-S 'to expect'	*tiki-*$_2$	{CONJ.2 Aktprf.none +refl}
NU-GALĖTI 'to defeat'	*gali-*	{CONJ.2 Aktprf.*nu* −refl}
PA-ILSĖTI 'to rest'	*ilsi-*	{CONJ.2 Aktprf.*pa* −refl}
AP-DAUŽYTI 'to damage, beat'	*dauž-*$_1$	{CONJ.3 Aktprf.*ap* −refl}
AP-SI-DAUŽYTI 'to bang about'	*dauž-*$_2$	{CONJ.3 Aktprf.*ap* +refl}
MATYTI 'to see'	*mat-*$_1$	{CONJ.3 Aktprf.none −refl}
MATYTI-S 'to meet'	*mat-*$_2$	{CONJ.3 Aktprf.none +refl}
NU-KRAPŠTYTI 'to pull off'	*krapšt-*	{CONJ.3 Aktprf.*nu* −refl}
RODYTI 'to show'	*rod-*$_1$	{CONJ.3 Aktprf.none −refl}
PA-RODYTI 'to show'	*rod-*$_2$	{CONJ.3 Aktprf.*pa* −refl}
RODYTI-S 'to show up'	*rod-*$_3$	{CONJ.3 Aktprf.none +refl}
PA-SI-RODYTI 'to appear'	*rod-*$_4$	{CONJ.3 Aktprf.*pa* +refl}

The composites defined by (18) are listed in (19). These composites serve as FERs in the simple inflection of unprefixed reflexives. Thus, the content and form cells in part (b) of Table 7.19 are realized through the application of the FER ([[-si]] ∘ [[-o]]) in (19c), a rule of type (R_{REFL} ∘ R_{TERM}).

(17)   Rules of type R_{REFL}: simple rules realizing reflexiveness
    a. [[-si]] : [V, {+refl} : -*si*]
    b. [[-s]] : [V, {pl +refl} : X*e* → X*ės*]

Table 7.18 *Present indicative forms (simple and negative continuative) of four Lithuanian verbs*

		RODYTI 'to show'	PA-RODYTI 'to show'	RODYTI-S 'to show up'	PA-SI-RODYTI 'to appear'
Simple	1SG	*rodau*	*pa-rodau*	*rodau-si*	*pa-si-rodau*
	2SG	*rodai*	*pa-rodai*	*rodai-si*	*pa-si-rodai*
	3SG	*rodo*	*pa-rodo*	*rodo-si*	*pa-si-rodo*
	1PL	*rodome*	*pa-rodome*	*rodomė-s*	*pa-si-rodome*
	2PL	*rodote*	*pa-rodote*	*rodotė-s*	*pa-si-rodote*
	3PL	*rodo*	*pa-rodo*	*rodo-si*	*pa-si-rodo*
Negative continuative	1SG	*ne-be-rodau*	*ne-be-pa-rodau*	*ne-be-si-rodau*	*ne-be-pa-si-rodau*
	2SG	*ne-be-rodai*	*ne-be-pa-rodai*	*ne-be-si-rodai*	*ne-be-pa-si-rodai*
	3SG	*ne-be-rodo*	*ne-be-pa-rodo*	*ne-be-si-rodo*	*ne-be-pa-si-rodo*
	1PL	*ne-be-rodome*	*ne-be-pa-rodome*	*ne-be-si-rodome*	*ne-be-pa-si-rodome*
	2PL	*ne-be-rodote*	*ne-be-pa-rodote*	*ne-be-si-rodote*	*ne-be-pa-si-rodote*
	3PL	*ne-be-rodo*	*ne-be-pa-rodo*	*ne-be-si-rodo*	*ne-be-pa-si-rodo*

Table 7.19 *The morphotactics of five Lithuanian verb forms from Table 7.18*

(a)	Content cell: Form cell: ⎯ FER → Realized cell:	⟨RODYTI, {pos ind prs 1sg}⟩ ⟨*rod*-₁, {CONJ.3 Aktprf.none −refl ind prs 1sg}⟩ [**-au**] ⟨*rodau*, {CONJ.3 Aktprf.none −refl pos ind prs 1sg}⟩	'I show' (= (16a), a rule of type R_{TERM})
(b)	Content cell: Form cell: ⎯ FER → Realized cell:	⟨RODYTI-S, {pos ind prs 3sg}⟩ ⟨*rod*-₂, {CONJ.3 Aktprf.none +refl pos ind prs 3sg}⟩ [[**-si**] ∘ [**-o**]] ⟨*rodosi*, {CONJ.3 Aktprf.none +refl pos ind prs 3sg}⟩	's/he shows up' (= (19c), a rule of type (R_{REFL} ∘ R_{TERM}))
(c)	Content cell: Form cell: ⎯ FER → Realized cell:	⟨PA-RODYTI, {neg cnt ind prs 3sg}⟩ ⟨*rod*-₃, {CONJ.3 neg cnt Aktprf.**pa** −refl ind prs 3sg}⟩ ((([[**ne-**] ∘ [**be-**]) ∘ [**pa-**]) ∘ [**-o**]]) ⟨*nebeparodo*, {CONJ.3 neg cnt Aktprf.**pa** −refl ind prs 3sg}⟩	's/he isn't showing' (= (22m), a rule of type (R_{PREF} ∘ R_{TERM}))
(d)	Content cell: Form cell: ⎯ FER → Realized cell:	⟨PA-SI-RODYTI, {pos ind prs 1pl}⟩ ⟨*rod*-₄, {CONJ.3 Aktprf.**pa** +refl pos ind prs 1pl}⟩ ([[**-si**] Ⓐ [[**pa-**]) ∘ ([**-me**] ∘ [**-o**]]) ⟨*pasirodome*, {CONJ.3 Aktprf.**pa** +refl pos ind prs 1pl}⟩	'we appear' (= (25d), a rule of type ((R_{REFL} Ⓐ R_{PREF}) ∘ R_{TERM}))
(e)	Content cell: Form cell: ⎯ FER → Realized cell:	⟨PA-SI-RODYTI, {neg cnt ind prs 3sg}⟩ ⟨*rod*-₄, {CONJ.3 neg cnt Aktprf.**pa** +refl ind prs 3sg}⟩ ([[**-si**] Ⓐ (([**ne-**] ∘ [**be-**]) ∘ [**pa-**]) ∘ [**-o**]]) ⟨*nebepasirodo*, {CONJ.3 neg cnt Aktprf.**pa** +refl ind prs 3sg}⟩	's/he isn't appearing' (= (25m), a rule of type ((R_{REFL} Ⓐ R_{PREF}) ∘ R_{TERM}))

208 *Rule Aggregation*

(18) FER pattern for unprefixed reflexives
Where R_{TERM} is a termination rule (any of (16a–c,f,g)) and R_{REFL} is a reflexive rule, ($R_{REFL} \circ R_{TERM}$) is a FER.

(19) Composite rules of type ($R_{REFL} \circ R_{TERM}$) defined by (18)
   a. ([[-si]] ∘ [[-au]]) : [V, {CONJ.3 +refl 1sg} : *-ausi*]
   b. ([[-si]] ∘ [[-ai]]) : [V, {CONJ.3 +refl 2sg} : *-aisi*]
   c. ([[-si]] ∘ [[-o]]) : [V, {CONJ.3 +refl} : *-osi*]
   d. ([[-s]] ∘ ([[-me]] ∘ [[-o]])) : [V, {CONJ.3 +refl 1pl} : *-omės*]
   e. ([[-s]] ∘ ([[-te]] ∘ [[-o]])) : [V, {CONJ.3 +refl 2pl} : *-otės*]

The definition of the prefixed forms in Table 7.18 involves the prefixation rules in (20); these are rules of type R_{PREF}. Three simple prefixation rules are relevant for defining the forms in Table 7.18: the negative prefix rule [[**ne-**]], the continuative prefix rule [[**be-**]], and the Aktionsart prefix rule [[**pa-**]]. The [[**ne-**]] rule composes with both [[**be-**]] and [[**pa-**]] (as in (20d) and (20e)), and the negative continuative composite ([[**ne-**]] ∘ [[**be-**]]) composes with [[**pa-**]] (as in (20f)). In accordance with the FER pattern (21), rules of type P_{PREF} compose with rules of type R_{TERM} to yield composites such as those in (22); these are the FERs for the prefixed nonreflexive verb forms in Table 7.18. Thus, the content and form cells in part (c) of Table 7.19 are realized through the application of the FER ((([[**ne-**]] ∘ [[**be-**]]) ∘ [[**pa-**]]) ∘ [[-o]]) in (22m), a rule of type ($R_{PREF} \circ R_{TERM}$).

(20) Rules of type R_{PREF}: prefixational rules unspecified for reflexiveness (simple and composite)
   a. [[**ne-**]] : [V, {neg} : *ne-*]
   b. [[**be-**]] : [V, {cnt} : *be-*]
   c. [[**pa-**]] : [V, {Aktprf.**pa**} : *pa-*]
   d. ([[**ne-**]] ∘ [[**be-**]]) : [V, {neg cnt} : *nebe-*]
   e. ([[**ne-**]] ∘ [[**pa-**]]) : [V, {neg Aktprf.**pa**} : *nepa-*]
   f. (([[**ne-**]] ∘ [[**be-**]]) ∘ [[**pa-**]]) : [V, {neg cnt Aktprf.**pa**} : *nebepa-*]

(21) FER pattern for prefixed nonreflexives
Where R_{TERM} is a termination rule (any of (16a–c, f, g)) and R_{PREF} is a prefixational rule, ($R_{PREF} \circ R_{TERM}$) is a FER.

(22) Composite rules of type ($R_{PREF} \circ R_{TERM}$) defined by (21)
   a. ([[**pa-**]] ∘ [[-au]]) :   [V, {CONJ.3 Aktprf.**pa** 1sg} : X→ *pa-X-au*]
   b. ([[**pa-**]] ∘ [[-ai]]) :   [V, {CONJ.3 Aktprf.**pa** 2sg} : X→ *pa-X-ai*]
   c. ([[**pa-**]] ∘ [[-o]]) :   [V, {CONJ.3 Aktprf.**pa**} : X→ *pa-X-o*]

7.2 Lithuanian   209

    d. $(\llbracket\textbf{pa-}\rrbracket \circ (\llbracket\textbf{-me}\rrbracket \circ \llbracket\textbf{-o}\rrbracket))$:   [V, {CONJ.3 Aktprf.**pa** 1pl} :
                                                                                                X→ *pa-X-ome*]
    e. $(\llbracket\textbf{pa-}\rrbracket \circ (\llbracket\textbf{-te}\rrbracket \circ \llbracket\textbf{-o}\rrbracket))$:   [V, {CONJ.3 Aktprf.**pa** 2pl} :
                                                                                                 X→ *pa-X-ote*]
    f. $(((\llbracket\textbf{ne-}\rrbracket \circ \llbracket\textbf{be-}\rrbracket) \circ \llbracket\textbf{-au}\rrbracket))$:   [V, {CONJ.3 neg cnt 1sg} :
                                                                                                 X→ *nebe-X-au*]
    g. $(((\llbracket\textbf{ne-}\rrbracket \circ \llbracket\textbf{be-}\rrbracket) \circ \llbracket\textbf{-ai}\rrbracket))$:   [V, {CONJ.3 neg cnt 2sg} :
                                                                                                 X→ *nebe-X-ai*]
    h. $(((\llbracket\textbf{ne-}\rrbracket \circ \llbracket\textbf{be-}\rrbracket) \circ \llbracket\textbf{-o}\rrbracket))$:   [V, {CONJ.3 neg cnt} :
                                                                                                 X→ *nebe-X-o*]
    i. $(((\llbracket\textbf{ne-}\rrbracket \circ \llbracket\textbf{be-}\rrbracket) \circ (\llbracket\textbf{-me}\rrbracket \circ \llbracket\textbf{-o}\rrbracket)))$: [V, {CONJ.3 neg cnt 1pl} :
                                                                                                 X→ *nebe-X-ome*]
    j. $(((\llbracket\textbf{ne-}\rrbracket \circ \llbracket\textbf{be-}\rrbracket) \circ (\llbracket\textbf{-te}\rrbracket \circ \llbracket\textbf{-o}\rrbracket)))$: [V, {CONJ.3 neg cnt 2pl} :
                                                                                                 X→ *nebe-X-ote*]
    k. $((((\llbracket\textbf{ne-}\rrbracket \circ \llbracket\textbf{be-}\rrbracket) \circ \llbracket\textbf{pa-}\rrbracket) \circ \llbracket\textbf{-au}\rrbracket))$: [V, {CONJ.3 neg cnt Aktprf.**pa** 1sg} :
                                                                                                 X→ *nebepa-X-au*]
    l. $((((\llbracket\textbf{ne-}\rrbracket \circ \llbracket\textbf{be-}\rrbracket) \circ \llbracket\textbf{pa-}\rrbracket) \circ \llbracket\textbf{-ai}\rrbracket))$: [V, {CONJ.3 neg cnt Aktprf.**pa** 2sg} :
                                                                                                 X→ *nebepa-X-ai*]
    m. $((((\llbracket\textbf{ne-}\rrbracket \circ \llbracket\textbf{be-}\rrbracket) \circ \llbracket\textbf{pa-}\rrbracket) \circ \llbracket\textbf{-o}\rrbracket))$: [V, {CONJ.3 neg cnt Aktprf.**pa**} :
                                                                                                 X→ *nebepa-X-o*]
    n. $((((\llbracket\textbf{ne-}\rrbracket \circ \llbracket\textbf{be-}\rrbracket) \circ \llbracket\textbf{pa-}\rrbracket) \circ$ [V, {CONJ.3 neg cnt Aktprf.**pa** 1pl} :
        $(\llbracket\textbf{-me}\rrbracket \circ \llbracket\textbf{-o}\rrbracket))$:   X→ *nebepa-X-ome*]
    o. $((((\llbracket\textbf{ne-}\rrbracket \circ \llbracket\textbf{be-}\rrbracket) \circ \llbracket\textbf{pa-}\rrbracket) \circ$ [V, {CONJ.3 neg cnt Aktprf.**pa** 2pl} :
        $(\llbracket\textbf{-te}\rrbracket \circ \llbracket\textbf{-o}\rrbracket))$:   X→ *nebepa-X-ote*]
    etc.

Additional prefixation rules are necessary to account for prefixed reflexive forms. Each of these additional rules is a rule of type (R_{REFL} Ⓐ R_{PREF}), the aggregation of $\llbracket\textbf{-si}\rrbracket$ with a rule of type R_{PREF}, such as the rule aggregations in (23); the aggregation of $\llbracket\textbf{-si}\rrbracket$ with a prefixation rule R entails the suffixation of *-si* to the simple or composite prefix introduced by R. In accordance with the FER pattern in (24), the rule aggregations in (23) compose with the rules of type R_{TERM} in (16a–c,f,g) to yield composites such as those in (25); these composite rules of type ((R_{REFL} Ⓐ R_{PREF}) $\circ$ R_{TERM}) are the FERs for the prefixed reflexive verb forms in Table 7.18. Thus, the content and form cells in parts (d) and (e) of Table 7.19 are realized through the application of the FERs $((\llbracket\textbf{-si}\rrbracket$ Ⓐ $\llbracket\textbf{pa-}\rrbracket) \circ (\llbracket\textbf{-me}\rrbracket \circ \llbracket\textbf{-o}\rrbracket))$ in (25d) and $((\llbracket\textbf{-si}\rrbracket$ Ⓐ $((\llbracket\textbf{ne-}\rrbracket \circ \llbracket\textbf{be-}\rrbracket) \circ \llbracket\textbf{pa-}\rrbracket)) \circ \llbracket\textbf{-o}\rrbracket)$ in (25m).

(23)   Rule aggregations of type (R_{REFL} Ⓐ R_{PREF})
        a. $(\llbracket\textbf{-si}\rrbracket$ Ⓐ $\llbracket\textbf{ne-}\rrbracket)$:   [V, {neg +refl} : *nesi-*]
        b. $(\llbracket\textbf{-si}\rrbracket$ Ⓐ $\llbracket\textbf{be-}\rrbracket)$:   [V, {cnt +refl} : *besi-*]
        c. $(\llbracket\textbf{-si}\rrbracket$ Ⓐ $\llbracket\textbf{pa-}\rrbracket)$:   [V, {Aktprf.**pa** +refl} : *pasi-*]
        d. $(\llbracket\textbf{-si}\rrbracket$ Ⓐ $(\llbracket\textbf{ne-}\rrbracket \circ \llbracket\textbf{be-}\rrbracket))$:   [V, {neg cnt +refl} : *nebesi-*]

210 *Rule Aggregation*

      e. (⟦-si⟧ Ⓐ (⟦ne-⟧ ∘ ⟦pa-⟧)) :   [V, {neg Aktprf.*pa* +refl} : *nepasi-*]
      f. (⟦-si⟧ Ⓐ ((⟦ne-⟧ ∘ ⟦be-⟧) ∘   [V, {neg cnt Aktprf.*pa* +refl} :
         ⟦pa-⟧)) :   *nebepasi-*]

(24)   FER pattern for prefixed reflexives
        Where R_{TERM} is a termination rule (any of (16a–c,f,g)) and
        (R_{REFL} Ⓐ R_{PREF}) is a rule aggregation in (23), ((R_{REFL} Ⓐ R_{PREF}) ∘ R_{TERM}) is
        a FER.

(25)   Composite rules of type ((R_{REFL} Ⓐ R_{PREF}) ∘ R_{TERM}) defined by (24)
      a. ((⟦-si⟧ Ⓐ ⟦pa-⟧) ∘ ⟦-au⟧) : [V, {CONJ.3 Aktprf.**pa** +refl 1sg} :
                                            X→ *pasi-X-au*]
      b. ((⟦-si⟧ Ⓐ ⟦pa-⟧) ∘ ⟦-ai⟧) : [V, {CONJ.3 Aktprf.**pa** +refl 2sg} :
                                            X→ *pasi-X-ai*]
      c. ((⟦-si⟧ Ⓐ ⟦pa-⟧) ∘ ⟦-o⟧) :   [V, {CONJ.3 Aktprf.**pa** +refl} :
                                            X→ *pasi-X-o*]
      d. ((⟦-si⟧ Ⓐ ⟦pa-⟧) ∘ (⟦-me⟧ ∘ [V, {CONJ.3 Aktprf.**pa** +refl 1pl} :
         ⟦-o⟧)) :   X→ *pasi-X-ome*]
      e. ((⟦-si⟧ Ⓐ ⟦pa-⟧) ∘ (⟦-te⟧ ∘   [V, {CONJ.3 Aktprf.**pa** +refl 2pl} :
         ⟦-o⟧)) :   X→ *pasi-X-ote*]
      f. ((⟦-si⟧ Ⓐ (⟦ne-⟧ ∘ ⟦be-⟧)) ∘   [V, {CONJ.3 neg cnt +refl 1sg} :
         ⟦-au⟧) :   X→ *nebesi-X-au*]
      g. ((⟦-si⟧ Ⓐ (⟦ne-⟧ ∘ ⟦be-⟧)) ∘   [V, {CONJ.3 neg cnt +refl 2sg} :
         ⟦-ai⟧) :   X→ *nebesi-X-ai*]
      h. ((⟦-si⟧ Ⓐ (⟦ne-⟧ ∘ ⟦be-⟧)) ∘   [V, {CONJ.3 neg cnt +refl} :
         ⟦-o⟧) :   X→ *nebesi-X-o*]
      i. ((⟦-si⟧ Ⓐ (⟦ne-⟧ ∘ ⟦be-⟧)) ∘   [V, {CONJ.3 neg cnt +refl 1pl} :
         (⟦-me⟧ ∘ ⟦-o⟧)) :   X→ *nebesi-X-ome*]
      j. ((⟦-si⟧ Ⓐ (⟦ne-⟧ ∘ ⟦be-⟧)) ∘   [V, {CONJ.3 neg cnt +refl 2pl} :
         (⟦-te⟧ ∘ ⟦-o⟧)) :   X→ *nebesi-X-ote*]
      k. ((⟦-si⟧ Ⓐ ((⟦ne-⟧ ∘ ⟦be-⟧) ∘ [V, {CONJ.3 neg cnt Aktprf.**pa** +refl 1sg} :
         ⟦pa-⟧)) ∘ ⟦-au⟧) :   X→ *nebepasi-X-au*]
      l. ((⟦-si⟧ Ⓐ ((⟦ne-⟧ ∘ ⟦be-⟧) ∘ [V, {CONJ.3 neg cnt Aktprf.**pa** +refl 2sg} :
         ⟦pa-⟧)) ∘ ⟦-ai⟧) :   X→ *nebepasi-X-ai*]
      m. ((⟦-si⟧ Ⓐ ((⟦ne-⟧ ∘ ⟦be-⟧) ∘ [V, {CONJ.3 neg cnt Aktprf.**pa** +refl} :
         ⟦pa-⟧)) ∘ ⟦-o⟧) :   X→ *nebepasi-X-o*]
      n. ((⟦-si⟧ Ⓐ ((⟦ne-⟧ ∘ ⟦be-⟧) ∘ [V, {CONJ.3 neg cnt Aktprf.**pa** +refl 1pl} :
         ⟦pa-⟧)) ∘ (⟦-me⟧ ∘ ⟦-o⟧)) : X→ *nebepasi-X-ome*]
      o. ((⟦-si⟧ Ⓐ ((⟦ne-⟧ ∘ ⟦be-⟧) ∘ [V, {CONJ.3 neg cnt Aktprf.**pa** +refl 2pl} :
         ⟦pa-⟧)) ∘ (⟦-te⟧ ∘ ⟦-o⟧)) : X→ *nebepasi-X-ote*]
      etc.

The analysis proposed here for the variety of forms in Table 7.18 involves the four types of FERs in Table 7.20. Unprefixed nonreflexive forms are defined by FERs of type R_{TERM}; prefixed nonreflexive forms are defined by the rules of type

7.3 Discussion   211

Table 7.20 *FERs for the verb forms in Table 7.18*

(where R_{TERM} is a termination rule; R_{PREF}, a prefixation rule; and R_{REFL}, a reflexive rule)

	For unprefixed forms	For prefixed forms
For nonreflexive forms	e.g. *rodau* 'I show': rules of type R_{TERM} (= (16))	e.g. *ne-be-rodau* 'I no longer show': composites of type $(R_{PREF} \circ R_{TERM})$ (= (22))
For reflexive forms	e.g. *rodau-si* 'I show up': composites of type $(R_{REFL} \circ R_{TERM})$ (= (19))	e.g. *ne-be-si-rodau* 'I no longer show up': composites of type $((R_{REFL} \text{Ⓐ} R_{PREF}) \circ R_{TERM})$ (= (25))

$(R_{PREF} \circ R_{TERM})$ determined by the FER pattern in (21). Unprefixed reflexives are defined by the rules of type $(R_{REFL} \circ R_{TERM})$ determined by the FER pattern in (18); and prefixed reflexives, by the rules of type $((R_{REFL} \text{Ⓐ} R_{PREF}) \circ R_{TERM})$ determined by the FER pattern in (24). In this analysis, the rule introducing the reflexive affix is uniformly suffixational and is therefore canonical with respect to the affix directionality criterion; at the same time, this rule is noncanonical with respect to the stem operand criterion, since it may operate either on a stem (in unprefixed reflexive forms) or on a prefix (in prefixed reflexive forms).

7.3 Discussion

According to the analyses proposed here, the inflection of Noon adjectives and Lithuanian verbs is morphotactically canonical insofar as it conforms to the affix directionality criterion: the consonantal marker rules in Noon are uniformly prefixational, and the reflexive affix rule in Lithuanian is invariably suffixational. At the same time, the proposed analyses represent the inflection of Noon and Lithuanian as morphotactically noncanonical insofar as they deviate from the stem operand criterion. In the proposed analysis of Noon, the aggregation of a consonantal marker rule R_2 with a positional formative rule R_1 causes the prefix introduced by R_2 to attach to the suffix introduced by R_1; in the proposed analysis of Lithuanian, the aggregation of the rule R_2 of reflexive suffixation with a rule R_1 of verb prefixation causes the suffix introduced by R_2 to attach to the prefix introduced by R_1.

If one wished to develop analyses of Noon and Lithuanian that conformed to the stem operand criterion, one would seemingly need to postulate two separate rules – one prefixational and one suffixational – for each consonantal marker in Noon as well as for the Lithuanian reflexive affix. Pursuing the idea of stipulating affixal exponence separately from prefixal or suffixal directionality (Stump 1993; Luís & Spencer 2005; Spencer 2005), one might say that the Noon consonantal markers and the Lithuanian reflexive affix each correspond to a single exponence specification corresponding to a pair of contrasting rules specifying affix directionality. This sort of analysis would allow one to maintain that the Noon consonantal markers and the Lithuanian reflexive affix are canonical with respect to the stem operand criterion, since the rules introducing them would always operate on a stem; at the same time, this sort of analysis would be inherently noncanonical with respect to the affix directionality criterion.

To be sure, there are cases in which the same affix has both prefixal and suffixal instances; I shall call such cases **true ambifixes** (Hamp 1959) in order to distinguish them from instances of affix counterposition. In order to account for true ambifixes, it is desirable to distinguish affix exponence from affix directionality. Luís & Spencer 2005 and Spencer 2005 propose a plausible analysis of this sort for pronominal object affixes in European Portuguese. Consider likewise the case of Gurma gender-class affixes.

In Gurma (Gur; Burkina Faso), indefinite nouns exhibit suffixes indicating their number and gender; definite nouns exhibit these same suffixes, but also exhibit prefixes expressing definiteness, number, and gender. In many but not all cases, a noun's definite prefix is segmentally identical to its number/gender suffix; the examples in Table 7.21 illustrate.[11] Note that in their definite forms, Gurma nouns generally exhibit the eight tone patterns in Table 7.22; a noun's singular and plural forms may or may not exhibit the same tone pattern, and members of the same gender class may differ in their tone patterns – see Beckett (1974: 66ff.) and Naba (1994: 127ff.) for details.

In a formal model of Gurma noun inflection, one might propose three groups of rules: rules in Group I specify gender-class prefixes (or the overriding absence of a prefix in gender class 9); rules in Group II specify gender-class suffixes (or the overriding absence of a suffix in singular forms in gender class 9); and rules in Group III specify a form's tone pattern. Most of the rules in these groups may be defined as in Table 7.23. Certain rules, however, specify affix exponence and affix directionality separately. Each of the rules in Table 7.24 specifies a constant exponent, but may function either as a

---

[11] Table 7.21 presents the principal patterns of Gurma gender-class morphology; for discussion of some lexical and dialectal deviations from these patterns, see Beckett (1974: 54ff.).

Table 7.21 *The principal patterns of Gurma gender-class morphology*

(Tone markers are as in Table 7.22.)

Gender class		Singular		Plural		Examples		
		Prefix	Suffix	Prefix	Suffix	Singular	Plural	
GC1	a	o-	-o	bi-	-ba	ō-bádī-ō	bī-bádī-bā	'the chief/s'
	b	o-	-o	a-	-a	ó-wāb-ō	á-wāb-ā	'the cripple/s'
GC2		o-	-u	i-	-i	ó-ŋuáb-ō	í-ŋuáb-ī	'the goat/s'
GC3		o-	-bu	i-	-i	ŏ-piĕm-ū	ī-piĕm-ī	'the arrow/s'
GC4		o-	-gu	i-	-di	ŏ-sáam-bū	ī-sáam-dī	'the shea tree/s'
GC5		o-	-gu	ti-	-di	ó-dúu-gú	tí-dúu-dí	'the locust bean pod/s'
GC6	a	li-	-li	a-	-la	lí-tí-lī	ā-tí-lā	'the book/s'
	b	li-	-li	a-	-na	lí-cáa-lī	ā-cáa-nā	'the well/s'
GC7		gi-	-ga	mu-	-mu	gī-jū-gā	mú-jū-mú	'the knife/knives'
GC8		mi-	-ma	(noncount)		mī-tá-mā		'the soil'
GC9		none	none	none	-mba	mobili	mobili-mba	'the automobile/s'

(Beckett 1974)

Table 7.22 *Tone patterns of Gurma nouns*

(− = mid tone; ′ = high tone; ″ = very high tone)

Pattern A	− ′ −	Pattern E	′ − ′
Pattern B	′ − −	Pattern F	′ ′ ′
Pattern C	′ ′ −	Pattern G	″ − −
Pattern D	− − −	Pattern H	″ ″ −

(Beckett 1974)

Table 7.23 *Rules in Groups I–III in the inflection of Gurma nouns*

Group I	⟦**gi-**⟧ :	[N, {gc7 sg +def} : *gi-*]	⟦**bi-**⟧ :	[N, {gc1a pl +def} : *bi-*]
	⟦**mi-**⟧ :	[N, {gc8 sg +def} : *mi-*]	⟦**ti-**⟧ :	[N, {gc5 pl +def} : *ti-*]
	⟦id.fcn⟧$_1$:	[N, {gc9 sg/pl +def} : X → X]	⟦**a-**⟧ :	[N, {gc6 pl +def} : *a-*]
Group II	⟦**-u**⟧ :	[N, {gc3 sg} : *-u*]	⟦**-ba**⟧ :	[N, {gc1a pl} : *-ba*]
	⟦**-bu**⟧ :	[N, {gc4 sg} : *-bu*]	⟦**-di**⟧ :	[N, {gc4/5 pl} : *-di*]
	⟦**-gu**⟧ :	[N, {gc5 sg} : *-gu*]	⟦**-la**⟧ :	[N, {gc6a pl} : *-la*]
	⟦**-ga**⟧ :	[N, {gc7 sg} : *-ga*]	⟦**-na**⟧ :	[N, {gc6b pl} : *-na*]
	⟦**-ma**⟧ :	[N, {gc8 sg} : *-ma*]	⟦**-mba**⟧ :	[N, {gc9 pl} : *-mba*]
	⟦id.fcn⟧$_2$:	[N, {gc9 sg} : X → X]		
Group III	⟦A⟧ :	[N, {TONE.A} : − ′ −]	⟦E⟧ :	[N, {TONE.E} : ′ − ′]
	⟦B⟧ :	[N, {TONE.B} : ′ − −]	⟦F⟧ :	[N, {TONE.F} : ′ ′ ′]
	⟦C⟧ :	[N, {TONE.C} : ′ ′ −]	⟦G⟧ :	[N, {TONE.G} : ″ − −]
	⟦D⟧ :	[N, {TONE.D} : − − −]	⟦H⟧ :	[N, {TONE.H} : ″ ″ −]

prefixational rule in Group I or as a suffixational rule in Group II (subject to the condition that as a member of Group I, it must realize definiteness); thus, the exponents introduced by the rules in Table 7.24 are true ambifixes.

In this sort of system, each noun has a FER of the type ($R_{III} \circ (R_{II} \circ R_I)$), where R_n represents a rule in Group *n*. The singular Class 7 noun *gī-jū-gā* 'the knife' is defined by the composite rule (⟦D⟧ ∘ (⟦**-ga**⟧ ∘ ⟦**gi-**⟧)), as in part (a) of Table 7.25. The corresponding plural noun *mú-jū-mú* 'the knives' in part (b) is defined by the composite (⟦E⟧ ∘ (⟦**mu**⟧$_{II}$ ∘ ⟦**mu**⟧$_I$)); here, the same rule ⟦**mu**⟧ applies twice, once as a Group I rule effecting prefixation, and again as a Group II rule effecting suffixation. Thus, ⟦**mu**⟧ is a truly ambifixal rule in whose formulation the relations of affix exponence and affix directionality are plausibly distinguished.

One might try to argue that the Noon and Lithuanian cases are not different from the Gurma case – that all three involve rules that specify a single relation

7.3 Discussion   215

Table 7.24 *Rules belonging to both Groups I and II in the inflection of Gurma nouns*

Affix exponence		Affix directionality	
⟦o⟧ : [N, {sg αdef} :	As members of	As members of Group II,
X → f (o, X)]	Group I, defined	defined only if f is the suffixing
⟦li⟧ : [N, {gc6 sg αdef} :	only if	operation.
X → f (li, X)]	(i) α = + and	
⟦a⟧ : [N, {gc1b pl αdef} :	(ii) f is the	
X → f (a, X)]	prefixing	
⟦i⟧ : [N, {pl αdef} :	operation.	
X → f (i, X)]		
⟦mu⟧ : [N, {gc7 pl αdef} :		
X → f (mu, X)]		

Table 7.25 *The morphotactics of two Gurma noun forms from Table 7.21*

(a)	Content cell:	⟨JU, {gc7 sg +def}⟩	'the knife'
	Form cell:	⟨ju, {gc7 sg +def TONE.D}⟩	
	|		
	FER	(⟦D⟧ ∘ (⟦-ga⟧ ∘ ⟦gi-⟧))	
	↓		
	Realized cell:	⟨gījūgā, {gc7 sg +def TONE.D}⟩	
(b)	Content cell:	⟨JU, {gc7 pl +def}⟩	'the knives'
	Form cell:	⟨ju, {gc7 pl +def TONE.E}⟩	
	|		
	FER	(⟦E⟧ ∘ (⟦mu⟧$_{II}$ ∘ ⟦mu⟧$_{I}$))	
	↓		
	Realized cell:	⟨mújūmú, {gc7 pl +def TONE.E}⟩	

of affix exponence but two relations of affix directionality, one prefixational, the other suffixational. Careful consideration, however, reveals that the Noon and Lithuanian cases are different from the Gurma case. The difference boils down to this: instances of affix counterposition (e.g. those of Noon and Lithuanian) possess a defining signature which true ambifixes (e.g. those of Gurma) lack.

Consider first the reflexive affix in Lithuanian. According to the aggregation analysis, the rule that suffixes the reflexive affix (repeated here in (26)) composes with the rule introducing the subject-agreement termination in a form such as *rodau-si* 'I show up' and aggregates with the rule introducing the prefix sequence in *ne-be-si-rodau* 'I no longer show up'. Now, suppose that, exploiting the idea of alternative relations of affix directionality, one replaced rule (26) with (27); the two directionalities in (27) would then make it possible to dispense with the idea that (26) aggregates with the rule introducing a prefixed verb form's prefix cluster.

(26)   The Lithuanian reflexive rule under the aggregation approach:
⟦-si⟧ : [V, {+refl} : -si]

(27)   The Lithuanian reflexive rule ⟦si⟧ under the ambifixal approach:
Affix exponence: [V, σ : X → f(si, X)], where {+refl} ⊆ σ
Affix directionality: a.   f is the prefixing operation if σ is not disjoint from {neg cnt Aktprf.α}
                          b.   otherwise, f is the suffixing operation.

The choice between the aggregation analysis and the ambifixal analysis at first seems like a toss-up. The aggregation analysis is canonical with respect to the affix directionality criterion (the reflexive affix rule is always suffixational) but noncanonical with respect to the stem operand criterion (the reflexive affix rule operates on a stem in some cases but on a prefix in others); the ambifixal analysis is canonical with respect to the stem operand criterion (the reflexive affix rule always operates on a stem) but noncanonical with respect to the affix directionality criterion (the reflexive affix rule is sometimes prefixational and sometimes suffixational). But there is additional evidence that tips the balance in favor of the aggregation analysis.

First, the aggregation analysis avoids the need to say that the content expressed by the reflexive affix varies with its directionality: according to (26), the reflexive affix always expresses exactly the content {+refl}. In the ambifixal analysis in (27), by contrast, the reflexive affix must always be associated with one or more of {neg}, {cnt}, and {Aktprf.α} (for some choice of α) when it is affixed as a prefix, but never when it is affixed as a suffix.

Second, the ambifixal analysis portrays it as a coincidence that (i) when it appears prefixally, *si-* is always preceded by one to three more peripheral prefixes and (ii) the extra content realized by the prefixal directionality of *si-* always duplicates content realized by this more peripheral prefix sequence. In the aggregation analysis, by contrast, the definition of aggregation entails that *-si* will follow a prefix whenever ⟦-si⟧ is aggregated, and there is no need for the content expressed by ⟦-si⟧ to duplicate the content of the prefixation rule with which it is aggregated.

Consider now the consonantal marker rules in Noon. These are exemplified by the two instances of *w-* in *w-i-yak-w-ii* 'big (singular, definite, noun class 1, location 1)'. According to the analysis proposed above, the rule that prefixes the singular consonantal marker *w-* of noun class 1 (repeated here in (28a)) applies twice in the definition of this form, once in composition with the rule (28b) that introduces the prefixal formative *-i* and again in aggregation with the rule (28c) that introduces the positional formative *-ii* indexed for location 1 (near the speaker). Now, suppose that one wanted to exploit the idea of alternative relations of affix directionality, as in the case of the Gurma affixes in Table 7.24. In that case, one might replace rule (28a) with (29); the two directionalities in (29) would then make it possible to dispense with the idea that (28a) aggregates with (28c).

(28) The aggregation approach to Noon adjective inflection
    a. Consonantal marker rule: ⟦**w-**⟧ : [Nom, {–dim –anim sg nc1} : *w*-]
    b. Prefixal formative rule: ⟦**i-**⟧ :   [A, { } : *i*-]
    c. Positional formative rule: ⟦**-ii**⟧ : [Nom, {definite loc1} : *-ii*]

(29) The ambifixal approach to Noon adjective inflection
Consonantal marker rule ⟦**w**⟧
Affix exponence: [Nom, {–dim –anim sg nc1 αdefinite} : X→ $f(w, X)$]
Affix directionality: a. *f* is the prefixing operation
                         b. *f* is the suffixing operation, provided that α = +.

The aggregation analysis is clearly the preferable analysis for reasons similar to what was seen for Lithuanian. First, the aggregation analysis avoids the need to say that the content expressed by *w-* varies with its directionality. In the ambifixal analysis, by contrast, suffixal *-w* (unlike prefixal *w-*) must express definiteness, as in directionality (29b); otherwise, suffixal *-w* would wrongly appear in indefinite forms.

Second, the ambifixal analysis portrays it as a coincidence that (i) when it appears suffixally, *-w* is always followed by another suffix and (ii) the extra content realized by the suffixal directionality of *-w* always duplicates part of the content realized by the more peripheral suffix (be it the location 1 suffix *-ii*, the location 2 suffix *-um*, or the location 3 suffix *-aa*). In the aggregation analysis, by contrast, the definition of aggregation entails that *w-* will precede a suffix whenever ⟦**w-**⟧ is aggregated, and there is no need for the content expressed by ⟦**w-**⟧ to duplicate the content of the suffixation rule with which it is aggregated.

I conclude that in theoretical terms, true ambifixes and affix counterpositions are distinct phenomena. Affix counterpositions possess a defining signature, which true ambifixes always lack.

218 *Rule Aggregation*

Table 7.26 *Italian pronominal affixes*

Type 1		Type 2	Type 3	Type 4		Type 5	Type 6
Acc or Dat		Locative	Reflexive	Acc.3		Impersonal	Partitive
1sg	mi_1	ci_2	si_3	masc sg	lo_4	si_5	ne_6
2sg	ti_1			fem sg	la_4		
Dat 3sg masc	gli_1			masc pl	li_4		
Dat 3sg fem	le_1			fem pl	le_4		
1pl	ci_1						
2pl	vi_1						

(cf. Monachesi 1999: 23)

That said, there are systems in which a pattern of true ambifixation interacts with a pattern of rule aggregation. A case in point is that of Italian pronominal affixes.[12]

7.4 The Interaction of Aggregation with True Ambifixation in Italian

In Italian, verbs exhibit the system of pronominal affixes in Table 7.26. These affixes are ordinarily prefixed to the verb (as in (30a)), but they are suffixed to nonfinite forms (as in (30b)) and to imperatives (as in (30c)). The examples in (30) therefore embody true ambifixation.

(30) a. *Martina   lo   legge.*
           Martina   3SG.ACC.MASC   reads
           'Martina reads it.'
      b. *Visto-lo,   fu   facile decidere.*
           seen-3SG.ACC.MASC   was   easy   to.decide
           'Having seen it, it was easy to decide.'
      c. *Leggi-lo!*
           read.IMPERATIVE-3SG.ACC.MASC
           'Read it!'

(Monachesi 1995: 47)

The numeral subscript on each affix in Table 7.26 indicates the affix type to which it belongs. Type membership determines the way in which one pronominal affix may combine with another: when a Type m affix Af_m combines with

---

[12] The Italian pronominal affixes have traditionally been regarded as clitics, but a range of criteria suggests that they are indeed affixal in status; see Monachesi (1995: chapter 3; 1999: chapter 2). Note that conventionally, pronominal prefixes are written separately from the following verb form.

a Type n affix Af_n, Af_m precedes Af_n if $m < n$; affixes belonging to the same type do not combine. According to Monachesi (1995: 102ff.), the usual combinations of pronominal affixes are the pairs in Table 7.27. Note that although combined pronominal affixes are normally written apart (*me lo dà* 'he gives it to me'), $glie_1$ is conventionally written together with the following affix (*glielo do* 'I give it to him').

The combinations in Table 12.10 exhibit two important morphotactic characteristics. First, certain affixes assume an alternate form when they combine with certain other following affixes. Most prominently, the affixes in Types 1–3 and 5 assume an alternate form when they combine with an affix from Type 4 or 6; specifically, mi_1, ti_1, ci_1, vi_1, ci_2, si_3, and si_5 assume the forms me_1, te_1, ce_1, ve_1, ce_2, se_3, and se_5. In each of these cases, an affix in /i/ simply has an alternate, combining form in /e/, but there are other alternations that do not conform to this pattern. When the third-person singular dative affixes gli_1 and le_1 combine with an affix from Type 4 or 6, they both appear as $glie_1$, in effect neutralizing the gender distinction between masculine gli_1 and feminine le_1; that is, the alternate form is in this instance syncretic. Finally, when si_3 is followed by si_5, the first *si* assumes the form *ci*. These alternations cannot be straightforwardly attributed to ordinary principles of Italian phonology, but are plausibly seen as allomorphic in nature (Anderson 1995; Monachesi 1995: 43–46; 1999: 28–31).

Second, the affix combinations in Table 12.10 exhibit the same relative order whether they precede the verb stem or follow it. For example, the relative ordering of the affixes in the combination me_1 lo_4 remains the same whether the combination appears prefixally (as in (31a)) or suffixally (as in (31b)). This is evidence that when two pronominal affixes appear in succession, one affix has the other affix as its operand; that is, this is evidence that the rules by which a sequence of two pronominal affixes is realized stand in a relation of aggregation.

(31) a. *Me   lo   da-te.*
DAT:1SG   ACC:3SG.MASC   give-SBJ:2PL
'You give it to me.'
b. *Da-te-me-lo!*
give-SBJ:2PL-DAT:1SG-ACC:3SG.MASC
'Give it to me!'

(Crysmann & Bonami 2016: 330)

As in the analysis of Gurma noun-class markings, the ambifixal status of the Italian pronominal affixes may be accounted for by drawing a distinction between exponence and (prefixal or suffixal) directionality, as in (32). Each of the rules of exponence in (32a) introduces an affix whose prefixal or suffixal directionality is determined by the directionality rule in (32b). Thus, by (32b), each of the rules of exponence in (32a) is instantiated by (i) a suffixation rule in

Table 7.27 Possible combinations of Italian pronominal affixes

	Type of second affix					
Type of first affix	2	3	4			
					5	6
1	$mi_1\ ci_2$	$mi_1\ si_3$	$me_1\ lo_4$	$me_1\ la_4$	$me_1\ li_4$	$me_1\ le_4$	$mi_1\ si_5$	$me_1\ ne_6$
	$ti_1\ ci_2$	$ti_1\ si_3$	$te_1\ lo_4$	$te_1\ la_4$	$te_1\ li_4$	$te_1\ le_4$	$ti_1\ si_5$	$te_1\ ne_6$
	$gli_1\ ci_2$	$gli_1\ si_3$	$glie_1lo_4$	$glie_1la_4$	$glie_1li_4$	$glie_1le_4$	$gli_1\ si_5$	$glie_1ne_6$
	$le_1\ ci_2$	$le_1\ si_3$					$le_1\ si_5$	
		$ci_1\ si_3$	$ce_1\ lo_4$	$ce_1\ la_4$	$ce_1\ li_4$	$ce_1\ le_4$	$ci_1\ si_5$	$ce_1\ ne_6$
	$vi_1\ ci_2$	$vi_1\ si_3$	$ve_1\ lo_4$	$ve_1\ la_4$	$ve_1\ li_4$	$ve_1\ le_4$	$vi_1\ si_5$	$ve_1\ ne_6$
2		$ci_2\ si_3$	$ce_2\ lo_4$	$ce_2\ la_4$	$ce_2\ li_4$	$ce_2\ le_4$	$ci_2\ si_5$	$ce_2\ ne_6$
3			$se_3\ lo_4$	$se_3\ la_4$	$se_3\ li_4$	$se_3\ le_4$	$ci_3\ si_5$	$se_3\ ne_6$
4				$la_4\ si_5$	$li_4\ si_5$		$lo_4\ si_5$	
5								$se_5\ ne_6$

220

7.4 Aggregation and True Ambifixation in Italian   221

which α = imperative or nonfinite and (ii) a prefixation rule in which α = ∅; the Type 1 rule ⟦mi₁⟧, for example, is instantiated by the two rules in (33), and the Type 4 rule ⟦lo₄⟧, by the two rules in (34).

(32)   Exponence/directionality rules for Italian pronominal affixes (in which α = imperative, nonfinite, or ∅).
    a. **Exponence** Type 1 ⟦mi₁⟧ : [V, {{obj 1sg} α} : X → f (mi, X)]
                           ⟦ti₁⟧ : [V, {{obj 2sg} α} : X → f (ti, X)]
                           ⟦gli₁⟧ : [V, {{obj dat 3sg masc} α} : X → f (gli, X)]
                           ⟦le₁⟧ : [V, {{obj dat 3sg fem} α} : X → f (le, X)]
                           ⟦ci₁⟧ : [V, {{obj 1pl} α} : X → f (ci, X)]
                           ⟦vi₁⟧ : [V, {{obj 2pl} α} : X → f (vi, X)]
               Type 2 ⟦ci₂⟧ : [V, {loc α} : X → f (ci, X)]
               Type 3 ⟦si₃⟧ : [V, {{obj refl} α} : X → f (si, X)]
               Type 4 ⟦lo₄⟧ : [V, {{obj acc 3sg masc} α} : X → f (lo, X)]
                           ⟦la₄⟧ : [V, {{obj acc 3sg fem} α} : X → f (la, X)]
                           ⟦li₄⟧ : [V, {{obj acc 3pl masc} α} : X → f (li, X)]
                           ⟦le₄⟧ : [V, {{obj acc 3pl fem} α} : X → f (le, X)]
               Type 5 ⟦si₅⟧ : [V, {{sbj imps} α} : X → f (si, X)]
               Type 6 ⟦ne₆⟧ : [V, {{part} α} : X → f (si, X)]
    b. **Directionality** If α = imp or –fin, f = suffix; otherwise, f = prefix.

(33)   The suffixational and prefixational instantiations of the ⟦mi₁⟧ rule
    a.   ⟦-mi₁⟧ : [V, {{obj 1sg} imperative/nonfinite} : -mi]
    b.   ⟦mi-₁⟧ : [V, {{obj 1sg}} : mi-]

(34)   The suffixational and prefixational instantiations of the ⟦lo₄⟧ rule
    a.   ⟦-lo₄⟧ : [V, {{obj acc 3sg masc} imperative/nonfinite} : -lo]
    b.   ⟦lo-₄⟧ : [V, {{obj acc 3sg masc}} : lo-]

Each of the rules in (32a) also has a special aggregative instantiation – the version R_{aggr} of the rule that is employed as the first member of an aggregation of the type (R_{aggr} Ⓐ R_{pron}), for some rule R_{pron} of pronominal affixation. Several of these aggregative instantiations specify exponence relations that differ from those in (32a); these are the aggregative instantiations in (35). For each of the pronominal affix rules of Types 4 and 6 in (32a), the aggregative instantiation is identical to the corresponding prefixational instantiation specified by (32b).

(35)   Aggregative instantiations that specify exponence relations distinct from those in (32a)
    Type 1   ⟦me-₁⟧ : [V, {{obj 1sg}} : me-]
                               ⟦te-₁⟧ : [V, {{obj 2sg}} : te-]
                               ⟦glie-₁⟧ : [V, {{obj dat 3sg}} : glie-]
                               ⟦ce-₁⟧ : [V, {{obj 1pl}} : ce-]
                               ⟦ve-₁⟧ : [V, {{obj 2pl}} : ve-]

222 *Rule Aggregation*

Table 7.28 *Rules of exponence for Italian pronominal affixes and their suffixational, prefixational, and aggregative instantiations*

	Rule of exponence	Instantiations		
		Suffixational	Prefixational	Aggregative
Type 1	⟦mi₁⟧	⟦-mi₁⟧	⟦mi-₁⟧	⟦me-₁⟧
	⟦ti₁⟧	⟦-ti₁⟧	⟦ti-₁⟧	⟦te-₁⟧
	⟦gli₁⟧	⟦-gli₁⟧	⟦gli-₁⟧	⟦glie-₁⟧
	⟦le₁⟧	⟦-le₁⟧	⟦le-₁⟧	⟦glie-₁⟧
	⟦ci₁⟧	⟦-ci₁⟧	⟦ci-₁⟧	⟦ce-₁⟧
	⟦vi₁⟧	⟦-vi₁⟧	⟦vi-₁⟧	⟦ve-₁⟧
Type 2	⟦ci₂⟧	⟦-ci₂⟧	⟦ci-₂⟧	⟦ce-₂⟧
Type 3	⟦si₃⟧	⟦-si₃⟧	⟦si-₃⟧	⟦se-₃⟧/⟦ci-₃⟧
Type 4	⟦lo₄⟧	⟦-lo₄⟧	⟦lo-₄⟧	= ⟦lo-₄⟧
	⟦la₄⟧	⟦-la₄⟧	⟦la-₄⟧	= ⟦la-₄⟧
	⟦li₄⟧	⟦-li₄⟧	⟦li-₄⟧	= ⟦li-₄⟧
	⟦le₄⟧	⟦-le₄⟧	⟦le-₄⟧	= ⟦le-₄⟧
Type 5	⟦si₅⟧	⟦-si₅⟧	⟦si-₅⟧	⟦se-₅⟧
Type 6	⟦ne₆⟧	⟦-ne₆⟧	⟦ne-₆⟧	= ⟦ne-₆⟧

Type 2   ⟦ce-₂⟧ : [V, {loc} : *ce-*]
Type 3   ⟦se-₃⟧ : [V, {{obj refl}} : *se-*]
              ⟦ci-₃⟧ : [V, {{obj refl}} : *ci-*]
Type 5   ⟦se-₅⟧ : [V, {{sbj imps}} : *se-*]

Each of the pronominal affix rules in (32a) therefore has the three instantiations in Table 7.28: (i) a suffixational instantiation, (ii) a prefixational instantiation, and (iii) an aggregative instantiation; for rules of Types 4 and 6, the prefixational and aggregative instantiations are the same.

Instantiations of the pronominal affix rules combine with one another by aggregation, in accordance with the pattern in (36), whose effect is to combine, by aggregation, the aggregative instantiation R_m of a pronominal affix rule of Type m with the prefixational or suffixational instantiation R_n of a pronominal affix rule of Type n (where $n > m$). For example, given the ⟦me-₁⟧ rule in (35) and the ⟦-lo₄⟧ rule in (34a), (36) defines the aggregation (⟦me-₁⟧ Ⓐ ⟦-lo₄⟧) in (37a); given the ⟦me-₁⟧ rule and the ⟦lo-₄⟧ rule in (34b), (36) defines the aggregation (⟦me-₁⟧ Ⓐ ⟦lo-₄⟧) in (37b).

(36)   Aggregations of pronominal affix rules
        Where R_m is the aggregative instantiation of a pronominal affix rule
        belonging to Type m, R_n is a prefixational or suffixational instantiation of a

pronominal affix rule belonging to Type n, and $1 \leq m < n \leq 6$, the aggregation (R_m Ⓐ R_n) is a pronominal affix rule.
Restriction: If R_m is of Type 3, then R_m is ⟦**se-3**⟧ unless R_n is ⟦**si-5**⟧, in which case R_m is ⟦**ci-3**⟧.

(37) Two aggregations defined by (36)
 a. (⟦**me-1**⟧ Ⓐ ⟦**-lo4**⟧) : [V, {{obj dat 1sg}{obj acc 3sg masc} imp/–fin} : -*me-lo*]
 b. (⟦**me-1**⟧ Ⓐ ⟦**lo-4**⟧) : [V, {{obj dat 1sg}{obj acc 3sg masc}} : *me-lo-*]

This analysis captures the interaction of ambifixation with aggregation in the morphotactics of Italian pronominal affixes. The verb form in (31b) inflects by means of the aggregation in (37a), and the verb form in (31a), by means of the aggregation in (37b). In both cases, the ⟦**me-1**⟧ rule in (35) (= the aggregative instantiation of the ambifix ⟦**mi1**⟧ in (32a)) is aggregated to an instantiation of the ambifix ⟦**lo4**⟧ in (32a). The most general formulation of the pattern of aggregation in (36) is one in which an aggregative instantiation aggregates with members of a class of rules some of which are prefixational instantiations of an ambifix and others of which are suffixational instantiations of an ambifix. Thus, it is desirable to assume that ($Rule_2$ Ⓐ $Rule_1$) is defined even if $Rule_1$ and $Rule_2$ are alike in their directionality.

7.5 Conclusion

Affix counterposition is a phenomenon with a highly distinctive signature. In the rule-combining approach to morphotactics, this phenomenon is modeled by rule aggregation, a mode of rule combination by which one rule operates on the affix defined by another rule. Because rules of exponence operate on stems in the default case, any rule aggregation (R_2 Ⓐ R_1) involves a deviation from the stem operand criterion: in the definition of (R_2 Ⓐ R_1), R_2 operates not on a stem but on the affix defined by R_1. At the same time, rule aggregation has the effect of bringing instances of affix counterposition into conformity with the affix directionality criterion: the directionality of the affix introduced by R_2 remains the same whether its operand is a stem or another rule's affix.

Cross-linguistically, aggregation is not an unusual mode of rule combination. As will be seen in the following chapter, it has more than one role in the inflectional morphotactics of verbs in Swahili.

8 Complex Morphotactic Interactions in Swahili

Within a single system of morphotactics, multiple patterns of rule combination may interact in complex ways. In this chapter, I demonstrate this fact by presenting a detailed analysis of a significant fragment of Swahili verb inflection in which simple rules, composite rules, and aggregated rules all enter into competition.[1] As the examples in Table 8.1 show, the Swahili system of verb inflection presents an extravaganza of deviations (some real, others merely apparent) from a number of canonical morphotactic criteria, including the rule independence criterion, the parallel sequence criterion, the unique sequence criterion, the stem operand criterion, the rule opposition criterion, and the affix directionality criterion.

The rule-combining approach to morphotactics, though it itself inherently deviates from the minimal rule criterion (Section 1.5.1), allows deviations from the last two of these criteria to be seen as merely apparent; moreover, it affords an explanatory way of modeling genuine deviations from the other canonical criteria. I shall argue that despite the morphotactic complexity of the Swahili conjugational system, the rule-combining approach to morphotactics makes it possible to model this system in a very simple way at the most general level. As I shall show, the rules of Swahili verb inflection fall into three groups (Groups III, II, and I) such that the definition of a verb form's morphotactics a composite of either the type ($R_{III} \circ R_{II}$) or the type (($R_{III} \circ R_{II}) \circ R_{I}$). The real complexity of the analysis resides in identifying the group membership of the system's simple rules and their many and varied combinations.

At the center of this discussion are three characteristics of the Swahili conjugational system: the polyfunctionality of verbal concords (Section 8.2), the expression of negation (Section 8.3), and the special marking of verb forms for a relativized argument (Section 8.4). I begin with a brief description of the wider morphosyntactic setting of these three characteristics.

---

[1] In this analysis, I have drawn upon several descriptions of Swahili grammar: Ashton (1947), Contini-Morava (2007), Loogman (1965), Mohammed (2001), and Steere (1919).

Table 8.1 *Real or apparent deviations from six criterial characteristics of canonical morphotactics in Swahili verb inflection*

Criterion	Real or apparent deviation
Rule independence criterion (Section 1.5.2)	The rule 〚**wa-**〛 expresses concord with a 3pl argument belonging to NC2, but its application depends on that of an accompanying rule to determine whether it expresses subject concord (*wa*lilala 'they slept') or concord with a pronominal object (*tuliwaamsha* 'we awakened them').
Parallel sequence criterion (Section 1.5.3)	The indicative negative rule 〚**ha-**〛 applies more peripherally than the subject concord rule (*ha*wakulala 'they didn't sleep') but the nonindicative negative rule 〚**si-**〛 applies less peripherally than the subject concord rule ([*watu*] *wasi*olala '[people] who don't sleep').
Unique sequence criterion (Section 1.5.4)	The 〚**wa-**〛 rule may apply before or after a tense rule (e.g. the past-tense rule 〚**li-**〛) depending on whether it expresses concord with a pronominal object (*tuliwaamsha* 'we awakened them') or with the subject (*walilala* 'they slept').
Stem operand criterion (Section 1.5.6)	The rule 〚**-ye**〛 expressing a 3sg relativized argument belonging to NC1 operates on the verb stem in tenseless positive forms ([*mtu*] *asomaye* '[person] who reads', stem *-soma*) but otherwise operates on the tense/negative prefix ([*mtu*] *aliyesoma* '[person] who read', [*mtu*] *asiyesoma* '[person] who doesn't read').
Rule opposition criterion (Section 1.5.9)	The portmanteau rule 〚**si-**〛, an expression of both indicative negation and 1sg subject agreement (*si-kulala* 'I didn't sleep'), is distributionally like two-rule sequences that spell out subject agreement and negation separately (*ha-wa-kulala* 'they didn't sleep').
Affix directionality criterion (Section 1.5.10)	The 3sg relative affix *ye* appears to be prefixed to the verb stem in some cases ([*mtu*] *aliyesoma* '[person] who read', stem *-soma*) but suffixed to it in others ([*mtu*] *asomaye* '[person] who reads').

8.1 The Morphotactics of Swahili Verb Inflection

The broader structural context in which these characteristics exist are no doubt familiar to many readers. As a Bantu language, Swahili possesses an array of noun classes whose effects pervade its entire inflectional system. The Swahili

Table 8.2 *Swahili noun classes*

Gender	Noun-class prefixes		Example
	Singular	Plural	
NC1+NC2	NC1: m- (~ mw- ~ mu-)	NC2: wa- (~ w-)	m-tu 'person', wa-tu 'people'
NC3+NC4	NC3: m- (~ mw- ~ mu-)	NC4: mi- (~ my-)	m-kate 'loaf', mi-kate 'loaves'
NC5+NC6	NC5: ji- (~ j- ~ –)	NC6: ma- (~ m-)	ji-we 'stone', ma-we 'stones'
NC7+NC8	NC7: ki- (~ ch-)	NC8: vi- (~ vy-)	ki-su 'knife', vi-su 'knives'
NC9+NC10	NC9: n- (~ ny- ~ m-)	NC10: n- (~ ny- ~ m-)	n-goma 'drum', n-goma 'drums'
NC11+NC10	NC11: u- (~ w- ~ uw-)	NC10: n- (~ ny- ~ m-)	w-embe 'razor', ny-embe 'razors'
NC14	NC14: u- (~ w- ~ uw-)		u-zee 'old age'

noun classes may be distinguished as in Table 8.2.[2] In this table, a count noun's gender is represented as a pairing NCx+NCy of noun classes such that the noun's singular and plural forms belong to NCx and NCy, respectively. Because noncount nouns don't distinguish singular and plural numbers, their gender is therefore an unpaired noun class (NC14).[3]

As Table 8.2 shows, each noun class is associated with a prefix. In the simplest cases, a noun exhibits the prefix associated with the noun class to which it belongs, as the examples in the table show. (The exact form of a noun-class prefix may naturally vary according to its phonological context; thus, the noun class 1 prefix is *m-* in *m-toto* 'child', *mw-* in *mw-ongo* 'liar', and *mu-* in *mu-umbaji* 'creator'.) There are, however, cases in which a noun simply seems to exhibit the wrong prefixes; for example, the singular noun *kipofu* 'blind man' (plural *vipofu*) belongs to noun class NC1 (plural NC2) despite exhibiting

---

[2] The numbering of Swahili noun classes in Table 8.2 stems ultimately from Meinhof (1906). Meinhof's system of numbering is intended to facilitate noun-class system comparisons across the Bantu languages; apparent gaps in the numbering of Swahili noun classes therefore reflect the fact that Swahili has lost noun-class distinctions that are preserved elsewhere in Bantu.

[3] Verbal nouns and locationally specified nouns have certain morphosyntactic characteristics comparable to those of the classes distinguished in Table 8.2; however, they also exhibit a number of special characteristics. I follow Contini-Morava (2007: 1150f.) in assuming that they do not constitute ordinary noun classes but embody orthogonal morphosyntactic subsystems.

ki- (plural *vi-*) rather than *m-* (plural *wa-*) as its prefix. Thus, a noun's prefix isn't always a reliable sign of its noun-class membership.

Definitive evidence of a noun's noun-class membership is provided by an expression that agrees with it by means of a concordial affix. Thus, in the sentence *Kipofu aliondoka* 'A blind man left', the concordial subject prefix *a-* on the verb form *aliondoka* '(s/he) left' reveals that *kipofu* belongs to NC1. In some cases, the concordial affixes take the same form as the corresponding noun-class prefix; thus, in *Watu watalala* 'people will sleep', the noun-class prefix of *wa-tu* 'people' (a member of NC2) is reflected by the NC2 subject concord *wa-* of the verb form *wa-talala* '(they) will sleep'. Often, however, the verbal concords for a given noun class differ from the noun-class prefix associated with that class; thus, in *Mtu atalala* 'a person will sleep', the noun-class prefix of *m-tu* 'person' (a member of NC1) differs from the corresponding NC1 subject concord *a-* of the verb form *a-talala* '(s/he) will sleep'. The inventory of Swahili verbal concords corresponding to the noun classes in Table 8.2 is listed in Table 8.3; these verbal concords include first- and second-person prefixes (singular and plural) as well as third-person prefixes distinguished according to gender as well as number.

8.1.1 The Polyfunctionality of the Verbal Concords in Swahili

The problem posed by the concordial prefixes in Table 8.3 is their polyfunctionality – the fact that they serve three distinct functions in the inflection of Swahili verbs. Their first function is to encode the properties of a verb's subject, as *tu-* expresses a first-person plural subject in (1a) and *ni-* expresses

Table 8.3 *Swahili verbal concords*

Person		Singular		Plural	
1		*ni-*		*tu-*	
2		SBJ *u-*, OBJ *ku-*		SBJ *m-*, OBJ *wa-*	
3	Gender				
	NC1+NC2	NC1:	SBJ *a-*, OBJ *m-*	NC2:	*wa-*
	NC3+NC4	NC3:	*u-*	NC4:	*i-*
	NC5+NC6	NC5:	*li-*	NC6:	*ya-*
	NC7+NC8	NC7:	*ki-*	NC8:	*vi-*
	NC9+NC10	NC9:	*i-*	NC10:	*zi-*
	NC11+NC10	NC11:	*u-*	NC10:	*zi-*
	NC14	NC14:	*u-*		

a first-person singular subject in (1b). Their second function is to encode the properties of verb's pronominal object, as *tu-* expresses a first-person plural object in (2a) and *ni-* expresses a first-person singular object in (2b). Most often, the prefix expressing a subject's person, number, and gender has the same form as the corresponding pronominal object prefix; in a few cases, however, they are different (specifically, in the second person singular and plural and in noun class 1), as Table 8.3 indicates.

(1)   a.   *tu-ta-soma*   b.   *ni-ta-soma*
              SBJ.1PL-FUT-read   SBJ.1SG-FUT-read
              'we will read'   'I will read'

(2)   a.   *a-ta-tu-piga*   b.   *a-ta-ni-piga*
              SBJ.NC1-FUT-OBJ.1PL-strike   SBJ.NC1-FUT-OBJ.1SG-strike'
              's/he will strike us'   's/he will strike me'

The verbal concords' third function relates specifically to the noun-class concords in the lower part of Table 8.3. In the morphology of relative verb forms, the noun-class concords specify the number and gender of the verb's relativized argument. In (3), for example, the suffix *-vyo* specifies that the relativized argument is plural and belongs to noun class 8 (hence to the gender NC7+NC8). This affix has two parts: the verbal concord *vi-* and a component *-o*, which Ashton (1947: 110ff.) labels 'the *o* of reference'. All of the relative affixes but two have this bipartite structure: the singular relative affix *-ye* for noun class 1 and the plural relative affix *-o* for noun class 2 do not. Although the remaining relative affixes do have a bipartite structure based on the appropriate verbal concord, this structure is often rendered less transparent as an effect of sandhi modifications. The full inventory of bipartite relative affixes is given in Table 8.4.

Table 8.4 *Swahili relative affixes for noun classes* NC3–NC14

	Verbal concords		Relative affixes			
Gender	Singular	Plural	Singular		Plural	
NC3+NC4	*u-*	*i-*	*-o*	(← *u-o*)	*-yo*	(← *i-o*)
NC5+NC6	*li-*	*ya-*	*-lo*	(← *li-o*)	*-yo*	(← *ya-o*)
NC7+NC8	*ki-*	*vi-*	*-cho*	(← *ki-o*)	*-vyo*	(← *vi-o*)
NC9+NC10	*i-*	*zi-*	*-yo*	(← *i-o*)	*-zo*	(← *zi-o*)
NC11+NC10	*u-*	*zi-*	*-o*	(← *u-o*)	*-zo*	(← *zi-o*)
NC14	*u-*		*-o*	(← *u-o*)		

(3)   vi-tabu   a-vi-taka-vyo
      NC8-book   SBJ.NC1-OBJ.NC8-want-REL.NC8
      'the books that s/he wants'

In Section 8.2, I show how principles of rule combination make it possible to give a precise account of the subject/object polyfunctionality of verbal concords in Swahili verbal morphotactics; in Section 8.4, I extend the proposed analysis to account for the use of the verbal concords in expressing the gender and number of a relative verb form's relativized argument. As we shall see, the polyfunctionality of the rules introducing the verbal concords in Table 8.3 engenders genuine deviations from the rule independence criterion and the unique sequence criterion.

8.1.2   The Morphotactics of Negation in Swahili Verb Inflection

The problems posed by verbal negation in Swahili are twofold. First, negation isn't always expressed in the same place in a verb form's morphotactics, contrary to the parallel sequence criterion. Second, the exponence of negation is complex: in one class of cases, negation is expressed cumulatively with subject agreement; in another class of cases, it is expressed cumulatively with tense; and in still other cases, its expression is cumulative with neither subject agreement nor tense. As a consequence, negative morphology gives rise to apparent deviations from the rule opposition criterion and to genuine instances of multiple exponence.

The negation of an indicative verb form is ordinarily effected by a rule 〚**ha-**〛 that introduces the prefix *ha-*; thus, alongside the positive form *tutasoma* 'we will read' in (1a) is the negative form *hatutasoma* 'we will not read' in (4a). This general pattern leads one to expect that the first-person singular form *nitasoma* 'I will read' in (1b) should have *hanitasoma as its negative counterpart, but it doesn't; instead, the corresponding negative form is the form *sitasoma* 'I will not read', as in (4b), in which the expected sequence of the negative prefix *ha-* and the first-person singular subject concord *ni-* is supplanted by the portmanteau prefix *si-*.[4]

(4)   a.   *ha-tu-ta-soma*   b.   *si-ta-soma*
           NEG-SBJ.1PL-FUT-read   NEG.1SG-FUT-read
           'we will not read'   'I will not read'

---

[4] For discussion of the complex correspondences of this portmanteau prefix across the Bantu languages, see Hyman 2018.

The morphotactics of negation is further complicated in two ways. First, there is a second negative prefix having the form *si-* that differs both paradigmatically and syntagmatically from the portmanteau prefix *si-*. Unlike the portmanteau prefix *si-*, which expresses both negation and first-person singular subject agreement in indicative forms such as (4b), this second negative *si-* doesn't express subject agreement, but appears in nonindicative contexts in the presence of any sort of subject, as for example in the prohibitive subjunctive form in (5b). The nonindicative negative *si-* also differs syntagmatically from the portmanteau negative *si-*: the former appears alongside a separate subject-agreement prefix (as in (5c)) while the latter never does (cf. (5d)), and the latter appears alongside a separate tense prefix (as in (4b)) while the former never does (cf. (5e)). That is, the portmanteau *si-* is paradigmatically opposed to the subject-agreement prefixes while the nonindicative *si-* is paradigmatically opposed to the tense prefixes, as in Figure 8.1.

(5) a. *u-ni-saidi-e*
         SBJ.2SG-OBJ.1SG-help-SBJV
         'help me'
     b. *u-si-ni-saidi-e*
         SBJ.2SG-NEG.NONIND-OBJ.1SG-help-SBJV
         'don't help me'
     c. *ili   ni-si-som-e*
         so.that SBJ.1SG-NEG.NONIND-read-SBJV
         'so that I don't read'
     d. **ni-si-ta-soma*
         SBJ.1SG-NEG.1SG-FUT-read
         Purportedly: 'I will not read'
     e. **ili   ni-si-ta-som-e*
         so.that SBJ.1SG-NEG.NONIND-FUT-read-SBJV
         Purportedly: 'so that I will not read'

A second additional complication in the morphotactics of negative indicative verb forms is the incidence of multiple exponence in negative past-tense forms. In each of the negative verb forms considered so far, negation has only a single exponent: the prefix *ha-* in (4a), the portmanteau

(i) portmanteau si_{-1} is paradigmatically opposed to subject-agreement prefixes, e.g. 1sg *ni-*;

(ii) nonindicative si_{-2} is paradigmatically opposed to tense prefixes, e.g. future-tense *ta-*.

(i)	*ni-*	*ta-*	*soma*	'I will read'
	si_{-1}	*ta-*	*soma*	'I will not read'
(ii)	*ni-*	si_{-2}	*some*	'so that I don't read'

Figure 8.1 *Two distinct patterns of paradigmatic opposition*

prefix *si-* in (4b), and the nonindicative prefix *si-* in (5b,c). In the past tense, however, negation involves the negative past-tense prefix *ku-* in addition to either *ha-* (as in (6b)) or *si-* (as in (7b)). These forms raise natural questions. What induces the application of ⟦**ha-**⟧ in *hatukusoma* 'we did not read' insofar as the application of ⟦**ku-**⟧ itself realizes negation? Why isn't **nikusoma* admissible as a nonredundant alternative to the multiple exponence of negation in *sikusoma* 'I did not read'? I return to these questions in Section 8.3, where I show how principles of rule combination make it possible to give a precise account of the morphotactics of negation in Swahili verb inflection.

(6) a. *tu-li-soma*   b. *ha-tu-ku-soma*
       1PL-PST-read   NEG-1PL-NEG.PST-read
       'we read'   'we did not read'

(7) a. *ni-li-soma*   b. *si-ku-soma*
       1SG-PST-read   NEG.1SG-NEG.PST-read
       'I read'   'I did not read'

8.1.3 The Morphotactics of Relative Verb Forms in Swahili

The problem posed by the morphotactics of relative verb forms is the fact that relative affixes appear to be suffixal in some forms but prefixal in others, contrary to the affix directionality criterion. At issue is a particular sort of relative clause structure that centers on a verb form inflected for the noun class of the verb's relativized argument.[5] A relative verb form's relative affix may encode a relativized subject (as in (8a)) or a relativized object (as in (8b)). If it encodes a relativized subject, that subject still triggers subject agreement morphology on the verb; if it encodes a relativized object, that object's person, number, and noun class are additionally coded by a pronominal object prefix

---

[5] Swahili also possesses a relative clause structure based on the proform *amba* (etymologically related to the verb *ambia* 'tell') in which the verb in the relative clause does not specify which of its arguments is relativized – in which it is the relative proform that bears the relative affix (see again Table 8.4) indicating the noun class of the relativized argument; (i) is an example of this structure.

(i)   *ki-ti*   *amba-cho*   *ki-me-vunjika*
       NC7-chair   REL.PRON-NC7   SBJ.NC7-CMPLTV-be.broken
       'the chair that is broken'

on the verb. Thus, the only difference between the relative verb forms in (8) and the simple indicative verb form in (9) is that the former exhibit relative affixes.

(8) a. *m-tu*   *a-li-ye-vi-taka*
       NC1-person   SBJ.NC1-PST-REL.NC1-OBJ.NC8-want
       'a person who wanted them'
    b. *vi-tabu*   *a-li-vyo-vi-taka*
       NC8-book   SBJ.NC1-PST-REL.NC8-OBJ.NC8-want
       'the books that s/he wanted'

(9) *A-li-vi-taka.*
    SBJ.NC1-PST-OBJ.NC8-want.
    'S/he wanted them.'

The relative affixes for noun classes 1 and 2 are *ye* and *o*, respectively. The remaining noun classes have relative affixes that result from combining the corresponding verbal concord with *o* ('the *o* of reference'), as seen above in Table 8.4. The relative affixes share an important peculiarity: the fact that they are sometimes preverbal (as in (8)) and sometimes postverbal (as in (10)). How is this apparently ambifixal nature to be accounted for in an explicit morphotactics for Swahili relative affixes? How, in particular, can one explain the fact that a relative verb form's relative affix is preverbal if and only if that form exhibits overt morphology for either tense or negation? In Section 8.4, I shall argue that this is a case of affix counterposition (Sections 1.5.6 and 2.4), whose deviation from the stem operand criterion has the effect of reconciling it with the affix directionality criterion.

(10) a. *m-tu*   *a-vi-taka-ye*
        NC1-person   SBJ.NC1-OBJ.NC8-want-REL.NC1
        'a person who wants them'
     b. *vi-tabu*   *a-vi-taka-vyo*
        NC8-book   SBJ.NC1-OBJ.NC8-want-REL.NC8
        'the books that s/he wants'

In order to account for the polyfunctionality of Swahili verbal concords, for the exponence of negation, and for the special morphotactics of relative verb forms, I now propose specific formulations of the rules of Swahili verb inflection, of the manners in which they combine, and of the ways in which they and their combinations enter into competition. I focus on the subject/object polyfunctionality of the verbal concords in Section 8.2; on the exponence of negation in Section 8.3; and on the morphotactics of relative verb forms in Section 8.4. The analyses presented in these sections are cumulative: the fragment of Swahili verb morphology presented in Section 8.2 (Fragment I, relating to the subject/object polyfunctionality of the verbal concords) is extended in Section 8.3 (where Fragment II incorporates Fragment I but further accounts for the exponence of negation) and again in Section 8.4 (where Fragment III incorporates Fragments II and I but further accounts for the morphotactics of relative verb forms).[6] Despite the fact that the final, fully cumulative analysis is quite complex in detail, the three fragments converge on what is, at a general level, a very simple analysis – one in which the rules of Swahili verb inflection fall into three groups (Groups I, II, and III) such that each verb form is defined either by a composite rule of the type ($R_{III} \circ R_{II}$) or by a nested composite rule of the type (($R_{III} \circ R_{II}) \circ R_{I}$).

8.2 The Subject/Object Polyfunctionality of Verbal Concords in Swahili Verb Morphology: Fragment I

In the analyses that I propose here and in Sections 8.3–8.4, rules of Swahili verb inflection fall into three groups; in Figure 8.2, the affixes of Swahili verb inflection are classified according to the rule group by which they are defined. All groups contain both simple rules and combined rules. The numbering of the three groups reflects the order in which a (simple or combined) member of one group combines with a (simple or combined) member of another group. Group III includes the rule ⟦**ha-**⟧ introducing the indicative negative prefix *ha-*, the rules introducing the subject concord prefixes, and combinations of these rules. Group II includes the rules introducing the tense prefixes, the rule introducing the nonindicative negative prefix *si-*, the rules introducing the relative affixes, and combinations of these rules. Group I includes the rules introducing the pronominal object prefixes.

The morphosyntactic property sets realized by the rules in Groups I–III are somewhat complex in their structure. Besides inflecting for mood, tense, and polarity, a Swahili verb inflects for subject agreement (indicating the subject's person and number, and in the third person, its noun class); a verb may also inflect for the person, number, and noun class of a pronominal object, and as we have seen, relative verb forms further inflect for the number and noun class

---

[6] The full analysis proposed here contrasts rather starkly with that proposed by Crysmann & Bonami (2016); see Section 12.5.1 for detailed discussion.

indicative negative prefix *ha-*	subject concord prefixes	tense prefixes; nonindicative negative prefix *si-*	preverbal relative affixes	pronominal object prefixes	verb root	final vowel	postverbal relative affixes
					verb stem		
portmanteau negative prefix *si-*							

Defining rule group:	Group III	Group II	Group I		Group II

Figure 8.2 *Individual affixes of Swahili verb inflection categorized according to the rule group by which they are defined*

of a relativized argument. In the preliminary Fragment I of Swahili verb inflection under scrutiny in this section, the morphosyntactic property sets of positive indicative verb forms include the properties in the 'Fragment I' row of Table 8.5. This system of property sets is extended in Sections 8.3–8.4 to additionally accommodate the properties associated with subjunctive, negative, and relative verb forms.

The morphosyntactic properties in Table 8.5 do not combine absolutely freely; instead, a well-formed morphosyntactic property set must conform to various property coöccurrence restrictions. For Fragment I, the relevant restrictions are those in (11). The notion 'extension' to which (11d–e) refer is defined recursively in (12); the 'atomic properties' in this analysis are those listed in Table 8.5.

(11) Property coöccurrence restrictions for Fragment I of Swahili verb inflection
    a. A well-formed property set includes at most one property from each of columns 1–9 of Table 8.5.
    b. In a well-formed property set, properties chosen from columns 4–6 belong to a nested set containing sbj.
    c. In a well-formed property set, properties chosen from columns 7–9 belong to a nested set containing obj.
    d. Where τ is a nested set {sbj} or {obj}, a well-formed extension of τ that includes nc1, nc3, nc5, nc7, nc9, nc11, or nc14 also includes 3sg.
    e. Where τ is a nested set {sbj} or {obj}, a well-formed extension of τ that includes nc2, nc4, nc6, nc8, or nc10 also includes 3pl.

(12) Set B is an ***extension*** of set A just in case
    a. for every atomic property p that is a member of A, p is a member of B; and
    b. for every set s that is a member of A, an extension of s is a member of B.

For the preliminary Fragment I of Swahili verb inflection under discussion in this section, the basic members of the three groups of rules of exponence are those in (13). For expository convenience, I employ three conventions in the representation of these rules. First, each rule label ⟦**x**⟧ carries an external, Roman-numeral subscript indicating its group membership; for example, the Group III rule introducing the negative prefix *ha-* has the label ⟦**ha-**⟧$_{III}$. Second, if a rule ⟦**x**⟧ introduces an affix **x** that expresses noun class n, I represent **x** with a bold subscript n; for instance, the Group III rule introducing the subject-agreement prefix *a-* for noun class 1 is labeled ⟦**a-₁**⟧$_{III}$. Third, I use the ⟦id.fcn⟧ label for rules that realize specific content through the application of an identity function; there are two such rules in (13), distinguished by their rule-group subscript: ⟦id.fcn⟧$_{I}$, ⟦id.fcn⟧$_{III}$.

Table 8.5 *Morphosyntactic properties for three cumulative fragments of Swahili verb inflection*

	1	2	3	4	5	6	7	8	9	10	11	12
	mood	polarity	tense, mood	{subject agreemt.}	person, number	noun class	{pron. object}	person, number	noun class	{relativized argument}	person, number	noun class
Fragment I (Section 8.2)	ind	pos	fut, pst, def. time	sbj	1sg, 1pl, 2sg, 2pl, 3sg, 3pl	nc1, nc2, nc3, nc4, nc5, nc6, nc7, nc8, nc9, nc10, nc11, nc14	obj	1sg, 1pl, 2sg, 2pl, 3sg, 3pl	nc1, nc2, nc3, nc4, nc5, nc6, nc7, nc8, nc9, nc10, nc11, nc14			
Additional properties in Fragment II (Section 8.3)	–ind	neg	sbjv									
Additional properties in Fragment III (Section 8.4)			–tense							rel	3sg, 3pl	nc1, nc2, nc3, nc4, nc5, nc6, nc7, nc8, nc9, nc10, nc11, nc14

8.2 *Subject/Object Polyfunctionality*   237

(13) Basic rules of exponence for Fragment I
    a. Group III
        Basic subject-agreement rules
            ⟦**u-**⟧$_{III}$: [V, {{sbj 2sg}} : *u-*]   e.g. *u-ta-ni-piga* 'you (sg.) will strike me'

            ⟦**m-**⟧$_{III}$: [V, {{sbj 2pl}} : *m-*]   *m-ta-ni-piga* 'you (pl.) will strike me'

            ⟦**a-$_1$**⟧$_{III}$: [V, {{sbj 3sg nc1}} : *a-*]   *a-ta-ni-piga* 's/he will strike me'

        Carrier rule for verbal concords expressing subject agreement
            ⟦id.fcn⟧$_{III}$: [V, {{sbj}} : X → X]   *ha-tu-ta-piga* 'we will not strike'

    b. Group II
        Basic tense rules
            ⟦**ta-**⟧$_{II}$: [V, {ind fut} : *ta-*]   *u-ta-m-piga* 'you (sg.) will strike him/her'

            ⟦**li-**⟧$_{II}$: [V, {pst} : *li-*]   *u-li-m-piga* 'you (sg.) struck him/her'

            ⟦**na-**⟧$_{II}$: [V, {def.time} : *na-*]   *u-na-m-piga* 'you (sg.) are striking him/her'

    c. Group I
        Basic pronominal-object rules
            ⟦**ku-**⟧$_{I}$: [V, {{obj 2sg}} : *ku-*]   *a-ta-ku-piga* 's/he will strike you (sg.)'

            ⟦**wa-**⟧$_{I}$: [V, {{obj 2pl}} : *wa-*]   *a-ta-wa-piga* 's/he will strike you (pl.)'

            ⟦**m-$_1$**⟧$_{I}$: [V, {{obj 3sg nc1}} : *m-*]   *u-ta-m-piga* 'you (sg.) will strike him/her'

        Carrier rule for verbal concords expressing a pronominal object
            ⟦id.fcn⟧$_{I}$: [V, {{obj}} : X → X]   *a-ta-tu-piga* 's/he will strike us'

In Fragment I, the basic rules of exponence in Group III express subject agreement; the basic rules in Group II express tense; and the basic rules in Group III express a pronominal object.

Not included among the basic rules in (13) are the "versatile" rules that introduce affixes that may serve both to express subject agreement and to express the properties of a pronominal object. The rules in (14) are all versatile in this way. The first-person singular ⟦**ni-**⟧ rule, for example, applies to express a first-person singular subject in the definition of forms such as *nitasoma* 'I will read' but also applies to express a first-person singular object in forms such as *atanipiga* 's/he will strike me'.

(14) Dependent argument-coding rules
    a. ⟦**ni-**⟧ :   [V, {{1sg}} : *ni-*]
    b. ⟦**tu-**⟧ :   [V, {{1pl}} : *tu-*]
    c. ⟦**wa-$_2$**⟧ :   [V, {{3pl nc2}} : *wa-*]
    d. ⟦**u-$_3$**⟧ :   [V, {{3sg nc3}} : *u-*]

e. ⟦i-₄⟧ : [V, {{3pl nc4}} : *i-*]
f. ⟦li-₅⟧ : [V, {{3sg nc5}} : *li-*]
g. ⟦ya-₆⟧ : [V, {{3pl nc6}} : *ya-*]
h. ⟦ki-₇⟧ : [V, {{3sg nc7}} : *ki-*]
i. ⟦vi-₈⟧ : [V, {{3pl nc8}} : *vi-*]
j. ⟦i-₉⟧ : [V, {{3sg nc9}} : *i-*]
k. ⟦zi-₁₀⟧ : [V, {{3pl nc10}} : *zi-*]
l. ⟦u-₁₁⟧ : [V, {{3sg nc11}} : *u-*]
m. ⟦u-₁₄⟧ : [V, {{3sg nc14}} : *u-*]

The versatility of the rules in (14) follows from the fact that these rules realize category-indeterminate properties (Section 2.1.1). For example, the property set {{1 sg}} realized by the application of ⟦ni-⟧ contains the set-based property {1 sg}, which is indeterminate with respect to its inflectional category. In the definition of some forms, ⟦ni-⟧ participates in the realization of the set-based property {sbj 1 sg} (which belongs to the inflectional category of subject agreement); in the definition of other forms, it participates in the realization of the set-based property {obj 1 sg} (which belongs to the inflectional category of pronominal object specification). In accordance with the Category Determination Principle (Section 2.1.1),[7] ⟦ni-⟧ always combines with a rule realizing a category-determinate property Q such that the unification [{1 sg} ⊔ Q] is itself a set-based property that is well-formed and category-determinate; the same is true of all of the other rules in (14).

Whether a versatile rule of this sort expresses subject agreement or the properties of a pronominal object thus depends on how it combines with other rules. To account for this fact, I assume that the rules in (14) are dependent rules that do not inherently belong to any of the three rule groups but may compose with the carrier rules given in (13) for Groups I and III,[8] that is, the

---

[7] Informally, the Category Determination Principle entails that a rule whose morphosyntactic content is ambiguous (because it contains a category-indeterminate property) is disambiguated by the first rule with which it composes. In more precise terms: if R is a rule of inflectional exponence that realizes a category-indeterminate property P, R always combines with a rule that realizes a set-based property Q such that the unification [P ⊔ Q] is a set-based property that is well-formed and category-determinate.

[8] In their account of the versatility of the affixes realized by the rules in (14), Crysmann & Bonami (2016: 356) resort to the postulation of orthogonal multiple inheritance from underspecified rule schemata; the form and content of the first-person singular affix *ni* is defined by an underspecified rule schema for exponence, while subject agreement and object agreement are associated with distinct affix positions by separate underspecified rule schemata for morphotactics. The analysis proposed here for the versatility of the rules in (14) doesn't rely on orthogonal multiple exponence, but simply appeals to rule composition, as in (15). See Section 12.5.1.

rules ⟦id.fcn⟧$_I$ and ⟦id.fcn⟧$_{III}$.[9] Their combination with these carrier rules conforms to the pair of patterns in (15).[10]

(15) Where R is a dependent argument-coding rule in (14),
    a. (R ∘ ⟦id.fcn⟧$_{III}$) is a subject-agreement rule in Group III and
    b. (R ∘ ⟦id.fcn⟧$_I$) is a pronominal-object rule in Group I.

The composite rules defined for Group III by (15a) are listed in (16); those defined for Group I by (15b) are listed in (17). Whether the dependent rules in (14) express properties of subject agreement or properties of a pronominal object depends on their carrier rule: when one of the dependent rules in (14) composes with the carrier rule ⟦id.fcn⟧$_{III}$ in (13a), its content unifies with the carrier rule's content {{sbj}}, producing a composite expressing subject agreement, as in (16); when that same dependent rule composes with the carrier rule ⟦id.fcn⟧$_I$ in (13c), its content unifies with the carrier rule's content {{obj}}, producing a composite expressing the properties of a pronominal object, as in (17).[11]

(16) Composite subject-agreement rules defined for Group III by (15a)
    a. (⟦**ni-**⟧ ∘ ⟦id.fcn⟧$_{III}$) :   [V, {{sbj 1sg}} : *ni-*]
    b. (⟦**tu-**⟧ ∘ ⟦id.fcn⟧$_{III}$) :   [V, {{sbj 1pl}} : *tu-*]
    c. (⟦**wa-$_2$**⟧ ∘ ⟦id.fcn⟧$_{III}$) :   [V, {{sbj 3pl nc2}} : *wa-*]
    d. (⟦**u-$_3$**⟧ ∘ ⟦id.fcn⟧$_{III}$) :   [V, {{sbj 3sg nc3}} : *u-*]
    e. (⟦**i-$_4$**⟧ ∘ ⟦id.fcn⟧$_{III}$) :   [V, {{sbj 3pl nc4}} : *i-*]
    f. (⟦**li-$_5$**⟧ ∘ ⟦id.fcn⟧$_{III}$) :   [V, {{sbj 3sg nc5}} : *li-*]
    g. (⟦**ya-$_6$**⟧ ∘ ⟦id.fcn⟧$_{III}$) :   [V, {{sbj 3pl nc6}} : *ya-*]
    h. (⟦**ki-$_7$**⟧ ∘ ⟦id.fcn⟧$_{III}$) :   [V, {{sbj 3sg nc7}} : *ki-*]
    i. (⟦**vi-$_8$**⟧ ∘ ⟦id.fcn⟧$_{III}$) :   [V, {{sbj 3pl nc8}} : *vi-*]

---

[9] One might object to the carrier rules ⟦id.fcn⟧$_{III}$ and ⟦id.fcn⟧$_I$ on the grounds that they are like zero affixes, but this is not an apt comparison. In a theory that allows them, the postulation of zero affixes is generally motivated by the observation that the absence of an affix from a certain position contrasts with overt affixes in that same position (e.g. *they have writt-en* vs. *they have knitt-ed* vs. *they have hit-∅*). But the application of ⟦id.fcn⟧$_{III}$ never yields the absence of a Group III affix, nor does the application of ⟦id.fcn⟧$_I$ ever yield the absence of a Group I affix, since ⟦id.fcn⟧$_{III}$ and ⟦id.fcn⟧$_I$ carry an overt rule from (14) in any form in whose definition they are ever involved. That is, the application of rules such as ⟦**a-$_1$**⟧$_{III}$ and ⟦**m-$_1$**⟧$_I$ in (13a,c) contrasts with that of composite rules such as (⟦**ni-**⟧ ∘ ⟦id.fcn⟧$_{III}$) and (⟦**ni-**⟧ ∘ ⟦id.fcn⟧$_I$), not with that of ⟦id.fcn⟧$_{III}$ and ⟦id.fcn⟧$_I$ on their own.

[10] In Section 8.4, the third-person dependent rules in (14) will also be seen to compose with a carrier rule in Group II to form composite rules introducing the relative affixes in Table 8.4.

[11] These distinct patterns of unification are guaranteed by the definition of unification in (25b) in Section 2.2, according to which the unification of a rule realizing property set τ_1 with a rule realizing property set τ_2 realizes the smallest well-formed extension of both τ_1 and τ_2, where 'smallest' means lowest in cardinality.

	j.	$(\llbracket \mathbf{i\text{-}_9} \rrbracket \circ \llbracket \text{id.fcn} \rrbracket_{\text{III}})$:	[V, {{sbj 3sg nc9}} : *i-*]
	k.	$(\llbracket \mathbf{zi\text{-}_{10}} \rrbracket \circ \llbracket \text{id.fcn} \rrbracket_{\text{III}})$:	[V, {{sbj 3pl nc10}} : *zi-*]
	l.	$(\llbracket \mathbf{u\text{-}_{11}} \rrbracket \circ \llbracket \text{id.fcn} \rrbracket_{\text{III}})$:	[V, {{sbj 3sg nc11}} : *u-*]
	m.	$(\llbracket \mathbf{u\text{-}_{14}} \rrbracket \circ \llbracket \text{id.fcn} \rrbracket_{\text{III}})$:	[V, {{sbj 3sg nc14}} : *u-*]

(17) Composite pronominal-object rules defined for Group I by (15b)

	a.	$(\llbracket \mathbf{ni\text{-}} \rrbracket \circ \llbracket \text{id.fcn} \rrbracket_{\text{I}})$:	[V, {{obj 1sg}} : *ni-*]
	b.	$(\llbracket \mathbf{tu\text{-}} \rrbracket \circ \llbracket \text{id.fcn} \rrbracket_{\text{I}})$:	[V, {{obj 1pl}} : *tu-*]
	c.	$(\llbracket \mathbf{wa\text{-}_2} \rrbracket \circ \llbracket \text{id.fcn} \rrbracket_{\text{I}})$:	[V, {{obj 3pl nc2}} : *wa-*]
	d.	$(\llbracket \mathbf{u\text{-}_3} \rrbracket \circ \llbracket \text{id.fcn} \rrbracket_{\text{I}})$:	[V, {{obj 3sg nc3}} : *u-*]
	e.	$(\llbracket \mathbf{i\text{-}_4} \rrbracket \circ \llbracket \text{id.fcn} \rrbracket_{\text{I}})$:	[V, {{obj 3pl nc4}} : *i-*]
	f.	$(\llbracket \mathbf{li\text{-}_5} \rrbracket \circ \llbracket \text{id.fcn} \rrbracket_{\text{I}})$:	[V, {{obj 3sg nc5}} : *li-*]
	g.	$(\llbracket \mathbf{ya\text{-}_6} \rrbracket \circ \llbracket \text{id.fcn} \rrbracket_{\text{I}})$:	[V, {{obj 3pl nc6}} : *ya-*]
	h.	$(\llbracket \mathbf{ki\text{-}_7} \rrbracket \circ \llbracket \text{id.fcn} \rrbracket_{\text{I}})$:	[V, {{obj 3sg nc7}} : *ki-*]
	i.	$(\llbracket \mathbf{vi\text{-}_8} \rrbracket \circ \llbracket \text{id.fcn} \rrbracket_{\text{I}})$:	[V, {{obj 3pl nc8}} : *vi-*]
	j.	$(\llbracket \mathbf{i\text{-}_9} \rrbracket \circ \llbracket \text{id.fcn} \rrbracket_{\text{I}})$:	[V, {{obj 3sg nc9}} : *i-*]
	k.	$(\llbracket \mathbf{zi\text{-}_{10}} \rrbracket \circ \llbracket \text{id.fcn} \rrbracket_{\text{I}})$:	[V, {{obj 3pl nc10}} : *zi-*]
	l.	$(\llbracket \mathbf{u\text{-}_{11}} \rrbracket \circ \llbracket \text{id.fcn} \rrbracket_{\text{I}})$:	[V, {{obj 3sg nc11}} : *u-*]
	m.	$(\llbracket \mathbf{u\text{-}_{14}} \rrbracket \circ \llbracket \text{id.fcn} \rrbracket_{\text{I}})$:	[V, {{obj 3sg nc14}} : *u-*]

Given this approach, the full exponence rules (FERs) for Fragment I can be characterized through the composition of rules from Groups I, II, and III, as in (18). (As will be seen, the two patterns in (18) extend without modification to Fragments II and III.)

(18) FER patterns for Fragments I, II, and III
Where R_{II} and R_{III} are the narrowest rules in Groups II and III that are applicable to the form cell $\langle Z, \sigma \rangle$,
  a. if there is no rule in Group I that is applicable to $\langle Z, \sigma \rangle$, then $(R_{\text{III}} \circ R_{\text{II}})$ is the FER for $\langle Z, \sigma \rangle$;
  b. if R_{I} is the narrowest rule in Group I that is applicable to $\langle Z, \sigma \rangle$, then $((R_{\text{III}} \circ R_{\text{II}}) \circ R_{\text{I}})$ is the FER for $\langle Z, \sigma \rangle$.

Examples of the FERs defined by (18) are the composite rules in (19). The FER (19a) defines forms such as *ninasoma* 'I am reading', as in part (a) of Table 8.6; here, the composite rule ($\llbracket \mathbf{ni\text{-}} \rrbracket \circ \llbracket \text{id.fcn} \rrbracket_{\text{III}}$) in (16a) expresses subject agreement. The FER (19b) defines forms such as *atampiga* 's/he will strike her/him', as in part (b) of Table 8.6; in this form, the subject properties and the pronominal object properties are respectively realized by the simple rules $\llbracket \mathbf{a\text{-}_1} \rrbracket_{\text{III}}$ and $\llbracket \mathbf{m\text{-}_1} \rrbracket_{\text{I}}$ in (13a,c). The FER (19c) defines forms such as *watawapiga* 'they will strike them', as in part (c) of Table 8.6; here, the dependent rule $\llbracket \mathbf{wa\text{-}_2} \rrbracket$ in (14c) figures in both the expression of subject agreement (by means of the composite rule ($\llbracket \mathbf{wa\text{-}_2} \rrbracket \circ \llbracket \text{id.fcn} \rrbracket_{\text{III}}$) in (16c)) and the expression of a pronominal object (by means of the composite rule ($\llbracket \mathbf{wa\text{-}_2} \rrbracket \circ \llbracket \text{id.fcn} \rrbracket_{\text{I}}$) in (17c)).

Table 8.6 *The morphotactics of three Swahili verb forms in Fragment I*

(a)	Form cell:	⟨*soma*, {ind pos def.time {sbj 1sg}}⟩	'I am reading'
	|		
	FER	((⟦**ni-**⟧ ∘ ⟦id.fcn⟧_{III}) ∘ ⟦**na-**⟧_{II})	(= (19a))
	↓		
	Realized cell:	⟨*ninasoma*, {ind pos def.time {sbj 1sg}}⟩	
(b)	Form cell:	⟨*piga*, {ind pos fut {sbj 3sg nc1} {obj 3sg nc1}}⟩	's/he will strike her/him'
	|		
	FER	((⟦**a-₁**⟧_{III} ∘ ⟦**ta-**⟧_{II}) ∘ ⟦**m-₁**⟧_I)	(= (19b))
	↓		
	Realized cell:	⟨*atampiga*, {ind pos fut {sbj 3sg nc1} {obj 3sg nc1}}⟩	
(c)	Form cell:	⟨*piga*, {ind pos fut {sbj 3pl nc2} {obj 3pl nc2}}⟩	'they will strike them'
	|		
	FER	((((⟦**wa-₂**⟧ ∘ ⟦id.fcn⟧_{III}) ∘ ⟦**ta-**⟧_{II}) ∘ (⟦**wa-₂**⟧ ∘ ⟦id.fcn⟧_I))	(= (19c))
	↓		
	Realized cell:	⟨*watawapiga*, {ind pos fut {sbj 3pl nc2} {obj 3pl nc2}}⟩	

(19) Some FERs defined by (18)
a.   ((⟦**ni-**⟧ ∘ ⟦id.fcn⟧_{III}) ∘ ⟦**na-**⟧_{II}) : [V, {def.time {sbj 1sg}} : *nina-*]
b.   ((⟦**a-₁**⟧_{III} ∘ ⟦**ta-**⟧_{II}) ∘ ⟦**m-₁**⟧_I) : [V, {ind fut {sbj 3sg nc1} {obj 3sg nc1}} : *atam-*]
c.   ((((⟦**wa-₂**⟧ ∘ ⟦id.fcn⟧_{III}) ∘ ⟦**ta-**⟧_{II}) ∘ (⟦**wa-₂**⟧ ∘ ⟦id.fcn⟧_I)) :
     [V, {ind fut {sbj 3pl nc2} {obj 3pl nc2}} : *watawa-*]

This way of accounting for the subject/object polyfunctionality of the rules in (14) correctly portrays these rules as deviations from the unique sequence criterion: each of the rules in (14) may join with other rules in more than one sequence, owing to the fact that it is a dependent rule whose carrier may belong either to Group III or to Group I.[12] The fact that the rules in (14) may express either properties of subject agreement or properties of a pronominal object is not attributed to their own formulation, but to the formulation of the carrier

---

[12] This analysis recalls the deviation from the unique sequence criterion seen in Limbu verb inflection in Section 3.2. There is, however, an important difference: in the deviation exhibited by Limbu *huʔr-u-ŋ-si-ŋ* 'I teach them', the two applications of the ⟦**-ŋ**⟧ rule realize the same morphosyntactic property {agt 1 sg} and thus constitute a case of multiple exponence; but in the deviation exhibited by Swahili *watawapiga* 'they will strike them', the two applications of the ⟦**wa-**⟧ rule participate in the realization of different properties (namely {sbj 3pl NC2} and {obj 3pl NC2}), and thus do not constitute a case of multiple exponence.

242 *Complex Morphotactic Interactions in Swahili*

rule with which they compose: in accordance with the Category Determination Principle, combination with the carrier rule [[id.fcn]]$_{III}$ in (13a) produces a composite rule expressing subject agreement, while combination with the carrier rule [[id.fcn]]$_{I}$ in (13c) produces a composite rule expressing the properties of a pronominal object.

8.3 The Morphotactics of Negation in Swahili Verb Morphology: Fragment II

Building on the foregoing analysis, I now examine a larger fragment of Swahili conjugational morphotactics. Fragment II includes negative forms and (nonindicative) subjunctive forms, so the morphosyntactic properties '–ind', 'neg', and 'sbjv' are now included in the relevant inventory of morphosyntactic properties. (See the 'Fragment II' row of Table 8.5.) With the inclusion of these additional properties, the property coöccurrence restrictions in (11) must now be supplemented with the restrictions in (20). According to (20a), subjunctive forms are necessarily nonindicative; according to (20b), indicative forms are all tensed forms (though, as we will see in Section 8.4, the reverse is not always true).

(20) Additional property coöccurrence restrictions for Fragment II of Swahili verb inflection
    a. A well-formed extension of {sbjv} is also an extension of {–ind}.
    b. A well-formed extension of {ind} is also an extension of a tense property set (either {fut}, {pst}, or {def.time}, in this fragment).

In order to account for negative and subjunctive forms, it is necessary to add some rules of exponence to Groups III and II; these are the additional rules in (21).

(21) Additional basic rules of exponence for Fragment II
    a. Group III
        Basic indicative negative rule
        [[**ha-**]]$_{III}$: [V, {ind neg} : *ha-*]   e.g. *ha-tu-ta-taka* 'we will not want'
        Portmanteau rule for indicative negation and first-person plural subject agreement
        [[**si-**]]$_{III}$: [V, {ind neg {sbj 1sg}} : *si-*] *si-ta-m-piga* 'I will not strike her/him'
    b. Group II
        Basic tense rules
        [[**ku-**]]$_{II}$: [V, {ind neg pst} : *ku-*]   *ha-tu-ku-taka* 'we did not want'
        [[**-i**]]$_{II}$: [V, {ind neg def.time} : *-i*]   *ha-tu-tak-i* 'we do not want'

Basic nonindicative negative rule
⟦si-⟧_II : [V, {–ind neg} : si-]   u-si-som-e 'do not read!'
Basic subjunctive rule
⟦-e⟧_II : [V, {sbjv} : -e]   u-ni-saidi-e 'help me!'

The basic rules of exponence in Fragment II are the result of combining the basic rules for Fragment I (i.e. the rules in (13)) with the basic rules in (21). Taken together, the basic members of Group III in (13a) and (21a) are quite varied. They include rules expressing indicative negation (⟦ha-⟧_III), subject agreement (⟦u-⟧_III, ⟦m-⟧_III, ⟦a-₁⟧_III), or both (⟦si-⟧_III). The basic members of Group II in (13b) and (21b) are similarly varied, since they include rules expressing tense (⟦ta-⟧_II, ⟦li-⟧_II, ⟦na-⟧_II), nonindicative negation (⟦si-⟧_II), tense cumulatively with (indicative) negation (⟦ku-⟧_II and ⟦-i⟧_II), and subjunctive mood (⟦-e⟧_II). The ⟦-i⟧_II and ⟦-e⟧_II rules in (21b) differ from the other basic members of Group II in that they introduce suffixes. I assume that these suffixes -i and -e induce the elision of a stem-final vowel (as in *ha-tu-tak-i* 'we do not want' [stem *-taka*], *u-ni-saidi-e* 'help me!' [stem *-saidia*]).[13] In addition to its basic members, Group II includes the composite rule in (22), which serves in the inflection of negative subjunctive forms such as *u-si-som-e* 'do not read!'.

(22)   (⟦si-⟧_II ∘ ⟦-e⟧_II) : [V, {–ind neg sbjv} : X → si-X-e]

Group III also includes composite rules – those in (16) and some new ones. The latter arise through the composition of the indicative negative ⟦ha-⟧_III rule with the basic subject-agreement rules in (13a) (i.e. with ⟦u-⟧_III, ⟦m-⟧_III, and ⟦a-₁⟧_III) and with the Group III composites in (16). Thus, the composite rules in Group III for Fragment II are those of Fragment I plus those in (23). Note that ⟦ha-⟧_III does not compose with ⟦ni-⟧_III; the portmanteau rule ⟦si-⟧_III in (21a) takes the place of this composite.

(23)   Indicative negative composite members of Group III
   a. (⟦ha-⟧_III ∘ (⟦tu-⟧ ∘ ⟦id.fcn⟧_III)) :   [V, {ind neg {sbj 1pl}} : hatu-]
   b. (⟦ha-⟧_III ∘ ⟦u-⟧_III) :   [V, {ind neg {sbj 2sg}} : hu-]
                                               (elision: ha-u- → hu-)
   c. (⟦ha-⟧_III ∘ ⟦m-⟧_III) :   [V, {ind neg {sbj 2pl}} : ham-]
   d. (⟦ha-⟧_III ∘ ⟦a-₁⟧_III) :   [V, {ind neg {sbj 3sg ncl}} : ha-]
                                               (elision: ha-a- → ha-)

---

[13] In the case of verbs borrowed from Arabic, the stem-final vowel is instead preserved in place of the suffixal -i or -e (as in *ha-wa-tubu* 'they do not repent', *u-si-tubu* 'do not repent!').

244 *Complex Morphotactic Interactions in Swahili*

e. $(\![\mathbf{ha\text{-}}]\!]_{\text{III}} \circ (\![\mathbf{wa\text{-}_2}]\!] \circ [\![\text{id.fcn}]\!]_{\text{III}}))$: [V, {ind neg {sbj 3pl nc2}} : *hawa-*]
f. $(\![\mathbf{ha\text{-}}]\!]_{\text{III}} \circ (\![\mathbf{u\text{-}_3}]\!] \circ [\![\text{id.fcn}]\!]_{\text{III}}))$: [V, {ind neg {sbj 3sg nc3}} : *hau-*]
g. $(\![\mathbf{ha\text{-}}]\!]_{\text{III}} \circ (\![\mathbf{i\text{-}_4}]\!] \circ [\![\text{id.fcn}]\!]_{\text{III}}))$: [V, {ind neg {sbj 3pl nc4}} : *hai-*]
h. $(\![\mathbf{ha\text{-}}]\!]_{\text{III}} \circ (\![\mathbf{li\text{-}_5}]\!] \circ [\![\text{id.fcn}]\!]_{\text{III}}))$: [V, {ind neg {sbj 3sg nc5}} : *hali-*]
i. $(\![\mathbf{ha\text{-}}]\!]_{\text{III}} \circ (\![\mathbf{ya\text{-}_6}]\!] \circ [\![\text{id.fcn}]\!]_{\text{III}}))$: [V, {ind neg {sbj 3pl nc6}} : *haya-*]
j. $(\![\mathbf{ha\text{-}}]\!]_{\text{III}} \circ (\![\mathbf{ki\text{-}_7}]\!] \circ [\![\text{id.fcn}]\!]_{\text{III}}))$: [V, {ind neg {sbj 3sg nc7}} : *haki-*]
k. $(\![\mathbf{ha\text{-}}]\!]_{\text{III}} \circ (\![\mathbf{vi\text{-}_8}]\!] \circ [\![\text{id.fcn}]\!]_{\text{III}}))$: [V, {ind neg {sbj 3pl nc8}} : *havi-*]
l. $(\![\mathbf{ha\text{-}}]\!]_{\text{III}} \circ (\![\mathbf{i\text{-}_9}]\!] \circ [\![\text{id.fcn}]\!]_{\text{III}}))$: [V, {ind neg {sbj 3sg nc9}} : *hai-*]
m. $(\![\mathbf{ha\text{-}}]\!]_{\text{III}} \circ (\![\mathbf{zi\text{-}_{10}}]\!] \circ [\![\text{id.fcn}]\!]_{\text{III}}))$: [V, {ind neg {sbj 3pl nc10}} : *hazi-*]
n. $(\![\mathbf{ha\text{-}}]\!]_{\text{III}} \circ (\![\mathbf{u\text{-}_{11}}]\!] \circ [\![\text{id.fcn}]\!]_{\text{III}}))$: [V, {ind neg {sbj 3sg nc11}} : *hau-*]

Exactly as in Fragment I, the FERs for Fragment II are characterized by the FER patterns in (18). Examples of the FERs that (18) defines for Fragment II are the composite rules in (24). The FER (24a) defines forms such as *hatutasoma* 'we will not read', as in part (a) of Table 8.7. Here, the Group III rule is the composite (23a) and the Group II rule is the future-tense rule $[\![\mathbf{ta\text{-}}]\!]_{\text{II}}$; because *hatutasoma* lacks a pronominal object, no Group I rule applies in this FER. The FER (24b) defines forms such as *hatukumpiga* 'we did not strike her/him' as in part (b) of Table 8.7, accounting for the multiple exponence of negation by means of the negative composite (23a) in Group III and the negative past-tense rule $[\![\mathbf{ku\text{-}}]\!]_{\text{II}}$ in Group II. The FER (24c) defines forms such as *sikumpiga* 'I didn't strike her/him' by means of a composite of three simple rules: the first-person singular negative portmanteau rule $[\![\mathbf{si\text{-}}]\!]_{\text{III}}$ in Group III, the negative past-tense rule $[\![\mathbf{ku\text{-}}]\!]_{\text{II}}$ in Group II, and the third-person singular (noun class 1) rule $[\![\mathbf{m\text{-}_1}]\!]_{\text{I}}$ in Group I; see part (c) of Table 8.7. The FERs (24d,e) define subjunctive forms such as *unisaidie* 'help me!' (in which $[\![\mathbf{\text{-}e}]\!]_{\text{II}}$ serves as the Group II rule) and *usinisaidie* 'don't help me!' (which the composite negative subjunctive rule $([\![\mathbf{si\text{-}}]\!]_{\text{II}} \circ [\![\mathbf{\text{-}e}]\!]_{\text{II}})$ in (22) serves as the Group II rule); see parts (d) and (e) of Table 8.7.

(24) Some FERs defined by (18)
 a. $(([\![\mathbf{ha\text{-}}]\!]_{\text{III}} \circ ([\![\mathbf{tu\text{-}}]\!] \circ [\![\text{id.fcn}]\!]_{\text{III}})) \circ [\![\mathbf{ta\text{-}}]\!]_{\text{II}})$: [V, {ind neg fut {sbj 1pl}} : *hatuta-*]
 b. $((([\![\mathbf{ha\text{-}}]\!]_{\text{III}} \circ ([\![\mathbf{tu\text{-}}]\!] \circ [\![\text{id.fcn}]\!]_{\text{III}})) \circ [\![\mathbf{ku\text{-}}]\!]_{\text{II}}) \circ [\![\mathbf{m\text{-}_1}]\!]_{\text{I}})$:
    [V, {ind neg pst {sbj 1pl} {obj 3sg nc1}} : *hatukum-*]
 c. $(([\![\mathbf{si\text{-}}]\!]_{\text{III}} \circ [\![\mathbf{ku\text{-}}]\!]_{\text{II}}) \circ [\![\mathbf{m\text{-}_1}]\!]_{\text{I}})$: [V, {ind neg pst {sbj 1sg} {obj 3sg nc1}} : *sikum-*]
 d. $(([\![\mathbf{u\text{-}}]\!]_{\text{III}} \circ [\![\mathbf{\text{-}e}]\!]_{\text{II}}) \circ ([\![\mathbf{ni\text{-}}]\!] \circ [\![\text{id.fcn}]\!]_{\text{I}}))$: [V, {–ind sbjv {sbj 2sg} {obj 1sg}} : X → *uni*-X-*e*]
 e. $(([\![\mathbf{u\text{-}}]\!]_{\text{III}} \circ ([\![\mathbf{si\text{-}}]\!]_{\text{II}} \circ [\![\mathbf{\text{-}e}]\!]_{\text{II}})) \circ ([\![\mathbf{ni\text{-}}]\!] \circ [\![\text{id.fcn}]\!]_{\text{I}}))$:
    [V, {–ind neg sbjv {sbj 2sg} {obj 1sg}} : X → *usini*-X-*e*]

This analysis accounts for two ways in which the morphotactics of Swahili negative verb forms apparently deviates from canonical criteria. First, it

8.3 Morphotactics of Negation   245

Table 8.7 *The morphotactics of five Swahili verb forms in Fragment II*

(a)	Form cell:	⟨*soma*, {ind neg fut {sbj 1pl}}⟩	'we will not read'
	|		
	FER	((⟦**ha-**⟧$_{III}$ ∘ (⟦**tu-**⟧ ∘ ⟦id.fcn⟧$_{III}$)) ∘ ⟦**ta-**⟧$_{II}$)	(= (24a))
	↓		
	Realized cell:	⟨*hatutasoma*, {ind neg fut {sbj 1pl}}⟩	
(b)	Form cell:	⟨*piga*, {ind neg pst {sbj 1pl} {obj 3sg ncl}}⟩	'we didn't strike her/him'
	|		
	FER	(((⟦**ha-**⟧$_{III}$ ∘ (⟦**tu-**⟧ ∘ ⟦id.fcn⟧$_{III}$)) ∘ ⟦**ku-**⟧$_{II}$) ∘ ⟦**m-₁**⟧$_{I}$)	(= (24b))
	↓		
	Realized cell:	⟨*hatukumpiga*, {ind neg pst {sbj 1pl} {obj 3sg ncl}}⟩	
(c)	Form cell:	⟨*piga*, {ind neg pst {sbj 1sg} {obj 3sg ncl}}⟩	'I didn't strike her/him'
	|		
	FER	((⟦**si-**⟧$_{III}$ ∘ ⟦**ku-**⟧$_{II}$) ∘ ⟦**m-₁**⟧$_{I}$)	(= (24c))
	↓		
	Realized cell:	⟨*sikumpiga*, {ind neg pst {sbj 1sg} {obj 3sg ncl}}⟩	
(d)	Form cell:	⟨*saidia*, {−ind pos sbjv {sbj 2sg} {obj 1sg}}⟩	'help me!'
	|		
	FER	((⟦**u-**⟧$_{III}$ ∘ ⟦**-e**⟧$_{II}$) ∘ (⟦**ni-**⟧ ∘ ⟦id.fcn⟧$_{I}$))	(= (24d))
	↓		
	Realized cell:	⟨*unisaidie*, {−ind pos sbjv {sbj 2sg} {obj 1sg}}⟩	
(e)	Form cell:	⟨*saidia*, {−ind neg sbjv {sbj 2sg} {obj 1sg}}⟩	'don't help me!'
	|		
	FER	((⟦**u-**⟧$_{III}$ ∘ (⟦**si-**⟧$_{II}$ ∘ ⟦**-e**⟧$_{II}$)) ∘ (⟦**ni-**⟧ ∘ ⟦id.fcn⟧$_{I}$))	(= (24e))
	↓		
	Realized cell:	⟨*usinisaidie*,{−ind neg sbjv {sbj 2sg} {obj 1sg}}⟩	

accounts for the fact that in Swahili, negative morphology does not conform to the parallel sequence criterion, according to which rules that express the same inflectional category canonically occupy the same position in any sequence of rule applications. In Swahili, negation is expressed sometimes by a Group III rule (as in *hatutasoma* 'we won't read', *sitasoma* 'I won't read'), sometimes by a Group II rule (as in *usinisaidie* 'don't help me'), and sometimes by both a Group III rule and a Group II rule (as in *hatukusoma* 'we didn't read', *sikusoma* 'I didn't read').

Second, the analysis proposed here accounts for an apparent deviation from the rule opposition criterion, according to which relations of paradigmatic opposition among rules of inflectional exponence are, canonically, relations among individual rules. In Swahili, the portmanteau ⟦si-⟧$_{III}$ rule introducing the first-person singular negative prefix *si-* in forms like *sitasoma* 'I won't read' apparently stands in paradigmatic opposition to the sequence of rules introducing the prefix string *ha-m-* in second-person plural negative forms like *hamtasoma* 'you (pl.) won't read'; but if the latter rules are assumed to constitute a composite rule (⟦ha-⟧$_{III}$ ∘ ⟦m-⟧$_{III}$), then the relation of paradigmatic opposition between ⟦si-⟧$_{III}$ and (⟦ha-⟧$_{III}$ ∘ ⟦m-⟧$_{III}$) actually conforms to the rule opposition criterion.[14]

The proposed analysis of negation in Swahili conjugation also accounts for issues relating to multiple exponence (Section 8.1.2). Consider first the form *hatukusoma* 'we didn't read'. What necessitates the appearance of the negative prefix *ha-* in this form given the presence of the negative past-tense prefix *ku-*? In the analysis proposed here, *hatukusoma* arises from the form cell (25), whose realization, in accordance with (18a), involves the narrowest applicable rules from Groups II and III. (Note that there is no rule in Group I that is applicable for the realization of (25).) The composite rule (⟦ha-⟧$_{III}$ ∘ (⟦tu-⟧ ∘ ⟦id.fcn⟧$_{III}$)) (= (23a)) overrides (⟦tu-⟧ ∘ ⟦id.fcn⟧$_{III}$) (= (16b)) as the narrowest applicable rule in Group III. Because the past-tense ⟦li-⟧$_{II}$ rule in (13b) isn't as narrowly applicable as the negative past-tense ⟦ku-⟧$_{II}$ rule in (21b), the latter is the only Group II rule applicable for the realization of (25). This fact has no effect on the choice of rule in Group III. That is, what necessitates the appearance of the negative prefix *ha-* in *hatukusoma* is the fact that (in accordance with (18a)) the FER for (25) is a two-rule composite (R_{III} ∘ R_{II}) such that each of R_{III} and R_{II} is the narrowest applicable rule in its group.

(25)   ⟨*soma*, {ind neg pst {sbj 1pl}}⟩

Now consider the form *sikusoma* 'I didn't read', in which negation is expressed cumulatively with first-person singular subject agreement by the prefix *si-* and cumulatively with past tense by the prefix *ku-*. What excludes the possibility of the nonredundant form **ni-ku-soma* (in which first-person singular subject agreement is expressed by *ni-*, as in positive forms) rather than the redundant form *si-ku-soma* as a realization for the form cell in (26)? The answer is that the portmanteau ⟦si-⟧$_{III}$ rule in (21a) overrides the composite

---

[14] This recalls the analysis of *audīminī* 'you are heard' in Section 5.2.1, where the apparent deviation of Latin *audiuntur* 'they are heard' from the rule opposition criterion is reconciled with it by analyzing (⟦-(u)r⟧ ∘ ⟦-unt⟧) as a composite rule that is paradigmatically opposed to the simple rule ⟦-minī⟧.

rule ($[\![$**ni**-$]\!]_{\text{III}} \circ [\![$id.fcn$]\!]_{\text{III}}$) in (16a) as the narrowest rule in Group III applicable for the realization of this cell, in accordance with (18a). As with (25), the negative past-tense $[\![$**ku**-$]\!]_{\text{II}}$ rule is the only Group II rule applicable for the realization of (26).

(26)   ⟨*soma*, {ind neg pst {sbj 1sg}}⟩

8.4   The Morphotactics of Relativization in Swahili Verb Morphology: Fragment III

I now extend the proposed fragment of Swahili verb inflection to include relative verb forms. In order to accommodate these in the analysis proposed in Sections 8.2–8.3, several additions are necessary. First, I assume the additional morphosyntactic properties '–tense' and 'rel' in the 'Fragment III' row of Table 8.5; the property '–tense' is associated with tenseless relative verb forms and the property 'rel' is associated with all relative verb forms. Combinations of the properties in Table 8.5 are subject to the revised set of property coöccurrence restrictions in (27), which subsume and extend those given above in (11) and (20). By restrictions (27e) and (27f), subjunctive verb forms and relative verb forms are both nonindicative; relative verb forms are seen as nonindicative insofar as they are never used on their own to perform the speech act of assertion in the way that indicative verb forms are. By restriction (27g), forms in this fragment that are specified as tenseless are relative, but by (27h), only negative relatives are necessarily specified as tenseless; that is, positive relatives may or may not express overt tense. Restrictions (27j,k) entail that just as the properties 'sbj' and 'obj' identify nested property sets encoding the person, number, and gender of a verb form's subject and pronominal object arguments, the property 'rel' identifies nested property sets encoding the person, number, and gender of a relative verb form's relativized argument. Restriction (27l) guarantees that the argument coded by a verb's relative morphology will likewise be coded by either its subject or its object morphology.

(27)   Property coöccurrence restrictions for Fragment III of Swahili verb inflection
    a. A well-formed property set includes at most one property from each of columns 1–12.
    b. In a well-formed property set, properties chosen from columns 4–6 belong to a nested set.
    c. In a well-formed property set, properties chosen from columns 7–9 belong to a nested set.
    d. In a well-formed property set, properties chosen from columns 10–12 belong to a nested set.

e. A well-formed extension of {sbjv} is also an extension of {−ind}.
f. A well-formed extension of {{rel}} is also an extension of {−ind}.
g. A well-formed extension of {−tense} is also an extension of {{rel}}.
h. A well-formed extension of {{rel} neg} is also an extension of {−tense}.
i. A well-formed extension of {ind} is also an extension of either {fut}, {pst}, or {def.time}.
j. Where τ is a nested set {sbj}, {obj}, or {rel}, a well-formed extension of τ that includes nc1, nc3, nc5, nc7, nc9, or nc11 also includes 3sg.
k. Where τ is a nested set {sbj}, {obj}, or {rel}, a well-formed extension of τ that includes nc2, nc4, nc6, nc8, or nc10 also includes 3pl.
l. For any noun class α, a well-formed extension of {{rel α}} is also an extension of either {{sbj α}} or {{obj α}}.

In Fragment III, three additional basic rules of exponence are necessary; these are all members of Group II, and are formulated in (28). The $[\![\text{taka-}]\!]_{II}$ rule expresses the future tense in relative verb forms. The basic rules encoding a relative verb form's relative argument are $[\![\text{-ye}_1]\!]_{II}$ and $[\![\text{-o}]\!]_{II}$. The $[\![\text{-ye}_1]\!]_{II}$ rule encodes a relativized argument belonging to noun class 1 through the suffixation of *-ye*; by contrast, $[\![\text{-o}]\!]_{II}$ is a default rule that encodes the presence of a relativized argument without expressing any particular noun class.

(28) Additional basic rules of exponence for Fragment III of Swahili verb inflection
Group II
Basic tense rule
   $[\![\text{taka-}]\!]_{II}$: [V, {{rel} fut} : *taka-*]   e.g. *a-taka-ye-soma* 'who will read'
Basic relativized-argument rule for noun class 1
   $[\![\text{-ye}_1]\!]_{II}$: [V, {−ind {rel 3sg nc1}} : *-ye*]   *a-taka-ye-soma* 'who will read'
Default relativized-argument rule and carrier rule for relativized-argument rules based on verbal concords
   $[\![\text{-o}]\!]_{II}$: [V, {−ind {rel}} : *-o*]   *wa-na-o-soma* 'who are reading'

In this extended fragment, I propose to treat relativized-argument rules (whether simple or combined) as rules of suffixation that participate in the definition of affix counterpositions in the presence of a tense/negation prefix; thus, the suffixational $[\![\text{-ye}_1]\!]_{II}$ rule in (28) is responsible both for the *-ye* suffix in the tenseless form *(mtu) asomaye* '(person) who reads' and for the *-ye* suffix that is counterposed to the tense prefix *taka-* in *(mtu) atakayesoma* '(person) who will read'. In order to accommodate this analysis, Group II includes a large number of aggregated rules. These are of two sorts: ***aggregated relativized-argument rules*** and ***aggregated relative tense/negation rules.*** Consider these in turn.

The dependent argument-coding rules that realize nonpersonal noun classes (= (14d–m)) aggregate with the default relativized-argument rule $[\![\text{-o}]\!]_{II}$ to produce aggregated relativized-argument rules, in accordance with the pattern in (29); like

8.4 Morphotactics of Relativization

their carrier rule $[\![\text{-o}]\!]_{\text{II}}$, these aggregated rules belong to Group II. The aggregated rules defined by (29) are listed in (30). For expository convenience, I abbreviate each of the aggregated rules in (30) as in the column to its right; these abbreviations highlight the fact that the rule aggregations in (30) define suffixational counterpositions. These aggregated rules are another instance of the versatility of the noun-class rules (14d–m). Each rule R in (14d–m) realizes a category-indeterminate property P; but in accordance with the Category Determination Principle, the corresponding aggregation (R Ⓐ $[\![\text{-o}]\!]_{\text{II}}$) in (30) realizes the well-formed, category-determinate property [P ⊔ {rel}].

(29) Where R is a dependent argument-coding rule in (14d–m), (R Ⓐ $[\![\text{-o}]\!]_{\text{II}}$) is a relativized-argument rule in Group II.

(30) Aggregated relativized-argument rules defined for Group II by (29)
      (NB: Sandhi is as indicated in Table 8.4.)

			Abbreviation:
a.	($[\![\text{u-}_3]\!]$ Ⓐ $[\![\text{-o}]\!]_{\text{II}}$) :	[V, {–ind {rel 3sg nc3}} : -o]	$[\![\text{-o}_3]\!]_{\text{II}}$:
b.	($[\![\text{i-}_4]\!]$ Ⓐ $[\![\text{-o}]\!]_{\text{II}}$) :	[V, {–ind {rel 3pl nc4}} : -yo]	$[\![\text{-yo}_4]\!]_{\text{II}}$:
c.	($[\![\text{li-}_5]\!]$ Ⓐ $[\![\text{-o}]\!]_{\text{II}}$) :	[V, {–ind {rel 3sg nc5}} : -lo]	$[\![\text{-lo}_5]\!]_{\text{II}}$:
d.	($[\![\text{ya-}_6]\!]$ Ⓐ $[\![\text{-o}]\!]_{\text{II}}$) :	[V, {–ind {rel 3pl nc6}} : -yo]	$[\![\text{-yo}_6]\!]_{\text{II}}$:
e.	($[\![\text{ki-}_7]\!]$ Ⓐ $[\![\text{-o}]\!]_{\text{II}}$) :	[V, {–ind {rel 3sg nc7}} : -cho]	$[\![\text{-cho}_7]\!]_{\text{II}}$:
f.	($[\![\text{vi-}_8]\!]$ Ⓐ $[\![\text{-o}]\!]_{\text{II}}$) :	[V, {–ind {rel 3pl nc8}} : -vyo]	$[\![\text{-vyo}_8]\!]_{\text{II}}$:
g.	($[\![\text{i-}_9]\!]$ Ⓐ $[\![\text{-o}]\!]_{\text{II}}$) :	[V, {–ind {rel 3sg nc9}} : -yo]	$[\![\text{-yo}_9]\!]_{\text{II}}$:
h.	($[\![\text{zi-}_{10}]\!]$ Ⓐ $[\![\text{-o}]\!]_{\text{II}}$) :	[V, {–ind {rel 3pl nc10}} : -zo]	$[\![\text{-zo}_{10}]\!]_{\text{II}}$:
i.	($[\![\text{u-}_{11}]\!]$ Ⓐ $[\![\text{-o}]\!]_{\text{II}}$) :	[V, {–ind {rel 3sg nc11}} : -o]	$[\![\text{-o}_{11}]\!]_{\text{II}}$:
j.	($[\![\text{u-}_{14}]\!]$ Ⓐ $[\![\text{-o}]\!]_{\text{II}}$) :	[V, {–ind {rel 3sg nc14}} : -o]	$[\![\text{-o}_{14}]\!]_{\text{II}}$:

In accordance with the pattern in (31), the relativized argument rules in Group II (including the basic rules $[\![\text{-ye}_1]\!]_{\text{II}}$ and $[\![\text{-o}]\!]_{\text{II}}$ in (28) as well as the aggregated rules in (30)) aggregate with Group II rules of tense and nonindicative negation to produce aggregated relative tense/negation rules; these are listed in Table 8.8. Like their component rules, all of the aggregated rules in Table 8.8 belong to Group II. Unlike the aggregations in (30) (which define suffixational counterpositions), the aggregations in Table 8.8 define prefixational counterpositions.

(31) Where R_1 is a rule of tense or nonindicative negation belonging to Group II (i.e. $[\![\text{li-}]\!]_{\text{II}}$ or $[\![\text{na-}]\!]_{\text{II}}$ in (13b), $[\![\text{taka-}]\!]_{\text{II}}$ in (28), or $[\![\text{si-}]\!]_{\text{II}}$ in (21b)) and R_2 is a (basic or aggregated) relativized-argument rule belonging to Group II, (R_2 Ⓐ R_1) is an aggregated relative tense/negation rule belonging to Group II.

It is worth taking a moment to notice how heterogeneous Group II has become. It includes

- simple rules of prefixation (e.g. the simple tense rules in (13b), (21b), and (28) and the simple rule $[\![\text{si-}]\!]_{\text{II}}$ of nonindicative negation in (21b));

250 *Complex Morphotactic Interactions in Swahili*

Table 8.8 *Aggregated relative tense/negation rules defined for Group II by (31)*

a.	Future tense+relativized argument rules	
	$(\llbracket\text{-ye}_1\rrbracket_{II} \circledA \llbracket\text{taka-}\rrbracket_{II})$:	[V, {–ind fut {rel 3sg nc1}} : *takaye-*]
	$(\llbracket\text{-o}\rrbracket_{II} \circledA \llbracket\text{taka-}\rrbracket_{II})$:	[V, {–ind fut {rel}} : *takao-*]
	$(\llbracket\text{-o}_3\rrbracket_{II} \circledA \llbracket\text{taka-}\rrbracket_{II})$:	[V, {–ind fut {rel 3sg nc3}} : *takao-*]
	$(\llbracket\text{-yo}_4\rrbracket_{II} \circledA \llbracket\text{taka-}\rrbracket_{II})$:	[V, {–ind fut {rel 3pl nc4}} : *takayo-*]
	$(\llbracket\text{-lo}_5\rrbracket_{II} \circledA \llbracket\text{taka-}\rrbracket_{II})$:	[V, {–ind fut {rel 3sg nc5}} : *takalo-*]
	$(\llbracket\text{-yo}_6\rrbracket_{II} \circledA \llbracket\text{taka-}\rrbracket_{II})$:	[V, {–ind fut {rel 3pl nc6}} : *takayo-*]
	$(\llbracket\text{-cho}_7\rrbracket_{II} \circledA \llbracket\text{taka-}\rrbracket_{II})$:	[V, {–ind fut {rel 3sg nc7}} : *takacho-*]
	$(\llbracket\text{-vyo}_8\rrbracket_{II} \circledA \llbracket\text{taka-}\rrbracket_{II})$:	[V, {–ind fut {rel 3pl nc8}} : *takavyo-*]
	$(\llbracket\text{-yo}_9\rrbracket_{II} \circledA \llbracket\text{taka-}\rrbracket_{II})$:	[V, {–ind fut {rel 3sg nc9}} : *takayo-*]
	$(\llbracket\text{-zo}_{10}\rrbracket_{II} \circledA \llbracket\text{taka-}\rrbracket_{II})$:	[V, {–ind fut {rel 3pl nc10}} : *takazo-*]
	$(\llbracket\text{-o}_{11}\rrbracket_{II} \circledA \llbracket\text{taka-}\rrbracket_{II})$:	[V, {–ind fut {rel 3sg nc11}} : *takao-*]
	$(\llbracket\text{-o}_{14}\rrbracket_{II} \circledA \llbracket\text{taka-}\rrbracket_{II})$:	[V, {–ind fut {rel 3sg nc14}} : *takao-*]
b.	Past tense+relativized argument rules	
	$(\llbracket\text{-ye}_1\rrbracket_{II} \circledA \llbracket\text{li-}\rrbracket_{II})$:	[V, {–ind pst {rel 3sg nc1}} : *liye-*]
	$(\llbracket\text{-o}\rrbracket_{II} \circledA \llbracket\text{li-}\rrbracket_{II})$:	[V, {–ind pst {rel}} : *lio-*]
	[and so on in parallel to (a), with $\llbracket\text{li-}\rrbracket_{II}$ substituted for $\llbracket\text{taka-}\rrbracket_{II}$.]	
c.	Definite time+relativized argument rules	
	$(\llbracket\text{-ye}_1\rrbracket_{II} \circledA \llbracket\text{na-}\rrbracket_{II})$:	[V, {–ind def.time {rel 3sg nc1}} : *naye-*]
	$(\llbracket\text{-o}\rrbracket_{II} \circledA \llbracket\text{na-}\rrbracket_{II})$:	[V, {–ind def.time {rel}} : *nao-*]
	[and so on in parallel to (a), with $\llbracket\text{na-}\rrbracket_{II}$ substituted for $\llbracket\text{taka-}\rrbracket_{II}$.]	
d.	Tenseless negation+relativized argument rules	
	$(\llbracket\text{-ye}_1\rrbracket_{II} \circledA \llbracket\text{si-}\rrbracket_{II})$:	[V, {–ind neg –tense {rel 3sg nc1}} : *siye-*]
	$(\llbracket\text{-o}\rrbracket_{II} \circledA \llbracket\text{si-}\rrbracket_{II})$:	[V, {–ind neg –tense {rel}} : *sio-*]
	[and so on in parallel to (a), with $\llbracket\text{si-}\rrbracket_{II}$ substituted for $\llbracket\text{taka-}\rrbracket_{II}$.]	

- simple rules of suffixation (e.g. the negative definite time rule $\llbracket\text{-i}\rrbracket_{II}$ and subjunctive rule $\llbracket\text{-e}\rrbracket_{II}$ in (21b) and the simple relativized-argument rules $\llbracket\text{-ye}_1\rrbracket_{II}$ and $\llbracket\text{-o}\rrbracket_{II}$ in (28));
- the composite negative subjunctive rule ($\llbracket\text{si-}\rrbracket_{II} \circ \llbracket\text{-e}\rrbracket_{II}$) in (22), which involves both prefixation and suffixation;
- the aggregated relativized-argument rules in (30), which are suffixational; and
- the aggregated relative tense/negation rules in Table 8.8, which are prefixational.

All of these rules are in paradigmatic opposition, and a single principle – Pāṇini's principle – suffices to resolve all instances of competition among them.

8.4 *Morphotactics of Relativization* 251

A couple of additional features of the proposed account of relative verb forms should be carefully noted. First, the ⟦**ta-**⟧$_{II}$ rule in (13b) is not applicable in the realization of relative verb forms because it realizes indicative mood as well as future tense; recall again that relative verb forms are nonindicative. Second, the basic relativized argument rule ⟦**-o**⟧$_{II}$ in (28) is, again, a default rule that doesn't express any particular noun class, but it does apply by default in the realization of a plural relativized argument of noun class 2; this is because neither the relativized-argument rules in (28) nor the aggregated relativized-argument rules in (30) include a dedicated rule for noun class 2. The aggregations of ⟦**-o**⟧$_{II}$ in Table 8.8 (namely (⟦**-o**⟧$_{II}$ ⓐ ⟦**taka-**⟧$_{II}$), (⟦**-o**⟧$_{II}$ ⓐ ⟦**na-**⟧$_{II}$), (⟦**-o**⟧$_{II}$ ⓐ ⟦**li-**⟧$_{II}$), and (⟦**-o**⟧$_{II}$ ⓐ ⟦**si-**⟧$_{II}$)) are likewise default rules that do not express any noun class; as such, they are usually overridden by the other aggregations in Table 8.8, but they, too, apply by default in the expression of plural relativized arguments belonging to noun class 2, for which no dedicated aggregations exist in Table 8.8.

As before, the FERs for Fragment III are defined through the composition of rules from Groups I, II, and III, in accordance with the FER patterns in (18). Examples of the FERs that (18) defines for Fragment III are the composite rules in (32). The FER in (32a) defines tenseless positive verb forms such as *asomaye* '(person) who reads', as in part (a) of Table 8.9. The fact that the verb form is unspecified for either tense or negation allows ⟦**-ye$_1$**⟧$_{II}$, the basic relativized-argument rule for noun class 1, to operate directly on the verb stem *soma*; encoding the same person, number, and gender as the simple subject-agreement rule ⟦**a-$_1$**⟧$_{III}$, ⟦**-ye$_1$**⟧$_{II}$ here expresses a relativized subject.

(32)   Some FERs defined by (18)
    a. (⟦**a-$_1$**⟧$_{III}$ ∘ ⟦**-ye$_1$**⟧$_{II}$) : [V, {–ind –tns {sbj 3sg nc1} {rel 3sg nc1}} : X→ *a*-X-*ye*]
    b. (((⟦**wa-$_2$**⟧ ∘ ⟦id.fcn⟧$_{III}$) ∘ ⟦**-o**⟧$_{II}$) : [V, {–ind –tns {sbj 3pl nc2} {rel 3pl nc2}} : X→ *wa*-X-*o*]
    c. ((((⟦**tu-**⟧ ∘ ⟦id.fcn⟧$_{III}$) ∘ ⟦**-vyo$_8$**⟧$_{II}$) ∘ (⟦**vi-$_8$**⟧ ∘ ⟦id.fcn⟧$_I$)) : [V, {–ind –tns {sbj 1pl} {obj 3pl nc8} {rel 3pl nc8}} : X→ *tuvi*-X-*vyo*]
    d. ((((⟦**tu-**⟧ ∘ ⟦id.fcn⟧$_{III}$) ∘ (⟦**-vyo$_8$**⟧$_{II}$ ⓐ ⟦**li-**⟧$_{II}$)) ∘ (⟦**vi-$_8$**⟧ ∘ ⟦id.fcn⟧$_I$)) : [V, {–ind pst {sbj 1pl} {obj 3pl nc8} {rel 3pl nc8}} : *tulivyovi*-]
    e. ((((⟦**tu-**⟧ ∘ ⟦id.fcn⟧$_{III}$) ∘ (⟦**-vyo$_8$**⟧$_{II}$ ⓐ ⟦**si-**⟧$_{II}$)) ∘ (⟦**vi-$_8$**⟧ ∘ ⟦id.fcn⟧$_I$)) : [V, {–ind neg –tns {sbj 1pl} {obj 3pl nc8} {rel 3pl nc8}} : *tusivyovi*-]

The FER in (32b) defines tenseless positive forms such as *wasomao* '(people) who read', as in part (b) of Table 8.9. In this form, the composite subject-agreement rule (⟦**wa-$_2$**⟧ ∘ ⟦id.fcn⟧$_{III}$) expresses noun class 2; because there is no dedicated relativized-argument rule for noun class 2, the default

Table 8.9 *The morphotactics of five Swahili verb forms in Fragment III*

(a)	Form cell:	⟨-*soma*, {–ind pos –tns {sbj 3sg nc1} {rel 3sg nc1}}⟩	'(person) who reads (tenseless)'
	FER ↓	($[\![\mathbf{a\text{-}1}]\!]_{\mathrm{III}} \circ [\![\mathbf{\text{-}ye_1}]\!]_{\mathrm{II}}$)	(= (32a))
	Realized cell:	⟨*asomaye*, {–ind pos –tns {sbj 3sg nc1} {rel 3sg nc1}}⟩	'(people) who read (tenseless)'
(b)	Form cell:	⟨-*soma*, {–ind pos –tns {sbj 3pl nc2} {rel 3pl nc2}}⟩	
	FER ↓	(($[\![\mathbf{wa\text{-}2}]\!] \circ [\![\mathrm{id.fcn}]\!]_{\mathrm{III}}) \circ [\![\mathbf{\text{-}o}]\!]_{\mathrm{II}}$)	(= (32b))
	Realized cell:	⟨*wasomao*, {–ind pos –tns {sbj 3pl nc2} {rel 3pl nc2}}⟩	
(c)	Form cell:	⟨-*soma*, {–ind pos –tns {sbj 1pl} {obj 3pl nc8} {rel 3pl nc8}}⟩	'(books) which we read (tenseless)'
	FER ↓	(((($[\![\mathbf{tu\text{-}}]\!] \circ [\![\mathrm{id.fcn}]\!]_{\mathrm{III}}) \circ [\![\mathbf{\text{-}vyo_8}]\!]_{\mathrm{II}}) \circ ([\![\mathbf{vi\text{-}8}]\!] \circ [\![\mathrm{id.fcn}]\!]_{\mathrm{I}})$)	(= (32c))
	Realized cell:	⟨*tuvisomavyo*, {–ind pos –tns {sbj 1pl} {obj 3pl nc8} {rel 3pl nc8}}⟩	'(books) which we read (past)'
(d)	Form cell:	⟨-*soma*, {–ind pos pst {sbj 1pl} {obj 3pl nc8} {rel 3pl nc8}}⟩	
	FER ↓	(((($[\![\mathbf{tu\text{-}}]\!] \circ [\![\mathrm{id.fcn}]\!]_{\mathrm{III}}) \circ ([\![\mathbf{\text{-}vyo_8}]\!]_{\mathrm{II}} \textcircled{A} [\![\mathbf{li\text{-}}]\!]_{\mathrm{II}})) \circ ([\![\mathbf{vi\text{-}8}]\!] \circ [\![\mathrm{id.fcn}]\!]_{\mathrm{I}})$)	(= (32d))
	Realized cell:	⟨*tulivyovisoma*, {–ind pos pst {sbj 1pl} {obj 3pl nc8} {rel 3pl nc8}}⟩	'(books) which we do not read (tenseless)'
(e)	Form cell:	⟨-*soma*, {–ind neg –tns {sbj 1pl} {obj 3pl nc8} {rel 3pl nc8}}⟩	
	FER ↓	(((($[\![\mathbf{tu\text{-}}]\!] \circ [\![\mathrm{id.fcn}]\!]_{\mathrm{III}}) \circ ([\![\mathbf{\text{-}vyo_8}]\!]_{\mathrm{II}} \textcircled{A} [\![\mathbf{si\text{-}}]\!]_{\mathrm{II}})) \circ ([\![\mathbf{vi\text{-}8}]\!] \circ [\![\mathrm{id.fcn}]\!]_{\mathrm{I}})$)	(= (32e))
	Realized cell:	⟨*tusivyovisoma*, {–ind neg –tns {sbj 1pl} {obj 3pl nc8} {rel 3pl nc8}}⟩	

N.B. $[\![\mathbf{\text{-}vyo_8}]\!]$ is the aggregation ($[\![\mathbf{vi\text{-}8}]\!] \textcircled{A} [\![\mathbf{\text{-}o}]\!]_{\mathrm{II}}$).

relativized-argument rule ⟦-o⟧$_{II}$ instead applies, operating directly on the verb stem *soma* to express a relativized subject.

The FER in (32c) defines tenseless positive forms such as *tuvisomavyo* '(books) which we read', in which the aggregated relativized-argument rule ⟦-vyo$_8$⟧$_{II}$ matches the person, number, and gender of the composite pronominal-object rule (⟦**vi-$_8$**⟧ ∘ ⟦id.fcn⟧$_I$) and therefore expresses a relativized object, as in part (c) of Table 8.9.

The FER in (32d) defines positive past-tense forms such as *tulivyovisoma* '(books) which we read'. Here, the aggregated relativized-argument rule ⟦-vyo$_8$⟧$_{II}$ (which again expresses a relativized object) is itself aggregated with the past-tense rule ⟦li-⟧$_{II}$ to produce the aggregated relative tense rule (⟦-vyo$_8$⟧$_{II}$ Ⓐ ⟦li-⟧$_{II}$), as in part (d) of Table 8.9.

The FER in (32e) defines tenseless negative forms such as *tusivyovisoma* '(books) which we do not read'. In this instance, ⟦-vyo$_8$⟧$_{II}$ (once again expressing a relativized object) is aggregated with the nonindicative negative rule ⟦si-⟧$_{II}$ to produce the negative relativized-argument rule (⟦-vyo$_8$⟧$_{II}$ Ⓐ ⟦si-⟧$_{II}$), as in part (e) of Table 8.9.

8.5 Discussion and Conclusions

The analysis of the Swahili conjugational system presented cumulatively in Fragments I, II, and III draws attention to the fact that Swahili verbs are highly uniform in their morphotactic characteristics. In accordance with the FER patterns in (18), all three fragments consist of finite forms whose FERs are either of the type ($R_{III} \circ R_{II}$) or of the type (($R_{III} \circ R_{II}$) ∘ R_I), where R_I, R_{II}, and R_{III} are rules belonging to Groups I, II, and III, respectively. As Table 8.10 shows, this is the case whether a verb form is indicative, subjunctive, or relative and whether it is positive or negative.

The proposed analysis elucidates the ways in which this system deviates from certain canonical morphotactic criteria but also reveals the ways in which, contrary to first impressions, it actually conforms to some criteria.

According to the rule independence criterion, a rule's operation on a stem is conditioned only by that stem's characteristics, and hence is not directly sensitive to the concurrent application of some other rule. In the inflection of Swahili verbs, however, there are many dependent/carrier relations: the argument-coding rules in (14) only apply in combination with one of three carrier rules (the Group III carrier rule ⟦id.fcn⟧$_{III}$ in (13a), the Group II carrier rule ⟦-o⟧$_{II}$ in (28), or the Group I carrier rule ⟦id.fcn⟧$_I$ in (13c)); the specific

Table 8.10 *FERs are of either the type* $(R_{III} \circ R_{II})$ *or the type* $((R_{III} \circ R_{II}) \circ R_I)$ *in the morphotactics of Swahili verbs*

R_I, R_{II}, and R_{III} are rules belonging to Groups I, II, and III, respectively.
R_{SBJ} is a (simple or composite) subject-agreement rule.
R_{TNS} is a simple tense rule.
R_{OBJ} is a (simple or composite) pronominal object rule.
R_{REL} is a (simple or aggregated) relativized-argument rule.

	Positive forms			Negative forms		
	R_{III}	R_{II}	R_I	R_{III}	R_{II}	R_I
Indicative	R_{SBJ}	R_{TNS}	(R_{OBJ})	$\left\{\begin{array}{l}(ha_{III} \circ R_{SBJ}) \\ si_{III}\end{array}\right\}$	R_{TNS}	(R_{OBJ})
Subjunctive	R_{SBJ}	$[\text{-e}]_{II}$	(R_{OBJ})	R_{SBJ}	$([\textbf{si-}]_{II} \circ [\textbf{-e}]_{II})$	(R_{OBJ})
Relative	R_{SBJ}	$\left\{\begin{array}{l} R_{REL} \\ (R_{REL} \circledA R_{TNS}) \end{array}\right\}$	(R_{OBJ})	R_{SBJ}	$(R_{REL} \circledA [\textbf{si-}]_{II})$	(R_{OBJ})

8.5 Discussion and Conclusions   255

property set realized by each of the rules in (14) depends entirely on the unification of its content with that of a carrier rule.

We have already seen how the proposed analysis models the deviation from the unique sequence criterion in the morphotactics of argument coding (Section 8.2); cf. again the fact that the ⟦**wa-₂**⟧ rule applies both before and after the future-tense rule ⟦**ta-**⟧$_{II}$ in the analysis of *watawapiga* 'they will strike them' in part (c) of Table 8.6. We have likewise seen how the proposed analysis models the deviation from the parallel sequence criterion in the morphotactics of negation (Section 8.3); cf. again the fact that negation may be expressed by a Group III rule, by a Group II rule, or by both the Group III and the Group II rule in certain composites, as in the analyses in Table 8.7.

According to the stem operand criterion, the formal operation associated with a morphological rule is an operation on stems. Each of the aggregations in (30) and Table 8.8 is a case in which a rule deviates from this criterion, operating on an affix rather than on a stem. The Swahili facts are doubly interesting in this regard insofar as most of the rules in Table 8.8 involve nested aggregations – the suffixation of a prefixed suffix to a prefix, for example *-livyo*: (((⟦**vi-₈**⟧ Ⓐ ⟦**-o**⟧$_{II}$) Ⓐ ⟦**li-**⟧$_{II}$).

The Swahili relativized-argument rules seem to introduce affixes that are sometimes prefixal and sometimes suffixal, contrary to the affix directionality criterion. The argument-coding rule ⟦**vi-₈**⟧ in (14i) introduces a prefix in the definition of *tu-ta-vi-soma* 'we will read them' but seems also to introduce a suffix in the definition of the tenseless relative form *tuvisomavyo* (← *tu-vi-soma-vi-o*) '(books) that we read'; the relativized-argument rule ⟦**-ye₁**⟧$_{II}$ in (28) introduces a suffix in the definition of the tenseless relative form *a-some-ye* '(person) who reads' but seems to introduce a prefix in *a-taka-ye-soma* '(person) who will read'. Although the aggregation operation inherently deviates from the stem operand criterion, it also allows us to maintain that the dependent argument-coding rules in (14) are uniformly prefixational and that the simple and aggregated relativized-argument rules in (28) and (30) are uniformly suffixational: in *tuvisomavyo*, the second *vi-* isn't suffixed to the verb, but is instead (through aggregation) prefixed to the suffix *-o*; in *a-taka-ye-soma*, *-ye* isn't prefixed to the verb, but is instead (through aggregation) suffixed to the prefix *taka-*. Swahili verb morphology is therefore canonical with respect to the affix directionality criterion.

We have already seen (Section 8.3) that the Swahili pattern of negative inflection apparently deviates from the rule opposition criterion, since the application of the first-person singular negative portmanteau rule ⟦**si-**⟧$_{III}$ (as in *si-tasoma* 'I won't read') is paradigmatically opposed to the application of the indicative negative rule $[\![\mathbf{ha\text{-}}]\!]_{\mathrm{III}}$ together with a subject-agreement rule (e.g. with the second-person plural $[\![\mathbf{m\text{-}}]\!]_{\mathrm{III}}$ rule in *ha-m-tasoma* 'you (pl.) won't read') but that this deviation becomes merely apparent if we assume that what looks like the opposition of one rule to two rules is actually the opposition of one rule to another, composite rule (e.g to $([\![\mathbf{ha\text{-}}]\!]_{\mathrm{III}} \circ [\![\mathbf{m\text{-}}]\!]_{\mathrm{III}})$).

The patterns of relative inflection seen in this section also present a more extreme case in which one rule is opposed to combinations of as many as three rules; for instance, the past-tense rule $[\![\mathbf{li\text{-}}]\!]_{\mathrm{II}}$, the aggregated relativized-argument rule $([\![\mathbf{vi\text{-}_8}]\!] \circledA [\![\mathbf{\text{-}o}]\!]_{\mathrm{II}})$, and the aggregated relative tense rule $(([\![\mathbf{vi\text{-}_8}]\!] \circledA [\![\mathbf{\text{-}o}]\!]_{\mathrm{II}}) \circledA [\![\mathbf{li\text{-}}]\!]_{\mathrm{II}})$ all stand in paradigmatic opposition as members of Group II. Thus, the proposed analysis explains the relation of mutual exclusion that exists among simple or aggregated relativized-argument rules, rules of tense and nonindicative negation, and aggregated relative tense/negation rules. A relative suffix never appears in postverbal position if there is overt morphology for tense or negation in preverbal position: this mutual exclusion is a consequence of the fact that the rules of relative suffixation in (28) and (30) belong to Group II, the same group as the rules of tense and nonindicative negation in (13b), (21b), and (28); all of these rules are in paradigmatic opposition to one another. To be sure, the rules of relative suffixation may combine with the rules of tense and nonindicative negation (as in Table 8.8), but their mode of combination is aggregation rather than composition; as a consequence of this aggregation, a relative affix appears preverbally in any verb form in which it coincides with the appearance of tense or negative morphology. Because the aggregations in Table 8.8 also belong to Group II, they are in paradigmatic opposition to the rules of relative suffixation in (28) and (30). This analysis therefore correctly accounts for the fact that the same verb form never has two relative suffixes, one in preverbal position and the other in postverbal position; this is a consequence of Pāṇini's principle, which entails that the competition of an aggregated relative tense/negation rule with a (simple or aggregated) relativized-argument rule is always resolved in favor of the former rule. Finally, this analysis accounts for the fact that when they are in preverbal position, the relative affixes are always immediately preceded by a prefix expressing tense or negation: this is because relative affixes only end up in preverbal position as a consequence of the aggregation of a rule of relative suffixation with a rule of tense or negation, as in Table 8.8.

Interestingly, the analysis of Swahili verb inflection presented here derives additional support from the domain of phonology. As Barrett-Keach (1986) has observed, polysyllabic verb forms in Swahili tend to consist of two phonological words, each with its own penultimate stress. The boundary between the two phonological words is after the tense prefix in (33a) and after the counterposed relative suffix in (33b).

(33) a. *à-na-* | *ni-píga*
SBJ.NC1-DEF.TIME | OBJ.1SG-strike
's/he strikes me'
b. *m-tu*   *a-nà-ye-* | *ni-píga*
NC1-person   SBJ.NC1-DEF.TIME-REL.NC1 | OBJ.1SG-strike
'the person who strikes me'

In both of the instances in (33), the verb form's first phonological word is a composite prefix defined by a composite rule of the type ($R_{III} \circ R_{II}$): the composite rule (34a) defines the composite prefix *ana-* in (33a) and the composite rule (34b) defines the composite prefix *anaye-* in (33b). Thus, the interface of Swahili morphotactics with the phonology of the language may be assumed to conform to the general patterns in (35), however these are to be formulated.

(34) a. $(\llbracket \mathbf{a\text{-}_1} \rrbracket_{III} \circ \llbracket \mathbf{na\text{-}} \rrbracket_{II}) : [V, \{\{sbj\ 3sg\ nc1\}\ def.time\} : ana\text{-}]$
b. $(\llbracket \mathbf{a\text{-}_1} \rrbracket_{III} \circ (\llbracket \text{-}\mathbf{ye} \rrbracket_{II} \circledA \llbracket \mathbf{na\text{-}} \rrbracket_{II})) :$
    $[V, \{\{sbj\ 3sg\ nc1\}\ \{rel\ 3sg\ nc1\}\ \text{–ind}\ def.time\} : anaye\text{-}]$

(35) Interface patterns between Swahili morphotactics and phonology
a. By default, a phonological word has stress on its penultimate syllable.
b. Where ($R_{III} \circ R_{II}$) is the rule [V, σ: *x*-], both *x*- and the operand of ($R_{III} \circ R_{II}$) constitute phonological words.

Summarizing, the inflectional morphotactics of Swahili verbs presents a number of real and apparent deviations from canonical morphotactic criteria. Deviating from both the rule independence criterion and the unique sequence criterion, the argument-coding rules in (14) depend for their application on their composition with the three carrier rules in Groups III, II, and I, and it is their composition with one or another of these rules that determines the morphosyntactic property that they express. The expression of negation deviates from the parallel sequence criterion. Both the formation of the relativized argument rules in (30) and the combination of these rules in Table 8.8 involve aggregation, and thus deviate from the stem operand criterion; at the same time, these aggregations reconcile both the formation and the combination of the relativized argument rules with the affix directionality criterion. The numerous apparent deviations from the rule opposition criterion are reconciled with it by the relations of composition and aggregation in the proposed analysis. At the most general level, all of the rules proposed in this analysis correlate with three groups, such that all of the relevant word forms are defined by FERs of either type ($R_{III} \circ R_{II}$) or type (($R_{III} \circ R_{II}) \circ R_I$).

The Swahili analysis developed here shows that the same basic rules may compose in different ways to realize different content. For instance, the composite rules in (36) involve the same basic rules but these are composed in different ways; rule (36a) is therefore the FER for the verb form *wananipiga* 'they hit me', while rule (36b) is the FER for the verb form *ninawapiga* 'I hit them'. Although both of the composite rules in (36) involve the same basic rules, these are composed in different linear orders.

(36)   a. $((([\![\mathbf{wa\text{-}2}]\!] \circ [\![\mathrm{id.fcn}]\!]_{III}) \circ [\![\mathbf{na\text{-}}]\!]_{II}) \circ ([\![\mathbf{ni\text{-}}]\!] \circ [\![\mathrm{id.fcn}]\!]_{I}))$
       b. $((([\![\mathbf{ni\text{-}}]\!] \circ [\![\mathrm{id.fcn}]\!]_{III}) \circ [\![\mathbf{na\text{-}}]\!]_{II}) \circ ([\![\mathbf{wa\text{-}2}]\!] \circ [\![\mathrm{id.fcn}]\!]_{I}))$

The next chapter focuses on a surprising characteristic of the Murrinhpatha system of verbal morphotactics: the fact that it allows the same basic rules to compose in the same linear order but with different hierarchical groupings to express different content.

9 *The Nonassociativity of Rule Composition in Murrinhpatha*

In Chapter 6, we saw that the same rules may express different content if they enter into different holistic combinations. There are also cases in which the same rules express different content depending on the order in which they compose. We saw evidence of this in Swahili, where the forms *tuliwapiga* 'we struck them' and *walitupiga* 'they struck us' are defined by the same simple rules composed in two different ways; in this chapter, I examine a second case of this sort from Murrinhpatha. In approaching this second case, it is useful to compare rule composition in morphology with function composition in mathematics.

In most ways, composition is comparable across these two domains. There is, however, an important difference. In mathematics, function composition is associative. That is, for any mathematical functions f, g, and h such that $(h \circ (g \circ f))$ is defined for x, $(h \circ (g \circ f))(x) = ((h \circ g) \circ f)(x)$. (Given this fact, multiple composed functions are sometimes represented without binary parenthesization in mathematics: $(h \circ g \circ f)$.) The formal operation defined by the composition of multiple morphological rules is likewise associative. But the content realized by the composition of multiple rules is not always associative. In particular, it may be nonassociative if one of the rules realizes a set-based property that is category-indeterminate (Section 2.1.1). I explain this difference in Section 9.1. In Section 9.2, I examine the system of verb inflection of Murrinhpatha (Southern Daly; Northern Territory, Australia); as I show in Section 9.3, the morphotactics of this system is structured so as to exploit the nonassociativity of rule composition.

9.1   Rule Composition Is Nonassociative

In Section 8.2, the polyfunctionality exhibited by most verbal concords in Swahili is modeled by defining these concords as realizing category-indeterminate properties; for example, the first-person singular rule ⟦**ni-**⟧ in (1) is formulated as realizing the property set {{1 sg}}, whose set-based property {1 sg} is indeterminate with respect to whether it belongs to the category of subject agreement or to that of pronominal object specification. In accordance with the Category Determination Principle (Section 2.1.1), the category-indeterminate property {1 sg} unifies with a category-determinate property Q expressed by the rule with which ⟦ni-⟧ combines; the resulting unification [{1 sg} ⊔ Q] is itself category-determinate. In particular, the rule ⟦ni-⟧ composes with the ⟦id.fcn⟧$_{III}$ rule in (2a) to produce (2b), a rule expressing the category-determinate property of first-person singular subject agreement; or it composes with the ⟦id.fcn⟧$_I$ rule in (3a) to produce (3b), a rule expressing the category-determinate property of first-person singular pronominal object specification.

(1)   ⟦**ni-**⟧ : [V, {{1sg}} : *ni-*]

(2)   a.   ⟦id.fcn⟧$_{III}$: [V, {{sbj}} : X → X]
      b.   (⟦**ni-**⟧ ∘ ⟦id.fcn⟧$_{III}$) : [V, {{sbj 1sg}} : *ni-*]

(3)   a.   ⟦id.fcn⟧$_I$: [V, {{obj}} : X → X]
      b.   (⟦**ni-**⟧ ∘ ⟦id.fcn⟧$_I$) : [V, {{obj 1sg}} : *ni-*]

The assumption that a rule may express a category-indeterminate property has interesting consequences for the composition of rules and for the concomitant unification of the property sets that they realize – specifically, it entails that neither rule composition nor property-set unification is always associative. Consider a hypothetical illustration. Suppose that rules R_1, R_2, and R_3 are as in (4a–c) and that (in accordance with the Category Determination Principle; Section 2.1.1) the composite rules ($R_1 \circ R_2$) and ($R_2 \circ R_3$) are as in (4d,e). In that case, (($R_1 \circ R_2) \circ R_3$) realizes the property set [[$\sigma_1 \sqcup \sigma_2] \sqcup \sigma_3$], which contains the set-based property [$P_1 \sqcup P_2$] (a member of CATEGORY$_1$), but ($R_1 \circ (R_2 \circ R_3)$) instead realizes the property set [$\sigma_1 \sqcup [\sigma_2 \sqcup \sigma_3$]], which contains the set-based property [$P_2 \sqcup P_3$] (a member of CATEGORY$_3$). The nonassociativity of rule composition in (5a) reflects the fact that because σ_2 contains the category-indeterminate property P_2, the unification of σ_1, σ_2, and σ_3 is itself nonassociative, as in (5b).

(4)   a. R_2 realizes a property set σ_2 containing a set-based property P_2 that is category-indeterminate.
      b. R_1 realizes a property set σ_1 containing a set-based property P_1 that belongs to CATEGORY$_1$.
      c. R_3 realizes a property set σ_3 containing a set-based property P_3 that belongs to CATEGORY$_3$ ($\neq$ CATEGORY$_1$).
      d.   The composite ($R_1 \circ R_2$) realizes the unification [$\sigma_1 \sqcup \sigma_2$], which contains the set-based property [$P_1 \sqcup P_2$], a member of CATEGORY$_1$.
      e.   The composite ($R_2 \circ R_3$) realizes the unification [$\sigma_2 \sqcup \sigma_3$], which contains the set-based property [$P_2 \sqcup P_3$], a member of CATEGORY$_3$.

(5) a. $((R_1 \circ R_2) \circ R_3) \neq (R_1 \circ (R_2 \circ R_3))$
     b. $[[\sigma_1 \sqcup \sigma_2] \sqcup \sigma_3] \neq [\sigma_1 \sqcup [\sigma_2 \sqcup \sigma_3]]$.

This is a striking fact, because the composition of rules that realize property sets none of whose members is category-indeterminate is invariably associative, as is the unification of the property sets that they realize. Consider, for example, the Swahili verb form in (6). According to the analysis in Section 8.2, the full exponence rule (FER) for this verb form is (7), the composite of the three rules in (8).

(6) *a-li-ku-piga*
     SBJ.3SG.NC1-PST-OBJ.2SG-strike
     'S/he struck you (sg.).'

(7) FER for (6): $(([\![a\text{-}_1]\!]_{III} \circ [\![li\text{-}]\!]_{II}) \circ [\![ku\text{-}]\!]_{I})$:
     [V, {{sbj 3sg nc1} pst {obj 2sg}} : *aliku-*]

(8) The component rules of the FER in (7)
     a. $[\![a\text{-}_1]\!]_{III}$: [V, {{sbj 3sg nc1}} : *a-*]
     b. $[\![li\text{-}]\!]_{II}$: [V, {pos pst} : *li-*]
     c. $[\![ku\text{-}]\!]_{I}$: [V, {{obj 2sg}} : *ku-*]

Because none of the three component rules in (8) realizes a category-indeterminate property, the composition of these rules in (7) is associative – that is,

$(([\![a\text{-}_1]\!]_{III} \circ [\![li\text{-}]\!]_{II}) \circ [\![ku\text{-}]\!]_{I}) = ([\![a\text{-}_1]\!]_{III} \circ ([\![li\text{-}]\!]_{II} \circ [\![ku\text{-}]\!]_{I}))$.

By the same token, the unification of the property sets realized by the rules in (8) is associative:

[[{{sbj 3sg nc1}} ⊔ {pos pst}] ⊔ {{obj 2sg}}]
 = [{{sbj 3sg nc1}} ⊔ [{pos pst} ⊔ {{obj 2sg}}]].

The Murrinhpatha system of verb inflection is of particular interest because its morphotactics exploits the possibility of nonassociativity in its patterns of rule composition and in the corresponding patterns of property-set unification.[1]

---

[1] One (admittedly rather indirect) inspiration for the morphotactic analysis of Murrinhpatha number concord proposed here is the syntactic and semantic analysis of English control verbs developed by Bach (1979).

9.2 Murrinhpatha Verb Inflection

Murrinhpatha conjugation expresses both subject and object concord in the context of a rich system of verb classification (Nordlinger 2010, 2015; Nordlinger & Caudal 2012; Mansfield 2019; Nordlinger & Mansfield 2021). In this system, most verb forms are compound, involving both a classifier stem (CS) and a lexical stem (LS); for example, the verb forms in (9) have *ba* as their classifier stem and *ngkardu* as their lexical stem.

(9) a. *ba-m-ngkardu*
CS:3.SINGULAR'.SEE(13)-NFUT-LS:see
'He/she saw her/him.'
b. *ba-m-ngintha-ngkardu*
CS:3.SINGULAR'.SEE(13)-NFUT-DNS.FEMALE-LS:see
'They (two female nonsiblings) saw her/him.'

(Nordlinger 2010)

In the verbal template that she proposes for the description of Murrinhpatha verb inflection, Nordlinger (2015: 495) situates a verb's classifier stem in position 1 and its lexical stem in position 5 (Table 9.1). Within this template, subject concord is marked in three positions: it is always part of the content expressed in position 1 by a verb form's inflected classifier stem, and subject number and gender may additionally be encoded both in position 2 and, after the verb's lexical stem, in position 8. Object concord is also expressed in positions 2 and 8. Thus, an important feature of Murrinhpatha verb inflection is the competition of subject concord and object concord for these two positions. In neither of these positions are both subject and object concord expressed cumulatively.

In the fragment of Murrinhpatha verb morphology on which I focus in this chapter, my concern is with the morphotactics of the formatives appearing in

Table 9.1 *The Murrinhpatha verbal template*

1	2	3	4	5	6	7	8	9
Classifier stem encoding subject concord *and* tense/aspect/mood	Subject number *or* object concord	Reflexive/reciprocal	Incorporated bodypart	Lexical stem	Tense/aspect/mood	Adverbial	Subject number *or* object number	Adverbial

(Nordlinger 2015: 495)

positions 1, 2, 5, and 8 in Nordlinger's template; these are what demonstrate the nonassociativity of Murrinhpatha verb inflection. Though I will not discuss the formatives occupying the unshaded positions in Table 9.1 (i.e. positions 3, 4, 6, 7, and 9), there is no obstacle to expanding the analysis presented here to accommodate the morphotactics of those formatives as well.

In this section, I discuss the morphotactics of concord in Murrinhpatha verb inflection. First, I discuss the expression of subject concord in a verb's classifier stem (Section 9.2.1). Then I examine the set of concordial suffixes appearing in positions 2 and 8 (Section 9.2.2). I discuss the joint expression of subject person and number by a verb form's classifier inflection and its subject-number suffix (Section 9.2.3) and the joint expression of object person and number by suffixes appearing in positions 2 and 8 (Section 9.2.4). Finally, I detail the full morphotactic complexity of Murrinhpatha subject concord, taking account of its interaction with the simpler morphotactics of object concord (Section 9.2.5). In the following section (Section 9.3), I present a rule-combining analysis of the morphotactic patterns described in Section 9.2. I summarize the wider implications of this analysis in Section 9.4.

9.2.1   Classifier Inflection in Murrinhpatha Verbs

The classifiers employed in the inflection of Murrinhpatha verbs constitute a closed class with thirty-eight members. A given classifier has its own full paradigm of forms; for instance, the classifier SEE(13) employed in (9) has the paradigm in Table 9.2. (The significance of the prime notation in the 'Number' column of this table is explained in Section 9.2.3.) A given classifier exhibits different stems in different parts of its paradigm; in Table 9.2, for example, the classifier SEE(13) exhibits the default stem *ba*, the apical stem *da*, the front stem *be*, and the apical front stem *de*. (The terminology here is that of Mansfield 2019.) A verb's classifier inflects for subject concord, tense, aspect, and mood. In the inflection of the classifier SEE(13) in Table 9.2, the exponent of subject concord is either a prefix or (in Singular′ forms) the significative absence of a prefix, this accompanied in the second person by the use of an apical stem; tense, aspect, and mood are expressed suffixally (e.g. by the nonfuture[2] tense suffix *-m*), by stem choice (e.g. by the choice of a front stem in the past tenses), or by a special subject prefix (as in the 1 INCL future form *pu-ba* and in the form *ku-ba* of the third-person Dual′ and Plural′ future irrealis).

---

[2] Concerning the temporal and aspectual underspecificity of the Murrinhpatha nonfuture tense, see Nordlinger & Caudal (2012).

Table 9.2 *The inflection of the classifier* SEE*(13) (default stem* ba-*) in Murrinhpatha*

(∅- = significative absence of a prefix)

Number	Person	Nonfuture	Past Impf.	Future	Future Irrealis	Past Irrealis
Singular′	1	∅-ba-m	∅-be	∅-ba	∅-ba	∅-be
	2	∅-da-m	∅-de	∅-da	∅-da	∅-de
	3	∅-ba-m	∅-be	∅-ba	∅-ba	∅-be
1 INCL		thu-ba-m	thu-be	pu-ba	pu-ba	thu-be
Dual′	1	ngu-ba-m	ngu-be	ngu-ba	ngu-ba	ngu-be
	2	nu-ba-m	nu-be	nu-ba	nu-ba	nu-be
	3	pu-ba-m	pu-be	pu-ba	ku-ba	pu-be
Plural′	1	ngu-ba-m	ngu-be	ngu-ba	ngu-ba	ngu-be
	2	nu-ba-m	nu-be	nu-ba	nu-ba	nu-be
	3	pu-ba-m	pu-be	pu-ba	ku-ba	pu-be

(cf. Blythe et al. 2007: 9; Mansfield 2019: 249)

Different classifiers may exhibit different conjugations; for instance, the inflection of the classifier SAY(34) in Table 9.3 differs from that of SEE(13) in Table 9.2.

Every lexical verb stem requires an accompanying classifier stem. Most of the classifiers likewise require an accompanying lexical stem, but eleven of the classifiers also function as verbs independently of any lexical stem; see Blythe et al. (2007), Nordlinger & Caudal (2012), and Mansfield (2019) for examples.

9.2.2 Concordial Exponents in Murrinhpatha Verb Forms

In discussing concordial morphology in Murrinhpatha verb forms, it is useful to maintain a careful terminological distinction between subject-agreement (SBJ.AGR) exponents, subject number (SBJ.NUM) suffixes, object agreement (OBJ.AGR) suffixes, object number (OBJ.NUM) suffixes, and the DNS/PNS suffixes (where DNS = 'dual nonsibling' and PNS = 'paucal nonsibling'). Consider this fivefold distinction, schematized in Table 9.4.

As was seen in Section 9.2.1, SBJ.AGR exponents are part of the inflection of a verb form's classifier stem; in the inflection of the SEE(13) classifier (Table 9.2), a SBJ.AGR exponent may be a prefix (e.g. the prefix *ngu-* in the first-person Dual′/Plural′ forms) or (in the Singular′) the significative absence of a prefix (e.g. the absence of a prefix in the first-person Singular′ nonfuture

Table 9.3 *The inflection of the classifier* SAY(34) *(default stem* ma-*)
in Murrinhpatha*

(∅- = significative absence of a prefix)

Number	Person	Nonfuture	Past Impf.	Future	Future Irrealis	Past Irrealis
Singular'	1	nga-ma-m	∅-me	nga-ma	nga-ma	∅-mi ~ ngi-mi
	2	∅-na-m	∅-ne	tha-ma	tha-ma	∅-ni
	3	∅-ma-m	∅-me	pa-ma	ka-ma	∅-mi
1 INCL		tha-ma-m	thu-me	pa-ma	pa-ma	thu-mi
Dual'	1	nga-ma-m	ngu-me	nguye-ma ~ ngiye-ma	nguye-ma	ngu-mi
	2	na-ma-m	nu-me	nuye-ma	nuye-ma	nu-mi
	3	pa-ma-m	pu-me	puye-ma ~ piye-ma	kuye-ma	pu-mi
Plural'	1	nga-ma-m	ngu-me	nguye-ma ~ ngiye-ma	nguye-ma	ngu-mi
	2	na-ma-m	nu-me	nuye-ma ~ niye-ma	nuye-ma	nu-mi
	3	pa-ma-m	pu-me	puye-ma ~ piye-ma	kuye-ma	pu-mi

(cf. Blythe et al. 2007: 21; Mansfield 2019: 247)

form *bam*), possibly in combination with the choice of a special classifier stem (e.g. the choice of the apical stem in *da-* in the second-person Singular' forms).

The SBJ.NUM suffixes listed in Table 9.4 distinguish dual and paucal number, and additionally specify both the sex of their referents[3] and whether or not their referents are siblings of each other.[4] They are morphotactically heterogeneous, in that *-ka* is restricted to position 2 in the template in Table 9.1; *-ngime* and *-neme* are restricted to position 8; and *-ngintha* and *-nintha* appear sometimes in position 2 and sometimes in position 8, subject to the restrictions to be discussed in Section 9.2.5. The prefixes *-ngime* and *-neme* may be used to refer to a first-person inclusive subject, but *-ka*, *-ngintha*, and *-nintha* are not.

---

[3] Female is the default, being used for groups of mixed gender (Mansfield 2019: 141).
[4] This sibling/nonsibling distinction is typologically unusual in inflectional systems; see Rácz et al. (2018) for discussion.

Table 9.4 *Five distinct types of concordial exponents in Murrinhpatha verb inflection*

	Realization	Content	Morphotactics
subject-agreement (SBJ. AGR) exponents	prefix, absence of prefix, stem choice	properties of person, number	part of a verb form's classifier stem
subject number (SBJ.NUM) suffixes	-ka -ngintha -nintha -ngime -neme	DS (dual sibling) or PNS (paucal nonsibling) DNS (dual nonsibling), female DNS (dual nonsibling), male PNS (paucal nonsibling), female (possibly 1 INCL) PNS (paucal nonsibling), male (possibly 1 INCL)	position 2 in Table 9.1 positions 2, 8 positions 2, 8 position 8 position 8
object agreement (OBJ. AGR) suffixes	-nhi -ngi -nganku -ngan -nhi -nanku -nan -(wu)nku -(wu)n	first-person, inclusive first-person, singular first-person, dual/PNS, exclusive first-person, PS (paucal sibling) or plural, exclusive second-person, singular second-person, dual/PNS second-person, PS/plural third-person, dual/PNS third-person, PS/plural	all position 2
object number (OBJ.NUM) suffixes	-ngintha -nintha -ngime -neme	(as above) (as above) (as above) (as above)	all position 8
DNS/PNS suffixes	-ngintha, -nintha, -ngime, -neme (as either SBJ.NUM or OBJ.NUM affixes)		

The OBJ.AGR suffixes listed in Table 9.4 appear in position 2 in the template in Table 9.1. Note that the *wu-* portion of the prefixes *(wu)nku-* and *(wu)n-* only appears in forms in the nonfuture tense.

The OBJ.NUM suffixes listed in Table 9.4 are identical in form to the last four SBJ.NUM suffixes in the table, whose content they share except insofar as they code object rather than subject properties. They differ morphotactically from their SBJ.NUM counterparts in the sense that they are all restricted to position 8.

The fact that the DNS suffixes *-ngintha*, *-nintha* and the PNS suffixes *-ngime*, *-neme* are versatile, serving in some instances as SBJ.NUM suffixes and in other instances as OBJ.NUM suffixes, plays a central role in the nonassociativity of Murrinhpatha verb inflection. When I wish to refer to the DNS suffixes *-ngintha*, *-nintha* and the PNS suffixes *-ngime*, *-neme* independently of their particular use as either SBJ.NUM suffixes or OBJ.NUM suffixes, I shall refer to them as the DNS/PNS suffixes.

9.2.3   The Joint Expression of a Subject's Person and Number in a Murrinhpatha Verb Form

When a verb form's subject is singular, PS, or plural, the person and number of its subject are expressed by the inflection of its classifier stem; but when a verb form's subject is dual or PNS, the person and number of its subject are expressed jointly, by the inflection of its classifier stem together with its SBJ.NUM suffix. When a Singular' classifier appears without a SBJ.NUM suffix, the subject is singular, as in (10a). When a Singular' or Dual' classifier appears with a DNS SBJ.NUM suffix, the subject is DNS, as in (10b,c); as these two examples suggest, the preference is for the classifier stem accompanying a DNS SBJ.NUM suffix to be Singular' in the absence of object concord (as in (10b)) but to be Dual' in the presence of object concord (as in (10c)). I will return to the morphotactic difference between (10b) and (10c) in Section 9.2.5.

(10) a. *ba-m-ngkardu*
CS:3.SINGULAR'.SEE(13)-NFUT-LS:see
'He/she saw her/him.'
b. *ba-m-ngintha-ngkardu*
CS:3.SINGULAR'.SEE(13)-NFUT-DNS.FEMALE-LS:see
'They (two female nonsiblings) saw her/him.'
c. *pu-ba-m-ngi-ngkardu-ngintha*
CS:3.DUAL'-SEE(13)-NFUT-OBJ.1SG-LS:see-DNS.FEMALE
'They (two female nonsiblings) saw me.'
d. *pu-ba-m-ka-ngkardu*
CS:3.DUAL'-SEE(13)-NFUT-SBJ.DS/PNS.NFUT-LS:see
'They (two siblings) saw her/him.'

e. *pu-ba-ngkardu*
   CS:3.DUAL′-SEE(13).FUT-LS:see
   'They (two siblings) will see her/him.'
f. *pu-ba-m-ka-ngkardu-ngime*
   CS:3.DUAL′-SEE(13)-NFUT-SBJ.DS/PNS.NFUT-LS:see-PNS.FEMALE
   'They (paucal female nonsiblings) saw her/him.'
g. *pu-ba-m-ngkardu*
   CS:3.PLURAL′-SEE(13)-NFUT-LS:see
   'They saw her/him.'

(Nordlinger 2010)

When a Dual′ classifier appears with the DS/PNS SBJ.NUM suffix -*ka* on its own (only in the nonfuture tense) or without any SBJ.NUM suffix (in the other tenses, sometimes also in the nonfuture tense), the subject refers to dual siblings, as in (10d,e); but when a Dual′ classifier appears with a PNS SBJ.NUM suffix (sometimes with the -*ka* suffix, in the nonfuture tense), the subject is PNS, as in (10f). (As will be seen in Section 9.2.5, the morphotactics of forms with a Dual′ classifier is complicated by the fact that the appearance of an OBJ.AGR suffix pre-empts that of the -*ka* suffix.) Finally, when a Plural′ classifier appears (always without a SBJ.NUM suffix), the subject is PS or plural, as in (10g).

Thus, the significance of the prime notation in Tables 9.2 and 9.3 may be summarized as in Table 9.5. A Singular′ classifier may be seen as signaling a subject that is singular by default, but DNS in the marked case; a Dual′ classifier may be seen as signaling a subject that is dual by default, but PNS in the marked case; and a Plural′ classifier may be seen as signaling a subject that is PS or plural.

9.2.4 The Joint Expression of an Object's Person and Number in a Murrinhpatha Verb Form

Just as the person and number of a verb form's subject is expressed jointly by its classifier stem and its SBJ.NUM suffix(es) (if any), so the person and number of a verb form's object is expressed jointly by its OBJ.AGR suffix and its OBJ.NUM

Table 9.5 *The encoding of subject number in the Murrinhpatha verb*

Classifier stem	SBJ.NUM suffix(es)	Subject number
Singular′	none	SG, e.g. (10a)
Singular′	DNS suffix -*nginthal*/-*nintha*	DNS, e.g. (10b)
Dual′	DNS suffix -*nginthal*/-*nintha*	DNS, e.g. (10c)
Dual′	(DS/PNS suffix -*ka*)	DS, e.g. (10d, e)
Dual′	(DS/PNS suffix -*ka*,) PNS suffix -*ngime*/-*neme*	PNS, e.g. (10f)
Plural′	none	PS/PL, e.g. (10g)

(Nordlinger 2010: 327; Nordlinger & Mansfield 2021)

suffix (if any). Third-person singular objects are not marked on the verb. Otherwise, objects are marked by an OBJ.AGR suffix in position 2 in Nordlinger's template. If the object is DNS (but not first-person inclusive), that fact is additionally marked by the appearance of *-ngintha* or *-nintha* in position 8; if the object is PNS (even if it is first-person inclusive), that fact is additionally marked by the appearance of *-ngime* or *-neme* in position 8. These facts are summarized in Table 9.6.

9.2.5 The Complex Morphotactics of Subject Concord in Murrinhpatha Verb Forms

While the morphotactics of object concord is comparatively straightforward in Murrinhpatha verb inflection, that of subject concord is complicated. The SBJ. NUM suffixes are of three types. In nonfuture forms, the DS/PNS suffix *-ka* only appears in position 2, and it is prevented from appearing in that position by the presence of an OBJ.AGR suffix in that position. For example, the SBJ.NUM suffix *-ka* appears in position 2 in (10d), where it encodes a dual sibling subject; but if a dual sibling object is encoded in position 2, as in (11), *-ka* is absent.

(11)   *pu-bam-nganku-ngkardu*
       CS:3.DUAL'-SEE(13).NFUT-OBJ.1DS.EXCL-LS:see
       'They (two siblings) saw us (two excl siblings)'

If a verb form's SBJ.NUM suffix is a DNS suffix (*-ngintha* (f) or *-nintha* (m)), this appears in position 2 provided that it isn't prevented from doing so by an OBJ.AGR suffix; thus, *-ngintha* appears in position 2 in (10b). But in the presence of an OBJ.AGR suffix in position 2, the DNS SBJ.NUM suffix must instead appear in position 8; thus, *-ngintha* appears in position 8 in (10c). Nordlinger & Mansfield (2021) show that in a verb form with a DNS SBJ.NUM suffix, the inflection of the classifier stem tends to covary with the position of the SBJ.NUM suffix: if the SBJ.NUM suffix appears in position 2, a Singular' classifier is used, but if the SBJ.NUM suffix appears in position 8, a Dual' classifier is preferred (though the possibility of a Singular' classifier seems not to be categorically excluded); the examples in (10b,c) reflect this covariation.

Finally, if a verb form's SBJ.NUM suffix is a PNS suffix (*-ngime* (f) or *-neme* (m)), this can only appear in position 8, as in (10f).

The morphotactics of the SBJ.NUM suffixes might therefore be schematized as in Table 9.7.

The use of the SBJ.NUM suffixes in Table 9.7 raises two questions. First, if a verb's subject and its object both call for a DNS/PNS suffix in position 8, which demand is satisfied and which goes unsatisfied? Second, given that a DNS/PNS suffix in position 8 may distinguish either a subject's number or an object's number, doesn't this give rise to ambiguities? Consider each of these questions in turn.

Table 9.6 *Direct-object suffixes in Murrinhpatha*

Position		First person					Second person			Third person	
		Inclusive		Exclusive							
		2	8	2	8	2	8	2*	8		
Singular											
DNS	male	-nhi	—	-nganku	-nintha	-nhi	-nanku	-nintha	—(wu)nku	-nintha	
	female	-nhi	—	-nganku	-ngintha		-nanku	-ngintha	-(wu)nku	-ngintha	
DS		-nhi	—	-nganku	—		-nanku	—	-(wu)nku	—	
PNS	male	-nhi	-neme	-nganku	-neme		-nanku	-neme	-(wu)nku	-neme	
	female	-nhi	-ngime	-nganku	-ngime		-nanku	-ngime	-(wu)nku	-ngime	
PS		-nhi	—	-ngan	—		-nan	—	-(wu)n	—	
Plural		-nhi	—	-ngan	—		-nan	—	-(wu)n	—	

* The suffixes in this column include *wu* in the nonfuture. — = no OBJ.AGR or OBJ.NUM suffix is eligible to appear.

(Nordlinger 2015: 505)

Table 9.7 *The morphotactics of the Murrinhpatha SBJ.NUM suffixes*

Classifier stem	Subject properties		First-person inclusive forms		First-person exclusive and second- and third-person forms	
			Position 2	Position 8	Position 2	Position 8
Singular′	SG		—	—	—	—
Singular′	DNS	male	—	—	-nintha	-nintha
		female	—	—	-ngintha	-ngintha
Singular′* or Dual′	DNS	male	—	—	(if occupied by OBJ.AGR suffix)	—
		female	—	—	(if occupied by OBJ.AGR suffix)	—
Dual′	DS		—	—	-ka**	—
Dual′	PNS	male	—	-neme	-ka**	-neme
		female	—	-ngime	-ka**	-ngime
Plural′	PS/PL		—	—	—	—

* Possible but dispreferred. ** Only in the nonfuture tense and only present in the absence of an OBJ.AGR suffix in position 2. — = no SBJ.NUM suffix is eligible to appear.
(cf. Nordlinger 2015: 495–504)

Suppose first that a verb's subject and its object both call for a DNS/PNS suffix in position 8; which of the two demands is satisfied at the expense of satisfying the other? As Nordlinger (2015: 507) shows, the object's demand takes priority. Consider, for example, the expression of the meaning 'they (PNS male) saw us (PNS female exclusive).' The expression of the subject would seemingly call for the appearance of the suffix *-neme* in position 8; cf. Table 9.7. By contrast, the expression of the object would seemingly require the suffix *-ngime* to appear in position 8; cf. Table 9.6. It is the fulfillment of the latter of these requirements that takes precedence: the target meaning is expressed as *pu-bam-nganku-ngkardu-ngime*, with *-ngime* rather than *-neme* in position 8.

Consider now the fact that in position 8, the DNS suffixes *-ngintha* (f)/*-nintha* (m) and the PNS suffixes *-ngime* (f)/*-neme* (m) sometimes refer to a verb's subject and sometimes to its object; in view of this fact, one might expect that ambiguities will sometimes arise, and indeed they do. Nordlinger (2015) cites several such examples, including (12), whose gloss is ambiguous with respect to whether the PNS suffix *-ngime* refers to the form's subject or to its object. Among the interpretations of the verb form in (12) are those listed in (13a–e). For interpretations (13a,b), (12) is glossed as in (12a): here, the subject is (13a) plural or (13b) PS and the PNS suffix *-ngime* refers to the object. For interpretations (13c–e), (12) is glossed as in (12b). In interpretation (13c), the subject is DS, the appearance of the OBJ.AGR suffix *nganku* in position 2 blocks that of the DS/PNS SBJ.NUM suffix *-ka*, and the PNS suffix *-ngime* refers to the object. For interpretation (13d), the object is DS, hence the PNS suffix *-ngime* refers to the subject. For interpretation (13e), the subject and object are both PNS, and the PNS suffix *-ngime* refers to the object, blocking the appearance of the PNS suffix *-ngime* (f)/*-neme* (m) that the subject would otherwise call for in position 8.

(12)   *pu-ba-m-nganku-ngkardu-ngime*
      a.   CS:3.PLURAL′-SEE(13)-NFUT-OBJ.1DU/PNS.EXCL-LS:see-PNS.
           FEMALE
      b.   CS:3.DUAL′-SEE(13)-NFUT-OBJ.1DU/PNS.EXCL-LS:see-PNS.
           FEMALE

(Nordlinger 2015: 507)

(13)   Interpretations of (12)
      a, b.   'They ((a) PL *or* (b) PS) saw us (PNS exclusive female).'
      c.   'They (DS) saw us (PNS exclusive female)'
      d.   'They (PNS female) saw us (DS exclusive).'
      e.   'They (PNS) saw us (PNS exclusive female).'

To summarize, an analysis of the morphotactics of the Murrinhpatha system of verb inflection must account for the five morphotactic facts in (14).

(14) Morphotactic facts about Murrinhpatha verb inflection
   a. The DNS suffixes -ngintha (f)/-nintha (m) and the PNS suffixes -ngime (f)/-neme (m) refer to the subject in some verb forms and to the object in others.
   b. In verb forms in which a DNS suffix (-ngintha (f) or -nintha (m)) refers to the subject, it may appear in two alternative positions: in position 2 if there is no accompanying OBJ.AGR suffix and in position 8 if there is an accompanying OBJ.AGR suffix (which itself occupies position 2).
   c. When a DNS suffix appears as a SBJ.NUM suffix in position 2, it is accompanied by a Singular′ classifier stem, but when it appears in position 8, the accompanying classifier stem is either Singular′ (dispreferred) or Dual′.
   d. Within a verb form, the DS/PNS suffix -ka is absent in the presence of an OBJ.AGR suffix.
   e. If the realization of a given form is compatible with the appearance of either an OBJ.NUM suffix or a SBJ.NUM suffix, it is the OBJ.NUM suffix that is used, excluding the appearance of the SBJ.NUM suffix.

9.3 A Rule-combining Morphotactic Analysis of Murrinhpatha Verbs

The rule-combining approach to exponence-driven morphotactics affords a streamlined account of all of the facts in (14). I demonstrate this by analyzing a fragment of Murrinhpatha verb morphology comprising nonfuture-tense forms with third-person subjects. In order to simplify the exposition of this analysis, I restrict my attention to the compound verb 'see' based on the classifier SEE(13) and to the simple verb 'say' based on the classifier SAY (34). These classifiers have the default stems *ba* and *ma* (respectively), to which to the suffix *-m* is added in all nonfuture-tense forms. In order to avoid repeated reference to the rule of *-m* suffixation, I shall make the expositorily simplifying assumption that these classifiers have *bam* and *mam* as nonfuture-tense stems; no part of the analysis hinges crucially on this assumption.

Because compound verb forms are based on a classifier stem and a lexical stem in Murrinhpatha, I assume that each rule of affixation takes either the classifier stem or the lexical stem as its operand. For clarity, I accordingly mark each rule's label with a subscript (C or L) indicating the type of operand that it takes; for example, 〚**-ngi$_C$**〛 suffixes *-ngi* to a verb's classifier stem, while 〚**-ngime$_L$**〛 suffixes *-ngime* to a verb's lexical stem. I additionally assume that the result of attaching an affix to a classifier stem or lexical stem itself constitutes a stem of the same type. Where CS is a classifier stem and LS is a lexical stem, I further assume the following convention.

(15) Compound verb convention
   a. If a classifier-operand rule R_C operates on CS to yield CS′, R_C likewise operates on the compound CS|LS to yield CS′|LS.

274 *Nonassociativity of Rule Composition in Murrinhpatha*

  b. If a lexical-operand rule R_L operates on LS to yield LS', R_L likewise operates on the compound CS|LS to yield CS|LS'. Thus,
  c. the composite rule ($R_L \circ R_C$) operates on the compound CS|LS to yield the compound CS'|LS'.

The fragment's simple rules of inflectional exponence are those in (16); these are sorted into three groups. The Group I rules introduce SBJ.AGR exponents, serving in this way to inflect a verb's classifier stem. For expository clarity, I use subscripts to distinguish Group I rules according to whether the subject to which they refer is Singular', Dual', or Plural': ⟦id.fn$_C$⟧$_{SG}$, ⟦**pu-**$_C$⟧$_{DU}$, ⟦**pu-**$_C$⟧$_{PL}$. I additionally assume that where a verbal lexeme is associated with classifier n, the property sets realized by its forms include the morphomic property 'clf.n'; thus, the Group I rules in the fragment under consideration apply to verbs associated with classifier 13.

(16) Simple rules of inflectional exponence for a fragment of Murrinhpatha verb morphology

Group I   ⟦id.fn$_C$⟧$_{SG}$:   [V, {{sbj 3 sg/dns} clf.13} : CS → CS]
(SBJ.AGR rules):

         ⟦**pu-**$_C$⟧$_{DU}$:   [V, {{sbj 3 du/pns} clf.13} : *pu*-]
         ⟦**pu-**$_C$⟧$_{PL}$:   [V, {{sbj 3 ps/pl} clf.13} : *pu*-]

Group II (suffixation to the lexical stem):
DNS rules   ⟦**-ngintha**$_L$⟧ :   [V, {{dns female}} : *-ngintha*]
         ⟦**-nintha**$_L$⟧ :   [V, {{dns male}} : *-nintha*]
PNS rules   ⟦**-ngime**$_L$⟧ :   [V, {{pns female}} : *-ngime*]
         ⟦**-neme**$_L$⟧ :   [V, {{pns male}} : *-neme*]

Group III (suffixation to the classifier stem):
OBJ.AGR rules   ⟦**-ngi**$_C$⟧ :   [V, {{obj 1 sg} : *-ngi*]
         ⟦**-nganku**$_C$⟧ :   [V, {{obj 1 du/pns excl}} : *-nganku*]
         ⟦**-nhi**$_C$⟧ :   [V, {{obj 2 sg} : *-nhi*]
         ⟦**-nanku**$_C$⟧ :   [V, {{obj 2 du/pns}} : *-nganku*]
SBJ.NUM rule   ⟦**-ka**$_C$⟧ :   [V, {{sbj ds/pns}{obj none} –fut} : *-ka*]
DNS rules   ⟦**-ngintha**$_C$⟧ :   [V, {{dns female}} : *-ngintha*]
         ⟦**-nintha**$_C$⟧ :   [V, {{dns male}} : *-nintha*]

The Group II rules in (16) define suffixes that inflect a verb's lexical stem; these include the DNS rules ⟦**-ngintha**$_L$⟧ and ⟦**-nintha**$_L$⟧ and the PNS rules ⟦**-ngime**$_L$⟧ and ⟦**-neme**$_L$⟧. The Group III rules define suffixes that inflect a verb's classifier stem; these include OBJ.AGR rules, the SBJ.NUM rule ⟦**-ka**$_C$⟧, and the DNS rules ⟦**-ngintha**$_C$⟧ and ⟦**-nintha**$_C$⟧.

Note that the DNS/PNS rules in Group II of (16) serve to express subject number in the realization of some verb forms and to express object number in the realization of others. As a consequence, the rules in (16) deviate massively from the parallel sequence criterion (Section 1.5.3): rules realizing subject

9.3 Rule combining Morphotactic Analysis of Verbs

properties appear in all three rule groups and rules realizing object properties appear in Groups II and III.

The rules introducing the DNS suffixes *-ngintha* (f) and *-ngintha* (m) have a special status in this system of rules: they may serve either as classifier-operand rules in Group III or as lexical-operand rules in Group II. Thus, the rules 〚**-ngintha$_L$**〛 and 〚**-ngintha$_C$**〛 may be seen as instances of the rule schema (17a); similarly, the rules 〚**-nintha$_L$**〛 and 〚**-nintha$_C$**〛 may be seen as instances of the rule schema (17b). As will be seen below, this special status accounts for fact (14b) – the fact that *-ngintha* and *-nintha* may serve as SBJ. NUM suffixes in both position 2 and position 8.

(17)   Rule schemata for the DNS suffixes
       a.   〚**-ngintha$_{C/L}$**〛 :   [V, {{dns female}} : *-ngintha*]
       b.   〚**-nintha$_{C/L}$**〛 :   [V, {{dns male}} : *-nintha*]

The proposed analysis accounts for fact (14a) without resorting to one set of DNS/PNS rules to express subject number and a second, essentially duplicate set of DNS/PNS rules to express object number; in this analysis, the DNS/PNS rules in Group II and the DNS rules in Group III realize set-based properties that are category-indeterminate, serving both to express subject number in the realization of some verb forms and to express object number in the realization of others. In accordance with the Category Determination Principle, the DNS/PNS rules are always dependent: whether they express subject number or object number depends on the carrier rule with which they combine. Thus, in each of the three types of rule in (18)–(20), a DNS/PNS rule combines with a carrier rule that determines its status as an expression of subject number or object number. When a Group II rule composes with an OBJ.AGR rule, as in (18), it expresses object number. This is in accordance with the definition of rule composition; thus, (〚**-ngintha$_L$**〛 ○ 〚**-nganku$_C$**〛) expresses the unification of {{dns female}} with {{obj 1 du/pns excl}} (= {{obj 1 dns excl female}}).[5] When a SBJ.AGR rule composes with a Group II rule, as in (19), the Group II rule instead expresses subject number, again in accordance with the definition of rule composition; thus, (〚**pu-$_C$**〛$_{DU}$ ○ 〚**-ngintha$_L$**〛) expresses the unification of {{sbj 3 du/pns} clf.13} with {{dns female}} (= {{sbj 3 dns female} clf.13}). (Among the composite rules in (19), those in (19e) are dispreferred, a point to which I return below.) Finally, when the SBJ.AGR rule 〚id.fcn$_C$〛$_{SG}$ composes with a DNS rule in Group III, as in (20), the DNS rule again expresses subject number. I shall refer to the rules in (18)–(20) as ***category-determining composites***, since each determines a DNS/PNS rule's category-indeterminate agreement property.

---

[5] In Murrinhpatha, the dual property DU is interpretable as the disjunction DS/DNS.

(18) Category-determining composites of type (R_DNS/PNS ∘ R_OBJ.AGR), pattern (Group II ∘ Group III)

  a. ([[-ngintha_L] ∘ [[-ngankuc_C]]) : [V, {{obj 1 dns excl female}} : CSILS → CS-*ngankul*LS-*ngintha*]
  b. ([[-nintha_L] ∘ [[-ngankuc_C]]) : [V, {{obj 1 dns excl male}} : CSILS → CS-*ngankul*LS-*nintha*]
  c. ([[-ngime_L] ∘ [[-ngankuc_C]]) : [V, {{obj 1 pns excl female}} : CSILS → CS-*ngankul*LS-*ngime*]
  d. ([[-neme_L] ∘ [[-ngankuc_C]]) : [V, {{obj 1 pns excl male}} : CSILS → CS-*ngankul*LS-*neme*]
  e. ([[-ngintha_L] ∘ [[-nankuc_C]]) : [V, {{obj 2 dns female}} : CSILS → CS-*nankul*LS-*ngintha*]
  f. ([[-nintha_L] ∘ [[-nankuc_C]]) : [V, {{obj 2 dns male}} : CSILS → CS-*nankul*LS-*nintha*]
  g. ([[-ngime_L] ∘ [[-nankuc_C]]) : [V, {{obj 2 pns female}} : CSILS → CS-*nankul*LS-*ngime*]
  h. ([[-neme_L] ∘ [[-nankuc_C]]) : [V, {{obj 2 pns male}} : CSILS → CS-*nankul*LS-*neme*]

(19) Category-determining composites of type (R_SBJ.AGR ∘ R_DNS/PNS), pattern (Group I ∘ Group II)

  a. ([**pu-c**]_DU ∘ [[-ngintha_L]]) : [V, {{sbj 3 dns female} clf.13} : CSILS → *pu*-CSILS-*ngintha*]
  b. ([**pu-c**]_DU ∘ [[-nintha_L]]) : [V, {{sbj 3 dns male} clf.13} : CSILS → *pu*-CSILS-*nintha*]
  c. ([**pu-c**]_DU ∘ [[-ngime_L]]) : [V, {{sbj 3 pns female} clf.13} : CSILS → *pu*-CSILS-*ngime*]
  d. ([**pu-c**]_DU ∘ [[-neme_L]]) : [V, {{sbj 3 pns male} clf.13} : CSILS → *pu*-CSILS-*neme*]
  e. Dispreferred composites:
     ([id.fnc_C]_SG ∘ [[-ngintha_L]]) : [V, {{sbj 3 dns female} clf.13} : CSILS → CSILS-*ngintha*]
     ([id.fnc_C]_SG ∘ [[-nintha_L]]) : [V, {{sbj 3 dns male} clf.13} : CSILS → CSILS-*nintha*]

(20) Category-determining composites of type ([[id.fnc_C]_SG ∘ R_DNS), pattern (Group I ∘ Group III)

  a. ([id.fnc_C]_SG ∘ [[-ngintha_C]]) : [V, {{sbj 3 dns female} clf.13} : CSILS → CS-*nginthal*LS]
  b. ([id.fnc_C]_SG ∘ [[-nintha_C]]) : [V, {{sbj 3 dns male} clf.13} : CSILS → CS-*ninthal*LS]

9.3 Rule combining Morphotactic Analysis of Verbs

The simple rules in (16) and the category-determining composites in (18)–(20) determine FERs for the fragment of Murrinhpatha verb inflection in accordance with the four general FER patterns listed in (21).

(21) Four general FER patterns for a fragment of Murrinhpatha verbal morphotactics
  a. The simple rule pattern, consisting of a single Group I rule
  b. The two-rule pattern, consisting of a (Group I ∘ Group III) composite
  c. The nested pattern consisting of a ((Group I ∘ Group II) ∘ Group III) composite
  d. The nested pattern consisting of a (Group I ∘ (Group II ∘ Group III)) composite

The patterns in (21) are morphotactically quite simple: each FER is either a simple rule from Group I, the composite of a Group I rule with a Group III rule, or a nested composite of three simple rules, one from each of Groups I–III. Note that the ways in which rules enter into these combinations are quite restricted:

- No rule composes with another rule from the same group.
- Every FER consists of or contains a Group I rule.
- When a Group I rule R_I enters into composition with another rule R_X, R_I must be the "outer" member of the resulting composite: (R_I ∘ R_X).
- When a Group III rule R_{III} enters into composition with another rule R_X, R_{III} must be the "inner" member of the resulting composite: (R_X ∘ R_{III}).
- The DNS/PNS rules are invariably dependent. If a DNS/PNS rule serves as an OBJ.NUM rule, it composes with its carrier rule (an OBJ.AGR rule in Group III), as in (18). If a DNS/PNS rule serves as a SBJ.NUM rule, its carrier rule composes with it. In such cases, the carrier rule is a SBJ.AGR rule in Group I and the SBJ.NUM rule is either a lexical-operand rule in Group II (as in (19)) or a classifier-operand rule in Group III (as in (20)).
- Any FER containing a Group II rule contains a Group III rule, while the reverse is not always true.

Consider some different types of FERs conforming to the four patterns in (21).

9.3.1 FERs Conforming to the Simple Rule Pattern (21a)

FERs conforming to the simple rule pattern (21a) are of a single type: they consist of a single SBJ.AGR rule (that is, a single Group I rule). These are the

278 *Nonassociativity of Rule Composition in Murrinhpatha*

Table 9.8 *The morphotactics of Murrinhpatha* pu-bam-ngkardu
'they saw her/him' (= (10g))

Content cell:	⟨NGKARDU, {{sbj 3 ps}{obj 3 sg} –fut clf.13}⟩
Form cell:	⟨bam|ngkardu, {{sbj 3 ps}{obj none} –fut clf.13}⟩
|	
FER	$[\![\mathbf{pu}\text{-}_C]\!]_{PL}$ (from Group I in (16))
↓	
Realized cell:	⟨pu-bam|ngkardu, {{sbj 3 ps}{obj none} –fut clf.13}⟩

FERs for verb forms such as (10a) *bam-ngkardu* 's/he saw her/him' (defined by the Group I rule $[\![\text{id.fnc}_C]\!]_{SG}$ in (16)) and (10g) *pu-bam-ngkardu* 'they saw her/him' (defined by the Group I rule $[\![\mathbf{pu}\text{-}_C]\!]_{PL}$ in (16)). These are forms that lack[6] object concord and have a subject that is singular, PS, or plural. Treated as having a paucal-sibling subject, the form (10g) *pu-bam-ngkardu* 'they saw her/him' has the analysis in Table 9.8.

9.3.2   FERs Conforming to the Two-rule Pattern (21b)

FERs conforming to the two-rule pattern (21b) are of the three types in Table 9.9, all of which take the form of a (Group I ∘ Group III) composite.

In the nonfuture tense, verb forms that lack object concord and have a DS/PNS subject involve the SBJ.NUM rule $[\![\text{-}\mathbf{ka}_C]\!]$ in Group III. The FERs defining such verb forms are of the first type in Table 9.9, according to which the SBJ.AGR rule $[\![\mathbf{pu}\text{-}_C]\!]_{DU}$ in Group I composes with $[\![\text{-}\mathbf{ka}_C]\!]$ to produce the FER in (22). In this FER, the content of $[\![\text{-}\mathbf{ka}_C]\!]$ specifies the absence of overtly realized object properties; this accounts for the absence of *-ka* from forms with overt object concord (fact (14d)).[7] The morphotactics of the verb form

---

[6] A verb form lacks object concord either because it doesn't have an object or because its object is third-person singular and is therefore not overtly expressed in the verb form's morphology.

[7] This analysis does not exclude the possibility that *-ka* might coincide with overtly unrealized object properties. I assume that overtly unrealized properties are properties that are present in a content cell but absent from the corresponding form cell as an effect of the property mapping relating the former to the latter (Section 2.1). This means that the content cell of a Murrinhpatha verb form such as (i) specifies third-person singular object properties, but that that these properties are absent from the corresponding form cell and therefore do not exclude the presence of *-ka* in (i).

9.3 Rule combining Morphotactic Analysis of Verbs

Table 9.9 *The three types of composite FERs conforming to the two-rule pattern (Group I ∘ Group III) in (21b)*

Type	Examples	
($R_{SBJ.AGR}$ ∘ [[-**ka**$_C$]])	([[**pu**-$_C$]]$_{DU}$ ∘ [[-**ka**$_C$]])	(= (22))
([[id.fcn$_C$]]$_{SG}$ ∘ R_{DNS})	([[id.fcn$_C$]]$_{SG}$ ∘ [[-**nginthac**$_C$]])	(= (20a))
	([[id.fcn$_C$]]$_{SG}$ ∘ [[-**nintha**$_C$]])	(= (20b))
($R_{SBJ.AGR}$ ∘ $R_{OBJ.AGR}$)	([[id.fcn$_C$]]$_{SG}$ ∘ [[-**ngi**$_C$]])	(= (23a))
	([[id.fcn$_C$]]$_{SG}$ ∘ [[-**nganku**$_C$]])	(= (23d))
	([[**pu**-$_C$]]$_{DU}$ ∘ [[-**nhi**$_C$]])	(= (23h))
	([[**pu**-$_C$]]$_{PL}$ ∘ [[-**nanku**$_C$]])	(= (23l))
	etc.	

Table 9.10 *The morphotactics of Murrinhpatha pu-bam-ka-ngkardu 'they (two siblings) saw her/him' (= (10d))*

Content cell:	⟨NGKARDU, {{sbj 3 ds}{obj 3 sg} –fut clf.13}⟩
Form cell:	⟨bam|ngkardu, {{sbj 3 ds}{obj none} –fut clf.13}⟩
|	
FER	([[**pu**-$_C$]]$_{DU}$ ∘ [[-**ka**$_C$]]) (= (22), type ($R_{SBJ.AGR}$ ∘ [[-**ka**$_C$]]))
↓	
Realized cell:	⟨*pu-bam-ka|ngkardu*, {{sbj 3 ds}{obj none} –fut clf.13}⟩

(10d) *pu-bam-ka-ngkardu* 'they (two siblings) saw her/him' is therefore defined by the application of (22), as in Table 9.10.

(22)   FER of type ($R_{SBJ.AGR}$ ∘ [[-**ka**$_C$]])
       ([[**pu**-$_C$]]$_{DU}$ ∘ [[-**ka**$_C$]]) : [V, {{sbj 3 ds/pns}{obj none} –fut clf.13} :
       CS → *pu*-CS-*ka*]

Forms that lack object concord whose subject is DNS are defined by a FER of the second type in Table 9.9. In these FERs, the category-indeterminate rules in Group III are combined with SBJ.AGR rules in Group I (as in (20)); as a

(i)   *pu-bam-ka-ngkardu*
      CS:3.DUAL'-SEE(13).NFUT-SBJ.DS/PNS.NFUT-LS:see
      'They (two siblings) saw her/him.'

Table 9.11 *The morphotactics of Murrinhpatha* bam-ngintha-ngkardu *'they (two female nonsiblings) saw her/him'* (= (10b))

Content cell:	⟨NGKARDU, {{sbj 3 dns female}{obj 3 sg} –fut clf.13}⟩
Form cell:	⟨bam|ngkardu, {{sbj 3 dns female}{obj none} –fut clf.13}⟩
|	
FER	([id.fcn$_C$]$_{SG}$ ∘ [[-ngintha$_C$]]) (= (20a), type ([id.fcn$_C$]$_{SG}$ ∘ R$_{DNS}$))
↓	
Realized cell:	⟨bam-ngintha|ngkardu, {{sbj 3 dns female}{obj none} –fut clf.13}⟩

Table 9.12 *The morphotactics of Murrinhpatha* pu-bam-nganku-ngkardu *'they (two siblings) saw us (two excl siblings)'* (= (11))

Form cell:	⟨bam|ngkardu, {{sbj 3 ds}{obj 1 ds excl} –fut clf.13}⟩
|	
FER	([[**pu**-$_C$]]$_{DU}$ ∘ [[**-nganku**$_C$]]) (= (23e), type (R$_{SBJ.AGR}$ ∘ R$_{OBJ.AGR}$))
↓	
Realized cell:	⟨*pu-bam-nganku*|*ngkardu*, {{sbj 3 ds}{obj 1 ds excl} –fut clf.13}⟩

consequence, the Group III rules function as SBJ.NUM rules in these FERs. According to the definition of this FER pattern in (20), the SBJ.AGR rule [id.fcn$_C$]$_{SG}$ composes with a classifier-operand rule introducing a DNS suffix (i.e. [[-ngintha$_C$]] or [[-nintha$_C$]]); the category-determining composites in (20) affix a DNS suffix to the classifier stem (in effect placing the suffix in position 2 in Nordlinger's template in Table 9.1). Thus, the morphotactics of the form (10b) *bam-ngintha-ngkardu* 'they (two female nonsiblings) saw her/him' is defined by means of the composite rule ([id.fcn$_C$]$_{SG}$ ∘ [[-ngintha$_C$]]), as in Table 9.11.

Some two-rule composites serve as FERs for forms that have object concord. If a form has object concord and neither its subject nor its object is DNS or PNS, then it is defined by a FER of type (R$_{SBJ.AGR}$ ∘ R$_{OBJ.AGR}$), the third type in Table 9.9. In accordance with this type, the classifier rules from Group I compose with the OBJ.AGR rules from Group III to yield the numerous composites in (23). The form (11) *pu-bam-nganku-ngkardu* 'they (two siblings) saw us (two excl siblings)' is thus defined by means of the two-rule FER ([[**pu**-$_C$]]$_{DU}$ ∘ [[**-nganku**$_C$]]), as in Table 9.12.

(23) FERs of type ($R_{SBJ.AGR} \circ R_{OBJ.AGR}$)

a. ([id.fcnc]$_{SG}$ ∘ [**-ngi**$_{C}$]) : [V, {{sbj 3 sg/dns}{obj 1 sg} clf.13} : CSILS → CS-*ngi*ILS]
b. ([**pu-**$_{C}$]$_{DU}$ ∘ [**-ngi**$_{C}$]) : [V, {{sbj 3 du/pns}{obj 1 sg} clf.13} : CSILS → *pu*-CS-*ngi*ILS]
c. ([**pu-**$_{C}$]$_{PL}$ ∘ [**-ngi**$_{C}$]) : [V, {{sbj 3 ps/pl}{obj 1 sg} clf.13} : CSILS → *pu*-CS-*ngi*ILS]
d. ([id.fcnc]$_{SG}$ ∘ [**-ngankul**$_{C}$]) : [V, {{sbj 3 sg/dns}{obj 1 du/pns excl} clf.13} : CSILS → CS-*ngankul*ILS]
e. ([**pu-**$_{C}$]$_{DU}$ ∘ [**-ngankul**$_{C}$]) : [V, {{sbj 3 du/pns}{obj 1 du/pns excl} clf.13} : CSILS → *pu*-CS-*ngankul*ILS]
f. ([**pu-**$_{C}$]$_{PL}$ ∘ [**-ngankul**$_{C}$]) : [V, {{sbj 3 ps/pl}{obj 1 du/pns excl} clf.13} : CSILS → *pu*-CS-*ngankul*ILS]
g. ([id.fcnc]$_{SG}$ ∘ [**-nhi**$_{C}$]) : [V, {{sbj 3 sg/dns}{obj 2 sg} clf.13} : CSILS → CS-*nhi*ILS]
h. ([**pu-**$_{C}$]$_{DU}$ ∘ [**-nhi**$_{C}$]) : [V, {{sbj 3 du/pns}{obj 2 sg} clf.13} : CSILS → *pu*-CS-*nhi*ILS]
i. ([**pu-**$_{C}$]$_{PL}$ ∘ [**-nhi**$_{C}$]) : [V, {{sbj 3 ps/pl}{obj 2 sg} clf.13} : CSILS → *pu*-CS-*nhi*ILS]
j. ([id.fcnc]$_{SG}$ ∘ [**-nankul**$_{C}$]) : [V, {{sbj 3 sg/dns}{obj 2 du/pns} clf.13} : CSILS → CS-*nankul*ILS]
k. ([**pu-**$_{C}$]$_{DU}$ ∘ [**-nankul**$_{C}$]) : [V, {{sbj 3 du/pns}{obj 2 du/pns} clf.13} : CSILS → *pu*-CS-*nankul*ILS]
l. ([**pu-**$_{C}$]$_{PL}$ ∘ [**-nankul**$_{C}$]) : [V, {{sbj 3 ps/pl}{obj 2 du/pns} clf.13} : CSILS → *pu*-CS-*nankul*ILS]

9.3.3 FERs Conforming to the Nested Pattern (21c)

Certain FERs in the fragment under consideration involve the nested composition of three rules in the ((Group I ∘ Group II) ∘ Group III) pattern in (21c). In these FERs, the category-indeterminate rules in Group II are first combined with SBJ.AGR rules in Group I (as in (19)); as a consequence, the Group II rules function as SBJ.NUM rules in these FERs. FERs conforming to this pattern are of the two types in Table 9.13.

In the nonfuture tense, verb forms that lack object concord and have a PNS subject involve both a PNS rule from Group II and the SBJ.NUM rule $[\![\text{-ka}_C]\!]$ from Group III. The FERs defining such verb forms are of the first type in Table 9.13. In accordance with this type, the category-determining composites in (19c,d) compose with $[\![\text{-ka}_C]\!]$ to produce the FERs in (24). The form (10f) *pu-bam-ka-ngkardu-ngime* 'they (paucal female nonsiblings) saw her/him' is defined by means of the composite rule (24b) as in Table 9.14; this FER suffixes *-ka* to a verb form's classifier stem, suffixes *-ngime* to its lexical stem, and prefixes *pu-* to its classifier stem.

(24) FERs of type $((R_{\text{SBJ.AGR}} \circ R_{\text{PNS}}) \circ [\![\text{-ka}_C]\!])$
  a. $(([\![\text{pu-}_C]\!]_{\text{DU}} \circ [\![\text{-neme}_L]\!]) \circ [\![\text{-ka}_C]\!])$: [V, {{sbj 3 pns male}{obj none} –fut clf.13} : CS|LS → *pu*-CS-*ka*|LS-*neme*]
  b. $(([\![\text{pu-}_C]\!]_{\text{DU}} \circ [\![\text{-ngime}_L]\!]) \circ [\![\text{-ka}_C]\!])$: [V, {{sbj 3 pns female}{obj none} –fut clf.13} : CS|LS → *pu*-CS-*ka*|LS-*ngime*]

If a form has an OBJ.AGR suffix but has a DNS/PNS suffix serving as a SBJ.NUM suffix, then it is defined by a FER of the second type in Table 9.13. In

Table 9.13 *The two types of composite FERs conforming to the nested pattern ((Group I ∘ Group II) ∘ Group III) in (21c)*

Type	Examples	
$((R_{\text{SBJ.AGR}} \circ R_{\text{PNS}}) \circ [\![\text{-ka}_C]\!])$	$(([\![\text{pu-}_C]\!]_{\text{DU}} \circ [\![\text{-neme}_L]\!]) \circ [\![\text{-ka}_C]\!])$	(= (24a))
	$(([\![\text{pu-}_C]\!]_{\text{DU}} \circ [\![\text{-ngime}_L]\!]) \circ [\![\text{-ka}_C]\!])$	(= (24b))
$((R_{\text{SBJ.AGR}} \circ R_{\text{DNS/PNS}}) \circ R_{\text{OBJ.AGR}})$	$(([\![\text{pu-}_C]\!]_{\text{DU}} \circ [\![\text{-nintha}_L]\!]) \circ [\![\text{-ngi}_C]\!])$	(= (26a))
	$(([\![\text{pu-}_C]\!]_{\text{DU}} \circ [\![\text{-nintha}_L]\!]) \circ [\![\text{-nganku}_C]\!])$	(= (26f))
	$(([\![\text{pu-}_C]\!]_{\text{DU}} \circ [\![\text{-ngime}_L]\!]) \circ [\![\text{-nhi}_C]\!])$	(= (26k))
	$(([\![\text{pu-}_C]\!]_{\text{DU}} \circ [\![\text{-neme}_L]\!]) \circ [\![\text{-nanku}_C]\!])$	(= (26p))
	etc.	

9.3 Rule combining Morphotactic Analysis of Verbs   283

Table 9.14 *The morphotactics of Murrinhpatha* pu-bam-ka-ngkardu-ngime *'they (paucal female nonsiblings) saw her/him' (= (10f))*

Content cell:	⟨NGKARDU, {{sbj 3 pns female}{obj 3 sg} –fut clf.13}⟩
Form cell:	⟨bam|ngkardu, {{sbj 3 pns female}{obj none} –fut clf.13}⟩
|	
FER	((⟦**pu**-$_C$⟧$_{DU}$ ∘ ⟦-**ngime**$_L$⟧) ∘ ⟦-**ka**$_C$⟧) (= (24b), type
↓	(($R_{SBJ.AGR}$ ∘ R_{PNS}) ∘ ⟦-**ka**$_C$⟧))
Realized cell:	⟨pu-bam-ka|ngkardu-ngime, {{sbj 3 pns female}{obj none} –fut clf.13}⟩

Table 9.15 *The morphotactics of Murrinhpatha* pu-bam-ngi-ngkardu-ngintha *'they (two female nonsiblings) saw me' (= (10c))*

Form cell:	⟨bam|ngkardu, {{sbj 3 dns female}{obj 1 sg} –fut clf.13}⟩
|	
FER	((⟦**pu**-$_C$⟧$_{DU}$ ∘ ⟦-**ngintha**$_L$⟧) ∘ ⟦-**ngi**$_C$⟧) (= (26a), type
↓	(($R_{SBJ.AGR}$ ∘ R_{DNS}) ∘ $R_{OBJ.AGR}$))
Realizedcell:	⟨pu-bam-ngi|ngkardu-ngintha, {{sbj 3 dns female}{obj 1 sg} –fut clf.13}⟩

accordance with this type, the category-determining composites in (19) compose with the OBJ.AGR rules in Group III to produce the sixteen FERs listed in (25).[8] The form (10c) *pu-bam-ngi-ngkardu-ngintha* 'they (two female nonsiblings) saw me' is defined by the composite FER (25a), which instantiates the pattern ((Group I ∘ Group II) ∘ Group III) by suffixing *-ngi* to the classifier stem, suffixing *-ngintha* to the lexical stem, and prefixing *pu-* to the classifier stem, as in Table 9.15.

---

[8] In (25), I omit the composites of the dispreferred rules in (19e) with the OBJ.AGR rules. Such composites should be assumed to exist alongside those in (26), but as dispreferred options.

(25) Composite FERs of type ((R_SBJ.AGR ∘ R_DNS/PNS) ∘ R_OBJ.AGR), pattern ((Group I ∘ Group II) ∘ Group III)

a. (([**pu-c**]_DU ∘ [**-ngintha**_L]) ∘ [**-ngi**_C]) : [V, {{sbj 3 dns female}{obj 1 sg} clf.13} : CSILS → *pu-*CS*-ngi*ILS*-ngintha*]
b. (([**pu-c**]_DU ∘ [**-nintha**_L]) ∘ [**-ngi**_C]) : [V, {{sbj 3 dns male}{obj 1 sg} clf.13} : CSILS → *pu-*CS*-ngi*ILS*-nintha*]
c. (([**pu-c**]_DU ∘ [**-ngime**_L]) ∘ [**-ngi**_C]) : [V, {{sbj 3 pns female}{obj 1 sg} clf.13} : CSILS → *pu-*CS*-ngi*ILS*-ngime*]
d. (([**pu-c**]_DU ∘ [**-neme**_L]) ∘ [**-ngi**_C]) : [V, {{sbj 3 pns male}{obj 1 sg} clf.13} : CSILS → *pu-*CS*-ngi*ILS*-neme*]
e. (([**pu-c**]_DU ∘ [**-ngintha**_L]) ∘ [**-nganku**_C]) : [V, {{sbj 3 dns female}{obj 1 du/pns excl} clf.13} : CSILS → *pu-*CS*-ngankul*LS*-ngintha*]
f. (([**pu-c**]_DU ∘ [**-nintha**_L]) ∘ [**-nganku**_C]) : [V, {{sbj 3 dns male}{obj 1 du/pns excl} clf.13} : CSILS → *pu-*CS*-ngankul*LS*-nintha*]
g. (([**pu-c**]_DU ∘ [**-ngime**_L]) ∘ [**-nganku**_C]) : [V, {{sbj 3 pns female}{obj 1 du/pns excl} clf.13} : CSILS → *pu-*CS*-ngankul*LS*-ngime*]
h. (([**pu-c**]_DU ∘ [**-neme**_L]) ∘ [**-nganku**_C]) : [V, {{sbj 3 pns male}{obj 1 du/pns excl} clf.13} : CSILS → *pu-*CS*-ngankul*LS*-neme*]
i. (([**pu-c**]_DU ∘ [**-ngintha**_L]) ∘ [**-nhi**_C]) : [V, {{sbj 3 dns female}{obj 2 sg} clf.13} : CSILS → *pu-*CS*-nhi*ILS*-ngintha*]
j. (([**pu-c**]_DU ∘ [**-nintha**_L]) ∘ [**-nhi**_C]) : [V, {{sbj 3 dns male}{obj 2 sg} clf.13} : CSILS → *pu-*CS*-nhi*ILS*-nintha*]
k. (([**pu-c**]_DU ∘ [**-ngime**_L]) ∘ [**-nhi**_C]) : [V, {{sbj 3 pns female}{obj 2 sg} clf.13} : CSILS → *pu-*CS*-nhi*ILS*-ngime*]
l. (([**pu-c**]_DU ∘ [**-neme**_L]) ∘ [**-nhi**_C]) : [V, {{sbj 3 pns male}{obj 2 sg} clf.13} : CSILS → *pu-*CS*-nhi*ILS*-neme*]
m. (([**pu-c**]_DU ∘ [**-ngintha**_L]) ∘ [**-nanku**_C]) : [V, {{sbj 3 dns female}{obj 2 du/pns} clf.13} : CSILS → *pu-*CS*-nankul*LS*-ngintha*]
n. (([**pu-c**]_DU ∘ [**-nintha**_L]) ∘ [**-nanku**_C]) : [V, {{sbj 3 dns male}{obj 2 du/pns} clf.13} : CSILS → *pu-*CS*-nankul*LS*-nintha*]
o. (([**pu-c**]_DU ∘ [**-ngime**_L]) ∘ [**-nanku**_C]) : [V, {{sbj 3 pns female}{obj 2 du/pns} clf.13} : CSILS → *pu-*CS*-nankul*LS*-ngime*]
p. (([**pu-c**]_DU ∘ [**-neme**_L]) ∘ [**-nanku**_C]) : [V, {{sbj 3 pns male}{obj 2 du/pns} clf.13} : CSILS → *pu-*CS*-nankul*LS*-neme*]

9.3 Rule combining Morphotactic Analysis of Verbs 285

Table 9.16 *The morphotactics of Murrinhpatha*
pu-bam-nganku-ngkardu-ngime *'they (two siblings) saw us (paucal exclusive female nonsiblings)' (= (12b))*

Form cell:	⟨bam|ngkardu, {{sbj 3 ds}{obj 1 pns excl female} –fut clf.13}⟩
↓ FER ↓	($[\![\mathbf{pu}\text{-}_\mathrm{C}]\!]_\mathrm{DU} \circ ([\![\text{-}\mathbf{ngime}_\mathrm{L}]\!] \circ [\![\text{-}\mathbf{nganku}_\mathrm{C}]\!]))$ (= (26c), type $(R_\mathrm{SBJ.AGR} \circ (R_\mathrm{PNS} \circ R_\mathrm{OBJ.AGR})))$
Realized cell:	⟨pu-bam-nganku|ngkardu-ngime, {{sbj 3 ds}{obj 1 pns excl female} –fut clf.13}⟩

9.3.4 FERs Conforming to the Nested Pattern (21d)

In contrast to the FERs discussed in Section 9.3.3, certain other FERs in the fragment under consideration involve the nested composition of three rules in the (Group I ∘ (Group II ∘ Group III)) pattern in (21d). In these FERs, the category-indeterminate rules in Group II are first combined with OBJ.AGR rules in Group III (as in (18)); as a consequence, the Group II rules function as OBJ.NUM rules in these FERs. FERs conforming to this pattern are of a single type – the result of composing a SBJ.AGR rule with any of the category-determining composites in (18) (which belong to the type $(R_\mathrm{DNS/PNS} \circ R_\mathrm{OBJ.AGR}))$. If a verb form in the fragment under consideration has a DNS or PNS object, then it is defined by a FER of this type. Some examples of FERs of this type are those in (26), which exemplify the pattern with the Group I rule $[\![\mathbf{pu}\text{-}_\mathrm{C}]\!]_\mathrm{DU}$. (Sets of FERs parallel to those in (26) arise by composing the Group I rules $[\![\text{id.fcn}_\mathrm{C}]\!]_\mathrm{SG}$ and $[\![\mathbf{pu}\text{-}_\mathrm{C}]\!]_\mathrm{PL}$ with the composite rules in (18).) The form (12b) *pu-bam-nganku-ngkardu-ngime* 'they (two siblings) saw us (paucal exclusive female nonsiblings)' is defined by the composite FER (26c), which instantiates the pattern (Group I ∘ (Group II ∘ Group III)) by suffixing *-nganku* to the classifier stem, suffixing *-ngime* to the lexical stem, and prefixing *pu-* to the classifier stem, as in Table 9.16.

(26) Composite FERs of type ($R_{SBJ.AGR} \circ (R_{DNS/PNS} \circ R_{OBJ.AGR})$), pattern (Group I ∘ (Group II ∘ Group III))

a. (([**pu**-c]$_{DU}$ ∘ ([-**nginθa**$_L$] ∘ [-**nganku**$_C$])) : [V, {{sbj 3 du/pns}{obj 1 dns excl female} clf.13} : CSILS → *pu*-CS-*nganku*ILS-*nginθa*]

b. (([**pu**-c]$_{DU}$ ∘ ([-**ninθa**$_L$] ∘ [-**nganku**$_C$])) : [V, {{sbj 3 du/pns}{obj 1 dns excl male} clf.13} : CSILS → *pu*-CS-*nganku*ILS-*ninθa*]

c. (([**pu**-c]$_{DU}$ ∘ ([-**ngime**$_L$] ∘ [-**nganku**$_C$])) : [V, {{sbj 3 du/pns}{obj 1 pns excl female} clf.13} : CSILS → *pu*-CS-*nganku*ILS-*ngime*]

d. (([**pu**-c]$_{DU}$ ∘ ([-**neme**$_L$] ∘ [-**nganku**$_C$])) : [V, {{sbj 3 du/pns}{obj 1 pns excl male} clf.13} : CSILS → *pu*-CS-*nganku*ILS-*neme*]

e. (([**pu**-c]$_{DU}$ ∘ ([-**nginθa**$_L$] ∘ [-**nanku**$_C$])) : [V, {{sbj 3 du/pns}{obj 2 dns female} clf.13} : CSILS → *pu*-CS-*nanku*ILS-*nginθa*]

f. (([**pu**-c]$_{DU}$ ∘ ([-**ninθa**$_L$] ∘ [-**nanku**$_C$])) : [V, {{sbj 3 du/pns}{obj 2 dns male} clf.13} : CSILS → *pu*-CS-*nanku*ILS-*ninθa*]

g. (([**pu**-c]$_{DU}$ ∘ ([-**ngime**$_L$] ∘ [-**nanku**$_C$])) : [V, {{sbj 3 du/pns}{obj 2 pns female} clf.13} : CSILS → *pu*-CS-*nanku*ILS-*ngime*]

h. (([**pu**-c]$_{DU}$ ∘ ([-**neme**$_L$] ∘ [-**nanku**$_C$])) : [V, {{sbj 3 du/pns}{obj 2 pns male} clf.13} : CSILS → *pu*-CS-*nanku*ILS-*neme*]

9.3 Rule combining Morphotactic Analysis of Verbs   287

Table 9.17 *Where* R *is a DNS rule instantiating* ⟦-ngintha$_{C/L}$⟧ *or* ⟦-nintha$_{C/L}$⟧, R *enters into one of three patterns of composition*

	R is	R$_{SBJ.AGR}$ (a Group I rule) composes with R, so that R serves as a SBJ.NUM rule	R composes with R$_{OBJ.AGR}$ (a Group III rule), so that R serves as an OBJ.NUM rule
(A)	a lexical-operand rule in Group II	pattern (Group I ∘ Group II)	pattern (Group II ∘ Group III)
(B)	a classifier-operand rule in Group III	pattern (Group I ∘ Group III)	Excluded: No rule composes with another rule from the same group

9.3.5 Accounting for the Morphotactic Facts in (14)

Consider again the remarkable morphotactic facts listed in (14). According to (14a), the DNS suffixes *-ngintha* (f)/*-nintha* (m) and the PNS suffixes *-ngime* (f)/*-neme* (m) refer to the subject in some verb forms and to the object in others. The proposed analysis accounts for this fact by means of the simple rules in Group II of (16), which are neutral with respect to whether they characterize the realization of subject properties or that of object properties; each of these rules is a dependent rule realizing a category-indeterminate property whose carrier rule determines the subject or object reference of this property, in accordance with the Category Determination Principle.

The proposed analysis also accounts for (14b) – the fact that in verb forms in which a DNS suffix (*-ngintha* (f) or *-nintha* (m)) refers to the subject, it appears in position 2 if there is no accompanying OBJ.AGR suffix and in position 8 if there is one. Recall that each of the schemata in (17) is instantiated by both a lexical-operand rule and a classifier-operand rule. As (18)–(20) show, the rules instantiating the schemata in (17) enter into the three patterns of composition in Table 9.17. As lexical-operand rules in Group II, ⟦-ngintha$_L$⟧ and ⟦-nintha$_L$⟧ may introduce suffixes into position 8 in two ways, as part (A) of Table 9.17 shows. On one hand, a SBJ.AGR rule in Group I may compose with ⟦-ngintha$_L$⟧ or ⟦-nintha$_L$⟧ to instantiate the pattern (Group I ∘ Group II), in which case the suffixes that they introduce serve as SBJ.NUM suffixes, as in (19); alternatively, they may compose with an OBJ.AGR rule belonging to Group III to yield the pattern (Group II ∘ Group III), in which case the suffixes that they introduce serve as OBJ.NUM suffixes, as in (18). But as classifier-operand rules belonging to Group III, ⟦-ngintha$_C$⟧ and ⟦-nintha$_C$⟧ may only introduce suffixes into position 2 in one way, as part (B) of Table 9.17 shows: the SBJ.AGR rule ⟦id.fcn$_C$⟧$_{SG}$ composes with them to yield the pattern (Group I ∘ Group III); in this case, the suffixes that they introduce are necessarily SBJ.NUM suffixes, as in (20). Composites fitting the (Group I ∘ Group III) pattern do not combine with the rules that introduce OBJ.AGR suffixes, because they, like ⟦-ngintha$_C$⟧ and ⟦-nintha$_C$⟧, are all Group III rules.

The proposed analysis accounts for (14c) – the fact that (i) when a DNS suffix appears as a SBJ.NUM suffix in position 2, it is accompanied by a Singular′ classifier stem, but (ii) when it appears in position 8, the accompanying classifier stem is either Singular′ (dispreferred) or Dual′. On one hand, the rule type in (20) only combines the DNS rules ⟦-ngintha$_C$⟧ and ⟦-nintha$_C$⟧ with the Singular′ classifier rule ⟦id.fcn$_C$⟧$_{SG}$; FERs of this type place a DNS SBJ.NUM suffix in position 2. On the other hand, the FER patterns of the type ((R$_{SBJ.AGR}$ ∘ R$_{DNS/PNS}$) ∘ R$_{OBJ.AGR}$) place a DNS SBJ.NUM suffix in position 8, and these may combine the DNS rules ⟦-ngintha$_L$⟧ and ⟦-nintha$_L$⟧ with either the Singular′ classifier rule ⟦id.fcn$_C$⟧$_{SG}$ or the Dual′ classifier rule ⟦pu-$_C$⟧$_{DU}$. The dispreference for the composites in (19e) may reflect the fact that the exclusion of these composites simplifies the patterns of rule composition in which the DNS rules introducing -ngintha and -nintha participate. In the preferred patterns, the Singular′ SBJ.AGR rule ⟦id.fcn$_C$⟧$_{SG}$ only composes with DNS rules taking a classifier operand (= ⟦-ngintha$_C$⟧ and ⟦-nintha$_C$⟧), as in (20), while the Dual′ SBJ.AGR rule ⟦pu-$_C$⟧$_{DU}$ only composes with DNS rules taking a lexical operand (= ⟦-ngintha$_L$⟧ and ⟦-nintha$_L$⟧), as in (19a,b); in addition, the preferred patterns in (19a,b) form a single pattern of combination with (19c,d) – a pattern in which the Dual′ SBJ.AGR rule is the only SBJ.AGR rule that composes directly with a SBJ.NUM rule in Group II.

The proposed analysis accounts for fact (14d) – that within a verb form, the DS/PNS suffix -ka is absent in the presence of an OBJ.AGR suffix. This is guaranteed by the definition of ⟦-ka$_C$⟧ in (16), according to which ⟦-ka$_C$⟧ realizes the property {obj none}.

Finally, the proposed analysis affords a way of explaining (14e) – the fact that if the realization of a given form is compatible with the appearance of either an OBJ.NUM suffix or a SBJ.NUM suffix, it is the OBJ.NUM suffix that is used, excluding the appearance of the SBJ.NUM suffix. In the context of the proposed system, fact (14e) can be restated as a preference affecting verb forms whose properties are realizable both by a FER of the type ((R$_{SBJ.AGR}$ ∘ R$_{DNS/PNS}$) ∘ R$_{OBJ.AGR}$) and by a FER of type (R$_{SBJ.AGR}$ ∘ (R$_{DNS/PNS}$ ∘ R$_{OBJ.AGR}$)): when FERs of these two types enter into competition for the realization of some form, it is the rule of the latter type that wins.

The form cell in (27) corresponds to a verb form of this sort: logically, it could be realized by either of the FERs in (28). Neither of these rules overrides

9.3 Rule combining Morphotactic Analysis of Verbs 289

the other, so Pāṇini's principle cannot resolve the competition between them; but according to fact (14e), (28b) prevails, so that (27) is realized by the verb form *pu-bam-nganku-ngkardu-ngime* rather than by the form *pu-bam-nganku-ngkardu-neme*. Rule (28a) and indeed all of the fragment's rules of type (($R_{SBJ.AGR}$ ° $R_{DNS/PNS}$) ° $R_{OBJ.AGR}$) create a discontinuity, causing an OBJ.AGR suffix to intervene linearly between two exponents of a subject's properties; by contrast, neither rule (28b) nor any other rule of type ($R_{SBJ.AGR}$ ° ($R_{DNS/PNS}$ ° $R_{OBJ.AGR}$)) engenders this kind of discontinuity (granting, of course, that a verb's lexical stem in any case intervenes between an OBJ.AGR suffix and an OBJ.NUM suffix). Thus, one might speculatively entertain a processing explanation for the fact that (28b) prevails over (28a) in the realization of (27): the forms defined by (28b) are more transparent in the sense that in their morphology, a linear sequence of subject-coding affixes is not interrupted by an object-coding affix. Note that this is not to say that an object-coding affix must never interrupt two subject-coding affixes; it clearly can, as in the forms defined by the composites in (26). But if there are two alternative rules available to realize a cell's content neither of which overrides the other but only one of which entails the interruption of a sequence of subject affixes by an object affix, the one that doesn't result in interruption is favored, seemingly for that very reason.

(27) ⟨ngkardu, {{sbj 3 pns male}{obj 1 pns excl female} –fut clf.13}⟩
      'They (paucal nonsibling male) saw us (paucal nonsibling exclusive female).'

(28) Alternative FERs for the realization of (27)
      a. FER of type (($R_{SBJ.AGR}$ ° $R_{DNS/PNS}$) ° $R_{OBJ.AGR}$),
          pattern ((Group I ° Group II) ° Group III)

          ((⟦**pu**-C⟧$_{DU}$ ° ⟦**-neme**$_L$⟧) ° ⟦**-nganku**$_C$⟧) :
            [V, {{sbj 3 pns male}{obj 1 du/pns excl} clf.13} : CS|LS →
                                                pu-CS-*nganku*|LS-*neme*]
      b. FER of type ($R_{SBJ.AGR}$ ° ($R_{DNS/PNS}$ ° $R_{OBJ.AGR}$)),
          pattern (Group I ° (Group II ° Group III))

          (⟦**pu**-C⟧$_{DU}$ ° (⟦**-ngime**$_L$⟧ ° ⟦**-nganku**$_C$⟧)) :
            [V, {{sbj 3}{obj 1 pns excl female} clf.13} : CS|LS →
                                                pu-CS-*nganku*|LS-*ngime*]

9.3.6 The Nonassociativity of Rule Composition in Murrinhpatha
According to the analysis embodied by the FERs in (25) and (26), Murrinhpatha verb inflection depends on the nonassociativity of rule composition. Thus, each of the FERs in the first column of Table 9.18 follows the FER

pattern ((Group I ∘ Group II) ∘ Group III), and the corresponding rule in the second column follows the pattern (Group I ∘ (Group II ∘ Group III)); yet, no two rules in Table 9.18 express the same content, as the extensional definitions in (25) and (26) show.

The nonassociativity exemplified in Table 9.18 accurately accounts for the observed ambiguity of certain forms. Consider again the verb form in (12). As Table 9.19 shows, the proposed system of rules and combinations correctly defines this form as the realization of a variety of meanings. Note that this variety is partly a result of the fact that certain affixes are inherently ambiguous. For example, the Dual' classifier rule 〚**pu**-$_C$〛$_{DU}$ and the Plural' classifier rule 〚**pu**-$_C$〛$_{PL}$ both introduce an affix having the form *pu-*; by the same token, the OBJ.AGR rule 〚-**nganku**$_C$〛 expresses a first-person exclusive object that is either dual or PNS. But the variety of meanings in Table 9.19 is also an effect of the fact that two different types of FERs are capable of defining this form. These are the type ((Group I ∘ Group II) ∘ Group III), here exemplified by the FER (25g), and the type (Group I ∘ (Group II ∘ Group III)), here exemplified by (26c). Although (25g) and (26c) are composites of the same three rules and although they both define the form (12) *pu-bam-nganku-ngkardu-ngime*, they associate it with different content. Because the SBJ.AGR rule 〚**pu**-$_C$〛$_{DU}$ first composes with 〚-**ngime**$_L$〛 in (((〚**pu**-$_C$〛$_{DU}$ ∘ 〚-**ngime**$_L$〛) ∘ 〚-**nganku**$_C$〛) (= (25g)), the paucal nonsibling female properties expressed by 〚-**ngime**$_L$〛 are, in this FER, properties associated with the subject. But because 〚-**ngime**$_L$〛 first composes with the OBJ.AGR rule 〚-**nganku**$_C$〛 in (〚**pu**-$_C$〛$_{DU}$ ∘ (〚-**ngime**$_L$〛 ∘ 〚-**nganku**$_C$〛)) (= (26c)), the paucal nonsibling female properties expressed by 〚-**ngime**$_L$〛 are, here, properties associated with the object. The ambiguity of the verb form in (12) provides compelling evidence in favor of the rule-combining approach to morphotactics, since it demonstrates that Murrinhpatha verb inflection exploits the nonassociative property of rule composition.

9.3.7   Extending the Analysis of Murrinhpatha Verbal Morphotactics

Up to this point, the morphotactic analysis proposed here for Murrinhpatha verb inflection has focused on **compound verbs**, which involve both a classifier stem and a lexical stem. But the logic of this analysis extends to the small number of classifier stems that also frequently serve on their own as **simple verbs**. Consider, as an example, the classifier SAY(34) (default stem *ma-*), whose classifier stem paradigm is given above in Table 9.3. In order to incorporate this verb into the morphotactic analysis of third-person nonfuture forms proposed above, Group I must be assumed to include the three rules in (29); the first of these is an extension of the rule 〚id.fcn$_C$〛$_{SG}$ in (16).

Table 9.18 *Composite rule pairs demonstrating the nonassociativity of rule composition in Murrinhpatha*

	Composite FER conforming to the pattern ((Group I ∘ Group II) ∘ Group III)		Composite FER conforming to the pattern (Group I ∘ (Group II ∘ Group III))
(25e)	(([pu-c]_DU ∘ [-nintha_L]) ∘ [-nganku_C])	(26a)	([pu-c]_DU ∘ ([-nintha_L] ∘ [-nganku_C]))
(25f)	(([pu-c]_DU ∘ [-nintha_L]) ∘ [-nganku_C])	(26b)	([pu-c]_DU ∘ ([-nintha_L] ∘ [-nganku_C]))
(25g)	(([pu-c]_DU ∘ [-ngime_L]) ∘ [-nganku_C])	(26c)	([pu-c]_DU ∘ ([-ngime_L] ∘ [-nganku_C]))
(25h)	(([pu-c]_DU ∘ [-neme_L]) ∘ [-nganku_C])	(26d)	([pu-c]_DU ∘ ([-neme_L] ∘ [-nganku_C]))
(25m)	(([pu-c]_DU ∘ [-nintha_L]) ∘ [-nanku_C])	(26e)	([pu-c]_DU ∘ ([-nintha_L] ∘ [-nanku_C]))
(25n)	(([pu-c]_DU ∘ [-nintha_L]) ∘ [-nanku_C])	(26f)	([pu-c]_DU ∘ ([-nintha_L] ∘ [-nanku_C]))
(25o)	(([pu-c]_DU ∘ [-ngime_L]) ∘ [-nanku_C])	(26g)	([pu-c]_DU ∘ ([-ngime_L] ∘ [-nanku_C]))
(25p)	(([pu-c]_DU ∘ [-neme_L]) ∘ [-nanku_C])	(26h)	([pu-c]_DU ∘ ([-neme_L] ∘ [-nanku_C]))

Table 9.19 *The ambiguity of the verb form in (12)*

Interpretation	Corresponding value of σ
(a) 'They (PNS female) saw us (DS excl.).'	{{sbj 3 pns female}{obj 1 ds excl} –fut clf.13}
(b) 'They (DS) saw us (PNS excl. female).'	{{sbj 3 ds}{obj 1 pns excl female} –fut clf.13}
(c) 'They (PNS male) saw us (PNS excl. female).'	{{sbj 3 pns male}{obj 1 pns excl female} –fut clf.13}
(d) 'They (PL) saw us (PNS excl. female).'	{{sbj 3 pl}{obj 1 pns excl female} –fut clf.13}
(e) 'They (PS) saw us (PNS excl.female).'	{{sbj 3 ps}{obj 1 pns excl female} –fut clf.13}

FER realizing the form cell ⟨*bamIngkardu*, σ⟩ as ⟨*pu-bam-nganku-ngkardu-ngime*, σ⟩

For interpretation (a) :	(([**pu**-C]DU ° [[-**ngime**L]] ° [[-**nganku**C]])	(= (25g))
For interpretations (b), (c) :	([**pu**-C]DU ° ([[-**ngime**L]] ° [[-**nganku**C]])	(= (26c))
For interpretations (d), (e):	([**pu**-C]PL ° ([[-**ngime**L]] ° [[-**nganku**C]]))	

9.3 Rule combining Morphotactic Analysis of Verbs 293

Table 9.20 *The morphotactics of the Murrinhpatha forms (30a,c)*

(a)	Form cell:	⟨*mam*, {{sbj 3 sg}{obj none} –fut clf.34}⟩ 's/he said'	
	|		
	FER	[[id.fnc$_C$]]$_{SG}$	(= (29a))
	↓		
	Realized cell:	⟨*mam*, {{sbj 3 sg}{obj none} –fut clf.34}⟩	
(b)	Form cell:	⟨*mam*, {{sbj 3 dns female}{obj none} –fut clf.34}⟩ 'they (DNS female) said'	
	|		
	FER	([[id.fnc$_C$]]$_{SG}$ ∘ [[**-ngintha**$_C$]])	(type ([[id.fnc$_C$]]$_{SG}$ ∘ R$_{DNS}$))
	↓		
	Realized cell:	⟨*mam-ngintha*, {{sbj 3 dns female}{obj none} –fut clf.34}⟩	

(29) Group I (SBJ.AGR rules)
     a. [[id.fnc$_C$]]$_{SG}$: [V, {{sbj 3 sg/dns} clf.13/34} : CS → CS]
     b. [[**pa**-$_C$]]$_{DU}$: [V, {{sbj 3 du/pns} clf.34} : *pa*-]
     c. [[**pa**-$_C$]]$_{PL}$: [V, {{sbj 3 ps/pl} clf.34} : *pa*-]

Just as a Group I rule may serve on its own as the FER for a compound verb form (as e.g. in Table 9.8), a Group I rule may likewise serve as the FER for a simple verb form, as in (30a,b); the morphotactic definition of (30a) in part (a) of Table 9.20 illustrates. Similarly, just as two-rule composites of the type ([[id.fnc$_C$]]$_{SG}$ ∘ R$_{DNS}$) may serve as FERs for compound verb forms (as e.g. in Table 9.11), so may they likewise serve as FERs for simple verb forms such as (30c), whose morphotactic definition is given in part (b) of Table 9.20.

(30) a. *mam*
          CS:3.SINGULAR′.SAY(34).NFUT
          's/he said'
     b. *pa-mam*
          CS:3.PLURAL′-SAY(34).NFUT
          'they (pl) said'
     c. *mam-ngintha*
          CS:3.SINGULAR′.SAY(34).NFUT-DNS.FEMALE
          'they (DNS female) said'

Compound verbs and simple verbs do, however, differ with respect to the object arguments for whose properties they inflect. The object properties for which a compound verb inflects may be those of a direct object (as in (10c)) or those of an oblique object (as in (31));[9] but because simple verbs seem not to take direct objects, they only inflect for the properties of an oblique object (as

---

[9] The glossing of example (31) is based on the number categories proposed by Nordlinger (2015); compare the 'broad paucal' of Mansfield (2019: 141).

Table 9.21 *The morphotactics of the Murrinhpatha forms (32a) and (34)*

(a)	Form cell:	⟨*mam*, {{sbj 3 sg}{obj none}{obl 1 sg} –fut clf.34}⟩ 's/he said to me'		
	|			
	FER	($[\![$id.fnc$_C]\!]_{SG}$ ∘ $[\![$**-nga**$_C]\!]$)	(type ($R_{SBJ.AGR}$ ∘ $R_{OBL.AGR}$))	
	↓			
	Realized cell:	⟨*mam-nga*, {{sbj 3 sg}{obj none}{obl 1 sg} –fut clf.34}⟩		
(b)	Form cell:	⟨*bam|ngkardu*, {{sbj 3 sg}{obj 1 sg} –fut clf.13}⟩ 's/he saw me'		
	|			
	FER	($[\![$id.fnc$_C]\!]_{SG}$ ∘ $[\![$**-ngi**$_C]\!]$)	(= (23a), type ($R_{SBJ.AGR}$ ∘ $R_{OBJ.AGR}$))	
	↓			
	Realized cell:	⟨*bam-ngi|ngkardu*, {{sbj 3 sg}{obj 1 sg} –fut clf.13}⟩		

in (32) and (33)). Even so, there is an apparent morphotactic parallelism between direct-object suffixes (OBJ.AGR suffixes such as the first-person singular suffix *-ngi* in (34), an expression of the $[\![$**-ngi**$_C]\!]$ rule in (16)) and oblique-object suffixes (OBL.AGR suffixes such as the first-person singular suffix *-nga* in (32)). I therefore assume that the rules introducing OBJ.AGR and OBL.AGR suffixes are alike in belonging to Group III. Thus, if the OBL.AGR rule $[\![$**-nga**$_C]\!]$ is as in (35), the morphotactic definitions of (32a) and (34) are parallel, as in Table 9.21; both involve FERs conforming to the pattern (Group I ∘ Group III).

(31)   *pani-wurra-thurrk-nintha-nu*
       CS:3.SINGULAR'.BE(4).FUT-3.DUAL'.OBL-LS:dive-DNS.MALE-FUT
       'he will dive in for the two of them'
                                                    (Mansfield 2019: 160)

(32)   a. *mam-nga*
           CS:3.SINGULAR'.SAY(34).NFUT-OBL:1SG
           's/he said to me'
       b. *pa-mam-nga*
           CS:3.PLURAL'-SAY(34).NFUT-OBL:1SG
           'they (pl) said to me'

(33)   a. *mam-ngarra*
           CS:3.SINGULAR'.SAY(34).NFUT-OBL:1PL
           's/he said to us (pl)'
       b. *pa-mam-ngarra*
           CS:3.PLURAL'-SAY(34).NFUT-OBL:1PL
           'they (pl) said to us (pl)'

9.3 Rule combining Morphotactic Analysis of Verbs 295

(34) *bam-ngi-ngkardu*
       CS:3.SINGULAR'.SEE(13).NFUT-OBJ.1SG-LS:see
       's/he saw me'

(35) Group III
       OBL.AGR rule   〚-nga_C〛 : [V, {{obl 1 sg}} : *-nga*]

In the inflection of compound verb forms, DNS/PNS rules applying as members of Group II operate on a verb's lexical stem in order to specify subject or direct-object number; they may likewise specify the number of a compound verb's oblique object, as in (31). These same rules also apply in the inflection of a simple verb in order to specify the number of its subject (as in (36)) or of its oblique object (as in (37)). In order to account for this fact, it is natural to assume that a simple verb's classifier stem simultaneously functions as a lexical stem, and thus as a possible operand for the Group II rules. In this way, the morphotactics of (36a) and (37a) may be defined as in Table 9.22 (in which I assume the definition of the first-person dual oblique rule 〚-ngarru_C〛 in (38)). As the analyses in Table 9.22 show, nonassociativity also plays a role in the inflection of simple verb forms. When a SBJ.AGR rule directly composes with a Group II rule, the Group II rule specifies subject number, as in part (a) of Table 9.22; here, ((〚**pa**-_C〛_DU ∘ 〚-**nginthaL**〛) ∘ 〚-**nga_C**〛) instantiates the pattern ((Group I ∘ Group II) ∘ Group III), in which (〚**pa**-_C〛_DU ∘ 〚-**nginthaL**〛) is a category-determining composite. But when a Group II rule composes directly with an OBL.AGR rule, the Group II rule specifies the number of the oblique object, as in part (b) of Table 9.22; here (〚id.fcn_C〛_SG ∘ (〚-**nginthaL**〛 ∘ 〚-**ngarru_C**〛)) instantiates the pattern (Group I ∘ (Group II ∘ Group III)), in which (〚-**nginthaL**〛 ∘ 〚-**ngarru_C**〛) is a category-determining composite.

(36) a. *pa-mam-nga-ngintha*
          CS:3.DUAL'-SAY(34).NFUT-OBL:1SG-DNS.FEMALE
          'they (DNS female) said to me'
      b. *pa-mam-ngarra-ngintha*
          CS:3.DUAL'-SAY(34).NFUT-OBL:1PL-DNS.FEMALE
          'they (DNS female) said to us (pl)'

(37) a. *mam-ngarru-ngintha*
          CS:3.SINGULAR'.SAY(34).NFUT-OBL:1DU-DNS.FEMALE
          's/he said to us (DNS female)'
      b. *pa-mam-ngarru-ngintha*
          CS:3.PLURAL'-SAY(34).NFUT-OBL:1DU-DNS.FEMALE
          'they (pl) said to us (DNS female)'

(38) 〚-**ngarru_C**〛 : [V, {{obl 1 du}} : *-ngarru*]

Table 9.22 *The morphotactics of the Murrinhpatha forms (36a) and (37a)*

(a)	Form cell:	⟨*mam*, {{sbj 3 dns female}{obj none}{obl 1 sg} –fut clf.34}⟩	'they (DNS female) said to me'
	↓ FER	(([**pa**-c]$_{DU}$ ° [**-ngintha**$_L$]) ° [**-nga**$_C$])	
	Realized cell:	⟨*pa-mam-nga-ngintha*, {{sbj 3 dns female}{obj none}{obl 1 sg} –fut clf.34}⟩	(type ((R$_{SBJ.AGR}$ ° R$_{DNS}$) ° R$_{OBL.AGR}$))
(b)	Form cell:	⟨*mam*, {{sbj 3 sg}{obj none}{obl 1 dns female} –fut clf.34}⟩	's/he said to us (DNS female)'
	↓ FER	([id.fcn$_C$]$_{SG}$ ° ([**-ngintha**$_L$] ° [**-ngarru**$_C$]))	
	Realized cell:	⟨*mam-ngarru-ngintha*, {{sbj 3 sg}{obj none}{obl 1 dns female} –fut clf.34}⟩	(type (R$_{SBJ.AGR}$ ° (R$_{DNS}$ ° R$_{OBL.AGR}$)))

9.4 Conclusion

The formal properties of rule composition entail that given three inflectional rules R_1, R_2, and R_3, the composite $((R_3 \circ R_2) \circ R_1)$ may realize different content from the composite $(R_3 \circ (R_2 \circ R_1))$, and the evidence discussed in this chapter shows that Murrinhpatha morphology exploits this possibility. In particular, the Group II rules that define DNS/PNS suffixes for a verb's lexical stem act as SBJ.NUM rules in the FER pattern ((Group I ∘ Group II) ∘ Group III) but as OBJ.NUM rules in the FER pattern (Group I ∘ (Group II ∘ Group III)). This chameleon characteristic of the Group II rules stems from the fact that they realize set-based properties that are category-indeterminate; it is this category indeterminacy that (together with the Category Determination Principle) allows these rules to act as SBJ.NUM rules when a SBJ.AGR rule composes with them but to act instead as OBJ.NUM rules when they compose with an OBJ.AGR rule. This analysis further provides a simple and economical account for widely observed patterns of ambiguity in Murrinhpatha verb morphology.

In the following chapter, I discuss another property exhibited by certain composite rules: the fact that sometimes, the domain-of-definition of the composite $(R_2 \circ R_1)$ is identical to that of R_1. This scenario is a rule-combining characterization of the phenomenon of potentiation (Williams 1981). I also discuss the opposite phenomenon, in which the combination of R_2 with R_1 has a domain-of-definition that is disjoint from that of R_1; this is the phenomenon of counterpotentiation.

10 *Potentiation and Counterpotentiation*

Many of the morphotactic phenomena that I have examined up to this point have fallen within the domain of inflection; but the rule-combining approach to morphotactics has important implications for derivational morphology as well. A familiar feature of derivational morphology is what Williams (1981) calls "potentiation" – the reliable creation of new contexts for the addition of some affix by the prior addition of some other affix; in English, *-able* potentiates *-ity*, consistently creating new contexts for its addition (*rely* → *reliable* → *reliability*). What is less familiar is the reverse phenomenon of counterpotentiation – the licensing of an affix by the subsequent addition of some other affix. In English, it is common for the suffix *-al* to follow the suffix *-ic*, as reflected by the pattern of *cycle* → *cyclic* → *cyclical, satire* → *satiric* → *satirical*, and so on. Yet, *-ic* doesn't potentiate *-al*, as the absence of adjectives such as *scenical and *basical shows. Moreover, *-al* sometimes counterpotentiates *-ic*, allowing it to attach to certain stems provided that *-al* attaches to the result (*nonsense, type, whimsy* → *nonsensic, *typic, *whimsic → *nonsensical, typical, whimsical*). As this kind of evidence shows, facilitatory relations among derivational rules are sometimes "outward" and sometimes "inward." In instances of potentiation, the application of an inner rule facilitates that of an outer rule, while in instances of counterpotentiation, the application of an outer rule facilitates that of an inner rule. In this chapter, I show that facilitatory relations of these two sorts can be straightforwardly modeled as involving distinct modes of rule combination. In Section 10.1, I draw on evidence from English to show that the potentiation of one rule by another can be seen as a particular kind of rule composition; in Section 10.2, I use English evidence to show that counterpotentiation involves a kind of rule combination distinct from composition. Potentiation enhances canonical conformity to the intermediate well-formedness criterion (Section 1.5.7); counterpotentiation, by contrast, is a kind of deviation from conformity to this criterion. In

Section 10.3, I argue that true instances of parasynthesis are instances of counterpotentiation.

10.1 Rule Composition and Potentiation

In a language's derivational morphology, it is common for the lexemes derived by means of a given rule to be alike in their capacity to serve as bases for the subsequent application of some other particular rule. For instance, deverbal adjectives derived by means of the English [[-**able**]] rule tend, as a class, to be available as bases for the subsequent application of the nominalizing [[-**ity**]] rule; thus, each of the *-able* derivatives in (1) has a corresponding *-ity* derivative. Williams (1981: 249f.) refers to the relation between the inner rule and the outer rule as one of ***potentiation***.

(1) Some derived adjectives in *-able* and their *-ity* nominalizations

Verb stem	Adjective stem	Noun stem
accept	*acceptable*	*acceptability*
believe	*believable*	*believability*
derive	*derivable*	*derivability*
rely	*reliable*	*reliability*
reuse	*reusable*	*reusability*
vary	*variable*	*variability*

What is interesting about potentiation is that it may identify pockets of high productivity in the domain of a rule whose application is, on the whole, not especially productive. For example, the [[-**ity**]] rule is not especially productive on its own; in my speech, for example, the *-ity* derivatives in (2) all exist but those in (3) do not. In some cases, the lack of an *-ity* derivative can be attributed to blocking; for instance, the absence of *calmity, *candidity, and *skepticality might be attributed to the existence of *calm* (noun), *candor*, and *skepticism*. But blocking cannot account for the absence of all of the candidate *-ity* derivatives in (3). To be sure, most of the adjectives in (3) have nominalizations in *-ness*, but nominalizations in *-ness* don't necessarily exclude the possibility of parallel nominalizations in *-ity*, since most of the adjectives in (2) also have nominalizations in *-ness* (e.g. *curiousness, obscureness, scarceness*). Moreover, there is no obvious semantic explanation for the lack of *-ity* derivatives in (3), given the semantic proximity of the target meanings of *compactity, *exemptity, and *rudity (for example) to the meanings of *density, immunity*, and *vulgarity*. One might argue that *weirdity is excluded by a requirement that *-ity* attach to bases of Romance origin, but the incidence of *oddity* casts doubt on the existence of such a requirement.

(2) Adjective stems with -*ity* nominalizations

civil	civility
curious	curiosity
dense	density
immune	immunity
obscure	obscurity
original	originality
scarce	scarcity
serene	serenity
tranquil	tranquility
vulgar	vulgarity

(3) Adjective stems lacking -*ity* nominalizations

calm	(*calmity)
candid	(*candidity)
compact	(*compactity)
exempt	(*exemptity)
fierce	(*fiercity)
gracious	(*graciosity)
quiet	(*quietity)
rude	(*rudity)
skeptical	(*skepticality)
weird	(*weirdity)

Aronoff (1976: 62f.) argues that the potentiation of rule R_2 by rule R_1 is accounted for in the formulation of R_2 by a positive condition on the morphology of the bases on which R_2 operates. For example, he proposes (4) as a formulation of the negative 〚**un-**〛 rule, in which the list (4b) identifies bases whose morphology specifically potentiates the 〚**un-**〛 rule.

(4) Rule of negative *un#* (Aronoff 1976: 63)
    a. $[X]_{Adj} \rightarrow [un\#[X]_{Adj}]_{Adj}$
       semantics (roughly) un#X = not X
    b. Forms of the base
       1. $X_V$en (where *en* is the marker for past participle)
       2. X_V#ing
       3. X_V#able
       4. X+y   (worthy)
       5. X+ly   (seemly)
       6. X#ful   (mindful)
       7. X-al   (conditional)
       8. X#like   (warlike)

Positive conditions such as those in (4b) can be formulated as properties of rule combinations. For example, the fact that the 〚**-able**〛 rule potentiates the 〚**-ity**〛 rule can be accounted for by the stipulation that the composed rule (〚**-ity**〛 ∘ 〚**-able**〛) has the same domain-of-definition as the 〚**-able**〛 rule. By definition, the domain-of-definition of (〚**-ity**〛 ∘ 〚**-able**〛) is a subset of that of the 〚**-able**〛 rule; the stipulation that (〚**-ity**〛 ∘ 〚**-able**〛) has the same domain-of-definition as the 〚**-able**〛 rule therefore amounts to the stipulation that 〚**-ity**〛 applies to every ⟨lexeme, stem, lexicosemantic category⟩ triplet defined by 〚**-able**〛. This stipulation accounts for the fact that the 〚**-ity**〛 rule is uniformly productive in (1) notwithstanding the patchiness of its productivity in (2)–(3). We might represent a composed rule ($R_2 \circ R_1$) that is defined for every member

10.1 Rule Composition and Potentiation

of the domain-of-definition of R_1 as $(R_2 ⓟ R_1)$, where the ***potentiation operator*** ⓟ is defined as in (5) and the rule combination $(R_2 ⓟ R_1)$ is itself simply called a potentiation.[1]

(5) Given two rules R_1 and R_2, $(R_2 ⓟ R_1)$ represents $(R_2 \circ R_1)$ if and only if for every member x of the domain-of-definition of R_1, the result of applying R_1 to x is a member of the domain-of-definition of R_2. $(R_2 ⓟ R_1)$ is otherwise undefined.

    Examples: $(⟦\text{-ity}⟧ ⓟ ⟦\text{-able}⟧) = (⟦\text{-ity}⟧ \circ ⟦\text{-able}⟧)$, since the domain-of-definition of $(⟦\text{-ity}⟧ \circ ⟦\text{-able}⟧)$ is that of ⟦**-able**⟧; $(⟦\text{-al}⟧ ⓟ ⟦\text{-ic}⟧)$ is undefined, given *basical, *ionical, etc.

This use of rule combination to model the phenomenon of potentiation is reminiscent of the use of subrules for a similar purpose by Bochner (1993). Bochner formulates the ⟦**-ity**⟧ rule as in (6a). The rule in (6b) is a subrule of (6a). On first consideration, a grammar incorporating both of these rules might seem redundant, since the pattern in (6a) apparently entails the pattern in (6b). But as Bochner observes, (6a), on its own, implies that the word pairs *sane/sanity* and *acceptable/acceptability* should be equally "costly" to learn; but given that (6b) is much more productive than (6a), the coexistence of (6a) and (6b) predicts that word pairs like *acceptable/acceptability* should be much less costly to learn than word pairs like *sane/sanity*. This same reasoning holds true of the potentiation $(⟦\text{-ity}⟧ ⓟ ⟦\text{-able}⟧)$. Where the simple rules ⟦**-able**⟧ and ⟦**-ity**⟧ are defined as in (7) and (8), the potentiation $(⟦\text{-ity}⟧ ⓟ ⟦\text{-able}⟧)$ has the definition in (9), where the domain-of-definition $μ_7$ of $(⟦\text{-ity}⟧ ⓟ ⟦\text{-able}⟧)$ is identical to that of ⟦**-able**⟧. Thus, even if $μ_8$ is a very restricted subset of the set of ⟨lexeme, stem, lexicosemantic category⟩ triplets of the type ⟨L, Z, Adj⟩ (so that overall, ⟦**-ity**⟧ is comparatively unproductive), (9) nevertheless entails that $μ_8$ subsumes the full set ξ of triplets of the type ⟨L, X*able*, Adj⟩ derived by ⟦**-able**⟧ (so that notwithstanding its limited productivity overall, ⟦**-ity**⟧ applies with full productivity to members of ξ).

(6) a. $\begin{bmatrix} /X/ \\ A \\ Z \end{bmatrix} \leftrightarrow \begin{bmatrix} /Xity/ \\ N \\ \text{STATE of being Z} \end{bmatrix}$

    b. $\begin{bmatrix} /Xable/ \\ A \\ \text{ABLE to be Zed} \end{bmatrix} \leftrightarrow \begin{bmatrix} /Xability/ \\ N \\ \text{STATE of being ABLE to be Zed} \end{bmatrix}$

(Bochner 1993: 88)

---

[1] The potentiation operator might be thought of as reifying the phenomenon of "embedded productivity" discussed by Booij (2010: 47–50).

(7)   [[-able]] : [μ₇ ⇒ Adj : -able]

Representative members of μ₇: ⟨L, *believe*, Verb⟩, ⟨L, *rely*, Verb⟩

(8)   [[-ity]] : [μ₈ ⇒ Noun : -ity]

Representative members of μ₈: ⟨L, *serene*, Adj⟩, ⟨L, *believable*, Adj⟩, ⟨L, *reliable*, Adj⟩

(9)   ([[-ity]] ⓟ [[-able]]) : [μ₇ ⇒ Noun : -ability] (where μ₇ is as in (7))

The rule-combining formalism of (7)–(9) makes it possible to model the potentiation of [[-ity]] by [[-able]] with full explicitness by overtly identifying the domain-of-definition μ₇ of the potentiation ([[-ity]] ⓟ [[-able]]) with that of its potentiating member [[-able]].

10.2 Counterpotentiation

A canonical characteristic of derivational morphotactics is conformity to the intermediate well-formedness criterion, which entails that for any triplet ⟨L, Z, C⟩ (where L is the base lexeme with stem Z belonging to category C), if the application of a derivational rule to ⟨L, Z, C⟩ is well-formed, then ⟨L, Z, C⟩ is itself well-formed. Conformity to this canonical characteristic is widely observable; some examples are given in Table 10.1.

Ordinarily, ill-formedness is expected to be a persistent characteristic of linguistic expressions: if an expression Z is ill-formed, the operation of a rule on Z isn't expected to be able to convert it into a well-formed expression. Yet, there are instances in which this expectation seems not to be confirmed; some apparent

Table 10.1 *Examples of conformity to the intermediate well-formedness criterion*

Derivational rule	Well-formed triplet to which the rule applies		Well-formed triplet resulting from the rule's application
[[-ion]] :	⟨L, *create*, Verb⟩	→	⟨L, *creation*, Noun⟩
[[-ity]] :	⟨L, *active*, Adj⟩	→	⟨L, *activity*, Noun⟩
[[-ize]] :	⟨L, *formal*, Adj⟩	→	⟨L, *formalize*, Verb⟩
[[-ness]] :	⟨L, *gracious*, Adj⟩	→	⟨L, *graciousness*, Noun⟩
[[-ous]] :	⟨L, *injury*, Noun⟩	→	⟨L, *injurious*, Adj⟩

Table 10.2 *Apparent examples of "nonpersistent ill-formedness" in English derivation*

Derivational rule	Triplet involving an ill-formed stem to which the rule apparently applies		Well-formed triplet resulting from the rule's application
⟦-al⟧ :	⟨L, *whimsic, Adj⟩	→	⟨L, whimsical, Adj⟩
	(cf. ⟨L, cyclic, Adj⟩		⟨L, cyclical, Adj⟩)
⟦-ian⟧ :	⟨L, *beautic, Adj⟩	→	⟨L, beautician, Noun⟩
	(cf. ⟨L, academic, Adj⟩		⟨L, academician, Noun⟩)
⟦-ic⟧ :	⟨L, *cannibalist, Noun⟩	→	⟨L, cannibalistic, Adj⟩
	(cf. ⟨L, capitalist, Noun⟩		⟨L, capitalistic, Adj⟩)
⟦-ion⟧ :	⟨L, *explanate, Verb⟩	→	⟨L, explanation, Noun⟩
	(cf. ⟨L, hyphenate, Verb⟩		⟨L, hyphenation, Noun⟩)
⟦-ory⟧ :	⟨L, *exposit, Verb⟩	→	⟨L, expository, Adj⟩
	(cf. ⟨L, mandate, Verb⟩		⟨L, mandatory, Adj⟩)

examples of such "nonpersistent ill-formedness" are given in Table 10.2. What is to be made of these in a formal account of English derivation?

Well-formed derivatives such as those in Table 10.2 involve counterpotentiation (Section 2.5), a special mode of rule combination whose properties I now examine in detail. Counterpotentiation and potentiation are both types of rule combination in which the application of one rule facilitates that of another rule. Potentiation, in particular, involves outward facilitation: the domain-of-definition of the potentiation ($R_2 \circledP R_1$) is the same as that of R_1, so that if R_1 can apply to a given ⟨lexeme, stem, lexicosemantic category⟩ triplet, then ($R_2 \circledP R_1$) can apply to that triplet as well; the application of R_1 potentiates that of R_2. Counterpotentiation, by contrast, involves inward facilitation, such that the applicability of derivational rule R_1 to a particular ⟨lexeme, stem, lexicosemantic category⟩ triplet is seemingly licensed only by the subsequent application of another derivational rule R_2. The examples in Table 10.3 illustrate. Whereas CYCLICAL and HISTORICAL arise from CYCLE and HISTORY via CYCLIC and HISTORIC through the successive application of the derivational rules ⟦-ic⟧ and ⟦-al⟧, WHIMSICAL and NONSENSICAL seem to arise directly from WHIMSY and NONSENSE without any mediating lexemes having stems in -*ic* (*WHIMSIC, *NONSENSIC), apparently through the combined application of ⟦-ic⟧ and ⟦-al⟧. It's not that ⟦-ic⟧ potentiates ⟦-al⟧; it doesn't, as cases such as BASE → BASIC → *BASICAL show. Instead, it is as though the application of ⟦-ic⟧ to ⟨L, whimsy, Noun⟩ is only defined if ⟦-al⟧ applies subsequently. In such

304 *Potentiation and Counterpotentiation*

Table 10.3 *Counterpotentiation of* [[-ic]] *by* [[-al]]

Base lexeme's stem	Stem arising through the application of [[-ic]]	Stem arising through the subsequent application of [[-al]]
cycle	cyclic	cyclical
history	historic	historical
whimsy	*whimsic	whimsical
nonsense	*nonsensic	nonsensical

instances, R_2 combines with R_1 by means of the ***counterpotentiation operator*** [CP]$_n$, whose interpretation (repeated from Section 2.5) is as in (10).

(10)   Counterpotentiation
    a. Let R_1 be the derivational rule [$\mu_1 \Rightarrow D : X \rightarrow f_1(X)$], whose domain-of-definition μ_1 is a subset of some set $\mathbb{C}$ of ⟨lexeme, stem, lexicosemantic category⟩ triplets, so that R_1 is a partial function from $\mathbb{C}$ to the set $\mathbb{D}$ of triplets of the type ⟨lexeme, stem, D⟩.
    b. Let R_2 be a derivational rule [$\mu_2 \Rightarrow E : X \rightarrow f_2(X)$] that defines members of the set $\mathbb{E}$ of triplets of type ⟨lexeme, stem, E⟩.
    c. In that case, the counterpotentiation

$$(R_2 \; \boxed{CP}_n \; R_1) : [\mu_n \Rightarrow E : X \rightarrow f_2(f_1(X))]$$

is a partial function from $\mathbb{C}$ to $\mathbb{E}$ whose domain-of-definition μ_n is disjoint from the domain-of-definition μ_1 of R_1.

If the derivational rules [[-ic]] and [[-al]] are defined as in (11) and (12), the counterpotentiation ([[-al]] [CP]$_{13}$ [[-ic]]) has the definition in (13) – a partial function from triplets of the type ⟨L, Z, Noun⟩ (in which lexeme L has stem Z and belongs to category Noun) to triplets of the type ⟨L, Zical, Relational Adj⟩.

(11)   [[-ic]] : [$\mu_{11} \Rightarrow$ Relational Adj : *-ic*]

    Representative members of μ_{11}: ⟨L, *scene*, Noun⟩, ⟨L, *cycle*, Noun⟩

(12)   [[-al]] : [$\mu_{12} \Rightarrow$ Relational Adj : *-al*]

    Representative members of μ_{12}:
       ⟨L, *tribe*, Noun⟩, ⟨L, *transcendent*, Adj⟩, ⟨L, *cyclic*, Relational Adj⟩

(13)   ([[-al]] [CP]$_{13}$ [[-ic]]) : [$\mu_{13} \Rightarrow$ Relational Adj : *-ic-al*], where μ_{13} is disjoint from μ_{11}.

    Representative members of μ_{13}: ⟨L, *whimsy*, Noun⟩, ⟨L, *nonsense*, Noun⟩
                                           (cf. **whimsic, *nonsensic*)

Although ⟦-ic⟧ and (⟦-al⟧ $\boxed{\text{CP}}_{13}$ ⟦-ic⟧) are both partial functions from the set of ⟨lexeme, stem, Noun⟩ triplets to the set of ⟨lexeme, stem, Relational Adj⟩ triplets, the definition in (13) entails that ⟦-ic⟧ and (⟦-al⟧ $\boxed{\text{CP}}_{13}$ ⟦-ic⟧) have disjoint domains-of-definition. For this reason, the counterpotentiation (⟦-al⟧ $\boxed{\text{CP}}_{13}$ ⟦-ic⟧) cannot be equated with the composite (⟦-al⟧ ∘ ⟦-ic⟧): the domain-of-definition of (⟦-al⟧ ∘ ⟦-ic⟧) is a subset of that of ⟦-ic⟧ (= μ_{11}), but the domain-of-definition μ_{13} of (⟦-al⟧ $\boxed{\text{CP}}_{13}$ ⟦-ic⟧) is, again, disjoint from that of ⟦-ic⟧. The domain-of-definition of (⟦-al⟧ $\boxed{\text{CP}}_{13}$ ⟦-ic⟧) includes the triplets ⟨L, *whimsy*, Noun⟩ and ⟨L, *nonsense*, Noun⟩, neither of which is in the domain-of-definition of ⟦-ic⟧, nor, therefore, in that of (⟦-al⟧ ∘ ⟦-ic⟧).

Potentiation and counterpotentiation both relate the domain-of-definition of rule R_1 to that of the combination of some other rule R_2 with R_1. The potentiation (R_2 ⓟ R_1) is that combination of R_2 with R_1 whose domain-of-definition is the same as that of R_1; the counterpotentiation (R_2 $\boxed{\text{CP}}_n$ R_1) is a combination of R_2 with R_1 whose domain-of-definition μ_n is disjoint from that of R_1.

As was observed in Section 2.5, counterpotentiations are of at least two types. First, pleonastic counterpotentiations are cases in which R_1, R_2, and (R_2 $\boxed{\text{CP}}_n$ R_1) have the same range and domain but have disjoint domains-of-definition. For example, ⟦-en⟧, ⟦en-⟧, and (⟦en-⟧ $\boxed{\text{CP}}_{62}$ ⟦-en⟧) all derive causative verbs from adjectives and nouns, but not the same adjectives and nouns: ⟦-en⟧ derives SWEETEN and STRENGTHEN, ⟦en-⟧ derives ENABLE and ENCOURAGE, and (⟦en-⟧ $\boxed{\text{CP}}_{62}$ ⟦-en⟧) derives EMBOLDEN and ENLIGHTEN.

Second, there are counterpotentiations that are compositionally motivated. These are cases in which the two rules R_1 and R_2 that enter into a composite (R_2 ∘ R_1) also enter into a counterpotentiation (R_2 $\boxed{\text{CP}}_n$ R_1) with a disjoint domain-of-definition. A compositionally motivated counterpotentiation (R_2 $\boxed{\text{CP}}_n$ R_1) may itself be of either of two types: on one hand, its domain-of-definition μ_n may differ from that of the composite (R_2 ∘ R_1) in lexically arbitrary ways, as in the morphotactics of derivatives in *-ical*, *-istic*, and *-ician* (Section 10.2.1); on the other hand, there may be a systematic grammatical difference between its domain-of-definition μ_n and that of the composite (R_2 ∘ R_1), as in the morphotactics of derivatives in *-ation* and *-ative* (Section 10.2.2).

10.2.1 Compositionally Motivated Counterpotentiations and Composites Whose Domains-of-definition Differ in a Lexically Arbitrary Way

Consider the difference between the counterpotentiation (⟦-al⟧ $\boxed{\text{CP}}_{13}$ ⟦-ic⟧) and the composite (⟦-al⟧ ∘ ⟦-ic⟧). The counterpotentiation (⟦-al⟧ $\boxed{\text{CP}}_{13}$ ⟦-ic⟧) accounts for the relation between ⟦-ic⟧ and ⟦-al⟧ in cases such as WHIMSICAL and NONSENSICAL – specifically, it accounts for the absence of the expected intermediate derivatives *WHIMSIC and *NONSENSIC. By contrast, the composite rule ([[-al]] ∘ [[-ic]]) accounts for the coexistence of HISTORICAL and CYCLICAL with the intermediate derivatives HISTORIC and CYCLIC. The domain-of-definition of ([[-al]] $\boxed{CP}_{13}$ [[-ic]]) and that of ([[-al]] ∘ [[-ic]]) are disjoint sets of triplets of the same type ⟨L, Z, Noun⟩; thus, it is a lexically arbitrary fact that ⟨L, *cycle*, Noun⟩ belongs to the domain-of-definition of ([[-al]] ∘ [[-ic]]) but that ⟨L, *whimsy*, Noun⟩ instead belongs to the domain-of-definition of ([[-al]] $\boxed{CP}_{13}$ [[-ic]]).

One might question the notion that HISTORIC is an intermediate derivative of HISTORICAL on the grounds that it seems wrongly to imply that the meaning of HISTORICAL ('pertaining to history') derives from that of HISTORIC ('whose incidence in history is of high importance'), but this is not a reasonable objection. As noted in Section 2.1.2, the meaning of a derived lexeme needn't be fully determined by the rule(s) defining its derivation, but may depend on a conventional pragmatic specialization agreed upon by language users. The adjectives HISTORIC and HISTORICAL have come to be reserved for expressing divergent meanings, but this doesn't alter the fact that the [[-al]] rule in (12) deduces the characteristics of HISTORICAL in (14) from those of HISTORIC in (15). By relating HISTORICAL to HISTORIC, the [[-al]] rule simplifies the lexical representation of HISTORICAL; it does not, however, account for the fine semantic difference between HISTORIC and HISTORICAL, which must be lexically specified.

(14) Some characteristics of the lexeme HISTORICAL
 a. Stem: *historical*
 b. Lexicosemantic category: Relational adjective (related to HISTORY)

(15) Some characteristics of the lexeme HISTORIC
 a. Stem: *historic*
 b. Lexicosemantic category: Relational adjective (related to HISTORY)

A similar case of counterpotentiation in coexistence with composition involves adjectives in *-istic*, such as those in Table 10.4. The suffixation of *-istic* is analyzable as the effect of two successive rules in derivations such as CAPITAL → CAPITALIST → CAPITALISTIC and NATIONAL → NATIONALIST → NATIONALISTIC; but adjectives in *-istic* also sometimes exhibit the "nonpersistent ill-formedness" exemplified by CANNIBALISTIC, CHARACTERISTIC, PROBABILISTIC, and SIMPLISTIC, which seem to imply the intermediate lexemes *CANNIBALIST, *CHARACTERIST, *PROBABILIST, and *SIMPLIST, none of which is in general use.

Table 10.4 *Counterpotentiation of* 〚-**ist**〛 *by* 〚-**ic**〛

Base lexeme's stem	Stem arising through the application of 〚-**ist**〛	Stem arising through the subsequent application of 〚-**ic**〛
capital	*capitalist*	*capitalistic*
national	*nationalist*	*nationalistic*
cannibal	**cannibalist*	*cannibalistic*
character	**characterist*	*characteristic*
probable	**probabilist*	*probabilistic*
simple	**simplist*	*simplistic*

Cases of this sort are complicated by the versatility of the 〚-**ist**〛 rule. In its most general formulation in (16), this rule operates on a nominal or adjectival stem to yield a nominal or adjectival stem. For example, the application of 〚-**ist**〛 derives the personal noun ARTIST from the noun ART; but it also derives CAPITALIST and NATIONALIST – each of which can function as either a personal noun (*He's a capitalist and a nationalist*) or an adjective (*a capitalist economy, nationalist fervor*) – from the noun CAPITAL and the adjective NATIONAL, respectively. Partly as a consequence of this versatility, the result of applying 〚-**ic**〛 to a base in *-ist* may approximate the meaning of that base or may differ from it. An adjective in *-ist* and its counterpart in *-istic* are typically quite close in their use: *capitalist economy ~ capitalistic economy*. By contrast, the meaning of the noun JOURNALIST is not obviously a necessary component of the meaning of JOURNALISTIC; on the contrary, the semantic relation between JOURNAL and JOURNALISTIC is similar to the relation between SCULPTURE and SCULPTURAL, in which the meaning of SCULPTOR has at most an indirect role. More to the point, the adjective JOURNALISTIC fulfills the same lexical relation to the disciplinary noun JOURNALISM as the adjective LITERARY does to the disciplinary noun LITERATURE: in both cases, the adjective's meaning is not simply realized by the sum of its morphological parts, but depends crucially on its lexical status as the adjectival counterpart of a corresponding disciplinary noun. While the stem of JOURNALISTIC, its category membership, and its relatedness to the lexeme JOURNAL are all deducible from its base JOURNALIST through the mediation of the 〚-**ic**〛 rule, its meaning is governed by its participation in a particular lexical relation.

(16)   〚-**ist**〛 : [$\mu_{16} \Rightarrow$ Noun/Adj : *-ist*]

Representative members of μ_{16}: ⟨L, *art*, Noun⟩, ⟨L, *national*, Adj⟩

If the derivational rule ⟦-ist⟧ is defined as in (16) and the derivational rule ⟦-ic⟧ is defined as in (11), the composite (⟦-ic⟧ ∘⟦-ist⟧) accounts for the coexistence of ARTIST and ARTISTIC, NATIONALIST and NATIONALISTIC, and COMMUNIST and COMMUNISTIC; at the same time, the counterpotentiation (⟦-ic⟧ $\boxed{\text{CP}}_{17}$ ⟦-ist⟧) in (17) accounts for the existence of CANNIBALISTIC and PROBABILISTIC in the absence of *CANNIBALIST and *PROBABILIST. The domain-of-definition of (⟦-ic⟧ $\boxed{\text{CP}}_{17}$ ⟦-ist⟧) and that of (⟦-ic⟧ ∘ ⟦-ist⟧) are disjoint sets of triplets of the types ⟨L, Z, Noun⟩ and ⟨L, Z, Adj⟩; here again, it is a lexically arbitrary fact that ⟨L, *capital*, Noun⟩ and ⟨L, *national*, Adj⟩ belong to the domain-of-definition of (⟦-ic⟧ ∘ ⟦-ist⟧) but that ⟨L, *cannibal*, Noun⟩ and ⟨L, *probable*, Adj⟩ instead belong to the domain-of-definition of (⟦-ic⟧ $\boxed{\text{CP}}_{17}$ ⟦-ist⟧).

(17)   (⟦-ic⟧ $\boxed{\text{CP}}_{17}$ ⟦-ist⟧) : [μ_{17} ⇒ Adj : -*ist-ic*], where μ_{17} is disjoint from μ_{16}.

Representative members of μ_{17}: ⟨L, *cannibal*, Noun⟩, ⟨L, *probable*, Adj⟩
(cf. *cannibalist, *probabilist)

A striking instance in which the domain-of-definition of a counterpotentiation differs in a lexically arbitrary way from that of the corresponding composite rule involves derivatives in -*ician*. At issue here are the three simple rules in (18)–(20).

(18)   ⟦-ic⟧$_N$: [μ_{18} ⇒ Noun : -*ic*]

Representative members of μ_{18}: ⟨L, *log*-, Noun⟩, ⟨L, *rhetor*-, Noun⟩
The function of ⟦-ic⟧$_N$ is thematizing rather than derivational.

(19)   ⟦-s⟧$_N$: [μ_{19} ⇒ Noun : -*s*]

Representative members of μ_{19}: ⟨L, *politic*-, Noun⟩, ⟨L, *phonetic*-, Noun⟩
The function of the composite rule (⟦-s⟧$_N$ ∘ ⟦-ic⟧$_N$) is thematizing rather than derivational.

(20)   ⟦-ian⟧ : [μ_{20} ⇒ Noun/Adj : -*ian*]

The ⟦-ian⟧ rule has a derivational function for some members of μ_{20} (e.g. ⟨L, *Paris*, Noun⟩, ⟨L, *reptile*, Noun⟩) but a thematizing function for others (e.g. ⟨L, *amphib*-, Noun⟩, ⟨L, *pedestr*-, Noun⟩).

The ⟦-ic⟧$_N$ rule in (18) must be distinguished from the adjective-forming ⟦-ic⟧ rule in (11), since it defines the stems of nouns denoting spheres of specialized human endeavor, such as those in (21a). The ⟦-ic⟧$_N$ rule is essentially thematizing in function (Section 2.1.2): it defines the form of a lexeme's stem from a substem of that lexeme, applying (for example) to the triplet ⟨LOGIC, *log*-, Noun⟩ to yield the triplet ⟨LOGIC, *logic*, Noun⟩; here and in

Table 10.5 *Some derivative stems in* -ian

amphibian	grammarian	Parisian
Bohemian	historian	pedestrian
centenarian	libertarian	reptilian
civilian	librarian	totalitarian
comedian	mammalian	tragedian
Egyptian	Martian	vegetarian

general, it serves unproductively to define the stems of nouns of Latin or Greek origin. In some instances, the stem of a noun denoting a sphere of endeavor is defined by the composite rule ($[\![$-s$]\!]_N \circ [\![$-ic$]\!]_N$), where $[\![$-s$]\!]_N$ is the thematizing rule in (19); for example, ($[\![$-s$]\!]_N \circ [\![$-ic$]\!]_N$) applies to ⟨POLITICS, *polit-*, Noun⟩ to yield ⟨POLITICS, *politics*, Noun⟩, and similarly for the other nouns in (21b).

(21) Nouns naming spheres of specialized human endeavor
 a. Having stems in -*ic*: LOGIC, MAGIC, MUSIC, PHYSIC 'medicine' (archaic), RHETORIC
 b. Having a stem in -*ic* extended by -*s*: ACADEMICS, BIOMETRICS, ESTHETICS, MECHANICS, OBSTETRICS, OPTICS, PEDIATRICS, PHONETICS, POLITICS, SEMIOTICS, STATISTICS

The $[\![$-ian$]\!]$ rule in (20) is quite versatile, serving to derive a large number of denominal forms that may be employed either as adjectives or as animate nouns; it also serves a thematizing function for many adjectives and animate nouns. The examples in Table 10.5 reveal some of the versatility of $[\![$-ian$]\!]$: derivatives in -*ian* include adjectives and demonyms derived from place names (EGYPTIAN); adjectives and personal nouns referring to ages (CENTENARIAN); adjectives and personal nouns relating to ideologies (LIBERTARIAN); adjectives and nouns relating to natural classifications (REPTILIAN).

An important peculiarity of the $[\![$-ian$]\!]$ rule is that when the base on which it operates denotes a sphere of specialized human endeavor, the derivative in -*ian* tends to be a noun referring to a person engaged in that sphere; for example, *collegian, comedian, custodian, grammarian, historian, librarian, theologian, tragedian,* and *veterinarian* are used as personal nouns, not as adjectives. (Contrast *They're obviously reptilian* with **They're obviously grammarian.*) An effect of this fact is that derivatives defined by the composite (22) are nouns referring to human specialists (Marchand 1966: 236f.; Dixon 2014: 316); the examples in Table 10.6 illustrate. None of the derivatives in Table 10.6 functions as an adjective; contrast *The species was definitely reptilian* and **The transcription was definitely phonetician.*

310 *Potentiation and Counterpotentiation*

Table 10.6 *Some derivative stems defined by the composite* ($[\![\text{-ian}]\!] \circ [\![\text{-ic}]\!]_N$)

academician	*musician*	*physician*
clinician	*obstetrician*	*politician*
esthetician	*optician*	*rhetorician*
logician	*pediatrician*	*statistician*
magician	*phonetician*	*tactician*

Table 10.7 *Instances of the counterpotentiation (23)*

Members of the domain-of-definition μ_{23} of (23)	Result of applying (23)
⟨L, *beauty*, Noun⟩	⟨L, *beautician*, Noun[specialist]⟩
⟨L, *cosmet-*, Noun⟩	⟨L, *cosmetician*, Noun[specialist]⟩
⟨L, *dialect*, Noun⟩	⟨L, *dialectician*, Noun[specialist]⟩
⟨L, *diet*, Noun⟩	⟨L, *dietitian*, Noun[specialist]⟩
⟨L, *electr-*, Noun⟩	⟨L, *electrician*, Noun[specialist]⟩
⟨L, *mort-*, Noun⟩	⟨L, *mortician*, Noun[specialist]⟩

(22)   ($[\![\text{-ian}]\!] \circ [\![\text{-ic}]\!]_N$) : [$\mu_{22} \rightarrow$ Noun[specialist] : *-ic-ian*] where the domain-of-definition μ_{22} is a subset of μ_{18}.

        Representative members of μ_{22}: ⟨L, *log-*, Noun⟩, ⟨L, *rhetor-*, Noun⟩

Alongside the composite ($[\![\text{-ian}]\!] \circ [\![\text{-ic}]\!]_N$) is the counterpotentiation (23), which derives the specialist nouns in Table 10.7 from nouns whose triplets are, as a lexically arbitrary fact, absent from the domain-of-definition μ_{22} of composite (22). Every member of the domain-of-definition μ_{22} of composite (22) is also a member of the domain-of-definition μ_{18} of the $[\![\text{-ic}]\!]_N$ rule in (18); but the $[\![\text{-ic}]\!]_N$ rule doesn't apply to any of the triplets in Table 10.7, hence the nonexistence of the lexemes *BEAUTIC(S), *COSMETIC(S), *DIALECTIC(S), *DIETIC(S), *ELECTRIC(S), and *MORTIC(S) as names for spheres of specialized human endeavor. Cosmetics are, of course, a kind of stuff, but *cosmetics* is not a synonym for *cosmetology*; yet, a specialist in cosmetology is sometimes called a *cosmetician*. And while dialectics is a discipline in philosophy, *dialectics* is not a synonym for *dialectology*; yet, *dialectician* is used to refer not only to specialists in philosophical dialectics but also to dialectologists. *Dietetics* (not **dietics*) refers to the study of diet and nutrition, but a specialist in this area is called a *dietitian* (sic) rather than a **dietetician*. (The spelling of *dietetics* may have some role in explaining the spelling of *dietitian*, though *dietician* is also an accepted spelling.) **Electric(s)* is not[2] a noun meaning 'the study or science of electricity', but the fact that *electric* exists as an adjective might be taken as evidence that ⟦**-ian**⟧ may apply to adjectives in *-ic* (which involve the adjective-deriving ⟦**-ic**⟧ rule in (11)) as well as to nouns in *-ic* (which involve the noun-deriving ⟦**-ic**⟧$_N$ rule in (18)).

(23)   (⟦**-ian**⟧ $\boxed{CP}_{23}$ ⟦**-ic**⟧$_N$) : [$\mu_{23} \rightarrow$ Noun[specialist] : *-ic-ian*], where the domain-of-definition μ_{23} is disjoint from the domain-of-definition μ_{18} of ⟦**-ic**⟧$_N$.
Representative members of μ_{23}: ⟨L, *beauty*, Noun⟩, ⟨L, *mort-*, Noun⟩

10.2.2   Compositionally Motivated Counterpotentiations and Composites Whose Domains-of-definition Differ Systematically

The counterpotentiations (24a–c) discussed above have domains-of-definition that differ in lexically arbitrary ways from those of the corresponding composites in (25). There are, however, cases in which the domains-of-definition of ($R_2 \circ R_1$) and (R_2 $\boxed{CP}_n$ R_1) differ in a systematic way. An example from English is the pair of derivational rule combinations which both have the effect of suffixing *-ation*. One of these rule combinations is the potentiation (⟦**-ion**⟧ ⓟ ⟦**-ate**⟧); the other is the counterpotentiation (⟦**-ion**⟧ $\boxed{CP}_{30}$ ⟦**-ate**⟧). In both of these combinations, ⟦**-ion**⟧ is the rule producing deverbal nominalizations in *-ion* (e.g. COMPRESSION, FUSION, SELECTION; this rule is formulated in (26)). Accordingly, the combinations (⟦**-ion**⟧ ⓟ ⟦**-ate**⟧) and (⟦**-ion**⟧ $\boxed{CP}_{30}$ ⟦**-ate**⟧) both define nominalizations in *-ation*. They differ, however, in that they involve systematically different domains-of-definition.

(24)   a.   (⟦**-al**⟧ $\boxed{CP}_{13}$ ⟦**-ic**⟧)   (25)   a.   (⟦**-al**⟧ ∘ ⟦**-ic**⟧)
       b.   (⟦**-ic**⟧ $\boxed{CP}_{17}$ ⟦**-ist**⟧)   b.   (⟦**-ic**⟧ ∘ ⟦**-ist**⟧)
       c.   (⟦**-ian**⟧ $\boxed{CP}_{23}$ ⟦**-ic**⟧$_N$)   c.   (⟦**-ian**⟧ ∘ ⟦**-ic**⟧$_N$)

(26)   ⟦**-ion**⟧ : [$\mu_{26} \Rightarrow$ Noun : *-ion*]

Representative members of μ_{26}: ⟨L, *compress*, Verb⟩, ⟨L, *fuse*, Verb⟩, ⟨L, *select*, Verb⟩

The domain-of-definition of (⟦**-ion**⟧ ⓟ ⟦**-ate**⟧) is identical to that of the ⟦**-ate**⟧ rule in (27). The ⟦**-ate**⟧ rule derives verbs in *-ate* from nouns and adjectives, as in Table 10.8; it also serves the thematizing function (Section 2.1) for verbs such as those in Table 10.9 (reflecting its origins in the perfect passive participial morphology of Latin first-conjugation verbs, e.g. *celebrāt-us*, *locāt-us*,

---

[2] *Electrics* is, of course, used with other meanings (e.g. as shorthand for 'electric cars' or to mean 'the wiring of a house').

312 *Potentiation and Counterpotentiation*

Table 10.8 *Derivative verb stems in* -ate

Denominal			Deadjectival
assassinate	*hyphenate*	*oxygenate*	*activate*
chlorinate	*liquidate*	*pollinate*	*alienate*
filtrate	*motivate*	*pulsate*	*authenticate*
fluoridate	*notate*	*salivate*	*captivate*
gradate	*orchestrate*	*ulcerate*	*domesticate*
hydrogenate	*originate*	*vaccinate*	*validate*

Table 10.9 *Verb stems in which* [[-**ate**]] *serves a thematizing function*

accelerate	*elaborate*	*insinuate*	*regulate*
celebrate	*evacuate*	*legislate*	*saturate*
culminate	*fascinate*	*locate*	*suffocate*
educate	*hallucinate*	*mutate*	*tolerate*

mūtāt-us). In other words, the domain μ_{27} of [[-**ate**]] includes noun triplets of the type ⟨L, stem, Noun⟩ (as in (28a)), adjective triplets of the type ⟨L, stem, Adj⟩ (as in (28b)), and for verbs that are thematized by [[-**ate**]], verb triplets of type ⟨L, substem, Verb⟩ (as in (28c)). Because the combination ([[-**ion**]] ⓟ [[-**ate**]]) is a potentiation, every verbal derivative in -*ate* in Table 10.8 has a nominalization in -*ation*, as do verbs such as those in Table 10.9 for which [[-**ate**]] has a thematizing function. Thus, the potentiation ([[-**ion**]] ⓟ [[-**ate**]]) applies to the triplets in (28) to yield the corresponding nominalizations in (29).

(27)   [[-**ate**]] : [μ_{27} ⇒ Verb : -*ate*]

The [[-**ate**]] rule has a derivational function for nominal and adjectival members of μ_{27} (e.g. ⟨L, *assassin*, Noun⟩, ⟨L, *hyphen*, Noun⟩, ⟨L, *active*, Adj⟩, ⟨L, *domestic*, Adj⟩) but a thematizing function for verbal members of μ_{27} (e.g. ⟨L, *insinu-*, Verb⟩, ⟨L, *evacu-*, Verb⟩).

(28)   a.   ⟨L, *hyphen*, Noun⟩   (29)   a.   ⟨L, *hyphenation*, Noun⟩
       b.   ⟨L, *active*, Adj⟩   b.   ⟨L, *activation*, Noun⟩
       c.   ⟨L, *insinu-*, Verb⟩   c.   ⟨L, *insinuation*, Verb⟩

The domain-of-definition μ_{30} of the counterpotentiation ([[-**ion**]] $\boxed{\text{CP}}_{30}$ [[-**ate**]]) defined in (30) is systematically disjoint from the domain-of-definition μ_{27} of [[-**ate**]] in (27) and of the potentiation ([[-**ion**]] ⓟ [[-**ate**]]). The domain-of-definition μ_{30} includes many triplets of the type ⟨L, stem, Verb⟩ (e.g. ⟨L, *admire*, Verb⟩, ⟨L, *cancel*, Verb⟩, ⟨L, *vary*, Verb⟩, all involving verbs

10.2 Counterpotentiation   313

Table 10.10 *Instances in which ([[-**ion**]] $\boxed{\text{CP}}_{30}$ [[-ate]]) applies to a ⟨lexeme, stem, Verb⟩ triplet*

Verb stem X / *X-*ate*	Stem of resulting nominalization	Verb stem X / *X-*ate*	Stem of resulting nominalization
accuse/*accusate	*accusation*	*flirt/*flirtate*	*flirtation*
cancel/*cancellate	*cancellation*	*fragment/ *fragmentate*	*fragmentation*
conserve/ *conservate	*conservation*	*imagine/ *imaginate*	*imagination*
continue/*continuate	*continuation*	*observe/ *observate*	*observation*
converse/ *conversate	*conversation*	*realize/*realizate*	*realization*
expect/*expectate	*expectation*	*starve/*starvate*	*starvation*

Table 10.11 *Instances in which ([[-**ion**]] $\boxed{\text{CP}}_{30}$ [[-ate]]) applies to a ⟨lexeme, stem, Noun⟩ triplet*

Noun stem X with no verb stem *X-*ate*	Corresponding nominalization	Noun stem X with no verb stem *X-*ate*	Corresponding nominalization
argument/ *argumentate	*argumentation*	*pigment/*pigmentate*	*pigmentation*
forest/*forestate	*forestation*	*public/*publicate*	*publication*
instrument/ *instrumentate	*instrumentation*	*sediment/*sedimentate*	*sedimentation*

that are not thematized by [[-**ate**]]) as well as a limited number of triplets of the type ⟨L, stem, Noun⟩ (e.g. ⟨L, *argument*, Noun⟩, ⟨L, *instrument*, Noun⟩; cf. Plag 2003: 90f.). Thus, the counterpotentiation ([[-**ion**]] $\boxed{\text{CP}}_{30}$ [[-**ate**]]) defines nominalizations in *-ation* for verbs such as those in Table 10.10 and for nouns such as those in Table 10.11, applying to triplets such as those in (31) to yield the corresponding nominalizations in (32). (This counterpotentiation thus reflects the use of [[-**ate**]] in forming combining stems; Section 2.1.2.)

(30)   ([[-**ion**]] $\boxed{\text{CP}}_{30}$ [[-**ate**]]) : [$\mu_{30} \Rightarrow$ Noun : *-ation*], where μ_{30} is disjoint from μ_{27}.

Representative members of μ_{30}: ⟨L, *admire*, Verb⟩, ⟨L, *instrument*, Noun⟩
(cf. **admirate*, **instrumentate*)

314   *Potentiation and Counterpotentiation*

Table 10.12 *Adjectives derived by ([[-ive]] ∘ [[-ate]]) from verbs thematized by* [[-ate]]

Thematized verb stem X-*ate*	Adjective stem	Thematized verb stem X-*ate*	Adjective stem
appreciate	*appreciative*	*innovate*	*innovative*
associate	*associative*	*manipulate*	*manipulative*
cooperate	*cooperative*	*narrate*	*narrative*
evaluate	*evaluative*	*predicate*	*predicative*
illustrate	*illustrative*	*relate*	*relative*
imitate	*imitative*	*speculate*	*speculative*

(31) a. ⟨L, *admire*, Verb⟩   (32) a. ⟨L, *admiration*, Noun⟩
      b. ⟨L, *instrument*, Noun⟩   b. ⟨L, *instrumentation*, Noun⟩

As these examples show, the makeup of the domain-of-definition μ_{27} of the potentiation ([[-ion]] ⓟ [[-ate]]) differs systematically from that of the domain-of-definition μ_{30} of the counterpotentiation ([[-ion]] $\boxed{\text{CP}}_{30}$ [[-ate]]): μ_{27} contains adjective triplets and substem triplets for verbs thematized by [[-ate]]; by contrast, μ_{30} lacks both of these, instead showing verbal triplets for verbs not thematized by [[-ate]]. The limited sense in which the domains-of-definition of μ_{27} and μ_{30} might be claimed to differ in a lexically arbitrary way is with respect to the nominal triplets that they contain (e.g. ⟨L, *hyphen*, Noun⟩ vs. ⟨L, *instrument*, Noun⟩).

The potentiation ([[-ion]] ⓟ [[-ate]]) and its paired counterpotentiation ([[-ion]] $\boxed{\text{CP}}_{30}$ [[-ate]]) are paralleled by other pairs involving derivational rules other than [[-ion]]. For instance, the derivational rule [[-ive]] in (33) gives rise to the composite in (34) and to the counterpotentiation in (35). The domains-of-definition of the composite (34) and the counterpotentiation (35) are systematically different. The domain-of-definition μ_{34} to which composite (34) applies includes triplets appropriate for verbs that are thematized by [[-ate]], for which it defines derivative adjectives such as those in Table 10.12. By contrast, the domain-of-definition μ_{35} to which the counterpotentiation (35) applies instead includes triplets for verbs not thematized by [[-ate]] to produce derivative adjectives such as those in Table 10.13.

(33)   [[-ive]] : [μ_{33} ⇒ Adj : *-ive*]

       Representative members of μ_{33}: ⟨L, *repress*, Verb⟩, ⟨L, *invent*, Verb⟩

Table 10.13 *Adjectives derived by (〚-ive〛 $\boxed{CP}_{35}$ 〚-ate〛) from verbs not thematized by* 〚**-ate**〛

Verb stem X / *X-*ate*	Adjective stem	Verb stem X / *X-*ate*	Adjective stem
affirm/*affirmate	affirmative	imagine/*imaginate	imaginative
augment/*augmentate	augmentative	inform/*informate	informative
compare/*comparate	comparative	preserve/*preservate	preservative
conserve/*conservate	conservative	provoke/*provocate	provocative
exploit/*exploitate	exploitative	represent/*representate	representative
figure/*figurate	figurative	talk/*talkate	talkative

(34) (〚-ive〛 ∘ 〚-ate〛) : [μ_{34} ⇒ Adj : *-ative*]

    Representative members of μ_{34}:
        ⟨L, *valid*, Adj⟩, ⟨L, *ulcer*, Noun⟩   (cf. *validate, ulcerate*)
        ⟨L, *appreci-*, Verb⟩, ⟨L, *recuper-*, Verb⟩   (cf. *appreciate, recuperate*)

(35) (〚-ive〛 $\boxed{CP}_{35}$ 〚-ate〛) : [μ_{35} ⇒ Adj : *-ative*], where μ_{35} is disjoint from μ_{27}

    Representative members of μ_{35}: ⟨L, *perform*, Verb⟩, ⟨L, *explore*, Verb⟩
                                       (cf. **performate, *explorate*)

10.3 Affixal Discontinuity, Parasynthesis, Synaffixes, and Domains-of-definition

Affixal discontinuities are of two types. On one hand, there are individual affixes that are discontinuous; these are uncontroversially circumfixal. On the other hand, there are affix combinations whose component affixes are discontinuous but jointly serve a single function; these are sometimes referred to as circumfixes, but less aptly, since their distinct affixes – typically, a prefix and a suffix – also appear independently in some words, where they have their own individual functions. I shall refer to affixal discontinuities of the former type as true circumfixes and to those of the latter type as instances of parasynthesis (Plag 2003: 40; Bauer et al. 2013: 500–503; Bauer 2014: 126–128).[3] Notwithstanding their comparative typological rarity, rules that define true circumfixes are fairly unremarkable: these are simple rules whose operation on a given stem involves

---

[3] Štekauer et al. (2012: 203ff.) maintain a similar terminological distinction between circumfixation and prefixal-suffixal derivation.

Table 10.14 *Circumfixal ordinal marking Kanuri*

Cardinal	Ordinal	
tiló	kə́n-tiló-mi	'one / first'
fíndi	kə́n-fíndi-mi	'twenty / twentieth'
fíndin tilôn	kə́n-fíndin tilôn-mi	'twenty-one / twenty-first'

Hutchison (1981: 76–77, 202–203); Cyffer (2007: 1106–1107); Stump (2010)

the introduction of a single, discontinuous marking. Rules that define parasyntheses, on the other hand, are remarkable in that they are rule combinations whose component rules serve a joint function. Consider first an example of true circumfixation, that of ordinal marking in Kanuri (Nilo-Saharan; Nigeria, Niger, Chad, Cameroon). In Kanuri, an ordinal numeral is derived from the corresponding cardinal through the circumfixation of *kə́n-__-mi*, as in Table 10.14. This marking is not synchronically the effect of a composite rule combining a prefixational 〚**kə́n-**〛 rule with a suffixational 〚**-mi**〛 rule; rather, it is the effect of the simple rule (38).

(38) 〚X → **kə́n-X-mi**〛 : [μ_{38} ⇒ Ordinal num : X → *kə́n-X-mi*]
      Members of μ_{38} are of the type ⟨lexeme, stem, Cardinal num⟩.

By contrast, the affixal marking of *embolden* is not an effect of circumfixation; rather, it is an instance of parasynthesis. In parasynthesis, two logically separable morphological operations combine in the definition of a single word-formation pattern. In the parasynthetic compound *ring-tailed* 'having a ringed tail', the compounding of *ring* with *tail* operates conjointly with the suffixation of *-ed*; it is not plausible to think of *ring-tailed* as the result of compounding the noun *ring* with an adjective *tailed* 'having a tail', nor is it plausible to think of it as the result of suffixing *-ed* to a noun-noun compound *ring-tail*. Similarly, it is not plausible to think of the parasynthetic derivative *em-bold-en* as the result of prefixing *en-* to an otherwise nonoccurring verb **bolden* (cf. *sweeten*), nor as the result of suffixing *-en* to an otherwise nonoccurring verb **embold* (cf. *enable*); instead, *bold* becomes a verb stem as a joint effect of the affixation of *en-* and *-en*.

Parasynthetic derivation is sometimes thought of in fairly restrictive terms as always involving the simultaneous use of a prefix and a suffix (Bauer et al. 2013: 500); but parasynthetic derivation might also be seen as a more general phenomenon that involves the simultaneous use of two derivational markings of any sort. Bauer 1988 refers to such patterns as "synaffixes." English examples include the two-suffix combination *-ist-ic* in *characteristic*

10.3 Affixal Discontinuity and Parasynthesis

(*characterist*) and the combination of ablaut and consonant gradation in *bath* /bæθ/ → *bathe* /beɪð/ (cf. ablaut alone in *food* → *feed* and consonant gradation alone in *wreath* → *wreathe*); Štekauer et al. (2012: 210–212) likewise cite instances of prefixal-infixal and infixal-suffixal derivation.

True instances of parasynthetic derivation are instances of counterpotentiation (Section 10.2) rather than of rule composition. In order to appreciate the validity of this claim, it is important to be careful about distinguishing true instances of parasynthetic derivation from merely apparent instances.

One apparent instance of parasynthesis is the verb *decaffeinate* 'to remove the caffeine from', in the definition of whose form the reversative ⟦**de-**⟧ rule and the causative ⟦**-ate**⟧ rule in some sense operate simultaneously on the noun stem *caffeine*. Although ⟦**de-**⟧ and ⟦**-ate**⟧ do not always accompany each other (compare *devein* from *vein* and *hyphenate* from *hyphen*), they do not seem to play separable roles in the derivation of *decaffeinate*, given the absence of **decaffeine* and the nonexistence or comparative infrequency of *caffeinate*. Yet, as Masini & Iacobini (2018) and Iacobini (2020) observe, missing intermediate derivatives such as *caffeinate* 'infuse with caffeine' are potential words, for whose absence or infrequency a pragmatic explanation is perfectly possible. But in cases of true parasynthesis, they argue, the parasynthetic derivation has the effect of blocking a synonymous intermediate form, as *embolden* blocks both **bolden* and **embold* as causative verbs; in the terminology of Rainer (2012), blocked forms like **bolden* and **embold* are virtual but not potential words.

Tying parasynthetic derivation to blocking helps distinguish true parasyntheses such as *embolden* from merely apparent parasyntheses such as *decaffeinate*, but it raises another problem – that of distinguishing cases such as *whimsical* (which seemingly blocks the intermediate synonym **whimsic*) from cases such as *cyclical* (which, for some reason, does not block the intermediate synonym *cyclic*). If *whimsical* is a parasynthesis that blocks the intermediate synonym **whimsic*, why doesn't *cyclical* block *cyclic* in a similar fashion?

This problem can be resolved by recognizing that *embolden* and *whimsical* are parasyntheses because the rule combinations that define them are counterpotentiations; *decaffeinate* and *cyclical*, by contrast, are not parasyntheses because the rule combinations that define them are composites rather than counterpotentiations. The ⟦**-ate**⟧ rule applies to noun triplets such as those in (39) to produce causative verb triplets such as those in (40); the triplet ⟨L, *caffeinate*, causative verb⟩, though merely potential, is within the domain-of-definition of the reversative ⟦**de-**⟧ rule, which defines both of the derivative verbs in (41). Alternatively, the composite rule (⟦**de-**⟧ ∘ ⟦**-ate**⟧)

318   *Potentiation and Counterpotentiation*

derives the verbs in (41) directly from the nouns in (39) – a derivation that is more compatible with the merely potential status of (40a).[4]

(39)   a.   ⟨L, *caffeine*, noun⟩
         b.   ⟨L, *oxygen*, noun⟩

(40)   a.   ⟨L, *caffeinate*, causative verb⟩   (potential)
         b.   ⟨L, *oxygenate*, causative verb⟩   (actual)

(41)   a.   ⟨L, *decaffeinate*, reversative causative verb⟩   (actual)
         b.   ⟨L, *deoxygenate*, reversative causative verb⟩   (actual)

Unlike the ([[de-]] ∘ [[-ate]]) rule, the combination of [[en-]] with [[-en]] is not a composite – it is a counterpotentiation ([[en-]] $\boxed{\text{CP}}_{62}$ [[-en]]) whose domain-of-definition μ_{62} is disjoint from those of both [[en-]] and [[-en]]. (See Section 2.5.) For example, μ_{62} includes the triplet in (42a) but not those in (42b,c); the domain-of-definition of [[en-]] includes the triplet in (42b) but not those in (42a, c); and the domain-of-definition of [[-en]] includes the triplet in (42c) but not those in (42a,b). From (42a), ([[en-]] $\boxed{\text{CP}}_{62}$ [[-en]]) defines the derivative verb in (43); while the inclusion of ⟨L, *caffeine*, noun⟩ in the domain-of-definition of the composite ([[de-]] ∘ [[-ate]]) licenses *caffeinate* as a potential verb form, the inclusion of ⟨L, *bold*, Adj⟩ in the domain-of-definition of the counterpotentiation ([[en-]] $\boxed{\text{CP}}_{62}$ [[-en]]) licenses neither *bolden nor *embold as potential verb forms. These forms are "blocked" precisely by the fact that (42a) is absent from the domains-of-definition of both [[en-]] and [[-en]].

(42)   a.   ⟨L, *bold*, Adj⟩
         b.   ⟨L, *able*, Adj⟩
         c.   ⟨L, *sweet*, Adj⟩

(43)   ⟨L, *embolden*, causative verb⟩

The rules [[-ic]] and [[-al]] combine both as the composite ([[-al]] ∘ [[-ic]]) and as the counterpotentiation ([[-al]] $\boxed{\text{CP}}_{13}$ [[-ic]]). Both the [[-ic]] rule and the composite ([[-al]] ∘ [[-ic]]) have the triplet (44a) in their domain-of-definition, and thus define both (44b) and (44c). Although the domain-of-definition of the counterpotentiation ([[-al]] $\boxed{\text{CP}}_{13}$ [[-ic]]) includes the triplet (45a), that of [[-ic]] does not; ([[-al]] $\boxed{\text{CP}}_{13}$ [[-ic]]) therefore applies to (45a) to derive (45b), but

---

[4] Under the assumptions of Construction Morphology, Booij (2010: 44) makes a similar argument for the postulation of a unified schema [*de* [[x]$_N$ *ate*]$_V$]$_V$, essentially the equivalent of the composite rule ([[de-]] ∘ [[-ate]]). See Section 12.2 for discussion of the similarities between schema unification and rule composition.

nothing licenses *whimsic* as a potential adjective. It is "blocked" because (45a) is absent from the domain-of-definition of ⟦**-ic**⟧.

(44) a. ⟨L, *cycle*, Noun⟩
b. ⟨L, *cyclic*, Adj⟩
c. ⟨L, *cyclical*, Adj⟩

(45) a. ⟨L, *whimsy*, Noun⟩
b. ⟨L, *whimsical*, Adj⟩

The phenomenon of parasynthesis constitutes an important piece of evidence in favor of defining a rule of derivational exponence not merely in terms of its domain of application (e.g. nouns, transitive verbs) but in terms of its domain-of-definition – the precise set of triplets for which its application supplies a value. The distinction between

$(R_2 \circ R_1)$, i.e. the composite of rule R_2 with rule R_1,
$(R_2 \; \textcircled{P} \; R_1)$, i.e. the potentiation of R_2 by R_1, and
$(R_2 \; \boxed{\text{CP}}_n \; R_1)$, i.e. the counterpotentiation of R_1 by R_2,

can only be drawn by reference to the domains-of-definition of R_1 and R_2. Thus, if the derivational rules R_1 and R_2 are defined as in (46), the composite $(R_2 \circ R_1)$ is only defined if the domain-of-definition μ_1 of R_1 includes at least one triplet t such that the result of applying R_1 to t belongs to the domain-of-definition μ_2 of R_2; the potentiation $(R_2 \; \textcircled{P} \; R_1)$ is only defined if every triplet t in the domain-of-definition μ_1 of R_1 is such that the result of applying R_1 to t belongs to the domain-of-definition μ_2 of R_2; and the counterpotentiation $(R_2 \; \boxed{\text{CP}}_n \; R_1)$ is only defined if its domain-of-definition μ_n is disjoint from the domain-of-definition μ_1 of R_1.

(46) Two hypothetical rules of derivational exponence
a. $R_1 : [\mu_1 \Rightarrow D : f_1]$
b. $R_2 : [\mu_2 \Rightarrow D : f_2]$

10.4 Conclusion

Potentiation and counterpotentiation are modes of rule combination that express facilitatory relations between derivational rules: potentiation is a mode of rule combination expressing an outward relation (⟦**-able**⟧ potentiates ⟦**-ity**⟧ in the definition of *reliability*), while counterpotentiation is a mode of rule combination expressing an inward relation (⟦**-ian**⟧ counterpotentiates ⟦**-ic**⟧ in the definition of *beautician*). Potentiation and counterpotentiation are like other modes of rule combination in the sense that they are local: when two rules ⟦x⟧ and ⟦y⟧ combine in some way, whether by composition, holistic combination, aggregation, potentiation, or counterpotentiation, the resulting combination is one in which ⟦x⟧ and ⟦y⟧ are adjacent in their application. On the other hand, potentiation and counterpotentiation seem to differ from other modes of rule combination in that they are always minimal – that is, to judge from the examples considered here, they always express relations between simple rules rather than between rules one or both of which are themselves combinations. Logically, one could imagine a relation of potentiation or counterpotentiation involving two rules either or both of which are combinations of simpler rules, but I know of no clear evidence of this kind.

In this chapter and those that precede it, empirical evidence has been shown to favor a rule-combining approach to morphotactics in which rules of exponence enter into various modes of binary combination: rules of inflectional exponence enter into relations of composition, holistic combination, and aggregation; rules of derivational exponence enter into relations of composition (including potentiation), holistic combination, and counterpotentiation. On first consideration, this conception of morphotactics might appear to be complicated. But rule combination actually contributes to a system's structural simplicity, making it possible for a comparatively small number of simple morphological rules to express a wide variety of lexicogrammatical distinctions by virtue of the ways in which they combine. Moreover, as I show in the next chapter, rule combinations make a language's morphology simpler to process, and they provide a basis for historical simplifications of various kinds.

11 *Rule Combinations and Morphological Simplicity*

In this chapter, I examine the relation between rule combination and morphological simplicity. On first consideration, rule combinations seem to be the opposite of simple: they are bigger, more complicated rules made up of smaller, simpler ones. Yet, we have already seen an important way in which combinability affords a kind of economy in a language's inventory of simple rules of exponence: combining the same simple rules in different ways gets more mileage out of them, allowing them to express a variety of differences of content. In Swahili, for example, the [[**vi-**$_8$]] rule simply expresses noun class 8, but in combination with the right rules, it more specifically expresses either agreement with a subject belonging to noun class 8 (as in *vi-lianguka* 'they (NC8) fell'), or a pronominal object belonging to noun class 8 (as in *tuli-vi-soma* 'we read them (NC8)'), or a relativized argument belonging to noun class 8 (as in *tuvisoma-vy-o* 'which (NC8) we read'). Here, I discuss two other respects in which rule combination can have simplifying effects.

Synchronically, rule combinations (like word combinations) are sometimes stored as formulaic units, and this fact contributes to a morphological system's processing simplicity, since accessing a stored rule combination directly is simpler than decomposing that combination into its component rules for separate lookup (Section 11.1). Stored, formulaic rule combinations may also contribute to diachronic simplifications of a language's morphology, since they are the locus of reanalyses that may eventuate in "affix telescoping," the development of a rule combination into a simple rule (Section 11.2). But affix telescoping is not a monolithic phenomenon; it involves the reduction of a rule combination's combinatory transparency along at least four dimensions. Thus, it is possible to find rule combinations that are progressing toward reanalysis as simple rules without yet having reached the point of reanalysis; I illustrate with examples from English.

11.1 Formulaic Rule Combinations

Logically, a rule combination could be either stored or assembled/decomposed "online" (e.g. in accordance with a stored FER pattern) as part of the production or interpretation of a complex word. If both possibilities exist, then it is important to determine what motivates the storage of a particular rule combination. In addressing this issue, it is instructive to compare rule combinations in morphology to word combinations in syntax. Each of the individual words in a syntactically complex expression is standardly assumed to correspond to an individual lexical entry; but it is also possible for a word combination to be a formulaic[1] unit possessing its own lexical entry (a stock example being the idiom *kick the bucket*). Formulaicity is itself a complex phenomenon; among the factors contributing to the formulaicity of word combinations are idiomaticity, conventionality, and frequency. A word combination's formulaicity is experimentally detectable; in research comparing the processing of such combinations with that of nonformulaic word combinations of comparable syntactic complexity, language users have been found to process formulaic combinations more quickly – evidence that such combinations need not be fully parsed, being instead accessed as stored wholes (Underwood et al. 2004; Arnon & Snider 2010; Tremblay et al. 2011; Conklin & Schmitt 2012; Carrol & Conklin 2020).

Drawing on evidence from Turkish, Durrant (2013, 2016), Özel et al. (2016), and Badrulhisham (2019) argue that in the morphological domain, an affix combination (or equivalently, in my view, the rule combination that defines it) may be a formulaic unit. It is reasonable to assume that as with word combinations, more than one factor may contribute to a rule combination's formulaicity. When rules enter into frequent composition, the resulting composite rule may be formulaic purely as an effect of its frequency, a consequence with observable psycholinguistic effects (Section 11.1.1). In addition, a rule combination may be formulaic because of its conventional character (e.g. the fact that it defines a language-specific pattern of affix ordering; Section 11.1.2), and a rule combination may be formulaic because it is semantically noncompositional (Section 11.1.3).

---

[1] Wray (2002: 9) characterizes a formulaic combination as "a sequence, continuous or discontinuous, of words or other elements, which is, or appears to be, prefabricated: that is, stored and retrieved whole from memory at the time of use, rather than being subject to generation or analysis by the language grammar."

11.1.1 Frequent Rule Combinations

Just as a frequently occurring sequence of words may be stored as a formulaic unit (Arnon & Snider 2010; Tremblay et al. 2011; Wray 2012), so may a frequently occurring sequence of affixes. Bilgin (2016) presents compelling experimental evidence to this effect from Turkish, a language rich in suffixal morphology. Drawing on a large list of Turkish suffix sequences of varying frequency, Bilgin constructed sets of words contrasting not with respect to the frequency of their stems nor with respect to the frequency of their individual suffixes, but with respect to the frequency of their specific suffix combinations. For instance, the verb form *gergedan-laş-tır-dı* 'caused to become a rhino' in (1a) has the infrequent nominal stem *gergedan-* and the frequent suffixes *-laş*, *-tır*, and *-dı* in the frequent combination *-laş-tır-dı*, while the gerund *antilop-laş-tır-ıp* 'having caused to become an antelope' in (1b) has the infrequent nominal stem *antilop-* and the frequent suffixes *-laş*, *-tır*, and *-ıp* in the infrequent combination *-laş-tır-ıp*. Thus, as far as frequency is concerned, (1a) and (1b) are alike in most ways: they involve stems and stem-affix combinations that are infrequent and suffixes that, taken individually, are frequent. There is, however, one important difference: (1a) involves a suffix sequence that is frequent, while (1b) involves a suffix sequence that is infrequent. This difference is represented schematically in Figures 11.1 and 11.2. Using such sets of words along with invented nonwords, Bilgin had native speakers carry out a lexical decision task; speakers reliably recognized real but infrequent words containing high-frequency suffix sequences more quickly than real but infrequent words containing low-frequency suffix sequences. These results suggest that high-frequency suffix sequences are formulaic sequences that are stored and rapidly accessed as wholes.

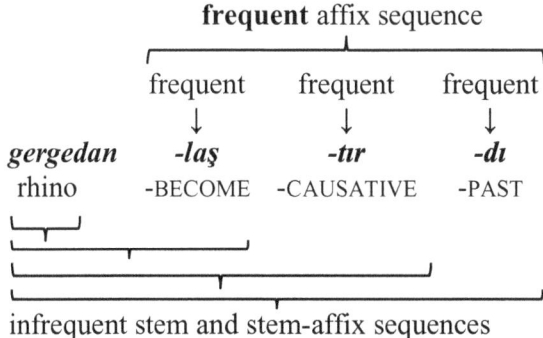

Figure 11.1 *The parts of the Turkish word form in (1a)*

324　*Rule Combinations and Morphological Simplicity*

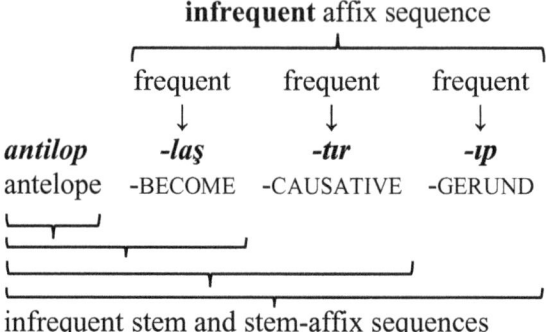

Figure 11.2　*The parts of the Turkish word form in (1b)*

(1)　a.　*gergedan-laş-tır-dı*
　　　　rhino-BECOME-CAUS-PAST
　　　　caused to become a rhino
　　b.　*antilop-laş-tır-ıp*
　　　　antelope-BECOME-CAUS-GERUND
　　　　having caused to become an antelope

When an affix sequence is formulaic, one can equally say that the rule combination that defines that sequence is formulaic; thus, Bilgin's results might be interpreted to mean that the stored composite ([[-dı]] ∘ ([[-tır]] ∘ [[-laş]])) is accessed in the recognition of the formulaic suffix sequence in (1a) and that accessing this composite facilitates recognition more rapidly than accessing its component rules [[-laş]], [[-tır]], and [[-dı]] in succession. The infrequency of the suffix sequence in (1b) makes it less likely that the composite ([[-ıp]] ∘ ([[-tır]] ∘ [[-laş]])) is stored, so that processing this sequence involves accessing the rules [[-laş]], [[-tır]], and [[-ıp]] separately from one another (or perhaps not fully composed, e.g. with ([[-tır]] ∘ [[-laş]]) separate from [[-ıp]]).

Many composite rules of inflectional exponence are highly frequent, a consequence of the fact that a language's morphosyntax requires words to be inflected according to the syntactic configuration in which they appear. Thus, while it is logically possible that inflectional rules could be combined online in accordance with a language's FER patterns, processing efficiency would favor the storage of frequent rule combinations, allowing them to be directly invoked as units in the production and comprehension of inflectionally complex forms.

One might be tempted to claim that the storage of a composite rule ([[y]] ∘ [[x]]) alongside the simple rules [[x]] and [[y]] constitutes a complication rather than a simplification, since it introduces redundancy into the system of stored rules. But if one assumes a pattern-matching evaluation metric (Bochner 1993; see also Section 1.3), the composite rule ($[\![y]\!] \circ [\![x]\!]$) is not costly to store, since it matches the patterns of the existing simple rules $[\![x]\!]$ and $[\![y]\!]$, stipulating only one novel piece of information – the order in which these rules compose. Moreover, storage of the composite rule ($[\![y]\!] \circ [\![x]\!]$) presumably enhances processing speed by eliminating the need to analyze it into its component rules in the production and interpretation of the forms that it defines.

11.1.2 Conventional Rule Combinations

Some word combinations are formulaic because they are the conventionally accepted way of expressing their content (Wray 2002: 72–75; Carrol & Conklin 2020): *take a walk*, *see a movie*, *watch TV*, *have a snack*, *get ready for school*, *sick and tired*, and so on. There are several kinds of rule combinations that might be said to be conventional in this sense: these include composite rules in which the order of composition is purely conventional; rule combinations whose mode of combination is something other than ordinary composition; and combinations of a dependent rule with a carrier rule.

When the morphology of an inflected word form is defined through the composition of two or more rules of inflectional exponence, the sequence of composition is in general conventional. For example, in the definition of the Latin verb form *vidē-t-ur* 's/he is seen' by the composite rule (2a), the order of composition of the two rules in (2b,c) is a matter of convention. In Sanskrit, the same content is expressed by *dṛś-yá-te*, whose definition involves what is essentially the opposite sequence of composition in (3a). To be sure, there are important cross-linguistic tendencies in the sequence in which inflectional rules are composed. Bybee (1985) provides evidence for a relevance principle according to which a verbal inflection of higher semantic relevance[2] is positioned closer to the verb stem than one of lower semantic relevance. Still, Bybee shows that this is only a statistical tendency, and one for the frequency of whose incidence historical processes afford a sufficient account. In other words, the sequence in which inflectional rules compose is not universally predictable from the content that they realize, being instead an effect of language-specific conventions. In view of this conventionality, composite rules such as (2a) and (3a) are likely to be stored as formulaic units.

---

[2] According to Bybee (1985: 4), "[t]he semantic relevance of an affix to a stem is the extent to which the meaning of the affix directly affects the meaning of the stem."

(2) Latin: a. (⟦-ur⟧ ∘ ⟦-t⟧) : [V, {{sbj 3 sg} pass} : -tur]
         b. ⟦-t⟧ : [V, {{sbj 3 sg}} : -t]
         c. ⟦-ur⟧ : [V, {pass} : -ur]

(3) Sanskrit: a. (⟦-te⟧ ∘ ⟦-yá⟧) : [V, {{sbj 3 sg} prs pass middle} : -yáte]
           b. ⟦-yá⟧ : [V, {prs pass} : -yá]
           c. ⟦-te⟧ : [V, {{sbj 3 sg} middle} : -te]

Although the sequence in which inflectional rules compose is largely conventional, the same cannot always be said of derivational rules. Consider, for example, the English potentiation in (4). This rule applies to the triplet ⟨L, *believe*, Verb⟩ to give the triplet ⟨L, *believability*, Noun⟩. The order in which the rules in (4b,c) compose in this case is not simply conventional: given their domains-of-definition, they can't compose in the opposite order.

(4)   (⟦-ity⟧ ⓟ ⟦-able⟧) : [μ_5 ⇒ Noun : *-ability*]   (where μ_5 is as in (5))

(5)   ⟦-able⟧ : [μ_5 ⇒ Adj : *-able*]
      Representative member of μ_5: ⟨L, *believe*, Verb⟩

(6)   ⟦-ity⟧ : [μ_6 ⇒ Noun : *-ity*]
      Representative member of μ_6: ⟨L, *serene*, Adj⟩

Even so, derivational rules sometimes combine in conventional ways. Hyman (2003) presents a striking example of this sort from Chichewa. In Chichewa, deverbal causative verbs are derived by means of the ⟦-its⟧ rule in (7), and deverbal applicative verbs by means of the ⟦-il⟧ rule in (8). Logically, these might be supposed to compose in either order, and one might expect that the order of composition would then correspond to the relative scope of causative and applicative semantics. Yet, as the examples in (9) show, the order of composition is invariably (⟦-il⟧ ∘ ⟦-its⟧), with ⟦-its⟧ as the inner rule and ⟦-il⟧ as the outer rule whether causation has wider or narrower scope than applicativization.[3] Thus, in (9a), applicativization has wider scope than causation: 'sticks' is the applied object of 'cause to cry'. In (9b), by contrast, causation has wider scope than applicativization: 'stir with a spoon' serves as a complement of 'cause'. In view of this conventionality, (⟦-il⟧ ∘ ⟦-its⟧) is plausibly seen as a stored formulaic unit in Chichewa.

(7)   ⟦-its⟧ : [μ_7 ⇒ Causative verb : *-its*]

(8)   ⟦-il⟧ : [μ_8 ⇒ Applicative verb : *-il*]

---

[3] The ⟦-its⟧ and ⟦-il⟧ rules may compose in the opposite order only if the reciprocalizing ⟦-an⟧ rule applies between them: (⟦-its⟧ ∘ (⟦-an⟧ ∘ ⟦-il⟧)); see Hyman (2003) for details.

(9) Chichewa (Hyman 2003: 248)
   a. Applicativized causative (where sticks are the instrument of causation)
      alenjé   a-ku-líl-íts-il-a   mwaná   ndodo
      hunters   3PL-PROG-cry-CAUS-APP-FV   child   sticks
      'the hunters are [making the child cry] with sticks'
   b. Causativized applicative (where a spoon is the instrument of stirring)
      alenjé   a-ku-tákás-its-il-a   mkází   mthíko
      hunters   3PL-PROG-stir-CAUS-APP-FV   woman   spoon
      'the hunters are making the woman [stir with a spoon]'

Given that rule composition is the canonical mode of rule combination, other modes of combination are inherently conventional and hence formulaic; thus, it is plausible to hypothesize that by their nature, rule aggregations and counterpotentiations must be stored. In many instances, these special modes of rule combination arise diachronically through reanalysis.

Thus, consider again the affix sequences appearing in Swahili relative verb forms such as those in (10). What is striking about such forms is the distribution of their relative affix, which appears before a verb stem marked for tense or negation but after a verb stem that is not so marked; thus, the relative affix *vyo* (coding a relativized argument belonging to noun class 8) appears before the verb stem marked with the future-tense prefix *taka-* in (10a) but after the tenseless affirmative verb stem in (10b).

(10) a. *a-taka-vyo-vi-soma*
         SBJ.NC1-FUT-REL.NC8-OBJ.NC8-read
         '(books) that s/he will read'
      b. *a-vi-soma-vyo*
         SBJ.NC1-OBJ.NC8-read-REL.NC8
         '(books) that s/he reads'

In the analysis of these facts in Section 8.4, the Swahili rules of relative affixation are shown to be fundamentally suffixational but capable of aggregating with a prefixational rule expressing tense or nonindicative negation; according to this analysis, the affix -*vyo* is suffixed to the verb stem in (10b), but is (as an effect of aggregation) suffixed to the prefix *taka-* in (10a). This means that the affix sequence *a-taka-vyo-vi-* is not defined by the simple composition of four rules, but by a complex rule combination in which ⟦**-vyo$_8$**⟧$_{II}$ is aggregated with ⟦**taka-**⟧$_{II}$, as in (11). This combination is a consequence of diachronic reanalysis. As Schadeberg (1989) observes, the future-tense prefix *taka-* in (10a) descends historically from the verb stem *taka* 'want' (which also remains as a verb in Swahili), so that etymologically, the relative affix -*vyo* in (10a) is suffixed to a verb stem, exactly as in (10b).

The reanalysis of *taka-* as a future-tense prefix in expressions such as (10a) engendered the special rule combination in (11) and others like it, whose conventionality would favor their storage as formulaic units.

(11) $(\llbracket \textbf{a-}_\textbf{1}\rrbracket_{\text{III}} \circ ((\llbracket \textbf{-vyo}_\textbf{8} \rrbracket_{\text{II}} \, Ⓐ \, \llbracket \textbf{taka-} \rrbracket_{\text{II}}) \circ (\llbracket \textbf{vi-}_\textbf{8} \rrbracket_{\text{I}} \circ \llbracket \text{id.fcn} \rrbracket_{\text{I}})))$

The patterns of rule aggregation in the inflection of Noon attributive adjectives (Section 7.1.2) and of Lithuanian reflexive verbs (Section 7.2.2) can likewise be seen as formulaic patterns of rule combination that have arisen through diachronic reanalysis; see Nevis & Joseph (1992) on Lithuanian and Greenberg (1977, 1978) and Harris (2017: 130–136) concerning the Atlantic-Congo languages. The Noon case is doubly interesting, since the formulaic pattern to which reanalysis has given rise involves both a special rule combination (that of aggregation) and what Harris (2017) calls periodic multiple exponence (Section 3.1); thus, in the definition of the adjectival form in (12a), the noun-class rule $\llbracket \textbf{w-} \rrbracket$ applies twice, once in composition with the $\llbracket \textbf{i-} \rrbracket$, and again in aggregation with $\llbracket \textbf{-ii} \rrbracket$, as in (12b).

(12)   a.   Noon   *w-i-yak-w-ii*
              NC1.SG-PFX-big-NC1.SG-DEF:LOC1
              'big (sg. def. near me)'
       b. $((\llbracket \textbf{w-} \rrbracket \circ \llbracket \textbf{i-} \rrbracket) \circ (\llbracket \textbf{w-} \rrbracket \, Ⓐ \, \llbracket \textbf{-ii} \rrbracket))$

Reanalysis is clearly implicated in the historical emergence of many instances of counterpotentiation. Recall from Section 10.2 that adjectives in *-ic* and their counterparts in *-ical* are of at least the four types exemplified in Table 11.1. In part (a) of the table are adjectives in *-ic* that lack any counterpart in *-ical* (evidence that the $\llbracket \textbf{-ic} \rrbracket$ rule does not potentiate the $\llbracket \textbf{-al} \rrbracket$ rule); in part (b) are adjective doublets in *-ic* and *-ical* that are essentially alike in meaning; in part (c) are adjective doublets in *-ic* and *-ical* whose meanings differ as a matter of lexical convention; and in part (d) are nonoccurring adjectives in *-ic* for which counterparts in *-ical* nevertheless exist.

The counterpotentiation ($\llbracket \textbf{-al} \rrbracket \, \boxed{\text{CP}}_{13} \, \llbracket \textbf{-ic} \rrbracket$) defines adjectives in *-ical* such as those in part (d) of Table 11.1; see again Section 10.2. The derivation of the *-ical* adjectives in parts (b) and (c) can be attributed to the composite rule ($\llbracket \textbf{-al} \rrbracket \circ \llbracket \textbf{-ic} \rrbracket$), and in view of the conventional semantic contrast between the *-ic* adjectives in part (c) and their *-ical* counterparts, the composite rule ($\llbracket \textbf{-al} \rrbracket \circ \llbracket \textbf{-ic} \rrbracket$) and the simple rule $\llbracket \textbf{-ic} \rrbracket$ can be seen as potentially having distinct derivational functions. Once it is possible to conceive of an adjective X-*ical* as deriving directly from a stem X, the path is open to attributing some such derivations to the counterpotentiation ($\llbracket \textbf{-al} \rrbracket \, \boxed{\text{CP}}_{13} \, \llbracket \textbf{-ic} \rrbracket$), whose domain-of-definition is disjoint from that of $\llbracket \textbf{-ic} \rrbracket$. This is a

Table 11.1 *Some Modern English adjectives in* -ic *and* -ical

a.	basic	* basical	c.	economic	economical
	Germanic	*Germanical		historic	historical
	ionic	*ionical		mythic	mythical
	psychotic	*psychotical		periodic	periodical
	specific	*specifical		theatric	theatrical
b.	conic	conical	d.	*biblic	biblical
	cyclic	cyclical		*canonic	canonical
	fanatic	fanatical		*farcic	farcical
	magic	magical		*nonsensic	nonsensical
	satiric	satirical		*quizzic	quizzical

kind of reanalysis. It is not that the composite rule ([[-al]] ∘ [[-ic]]) is itself reanalyzed as a counterpotentiation. Rather, it is that the class of adjectives in -*ical* is reanalyzed as arising both (i) from nouns that belong to the domain-of-definition of the [[-ic]] rule, via the composite ([[-al]] ∘ [[-ic]]), as in the case of *cycle* → *cyclic* → *cyclical*; and (ii) from other nouns, via the counterpotentiation ([[-al]] $\boxed{CP}_{13}$ [[-ic]]), as in the case of *bible* → *biblical* / **biblic*.

Reanalysis may likewise give rise to patterns of periodic multiple exponence that do not involve special rule combinations such as aggregation but instead simply involve ordinary rule composition; even so, such instances of rule composition are noncanonical, since they deviate from the unique sequence criterion (Section 1.5.4). Patterns of periodic multiple exponence might be seen as conventional (hence formulaic) whether or not they involve special rule combinations such as aggregation.

Pengo (S. Central Dravidian; India) presents a case of periodic multiple exponence involving only rule composition (Burrow & Bhattacharya 1970; Bybee 1985: 40f.; Steever 1993: 69–105; Harris 2017: 115–118). In Pengo, verb forms in the past and present perfect tenses inflect for subject agreement with respect to person and number, distinguishing inclusiveness in the first-person plural and gender in the third person; the past and present perfect forms of the verb HUṚ 'see' in Table 11.2 illustrate. In most present perfect forms, the subject-agreement suffix precedes the tense suffix -*na*; but in the first--person singular and the feminine and neuter forms of the third-person plural, the subject-agreement suffix appears twice, both before the perfect suffix and after it, as in the shaded cells of Table 11.2.[4]

---

[4] Steever (1993: 71) observes that although the present perfect forms in Table 12.1 are the most commonly used forms, the double agreement pattern in the shaded portion of the table

Table 11.2 *Past and present perfect forms of* HUṚ *'see' in Pengo*

			Singular	Plural
Past	1st		huṛ-t-aŋ	EXCL. huṛ-t-ap
				INCL. huṛ-t-as
	2nd		huṛ-t-ay	huṛ-t-ader
	3rd	m	huṛ-t-an	huṛ-t-ar
		f }	huṛ-t-at	huṛ-t-ik
		n		huṛ-t-iŋ
Perfect	1st		huṛ-t-aŋ-n-aŋ	EXCL. huṛ-t-ap-na
				INCL. huṛ-t-ah-na
	2nd		huṛ-t-ay-na	huṛ-t-ader-na
	3rd	m	huṛ-t-an-na	huṛ-t-ar-na
		f }	huṛ-t-at-na	huṛ-t-ik-n-ik
		n		huṛ-t-iŋ-n-iŋ

(Steever 1993: 70)

These synchronic facts are accounted for by the analysis of Pengo verb morphology sketched in (13)–(16). The simple rules in (13) include the preterite rule ⟦**-t**⟧ in (13a), the subject-agreement rules in (13b,c) (among which those in (13c) are "special" in that they participate in periodic multiple exponence), and the present-perfect rule ⟦**-na**⟧ in (13d). The tense rules both serve as carrier rules, but with an important difference. The preterite rule ⟦**-t**⟧ serves as a carrier for all of the subject-agreement rules in (13b,c); the present-perfect rule ⟦**-na**⟧, by contrast, only serves as a carrier for the "special" subject-agreement rules in (13c). Given this distinction, the simple rules in (13) participate in the definition of two distinct groups of carrier-dependent composites. The rules in (14) are composites of the subject-agreement rules in (13b,c) with the preterite rule ⟦**-t**⟧; these composites constitute Group 1. Together with the present-perfect rule ⟦**-na**⟧, the rules in (15) – composites of the "special" subject-agreement rules in (13c) with ⟦**-na**⟧ – constitute Group 2. The FER patterns in (16) accordingly define the FERs for the forms in Table 11.2 with reference to Groups 1 and 2.

---

sometimes shows up in other person/number combinations as well, the second-person plural being the only exception; by the same token, first-person singular forms and third-person plural feminine and neuter forms also sometimes show up without double agreement. For present purposes, I focus on the most common pattern.

11.1 Formulaic Rule Combinations

(13) Simple rules for Pengo verb inflection
    a. Preterite rule (used in the definition of both past-tense and present-perfect forms)
        ⟦-t⟧ :   [V, {pret} : -t]
    b. Subject-agreement rules
        ⟦-ay⟧ :   [V, {{sbj 2sg}} : -ay]
        ⟦-at⟧ :   [V, {{sbj 3sg}} : -at]
        ⟦-an⟧ :   [V, {{sbj 3sg masc}} : -an]
        ⟦-ap⟧ :   [V, {{sbj 1pl excl}} : -ap]
        ⟦-as⟧ :   [V, {{sbj 1pl incl}} : -as]
        ⟦-ader⟧ : [V, {{sbj 2pl}} : -ader]
        ⟦-ar⟧ :   [V, {{sbj 3pl masc}} : -ar]
    c. Special subject-agreement rules
        ⟦-aŋ⟧ :   [V, {{sbj 1sg}} : -aŋ]
        ⟦-ik⟧ :   [V, {{sbj 3pl fem}} : -ik]
        ⟦-iŋ⟧ :   [V, {{sbj 3pl neut}} : -iŋ]
    d. Present-perfect rule
        ⟦-na⟧ :   [V, {perf} : -na]

(14) Group 1 (= composites of the subject-agreement rules in (13b,c) with rule ⟦-t⟧ in (13a))
    (⟦-ay⟧ ∘ ⟦-t⟧) :   [V, {pret {sbj 2sg}} : -t-ay]
    (⟦-at⟧ ∘ ⟦-t⟧) :   [V, {pret {sbj 3sg}} : -t-at]
    (⟦-an⟧ ∘ ⟦-t⟧) :   [V, {pret {sbj 3sg masc}} : -t-an]
    (⟦-ap⟧ ∘ ⟦-t⟧) :   [V, {pret {sbj 1pl excl}} : -t-ap]
    (⟦-as⟧ ∘ ⟦-t⟧) :   [V, {pret {sbj 1pl incl}} : -t-as]
    (⟦-ader⟧ ∘ ⟦-t⟧) : [V, {pret {sbj 2pl}} : -t-ader]
    (⟦-ar⟧ ∘ ⟦-t⟧) :   [V, {pret {sbj 3pl masc}} : -t-ar]
    (⟦-aŋ⟧ ∘ ⟦-t⟧) :   [V, {pret {sbj 1sg}} : -t-aŋ]
    (⟦-ik⟧ ∘ ⟦-t⟧) :   [V, {pret {sbj 3pl fem}} : -t-ik]
    (⟦-iŋ⟧ ∘ ⟦-t⟧) :   [V, {pret {sbj 3pl neut}} : -t-iŋ]

(15) Group 2 (= the ⟦-na⟧ rule in (13d) and composites of the special subject-agreement rules in (13c) with ⟦-na⟧)
    (⟦-aŋ⟧ ∘ ⟦-na⟧) : [V, {perf {sbj 1sg}} : -aŋ]
    (⟦-ik⟧ ∘ ⟦-na⟧) : [V, {perf {sbj 3pl fem}} : -ik]
    (⟦-iŋ⟧ ∘ ⟦-na⟧) : [V, {perf {sbj 3pl neut}} : -iŋ]

(16) FER patterns for the Pengo verb forms in Table 11.2
    a. Where ⟨Z, σ⟩ is a past-tense form cell, the FER for ⟨Z, σ⟩ is the narrowest applicable rule in Group 1.
    b. Where ⟨Z, σ⟩ is a present-perfect form cell, the FER for ⟨Z, σ⟩ is $(R_2 \circ R_1)$, where R_1 and R_2 are, respectively, the narrowest applicable rules in Groups 1 and 2.

Table 11.3 *The morphotactics of two Pengo verb forms*

(a)	Form cell:	⟨huṛ, {{sbj 2sg} pret perf}⟩	'you (sg.) have seen'
	↓		
	FER	(⟦-na⟧ ∘ (⟦-ay⟧ ∘ ⟦-t⟧)) : [V, {pret perf {sbj 2sg}} : -tayna]	
	↓		
	Realized cell:	⟨huṛtayna, {{sbj 2sg} pret perf}⟩	
(b)	Form cell:	⟨huṛ, {{sbj 1sg} pret perf}⟩	'I have seen'
	↓		
	FER	((⟦-aŋ⟧ ∘ ⟦-na⟧) ∘ (⟦-aŋ⟧ ∘ ⟦-t⟧)) : [V, {pret perf {sbj 1sg}} : -taŋnaŋ]	
	↓		
	Realized cell:	⟨huṛtaŋnaŋ, {{sbj 1sg} pret perf}⟩	

Table 11.4 *Reconstructed serial verbs in Proto-Pengo*

		Singular		Plural
1		*huṛ -t-aŋ man-n-aŋ	excl	*huṛ -t-as man-n-as
			incl	*huṛ -t-ap man-n-ap
2		*huṛ -t-ay man-n-ay		*huṛ -t-ader man-n-ader
3	m	*huṛ -t-an man-n-an		*huṛ -t-ar man-n-ar
	f	*huṛ -t-at man-n-at		*huṛ -t-ik man-n-ik
	n			*huṛ -t-iŋ man-n-iŋ

(Steever 1993: 78)

In this analysis, the perfect forms *huṛtayna* 'you (sg.) have seen' and *huṛtaŋnaŋ* 'I have seen' have the morphotactic analyses in Table 11.3. Given that the second-person singular rule ⟦-ay⟧ is not a "special" subject-agreement rule, it only applies once in the definition of *huṛtayna*, as a dependent on the preterite rule ⟦-t⟧ (part (a) of Table 11.3). By contrast, the first-person singular rule ⟦-aŋ⟧ is a "special" subject-agreement rule; it therefore applies twice in the definition of *huṛtaŋnaŋ*, once as a dependent on the preterite rule ⟦-t⟧ and again as a dependent on the present-perfect rule ⟦-na⟧ (part (b) of Table 11.3).

Drawing on comparative evidence from Pengo's sister languages (Goṇḍi, Koṇḍa, Kūi, Kūvi, and Parji), Steever (1993: 78) suggests that the Pengo paradigm in Table 11.2 descends from a serial verb construction comprising a main verb in the past tense (with *-t*) and the auxiliary **man* 'be' in the nonpast tense (with *-n*), as in Table 11.4; these syntactic structures then undergo the series of historical changes exemplified in Table 11.5, eventuating in the morphotactic patterns of the Pengo present-perfect inflection.

11.1 Formulaic Rule Combinations

Table 11.5 *Univerbation and morphological simplification in Pengo*

2pl	3pl fem	Process
*huṛ -t-ader man-n-ader	*huṛ -t-ik man-n-ik	(Proto-Pengo reconstruction)
huṛ -t-ader-man-n-ader	huṛ -t-ik-man-n-ik	Auxiliary contraction
huṛ -t-ader-ma-n-ader	huṛ -t-ik-ma-n-ik	Nasal degemination
huṛ -t-ader-ma-n-a	—	Affix truncation
huṛ -t-ader-n-a	huṛ -t-ik-n-ik	Auxiliary verb deletion

(Steever 1993: 81f.)

The synchronic rule combinations embodying the (dependent ∘ carrier) patterns in (14) and (15) involve nothing more than ordinary rule composition, but their formulaicity is an effect not merely of frequency, but of the synthetic pattern of double agreement (16b) that resulted from the diachronic reanalysis of a serial-verb construction.

11.1.3 Semantically Noncompositional Rule Combinations

Idioms (e.g. *over the hill, sure as shooting*) are the clearest examples of formulaic language (Swinney & Cutler 1979; Gibbs & Gonzales 1985; Gibbs et al. 1989; Wray 2002: 4). If the meaning of a word combination isn't compositionally computable from the meanings of its component parts, language users must store that combination with its special meaning. In a language's morphotactics, a holistic rule combination – a combination that expresses content that cannot be attributed to either of its component rules – is similarly formulaic. For example, the Breton rule (17a) (= the FER for verb forms such as *kar-o-mp* 'we love') expresses the present indicative even though neither of the component rules in (17b,c) does: separately, these rules both apply in forms in other tenses (e.g. *kar-o-t* 'you [PL] will love', *kar-i-mp* 'we will love'). As was seen in Sections 6.1–6.2, Breton verb inflection presents a number of holistic combinations comparable to (17a); it is plausible to assume that in view of their lack of compositionality, such rule combinations are stored.

(17) a. Ⓢ$_{\{\text{ind prs}\}}$([[-**mp**]] ∘ [[-**o**]]) : [V, {ind prs 1pl} : -*omp*]
      b. [[-**o**]] : [V, { } : -*o*]
      c. [[-**mp**]] : [V, {1pl} : -*mp*]

Stored, formulaic rule combinations are themselves susceptible to diachronic reanalysis. Such reanalysis may eventuate in affix telescoping (van Marle 1990; Haspelmath 1995; Booij 2005: 273) – the change from a combination of affixational rules into a single, simple rule. Consider now the details of this sort of development.

11.2 Affix Telescoping

Rule combinations that undergo the process of affix telescoping do so as the effect of a decrease in what I shall call their **combinatory transparency**. Developing the ideas in Stump (2022), I assume that combinatory transparency is multifaceted, hence that a formulaic rule combination may exhibit varying degrees of combinatory transparency. Given a combination C of an outer rule R_2 with an inner rule R_1, the combinatory transparency of C is the extent to which C exhibits the four characteristics in (18).

(18)   Characteristics of combinatory transparency
Where C is a combination of rule R_2 with rule R_1, C is combinatorily transparent to the extent that it exhibits the following four characteristics:
   a. *Separability.* There is no necessary dependency between the application of R_1 and that of R_2.
   b. *Phonological transparency.* The form resulting from the application of C is the predicted combination of R_1's phonology with that of R_2.
   c. *Semantic transparency.* The content expressed by C is the combined content[5] expressed by rules R_1 and R_2.
   d. *Domain transparency.* If X is in the domain-of-definition of rule R_1 and the result of applying R_1 to X is in the domain-of-definition of rule R_2, then X is in the domain-of-definition of C.

The composite ($[\![\text{-ly}]\!] \circ [\![\text{-ish}]\!]$) in (19) possesses all four of these characteristics. First, it is separable (characteristic (18a)) because there is no direct dependency between the application of the rules $[\![\text{-ish}]\!]$ and $[\![\text{-ly}]\!]$ in (20) and (21): besides applying together in the derivation of word forms such as *fiendishly*, they also apply independently of one another in the derivation of various word forms (e.g. *fiendish* and *quickly*). The composite in (19) is also phonologically transparent (characteristic (18b)) because the form *fiendishly* that results from the application of (19) to the triplet ⟨L, *fiend*, N⟩ is the same as the form that results from the successive application of (20) and (21) to this triplet. The composite ($[\![\text{-ly}]\!] \circ [\![\text{-ish}]\!]$) exhibits semantic transparency (characteristic (18c)) because the content that it expresses in the definition of a word form such as *fiendishly* (that of a manner adverb related to the denotation of the base noun) is the combined content expressed by $[\![\text{-ish}]\!]$

---

[5] Stump (2017b, 2017c) argues that the manner of combination is unification rather than set union.

and ⟦**-ly**⟧. Finally, the composite (⟦**-ly**⟧ ∘ ⟦**-ish**⟧) exhibits domain transparency (characteristic (18d)), since its domain-of-definition is that of ⟦**-ish**⟧, that is, ⟦**-ish**⟧ potentiates ⟦**-ly**⟧.

(19)   (⟦**-ly**⟧ ∘ ⟦**-ish**⟧) : [μ_{20} ⇒ Manner Adv : *-ishly*]
        Representative member of μ_{20}: ⟨L, *fiend*, Noun⟩

(20)   ⟦**-ish**⟧ : [μ_{20} ⇒ Relational Adj : *-ish*]
        Representative member of μ_{20}: ⟨L, *fiend*, Noun⟩

(21)   ⟦**-ly**⟧ : [μ_{21} ⇒ Manner Adv : *-ly*]
        Representative members of μ_{21}: ⟨L, *quick*, Adj⟩, ⟨L, *fiendish*, Relational Adj⟩

If the process of affix telescoping is seen as the effect of a decrease in a rule combination's combinatory transparency, then this is clearly not a monolithic process but a diachronic correspondence whose starting point (22a) and endpoint (22c) are linked by the potentially complex transitional phase (22b); cf. Stump (2022).

(22)   The stages of affix telescoping
        a.   Starting point. Two successive rules of affixation constitute a formulaic combination.
        b.   Transitional phase. The combination exhibits an increasing deviation from the characteristics of combinatory transparency in (18).
        c.   Endpoint. The rule sequence is reanalyzed as a simple rule.

We have already seen examples at stage (22a), in which a rule combination is formulaic either

- by virtue of the sheer frequency of the affix sequence that it defines;
- because it embodies a special (not purely compositional) pattern, for example that of a holistic combination, an aggregation, or a counterpotentiation; or
- because it defines a noncanonical pattern, that of periodic multiple exponence.

In the transitional phase (22b) of the stages of affix telescoping, a rule combination exhibits an increasing degree of deviation from the characteristics of combinatory transparency in (18). Consider some examples of deviation from these characteristics.

A combination of rule R_2 with rule R_1 deviates from the characteristic (18a) of separability when the application of one rule develops some kind of dependency on that of the other rule. In the Tundra Nenets forms in (23), the nominative/accusative dual is expressed by two alternative rules whose choice depends on whether there is a following rule expressing a possessor: if there is, the 〚-xøyu〛 rule is used, as in (23b); otherwise, the 〚-xøh〛 rule is used, as in (23a) (Salminen 1997: 118). By the same token, the forms in (24) show that a second-person singular possessor is expressed by two alternative rules whose choice depends on whether there is a preceding rule of case suffixation: if there is, the 〚-tø〛 rule is used, as in (24b); otherwise (i.e. in the nominative singular, which is unmarked), the 〚-rø〛 rule is used, as in (24a) (Salminen 1997: 125). Thus, the composite (〚-tø〛 ∘ 〚-xøyu〛) in (24b) is not fully separable: the second-person singular possessor rule 〚-tø〛 doesn't apply on its own, but only in combination with 〚-xøyu〛 or with some other case rule, and the nominative/accusative dual rule 〚-xøyu〛 doesn't apply on its own, but only in combination with 〚-tø〛 or with some other possessor rule.

(23) a. the rule 〚-xøh〛
/ngøno-xøh/ (→ [ngønox°h])
boat-NOM/ACC.DU
'two boats'
b. the composite (〚-nø〛 ∘ 〚-xøyu〛)
/ngøno-xøyu-nø/ (→ [ngønoxøyun°])
boat-NOM/ACC.DU-POSS:1SG
'my two boats'

(Salminen 1997: 120, 126)

(24) a. the rule 〚-rø〛
/ngøno-rø/ (→ [ngønor°])
boat-POSS:2SG
'your (sg.) boat' (nom. sg.)
b. the composite (〚-tø〛 ∘ 〚-xøyu〛)
/ngøno-xøyu-tø/ (→ [ngønoxøyud°])
boat-NOM/ACC.DU-POSS:2SG
'your (sg.) two boats'

(Salminen 1997: 125f.)

A comparable example from English involves words of Latin origin containing the formative *-ific*. The large majority of these are nominalizations in *-ation*, in which *-ific* serves as a kind of combining form for the verb-deriving suffix *-ify*, as in (25); but as (26) shows, there are also a small number of adjectives in *-ific*, only some of which are derivatives of verbs in *-ify*. Thus, if a distinction is drawn between the rules 〚-ific〛 and 〚-ify〛, then the rule combination defining words in *-ification* is not fully separable, given that *-ific* is largely restricted to combinations with *-ation*.

(25) Nominalizations of verbs in *-ify*
amplification   *glorification*   *personification*
beautification *justification*   *purification*
clarification   *magnification*   *qualification*
exemplification *notification*   *ratification*
falsification   *nullification*   *simplification*

(26) Adjectives in *-ific*
beatific *honorific* *pacific*   *scientific* *specific*
calorific *horrific*   *prolific* *soporific*   *terrific*

A combination of two rules of affixation deviates from the characteristic (18b) of phonological transparency when the pronunciation of the combination takes on a special form. In my speech, for example, the suffix *-ful* loses its syllabicity in certain forms resulting from application the composite (⟦**-ly**⟧ ∘ ⟦**-ful**⟧). In general, these are forms in which *-ful* is preceded by an open unstressed syllable, as in *beautifully* /ˈbju.tɪ.fli/, *mercifully* /ˈmɝ.sɪ.fli/, and *powerfully* /ˈpaʊ.wɚ.fli/; in other contexts, *-ful* tends to retain its syllabicity, as in *delightfully* /dɪ.ˈlaɪt.fə.li/, *effortfully* /ˈɛ.fɚt.fə.li/, and *gleefully* /ˈgli.fə.li/. (Note, however, the loss of syllabicity in *awfully* /ˈɔ.fli/.)

As we have already seen (Chapter 7), holistic combinations are rule combinations that deviate from the characteristic (18c) of semantic transparency. We have also seen that counterpotentiations (Section 11.2) are rule combinations that deviate from the characteristic (18d) of domain transparency. A merely apparent sort of deviation from (18d) is that of a composite ($R_2 \circ R_1$) that applies to members of R_1's domain-of-definition to which R_1 has no history of applying; an example of this sort is the composite ((⟦**-ion**⟧ ∘ ⟦**-ate**⟧) ∘ ⟦**-ize**⟧), which facilitates the formation of nouns like *Walmartization* for which no corresponding verb in *-ize* is in regular use. Given that *Walmartize* is at least a potential verb, it would be inaccurate to say that *Walmartization* reflects a deviation from domain transparency; even so, the incidence of cases of this kind might be seen as a kind of baby step toward affix telescoping.

Once a rule combination has deviated sufficiently from combinatory transparency, it becomes a candidate for reanalysis as a simple rule, as in (22c). The central problem is therefore that of deciding what counts as a sufficient degree of deviation. This is, in fact, a question that arises fairly frequently in the analysis of a language's derivational morphology. In English morphology, it's a question that arises in connection with a number of suffixes, most prominently the suffixes *-ical*, *-istic*, *-ation*, and *-ician*. Though all of these surely arose historically as an effect of rule combination, what is their synchronic status in present-day English? Have they undergone affix telescoping to become simple affixes? I think that there are good reasons to conclude that although these combinations are on a path to affix telescoping, none of them has yet become a simple suffix. Consider each of them in turn in light of each of the four characteristics of combinatory transparency in (18).

11.2.1   -ic-al
Bauer et al. (2013: 289, 318–320) regard *-ical* as a telescoping of *-ic* and *-al*; that is, they treat *-ical* as a single suffix rather than as a synchronic combination of *-ic* and *-al*. In support of this analysis, they cite two kinds of evidence, showing in effect that *-ical* exhibits neither the characteristic of semantic transparency in (18c) nor that of domain transparency in (18d).

To be sure, the meaning of *historic* 'important as a part of history' is not a part of the meaning of *historical* 'pertaining to history', but this reflects a difference in lexical meaning (Section 2.1).[6] The rules ⟦**-ic**⟧ and ⟦**-al**⟧ themselves are very light in their semantic content, a fact reflected by the virtual synonymy of *cyclic* and *cyclical* or *satiric* and *satirical*. To argue that the combination of ⟦**-ic**⟧ and ⟦**-al**⟧ fails to exhibit semantic transparency, one would have to show that the content expressed by *-ical* in *cyclical* is not the same as the combination of the content of *-ic* in *cyclic* with that of *-al* in deadjectival derivatives such as *transcendental*; but this is not at all obvious.

The combination of ⟦**-ic**⟧ and ⟦**-al**⟧ does, however, deviate from combinatory transparency with respect to the characteristic of domain transparency. Note that there are two types of divergences from the pattern of *cycle*, *cyclic*, and *cyclical*: on one hand, there is no **basical* alongside *base* and *basic*; on the other hand, there is no **whimsic* alongside *whimsy* and *whimsical*. The absence of **basical* does not itself constitute a deviation from domain transparency, but simply shows that ⟦**-ic**⟧ does not potentiate ⟦**-al**⟧. By contrast, the absence of **whimsic* does signal a deviation from domain transparency. Even so, it is not clear that this deviation is sufficient evidence of affix telescoping; it might instead simply be seen as showing that ⟦**-ic**⟧ and ⟦**-al**⟧ enter into two combinations – a composite (⟦**-al**⟧ ∘ ⟦**-ic**⟧) that defines derivatives such as

---

[6] Marchand (1966: 185–188) and Dixon (2014: 251f.) identify a number of additional lexical semantic tendencies that distinguish the use of *-ic* and *-ical*.

cyclical and *historical* and a counterpotentiation (⟦-al⟧ CP₁₃ ⟦-ic⟧) that defines derivatives such as *whimsical* and *nonsensical*.

The conclusion that *-ical* is an expression of a synchronic combination of the ⟦-ic⟧ and ⟦-al⟧ rules is supported by characteristics of separability and phonological transparency in (18a,b). The combination of ⟦-ic⟧ and ⟦-al⟧ exhibits separability, as evidenced by derivatives such as *scenic* and *tribal*. It also exhibits phonological transparency, since (i) the pronunciation /ɪkəl/ of *-ical* in, for example, *whimsical* is the expected combination of the pronunciation /ɪk/ of *-ic* in, for example, *scenic* with the pronunciation /əl/ of *-al* in, for example, *tribal*; and (ii) the morphophonological and prosodic effects of *-ical* on the stem with which it joins (e.g. *sýntax* → *syntáct-ical*, /saɪkl/ → /sɪklɪkl/) are the same as are produced by the successive suffixation of *-ic* and *-al* (*sýntax* → *syntáct-ic* → *syntáctic-al*, /saɪkl/ → /sɪklɪk/ → /sɪklɪkl/).

In summary, a rule introducing *-ical* need not be stipulated separately from the rules ⟦-ic⟧ and ⟦-al⟧ since the phonological and semantic characteristics of *-ical* follow from the separable composite (⟦-al⟧ ∘ ⟦-ic⟧) and its deviation from domain transparency can be attributed to the coexisting counterpotentiation (⟦-al⟧ CP₁₃ ⟦-ic⟧).

11.2.2   *-ist-ic*

Bauer et al. (2013: 289, 321) suggest treating *-istic* as a simple suffix because of its lack of what I am calling domain transparency (characteristic (18d)). Note that there are two types of divergences from the pattern of *capital*, *capitalist*, and *capitalistic*: on the one hand, *racistic is not in use alongside *race* and *racist*; on the other hand, there is no *characterist alongside *character* and *characteristic*. The absence of *racistic is not obviously a deviation from domain transparency; it seems, if anything, to be a potential word (Section 1.5.7). On the other hand, *characterist is a definite deviation from domain transparency, but like *whimsic, it needn't be seen as sufficient evidence of affix telescoping, but may instead be seen as involving counterpotentiation. That is, ⟦-ic⟧ seems to combine with ⟦-ist⟧ in two ways: the composite (⟦-ic⟧ ∘ ⟦-ist⟧) defines derivatives such as *capitalistic* and *artistic* (which exhibit domain transparency) and the counterpotentiation (⟦-ic⟧ CP₁₇ ⟦-ist⟧) defines derivatives such as *characteristic* and *cannibalistic* (which deviate from domain transparency).

Other evidence provides further support for the assumption that *-istic* is a synchronic expression of rule combination. The combination of ⟦-ist⟧ and ⟦-ic⟧ exhibits separability (characteristic (18a)), as derivatives such as *pianist* and *scenic* show, and it exhibits phonological transparency (characteristic

(18b)), given that the pronunciation /ˈɪstɪk/ of *-istic* in e.g. *characteristic* is the expected combination of the pronunciation /ɪst/ of *-ist* in e.g. *pianist* with the pronunciation and prosodic effect /–́ɪk/ of *-ic* in e.g. *angélic*.

At the same time, the combination of ⟦**-ist**⟧ and ⟦**-ic**⟧ exhibits semantic transparency (characteristic (18c)) to only a limited extent. The issue is complicated by the versatility of the ⟦**-ist**⟧ rule, whose derivatives serve in some cases as either personal nouns or adjectives (e.g. *racist*: *those racists*, *as racist as ever*) and in other cases only as personal nouns (e.g. *artist*: *those artists*, **as artist as ever*). In those cases in which X*istic* can be seen as deriving from an adjective X*ist* (e.g. *capitalist* [*economy*], *fascist* [*ideology*]), X*istic* and X*ist* are very close in their meaning, so that the combination of ⟦**-ist**⟧ and ⟦**-ic**⟧ might be said to exhibit semantic transparency. But when the related form X*ist* is, unambiguously, a noun referring to a kind of person (e.g. *artist*, *novelist*), X*istic* differs from X*ist* in that its meaning does not imply reference to that kind of person. For instance, the semantic relation between *art* and *artistic* or between *novel* and *novelistic* is very much like the semantic relation between *sculpture* and *sculptural* (in which the meaning of *sculptor* has no direct role) or between *opera* and *operatic* (in which composers or performers of opera have no direct role). For that reason, the combination of ⟦**-ist**⟧ and ⟦**-ic**⟧ is less transparent semantically in forms such as *artistic*, which is semantically related to *art* more than to *artist*. At the same time, many adjectives in *-istic* are semantically related to nouns in *-ism*: *journalistic* 'pertaining to journalism', *cannibalistic* 'pertaining to cannibalism', and so on. In such cases of "cross-formation" (Becker 1993), the combination of ⟦**-ist**⟧ and ⟦**-ic**⟧ is less transparent semantically, since it defines forms whose meaning is lexically related to that of forms with contrasting morphology.

These facts suggest that *-istic* is not yet a telescoped affix, but that it is farther along the path toward that status than *-ical*.

11.2.3   *-at-ion*

Bauer et al. (2013: 201f.), Dixon (2014: 337–339), and Jackendoff & Audring (2020: 193) agree in regarding *-ation* as but one variant of a "multi-form suffix" having several additional realizations (*-(i)cation*, *-ion*, *-ition*, *-iation*, *-sion*, *-ution*, and *-tion*); they therefore seem to agree that in contemporary English, *-ation* does not express a combination of ⟦**-ate**⟧ and ⟦**-ion**⟧. Yet, the combination of ⟦**-ate**⟧ and ⟦**-ion**⟧ is combinatorially transparent with respect to at least two of the characteristics in (18). They clearly exhibit separability (characteristic (18a)), as derivatives such as *hyphenate* and *rebellion* show.

They also exhibit phonological transparency (characteristic (18b)). The latter fact is complicated by the prosodic and morphophonological modifications associated with ⟦-**ion**⟧: ⟦-**ion**⟧ imposes stem-final stress and causes the spirantization and palatalization of a stem-final /t/ with a concomitant loss of its own suffix-initial /j/ (e.g. *execute* /ˈɛksəkjut/ → *execution* /ɛksəˈkjuʃən/). But these modifications are fully in evidence in the pronunciation of *-ation* /ˈeʃən/.

In order to address the question of whether the combination of ⟦-**ate**⟧ and ⟦-**ion**⟧ exhibits the characteristics of semantic transparency and domain transparency in (18c,d), it is important to recall that ⟦-**ate**⟧ serves three different functions in English derivation (Sections 2.1.2 and 10.2.2): (i) ⟦-**ate**⟧ derives verbs from nouns and adjectives (e.g. *hyphen* → *hyphenate*, *active* → *activate*); (ii) ⟦-**ate**⟧ serves a thematizing function for verbs such as *insinuate*; and (iii) ⟦-**ate**⟧ serves to form a combining stem for the nominalization of verbs such as *vary* (→ *variation*, but *variate). In its true derivational function (i) and its thematizing function (ii), ⟦-**ate**⟧ potentiates the nominalizing rule ⟦-**ion**⟧. On the other hand, the counterpotentiation (⟦-**ion**⟧ $\boxed{\text{CP}}_{30}$ ⟦-**ate**⟧) defines nominalizations in which *-ate* serves function (iii). For verbs in which ⟦-**ate**⟧ serves function (i) or (ii), the composite (⟦-**ion**⟧ ∘ ⟦-**ate**⟧) is clearly domain transparent; for verbs in function (iii), the counterpotentiation (⟦-**ion**⟧ $\boxed{\text{CP}}_{30}$ ⟦-**ate**⟧) is, just as clearly, not domain transparent.

Whether these combinations of ⟦-**ate**⟧ and ⟦-**ion**⟧ are semantically transparent is a more delicate question. It is clear that *hyphenate* and *hyphen* differ in meaning, but part of this difference is a lexical matter. To *hyphenate* something means to interrupt it with one or more hyphens; but to *activate* something is to render it active or operative; to *assassinate* someone is to act against them as an assassin; to *orchestrate* a piece of music is to organize it for performance by an orchestra; and so on. The heterogeneousness of these meanings is a lexical matter; cf. Section 2.1. What these verbs in *-ate* have in common, semantically, is that they are all transitive verbs relating to actions in some way associated with the sense of the base lexeme from which they derive; no more semantic content than this need be specifically associated with the rule ⟦-**ate**⟧. Thus, the composite (⟦-**ion**⟧ ∘ ⟦-**ate**⟧) that defines derivatives such as *hyphenation* and the counterpotentiation (⟦-**ion**⟧ $\boxed{\text{CP}}_{30}$ ⟦-**ate**⟧) that defines derivatives such as *explanation* are both semantically transparent, but this transparency doesn't amount to much, given the semantic underspecification of the ⟦-**ate**⟧ rule.

These considerations suggest that *-ation* can be reasonably regarded as the expression of one or another synchronic combination of ⟦-**ate**⟧ and ⟦-**ion**⟧.

11.2.4 -ic-ian

The combination of ⟦**-ian**⟧ and ⟦**-ic**⟧$_N$ exhibits separability (characteristic (18a)), as the derivatives *grammarian* and *rhetoric* show; recall that the rule ⟦**-ic**⟧$_N$ derives a noun or noun stem in *-ic* (as in *music* or *physic-s*), and must therefore be distinguished from the rule ⟦**-ic**⟧ that derives adjectives like *scenic*.

Phonologically, the combination of ⟦**-ian**⟧ and ⟦**-ic**⟧$_N$ is not fully transparent, since the effect of ⟦**-ian**⟧ on the final /k/ of *-ic* (which it converts to /ʃ/, with loss of its own /j/) is not an effect that is otherwise observable with ⟦**-ian**⟧ (though ⟦**-ian**⟧ effects similar palatalizations of other obstruents, cf. *Parisian, Venetian, Martian*). Still, the stress pattern on nouns in *-ician* conforms to the general pattern of nouns in *-ian* (e.g. *beáuty* → *beaut-íc-ian*, *réptile* → *reptíl-ian*), contributing to its phonological transparency (characteristic (18b)).

The semantic transparency of the combination of ⟦**-ian**⟧ and ⟦**-ic**⟧$_N$ is complicated by a special peculiarity of ⟦**-ian**⟧ noted earlier (Section 10.2.1): although ⟦**-ian**⟧ ordinarily derives both nouns and adjectives (*Egyptians, Egyptian music*), it operates on a noun denoting a sphere of human activity to derive a noun denoting a practitioner of that activity (e.g. *grammar* → *grammarian*); a noun so derived cannot function as an adjective (**a grammarian article*). Once this peculiarity of ⟦**-ian**⟧ is taken into account – along with the fact that the *-ic* in *logic* and *phonetics* is that of the noun-forming ⟦**-ic**⟧$_N$ rule – it is apparent that *-ic-ian* possesses the characteristic (18c) of semantic transparency.

The absence of **beautic* alongside *beautician* reflects a deviation from domain transparency (characteristic (18d)), but needn't be seen as evidence that *-ic-ian* has telescoped into a simple affix. Instead, ⟦**-ic**⟧$_N$ and ⟦**-ian**⟧ seem to combine both as a composite (⟦**-ian**⟧ ∘ ⟦**-ic**⟧$_N$) and as a counterpotentiation (⟦**-ian**⟧ $\boxed{\text{CP}}_{23}$ ⟦**-ic**⟧$_N$), accounting for both *logician/logic* and *beautician/*beautic*; see Section 10.2.1.

Together, these facts suggest that *-ician* remains a formulaic affix sequence in contemporary English. Overall, the cases of English *-ical*, *-istic*, *-ation*, and *-ician* show that even if a rule combination doesn't possess all four of the characteristics of combinatory transparency in (18), it can't necessarily be assumed to have succumbed to affix telescoping. The clearest examples of affix telescoping are cases in which the decay of the characteristics in (18) has run its full course.

A case in point[7] is the English ⟦**-ate**⟧ rule. In Medieval Latin, many adjectives were converted to first-conjugation verbs with a causative meaning, for example *validus* 'strong, effective, valid' (stem *valid-*) → *validāre* 'to

---

[7] Stump (2022) discusses the English diminutive suffixes *-let* and *-ling* as fully realized instances of affix telescoping.

make valid' (stem *valid-ā-*, where *ā* is the theme vowel of the first conjugation). The perfect passive participle of such verbs had a stem in *-t*, for example *valid-ā-t-*, an expression of the Latin rule combination (⟦-t⟧ ∘ ⟦-ā⟧). Many Latin first-conjugation verbs were first borrowed into English in their perfect passive participial form, whose use was then extended to other verbal functions (Marchand 1966: 199ff.); the incidence of borrowed adjective/causative verb stem-pairs such as *valid-*/*validāt-* therefore led (⟦-t⟧ ∘ ⟦-ā⟧) to be reanalyzed as a simple derivational rule, preserved in Modern English as ⟦**-ate**⟧. The ⟦**-ate**⟧ rule is fully telescoped: because it is not separable into more basic rules, it cannot be said to exhibit phonological, semantic, or domain transparency. At the same time, the ⟦**-ate**⟧ rule has an important place in Modern English derivational morphology, having come to serve three distinct functions (Sections 2.1.2 and 10.2.2).

11.3   Conclusion

The evidence discussed here shows that morphological rule combinations are related to morphological simplicity in more than one way. Initially, one might expect that rule combinations could complicate a language's morphology. In fact, they contribute to its structural simplicity, making it possible to express diverse content with a small number of simple rules combined in various systematic ways. Moreover, they contribute to a morphological system's processing simplicity, allowing formulaic morphological patterns to be stored and accessed as units. The characteristics that contribute to a rule combination's formulaicity in a language's morphotactics are like those that contribute to a word combination's formulaicity in syntax; such characteristics include frequency, conventionality, and noncompositional content. Diachronically, formulaic rule combinations are themselves subject to simplifying changes whose ultimate effect is to telescope them into simple rules.

The rule-combining approach to exponence-driven morphotactics has important implications for morphological theory. On one hand, it suggests a number of ways in which existing theories might be enhanced. At the same time, it raises important questions about the viability of certain current approaches to modeling a language's morphotactics. I discuss these implications in the next chapter.

12 *Rule-combining Morphotactics and Morphological Theories*

Situating the rule-combining approach to morphotactics in a wider theoretical context, I summarize its implications for the architecture of Paradigm Function Morphology (Section 12.1) and for schema unification in Construction Morphology (Section 12.2). I further contrast the exponence-driven conception of morphotactics embodied by the rule-combining approach with the very different word-skeletal approach to morphotactics (Section 12.3), drawing attention to two advantages of the rule-combining approach. First, it affords a more parsimonious inventory of morphological operations than is assumed in Distributed Morphology (Section 12.4). Second, it avoids the cumbersome theoretical commitments of Information-based Morphology (the assumptions of position-based ordering, rule anchoring, and rule monopolism), which entail numerous complications in the analysis of a language's morphotactics. The distinct assumptions on which the rule-combining approach rests (those of combination-based ordering, unanchored rules, and rule pluralism) afford morphotactic analyses that are at once simpler and more explanatory (Section 12.5). I summarize in Section 12.6.

12.1 Paradigm Function Morphology

The rule-combining approach to morphotactics draws on the theoretical assumptions of Paradigm Function Morphology (PFM). This theory has evolved in numerous ways since its inception in Stump (1991); its most substantial evolutive change is the version articulated by Stump (2016), whose architecture rests on the distinction between content paradigms and form paradigms. The ideas developed here take this version as their context.

As noted in Section 2.2, the rule-combining approach to morphotactics constitutes a further step in the theory's growth. Following Anderson (1992), Stump (2001, 2016) assumes that rules of inflectional exponence are organized into ordered blocks such that rules belonging to the same block are mutually exclusive in their application and that the order of application of rules belonging to separate blocks is determined by the ordering of the blocks themselves. The rule-combining approach to morphotactics dispenses with the idea that an inflected word form is defined through the application of a string of rules, one from each ordered block. In the rule-combining approach, each inflected form is instead defined through the application of a single rule, its full exponence rule (FER), which may consist of smaller rules in combination.

Rules of exponence often fall into groups such that the members of one group combine in the same way with members of other groups; to this extent, rule groups may be seen as taking the place of rule blocks. But rule groups are not ordered; rules belonging to the same group may combine with other rules in more than one possible order. Moreover, the members of a given rule group may be heterogeneous in that some may be simple rules while others are themselves combinations, and such combinations may themselves involve different modes of combination.

The rule-combining approach to morphotactics therefore does not substantially change the theory of PFM presented in Stump (2016). It does, however, add a more refined architecture of rule interaction, in which rules of exponence may enter into various types of binary combinations which are themselves available for further combination. Consequently, each inflected word form is defined by a single FER, and each of a language's FERs acts as a subfunction of its paradigm function.

12.2 Construction Morphology

In Construction Morphology, morphological schemas enter into two kinds of combinations. Second-order schemas relate the words defined by one schema to those defined by a distinct schema (Booij 2010: 31ff.; Booij & Masini 2015; cf. the sister schemas of Jackendoff & Audring 2020: 107ff.); for example, the second-order schema in (1) expresses the nondirectional correspondence between nouns in *-ist* (*capitalist*, *altruist*) and nouns in *-ism* (*capitalism*, *altruism*). Construction Morphology also postulates unified schemas, which combine the effects of two smaller schemas into a larger, more specific schema (Booij 2010: 42ff., 163ff.; Kempf & Hartmann 2018). Unlike a second-order schema, which relates words instantiating schema$_1$ to distinct words instantiating schema$_2$, a unified schema defines words in which the effects of schema$_1$ and schema$_2$ are combined. For example, the Dutch schemas in (2) may be unified as (3).

(1) A second-order schema (Booij 2010: 33; Booij & Masini 2015: 50)
⟨[x-ism]$_{Ni}$ ↔ SEM$_i$⟩ ≈ ⟨[x-ist]$_{Nj}$ ↔ [person with property Y related to SEM$_i$]$_j$⟩

(2) Two schemas in Dutch derivational morphology
    a. [[X]$_V$ -*elijk*]$_A$
       Interpretation: (some function of X)
       e.g. *veracht-elijk* 'despicable'
    b. [*on*- [X]$_A$]$_A$
       Interpretation: 'not X'
       e.g. *on-rein* 'unclean'

(3) Unified schema for negative adjectives in Dutch
[*on*- [[X]$_V$ -*elijk*]$_A$]$_A$
Interpretation: 'not (some function of X)'
e.g. *on-aantrekk-elijk* 'unattractive'

Unified schemas are closely comparable to composite rules in the approach to morphotactics proposed here. Thus, given the rules in (4) and (5), the unified schema in (3) is like the composite rule in (6).

(4) ⟦**on-**⟧ : [μ_4 ⇒ Negative adj : *on-*]

    Representative member of μ_4: ⟨L, *rein*, Adj⟩

(5) ⟦**-elijk**⟧ : [μ_5 ⇒ Adj : *-elijk*]

    Representative member of μ_5: ⟨L, *veracht*, Verb⟩

(6) Composite of the rules in (4) and (5)
(⟦**on-**⟧ ∘ ⟦**-elijk**⟧) : [μ_6 ⇒ Negative adj : X → *on*-X-*elijk*]
(where the domain-of-definition μ_6 is the smallest set such that for each triplet t in μ_5, t belongs to μ_6 if and only if the result of applying ⟦**-elijk**⟧ to t belongs to μ_4)

    Representative members of μ_6: ⟨L, *aantrekk*, Verb⟩, ⟨L, *beschrijf*, Verb⟩

Two kinds of evidence have been cited to motivate the postulation of unified schemas in Construction Morphology: the fact that unified schemas make it possible to "bypass" intermediate derivatives that are not in actual use and the fact that a unified schema may express content that is not deducible from either of its component schemas. Booij (2018: 7) cites the Dutch examples in (7) as evidence of the first sort: although the base words in the middle column of (7) are well-formed and interpretable, they are not in actual use; thus, the common negative adjectives in (7) have plausibly arisen directly from the corresponding verbs as an effect of the unified schema (3).

(7)   Evidence for the unified schema (3)
      Verb   Base word   Negative adjective
      beschrijf 'describe' (*beschrijf-elijk*) *on-beschrijf-elijk* 'undescribable'
      doorgrond 'fathom' (*doorgrond-elijk*) *on-doorgrond-elijk* 'unfathomable'
      verget   'forget'   (*verget-elijk*)   *on-verget-elijk*   'unforgettable'
      verzett   'oppose'   (*verzett-elijk*)   *on-verzett-elijk*   'uncompromising'

As an example in which a unified schema possesses holistic semantics, Booij (2007: 40f.) cites the Dutch schema in (8), which combines the nominal schema [[X]$_A$ *heid*]$_N$ with the adjectival schema [[X]$_A$ *ig*]$_A$. Besides accounting for the fact that a noun having the form X-*ig-heid* may (as in (9a)) derive directly from an adjective X without implying that the intermediate adjective X-*ig* is anything more than a potential word, the postulation of the unified schema (8) also accounts for the fact that nouns in -*ig-heid* sometimes have special semantics not deducible from the component schemas [[A] *heid*]$_N$ and [[A] *ig*]$_A$; this semantic peculiarity – that of referring specifically to substances, as in (9b) – is associated directly with (8).

(8)   [[[X]$_A$ *ig*]$_A$ *heid*]$_N$

(9)   Evidence for schema unification (Booij 2007: 41)
           Adjective   Noun in -*ig-heid*
      a.   *flauw* 'silly'   *flauwigheid*   'silliness'
           mal   'silly'   *malligheid*   'silliness'
           naar   'nasty'   *narigheid*   'nastiness'
           slim   'smart'   *slimmigheid*   'smartness'
      b.   *glad*   'slippery'   *glad-ig-heid* 'slippery substance'
           nat   'wet'   *natt-ig-heid* 'wet substance'
           viez   'dirty'   *viez-ig-heid* 'dirty substance'
           zwart 'black'   *zwart-ig-heid* 'black substance'

Unified schemas that possess special semantics resemble the holistic combinations of Chapter 6. Two other kinds of rule combinations discussed here – aggregations and counterpotentiations – are not directly reformulable as unified schemas; this suggests that some schema combinations involve modes of combination different from ordinary unification. Consider first the Swahili rule in (10), an aggregation of the relativized-argument rule (11a) with the tense rule in (11b); in the analysis proposed in Chapter 8, (10) applies as part of the FER defining the verb form *a-taka-ye-soma* 'who will read'. Representing the rules in (11) as the schemas in (12), one might represent the aggregated rule in (10) as the aggregated schema in (13). The interpretation of (13) is the unification of the content of the schemas in (12), but the morphology defined by (13) is the aggregation of that of the schemas in (12).

348 *Rule combining Morphotactics*

(10) An aggregated rule of Swahili verb inflection
⟦**-ye₁**⟧₁₁ Ⓐ ⟦**taka-**⟧₁₁): [V, {–ind fut {rel 3sg nc1}} : *taka-ye-*]

(11) Two rules of Swahili verb inflection (from (28) in Section 8.4)
  a. ⟦**-ye₁**⟧₁₁ : [V, {–ind {rel 3sg nc1}} : *-ye*]
  b. ⟦**taka-**⟧₁₁ : [V, {{rel} fut} : *taka-*]

(12) Schemas corresponding to the rules in (11)
  a. [*taka-* [X]_V]_V
      Interpretation: {{rel} fut}
  b. [X *-ye*]
      Interpretation: {–ind {rel 3sg nc1}}

(13) Aggregation of schema (12b) with schema (12a)
  [*taka-ye-* [X]_V]_V
  Interpretation: {–ind fut {rel 3sg nc1}}

Consider likewise the ⟦**-ate**⟧ and ⟦**-ion**⟧ rules in (14) and (15). As was seen in Section 10.2.2, ⟦**-ate**⟧ and ⟦**-ion**⟧ combine in two ways. The potentiation (⟦**-ion**⟧ Ⓟ ⟦**-ate**⟧) in (16) derives nominalizations such as *hyphenation, activation*, and *insinuation* (each of which corresponds to a verb in *-ate*: *hyphenate, activate, insinuate*). It does not, however, derive nominalizations such as *admiration* and *instrumentation* (neither of which corresponds to a verb in *-ate*: **admirate, *instrumentate*); these nominalizations are instead derived by the counterpotentiation (⟦**-ion**⟧ [CP]₁₇ ⟦**-ate**⟧) in (17).

(14) ⟦**-ate**⟧ : [μ₁₄ ⇒ Verb : *-ate*]

  The ⟦**-ate**⟧ rule has a derivational function for nominal and adjectival members of μ₁₄ (e.g. ⟨L, *hyphen*, Noun⟩, ⟨L, *active*, Adj⟩) but a thematizing function for verbal members of μ₁₄ (e.g. ⟨L, *insinu-*, Verb⟩).

(15) ⟦**-ion**⟧ : [μ₁₅ ⇒ Noun : *-ion*]

  Representative members of μ₁₅: ⟨L, *compress*, Verb⟩, ⟨L, *fuse*, Verb⟩, ⟨L, *select*, Verb⟩

(16) (⟦**-ion**⟧ Ⓟ ⟦**-ate**⟧) : [X, μ₁₄ ⇒ Noun : *-ation*], where μ₁₄ is as in (14).

(17) (⟦**-ion**⟧ [CP]₁₇ ⟦**-ate**⟧) : [X, μ₁₇ ⇒ Noun : *-ation*], where μ₁₇ is disjoint from μ₁₄.

  Representative members of μ₁₇: ⟨L, *admire*, Verb⟩, ⟨L, *instrument*, Noun⟩ (cf. **admirate, *instrumentate*)

In order to account for this dual use of *-ation*, a schema-based approach requires the schemas in (18) to combine in two ways. On one hand, the schemas in (18) may unify as in (19), where the coindexing of the variable

12.3 Word skeletal vs. Exponence driven Morphotactics

'X_1' in (18a) and (19) reflects the potentiation of (18b) by (18a) (i.e. the "embedded productivity" of (18b); Booij 2010: 47ff.); on the other hand, the schemas in (18) may stand in the counterpotentiation relation in (20).

(18) Schemas corresponding to the rules in (14) and (15)
    a. $[[X_1]\text{ -}ate]_V$
        Interpretation: process related to X_1
    b. $[[X]_V\text{ -}ion]_N$
        Interpretation: action or result of X

(19) Unification of the schemas in (18)
     $[[[X_1]\text{ -}ate]_V\text{ -}ion]_N$
     Interpretation: action or result of process related to X_1

(20) Counterpotentiation of schema (18a) by schema (18b)
     $[[[X_2]_{V/N}\text{ -}ate]\text{ -}ion]_N$
     Interpretation: action or result of process related to X_2, where X_1 and X_2 range over disjoint sets

I see no clear obstacle to developing principles of schema combination closely comparable to the principles of rule combination proposed above.

12.3 Word-skeletal vs. Exponence-driven Morphotactics

Theories of morphotactics are of two types. A ***word-skeletal*** theory assumes that a language's grammar defines an abstract skeletal structure for each word form and provides means of fleshing out this structure with specific formatives. An ***exponence-driven*** theory assumes that a word form has no structure apart from what is conferred by the formatives of which it consists.

Word-skeletal theories of morphotactics take a variety of forms. One example is the 'syntax of words' theory proposed by Selkirk (1982), according to which the grammar of English generates structures like Figure 12.1a which it then endows with specific morphemes, as in Figure 12.1b. Distributed Morphology (Embick & Noyer 2001; Arregi & Nevins 2012) is also a

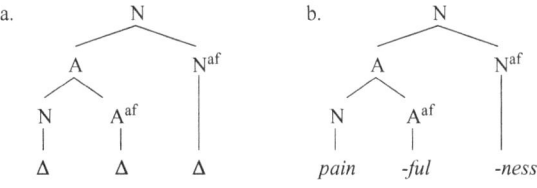

Figure 12.1 *Word skeleta in the 'syntax of words' theory of Selkirk (1982)*

word-skeletal theory, but one in which a word form's skeleton is not, in general, directly defined by constituent-structure rules but results from operations that manipulate constituent-structure trees originating in the language's syntax; here, too, the construction of a word form's skeleton logically precedes the process of "vocabulary insertion" that serves to flesh out its phonological form. The theory of Information-based Morphology (Crysmann & Bonami 2016) is a word-skeletal theory of a rather different sort, in which a language's morphology defines a template of indexed morph positions that serve as a scaffold for combining morphs to yield full word forms.

In exponence-driven theories of morphotactics, a word-form w arising through the application of a sequence S of rules of inflectional or derivational exponence has no complex structure that logically precedes the application of S – no vacant nodes, no indexed morph positions. What are taken for morph positions or affixal nodes in a word-skeletal theory are, in exponence-driven morphotactics, nothing more than an epiphenomenal effect of the application of rules of exponence.

Exponence-driven theories of morphotactics are of various types. Some assume that rules of exponence enter into combinations (Booij 2010; Jackendoff & Audring 2020), while others do not (Anderson 1992; Corbett & Fraser 1993).[1] Those that do assume the existence of rule combinations in general assume the morphotactic holism hypothesis (a combination of rules of exponence may possess characteristics that do not follow from the characteristics of its component rules; Section 1.2); by contrast, the rule-combining approach to morphotactics developed here is the only exponence-driven theory that additionally assumes the morphotactic variety hypothesis (rules of exponence enter into different kinds of combinations possessing different characteristics; Section 1.2).

One possible objection to the exponence-driven perspective is that it necessitates the abandonment of morphological templates, despite the extensive evidence that morphology is sometimes and somehow templatic. This is not a cogent objection. Morphological templates surely exist, but in the rule-combining approach to morphotactics, they exist as the emergent manifestation of patterns of rule combination. In a word form w that exhibits templatic morphology, that template doesn't constitute an aspect of w's structure that logically precedes the application of the combination C of rules that realizes w's morphology; rather, that template is an emergent manifestation of

---

[1] In its earliest incarnations, PFM did not overtly employ rule combinations, but in later versions (Stump 2017a–c, 2019a, 2019c, 2020a, 2021, 2022), rule combinations are explicitly postulated.

C itself. Templatic morphology exists because of the systematic ways in which rules of exponence combine with one another.

Two kinds of evidence favor the rule-combining approach to exponence-driven morphotactics over word-skeletal approaches to morphotactics. First, the rule-combining approach affords a more parsimonious inventory of morphological operations than is necessitated by the assumptions that underlie word-skeletal theories. Second, the dimensions of rule interaction afforded by the rule-combining approach make it possible to capture generalizations that remain elusive in word-skeletal theories. Consider these two sorts of evidence in greater detail.

12.4 A Parsimonious Inventory of Morphological Operations

The representations employed here for rules of inflectional and derivational exponence make essential use of operations. Recall from Section 2.1 that a rule of inflectional exponence has the form in (21), where τ is the property set realized by the rule, f is the operation by means of which τ is realized, and C is the category of forms on which f operates in default applications of the rule; a rule of derivational exponence has the form in (22), where μ is the rule's domain-of-definition, Q is the lexicosemantic category of the derivative lexeme, and f is the operation relating the stem of the base lexeme to that of the derivative lexeme. In either sort of rule, if f is a suffixation operation 'X → X-y' or a prefixation operation 'X → z-X', I have generally followed the abbreviatory convention of representing f simply as -y or as z-.

(21) Format for a rule of inflectional exponence: $[C, \tau : f\,]$

(22) Format for a rule of derivational exponence: $[\mu \Rightarrow Q : f\,]$

The most general representation of morphological rules must involve operations rather than just concatenations, since some morphology is nonconcatenative. But even in the domain of concatenative morphology, it is useful to think of rules as involving operations. Consider the contrast between rule composition and rule aggregation. Where 〚-y〛 and 〚z-〛 are as in (23) and (24), the composite (〚z-〛 ∘ 〚-y〛) is as in (25), whose operation on a stem *abc* prefixes z- to the result of suffixing -y to *abc*: z-*abc*-y. By contrast, the aggregation (〚z-〛 Ⓐ 〚-y〛) is as in (26), whose operation on a stem *abc* suffixes to *abc* the result of prefixing z- to -y: *abc*-z-y. Rules (23)–(26) are all concatenative. In (23), (25), and (26), the directionality of 〚-y〛 remains constant; it is a rule of suffixation. In (24)–(26), the directionality of 〚z-〛 remains constant;

it is a rule of prefixation. What distinguishes (25) from (26) is the prefixation operation's operand: in (25), the prefixation of z- operates on X-y; but in (26), it operates on -y. The distinction between composition and aggregation therefore hinges on reference to an operation and its operand.

(23)   ⟦-y⟧ : [C, ρ : X → suffix(y, X)]

(24)   ⟦z-⟧ : [C, σ : X → prefix(z, X)]

(25)   (⟦z-⟧ ∘ ⟦-y⟧) : [C, [ρ ⊔ σ] : X → prefix(z, suffix(y, X))]

(26)   (⟦z-⟧ Ⓐ ⟦-y⟧) : [C, [ρ ⊔ σ] : X → suffix(prefix(z, y), X)]

In a morphological framework based on operations, it is desirable to have a theory of morphological operations – of what they can and cannot do. The analyses proposed here are based on a rather conservative inventory of operations. Indeed, the simple morphological rules in these analyses are, in large part, rules performing operations of prefixation or suffixation. In a general theory of morphology, these operations should certainly be supplemented by a variety of additional nonconcatenative operations, including ablaut, consonant gradation, suprasegmental modification, reduplication, infixation, and subtraction. At the same time, once one adopts a rule-combining conception of morphotactics, phenomena that might be seen as requiring the postulation of more exotic morphological operations can be seen as involving more ordinary operations.

Word-skeletal approaches to morphotactics sometimes incorporate special operations whose sole motivation is to bring a superficially anomalous sequence of morphs into conformity with an apparently incompatible word skeleton. In Distributed Morphology, operations that copy or move affixes are special operations of this kind, as are "fission" and "fusion" operations that directly modify word skeleta. Zimmermann (2012, 2016) and van Driem (1996) postulate a process of affix copying to account for the pattern of multiple exponence exhibited by Limbu verb forms such as those in (27). But as was seen in Section 3.2, the forms in (27) involve nothing more than ordinary suffixation. They are not unusual because they involve an unusual operation, but rather because they involve an unusual pattern of rule combination, in which the same dependent rule (⟦-ŋ⟧ in (27a), ⟦-m⟧ in (27b)) piggybacks on more than one carrier rule in the definition of the same word form (the rules ⟦-u⟧ and ⟦-si⟧ in (27)).

(27)   Limbu (van Driem 1987: 367–374)
    a.   huʔr-u-ŋ-si-ŋ
        teach-PAT:3-AGT:1SG-PAT:3.NONSG-AGT:1SG
        'I teach them'

b. *a-huʔr-u-m-si-m*
    1-teach-PAT:3-AGT:1/2.PL-PAT:3.NONSG-AGT:1/2.PL
    'we (incl.) teach them'

Embick & Noyer (2001) and Šereikaitė (2017) appeal to an operation of Local Dislocation – and Arregi & Nevins (2012: 255), to a similar operation of reflexive metathesis – to account for the purported shift of the Lithuanian reflexive affix *-si-* from word-initial to post-prefix position in forms such as (28b). No such operation is necessary in the aggregation analysis presented in Section 7.2.2, in which the reflexive ⟦-**si**⟧ rule has suffixational directionality both in prefixless forms such as (29b) and in prefixed forms such as (28b). Here, too, a rule-combining approach to morphotactics simplifies the range of operations necessary for the definition of a language's morphology.

(28) a. *iš-laikau*
         PRF-preserve.1SG.PRS.IND
         'I preserve, withstand'
     b. *iš-si-laikau*
         PRF-REFL-preserve.1SG.PRS.IND
         'I hold my stand'

(29) a. *laikau*
         maintain.1SG.PRS.IND
         'I consider, maintain'
     b. *laikau-si*
         maintain.1SG.PRS.IND-REFL
         'I get along'

Often, the availability of special operations leaves word-skeletal approaches with an embarrassment of alternative analyses. For example, Nevins (2015) observes that the Swahili facts in (30)–(31) (cf. Section 8.3) can be analyzed in two different ways under the assumptions of Distributed Morphology. Assuming that Swahili syntax supplies a word skeleton of the type [NEG SBJ VERB], one can postulate (i) a prefix *si-* that is inserted from the list of "vocabulary items" into the NEG node provided that the following SBJ node is specified 'first-person singular', and (ii) a zero affix that is inserted from the list of "vocabulary items" into a first-person singular SBJ node provided that the preceding NEG node is occupied by *si-*. Either that, or one can postulate an operation that fuses NEG and first-person singular SBJ into a single portmanteau node into which *si-* alone is insertable. The problem here isn't that there's not enough evidence to motivate the choice between two (equally awkward) alternatives; the problem is the [NEG SBJ VERB] skeleton that is seen as necessitating this choice in the first place. Dispensing with the skeleton, one can simply say (as in Section 8.3) that the simple ⟦si-⟧~III~ rule in (31b) is paradigmatically opposed to the composite (⟦ha-⟧~III~ ∘ ⟦m-⟧~III~) rule in (30b). These are both just rules of prefixation. No zero affixes are involved, nor any fusion operation.

(30)   a.   *m-ta-soma*
              SBJ.2PL-FUT-read
              'you (pl.) will read'
     b.   *ha-m-ta-soma*
              NEG-SBJ.2PL-FUT-read
              'you (pl.) will not read'

(31)   a.   *ni-ta-soma*
              SBJ.1SG-FUT-read
              'I will read'
     b.   *si-ta-soma*   (*ha-ni-ta-soma)
              NEG.SBJ.1SG-FUT-read
              'I will not read'

12.5   Rule Combinations vs. Morph-position Templates

The rule-combining approach to exponence-driven morphotactics affords means of capturing morphological generalizations that are unavailable to word-skeletal theories. To show this, I now compare some of the analyses proposed in earlier chapters to word-skeletal analyses of the same data proposed by Crysmann and Bonami (2016) in the framework of Information-based Morphology (IbM), whose theory of morphotactics is precisely articulated and thus easy to compare. The key idea underlying the analyses proposed by Crysmann and Bonami is that a language's inflectional system defines its word forms as instantiations of a template of indexed morph positions. In particular, Crysmann and Bonami propose that templates possessing the characteristics in (32a) are fundamental to defining a language's inflectional morphotactics. Canonically, the morphs in a template of this sort are assumed to exhibit the characteristics of paradigmatic alignment (32b) and stable placement (32c); noncanonical paradigms exhibit deviations from these two characteristics.

(32)   Characteristics of IbM (Crysmann & Bonami 2016)
     a.   *Characteristics of templatic inflection* (p. 314)
          i.   Classes of lexemes are associated with a rigid sequence of positions for the realization of morphs.

12.5 Rule Combination vs. Morph-position Templates 355

      ii. Each position may be filled by at most one morph.
      iii. For each paradigm cell of each lexeme, the grammar specifies
          a. which morphs it consists of, and
          b. which position(s) these morphs may occur in.
  b. *Paradigmatic alignment of morphs* (p. 317)
      Within the paradigm of each lexeme, if two morphs are in paradigmatic opposition, they are syntagmatically equivalent.
  c. *Stable placement of morphs* (p. 319)
      Within the paradigm of a lexeme, for any pair of morphs m, m', the relative placement of m and m' is the same for all paradigm cells in which they co-occur: either m always precedes m' or m' always precedes m.

In IbM, rules of exponence (or "realization rules") are formalized as typed feature structures. For example, the realization rule defining the Swahili past-tense affix *li-* is represented as in Figure 12.2, where

- the 'morph set' feature MPH comprises a phonological form (the value of the 'phonology' feature PH) and a morph-position index (the value of the 'position class' feature PC);
- the 'morphosyntax under discussion' feature MUD specifies the content realized by the rule; and
- the 'morphosyntactic property set' feature MS specifies the full set of morphosyntactic properties of the word form in whose realization the rule applies; in Figure 12.2, this set is indexed as $\boxed{0}$.[2]

Typed feature structures are employed in IbM not only in the representation of rules of exponence, but also in the morphotactic representation of entire word forms. Thus, consider the Swahili relative verb form in (33). In the IbM analysis of Swahili presented by Crysmann and Bonami, this form has the feature structure in Figure 12.3. In this structure, the value of the topmost PH feature is the phonology of the word form as a whole. The value of the

$$\begin{bmatrix} \text{MPH} & \{[\begin{smallmatrix}\text{PH} & <\text{li}>\\ \text{PC} & 3\end{smallmatrix}]\} \\ \text{MUD} & \{[past]\} \\ \text{MS} & \boxed{0} \end{bmatrix}$$

Figure 12.2 *The realization rule introducing the Swahili past-tense affix* li *in an IbM analysis*

---

[2] C&B's distinction between a rule's MUD value and its MS value is closely comparable to the distinction (drawn by Noyer 1992) between primary and secondary exponence, that is, between what Stump (2001: 10f.) calls properties of content and properties of context. See Stump (2001: 156ff.) for arguments against the theoretical viability of this distinction.

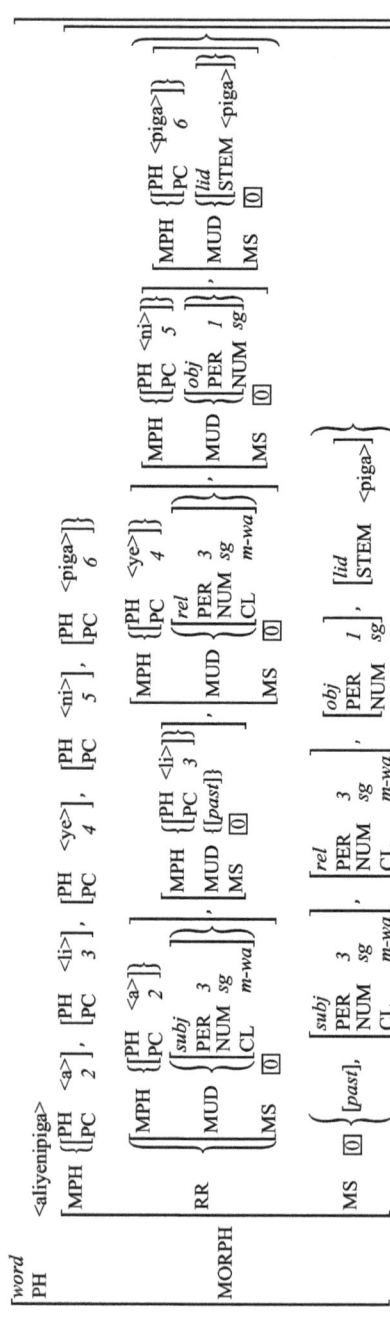

Figure 12.3 Feature structure of Swahili aliyenipiga 'who (sg.) struck me' in the IbM approach

12.5 Rule Combination vs. Morph-position Templates   357

'morphology' feature MORPH defines the word form's morphotactics as involving a morph set (the value of the feature MPH, which incorporates both a PH value and a PC value for each morph), a set of realization rules (the value of RR, one member of which is the rule in Figure 12.2), and a morphosyntactic property set (the value of MS). Note that the MPH values of the individual rules constituting the RR set are assembled as the members of the full word form's MPH set; similarly, each of the realization rules has a MS value that is coindexed with that of the word form as a whole. According to the IbM approach, the morphotactics of *aliyenipiga* is not exponence-driven, but instead embodies the skeletal structure of the word form's morph-set feature MPH (together with the principle that the members of the morph set are linearly ordered according to the numerical order of their morph-position indices).

(33)   *a-li-ye-ni-piga*
        SBJ.3SG.NC1-PST-REL.3SG.NC1-OBJ.1SG-strike
        'who (sg.) struck me'

Before proceeding, consider how starkly rules in the IbM approach differ from rules in the rule-combining approach. The *li-* rule in Figure 12.2 corresponds to the ⟦li-⟧$_{II}$ rule proposed in Section 8.2, repeated in (34). The feature structure in Figure 12.2 and the rule in (34) are alike in two respects (both specify the phonology of the *li-* affix and both specify its past-tense content), but from a formal perspective, they reflect very distinct theoretical architectures.

(34)   ⟦li-⟧$_{II}$: [V, {pst} : *li-*]

The rule in (34) is a function in the set of ⟨form, property set⟩ pairings. It therefore has an operand: the stem Z in the form/property-set pairing ⟨Z, σ⟩ to which the rule applies. The feature structure in Figure 12.2, by contrast, doesn't operate on anything, but is instead simply a declared association of particular properties of form and content with a particular morph position; specifically, it licenses the association of the past-tense morph *li* with morph position [3]. Related to this formal difference is the fact that the function (34) specifies the directionality of *li-*, identifying it as a prefix. The feature structure in Figure 12.2, by contrast, doesn't directly specify the prefixal directionality of *li-*, but instead identifies its position class membership as [PC 3]; thus, in the IbM analysis, *li* precedes the stem in the verb form *nilitaka* 'I wanted' only because it is specified as belonging to morph position [3], which happens to precede the stem's morph position [6].

358 *Rule combining Morphotactics*

The differences between the IbM approach and the rule-combining approach are even more dramatic in their definition of the morphotactics of the full word form in (33). In the IbM approach, the morphotactics of (33) is defined by a set of realization rules. Crucially, the members of the RR set in Figure 12.3 are not nested in smaller combinations, and because they are not functions, they are *a fortiori* not distinguished with respect to modes of combination such as composition or aggregation. Since the rules in this RR set don't have operands, the verb form's stem must itself be represented as a realization rule; this is the rightmost rule in the RR value of Figure 12.3.

In the rule-combining approach, the morphotactics of *aliyenipiga* is exponence-driven, an effect of the way in which the rules defining its inflectional exponents *a-*, *li-*, *ye-*, and *ni-* combine with one another – specifically, an effect of the fact that these rules combine as the FER in (35). All of the rule combinations in (35) are binary, joining one rule with another rule to form a larger rule. Because of this binariness, the combinations in (35) are nested combinations of the rules in (36); the nature and extent of this nesting is highlighted in Figure 12.4. In addition, each rule combination involves a specified mode of combination. The mode combination of ([[-ye₁]]_II Ⓐ [[li-]]_II) is aggregation; that of ([[a-₁]]_III ∘ ([[-ye₁]]_II Ⓐ [[li-]]_II)) is composition; and so on. The order and mode of a rule's combination determine both the relative sequence of the affix that it introduces and the content that it serves to express in that combination. The verb form's stem does not figure in the FER represented in (35)/Figure 12.4, since it instead serves as the operand of this FER.

(35)   The FER of Swahili *aliyenipiga* 'who (sg.) struck me'
        ((([[a-₁]]_III ∘ ([[-ye₁]]_II Ⓐ [[li-]]_II)) ∘ ([[ni-]] ∘ [[id.fcn]]_I)) :
                [V, {–ind pst {sbj 3sg nc1} {rel 3sg nc1} {obj 1sg}} : *aliyeni-*]

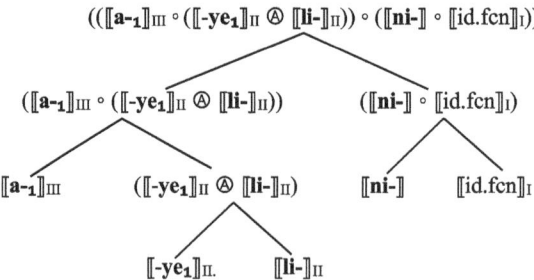

Figure 12.4 *Grouping of rules in the Swahili FER in (35)*

12.5 Rule Combination vs. Morph-position Templates

(36) The simple rules on which (35) is based
    a. $[\![\textbf{a-}_1]\!]_{\text{III}}$: [V, {{sbj 3sg nc1}} : *a-*]
    b. $[\![\textbf{li-}]\!]_{\text{II}}$: [V, {pst} : *li-*]
    c. $[\![\textbf{-ye}_1]\!]_{\text{II}}$: [V, {–ind {rel 3sg nc1}} : *-ye*]
    d. $[\![\textbf{ni-}]\!]$: [V, {{1sg}} : *ni-*]
    e. $[\![\text{id.fcn}]\!]_{\text{I}}$: [V, {{obj}} : X → X]

The IbM approach to morphotactics and the rule-combining approach therefore involve very different theoretical architectures. For purposes of comparison, the key architectural assumptions of the IbM approach are those in (37).

(37) Three architectural assumptions of the IbM approach to inflectional morphotactics
    a. The ***position-based ordering*** assumption: The morphs in a word form are individually associated with indexed morph positions, so that patterns of relative order and adjacency among a word form's morphs are predetermined by the strict linear ordering of the indexed morph positions with which they are associated.
    b. The ***rule anchoring*** assumption: Each fully instantiated[3] realization rule is anchored to a particular morph position.
    c. The ***rule monopolism*** assumption: In the RR set defining a word form's morphotactics, each of the word form's morphs has its own dedicated realization rule that specifies its phonological expression (as the rule's PH value), its sequencing (as the rule's PC value), and the content that it realizes (as the rule's MUD value).

To see the significance of these assumptions, consider again the IbM analysis of the Swahili relative verb form *aliyenipiga* 'who (sg.) struck me' in (33). The definition of this word form's morphotactics in Figure 12.3 conforms to the position-based ordering assumption because each of its five morphs is associated with a numbered morph position. The definition in Figure 12.3 likewise conforms to the rule anchoring assumption, since each realization rule is anchored to one of the five relevant morph positions. And it conforms to the rule monopolism assumption: in the RR set defining the morphotactics of the word form *a-li-ye-ni-piga*, each morph has a single dedicated rule that specifies that morph's phonological expression, its sequencing, and the content that it realizes.

In contrast to IbM, the rule-combining approach to morphotactics makes none of the three assumptions in (37), but instead makes the contrasting architectural assumptions in (38).

---

[3] In IbM, a fully instantiated realization rule is one that has explicit values for the MPH, MUD, and MS features; examples are the *li* rule in Figure 12.2 and the rules belonging to the RR set in Figure 12.3. A single fully instantiated rule may inherit its characteristics from several separate, underspecified rules that are not themselves fully instantiated.

(38) Three architectural assumptions of the rule-combining approach to morphotactics
  a. The **combination-based ordering** assumption: Because rules of inflectional exponence define operations on operands, patterns of relative order and adjacency among a word form's inflectional exponents depend on the operator/operand relations defined by the combinations into which those rules enter.
  b. The **unanchored rule** assumption: The rules defining a word form's inflectional exponents enter into binary combinations of various kinds, involving both different orders and different modes of combination.
  c. The **rule pluralism** assumption: In the definition of a word form's morphotactics, an affix's sequencing relative to other affixes and the content that it expresses may be jointly determined by a set of nested rules.[4]

The rule-combining approach makes no reference to indexed morph positions. Thus, in the rule-combining analysis of *aliyenipiga*, the word form's inflectional exponents are not individually associated with positions whose linear order is predetermined; instead, the patterns of relative order and adjacency exhibited by the word form's inflectional exponents depend on the ways in which rules combine in constituting the FER in (35)/Figure 12.4. Unanchored to particular morph positions, rules of inflectional exponence may combine with other rules in a variety of ways. The relative sequencing and (in one case) the content of the individual affixes in *aliyenipiga* are determined pluralistically rather than monopolistically. For example, the phonological form of *-ye*, its suffixal directionality, and the content that it realizes are all specified by the simple $[\![\text{-ye}_1]\!]_{II}$ rule in (36c), but its sequencing relative to other affixes depends on combined rules in which $[\![\text{-ye}_1]\!]_{II}$ is nested. The aggregated rule ($[\![\text{-ye}_1]\!]_{II}$ Ⓐ $[\![\text{li-}]\!]_{II}$) specifies *li-* as the operand to which *-ye* is suffixed. Beyond that, further aspects of the sequencing of *-ye* follow from those of the aggregated affix *liye-*, which depends on the aggregated rule ($[\![\text{-ye}_1]\!]_{II}$ Ⓐ $[\![\text{li-}]\!]_{II}$) for its prefixal directionality, on the composite rule ($[\![\text{a-}_1]\!]_{III}$ ∘ ($[\![\text{-ye}_1]\!]_{II}$ Ⓐ $[\![\text{li-}]\!]_{II}$)) for its sequencing after the subject-agreement

---

[4] Thus, the relative order of a set of inflectional affixes may vary either because the rules that define them combine in more than one order (as in the case of the Eastern Mari nominative forms *pört-βlak-em* and *pört-em-βlak* 'my houses'; Section 4.3) or because the rules that define them participate in more than one mode of combination (as in the case of the Swahili relative verb forms *a-vi-soma-vyo* '(books) that s/he reads' and *a-li-vyo-vi-soma* '(books) that she read'; Section 8.4). In the same way, the content expressed by an inflectional affix may vary either because the rule that defines it combines in more than one order (as in the case of the Swahili verb forms *wananipiga* 'they are striking me' and *ninawapiga* 'I am striking them'; Section 8.5) or because the rule that defines it participates in more than one mode of combination (as in the case of the Breton forms *kar-o-mp* 'we love', *kar-i-t* 'you (pl.) love', *kar-i-mp* 'we will love', *kar-o-t* 'you (pl.) will love'; Section 6.2).

12.5 Rule Combination vs. Morph-position Templates 361

prefix *a*-, and on the full FER in (35) for its sequencing before the object prefix *ni*-. Thus, every rule on the path from ⟦-**ye₁**⟧_II to the topmost FER in Figure 12.4 participates in determining the relative sequencing of -*ye* in *aliyenipiga*. Consider likewise the object prefix *ni*-. Its phonological form, its prefixal directionality, and part of its content (the fact that it expresses the first person singular) are specified by the simple ⟦**ni-**⟧ rule in (36d). The fact that *ni*- expresses object agreement is specified by the composite rule (⟦**ni-**⟧ ∘ ⟦id.fcn⟧_I), and the fact that *ni*- follows the combined prefix *aliye*- is in turn specified by the full FER in (35). Thus, every rule on the path from ⟦**ni-**⟧ to the topmost FER in Figure 12.4 participates in determining the relative sequencing of *ni*- in *aliyenipiga*, and two of these rules – the simple rule ⟦**ni-**⟧ and the composite rule (⟦**ni-**⟧ ∘ ⟦id.fcn⟧_I) – participate in determining the content that it expresses in this word. The full FER in (35) does specify the combined affix *aliyeni*- and the combined content that it realizes – the morphosyntactic property set {−ind pst {sbj 3sg nc1}{rel 3sg nc1}{obj 1sg}}) – but it is the smaller rules constituting the FER that jointly determine the form and content of the individual affixes in *aliyenipiga*, the patterns of sequencing that lead from the individual affixes in (36) to the combined affix *aliyeni*-, and the patterns of unification eventuating in the full morphosyntactic property set that *aliyeni*- realizes.

The assumptions in (37) seem to keep things orderly in the IbM analysis of (33), but even here, one can see an important difference between the IbM approach to morphotactics and the rule-combining approach. The IbM approach requires that the morphotactics of a full word form and the realization rules on which it depends be defined by typed feature structures of two distinct sorts. The morphotactics of the full word form *aliyenipiga* 'who (sg.) struck me' in (33) is defined by (i) the typed feature structure serving as the value of the 'morphology' feature MORPH in Figure 12.3 – a structure whose three constituents are a morph set (the value of the feature MPH), a set of fully instantiated realization rules (the value of RR), and a morphosyntactic property set (the value of MS). By contrast, each fully instantiated realization rule is defined by (ii) a typed feature structure whose three constituents are a morph set (e.g. the value of the MPH feature in Figure 12.2), a specification of the 'morphosyntax under discussion' (e.g. the value of the MUD feature in Figure 12.2), and a full morphosyntactic property set (e.g. the value of feature MS in Figure 12.2). This distinction between feature structures of types (i) and (ii) is an artifact of the IbM approach. No comparable distinction figures in the rule-combining approach to morphotactics, where a full word form's FER is the same type of rule as the individual inflectional rules on which it depends: each is a partial function in the set of ⟨form, property set⟩ pairings, and each

362 *Rule combining Morphotactics*

embodies the same format [C, τ : *f*] defined in Section 2.1.1 (in which τ is the property set representing the content realized by the rule, *f* is the morphological operation by means of which this content is realized, and C is the category of forms on which f operates in default uses of the rule); for instance, all of the simple and combined rules constituting the FER in Figure 12.4 are rules of the same type. Thus, rule-combining morphotactics affords a more parsimonious inventory of rule types than IbM.

Once one begins considering the full range of noncanonical morphotactic phenomena discussed in the preceding chapters, the differences between the IbM approach and the rule-combining approach grow even sharper. Adherence to the assumptions in (37) engenders cumbersome consequences for IbM analyses of these phenomena, but because the rule-combining approach does not make the assumptions in (37), it avoids these same cumbersome consequences. As a concrete basis for discussion, I focus on the analysis of Swahili relative verb forms (Section 12.5.1), Fula verbal concord (Section 12.5.2), and Eastern Mari noun inflection (Section 12.5.3), all topics that I have examined in preceding chapters and all of which are discussed by Crysmann & Bonami (2016). These topics provide good evidence of both the deleterious consequences of making the assumptions in (37) and the desirable effects of instead adopting the assumptions in (38).

12.5.1 *Analyzing Relative Verb Forms in Swahili*

As was seen in Section 8.4, the morphotactics of Swahili relative verb forms exhibits the defining signature of affix counterposition: the affix coding a verb's relativized argument (hereafter, the RA affix) follows the verb stem in the absence of a tense/negation prefix (as in (39)), but immediately follows the tense/negation prefix when one is present (as in (40)).

(39) a. *m-tu*   *a-ni-piga-ye*
        NC1-person   SBJ.NC1-OBJ.1SG-strike-REL.NC1
        'a person who strikes me'
     b. *vi-tabu*   *a-vi-soma-vyo*
        NC8-book   SBJ.NC1-OBJ.NC8-read-REL.NC8
        'the books that s/he reads'

(40) a. *m-tu*   *a-li-ye-ni-piga*
        NC1-person   SBJ.NC1-PST-REL.NC1-OBJ.1SG-strike
        'a person who struck me'
     b. *vi-tabu*   *a-li-vyo-vi-soma*
        NC8-book   SBJ.NC1-PST-REL.NC8-OBJ.NC8-read
        'the books that s/he read'

12.5 Rule Combination vs. Morph-position Templates   363

Table 12.1 *Analysis of the Swahili verb forms in (39) and (40) in the rule-combining approach to morphotactics*

Form	FER
a-ni-piga-ye 'who strikes me'	$((\llbracket \mathbf{a\text{-}1} \rrbracket_{\text{III}} \circ \llbracket \mathbf{\text{-}ye_1} \rrbracket_{\text{II}}) \circ (\llbracket \mathbf{ni\text{-}} \rrbracket \circ \llbracket \text{id.fcn} \rrbracket_{\text{I}}))$
a-vi-soma-vyo '(books) that s/he reads'	$((\llbracket \mathbf{a\text{-}1} \rrbracket_{\text{III}} \circ \llbracket \mathbf{\text{-}vyo_8} \rrbracket_{\text{II}}) \circ (\llbracket \mathbf{vi\text{-}8} \rrbracket \circ \llbracket \text{id.fcn} \rrbracket_{\text{I}}))$
a-li-ye-ni-piga 'who struck me'	$((\llbracket \mathbf{a\text{-}1} \rrbracket_{\text{III}} \circ (\llbracket \mathbf{\text{-}ye_1} \rrbracket_{\text{II}} \circledA \llbracket \mathbf{li\text{-}} \rrbracket_{\text{II}})) \circ (\llbracket \mathbf{ni\text{-}} \rrbracket \circ \llbracket \text{id.fcn} \rrbracket_{\text{I}}))$
a-li-vyo-vi-soma '(books) that s/he read'	$((\llbracket \mathbf{a\text{-}1} \rrbracket_{\text{III}} \circ (\llbracket \mathbf{\text{-}vyo_8} \rrbracket_{\text{II}} \circledA \llbracket \mathbf{li\text{-}} \rrbracket_{\text{II}})) \circ (\llbracket \mathbf{vi\text{-}8} \rrbracket \circ \llbracket \text{id.fcn} \rrbracket_{\text{I}}))$

Table 12.2 *The morphotactics of the Swahili relative forms* anipigaye *'who strikes me' and* aliyenipiga *'who (sg.) struck me'*

(a)	Form cell:	⟨*piga*, {–ind pos –tense {sbj 3sg nc1} {rel 3sg nc1} {obj 1sg}}⟩
	|	
	FER	$((\llbracket \mathbf{a\text{-}1} \rrbracket_{\text{III}} \circ \llbracket \mathbf{\text{-}ye_1} \rrbracket_{\text{II}}) \circ (\llbracket \mathbf{ni\text{-}} \rrbracket \circ \llbracket \text{id.fcn} \rrbracket_{\text{I}}))$
	↓	
	Realized cell:	⟨*anipigaye*, {–ind pos –tense {sbj 3sg nc1} {rel 3sg nc1} {obj 1sg}}⟩
(b)	Form cell:	⟨*piga*, {–ind pos pst {sbj 3sg nc1} {rel 3sg nc1} {obj 1sg}}⟩
	|	
	FER	$((\llbracket \mathbf{a\text{-}1} \rrbracket_{\text{III}} \circ (\llbracket \mathbf{\text{-}ye_1} \rrbracket_{\text{II}} \circledA \llbracket \mathbf{li\text{-}} \rrbracket_{\text{II}})) \circ (\llbracket \mathbf{ni\text{-}} \rrbracket \circ \llbracket \text{id.fcn} \rrbracket_{\text{I}}))$
	↓	
	Realized cell:	⟨*aliyenipiga*, {–ind pos pst {sbj 3sg nc1} {rel 3sg nc1} {obj 1sg}}⟩

In the rule-combining analysis of Swahili in Section 8.4, the FERs defining the verb forms in (39) differ from those defining the verb forms in (40) as in Table 12.1: the former simply involve the composition of a subject-concord rule with a relativized-argument rule, while the latter involve the composition of a subject-concord rule with the aggregation of a relativized-argument rule with a tense rule. In the forms defined by these FERs, the patterns of relative order and adjacency exhibited by the RA affix depend both on the simple rule defining that affix and on the nested combinations into which that rule enters. In the realization of the tenseless affirmative form cell in part (a) of Table 12.2, the composite $(\llbracket \mathbf{a\text{-}1} \rrbracket_{\text{III}} \circ \llbracket \mathbf{\text{-}ye_1} \rrbracket_{\text{II}})$ operates on the object-marked verb stem *-ni-piga*, to which *-ye* is therefore suffixed; here the relativized-argument rule $\llbracket \mathbf{\text{-}ye_1} \rrbracket_{\text{II}}$ takes *-ni-piga* as its operand. But in the realization of the past-tense form cell in part (b) of Table 12.2, the composite ($[\![$**a-₁**$]\!]_{\text{III}} \circ ([\![$**-ye₁**$]\!]_{\text{II}}$ Ⓐ $[\![$**li-**$]\!]_{\text{II}}))$ operates on the object-marked verb stem *-ni-piga*, to which the aggregated affix *li-ye-* is therefore prefixed; in the definition of this aggregated prefix, $[\![$**-ye₁**$]\!]_{\text{II}}$ takes the past-tense prefix *li-* as its operand. Thus, the RA affixes in (39) and (40) have a very different analysis from true ambifixes such as are found in Gurma noun-class morphology (Section 7.3); because they exhibit the defining signature of affix counterposition, the RA affixes in (40) involve rule aggregation, which ambifixes do not.

In IbM, by contrast, no distinction is drawn (or is even possible) between affix counterpositions and ambifixes. In their account of Swahili relative verb forms, Crysmann & Bonami (2016) propose the seven indexed morph positions in Figure 12.5. Each RA affix is situated within this template by two realization rules. One rule places a given RA affix in position [4] by default, but another rule instead places this affix in position [7] in affirmative tenseless forms.[5] For example, the *ye* affix in (40a) is associated with position [4] by the default rule in Figure 12.6a, while the same affix in (39a) is situated in position [7] by the overriding[6] rule in Figure 12.6b. To be sure, Crysmann and Bonami minimize redundancy in the formulation of the rules in Figure 12.6 by appealing to orthogonal multiple inheritance from underspecified rule schemas (p. 361): both rules in Figure 12.6 inherit the values of their MUD and PH features from an underspecified schema defining a single exponent form, but they differ with respect to the inheritance of their other feature values, inheriting them from distinct schemas associating them with distinct morph positions. Ultimately,

---

[5] Crysmann and Bonami incorrectly assert that a relative verb form's RA affix appears after the stem in the affirmative definite tense (2016: 360f.). In fact, the definite tense is overtly expressed by the prefix *na-* in relative verb forms, and the RA affix immediately follows this prefix, as in *anayesoma* 'who (sg.) is reading'. The RA affix appears after the verb stem in tenseless affirmative forms, as in (39). I have therefore corrected {*aff, def,* ...} to {*aff, –tense,* ...} in Figure 12.6b.

[6] In Crysmann and Bonami's framework, a rule filling one morph position overrides a competing but less specific rule filling another morph position, hence rule (b) overrides rule (a) in Figure 12.6; this recalls the notion of discontinuous bleeding first introduced by Noyer (1992). Moreover, Crysmann and Bonami assume an even more restrictive principle to the effect that the same MUD value cannot be realized more than once in the definition of the same word form. It remains to be seen how this latter assumption is to be reconciled with cases in which the same rule applies once in some forms but twice (expressing the same content redundantly) in others. We have seen several instances of this kind, for example the Limbu verb forms *huʔruŋ* 'I teach her/him' and *huʔruŋsiŋ* 'I teach them' (where the first-person singular agent rule $[\![$**-ŋ**$]\!]$ applies either once or twice; Section 3.2) and the Pengo verb forms *huṛtaŋ* 'I saw' and *huṛtaŋnaŋ* 'I have seen' (where the first-person singular subject rule $[\![$**-aŋ**$]\!]$ applies either once or twice; Section 11.1.2). In the rule-combining approach, the number of applications of Limbu $[\![$**-ŋ**$]\!]$ and Pengo $[\![$**-aŋ**$]\!]$ in a given verb form depends on the number of carrier rules that apply in that form.

12.5 Rule Combination vs. Morph-position Templates

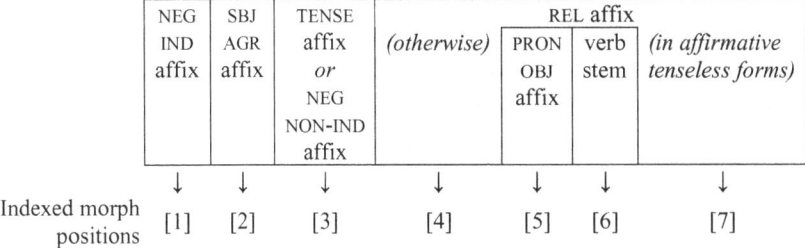

Figure 12.5 *Indexed morph positions for a fragment of Swahili verb morphology*
(cf. Crysmann & Bonami 2016: 318)

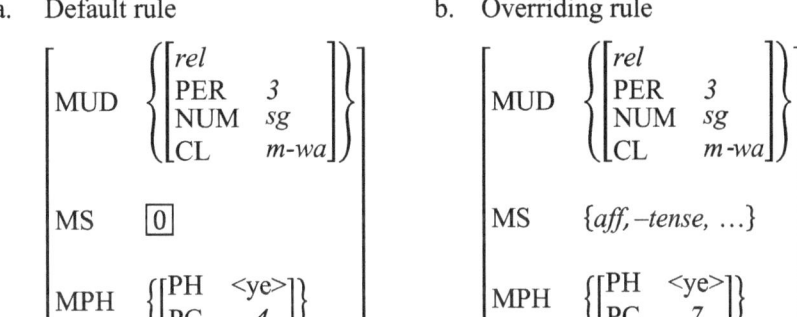

Figure 12.6 *Two fully instantiated rules defining the morphotactics of the Swahili RA affix* ye *in the IbM approach*
(cf. Crysmann & Bonami 2016: 361)

though, a fully instantiated rule of exponence has a MUD value, a MS value, and a MPH value (exactly as in Figure 12.3), and under full instantiation, the two rules for the affixation of *ye* are exactly as in Figure 12.6. In this way, the IbM analysis assigns the forms in (39) and (40) the morphotactic analyses in Table 12.3. According to this analysis, RA affixes are no different from true ambifixes such as those of Gurma noun-class inflection.

Here, then, is a case in which the rule anchoring assumption (37b) is cumbersome: it requires the same affix appearing in more than one indexed morph position to be defined by distinct rules, each anchored to a different position. The rule-combining approach, by contrast, is unencumbered in this respect: because the $[\![-\mathbf{ye_1}]\!]_\Pi$ rule isn't anchored to any position, it can place the relative affix *-ye* in more than one relative order, exactly as in the examples in (39a)/(40a)/Table 12.2. The precise relative order in which $[\![-\mathbf{ye_1}]\!]_\Pi$ places *-ye* depends on the manner in which $[\![-\mathbf{ye_1}]\!]_\Pi$ combines with other rules. Thus, in

Table 12.3 *Analysis of the Swahili verb forms in (39) and (40) in an IbM approach to morphotactics*

Indexed morph position:	[1]	[2]	[3]	[4]	[5]	[6]	[7]	Gloss
verb form in (39a)		*a-*			*ni-*	*piga*	*-ye*	'who strikes me'
verb form in (39b)		*a-*			*vi-*	*soma*	*-vyo*	'(books) that s/he reads'
verb form in (40a)		*a-*	*li-*	*ye-*	*ni-*	*piga*		'who struck me'
verb form in (40b)		*a-*	*li-*	*vyo-*	*vi-*	*soma*		'(books) that s/he read'

12.5 Rule Combination vs. Morph-position Templates 367

the rule-combining approach, the distribution of -*ye* is (contrary to the rule monopolism assumption (37c)) determined both by 〚-**ye₁**〛$_{II}$ and by the various combinations into which 〚-**ye₁**〛$_{II}$ enters, including (for example) the composition (〚**a-₁**〛$_{III}$ ∘ 〚-**ye₁**〛$_{II}$) in part (a) of Table 12.2 and the aggregation (〚-**ye₁**〛$_{II}$ Ⓐ 〚**li-**〛$_{II}$) in part (b) of Table 12.2. While the IbM approach treats -*ye* exactly as it would treat a true ambifix, the rule-combining approach treats -*ye* as a suffix in all of its uses, but one whose operand varies from use to use.

Besides requiring two (fully instantiated) rules for each RA affix, Crysmann and Bonami's analysis fails to express an evident generalization. In their analysis, the fact that a RA affix in position [4] is always immediately preceded by a tense/negation affix in position [3] is portrayed as a recurring coincidence. Certainly, the rules associating RA affixes with position [4] (e.g. rule (a) in Figure 12.6) only apply in verb forms that are tensed or negative (since otherwise they are overridden by rules associating RA affixes with position [7]); but the fact that the exponents of tense or negation are always situated in the immediately preceding position [3] follows by pure accident from the separate formulation of the rules defining the affixes of tense/negation.

This pattern is no accident in the rule-combining approach, in which a RA suffix can only appear preverbally through the aggregation of a rule of relative suffixation with a prefixational rule of tense or negation, in accordance with the pattern in (41) (repeated from Section 8.4). By the way aggregation is defined, the tense/negation affix with which a RA suffix aggregates immediately precedes it.

(41) Where R_1 is a rule of tense or nonindicative negation belonging to Group II and R_2 is a relativized-argument rule belonging to Group II, (R_2 Ⓐ R_1) is an aggregated relative tense/negation rule belonging to Group II.

The IbM analysis also treats it as a matter of coincidence that no verb has morphs in both positions [3] and [7] in the template in Figure 12.5. The MS value of each rule associating a RA affix with position [7] restricts this affix to affirmative tenseless forms; coincidentally, each rule that specifies tense or negation as part of its MUD value fills position [3]. In the rule-combining analysis, by contrast, the rules defining the simple affixes that Crysmann and Bonami associate with positions [3] and [7] are all in paradigmatic opposition to one another. Recall that in the analysis of Swahili verb inflection in Chapter 8, rules of inflectional exponence fall into the three groups in Table 12.4; the FER patterns for Swahili verb forms draw upon these three

368   *Rule combining Morphotactics*

Table 12.4 *Simple rules and rule combinations belonging to the three rule groups defining Swahili verb inflection*

Group III rules	Group II rules	Group I rules
• Indicative negative rule 〚ha-〛$_{III}$ • Subject concord prefix rules (R_{SBJ}) • Composite rules of the type (〚ha-〛$_{III}$ ∘ R_{SBJ}), where R_{SBJ} is a subject concord rule other than 1sg (〚ni-〛 ∘ 〚id.fcn〛$_{III}$) • Indicative 1sg negative rule 〚si-〛$_{III}$	• Tense affix rules (R_{TNS}) • Nonindicative negative rule 〚si-〛$_{II}$ • Subjunctive rule 〚-e〛$_{II}$ • Relative suffix rules (R_{REL}) • Negative subjunctive composite (〚si-〛$_{II}$ ∘ 〚-e〛$_{II}$) • Aggregated rules of the types (R_{REL} Ⓐ R_{TNS}) and (R_{REL} Ⓐ 〚si-〛$_{II}$)	Pronominal object prefix rules

groups as in (42). In this analysis, the simple rules that Crysmann and Bonami associate with positions [3] and [7] all belong to Group II, from which Pāṇini's principle forces the choice of a single member in the definition of any given form.

(42)   FER patterns for Fragments I, II, and III in Chapter 8 (Section 8.2)
       Where R_{II} and R_{III} are the narrowest rules in Groups II and III that are applicable to the form cell ⟨Z, σ⟩,
       a.   if there is no rule in Group I that is applicable to ⟨Z, σ⟩, then (R_{III} ∘ R_{II}) is the FER for ⟨Z, σ⟩;
       b.   if R_I is the narrowest rule in Group I that is applicable to ⟨Z, σ⟩, then ((R_{III} ∘ R_{II}) ∘ R_I) is the FER for ⟨Z, σ⟩.

Finally, the rule-combining approach avoids the superfluity of the seven indexed morph positions in Figure 12.5, no more than five of which are ever filled in a given verb form.

To reiterate the main point of this subsection: the rule anchoring assumption (37b) creates problems for Crysmann and Bonami's analysis of Swahili RA affixes, since it requires each RA affix to be introduced by two separate (fully instantiated) rules, one for position [4], the other for position [7]. The rule-combining approach encounters no such difficulty. Because this approach rejects the rule anchoring assumption, the same rule may define a RA affix in different relative orders. In general, the distribution of a RA affix α depends both on rule 〚α〛 (which specifies the phonology of α and determines its directionality as an affix) and on the manner in which 〚α〛 combines with other

12.5 Rule Combination vs. Morph-position Templates

rules (which determines both the identity of $[\![\alpha]\!]$'s operand X and the patterns of relative order and adjacency into which Xα itself enters); that is, the rule-combining approach also rejects the rule monopolism assumption (37c) in favor of the assumption (38c) of rule pluralism.

12.5.2 Analyzing Verbal Concord in Fula

Sometimes affix sequences have a default order to which certain specific combinations of affixes fail to conform. Recall from Section 4.1 that in the TAM group B in (43), a Fula verb form's subject-agreement suffix ordinarily precedes a pronominal object suffix (as in the lefthand column of Table 12.5), but in the particular case in which the first-person singular subject-agreement suffix -*mi* is accompanied by a singular personal pronominal object suffix (second-person singular -*maa* or third-person singular -*moo*), the object suffix precedes the subject-agreement suffix (as in the righthand column of Table 12.5).

(43)   Groups of tense/aspect/mood categories in Fula (Arnott 1970: 197ff.)

Group A
Subgroup (i):   General past, Emphatic past, General future, Vague future*, Desiderative*, Negative past, Negative future, Negative of quality
Subgroup (ii):   Stative-(i), Stative-(ii)*, Continuous-(i), Continuous-(ii)*

Group B: Relative past, Relative future, Subjunctive*

*Tenses that do not exhibit preterite forms (Arnott 1970: 216); cf. Section 2.4.

In the rule-combining analysis of these facts in Section 4.1, the rules at issue are the Series 5 subject-agreement rules and pronominal object rules exemplified in (44). The composition of these rules is regulated by the FER patterns in

Table 12.5 *Four Fula verb forms in the relative past active tense*

Subject agreement affix precedes pronominal object affix	Pronominal object affix precedes subject agreement affix
mballu-mi-ɓe-' help.TNS-SBJ.1SG-OBJ.3PL.NC2-FG 'I helped them'	*mballu-maa-mi-'* help.TNS-OBJ.2SG-SBJ.1SG-FG 'I helped you (sg.)'
mballu-daa-mo-' help.TNS-SBJ.2SG-OBJ.3SG.NC1-FG 'you (sg.) helped her/him'	*mballu-moo-mi-'* help.TNS-OBJ.3SG.NC1-SBJ.1SG-FG 'I helped her/him'

(Arnott 1970: Appendix 15)

370   *Rule combining Morphotactics*

Table 12.6 *Analysis of the verb forms in Table 12.5 in a rule-combining morphotactics*

($R_{OBJ} \circ R_{SBJ}$)	($R_{SBJ} \circ R_{OBJ}$)
($[\![\text{-ɓe}]\!] \circ [\![\text{-mi}]\!]$)	($[\![\text{-mi}]\!] \circ [\![\text{-maa}]\!]$)
mballu-mi-ɓe-'	*mballu-maa-mi-'*
'I helped them'	'I helped you'
($[\![\text{-mO}]\!] \circ [\![\text{-ɗaa}]\!]$)	($[\![\text{-mi}]\!] \circ [\![\text{-mO}]\!]$)
mballu-ɗaa-mo-'	*mballu-moo-mi-'*
'you helped her/him'	'I helped her/him'

(45), which allow the four verb forms in Table 12.5 to be defined by the four FERs in Table 12.6, each the composite of two rules. The position occupied by the suffix *-mi* relative to that of other suffixes in *mballu-mi-ɓe-'* 'I helped them', *mballu-maa-mi-'* 'I helped you', and *mballu-moo-mi-'* 'I helped her' depends on the order of $[\![\text{-mi}]\!]$'s combination. In the forms defined by ($[\![\text{-ɓe}]\!] \circ [\![\text{-mi}]\!]$), *-mi* precedes *-ɓe*, but in the forms defined by ($[\![\text{-mi}]\!] \circ [\![\text{-maa}]\!]$) and ($[\![\text{-mi}]\!] \circ [\![\text{-mO}]\!]$), *-mi* follows the pronominal object affix.[7]

(44) a. Series 5 subject-agreement rules (partial)
          $[\![\text{-mi}]\!]$:   [V, {{sbj 1 sg SER.5}} : -*mi*-$^{(\cdot)}$]
          $[\![\text{-ɗaa}]\!]$: [V, {{sbj 2 sg SER.5}} : -*ɗaa*]
          etc.
      b. Pronominal object rules (partial)
          $[\![\text{-maa}]\!]$: [V, {{obj 2 sg}} : -*maa*-$^{(\cdot)}$]
          $[\![\text{-mO}]\!]$:   [V, {{obj 3 sg nc1}} : -*mO'*][8]
          $[\![\text{-ɓe}]\!]$:   [V, {{obj 3 pl nc2}} : -*ɓe*-']
          etc.

(45) FER patterns for Fula nonpreterite relative past active forms
      Where R_{SBJ} is a subject-agreement rule in (44a) and R_{OBJ} is a pronominal object rule in (44b),
      a. ($R_{SBJ} \circ R_{OBJ}$) is a FER if R_{SBJ} = $[\![\text{-mi}]\!]$ and R_{OBJ} = $[\![\text{-maa}]\!]$ or $[\![\text{-mO}]\!]$;
      b. otherwise, ($R_{OBJ} \circ R_{SBJ}$) is a FER.

---

[7] In the analysis of Fula preterite verb forms in Section 2.4, FERs are based on two groups of rules, Groups I and II. I assume here that all of the rules referenced in (45) belong to Group II, including the Series 5 subject-agreement rules in (44a), the pronominal object rules in (44b), and the composite rules defined by (45) (e.g. the composite rules in Table 12.6).

[8] In (44), the diacritic -$^{(\cdot)}$ represents glottality if in word-final position and its absence otherwise. In (44b), *-mO'* represents *-moo* when followed by *-mi-'* and *-mo-'* otherwise; see Arnott (1970: 213ff.).

12.5 Rule Combination vs. Morph-position Templates 371

Crysmann and Bonami propose to account for the pattern exhibited by the forms in Table 12.5 by postulating four successive morph positions for the subject and object suffixes in these forms; these are positions [7] through [10] in Figure 12.7.[9] In indicative verb forms belonging to TAM group B in (43), second-person subject-agreement affixes occupy position [7]; all pronominal object affixes except *maa* and *mO* occupy position [10]; *maa* and *mO* occupy position [8]; and the subject-agreement affix *mi* occupies position [9]. In this way, the verb forms in Table 12.5 are analyzed as in Table 12.7.

Here, then, is another problem engendered by the rule anchoring assumption (37b): the need to anchor rules to a proliferation of different morph positions in order to get them to apply in the right order. None of the Fula verb forms at issue ever has affixes in more than two of positions [7] through [10]; thus, the word skeleton in Figure 12.7 is more intricate in structure than any of the word forms that actually instantiate it. Moreover, the IbM analysis portrays as pure coincidence both the fact that positions [7] and [9] are never both occupied in the same word form and the fact that positions [8] and [10] are likewise never both occupied.[10]

The rule-combining analysis of the morphotactic patterns in Table 12.5 represents these patterns with maximal simplicity, as involving either a default ($R_{OBJ} \circ R_{SBJ}$) pattern of rule composition or an overriding ($R_{SBJ} \circ R_{OBJ}$) pattern. This rule-combining analysis isn't open to IbM, since it runs contrary to the rule monopolism assumption (37c). For example, this analysis entails that the distribution of the first-person singular subject concord *-mi* depends both on the ⟦**-mi**⟧ rule in (44a) (which determines the concord's phonological shape and suffixal status) and on the combination into which this rule enters: combinations such as (⟦**-ɓe**⟧ ∘ ⟦**-mi**⟧) entail one pattern of relative order and combinations such as (⟦**-mi**⟧ ∘ ⟦**-maa**⟧) entail another, as in Table 12.6. In this way, the rule-combining approach avoids the superfluity of morph positions [7]–[10] in Figure 12.7.[11]

---

[9] Positions [1]–[6] in this table relate to the morphology of the preterite suffix *-nO* discussed in Section 2.4. Because this suffix exhibits the defining signature of affix counterposition, it presents precisely the same kinds of formal problems for IbM as the Swahili RA affixes.

[10] This kind of problem for template-based analyses was first pointed out by Stump (2001: 155f.) with reference to precisely this body of Fula evidence.

[11] A similar superfluity arises in the analysis that Crysmann and Bonami (2016: 364–368) propose for Italian pronominal affixes. In order to account for the full range of ordering relations among an Italian verb form's morphs, the assumptions in (37) make it necessary for them to assume a template that distinguishes twelve morph positions, even though no single word form ever exhibits morphs in more than five of these twelve positions. Compare the rule-combining approach to the Italian facts in Section 7.4; there, restrictions on the operator/operand relations in which rules of verb inflection participate are not attributed to a skeletal structure assumed to be shared by all verb forms.

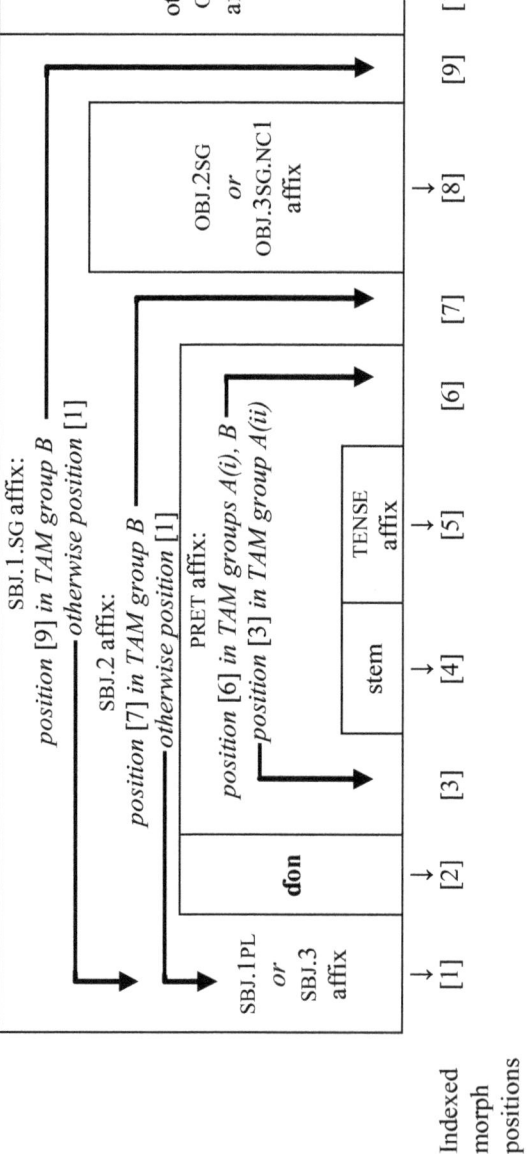

Figure 12.7 *Indexed morph positions for a fragment of Fula indicative verb morphology.*
(cf. Crysmann & Bonami 2016: 342)

12.5 Rule Combination vs. Morph-position Templates

Table 12.7 *Analysis of the verb forms in Table 12.5 in an IbM approach to morphotactics*

Tensed stem	Indexed positions for subject and object affixes				Gloss
	[7]	[8]	[9]	[10]	
mballu			mi	6e-'	'I helped them'
mballu	daa	mo-'			'you (sg.) helped her/him'
mballu		maa	mi-'		'I helped you (sg.)'
mballu		moo	mi-'		'I helped her/him'

12.5.3 Analyzing the Inflection of Eastern Mari Nouns

Morphotactic patterns vary in their length. In the rule-combining approach to morphotactics, the FERs of some inflected forms contain more rules than those of other inflected forms. Often, longer FERs have an annexational character: that is, a longer FER is defined as the result of combining a rule with a shorter FER. In such cases, in the longer FER manifests the patterns of relative order and adjacency determined by the shorter FER on which it is based. We saw a striking example of this in Eastern Mari.

Recall from Section 4.3 that in Eastern Mari, nouns inflect with up to three suffixes, one expressing plural number, another expressing case, and a third expressing the person and number of an associated possessor; recall, in addition, that of the six logically possible orderings of these three affixes in (46), only the three in (46a–c) are usual. Where only two affixes are involved, there are two logically possible orderings, as in each of (47)–(49); among these, (47b) is excluded. Not all orderings, however, are possible for all cases; instead, the orderings in (46b) and (48a) are usual only for the A cases in Figure 12.8 (repeated from Figure 4.1), and the orderings in (46c) and (48b) are usual only for the B cases.

(46)   a. $Af_{POSS} - Af_{PL} - Af_{CASE}$
             pört-em-βlak-ân 'of my houses'   (genitive)
             pört-em-βlak-eš 'to my houses'   (lative)
     b. $Af_{PL} - Af_{POSS} - Af_{CASE}$ (A cases)
             pört-βlak-em-ân 'of my houses'   (genitive)
     c. $Af_{PL} - Af_{CASE} - Af_{POSS}$ (B cases)
             pört-βlak-eš-em 'to my houses'   (lative)
     d.   *$Af_{POSS} - Af_{CASE} - Af_{PL}$
     e.   *$Af_{CASE} - Af_{POSS} - Af_{PL}$
     f.   *$Af_{CASE} - Af_{PL} - Af_{POSS}$

374 *Rule combining Morphotactics*

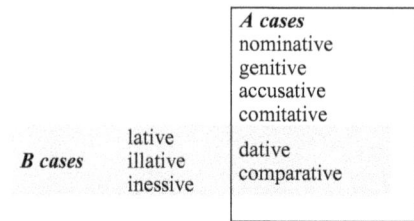

Figure 12.8 *The intersecting sets of A cases and B cases in Eastern Mari*

(47) a. $Af_{PL} - Af_{CASE}$
        pört-βlak-ǝn 'of houses' (genitive)
        pört-βlak-eš 'to houses' (lative)
      b. *$Af_{CASE} - Af_{PL}$

(48) a. $Af_{POSS} - Af_{CASE}$ (A cases)
        pört-em-ǝn 'of my house' (genitive)
      b. $Af_{CASE} - Af_{POSS}$ (B cases)
        pört-eš-em 'to my house' (lative)

(49) a. $Af_{POSS} - Af_{PL}$
        pört-em-βlak 'my houses' (nominative)
      b. $Af_{PL} - Af_{POSS}$
        pört-βlak-em 'my houses' (nominative)

In the rule-combining analysis of Eastern Mari nominal morphotactics presented in Section 4.3, the two-affix ordering patterns in (47a), (48), and (49) are accounted for by the two-rule composite FERs schematized in (50a), and the three-affix ordering patterns in (46a–c) are accounted for by the three-rule composite FERs schematized in (50b,c); the eight patterns defined in (50) are exemplified by the forms in Table 12.8. The three-rule composite FERs defined by (50b,c) are annexational: each arises from an existing two-rule composite FER (always one that expresses case) by composing it with another rule. In this way, the rule-combining analysis captures Luutonen's Variable Morphotactics Reduction Principle: every well-formed three-rule composite FER is defined on the basis of a well-formed two-rule composite FER, whose patterns of relative order and adjacency it preserves.

(50) FER patterns for Eastern Mari noun inflection
      Let R_{PL} be the rule of plural suffixation, R_{CASE} a rule of case suffixation, $R_{A.CASE}$ a rule of A case suffixation, $R_{B.CASE}$ a rule of B case suffixation, and R_{POSS} a rule of possessor suffixation.

12.5 Rule Combination vs. Morph-position Templates

Table 12.8 *Analysis of the Eastern Mari noun forms in (46)–(49) in the rule-combining approach to morphotactics*

Example			Composite type
(46a)	'of my houses'	pört-em-βlak-ǝn	((R_{CASE} ∘ R_{PL}) ∘ R_{POSS})
	'to my houses'	pört-em-βlak-eš	
(46b)	'of my houses'	pört-βlak-em-ǝn	(($R_{A.CASE}$ ∘ R_{POSS}) ∘ R_{PL})
(46c)	'to my houses'	pört-βlak-eš-em	((R_{POSS} ∘ $R_{B.CASE}$) ∘ R_{PL})
(47a)	'of houses'	pört-βlak-ǝn	(R_{CASE} ∘ R_{PL})
	'to houses'	pört-βlak-eš	
(48a)	'of my house'	pört-em-ǝn	($R_{A.CASE}$ ∘ R_{POSS})
(48b)	'to my house'	pört-eš-em	(R_{POSS} ∘ $R_{B.CASE}$)
(49a)	'my houses'	pört-em-βlak	(R_{PL} ∘ R_{POSS})
(49b)	'my houses'	pört-βlak-em	(R_{POSS} ∘ R_{PL})

a. Each of the following composites is a FER:
   i. (R_{CASE} ∘ R_{PL})   [for (47a)]
   ii. ($R_{A.CASE}$ ∘ R_{POSS})   [for (48a)]
   iii. (R_{POSS} ∘ $R_{B.CASE}$)   [for (48b)]
   iv. (R_{PL} ∘ R_{POSS})   [for (49a)]
   v. (R_{POSS} ∘ R_{PL})   [for (49b)]
b. The FER (R_{CASE} ∘ R_{PL}) in turn composes with R_{POSS} to form a FER: ((R_{CASE} ∘ R_{PL}) ∘ R_{POSS})   [for (46a)]
c. The FERs ($R_{A.CASE}$ ∘ R_{POSS}) and (R_{POSS} ∘ $R_{B.CASE}$) in turn compose with R_{PL} to form FERs:
   i. (($R_{A.CASE}$ ∘ R_{POSS}) ∘ R_{PL})   [for (46b)]
   ii. ((R_{POSS} ∘ $R_{B.CASE}$) ∘ R_{PL})   [for (46c)]

Crysmann and Bonami propose to account for the Eastern Mari facts by postulating five indexed morph positions, as in Figure 12.9. The position of the noun stem is fixed (position [1]), as are those of the plural affix (position [3]), the B case affixes (position [4]), and the A case affixes (position [5]). The possessor affixes, by contrast, may appear in position [5] in B case forms (where the case affix is instead in position [4]), in position [4] in A case forms (where the case affix is instead in position [5]), or – provided that the form is plural – in position [2] (in any of the cases). The patterns in (46a–c), (47a), (48), and (49) are thus given the IbM analyses in Table 12.9.

In Crysmann and Bonami's formalization of this template (p. 363), the distribution of the possessor-marking affixes is accounted for by the two underspecified realization-rule schemas in Figure 12.10. Fully instantiated

Table 12.9 *Analysis of the Eastern Mari noun forms in (46)–(49) in an IbM approach to morphotactics*

		Indexed morph position					
		[1]	[2]	[3]	[4]	[5]	Gloss
(46a)		pört	em	βlak		-ǝn	'of my houses'
			em	βlak	-eš		'to my houses'
(46b)		pört		βlak	em	-ǝn	'of my houses'
(46c)		pört		βlak	-eš	em	'to my houses'
(47a)		pört		βlak		-ǝn	'of houses'
		pört		βlak	-eš		'to houses'
(48a)		pört			em	-ǝn	'of my house'
(48b)		pört			-eš	em	'to my house'
(49a)		pört	em	βlak			'my houses'
(49b)	(i)	pört		βlak	em		'my houses'
	(ii)	pört		βlak		em	'my houses'

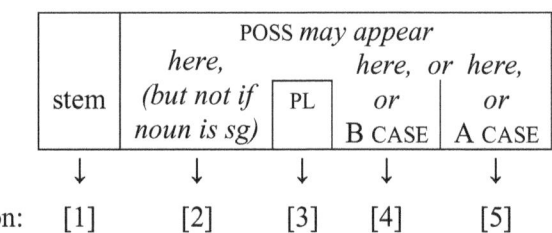

Figure 12.9 *Indexed morph positions for a fragment of Eastern Mari noun morphology*
(*cf.* Crysmann & Bonami 2016: 327)

rules for possessor-marking in general inherit the feature specifications of the schema in Figure 12.10a; in the inflection of a singular noun, a fully instantiated rule for possessor-marking must additionally inherit the feature specifications of the schema in Figure 12.10b, which excludes the possibility of associating possessor marking with morph position [2] in singular nouns. The net effect of this exclusion is that a possessive suffix cannot precede a B case suffix unless there is an intervening plural suffix.

The disjunctive PC values given by the underspecified realization-rule schemas in Figure 12.10 present another cumbersome consequence of the fundamental assumptions in (37). According to Crysmann and Bonami's

(a) $\begin{bmatrix} \text{MUD} & \{poss\} \\ \text{MPH} & \{[\text{PC} \quad 2 \vee 4 \vee 5]\} \end{bmatrix}$ (b) $\begin{bmatrix} \text{MS} & \left\{\begin{bmatrix} agr & \left\{\begin{bmatrix} \text{NUM} & sg \end{bmatrix}\right\} \end{bmatrix}\right\} \\ \text{MPH} & \{[\text{PC} \quad 4 \vee 5]\} \end{bmatrix}$

Figure 12.10 *Underspecified realization-rule schemas for possessor-marking rules in an IbM analysis of Eastern Mari noun inflection (Crysmann & Bonami 2016: 363)*

analysis, the availability of position [2] to a possessor affix depends on whether the word form being inflected is itself singular or plural. In view of this claimed dependency, the first-person singular possessor suffix *-em* must be assumed to occupy distinct positions in (51a) and (51b). In the nominative plural form (51a), it must occupy position [2], since this is the only one of the three positions in Figure 12.10a that precedes the position [3] occupied by the plural suffix. In the genitive singular form (51b), by contrast, *-em* can only occupy position [4], since position [2] is unavailable according to Figure 12.10b. There is, of course, no empirical evidence that *-em* occupies distinct positions in (51a) and (51b); rather, this conclusion is an artifact of the assumption (37a) of position-based ordering.[12]

(51) a. *pört-em-βlak*   b. *pört-em-ə̂n*
          house-POSS:1SG-PL   house-POSS:1SG-GEN
          'my houses'   'of my house'

In the rule-combining analysis, (51a) and (51b) are respectively defined by the FERs (52) and (53), according to which *-em* is the innermost suffix in both (51a) and (51b). According to the patterns of adjacency and relative order specified by (52) and (53), the possessor suffix *-em* is immediately preceded by the stem *pört-* in the definition of both (51a) and (51b); that is, *pört-* is the operand of ⟦**-em**⟧ in both instances in Table 12.10.

---

[12] A related problem arises in the analysis that Crysmann and Bonami propose for Italian pronominal affixes (Crysmann & Bonami 2016: 364–368): the ambifixal nature of the pronominal affixes requires them to postulate a morph-position template in which a verb's stem has two alternative positions: (i) a position near the end of the template in the default case, in which the verb stem is preceded by any pronominal affixes (as in *me lo date* 'you give it to me') and (ii) a template-initial position in nonfinite and imperative forms, in which the stem is followed by any pronominal affixes (as in *date-me-lo!* 'give it to me!'). This is an artifact of the assumptions in (37). Compare the rule-combining approach to Italian pronominal affixes in Section 7.4, in which this artifactual assumption has no counterpart: the aggregations (⟦**me-₁**⟧ Ⓐ ⟦**lo-₄**⟧) and (⟦**me-₁**⟧ Ⓐ ⟦**-lo₄**⟧) both simply take *date* as their operand, yielding *me lo date* in the one case and *date-me-lo!* in the other.

Table 12.10 *The morphotactics of the nouns in (51) in a rule-combining analysis of Eastern Mari*

(a)	Form cell:	⟨ pört-, {nom pl POSS:1sg} ⟩	'my houses'
	| FER ↓	([[-βlak]] ∘ [[-em]])	(= (52))
	Realized cell:	⟨ pörtemβlak, {nom pl POSS:1sg} ⟩	
(b)	Form cell:	⟨ pört-, {gen sg POSS:1sg} ⟩	'of my house'
	| FER ↓	([[-(ə)n]] ∘ [[-em]])	(= (53))
	Realized cell:	⟨ pörtemən, {gen sg POSS:1sg} ⟩	

(52)   ([[-βlak]] ∘ [[-em]]) : [N, {pl POSS:1sg} : -emβlak]

(53)   ([[-(ə)n]] ∘ [[-em]]) : [N, {gen POSS:1sg} : -emən]

The IbM analysis of Eastern Mari is also deficient in another respect. In this analysis, the three-affix sequences are not annexational in character; that is, two-affix sequences are not the definitional basis for three-affix sequences, nor are the rules that define three-affix sequences binarily grouped. For these reasons, the IbM analysis does not capture Luutonen's Variable Morphotactics Reduction Principle. Indeed, it must explicitly stipulate that the plural three-affix pattern exemplified by the plural lative form in (54) fails to correspond to a singular two-affix pattern (i.e. to the unacceptable pattern in (55)). This stipulation takes the form of the requirement (embodied by Figure 12.10b) that morph position [2] be unavailable in singular forms.

(54)   *pört-em-βlak-eš*
       house-my-PL-LAT
       'to my houses'

(55)   **pört-em-eš*
       house-my-LAT
       'to my house'

In order to exclude forms such as (55), the IbM approach must allow a morph position's availability for occupancy in a given word form to be stipulated to depend on that word form's full set of morphosyntactic properties. No comparable stipulation is necessary (or even possible) in the rule-combining analysis, in which (54) is defined by a three-rule composite of the type (($R_{B.CASE}$ ∘ R_{PL}) ∘

12.5 Rule Combination vs. Morph-position Templates

Table 12.11 *The purported structural ambiguity of dative nouns in an IbM approach to Eastern Mari morphotactics*

		Indexed morph position				
Gloss		[1]	[2]	[3]	[4]	[5]
'to a house'	i.	pört			lan	
	ii.	pört				lan
'to houses'	i.	pört		βlak	lan	
	ii.	pört		βlak		lan
'to my houses'	i.	pört	em	βlak	lan	
	ii.	pört	em	βlak		lan

R_{POSS}) (an instance of (50b)), which presupposes a corresponding two-rule composite of the type ($R_{B.CASE} \circ R_{PL}$) (an instance of (50.a.i). As for the ungrammatical form (55), it fails to conform to any of the FER patterns in (50).

A third problem for the IbM approach is that it treats possessor-marked nominative forms such as *pörtβlakem* 'my houses' as morphotactically ambiguous between the two possibilities represented by (i) and (ii) at the bottom of Table 12.9. And because the dative is both an A case and a B case (Figure 12.8), the IbM approach also treats dative forms such as *pörtlan* 'to a house', *pörtβlaklan* 'to houses', and *pörtemβlaklan* 'to my houses' as morphotactically ambiguous, since the dative suffix *-lan* in these word forms may be situated in either position [4] or position [5], as in Table 12.11. In the rule-combining approach, none of these nominative or dative forms is morphotactically ambiguous: they arise from the FERs ([[-em]] ∘ [[-βlak]]), ([[-lan]] ∘ [[-βlak]]), and ((([[-lan]] ∘ [[-βlak]]) ∘ [[-em]]), respectively. The ostensible structural ambiguity is an artifact of the position-based ordering assumption.

Summarizing, the architectural assumptions of IbM in (37) create problems. In one class of cases (as in Swahili), they require the same affix to be defined by two different rules because it appears in two different morph positions. In another class of cases (as in Fula), they require the postulation of a proliferation of morph positions in order to get anchored realization rules to apply in the proper order. And in a third class of cases (as in Eastern Mari), they entail the postulation of morphotactic contrasts that are purely artifactual. By rejecting these assumptions in favor of the architectural assumptions in (38), the rule-combining approach to morphotactics avoid all three sorts of problems.

Renewed consideration of the ten canonical morphotactic criteria proposed in Section 1.5 sheds additional light on the very different ways in which noncanonical morphotactic phenomena are approached under the assumptions of rule-combining morphology and those of IbM.

The main premise of the rule-combining approach is that there are various kinds of rule combinations; these are, inherently, deviations from the minimal rule criterion (Section 1.5.1). The postulation of such combinations makes it possible to model genuine deviations from some canonical criteria but also to reconcile various phenomena with the canonical criteria from which they only apparently deviate. Dependent/carrier relations of the sorts considered in Limbu (Section 3.2) and Sanskrit (Section 3.3) are genuine deviations from the rule independence criterion; the rule-combining approach models dependent/carrier relations as involving rules whose only use in a language's morphology is in composition with an appropriate carrier rule. Instances of holistic content of the kinds examined in Breton (Sections 6.1–6.2), Limbu (Section 6.3), and Old English (Section 6.4) genuinely deviate from the compositional content criterion; the rule-combining approach models holistic content by postulating holistic rule combinations involving a supplementary content operator.

The architecture of the IbM approach to morphotactics seems to elevate the minimal rule criterion, the rule independence criterion, and the compositional content criterion to the status of inviolable morphological principles. In view of this fact, it is not clear that this approach affords as direct an account of dependent/carrier relations or of holistic content as that proposed here.

The stem operand criterion, the integral stem criterion (Section 1.5.8), and the affix directionality criterion all presume that rules of morphology operate on things. According to the stem operand criterion, rules of morphology canonically operate on stems; according to the integral stem criterion, the characteristics of a whole stem are what canonically condition the application of a rule that operates on that stem; and according to the affix directionality criterion, a rule of affixation canonically positions an affix in a single way (prefixally or suffixally) with respect to the thing on which it operates. The rule-combining approach to morphotactics makes it possible to regard affix counterposition, an apparent deviation from the affix directionality criterion, as instead involving a deviation from the stem operand criterion – a deviation regularly possessing a defining signature. On the other hand, there are genuine deviations from the affix directionality criterion; in the rule-combining approach, these involve ambifixal rules of exponence that are associated with alternative directionalities (as in Gurma noun inflection, Section 7.3). The postulation of composite rules makes it possible to reconcile apparent

12.5 Rule Combination vs. Morph-position Templates

deviations from the integral stem criterion, as in the case of Sanskrit imperative inflection (Section 5.1).

In the IbM approach, realization rules don't operate on things; instead, they simply associate exponents with indexed morph positions. For this reason, the stem operand criterion, the integral stem criterion, and the affix directionality criterion are fundamentally incoherent under the IbM approach; the characteristics that they identify as canonical and the corresponding dimensions of morphotactic variation are not real in this approach. For example, it is unclear how to address issues of locality in the IbM approach, which seems not to provide any basis for articulating the locality issue that Sanskrit imperatives raise, much less for resolving that issue.

Similarly, the very notion of affix counterposition – a prefix followed by a suffix – is incoherent in the IbM approach, which accordingly affords no counterpart of rule aggregations for modeling the phenomena subsumed by that notion; where the rule-combining approach allows counterposed affixes to be distinguished from ambifixes (see Chapter 7), the IbM approach affords no such distinction.

A related deficiency of the IbM approach is that it cannot represent affix sequences as units; for instance, *aliye-* is not a unit in the representation of Swahili *aliyenipiga* 'who (sg.) struck me' in Figure 12.3. The rule-combining approach, by contrast, allows affix sequences to be treated as units. This is desirable for analyzing patterns of morphotactic distribution; for example, when the Lithuanian reflexive rule ⟦-si⟧ enters into aggregation (Section 7.2.2), its operand is a prefix that may be simple (as in *ne-si-lenkiu* 'I don't bow') or composite (as in *te-be-pa-si-tikiu* 'I still trust'). It is also desirable for capturing prosodic generalizations; for instance, the combined prefix *aliye-* introduced by the rule (⟦a-$_1$⟧$_{III}$ ∘ (⟦-ye$_1$⟧$_{II}$ Ⓐ ⟦li-⟧$_{II}$)) in (35)/Figure 12.4 functions as a domain of stress assignment in Swahili (Section 8.5).

12.5.4 Differences between FER Patterns and Templates

At the coarsest level of granularity, what distinguishes the exponence-driven, rule-combining approach to morphotactics from the word-skeletal, IbM approach is the fact that the former approach employs FER patterns while the latter employs morph-position templates. On first consideration, one might suppose that FER patterns are in fact very much like morph-position templates. For example, just as the IbM approach affords the templatic analysis of the seven Swahili verb forms in Table 12.12, the rule-combining approach affords the corresponding analysis in Table 12.13 (cf. Chapter 8). In both representations, columns list things that (i) are mutually exclusive and (ii) are alike in the

Table 12.12 *Templatic analysis of seven Swahili verb forms in an IbM approach*

	Indexed morph positions	[1]	[2]	[3]	[4]	[5]	[6]	[7]
tutampiga	'we will hit her/him'		*tu*	*ta*			*m*	*piga*
hatutampiga	'we will not hit her/him'	*ha*	*tu*	*ta*			*m*	*piga*
sitampiga	'I will not hit her/him'		*si*	*ta*			*m*	*piga*
atupigaye	'who (sg.) hits us'		*a*				*tu*	*piga*	*ye*
anayenipiga	'who (sg.) is hitting me'		*a*		*na*	*ye*	*ni*	*piga*
tukisomacho	'which (sg.) we read'		*tu*			*ki*	*soma*	*cho*
tutakachokisoma	'which (sg.) we will read'		*tu*	*taka*	*cho*	*ki*	*soma*

way in which they combine with things in other columns. The difference is that in Table 12.12, the columns are lists of morphs, while in Table 12.13, they are lists of rules. Should a FER pattern simply be seen as a morph-position template in whose columns the morphs have been replaced by the rules that define them? Tempting though it may be to think so, this is not an accurate characterization of a FER pattern.

Consider some of the fundamental ways in which FER patterns such as the ((Group III ∘ Group II) ∘ Group I) pattern in Table 12.13 differ from morph-position templates such as that in Table 12.12. First, *the columns in a morph-position template are occupied by single morphs. By contrast, the rule groups involved in a FER pattern may contain rule combinations as well as simple rules. Thus, while there is no nesting of morphs in a morph-position template, the rules constituting a FER are often clustered as nested rule combinations belonging to specific rule groups*. Consider, for example, the Group II column in Table 12.13. This includes simple prefixational rules such as ⟦**ta-**⟧$_{\text{II}}$, simple suffixational rules such as ⟦**-ye₁**⟧$_{\text{II}}$, suffixational aggregations such as ⟦**-cho₇**⟧$_{\text{II}}$ (= (⟦**ki-₇**⟧ Ⓐ ⟦**-o**⟧$_{\text{II}}$); cf. Section 8.4), and prefixational aggregations such as (⟦**-ye₁**⟧$_{\text{II}}$ Ⓐ ⟦**na-**⟧$_{\text{II}}$) and (⟦**-cho₇**⟧$_{\text{II}}$ Ⓐ ⟦**taka-**⟧$_{\text{II}}$). In the more extensive analysis of Swahili verb morphology in Chapter 8, Group II also includes the negative subjunctive composite (⟦**si-**⟧$_{\text{II}}$ ∘ ⟦**-e**⟧$_{\text{II}}$), which simultaneously involves both prefixation and suffixation; cf. Section 8.3. (See again Table 12.4.)

This difference between morph-position templates and FER patterns entails very different accounts of certain morphotactic phenomena. In the rule-combining approach to morphotactics, cases in which a simple, portmanteau rule is paradigmatically opposed to a composite rule (e.g. the cases in (56)) involve FERs in whose definition the simple rule and the composite rule are

Table 12.13 *A FER pattern instantiated by seven Swahili verb forms*

		b. FER pattern		
a.	Verb forms	((Group III	∘ Group II)	∘ Group I)
	tutampiga 'we will hit her/him'	(([**tu-**] ∘ [id.fcn]]$_{III}$)	∘ [**ta-**])	∘ [**m-**])
	hatutampiga 'we will not hit her/him'	((([**ha-**] ∘ ([**tu-**] ∘ [id.fcn]]$_{III}$))	∘ [**ta-**])	∘ [**m-**])
	sitampiga 'I will not hit her/him'	(([**si-**]	∘ [**ta-**])	∘ [**m-**])
	atupigaye 'who (sg.) hits us'	(([**a-**]	∘ [**-ye$_1$**])	∘ ([**tu-**] ∘ [id.fcn]]$_{I}$))
	anayenipiga 'who (sg.) is hitting me'	(([**a-**]	∘ ([**-ye$_1$**] Ⓐ [**na-**]))	∘ ([**ni-**] ∘ [id.fcn]]$_{I}$))
	tukisomacho 'which (sg.) we read'	(([**tu-**] ∘ [id.fcn]]$_{III}$	∘ [**-cho$_7$**])	∘ ([**ki$_7$-**] ∘ [id.fcn]]$_{I}$))
	tutakachokisoma 'which (sg.) we will read'	(([**tu-**] ∘ [id.fcn]]$_{III}$	∘ ([**-cho$_7$**] Ⓐ [**taka-**]))	∘ ([**ki$_7$-**] ∘ [id.fcn]]$_{I}$))

384   *Rule combining Morphotactics*

members of the same group. Such cases are awkward for the IbM approach, since a morph-position template must seemingly have two columns to accommodate a composite affix but needs only one column to accommodate a simple affix; the IbM approach must therefore somehow situate the simple affix in one of the two columns associated with the composite affix.

(56)   Simple, portmanteau rules in paradigmatic opposition to composite rules
    a.   Latin: 〚-**minī**〛 vs. (〚-(**u**)**r**〛 ∘ 〚-**unt**〛) in *audīminī* 'you are heard' vs. *audiuntur* 'they are heard' (Section 5.2.1)
    b.   Breton: 〚-**as**〛 vs. (〚-**mp**〛 ∘ ⑤$_{\{ind\}}$(〚-**o**〛 ∘ 〚-**j**〛)) in *kar-as* 's/he loved' vs. *kar-j-o-mp* 'we loved' (Section 6.2)
    c.   Swahili: 〚**si-**〛$_{III}$ vs. (〚**ha-**〛$_{III}$ ∘ (〚**tu-**〛 ∘ 〚id.fcn〛$_{III}$)) in *si-ta-soma* 'I will not read' vs. *hatutasoma* 'we will not read' (Section 8.3)

Postulating FER patterns also affords a straightforward account of cases in which the presence of one affix directly depends on that of an immediately adjacent affix. We have seen at least two kinds of cases of this sort in the inflectional domain: cases in which an affix is dependent on an adjacent carrier affix possessing the same directionality, and cases in which an affix is counterposed to an affix possessing the opposite directionality. Where a dependent rule and its carrier have the same directionality, the relation between the dependent affix and its carrier can be formalized as a relation of rule composition; thus, in the definition of the Limbu form *huʔruŋ* 'I teach her/him' (Section 3.2), the dependent rule (the first-person singular agent rule 〚-**ŋ**〛) composes with its carrier rule (the third-person patient rule 〚-**u**〛) to produce the composite (〚-**ŋ**〛 ∘ 〚-**u**〛). Crucially, this composite acts as a member of a single rule group in the FER for *huʔruŋ*: it belongs to the same group as 〚-**u**〛 on its own, which it overrides in any instance in which both are applicable. As for 〚-**ŋ**〛, it does not, on its own, belong to any rule group, but must be composed with a carrier rule; this accounts for the fact that in forms with a first-person singular agent, 〚-**ŋ**〛 does not apply if it is not composed with a carrier rule. Thus, in the case of *huʔnɛ* 'I teach you (sg.)', the lack of any applicable carrier rule precludes the application of 〚-**ŋ**〛. The IbM approach affords no direct way of accounting for this sort of dependency. The MS value of the *-ŋ* rule can be used to account for restrictions on its distribution, but this can only restrict its distribution on the basis of the morphosyntactic property set of the word form being realized, not on the basis of whether an appropriate carrier is available in the immediately preceding column of the template.

Consider now the case of affix counterpositions, whose signature pattern is one in which affix A exhibits a particular directionality D (prefixal or suffixal) with respect to a stem with which it joins, but in the presence of some affix

12.5 Rule Combination vs. Morph-position Templates

Table 12.14 *Examples of counterposition in four languages*

	[Suffix] not in counterposition	[Prefix-suffix] in prefixational counterposition	
Fula	*'o-warii*[*-no*] 's/he had come'	*'o-*[*ɗon-no*]*-wara'* 's/he was coming'	(Section 2.4)
Lithuanian	*lenkia*[*-si*] 's/he bows'	[*ne-si*]*-lenkia* 's/he doesn't bow'	(Section 7.2)
Swahili	*a-soma*[*-ye*] 'who reads'	*a-*[*taka-ye*]*-soma* 'who will read'	(Section 8.4)
	[Prefix] not in counterposition	[Prefix-suffix] in suffixational counterposition	
Noon	[*f-*]*i-yak* [NC2-]PFX-big 'big (indefinite)'	*f-i-yak-*[*f-um*] NC2-PFX-big-[NC2-LOCATION2] 'big (definite, near you)'	(Section 7.1)

B possessing the opposite directionality, A exhibits directionality D with respect to B, to which it is adjacent. We have seen several instances of affix counterposition, including those exemplified in Table 12.14.

In the rule-combining approach, instances of counterposition are formalized as instances of rule aggregation; thus, in the definition of the prefixational counterposition in Fula *'oɗonnowara'* 's/he was coming', the counterposition's suffix rule (the preterite rule 〚**-nO**〛) aggregates with the counterposition's prefix rule (the stative-(i)/continuous-(i) rule 〚**ɗon-**〛) to produce the aggregation (〚**-nO**〛 Ⓐ 〚**ɗon-**〛) in (57). Crucially, this aggregation acts as a member of a single rule group in the FER for *'oɗonnowara'*: it belongs to the rule group to which 〚**ɗon-**〛 and 〚**-nO**〛 both belong on their own and overrides them whenever it applies. The fact that (〚**-nO**〛 Ⓐ 〚**ɗon-**〛) overrides the simple rule 〚**-nO**〛 accounts for the fact that in preterite forms of the stative-(i)/continuous-(i) aspects (e.g. the form *'oɗonnowara'*), *-nO* is not suffixed to the stem. The fact that *-nO* is immediately preceded by *ɗon-* in such forms is directly entailed by the definition of aggregation.

(57) (〚**-nO**〛 Ⓐ 〚**ɗon-**〛) : [V, {stative-(i)/continuous-(i) pret} : *ɗonno-*]

The IbM analysis of Fula verbs schematized in Figure 12.7 portrays the latter fact as a coincidence. That is, the fact that *nO* is immediately preceded by *ɗon* in preterite forms of the stative-(i)/continuous-(i) aspects (e.g. the form 'odonnowara') is an accident of the fact that in the feature structure of such forms, the RR set includes both (a) a rule that associates the preterite affix *nO* with the MS value 'stative-(i)/continuous-(i)' and the PC value [3] and (b) a separate rule that associates the aspectual affix *don* with the MUD value 'stative-(i)/continuous-(i) and the PC value [2]. The affix whose MUD value satisfies the restriction on the other affix's MS value just happens to occupy the preceding morph position.

A second fundamental difference between FER patterns and morph-position templates is that *in a morph-position template, affixes in the same column are positioned in the same order relative to the position occupied by a word form's stem; in the columnar representation of a FER pattern's rule groups, by contrast, rules that operate on a stem by prefixation and rules that operate on a stem by suffixation may coexist in the same group and thus stand in paradigmatic opposition to one another.* In this way, the rule-combining approach avoids the need to resort to the kind of coincidental stipulation that the IbM approach cannot avoid. In the IbM approach to Swahili verb inflection schematized by the template in Figure 12.5, the fact that position [3] (before the verb stem) and position [7] (after the verb stem) are never both filled is, as we have seen (Section 12.5.1), an accident of the fact that the tense/negation rules that fill position [3] have a MUD value that is incompatible with the MS value of the RA affix rules that fill position [7]. In the rule-combining approach, by contrast, two rules' membership in the same rule-group suffices to predict the paradigmatic opposition of the affixes that they introduce even if these are not syntagmatically alike; thus, in Swahili, the rules defining tense/negation prefixes and the rules that define RA suffixes all belong to the same rule group (as does each aggregation of a rule of the latter sort with a rule of the former sort). No comparison of one rule's MUD value with another rule's MS value is necessary in order to establish their complementarity.

A third fundamental architectural difference between morph-position templates and FER patterns relates to instances of morphotactic ambiguity. *In every morph combination instantiating a morph-position template, morphs always stand in the same simple relation of linear concatenation. Yet, a language may possess FER patterns that specify the same linear order of rules but differ with respect to the ways in which these rules are binarily grouped or with respect to their mode of combination.*

Recall first that in the analysis of Murrinhpatha verbs in Section 9.3, evidence was given for the coexistence of the two FER patterns in (58). Recall that these patterns can be instantiated by the very same members of Groups I, II, and III; for example, the composite rule in (59a) instantiates (58a),

12.5 Rule Combination vs. Morph-position Templates

but the composite rule in (59b) instantiates (58b). The word forms defined by the rules in (59) are alike, but because of the difference in binary grouping between (59a) and (59b), the rules in (59) realize different content: (59a) defines *pu-bam-nganku-ngkardu-ngime* as a realization of the content 'They (PNS female) saw us (DS excl.)' (in which the paucal nonsibling female content of ⟦-ngime$_L$⟧ unifies with the subject properties expressed by ⟦pu-$_C$⟧$_{DU}$), but (59b) defines this same form as a realization of the content 'They (DS) saw us (PNS excl. female)' (in which the paucal nonsibling female content of ⟦-ngime$_L$⟧ instead unifies with the object properties expressed by ⟦-nganku$_C$⟧). Because there is no binary grouping of the positions in a morph-position template, it is not obvious how such a template might furnish an account of the ambiguity represented in (59).

(58) Two FER patterns in a rule-combining analysis of Murrinhpatha verb forms
    a. ((Group I ∘ Group II) ∘ Group III)
    b. (Group I ∘ (Group II ∘ Group III))

(59) Two Murrinhpatha rules instantiating the FER patterns in (58)
    a. ((⟦pu-$_C$⟧$_{DU}$ ∘ ⟦-ngime$_L$⟧) ∘ ⟦-nganku$_C$⟧)
    b. (⟦pu-$_C$⟧$_{DU}$ ∘ (⟦-ngime$_L$⟧ ∘ ⟦-nganku$_C$⟧))

A language may also possess FER patterns that differ with respect to binarily grouped rules' modes of combination. Consider, for example, the Old English verb forms in Table 12.15; the shaded forms, all second-person singular indicative forms in *-e-st*, conform to the morph-position template in Table 12.16. This template, however, conceals the differences among these forms.

In a rule-combining approach to Old English verb inflection (Section 6.4), the simple rules in (60) enter into two different holistic combinations, as in Table 12.17. The FER for the present-tense forms *singest* and *dēmest* is the holistic combination Ⓢ$_{\{prs\}}$(⟦-st⟧ ∘ ⟦-e⟧), whose addend is {prs}; this

Table 12.15 *Second-person singular indicative forms of three Old English verbs*

	SINGAN 'sing' (strong–3a)	DĒMAN 'judge' (weak–1)	LEORNIAN 'learn' (weak–2)
2sg prs ind	*sing-e-st*	*dēm-e-st*	*leorn-a-st*
2sg pst ind	*sung-e*	*dēmd-e-st*	*leornod-e-st*

388 *Rule combining Morphotactics*

Table 12.16 *Templatic analysis of the shaded verb forms in Table 12.15*

	Indexed morph positions		
[1]	[2]	[3]	
sing	e	st	'you (sg.) sing'
dēm	e	st	'you (sg.) judge'
dēmd	e	st	'you (sg.) judged'
leornod	e	st	'you (sg.) learned'

Table 12.17 *FERs of the shaded verb forms in Table 12.15*

singest, dēmest	Ⓢ$_{\{prs\}}$ ([-st] ∘ [-e])	:	[V, {ind prs 2 sg} : -est]
dēmdest, leornodest	Ⓢ$_{\{weak\ pst\}}$([-st] ∘ [-e])	:	[V, {weak ind pst 2 sg} : -est]

combination applies by default in the inflection of both strong and weak verbs but is overridden by the more specific rule (61) in the inflection of weak–2 verbs. The FER for the past-tense forms *dēmd-e-st* and *leornod-e-st* is the different holistic combination Ⓢ$_{\{weak\ pst\}}$([-st] ∘ [-e]), whose addend is {weak pst}; this applies by default in the inflection of weak verbs. Morph-position templates are not obviously suited to representing holistic content that morphs in different columns combine to express.

(60) [-e] : [V, { } : -e]
     [-st] : [V, {ind 2 sg} : -st]

(61) Ⓢ$_{\{weak\text{–}2\ prs\}}$([-st] ∘ [-a]) : [V, {weak–2 ind prs 2 sg} : -ast]

Ultimately, FER patterns and morph-position templates are not alike because they are intended to do different things. *A morph-position template is intended to abstract a skeletal structure valid for all inflected word forms belonging to some part of speech*; this is why morph templates tend to have more morph positions than are ever filled in any single word form and may include morph positions that are never both filled in the inflection of a single word form. *A FER pattern, by contrast, is more modestly intended to represent a pattern of rule combination shared by a particular class of word forms, not necessarily all of the word forms belonging to some part of speech.* A language's morphotactics may comprise various FER patterns for word forms belonging to the same part of speech and these may relate to each other in a variety of ways; they may be independent stipulations (e.g. the differently nested FER patterns for Murrinhpatha verbs in (59)), or one FER pattern may be defined as the result of annexing some group of rules to some other FER (e.g. the annexational FER patterns for Eastern Mari nouns in (50b,c)). A FER pattern specifies the order in which rules apply in the definition of some class of word forms, but it doesn't only specify order. It also specifies both the binary grouping of these rules and the mode of their combination. Specifications of these sorts determine the operator/operand relations by which a particular FER defines a particular word form's realization.

12.6 Conclusion

In this chapter, the rule-combining approach to morphotactics has been shown to have varied consequences for current theories of morphology. On the one hand, this approach is fully compatible with theories such as Paradigm Function Morphology and Construction Morphology, for both of which it has significant implications. In Paradigm Function Morphology, the postulation of FERs makes it unnecessary to regard a language's inflectional rules as constituting ordered blocks of rules such that the value of the language's paradigm function for some ⟨stem, property set⟩ pairing is the result of applying the most narrowly applicable rule from each block; instead, each of a language's FERs is a subfunction of its paradigm function, whose value in any given case is therefore the result of applying a single inflectional rule (Section 12.1). In Construction Morphology, schema unification has an effect that is closely comparable to that of rule composition; the rule-combining approach to morphotactics therefore suggests that schema unification should be seen as only one of several ways in which schemas might combine (Section 12.2).

The rule-combining approach to morphotactics entails that the arrangement of a complex word form's morphology is an effect of the ways in which rules of exponence combine with one another. This approach therefore casts doubt on the need to postulate abstract word skeleta that predefine the arrangement of a word form's morphotactics in advance of the application of any rule of exponence (Section 12.3). To this extent, the rule-combining approach casts doubt on morphological theories whose architecture necessitates the postulation of word skeleta, whether these be formalized as constituent structures defined by a language's syntax (as in Distributed Morphology) or as templates regulating the interaction of a language's rules of exponence (as in Information-based Morphology). In contrast to such theories, the rule-combining approach affords a parsimonious inventory of morphological operations (Section 12.4) and an explanatory and economical account of a range of noncanonical morphotactic phenomena (Section 12.5). The rule-combining approach to morphotactics allows a single rule of exponence to endow an exponent with different patterns of relative order and adjacency because of the different ways in which that rule combines with other rules; it makes no reference whatever to the plethora of indexed morph positions on which template-based analyses depend; and it avoids the postulation of structural distinctions that are purely artifactual.

13 Conclusions

In this concluding chapter, I discuss the general implications of the rule-combining approach to morphotactics developed in the course of the foregoing chapters. I summarize the numerous superficially problematic phenomena that the rule-combining approach resolves (Section 13.1), and I relate these phenomena to the variety of ways in which rule combinations may deviate from the canonical characteristics of a language's morphotactics (Section 13.2). Finally, I synopsize the set of formal definitions on which the rule-combining approach is based (Section 13.3).

13.1 Problematic Morphotactic Patterns and Their Resolution

Linguists have tended to equate a language's morphotactics with a set of ordering restrictions on morpheme sequences in that language. The evidence presented here suggests that a language's morphotactics can be more insightfully characterized as a system of principles by which its morphological rules combine with one another. This conception jettisons the cumbersome theoretical baggage associated with the morpheme concept and makes it possible to see clusters of morphological markings as the expression of rule combinations of various sorts. The modes of rule combination include composition (including potentiation), holistic combination, aggregation, and counterpotentiation. Each mode of combination allows some or all of the characteristics of a more complex rule to be deduced from the characteristics of simpler rules. By making recurrent use of a fixed set of combinatory patterns, a language's morphology may combine a small number of simple rules in a large number of ways to produce a system capable of expressing fine distinctions of content with considerable economy. The word forms defined by such a system do not embody word skeleta defined by the language's syntax or by the stipulation of a sequence of indexed morph positions; rather, their form is simply an expression of the way in which morphological rules combine and of each rule combination's domain-of-definition.

Postulating patterns of rule composition makes it possible to model a wide range of otherwise problematic morphotactic phenomena. In cases of carrier/dependent relations among rules of exponence, a dependent rule's sole use in a language's morphology is in composition with some member of a specific set of carrier rules. In some instances, the dependent rule composes with its carrier rule, as in Limbu agent concord (Section 3.2); in other instances, it is the carrier rule that composes with its dependent, as in the case of the Sanskrit union vowel (Section 3.3). Dependent/carrier relations entail periodic multiple exponence in cases in which (as in Limbu) the same dependent rule composes with more than one carrier rule in the definition of the same word form.

Rule composition makes it possible to model instances in which rules of inflectional exponence apply in an unexpected order in certain cases or in which they apply in more than one order. Rules of subject and object concord in Fula (Section 4.1) ordinarily compose in a default order, but certain particular rules of object concord compose with a particular rule of subject concord in the opposite order, overriding the default. In the inflection of Udmurt nouns (Section 4.2), rules of case inflection compose with rules of possessor marking in one order for one set of cases but in the opposite order for the complementary set of cases; here, neither order of composition clearly constitutes a default. Finally, in Eastern Mari noun inflection (Section 4.3), rules of case inflection, the rule of plural marking, and rules of possessor marking may compose in as many as three different orders as equally acceptable options.

In a framework in which rules may compose, apparent instances of nonlocal morphotactic conditioning can instead be seen as cases of local conditioning involving composite rules; Sanskrit imperative morphology (Section 5.1) exemplifies this possibility. By the same token, instances in which the application of one rule of exponence seems to stand in paradigmatic opposition to the application of a sequence of rules can instead be seen as the paradigmatic opposition of a simple rule to a single, composite rule; Latin, Limbu, and Sanskrit (Section 5.2) present cases of this sort, as does Swahili (Section 8.3).

The Category Determination Principle (Section 2.1.1) makes it possible to use rule composition to model the polyfunctionality of some inflectional rules. In Swahili (Section 8.2), several rules of verb inflection can be used in three ways: to express subject concord, pronominal object marking, or relativized-argument concord. On their own, these rules express set-based properties that are category-indeterminate; it is their composition with an appropriate carrier rule that fixes the category-determinate property that they serve to express in any given case. Murrinhpatha verb morphology (Sections 9.2–9.3) is remarkable for the way in which it exploits the Category Determination Principle to allow the very same rules to compose in the same linear order to express two different patterns of concord: a category-indeterminate rule of number concord expresses subject number when a category-determinate rule of subject agreement composes directly with it, but instead expresses object number when it itself composes with a category-determinate rule of object agreement. Thus, rule composition is nonassociative in Murrinhpatha verb inflection, a feature that allows the same rules to serve more than one function in the definition of a word form's morphology.

An important subtype of rule composition in many languages is that of potentiation: rule R_1 potentiates rule R_2 in exactly those cases in which the composite ($R_2 \circ R_1$) shares the domain-of-definition of R_1. An example is the English potentiation ([[-**ity**]] Ⓟ [[-**able**]]) (Section 10.1).

Composition is but one of the modes of rule combination that languages exploit. Many languages also exhibit holistic combinations – rule combinations whose content includes some parts that cannot be attributed to either of their component rules. Breton (Sections 2.3, 6.1, and 6.2), Limbu (Section 6.3), and Old English (Section 6.4) present numerous instances of this sort.

Languages also present cases of rule aggregation, a mode of rule combination in which one rule takes another rule's affix as its operand. Rule aggregation produces two sorts of affix counterposition: prefixation to a suffix (as in Noon [Section 7.1] and Swahili [Section 8.4]) and suffixation to a prefix (as in Fula [Section 2.4], Lithuanian [Section 7.2], and again Swahili [Section 8.4]). Unlike rule composition and holistic combination, aggregation seems to be limited to rules of inflection.

Finally, a language may exhibit counterpotentiation, a mode of rule combination that is in a way the opposite of potentiation: while the domain-of-definition of the potentiation (R_2 Ⓟ R_1) is identical to that of R_1, the domain-of-definition of the counterpotentiation (R_2 $\boxed{CP}_n$ R_1) is disjoint from that of R_1. English derivational morphology provides several examples of counterpotentiation, including cases involving "missing" intermediate derivatives (Section 10.2) and cases of parasynthesis (Section 10.3).

13.2 Canonical and Noncanonical Characteristics of a Language's Morphotactics

The problematic morphotactic phenomena at issue here can be seen as involving real or apparent deviations from the canonical characteristics of a language's morphotactics. A system of morphotactics should be seen as canonical to the extent that it exhibits three kinds of uniformity: definitional uniformity, interactive uniformity, and contrastive uniformity (Section 1.4). The individual rules in a morphotactic system are definitionally uniform if they are alike in their definition, as reflected by their conformity to four criteria (the minimal rule criterion, the stem operand criterion, the integral stem criterion, and the affix directionality criterion); rules that participate in the definition of the same word form are interactively uniform if they interact in the same way, as reflected by their conformity to four criteria (the rule independence criterion, the unique sequence criterion, the compositional content criterion, and the intermediate well-formedness criterion); and rules that express contrasting inflectional categories are contrastively uniform if there is a simple contrast in their application, as reflected by their conformity to two criteria (the parallel sequence criterion and the rule opposition criterion).

All rule combinations inherently deviate from the minimal rule criterion. Rule combinations also serve to model a number of other genuine deviations from the characteristics of canonical morphotactics; these include deviations from the rule independence criterion (Chapter 3), the unique sequence criterion (Chapters 3, 4, 7, 8), the parallel sequence criterion (Chapters 4, 8), the compositional content criterion (Chapter 6), the stem operand criterion (Chapters 7, 8), and the intermediate well-formedness criterion (Chapter 10). Other deviations sometimes prove to be merely apparent, ultimately conforming to canonical criteria if certain well-motivated assumptions are made; these include some apparent deviations from the integral stem criterion (Chapter 5), the rule opposition criterion (Chapters 5, 8), and the affix directionality criterion (Chapters 7, 8).

Composite rules enhance a morphotactic system's conformity to the integral stem criterion (as in the analysis of Sanskrit imperatives in Section 5.1) and to the rule opposition criterion (as in the analyses of Latin passives, Limbu preterites, and Sanskrit imperatives in Section 5.2). At the same time, composite rules afford a simple way of modeling deviations from the rule independence criterion (as in the analysis of Limbu agent concord in Section 3.2 and that of Sanskrit union vowels in Section 3.3), from the parallel sequence criterion (as in the analysis of Fula subject and object concord in Section 4.1 and that of Udmurt noun inflection in Section 4.2), and from the unique sequence criterion (as in the analysis of Eastern Mari noun inflection in Section 4.3).

Rule aggregations enhance a morphotactic system's conformity to the rule opposition criterion (as in the analysis of Swahili relative inflection, cf. Section 8.5) and to the affix directionality criterion (as in the analysis of Noon adjective inflection in Section 7.1, that of Lithuanian reflexive verbs in Section 7.2, and that of Swahili relative inflection in Section 8.4). At the same time, rule aggregations afford a simple way of modeling deviations from the stem operand criterion in these same cases.

Holistic rule combinations are the way in which deviations from the compositional content criterion are manifested (as in the analysis of Breton verb inflection in Sections 6.1–6.2, that of Limbu verb inflection in Section 6.3, and that of Old English verb inflection in Section 6.4). By the same token, counter-potentiations are the way in which deviations from the intermediate well-formedness criterion are manifested (as in the analyses of English derivational morphology in Chapter 10).

The four modes of rule combination proposed here lay a precise groundwork for understanding the nature of morphotactics. They elucidate the significance of the traditional analytic device of position-class templates. In the morphological literature, such templates have customarily been seen as columns of morphemes possessing three essential characteristics: (i) no morpheme appears in more than one column; (ii) no word form has more than one morpheme from any given column; and (iii) the order of morphemes in a word form corresponds to the order of their respective columns in the template. The rule-combining approach portrays such templates as an emergent property of language-specific patterns of rule combination but also correctly predicts that a language's patterns of rule combination may make it impossible to distill a template exhibiting all three of characteristics (i)–(iii). Instances in which a dependent rule composes with more than one carrier rule in the definition of the same word form (as in Limbu agent concord, Noon definite adjective inflection, and Swahili subject and object concord) are incompatible with the postulation of such templates, as are instances in which the same rule participates in both composition and aggregation (as in Fula preterite marking, Lithuanian reflexive marking, and Swahili relativized-argument concord).

The rule-combining approach to morphotactics also sheds new light on the nature of morphotactic complexity.[1] Traditionally, theorizing on morphotactic complexity has tended to focus on two dimensions of comparison: a morphological system's degree of synthesis and its degree of fusion. Under the assumptions of the rule-combining approach, new comparative criteria emerge. For example, morphotactic systems might be compared with respect

---

[1] Morphotactic complexity is but one aspect of the larger issue of morphological complexity. For a survey of current thought on the nature and dimensions of morphological complexity (see Stump 2017d) for a detailed and precise account of the complexity of inflection-class systems, see Stump & Finkel 2013.

to the extent that they appeal to modes of rule combination other than ordinary composition; on this view, a morphotactic system might be said to be more complex to the extent that it deviates from the compositional content criterion, the intermediate well-formedness criterion, and the stem operand criterion (deviations in which rules combine in relations of holistic combination, counterpotentiation, and aggregation, respectively).

Morphotactic systems might likewise be compared according to the extent to which they allow the same rules to enter into different combinations and according to the ways in which these alternative combinations differ from one another. In the Eastern Mari forms in (1), the dative case rule ⟦-lan⟧, the plural rule ⟦-βlak⟧, and first-person singular possessor rule ⟦-em⟧ enter into distinct combinations that express the same content; this pattern of optionality (different word forms/same content) might be seen as contributing in one way to the morphotactic complexity of Eastern Mari.

(1) (((⟦-lan⟧ ∘ ⟦-βlak⟧) ∘ ⟦-em⟧), as in *joltaš-em-βlak-lan* 'to my friends'
 (((⟦-lan⟧ ∘ ⟦-em⟧) ∘ ⟦-βlak⟧), as in *joltaš-βlak-em-lan* 'to my friends'
 (((⟦-em⟧ ∘ ⟦-lan⟧) ∘ ⟦-βlak⟧), as in *joltaš-βlak-lan-em* 'to my friends'

(cf. Section 4.3)

In the Swahili forms in (2), by contrast, (i) the past-tense rule ⟦li-⟧$_{II}$, (ii) the dependent argument-coding rules ⟦wa-$_2$⟧ (for noun class 2) and ⟦ni-⟧ (for first person singular), and (iii) the carrier rules ⟦id.fcn⟧$_{III}$ (for subject concord) and ⟦id.fcn⟧$_I$ (for the expression of a pronominal object) enter into distinct combinations to express distinct content; here, the possibility of exploiting the same rules to define words that contrast both in form and in meaning (different word forms/different content) might be seen as contributing in a different way to the morphotactic complexity of Swahili.

(2) (((⟦wa-$_2$⟧ ∘ ⟦id.fcn⟧$_{III}$) ∘ (⟦li-⟧$_{II}$ ∘ (⟦ni-⟧ ∘ ⟦id.fcn⟧$_I$))), as in *walinipiga* 'they struck me'
 (((⟦ni-⟧ ∘ ⟦id.fcn⟧$_{III}$) ∘ (⟦li-⟧$_{II}$ ∘ (⟦wa-$_2$⟧ ∘ ⟦id.fcn⟧$_I$))), as in *niliwapiga* 'I struck them'

(cf. Section 8.2)

In the ambiguous Murrinhpatha form in (3), the subject-agreement rule ⟦pu-$_C$⟧$_{DU}$, the paucal nonsibling female rule ⟦-ngime$_L$⟧, and the object-agreement rule ⟦-nganku$_C$⟧ enter into differently nested combinations that allow the same word form to express more than one content. This pattern (same word form/different content) might be seen as contributing in yet a different way to the morphotactic complexity of Murrinhpatha.

(3) *pubam-nganku-ngkardu-ngime*
(((〚**pu**-c〛_DU ∘ 〚-**ngime**_L〛) ∘ 〚-**nganku**_C〛): 'they (PNS female) saw us (DS excl.)'
(〚**pu**-c〛_DU ∘ (〚-**ngime**_L〛 ∘ 〚-**nganku**_C〛)): 'they (DS) saw us (PNS excl. female)'

(Section 9.3)

The alternative combinations of 〚**-ic**〛 and 〚**-ist**〛 in (4) present yet a different possibility, in which the same rules combine compositionally in one set of word forms but noncompositionally in another; this pattern surely contributes in a fourth way to the morphotactic complexity of English.

(4) (〚**-ic**〛 ∘ 〚**-ist**〛), as in *nationalistic*
(〚**-ic**〛 [CP]_17 〚**-ist**〛), as in *cannibalistic*

(cf. Section 10.2.1)

Although the contrasts of form and/or interpretation in (1)–(4) can be seen as manifestations of morphotactic complexity, they don't necessarily signify a higher degree of processing complexity, since the rule combinations in (1)–(4) may well be stored as formulaic units. Thus, even as it opens up new dimensions of morphotactic complexity, the rule-combining approach highlights the multifaceted nature of a language's morphotactics; complexity on one facet may well come with simplicity on another.

13.3 A Formal Synopsis of Rule Combinations

The theory of morphotactics proposed here is based on the principle that simple rules of exponence combine binarily to form more complex rules, which are in turn available for further binary combination. Such rule combinations inherently deviate from the minimal rule criterion, according to which rules of inflectional or derivational exponence are minimal (not analyzable into smaller, component rules of exponence).

I have argued that rules may combine in more than one way, with ordinary composition serving as the default mode of combination; that rule combinations are observable in both the inflectional and derivational domains; and that in the inflectional domain, the possibility of rule combination makes it possible to regard the definition of a given inflected word form as the expression of a single rule (a full exponence rule, or FER), often a rule of some complexity. The evidence favoring this conception of morphotactics is disparate, pervasive, and compelling. A synopsis of the kinds of rule combinations motivated here is given in the following subsections.

13.3.1 Composition (Operator ∘)

In informal terms, the composite of rule B with rule A is a rule whose application is the result of applying B to the result of applying A. In order to formalize this idea, it is important to distinguish the composition of inflectional rules from that of derivational rules.

Let R_1 and R_2 be the rules of inflectional exponence in (5).

(5) a. $R_1 : [C_1, \tau_1 : X \rightarrow f_1(X)]$

> (Where $\langle Z, \sigma \rangle$ is a ⟨stem, property set⟩ pairing, R_1 is applicable to $\langle Z, \sigma \rangle$ only if Z belongs to category C_1 and σ is an extension of τ_1; the result of applying R_1 to $\langle Z, \sigma \rangle$ is $\langle f_1(Z), \sigma \rangle$.)

b. $R_2 : [C_2, \tau_2 : X \rightarrow f_2(X)]$

> (Where $\langle Z, \sigma \rangle$ is a ⟨stem, property set⟩ pairing, R_2 is applicable to $\langle Z, \sigma \rangle$ only if Z belongs to category C_2 and σ is an extension of τ_2; the result of applying R_2 to $\langle Z, \sigma \rangle$ is $\langle f_2(Z), \sigma \rangle$.)

In that case, the ***composite inflectional rule*** $(R_2 \circ R_1)$ is that function F in the set of ⟨stem, property set⟩ pairings such that for any stem Z in the intersection $[C_2 \cap C_1]$ and any well-formed superset σ of the unification $[\tau_2 \sqcup \tau_1]$, $F(\langle Z, \sigma \rangle) = \langle f_2(f_1(Z)), \sigma \rangle$. Thus, $(R_2 \circ R_1)$ is the composite inflectional rule such that

$$(R_2 \circ R_1) = [[C_2 \cap C_1], [\tau_2 \sqcup \tau_1] : X \rightarrow f_2(f_1(X))].$$

> (Where $\langle Z, \sigma \rangle$ is a ⟨stem, property set⟩ pairing, $(R_2 \circ R_1)$ is applicable to $\langle Z, \sigma \rangle$ only if Z belongs to category $[C_2 \cap C_1]$ and σ is an extension of $[\tau_2 \sqcup \tau_1]$; the result of applying $(R_2 \circ R_1)$ to $\langle Z, \sigma \rangle$ is $\langle f_2(f_1(Z)), \sigma \rangle$.)

The preceding chapters present numerous examples of composition in inflection:

- Limbu: (dependent ∘ carrier) composites in verb inflection (Section 3.2)
- Sanskrit: (carrier ∘ dependent) composites in verb inflection (Section 3.3)
- Fula: default order of composition of subject and object concord overridden by its opposite (Section 4.1)
- Udmurt: complementary orders of composition of case and possessor marking (Section 4.2)
- Eastern Mari: alternative orders of composition of case, number, and possessor marking (Section 4.3)
- Sanskrit: composite imperative rules enhance locality (Section 5.1)
- Latin: passive portmanteau subject concord paradigmatically opposed to composite rules (Section 5.2)
- Limbu: override of composite rule by simple rule in verb inflection (Section 5.2.2.1)

13.3 A Formal Synopsis of Rule Combinations

- Sanskrit: override of simple rule by composite rule in imperatives (Section 5.2.2.2)
- Swahili: verbal concord involving the Category Determination Principle (Section 8.2)
- Swahili: negative portmanteau subject concord paradigmatically opposed to composite rules (Section 8.3)
- Murrinhpatha: nonassociative composition in verbal concord involving the Category Determination Principle (Section 9.3).

Let R_3 and R_4 be the rules of derivational exponence in (6).

(6)   a. $R_3 : [\mu_3 \Rightarrow D : X \rightarrow f_3(X)]$

(Where ⟨L, Z, C⟩ is a ⟨lexeme, stem, lexicosemantic category⟩ triplet, R_3 is applicable to ⟨L, Z, C⟩ only if ⟨L, Z, C⟩ belongs to its domain-of-definition μ_3; the result of applying R_3 to ⟨L, Z, C⟩ is ⟨L′, $f_3(Z)$, D⟩, where L′ is that lexeme of category D having $f_3(Z)$ as its default stem.)

       b. $R_4 : [\mu_4 \Rightarrow E : X \rightarrow f_4(X)]$

(Where ⟨L, Z, C⟩ is a ⟨lexeme, stem, lexicosemantic category⟩ triplet, R_4 is applicable to ⟨L, Z, C⟩ only if ⟨L, Z, C⟩ belongs to its domain-of-definition μ_4; the result of applying R_4 to ⟨L, Z, C⟩ is ⟨L′, $f_4(Z)$, D⟩, where L′ is that lexeme of category E having $f_4(Z)$ as its default stem.)

In that case, the **composite derivational rule** $(R_4 \circ R_3)$ is that function F in the set of ⟨lexeme, stem, lexicosemantic category⟩ triplets such that for any triplet t in the domain-of-definition μ_3, F(t) is the result of applying R_4 to the result of applying R_3 to t, if this is defined. F(t) is defined only if (a) t is in the domain-of-definition μ_3 of R_3 and (b) the result of applying R_3 to t is in the domain-of-definition μ_4 of R_4. The domain-of-definition of $(R_4 \circ R_3)$ is a subset of (potentially identical to) that of R_3. Thus, $(R_4 \circ R_3)$ is the composite derivational rule such that

$$(R_4 \circ R_3) = [\mu_0 \Rightarrow E : X \rightarrow f_4(f_3(X))],$$

where the domain-of-definition μ_0 is the smallest set such that for each triplet t in μ_3, t belongs to μ_0 if and only if the result of applying R_3 to t belongs to μ_4.

(Where ⟨L, Z, C⟩ is a ⟨lexeme, stem, lexicosemantic category⟩ triplet, $(R_4 \circ R_3)$ is applicable to ⟨L, Z, C⟩ only if ⟨L, Z, C⟩ belongs to its domain-of-definition μ_0; the result of applying $(R_4 \circ R_3)$ to ⟨L, Z, C⟩ is ⟨L′, $f_4(f_3(Z))$, E⟩, where L′ is that lexeme of category E having $f_4(f_3(Z))$ as its default stem.)

400 *Conclusions*

Chapters 10 and 11 present numerous examples of composition in English derivation: *decaffeinate* (Section 10.3); *cyclical*, etc. (Section 11.2.1); *artistic*, etc. (Section 11.2.2); *logician*, etc. (Section 11.2.4).

13.3.2   Potentiation (Operator Ⓟ)

In informal terms, the potentiation of rule B by rule A is a composite of B with A that has a defined value for every member of A's domain-of-definition. Thus, a composite derivational rule ($R_4 \circ R_3$) may be represented as the **potentiation** (R_4 Ⓟ R_3) if and only if it has the same domain-of-definition as R_3. Examples of potentiation in English: *acceptability*, etc. (Section 10.1); *hyphenation*, etc. (Sections 10.2.2 and 11.2.3).

13.3.3   Counterpotentiation (Operator $\boxed{CP}$)

In informal terms, the counterpotentiation of rule A by rule B is a rule R with the following characteristics: R's formal operation is the composite of B's formal operation with that of A; R's range is that of B; R's domain is that of A; but R's domain-of-definition is disjoint from that of A.

Let R_3 and R_4 be the derivational rules in (6). R_3 has the domain-of-definition μ_3, a subset of some set $\mathbb{C}$ of ⟨lexeme, stem, lexicosemantic category⟩ triplets, so that R_3 is a partial function from $\mathbb{C}$ to the set $\mathbb{D}$ of triplets of the type ⟨lexeme, stem, D⟩. R_4 defines members of the set $\mathbb{E}$ of triplets of the type ⟨lexeme, stem, E⟩. The **counterpotentiation** in (7) is a partial function from $\mathbb{C}$ to $\mathbb{E}$ whose domain-of-definition μ_6 is disjoint from the domain-of-definition μ_3 of R_3.

(7)   (R_4 $\boxed{CP}_6$ R_3) : [$\mu_6 \Rightarrow$ E : X $\rightarrow f_4(f_3(X))$]

Two types of counterpotentiation can be distinguished: pleonastic counterpotentiation and compositionally motivated counterpotentiation.

Pleonastic counterpotentiations are instances of (7) in which $\mathbb{D} = \mathbb{E}$ and μ_3, μ_4, and μ_6 are disjoint subsets of $\mathbb{C}$ (so that R_3, R_4, and (R_4 $\boxed{CP}_6$ R_3) are all partial functions from $\mathbb{C}$ to $\mathbb{E}$):

R_3 : [$\mu_3 \Rightarrow$ E : X $\rightarrow f_3(X)$]
R_4 : [$\mu_4 \Rightarrow$ E : X $\rightarrow f_4(X)$]
(R_4 $\boxed{CP}_6$ R_3) : [$\mu_6 \Rightarrow$ E : X $\rightarrow f_4(f_3(X))$].

Compositionally motivated counterpotentiations are instances of (7) in which ($R_4 \circ R_3$) and (R_4 $\boxed{CP}_6$ R_3) are both partial functions from $\mathbb{C}$ to $\mathbb{E}$:

13.3 A Formal Synopsis of Rule Combinations 401

$R_3 : [\mu_3 \Rightarrow D : X \rightarrow f_3(X)]$, where μ_3 is a subset of $\mathbb{C}$
$R_4 : [\mu_4 \Rightarrow E : X \rightarrow f_4(X)]$, where μ_4 is a subset of $\mathbb{D}$
$(R_4 \circ R_3) : [\mu_0 \Rightarrow E : X \rightarrow f_4(f_3(X))]$
$(R_4 \boxed{CP}_6 R_3) : [\mu_6 \Rightarrow E : X \rightarrow f_4(f_3(X))]$, where μ_6 is a subset of $\mathbb{C}$ disjoint from μ_3.

Examples of counterpotentiation in English: *embolden*, etc. (Section 2.5); *cannibalistic*, etc. (Sections 2.5, 10.2.1, and 11.2.2); *whimsical*, etc. (Sections 10.2.1 and 11.2.1); *beautician*, etc. (Sections 10.2.1 and 11.2.4); *accusation*, etc. (Sections 10.2.2 and 11.2.3). In nouns of the *accusation* type, counterpotentiation is the context in which 〚-ate〛 serves in the formation of a combining stem.

13.3.4 Content Supplementation (Operator Ⓢ)

In informal terms, a content supplementation of rule R is a rule whose formal properties are those of R but whose application realizes content that supplements that realized by R.

Where R_1 is the inflectional rule in (5a), the **inflectional content supplementation** Ⓢ$_\gamma(R_1)$ is such that

$$Ⓢ_\gamma(R_1) = [C_1, [\tau_1 \sqcup \gamma] : X \rightarrow f_1(X)].$$

Where R_3 is the derivational rule in (6a), the **derivational content supplementation** Ⓢ$_E(R_3)$ is such that

$$Ⓢ_E(R_3) = [\mu_3 \Rightarrow [D \cup E] : X \rightarrow f_3(X)].$$

Where R is a composite rule, Ⓢ$_\gamma(R)$ is a *holistic combination*; where R is a simple rule, Ⓢ$_\gamma(R)$ is a *solitary specialization*.

Examples of content supplementation:

- Breton: holistic combinations and solitary specializations in verb inflection (Section 6.2)
- Limbu: emergent supplementary content in verb inflection (Section 6.3)
- Old English: the same rules enter into contrasting holistic combinations (Section 6.4).

13.3.5 Aggregation (Operator Ⓐ)

In informal terms, aggregation may be described as follows. Where B is a rule whose formal operation is f and A is a rule whose formal operation is the suffixation (or prefixation) of x, the aggregation of B with A is a rule that realizes the same content as the composite of B with A but whose formal operation is the suffixation (or prefixation) of $f(x)$. Aggregation is the formal expression of affix counterposition (Sections 1.5.6 and 2.4).

Given the affixation operations f, g and the inflectional rules R_7 and R_8 in (8),

(8) a. $R_7 : [C_7, \tau_7 : X \to f(a, X)]$
     b. $R_8 : [C_8, \tau_8 : X \to g(b, X)]$,

the *aggregation* ($R_8 \circledA R_7$) is such that

$$(R_8 \circledA R_7) = [[C_8 \cap C_7], [\tau_8 \sqcup \tau_7] : X \to f(g(b, a), X)].$$

Although R_8 operates by default on a stem belonging to category C_8, this default is overridden when R_8 aggregates with R_7: in the aggregation, R_8 takes as its operand the affix a introduced by R_7.

Given that composition is the canonical mode of rule combination and that $(R_8 \circ R_7)$ is equivalent to $(R_8 \circledA R_7)$ whenever R_7 and R_8 are both prefixational or both suffixational, it is most usual to invoke aggregation in instances in which rules R_7 and R_8 differ in that one is prefixational and one is suffixational.[2] Thus, given the inflectional rules R_9 and R_{10} in (9),

(9) a. $R_9 : [C_9, \tau_9 : a\text{-}]$
     b. $R_{10} : [C_{10}, \tau_{10} : \text{-}b]$

the aggregation $(R_{10} \circledA R_9) = [[C_{10} \cap C_9], [\tau_{10} \sqcup \tau_9] : ab\text{-}]$ (a *prefixational aggregation*) and the aggregation $(R_9 \circledA R_{10}) = [[C_{10} \cap C_9], [\tau_{10} \sqcup \tau_9] : \text{-}ab]$ (a *suffixational aggregation*).

In the preceding chapters, several instances of affix counterposition are formalized as instances of rule aggregation:

- Fula: preterite verb inflection (Section 2.4)
- Noon: definite adjective inflection (Section 7.1)
- Lithuanian: reflexive verb inflection (Section 7.2)
- Italian: pronominal affixes on verbs (Section 7.4)
- Swahili: relative verb inflection (Section 8.4).

---

[2] Nevertheless, a rule may aggregate with members of a class of rules some of which are prefixational and others of which are suffixational; see again the discussion of Italian pronominal affixes in Section 7.4.

13.3.6 Inflectional Rule Combinations vs. Derivational Rule Combinations

According to the rule-combining approach to exponence-driven morphotactics, the ways in which rules of exponence combine depends on whether they are inflectional or derivational. Two derivational rules R_3, R_4 may combine in four different ways: they may form a composite rule ($R_4 \circ R_3$), a potentiation ($R_4 \; ⓟ \; R_3$), a counterpotentiation ($R_4 \; \boxed{CP}_6 \; R_3$), or a holistic combination $Ⓢ_E(R_4 \circ R_3)$. By definition, the domain-of-definition of a composite rule ($R_4 \circ R_3$) is a subset of (and possibly identical to) that of its inner member R_3. The domain-of-definition of a potentiation ($R_4 \; ⓟ \; R_3$) is identical to that of its inner member R_3; thus, a potentiation is a kind of composite rule. When a rule is defined as a potentiation rather than merely as a composite, its definition carries more information – specifically, it defines a context in which its outer rule R_4 is high in productivity, notwithstanding its potentially low productivity in other contexts. The domain-of-definition of a counterpotentiation ($R_4 \; \boxed{CP}_6 \; R_3$) is disjoint from that of its inner member R_3: if a ⟨lexeme, stem, lexicosemantic category⟩ triplet is in the domain-of-definition of R_3, it is absent from that of ($R_4 \; \boxed{CP}_6 \; R_3$), and vice versa. Nevertheless, the rules R_3 and ($R_4 \; \boxed{CP}_6 \; R_3$) have the same domain, being partial functions defined for different members of that domain. The domain-of-definition of a holistic combination $Ⓢ_E(R_4 \circ R_3)$ is a subset of that of R_3.

Two inflectional rules R_1, R_2 may combine in three different ways: they may form a composite rule ($R_2 \circ R_1$), a holistic combination $Ⓢ_\gamma(R_2 \circ R_1)$, or an aggregation ($R_2 \; Ⓐ \; R_1$). The application of a composite inflectional rule ($R_2 \circ R_1$) is like the successive application of rules R_1 and R_2 when not in combination: it realizes the same content by means of the same operator/operand relations. A holistic combination $Ⓢ_\gamma(R_2 \circ R_1)$ differs from the corresponding composite ($R_2 \circ R_1$): although it employs the same operator/operand relations, it realizes additional content. An aggregation ($R_2 \; Ⓐ \; R_1$) differs from the corresponding composite ($R_2 \circ R_1$) in the opposite way: although it realizes the same content, it does so by means of different operator/operand relations.

The similarities and differences among the different kinds of rule combination are summarized in Table 13.1.

13.3.7 The Category Determination Principle

A rule of inflectional exponence may realize a set-based morphosyntactic property P that is category-indeterminate. Rules of this kind are subject to the Category Determination Principle in (10).

Table 13.1 *How different combinations of two rules R_A, R_B differ from one another*
(Each shaded cell differs from the corresponding cell in the 'Composition' column.)

	Composition ($R_B \circ R_A$)	Holistic combination $\circledS_\gamma(R_B \circ R_A)$	Aggregation ($R_B \circledA R_A$)	Potentiation ($R_B \circledP R_A$)	Counterpotentiation ($R_B \boxed{CP}_n R_A$)
R_A and R_B may be inflectional	yes	yes	yes	no	no
R_A and R_B may be derivational	yes	yes	no	yes	yes
Content realized	X	X + γ	X	X	X
Operand of R_B in the combination's definition	stem defined by R_A's operation	stem defined by R_A's operation	affix defined by R_A	stem defined by R_A's operation	stem defined by R_A's operation
Domain-of-definition	subset of that of R_A	subset of that of R_A	subset of that of R_A	identical to that of R_A	disjoint from that of R_A

(10) Category Determination Principle (Section 2.1.1)
If R is a rule of inflectional exponence that realizes a category-indeterminate property P, R always combines with a rule that realizes a set-based property Q such that the unification [P ⊔ Q] is a set-based property that is well-formed and category-determinate.

Instances of rule composition or rule aggregation that involve this principle:

- Swahili: the polyfunctionality of noun-class concords (Sections 8.2 and 8.4)
- Murrinhpatha: nonassociative rule composition (Sections 9.1 and 9.3).

13.4 Looking Ahead

The approach to morphotactics synopsized here must naturally be seen as a work in progress; many refinements of this approach may well emerge as research continues. One important objective for future research is that of determining whether the proposed modes of rule combination must be supplemented with additional, possibly hybrid modes. Even so, the evidence and analyses presented here do converge on some certainties: that the morphotactic characteristics of natural languages involve rules, that simpler rules may enter into binary combinations yielding more complex rules, and that the economy of a language's morphotactics stems in part from the fact that there is more than one mode of rule combination.

References

Alhoniemi, Alho. (2010). *Marin kielioppi*, 2nd ed. Helsinki: Suomalais-Ugrilainen Seura.
Ambrazas, Vytautas, Emma Geniušienė, Aleksas Girdenis, Nijolė Sližienė, Dalija Tekorienė, Adelė Valeckienė, & Elena Valiulytė. (1997). *Lithuanian grammar*. Vilnius: Baltos lankos.
Anderson, Stephen R. (1992). *A-morphous morphology*. Cambridge: Cambridge University Press.
 (1995). Rules and constraints in describing the morphology of phrases. In A. Dainora, R. Hemphill, B. Luka, B. Need, & S. Pargman (eds.), *Papers from the 31st Regional Meeting of the Chicago Linguistic Society, volume 2: The parasession on clitics*. Chicago, IL: Chicago Linguistic Society, pp. 15–31.
Arkadiev, Peter. (2010). Notes on the Lithuanian restrictive. *Baltic Linguistics* 1, 9–49.
 (2011a). Aspect and actionality in Lithuanian on a typological background. In Daniel Petit, Claire Le Feuvre, & Henri Menantaud (eds.), *Langues baltiques, langues slaves*. Paris: CNRS Editions, pp. 61–92.
 (2011b). On the aspectual uses of the prefix be- in Lithuanian. *Baltic Linguistics* 2, 37–78.
 (2012a). "External" verbal prefixes in Lithuanian. Paper presented at the Scuola Normale Superiore di Pisa, December 14, 2012.
 (2012b). Stems in Lithuanian verbal inflection (with remarks on derivation). *Word Structure* 5(1), 7–27.
Arnon, Inbal & Neal Snider. (2010). More than words: Frequency effects for multi-word phrases. *Journal of Memory and Language* 62, 67–82.
Arnott, D. W. (1970). *The nominal and verbal systems of Fula*. Oxford: Oxford University Press.
Aronoff, Mark. (1976). *Word formation in generative grammar*. Cambridge, MA: MIT Press.
 (1994). *Morphology by itself*. Cambridge, MA: MIT Press.
Arregi, Karlos & Andrew Nevins. (2012). *Morphotactics: Basque auxiliaries and the structure of Spellout* (Studies in Natural Language and Linguistic Theory 86). Dordrecht: Springer.
Ashton, E. O. (1947). *Swahili grammar*, 2nd ed. Essex: Longman.
Bach, Emmon. (1979). Control in Montague Grammar. *Linguistic Inquiry* 10(4), 515–531.

Badrulhisham, Heikal. (2019). *Formulaicity of affixes in Turkish*. Master's thesis, Simon Fraser University.
Barrett-Keach, Camillia N. (1986). Word-internal evidence from Swahili for Aux/Infl. *Linguistic Inquiry* 17(3), 559–564.
Bauer, Laurie. (1988). A descriptive gap in morphology. In Geert Booij & Jaap van Marle (eds.), *Yearbook of morphology 1*. Dordrecht: Kluwer, pp. 17–27.
  (2014). Concatenative derivation. In Rochelle Lieber & Pavol Štekauer (eds.), *The Oxford handbook of derivational morphology*. Oxford: Oxford University Press, pp. 118–135.
Bauer, Laurie, Rochelle Lieber, & Ingo Plag. (2013). *The Oxford reference guide to English morphology*. Oxford: Oxford University Press.
Becker, Thomas. (1993). Back-formation, cross-formation, and "bracketing paradoxes" in paradigmatic morphology. In Geert Booij & Jaap van Marle (eds.), *Yearbook of morphology 1993*. Dordrecht: Springer, pp. 1–25.
Beckett, Eleanor. (1974). *A linguistic analysis of Gurma*. Master's thesis, University of British Columbia.
Bickel, Balthasar, Goma Banjade, Martin Gaenzle, Elena Lieven, Netra Prasad Paudyal, Ichchha Purna Rai, Manoj Rai, Novel Kishore Rai, & Sabine Stoll. (2007). Free prefix ordering in Chintang. *Language* 83, 43–73.
Bilgin, Orhan. (2016). *Frequency effects in the processing of morphologically complex Turkish words*. Master's thesis, Boğaziçi University.
Bisetto, Antonietta & Chiara Melloni. (2007). Parasynthetic compounding. *Lingue e Linguaggio* 7(2), 233–260.
Blythe, Joe, Rachel Nordlinger, & Nicholas Reid. (2007). *Murriny Patha finite verb paradigms*. Wadeye, NT: Unpublished MS.
Bochner, Harry. (1993). *Simplicity in generative morphology*. Berlin: Mouton de Gruyter.
Booij, Geert. (1979). Semantic regularities in word formation. *Linguistics* 17, 985–1001.
  (2005). *The grammar of words: An introduction to linguistic morphology*. Oxford: Oxford University Press.
  (2007). Construction Morphology and the lexicon. In Fabio Montermini, Gilles Boyé, & Nabil Hathout (eds.), *Selected proceedings of the 5th Décembrettes: Morphology in Toulouse*. Somerville, MA: Cascadilla Proceedings Project, pp. 34–44.
  (2010). *Construction Morphology*. Oxford and New York, NY: Oxford University Press.
  (2018). The construction of words: Introduction and overview. In Geert Booij (ed.), *The construction of words: Advances in Construction Morphology*. Berlin: Springer, pp. 3–16.
Booij, Geert & Francesca Masini. (2015). The role of second order schemas in the construction of complex words. In Laurie Bauer, Lívia Körtvélyessy, & Pavol Štekauer (eds.), *Semantics of complex words*. Cham: Springer, pp. 47–66.
Brook, George Leslie. (1955). *An introduction to Old English*. Manchester: Manchester University Press.

Brown, Dunstan, Marina Chumakina, & Greville G. Corbett (eds.) (2013). *Canonical morphology and syntax*. Oxford: Oxford University Press.

Burrow, Thomas & Bhattacharya, Sudhibhushan. (1970). *The Pengo language*. Oxford: Oxford University Press.

Bybee, Joan. (1985). *Morphology: A study of the relation between meaning and form*. Amsterdam: John Benjamins.

Carrol, Gareth & Kathy Conklin. (2020). Is all formulaic language created equal? Unpacking the processing advantage for different types of formulaic sequences. *Language and Speech* 63(1), 95–122.

Clark, Eve V. & Herbert H. Clark. (1979). When nouns surface as verbs. *Language* 55(4), 767–811.

Conklin, Kathy & Norbert Schmitt. (2012). The processing of formulaic language. *Annual Review of Applied Linguistics* 32, 45–61.

Contini-Morava, Ellen. (2007). Swahili morphology. In Alan S. Kaye (ed.), *Morphologies of Asia and Africa, vol. 2*. Winona Lake, IN: Eisenbrauns, pp. 1129–1158.

Corbett, Greville G. (2005). The canonical approach in typology. In Zygmunt Frajzyngier, Adam Hodges, & David S. Rood (eds.), *Linguistic diversity and language theories* (Studies in Language Companion Series 72). Amsterdam: John Benjamins, pp. 25–49.

(2015). Morphosyntactic complexity: A typology of lexical splits. *Language* 91, 145–193.

Corbett, Greville G. & Norman M. Fraser. (1993). Network Morphology: A DATR account of Russian nominal inflection. *Journal of Linguistics* 29, 113–142.

Corbin, Danielle. (1980). Contradictions et inadéquations de l'analyse parasynthétique en morphologie dérivationnelle. In A.-M. Dessaux-Berthonneau (ed.), *Théories linguistiques et traditions grammaticales*. Lille: Presses Universitaires de Lille, pp. 181–224.

Crysmann, Berthold & Olivier Bonami. (2016). Variable morphotactics in Information-based Morphology. *Journal of Linguistics* 52, 311–374.

Cyffer, Norbert. (2007). Kanuri morphology. In Alan S. Kaye (ed.), *Morphologies of Asia and Africa, vol. 2*. Winona Lake, IN: Eisenbrauns, pp. 1089–1126.

Dambriūnas, Leonardas, Antanas Klimas, & William R. Schmalstieg. (1972). *Introduction to modern Lithuanian*. New York, NY: Franciscan Fathers.

Darmesteter, Arsène. (1874). *Traité de la formation des mots composés dans la langue française comparée aux autres langues romanes et au latin*. Paris: Franck.

Deshpande, Madhav M. (1997). *Saṃskṛtasubodhinī: A Sanskrit primer*. Ann Arbor, MI: Center for South and Southeast Asian Studies, University of Michigan.

Dixon, R. M. W. (2014). *Making new words: Morphological derivation in English*. Oxford: Oxford University Press.

Durrant, Philip. (2013). Formulaicity in an agglutinating language: The case of Turkish. *Corpus Linguistics and Linguistic Theory* 9, 1–38.

(2016). Formulaicity within Turkish words. *Mersin Üniversitesi Dil ve Edebiyat Dergisi* 13(2), 35–52.

Embick, David & Rolf Noyer. (2001). Movement operations after syntax. *Linguistic Inquiry* 32(4), 555–595.

Fábregas, Antonio & Sergio Scalise. (2012). *Morphology: From data to theories*. Edinburgh: Edinburgh University Press.

Fradin, Bernard. (2003). *Nouvelles approches en morphologie*. Paris: Presses Universitaires de France.
Gazdar, Gerald, Ewan Klein, Geoffrey Pullum, & Ivan Sag. (1985). *Generalized phrase structure grammar*. Cambridge, MA: Harvard University Press.
Gibbs, Raymond W. & Gayle P. Gonzales. (1985). Syntactic frozenness in processing and remembering idioms. *Cognition* 20(3), 243–259.
Gibbs, Raymond W., Nandini P. Nayak, & Cooper Cutting. (1989). How to kick the bucket and not decompose: Analyzability and idiom processing. *Journal of Memory and Language* 28(5), 576–593.
Good, Jeff. (2016). *The linguistic typology of templates*. Cambridge: Cambridge University Press.
Greenberg, Joseph H. (1977). Niger-Congo noun class markers: Prefixes, suffixes, both, or neither. *Studies in African Linguistics* S7, 97–104.
  (1978). How does a language acquire gender markers? *Universals of human language, vol. 2*, ed. J. Greenberg, C. A. Ferguson, & Edith A. Moravcsik. Stanford: Stanford University Press, pp. 47–82.
Halle, Morris & Alec Marantz. (1993). Distributed Morphology and the pieces of inflection. In Kenneth Hale & Samuel J. Keyser (eds.), *The view from Building 20: Linguistic essays in honor of Sylvain Bromberger*. Cambridge, MA: MIT Press, pp. 111–176.
Hamp, E. P. (1959). Zuara Berber personals. *Bulletin of the School of Oriental and African Studies* 22(1), 140–141.
Hanks, Patrick. (2013). *Lexical analysis*. Cambridge, MA: MIT Press.
Harris, Alice C. (2017). *Multiple exponence*. Oxford: Oxford University Press.
Haspelmath, Martin. (1995). The growth of affixes in morphological reanalysis. In Geert Booij & Jaap van Marle (eds.), *Yearbook of morphology 1994*. Dordrecht: Kluwer, pp. 1–29.
Holvoet, Axel. (2020). *The middle voice in Baltic*. Amsterdam: John Benjamins.
Hutchison, John P. (1981). *A reference grammar of the Kanuri language*. Madison, WI: African Studies Program, University of Wisconsin and Boston: African Studies Center, Boston University.
Hyman, Larry. (2003). Suffix ordering in Bantu: A morphocentric approach. In Geert Booij & Jaap van Marle (eds.), *Yearbook of morphology 2002*. Dordrecht: Springer, pp. 245–281.
  (2018). The first person singular subject negative portmanteau in Luganda and Lusoga. *Berkeley Papers in Formal Linguistics*, 1(1), https://escholarship.org/uc/item/6qq6j48w.
Iacobini, Claudio. (2020). Parasynthesis in Morphology. In *Oxford Research Encyclopedia of Linguistics*, ed. by Mark Aronoff. Oxford: Oxford University Press, http://linguistics.oxfordre.com.
Jackendoff, Ray & Jenny Audring. (2020). *The texture of the lexicon*. Oxford: Oxford University Press.
Kempf, Luise & Stefan Hartmann. (2018). Schema unification and morphological productivity: A diachronic perspective. In Geert E. Booij (ed.), *The construction of words: Advances in Construction Morphology*. Berlin: Springer, pp. 441–474.
Kervella, Frañsez. (1976). *Yezhadur bras ar brezhoneg*. Brest: Al Liamm.

Kipacha, Ahmadi. (2006). The impact of the morphological alternation of subject markers on tense/aspect: The case of Swahili. In Laura J. Downing, Sabine Zerbian, & Lutz Marten (eds.), *Papers in Bantu grammar and description (ZAS Papers in Linguistics 43)*. Berlin: ZAS, pp. 81–96.
Lieber, Rochelle. (1992). *Deconstructing morphology: Word formation in syntactic theory*. Chicago, IL: University of Chicago Press.
  (2016). *English nouns: The ecology of nominalization*. Cambridge: Cambridge University Press.
Loogman, Alfons. (1965). *Swahili grammar and syntax*. Pittsburgh: Duquesne University Press.
Luís, Ana & Ryo Otoguro. (2004). Proclitic contexts and their effect on clitic placement. In Miriam Butt & Tracy Holloway King (eds.), *Proceedings of Lexical-Functional Grammar 2004*. Stanford: CSLI Publications, pp. 334–352.
  (2011). Inflectional morphology and syntax in correspondence: Evidence from European Portuguese. In Alexandra Galani, Glyn Hicks & George Tsoulas (eds.), *Morphology and its interfaces*. Amsterdam: John Benjamins, pp. 97–135.
Luís, Ana & Andrew Spencer. (2005). A paradigm function account of 'mesoclisis' in European Portuguese. In Geert Booij & Jaap van Marle (eds.), *Yearbook of morphology 2004*. Dordrecht: Springer, pp. 177–228.
Luutonen, Jorma. (1997). *The variation of morpheme order in Mari declension*. Helsinki: Suomalais-Ugrilainen Seura.
Maganga, Clement. (1990). *A study of the morphophonology of Standard Swahili, Kipemba, Kitumbatu and Kimakunduchi*. PhD dissertation, University of Dar es Salaam.
Mansfield, John. (2019). *Murrinhpatha morphology and phonology*. Boston, MA and Berlin: De Gruyter Mouton.
Mansfield, John, Sabine Stoll, & Balthasar Bickel. (2020). Category clustering: A probabilistic bias in the morphology of verbal agreement marking. *Language* 96(2), 255–293.
Marchand, Hans. (1966). *The categories and types of present-day English word-formation: A synchronic-diachronic approach*. University, AL: University of Alabama Press.
Masini, Francesca & Claudio Iacobini. (2018). Schemas and discontinuity in Italian: The view from Construction Morphology. In Geert Booij (ed.), *The construction of words*, 81–109. Dordrecht: Springer.
Matthews, Peter Hugoe. (1972). *Inflectional morphology: A theoretical study based on aspects of Latin verb conjugation*. Cambridge: Cambridge University Press.
  (1974). *Morphology: An introduction to the theory of word structure*. Cambridge: Cambridge University Press.
McIntosh, Mary. (1984). *Fulfulde syntax and verbal morphology*. London: Routledge & Kegan Paul.
Meier-Brügger, Michael. (2003). *Indo-European linguistics*, trans. by Charles Gertmenian. Berlin and New York: Walter de Gruyter.
Meinhof, Carl. (1906). *Grundzüge einer vergleichenden Grammatik der Bantusprachen*. Berlin: Reimer.

Mohammed, Mohammed Abdulla. (2001). *Modern Swahili grammar*. Nairobi, Kampala, and Dar es Salaam: East African Educational Publishers.

Monachesi, Paola. (1995). *A grammar of Italian clitics*. PhD dissertation, Tilburg University.

(1999). *A lexical approach to Italian cliticization*. Stanford: CSLI Publications.

Naba, Jean-Claude. (1994). *Le Gulmancema: Essai de systématisation*. Cologne: Rüdiger Köppe Verlag.

Nevins, Andrew. (2015). Lectures on postsyntactic morphology. Manuscript of July 21, 2015, LSA Summer Language Institute, University of Michigan.

Nevis, Joel A. & Brian D. Joseph. (1992). Wackernagel affixes: Evidence from Balto-Slavic. In Geert Booij & Jaap van Marle (eds.), *Yearbook of morphology 3*. Dordrecht: Kluwer, pp. 93–111.

Nordlinger, Rachel. (2010). Verbal morphology in Murrinh-Patha: Evidence for templates. *Morphology* 20, 321–341.

(2015). Inflection in Murrinh-Patha. In Matthew Baerman (ed.), *The Oxford handbook of inflection*. Oxford: Oxford University Press, pp. 491–519.

Nordlinger, Rachel & Patrick Caudal. (2012). The tense, aspect and modality system in Murrinh-Patha. *Australian Journal of Linguistics* 32, 113–173.

Nordlinger, Rachel & John Mansfield. (2021). Positional dependency in Murrinhpatha: Expanding the typology of non-canonical morphotactics. *Linguistics Vanguard* 7(1), 1–11.

Noyer, Robert Rolf. (1992). *Features, positions and affixes in autonomous morphological structure*. PhD dissertation, Massachusetts Institute of Technology.

Özel, Selma Ayşe, Yasin Bektaş, & Hakan Yilmazer. (2016). Formulaicity in Turkish: Evidence from the Turkish National Corpus. *Mersin Üniversitesi Dil ve Edebiyat Dergisi* 13(2), 1–33.

Pakerys, Jurgis. (2011). On derivational suffixes and inflection classes of verbs in Modern Lithuanian. *Lietuvių kalba* 5, 1–17.

(2021). Obligatory features of Lithuanian verbal inflection classes. In Peter Arkadiev, Jurgis Pakerys, Inesa Šeškauskienė, & Vaiva Žeimantienė (eds.), *Studies in Baltic and other languages. A Festschrift for Axel Holvoet on the occasion of his 65th birthday* (Vilnius University Open Series, vol. 16). Vilnius: Vilnius University Press, pp. 268–290.

Plag, Ingo. (2003). *Word-formation in English*. Cambridge: Cambridge University Press.

Quirk, Randolph & C. L. Wrenn. (1955). *An Old English grammar*. London: Methuen & Co.

Rácz, Péter, Alice Mitchell, & Joe Blythe. (2018). Egocentric and allocentric learning of social-indexical meaning in American English, Datooga, and Murrinhpatha. In T. T. Rogers, M. Rau, X. Zhu, & C. W. Kalish (eds.), *Proceedings of the 40th Annual Conference of the Cognitive Science Society*. Austin, TX: Cognitive Science Society, pp. 2303–2308.

Raffelsiefen, Renate. (1992). A nonconfigurational approach to morphology. In Mark Aronoff (ed.), *Morphology now*. Albany: SUNY Press, pp. 133–162.

Rainer, Franz. (2012). Morphological metaphysics: Virtual, potential, and actual words. *Word Structure* 5, 165–182.
Renou, Louis. (1996). *Grammaire sanscrite* (3rd ed., revised, corrected and augmented). Paris: Librairie d'Amérique et d'Orient, Jean Maisonneuve Successeur.
Salminen, Tapani. (1997). *Tundra Nenets inflection.* Helsinki: Suomalais-Ugrilainen Seura.
Scalise, Sergio. (1986). *Generative morphology*, 2nd ed. Dordrecht: Foris.
Schadeberg, Thilo C. (1989). The three relative constructions in Swahili (kisanifu). In Marie-Françoise Rombi (ed.), *Le swahili et ses limites: Ambigüité des notions reçues.* Paris: Editions Recherche sur les Civilisations, pp. 33–40.
Selkirk, Elisabeth O. (1982). *The syntax of words.* Cambridge, MA: MIT Press.
Šereikaitė, Milena. (2017). The reanalysis of Lithuanian reflexive -*si*-: A DM approach. In Aaron Kaplan et al. (eds.), *Proceedings of the 34th West Coast Conference on Formal Linguistics.* Somerville, MA: Cascadilla Proceedings Project, pp. 447–453.
Serrano-Dolader, D. (2015). Parasynthesis in Romance. In P. O. Müller, I. Ohnheiser, S. Olsen, & F. Rainer (eds.), *Word-formation: An international handbook of the languages of Europe, vol. 1.* Berlin: De Gruyter Mouton, pp. 524–536.
Sievers, Eduard & Albert S. Cook. (1903). *An Old English grammar*, 3rd ed. Boston, MA: Ginn.
Soukka, Maria. (2000). *A descriptive grammar of Noon: A Cangin language of Senegal.* Munich: Lincom Europa.
Spencer, Andrew. (2005). Inflecting clitics in Generalized Paradigm Function Morphology. *Lingue e Linguaggio* IV(2), 179–193.
 (2013). *Lexical relatedness: A paradigm-based model.* Oxford: Oxford University Press.
Spencer, Andrew & Gregory Stump. (2013). Hungarian pronominal case and the dichotomy of content and form in inflectional morphology. *Natural Language and Linguistic Theory* 31, 1207–1248.
Steere, Edward. (1919). *A handbook of the Swahili language as spoken at Zanzibar*, revised and enlarged by A. C. Madan. London: Society for Promoting Christian Knowledge.
Steever, Sanford B. (1993). *Analysis to synthesis: The development of complex verb morphology in the Dravidian languages.* Oxford and New York, NY: Oxford University Press.
Štekauer, Pavol, Salvador Valera, & Lívia Körtvélyessy. (2012). *Word-formation in the world's languages: A typological survey.* Cambridge: Cambridge University Press.
Stewart, Tom & Gregory Stump. (2007). Paradigm Function Morphology and the morphology/syntax interface. In Gillian Ramchand & Charles Reiss (eds.), *The Oxford handbook of linguistic interfaces.* Oxford: Oxford University Press, pp. 383–421.
Stump, Gregory. (1990). La morphologie bretonne et la frontière entre la flexion et la dérivation. *La Bretagne linguistique* 6, 185–237.
 (1991). A paradigm-based theory of morphosemantic mismatches. *Language* 67, 675–725.

(1993). Position classes and morphological theory. In Geert Booij & Jaap van Marle (eds.), *Yearbook of morphology 1992*. Dordrecht: Kluwer, pp. 129–180.

(2001). *Inflectional morphology: A theory of paradigm structure*. Cambridge: Cambridge University Press.

(2005). Delineating the boundary between inflection-class marking and derivational marking: The case of Sanskrit *-aya*. In Wolfgang U. Dressler, Dieter Kastovsky, Oskar E. Pfeiffer, & Franz Rainer (eds.), *Morphology and its demarcations*. Amsterdam: John Benjamins, pp. 293–309.

(2010). The derivation of compound ordinal numerals: Implications for morphological theory. *Word Structure* 3(2), 205–233.

(2012). The formal and functional architecture of inflectional morphology. In Angela Ralli, Geert Booij, Sergio Scalise, & Athanasios Karasimos (eds.), *Morphology and the architecture of grammar: On-line Proceedings of the Eighth Mediterranean Morphology Meeting (MMM8), Cagliari, Italy, 14–17 September 2011*, 254–270.

(2016). *Inflectional paradigms: Content and form at the syntax-morphology interface*. Cambridge: Cambridge University Press.

(2017a). Polyfunctionality and the variety of inflectional exponence relations. In Ferenc Kiefer, James P. Blevins, & Huba Bartos (eds.), *Perspectives on morphological organization: Data and analyses*. Leiden: Brill, pp. 11–30.

(2017b). Rule conflation in an inferential-realizational theory of morphotactics. *Acta Linguistica Academica* 64(1), 79–124.

(2017c). Rules and blocks. In Claire Bowern, Laurence Horn, & Raffaella Zanuttini (eds.), *On looking into words (and beyond)*. Berlin: Language Science Press, pp. 421–440.

(2017d). The nature and dimensions of complexity in morphology. *Annual Review of Linguistics* 3, 65–83.

(2019a). An apparently noncanonical pattern of morphotactic competition. In Franz Rainer, Francesco Gardani, Wolfgang Dressler, & Hans Christian Luschützky (eds.), *Competition in inflection and word-formation*. Berlin: Springer, pp. 259–278.

(2019b). Paradigm Function Morphology. In Jenny Audring & Francesca Masini (eds.), *The Oxford handbook of morphological theory*. Oxford: Oxford University Press, pp. 285–304.

(2019c). Some sources of apparent gaps in derivational paradigms. *Morphology* 29, 271–292.

(2020a). Complex exponents. In Lívia Körtvélyessy & Pavol Štekauer (eds.), *Complex words: Advances in morphology*. Cambridge: Cambridge University Press, pp. 159–174.

(2020b). Paradigm Function Morphology: Assumptions and innovations. In *Oxford Research Encyclopedia of Linguistics*, ed. by Mark Aronoff. Oxford: Oxford University Press, http://linguistics.oxfordre.com.

(2021). Conditional exponence. In Sedigheh Moradi, Marcia Haag, Janie Rees-Miller, & Andrija Petrovic (eds.), *All things morphology: Its independence and its interfaces*. Amsterdam: John Benjamins, pp. 255–278.

(2022). Rule combination, potentiation, affix telescoping. In Andrea Sims, Adam Ussishkin, Jeff Parker, & Samantha Wray (eds.), *Morphological typology and linguistic cognition*. Cambridge: Cambridge University Press, pp. 282–306.
Stump, Gregory & Raphael Finkel. (2013). *Morphological typology: From word to paradigm*. Cambridge: Cambridge University Press.
Swinney, David A. & Anne Cutler. (1979). The access and processing of idiomatic expressions. *Journal of Verbal Learning and Verbal Behavior* 18, 523–534.
Tremblay, Antoine, Bruce Derwing, Gary Libben, & Chris F. Westbury. (2011). Processing advantages of lexical bundles: Evidence from self-paced reading and sentence recall tasks. *Language Learning* 61, 569–613.
Trépos, Pierre. (1957). *Le pluriel breton*. Brest: Emgleo Breiz.
   (1968). *Grammaire bretonne* [1980 reprint]. Rennes: Ouest France.
Underwood, Geoffrey, Norbert Schmitt, & Adam Galpin. (2004). The eyes have it: An eye-movement study into the processing of formulaic sequences. In Norbert Schmitt (ed.), *Formulaic sequences: Acquisition, processing, and use*. Amsterdam: John Benjamins, pp. 153–172.
van Driem, George. (1987). *A grammar of Limbu*. Berlin and New York, NY: Mouton de Gruyter.
   (1996). A new analysis of the Limbu verb. In David Bradley (ed.), *Tibeto-Burman languages of the Himalayas*. Canberra: Pacific Linguistics, pp. 157–173.
van Marle, Jaap. (1990). Rule-creating creativity: Analogy as a synchronic morphological process. In W. U. Dressler, Hans C. Luschützky, Oskar E. Pfeiffer, & John R. Rennison (eds.), *Contemporary morphology*. Berlin: Mouton de Gruyter, pp. 267–273.
Whitney, William Dwight. (1885). *The roots, verb-forms, and primary derivatives of the Sanskrit language*. London: Trübner & Co.
   (1889). *Sanskrit grammar*, 2nd ed. Cambridge, MA: Harvard University Press.
Williams, Edwin. (1981). On the notions "lexically related" and "head of a word". *Linguistic Inquiry* 12, 245–274.
Winkler, Eberhard. (2001). *Udmurt*. Munich: Lincom Europa.
   (2011). *Udmurtische Grammatik*. Wiesbaden: Harrassowitz.
Wray, Alison. (2002). *Formulaic language and the lexicon*. Cambridge: Cambridge University Press.
   (2012). What do we (think we) know about formulaic language? An evaluation of the current state of play. *Annual Review of Applied Linguistics* 32, 231–254.
Zimmermann, Eva. (2012). Affix copying in Kiranti. In Enrico Boone, Kathrin Linke, & Maartje Schulpen (eds.), *Proceedings of the ConSOLE XIX*. Leiden: Leiden University, pp. 343–367.
   (2016). Copy affixes in Kiranti. In Katja Barnickel, Matías Guzmán Naranjo, Johannes Hein, Sampson Korsah, Andrew Murphy, Ludger Paschen, Zorica Puškar, & Joanna Zaleska (eds.), *Replicative processes in grammar*. Leipzig: Universität Leipzig, pp. 1–34.

Index

addend, 62
affix counterposition, 26–27, 66–76, 182–223, 384–386, see also aggregation
   distinct from ambifixation, 214–217
   in Fula, 66, 71–76, 384–386
   in Italian, 218–223
   in Lithuanian, 66, 198–211, 385
   in Noon, 190–193, 385
   in Swahili, 66, 247–251, 385
   prefixational counterposition, 26
   signature pattern, 26, 66, 182, 362, 384
   suffixational counterposition, 26
affix directionality criterion, 17, 394
   apparent deviation in Fula, 32, 76
   apparent deviation in Lithuanian, 193–211
   apparent deviation in Noon, 184–193
   apparent deviation in Swahili, 225, 231–233, 247–251, 255, 257
   defined, 32
   Gurma deviation from, 212–215
   Italian deviation from, 217–223
affix telescoping, 334–343
   English affix sequences that are not yet telescoped, 338–343
   English -*ate*, 342
   stages of, 335
affixal discontinuity, 315–319
aggregation, 384–386, see also affix counterposition
   aggregated rules vs ambifixal rules, 211–217
   and diachronic reanalysis, 66–68, 327–328
   characteristic of inflection, 76, 403–404
   conformity with affix directionality criterion, 66
   defined, 66–76, 183
   deviates from stem operand criterion, 66–76, 182–223, 247–251

   in Fula, 71–76
   in Italian, 217–223
   in Lithuanian, 198–211
   in Noon, 190–193
   in Swahili, 247–251, 347
   interaction with ambifixation in Italian, 217–223
   operator, 69, 401
   prefixational, 70, 183, 382, 402
   suffixational, 70, 183, 382, 402
Alhoniemi, Alho, 135
ambifix
   distinct from counterposed affix, 214–217
   in Gurma, 212–215
   interaction with aggregation in Italian, 217–223
Ambrazas, Vytautas, 193, 195–196
Anderson, Stephen, 16, 57, 219, 344, 350
Arkadiev, Peter, 194–198
Arnon, Inbal, 322
Arnott, D. W., 14, 30, 32, 71–73, 114, 369
Aronoff, Mark, 29, 125, 300
Arregi, Karlos, 3, 349, 353
Ashton, E. O., 14, 228
atomic property. See morphosyntactic property
Audring, Jenny, 340, 345, 350

Badrulhisham, Heikal, 322
Barrett-Keach, Camillia, 256
Bauer, Laurie, 9–10, 14, 28, 315–316, 338–340
Becker, Thomas, 340
Beckett, Eleanor, 212
Bickel, Balthasar, 21, 24, 113
Bilgin, Orhan, 323–324
blocking, 299, 317
Bochner, Harry, 7, 10, 14, 20, 301, 325

416 *Index*

Bonami, Olivier, 3, 219, 350, 354–357, 362, 364–368, 370–371, 375–377
Booij, Geert, 12–14, 20, 57, 333, 345–350
Breton
    fractional nouns, 63–65
    full exponence rules, 63, 166, 168–169, 171, 333
    holistic combination, 63, 160–171
    paradigm function, 167
    portmanteau suffixes, 160–163, 384
    solitary specialization, 63, 165–166
    verb inflection, 25–26, 62–63, 160–171, 333
Brown, Dunstan, 15
Bybee, Joan, 325, 329

canonical morphotactics, 15–32, see also minimal rule criterion, rule independence criterion, parallel sequence criterion, unique sequence criterion, compositional content criterion, stem operand criterion, intermediate well-formedness criterion, integral stem criterion, rule opposition criterion, affix directionality criterion
category clustering, 21, 113
Category Determination Principle
    and rule polyfunctionality, 392
    and the non-associativity of rule composition, 259–261
    defined, 44, 405
    in Murrinhpatha verb inflection, 287–292
    in Swahili verbal concord, 233–242, 249
category-determinate property. See morphosyntactic property
category-indeterminate property. See morphosyntactic property
cell. See content cell, form cell, realized cell
Chichewa
    formulaic suffix sequences, 326
Chumakina, Marina, 15
circumfix, 9, 182, 315–316
combinatory transparency, 334–335
    characteristics of, 334
    domain transparency, 334–335, 337–339, 341–343
    phonological transparency, 334, 337, 339–342
    semantic transparency, 334–335, 337–343
    separability, 334, 339–342
combining stem, 51–52, 77, 313, 341, 401

composition
    (carrier ∘ dependent) composites in Sanskrit, 96–111
    (dependent ∘ carrier) composites in Limbu, 86–96
    alternative orders of composition in Eastern Mari, 131–140
    characteristic of inflection and derivation, 54–61, 403–404
    complementary orders of composition in Udmurt, 121–131
    composite overrides simple rule in Sanskrit, 155–156
    composite rules opposed to portmanteau in Latin, 151–154
    composite rules opposed to portmanteau in Swahili, 242–247
    default order of composition overridden in Fula, 114–121
    defined, 54–61, 398–400
    enhances rule locality in Sanskrit, 141–149
    in English derivation, 315–319, 338–343
    non-associativity of rule composition, 259–261, 289–292
    of derivational rules, 56, 399
    of inflectional rules, 55, 398
    operator, 54, 398
    portmanteau overrides composite rule in Limbu, 154–155
compositional content criterion, 18, 61–66, 159–181, 394
    Breton deviation from, 25, 160–171
    defined, 24
    Limbu deviation from, 171–173
    Old English deviation from, 173–181
compounding, 8, 316
Construction Morphology, 12–13, 57, 345–349
content cell, 39, 101, 106–109, 148, 180, 207, 215, 278–279, 283
content paradigm, 39
content supplementation
    defined, 61–66, 401
    derivational, 63, 401
    emergent, 171–173, 176
    inflectional, 62, 401
    operator, 62, 401
contrastive uniformity, 18, 394
Corbett, Greville, 15, 350

counterpotentiation
  and diachronic reanalysis, 328–329
  characteristic of derivation, 77, 403–404
  compositionally motivated, 78–80, 305–315, 400
  defined, 77–80, 302, 400–401
  deviates from intermediate well-formedness criterion, 77–80
  in English derivation, 77–80, 302–315, 338–343
  operator, 77, 400
  pleonastic, 78–79, 305, 400
  use in forming a combining stem, 77, 313, 401
cross-formation, 340
Crysmann, Berthold, 3, 219, 350, 354–357, 362, 364–368, 370–371, 375–377

Dambriūnas, Leonardas, 195–198, 202–203
definitional uniformity, 17, 393
Deshpande, Madhav, 97, 99, 105
Distributed Morphology, 349, 351–354
Dixon, R. M. W., 28, 309, 340
domain of a function, 44
domain transparency
  separability, 335
domain-of-definition of a function, 44
Durrant, Philip, 322
Dutch
  derivational morphology, 9, 12–13, 345–347

Eastern Mari
  A cases vs B cases, 136, 374
  alternative orders of composition, 131–140
  annexational structure of FER patterns, 139, 373–374, 378, 389
  FER pattern for possessorless case-marked plurals, 135
  FER patterns for noun inflection, 374
  FER patterns for singular possessor-marked case forms, 136
  full exponence rules, 134–135, 137, 139, 361
  nominal inflection, 131–140, 373–379
  noun template, 376
  rule groups for noun inflection, 134
  three-rule FER patterns, 139
Embick, David, 3, 349, 353

English
  -abil-ity, 299–302, 326
  -at-ion, 311–315, 340–341
  beautician, 303, 310, 319, 342
  cannibalistic, 80, 303, 306–308, 339–340, 397
  conjugations, 44–46
  embolden, 9, 78, 305, 316–318
  formulaic affix sequences, 338–343
  -ful-ly, 337
  -ic-al, 303–305, 338–339
  -ic-ian, 308–310, 342–343
  -if-ic, 336–337
  -ish-ly, 334
  -ist-ic, 306–308, 339–340
  -iz-at-ion, 337
  stem-selection rule, 40–41
  thematizing use of *-ate*, 51, 308, 311, 341, 348
  thematizing use of *-ian*, 308
  thematizing use of *-ic*, 308
  thematizing use of *-ic-s*, 308
  true derivational use of *-ate*, 51, 308, 311, 341, 348
  true derivational use of *-ian*, 308
  use of *-ate* in forming a combining stem, 51, 313, 341, 401
  whimsical, 27–28, 35, 298, 303–305, 317–319, 338
European Portuguese
  pronominal objects, 119
evaluation metric
  pattern-matching, 10, 325
  symbol-counting, 10
exponence-driven morphotactics, 349–351
extension of a property set
  defined, 55

FER pattern, 59, see also *individual languages*
  different from template, 381–389
form cell, 39, 60, 74, 95, 101, 106–109, 119, 130, 148, 150, 171, 180, 192, 207, 215, 241, 245, 252, 278–280, 283, 285, 293–294, 296, 332, 363, 378
form correspondent, 40
form paradigm, 39
formulaic rule combination, 322–334
  conventional rule combination, 325–333
  frequent rule combination, 323–325

418 *Index*

formulaic rule combination (cont.)
    semantically noncompositional rule
        combination, 333
Fraser, Norman, 350
Fula
    affix counterposition in, 66, 71–76,
        384–386
    default order of composition overridden,
        114–121
    FER pattern for verb forms, 75, 119
    FER patterns for verb forms, 370
    full exponence rules, 73–74, 76, 91,
        119–120
    noun classes, 116
    preterite inflection, 71–76
    rule groups for verb inflection, 73–76, 385
    verb template, 372
    verbal concord, 114–121, 369–371
Full Exponence Principle, 59
full exponence rule (FER), see also *individual
    languages*
    defined, 4, 58
function
    partial, 42
    total, 42

Gazdar, Gerald, 55
Greenberg, Joseph, 68, 328
Gurma
    ambifixes, 212–215
    full exponence rules, 214
    gender classes, 212–214
    rule groups for noun inflection, 212–214

Harris, Alice, 67, 84, 328–329
Haspelmath, Martin, 333
holistic combination, 25, see also content
        supplementation
    characteristic of inflection and derivation,
        63, 403–404
    defined, 61–66, 166, 401
    deviates from compositional content
        criterion, 61–66, 159–181
    in Breton, 62–66, 160–171
    in Limbu, 171–173
    in Old English, 173–181, 387–388
Hyman, Larry, 326–327

Iacobini, Claudio, 9, 317
infix, 143, 317, 352

inflection-class function *ic*, 40
Information-based Morphology, 354–389
    analysis of Eastern Mari nouns, 373–379
    analysis of Fula verbal concord, 369–371
    analysis of Swahili relative verb forms,
        362–369
    position-based ordering, 359, 377, 379
    rule anchoring, 359, 365, 368, 371, 379
    rule monopolism, 359–360, 367, 369, 371
integral stem criterion, 17, 394
    apparent deviation in English, 29
    apparent deviation in Sanskrit, 141–149
    defined, 28
interactive uniformity, 17, 394
intermediate well-formedness criterion, 18,
        394
    defined, 27
    English deviation from, 27, 302–315
    potentiation enhances conformity,
        299–302
Italian
    full exponence rules, 221–223
    interaction of aggregation with true
        ambifixation, 217–223
    parasynthesis, 8–9
    pronominal affixes, 217–223

Jackendoff, Ray, 340, 345, 350

Kanuri
    circumfixation, 316
Kervella, F., 25, 62–63, 161
Körtvélyessy, Lívia, 317

Latin
    composite rules opposed to portmanteau
        -*minī*, 151–154, 384
    FER pattern for passive verb forms, 153
    formulaic suffix sequences, 326
    full exponence rules, 153
    passive verb forms, 30, 120, 151–154
    source of English -*ate*, 311, 342
Lieber, Rochelle, 16, 28, 50, 317, 338–340
Limbu, 384
    (dependent ∘ carrier) composites, 86–96
    FER pattern for verb forms, 94
    full exponence rules, 89, 91, 94
    holistic combinations, 171–173
    multiple exponence in, 89, 96, 352
    portmanteau -*mʔna*, 91–96

portmanteau -*mʔna* overrides composite rule, 154–155
rule groups for verb inflection, 88–94, 384
verb inflection, 86–96, 154–155, 171–173
Lithuanian
  affix counterposition in, 66, 198–211, 385
  Aktionsart prefix, 194–205, 208
  conjugations, 195, 198–203
  external vs internal prefixes, 195–198
  FER pattern for prefixed nonreflexives, 208
  FER pattern for prefixed reflexives, 210
  FER pattern for unprefixed reflexives, 208
  full exponence rules, 203, 207–208, 210–211
  inflection-class function *ic*, 205
  reflexive affix not ambifixal, 215–216
  reflexive verbs, 193–211
Luís, Ana, 11–12, 14, 212
Luutonen, Jorma, 135, 137–138, 374, 378

Mansfield, John, 21, 113, 262–264, 294
Marchand, Hans, 28, 309, 343
Masini, Francesca, 9, 317, 346
Matthews, P. H., 16, 84
minimal rule criterion, 17, 394
  all rule combinations deviate from, 20, 53, 156, 188, 380, 394, 397
  defined, 19
Monachesi, Paola, 218–219
morpheme, 4–5, 16, 85, 180, 391
morphological operations, 351–354
morphological processing, 289, 322–334, 397
morphomic property, 125, 274
morphosyntactic property
  atomic, 43
  set-based and category-determinate, 43
  set-based and category-indeterminate, 43, 403
morphotactic complexity, 397–403
morphotactic holism hypothesis
  defined, 8
  past work supporting, 8–15
morphotactic variety hypothesis
  defined, 8
morphotactics. See also canonical morphotactics, exponence-driven morphotactics, rule-combining morphotactics, word-skeletal morphotactics

as "regulatactics", 4
defined, 1
multiple exponence, 84–86, 111, 329, 335, 392
  in Limbu, 89, 96, 352
  in Noon, 85, 328
  in Pengo, 329–333
  in Swahili, 229–230, 244, 246
Murrinhpatha, 259–297
  category-indeterminate properties in, 275, 279, 282, 285, 287, 297, 393
  classifier conjugations, 264
  classifier stem, 14, 262, 265–271, 273–275, 280, 282, 285, 288, 290, 295
  compound verb, 290
  FER patterns for verb forms, 277, 279, 282
  full exponence rules, 277–285, 289–297
  lexical stem, 262, 264, 273–274, 283, 290, 295
  nested rule combinations, 282–285, 389, 396
  non-associative rule composition in, 289–292, 386–387
  rule groups for verb inflection, 274–280, 282–287, 289–295, 297, 386–387
  simple verb, 290
  verbal template, 262

Naba, Jean-Claude, 212
Nevins, Andrew, 3, 349, 353
Noon
  adjective inflection, 184–193
  affix counterposition in, 190–193, 385
  consonantal markers not ambifixal, 216
  FER pattern for definite adjectives, 191
  FER pattern for indefinite adjectives, 191
  formulaic affix sequences, 328
  full exponence rules, 192
  multiple exponence in, 85, 328
  noun classes, 185–186, 216
Nordlinger, Rachel, 14, 262–263, 267–272
Noyer, Rolf, 3, 349, 353

Old English
  full exponence rules, 174, 178–179
  holistic combinations, 173–181
  paradigm function, 178
  solitary specialization, 178
  strong vs weak verbs, 173–180
  verb inflection, 173–181, 387–388

operator/operand relations, 360, 389, 403
Özel, Selma Ayşe, 322

Pāṇini's principle, 30, 45, 148, 151, 154, 156, 158, 173, 250, 256, 289, 368
  defined, 43
paradigm. See content paradigm, form paradigm, realized paradigm
paradigm function, 40–69, 345, 389, see also *individual languages*
  defined, 41
Paradigm Function Morphology, 38, 57–59, 344–345, see also content cell, content paradigm, form cell, form paradigm, paradigm function, realized cell, realized paradigm
paradigmatic opposition, 10–11, 21–23, 29–32, 150–156, 230, 245–246, 250, 256, 351, 355, 367, 384, 392
  vs syntagmatic combination, 15
parallel sequence criterion, 18, 113, 394
  and category clustering, 21, 113
  defined, 21
  Eastern Mari deviation from, 131–135
  European Portuguese deviation from, 119
  Fula deviation from, 114–121
  Latin deviation from, 120
  Murrinhpatha deviation from, 274
  relates to inflection, 23
  Swahili deviation from, 225, 229
  Udmurt deviation from, 23, 121–131
parasynthesis, 8–10, 316–319
Pengo
  FER patterns for verb forms, 331
  formulaic affix sequences, 329–333
  full exponence rules, 332
  multiple exponence in, 329–333
  rule groups for verb inflection, 330–332
Plag, Ingo, 28, 313, 338–340
potentiation, 326
  characteristic of derivation, 403–404
  defined, 400
  in English derivation, 299–302, 340–341
  operator, 301, 400

Rainer, Franz, 28, 317
realized cell, 39, 60, 74, 95, 106–109, 120, 148, 171, 180, 192, 207, 215, 241, 245, 252, 278–280, 283, 285, 293–294, 296, 332, 363, 378

realized paradigm, 39
reanalysis, 66–68, 76, 160, 182, 321, 327–329, 333–334, 337
registered-to-vote-in function, 44
Renou, Louis, 97
rule
  carrier, 83–112
  dependent, 83–112
rule applies to vs rule operates on, 52
rule block, 11, 58, 115, 345
rule combination. See also aggregation, composition, counterpotentiation, holistic combination, potentiation
  and morphological simplicity, 321–343
  binariness of, 66, 320, 358, 360, 378, 386, 389, 397
  inner rule vs outer rule, 80
  nesting of, 233, 255, 277, 282–285, 358, 360, 363, 382, 389, 396
  stored, 322–334, see also formulaic rule combination
rule group, 345, 382, 386, see also *individual languages*
rule independence criterion, 17, 394
  defined, 20
  Limbu deviation from, 86–96
  Sanskrit deviation from, 96–111
  Swahili deviation from, 21, 225, 229, 253, 257
rule of derivational exponence, 46–53
  thematizing use, 51, 77
  true derivational use, 51, 77
  use in forming a combining stem, 51, 77, 313, 401
rule of inflectional exponence, 42–44
rule opposition criterion, 18, 150–156, 394
  apparent deviation in Latin, 30, 151–154
  apparent deviation in Limbu, 154–155
  apparent deviation in Sanskrit, 155–156
  apparent deviation in Swahili, 225, 229, 245, 255, 257
  defined, 29
rule-combining morphotactics, 5–8, 36–82, 391–405
  and Construction Morphology, 345–349
  and Distributed Morphology, 351–354
  and Information-based Morphology, 354–389
  and Paradigm Function Morphology, 57–59, 344–345